ABORIGINAL POPULATIONS

Social, Demographic, and Epidemiological Perspectives

CONTENTS

PART II: EPIDEMIOLOGICAL PERSPECTIVES

PART III: SOCIOLOGICAL PERSPECTIVES

PART IV: INTERNATIONAL PERSPECTIVES

PREFACE

In the early twenty-first century, Aboriginal concerns are at the forefront of
media attention and public discourse. Among academics, politicians, and
the Canadian public at large there is growing recognition of the important
contributions the First Peoples have made to the development of this
country as a prosperous and thriving nation. There is also growing sentiment that more can be done to help rectify past injustices toward this sector
of the Canadian family. Consequently, Canadians are keenly interested
in gaining a deeper understanding of Aboriginal conditions. The chapters in
this volume, originally presented at a symposium held at the University of
Alberta in October of 2008, provide a timely update on Canada's Aboriginal
peoples and future prospects in the new millennium. The symposium was
organized with the thought in mind that a comprehensive understanding of the social demographic transformations in the Canadian Aboriginal
population could be achieved through careful interdisciplinary analysis. The
overarching theme of this volume is that Canada's Aboriginal population has
reached a critical stage of transition, from a situation in the past characterized by delayed modernization, extreme socio-economic deficit, and minimal
control over their demography, to a point of social, political, economic, and

demographic ascendancy that, in total, present for this population a more
hopeful outlook for the future than was the case in the past. For certain,
one must acknowledge the serious socio-economic problems that must be
fully addressed and resolved over the course of the twenty-first century.
Appropriate policies must be formulated that would take into account
demographic, sociological, and epidemiological trends in historical and
contemporary perspectives. We have organized this volume in accordance
with these ideas. We include in this book research carried out by international experts of indigenous populations in the United States, Australia,
New Zealand, Russia, and the circumpolar North so as to provide a sense of
how Aboriginal conditions in these countries may complement or differ from
those faced by Canada's First Peoples.

ACKNOWLEDGEMENTS

We wish to acknowledge the financial support of the Social Sciences and Humanities Research Council of Canada (SSHRC) and the assistance provided by the departments of Sociology and Native Studies at the University of Alberta. We are also grateful to the Dean of Arts and the Population Research Laboratory at the University of Alberta for their support. We are especially grateful to the Society of Edmonton Demographers for having provided us with additional funding toward the publication of this volume. We also thank the discussants of the papers presented at the symposium for their valuable insights and observations, from which we have benefited in developing this volume: Drs. M.V. George, Christopher Fletcher, and Norbert Robitaille. Many thanks to Christine Whalen and Kamrul Islam for their expert and dedicated assistance throughout the planning and execution of the symposium, and to Kelly Gadzala for her editorial advice on an early version of this book. Finally, we wish to express our gratitude to Joanne Muzak for her careful copy editing and the expert involvement in the production of this volume by Linda Cameron and her staff at the University of Alberta Press.

INTRODUCTION

ABORIGINAL POPULATIONS: SOCIAL, DEMOGRAPHIC, AND EPIDEMIOLOGICAL PERSPECTIVES

Frank Trovato and Anatole Romaniuk

In this collection, we attempt to provide an up-to-date account of the social demography of the Canadian Aboriginal population based on historical and recent data, including information from the 2006 Census. Our main goals are as follows: (1) to review and extend the existing literature on the social demography of Aboriginal peoples in Canada so as to identify major demographic, sociological, and health trends in this population; (2) to examine how the Aboriginal population has been changing; (3) to point to relevant research and policies that might be required to meet the challenges Aboriginal peoples are likely to face over the course of the twenty-first century; (4) to present comparative selected research on Aboriginal peoples, including those of Australia, New Zealand, the United States, the Russian Federation, and Scandinavian countries.

DATA AND CONCEPTUAL ISSUES

Much of what is known about the social demography of Aboriginal peoples has been derived from Canadian censuses. Many of the works presented in this book rely on this important source. While censuses represent the most complete and consistent set of data concerning the Aboriginal peoples, it must be mentioned that such data have some limitations. For example, some Indian reserves refused to participate in various censuses, and in other cases a particular census was interrupted before completion. In 2006, there were 22 incompletely enumerated reserves, down from 30 in 2001 and 77 in 1996 (Gionet, 2008a). Another complexity inherent in the census data pertains to changes introduced over the years in defining Aboriginality in the census and the consequent difficulty in establishing who is an Aboriginal. In all censuses, except that of 1891, the Aboriginal population was counted through a question on ethnic origin, ancestry, or race. As a way to cover ambiguities arising out of potential inconsistencies with these practices, since 1996 the census has included questions on both identity (i.e., self-identity with respect to which group one identifies as being a member) as well as ancestry (i.e., ethnic origin). Since the 1986 Census, there has been a question included on multiple ethnic origins, allowing respondents to state more than one origin. Changes in the definition and methods of enumeration between censuses have introduced discontinuities in the time series that are difficult to explain.

These changes in the Canadian census mean that there are now different ways to count Aboriginals (i.e., Aboriginal identity; member of an Indian band/First Nation; Registered or Treaty Indian; and ethnic origin, including Aboriginal ancestries). Depending on which definition one uses, the numbers can vary considerably. In many statistical analyses, investigators focus on the Aboriginal identity variable alone, that is, on individuals who identify themselves as belonging to one or more of the following groups: North American Indian, Métis, or Inuit; Treaty Indian or Registered Indian as defined by the Indian Act; or members of an Indian band or First Nation. According to the 2006 Census, the Aboriginal identity population numbered 1,172,790, of which 698,025 were First Nations people, 389,780 were Métis, and 50,485 were Inuit. An additional 34,500 included multiple and other Aboriginal responses (i.e., persons who reported more than one Aboriginal identity group and those who reported being a Registered Indian and/or band member without reporting an Aboriginal identity).

Closely linked to these changes is the phenomenon of "ethnic mobility." In this introduction we limit ourselves to a description of the essential features of this concept, leaving the bulk of the details to the authors in this volume who concern themselves with this topic (see the chapters by Romaniuk; Guimond, Robitaille, & Senécal; Goldmann & Delic; and

Andersen). This term, ethnic mobility, refers to the tendency of persons to shift their identification from one ethnic category to another, such that when the question on ethnic identification in a census is observed over successive periods, there is either a decline or increase in the numbers of individuals who declare a given ethnic identity. Between 1986 and 2006, the Aboriginal identity population grew from 464,655 to 1,172,790, for an annual average rate of growth of 7.62% over this period. This large growth cannot be attributed to natural increase alone (excess of births over deaths), nor net international migration; therefore, ethnic mobility must be a key underlying factor.

An important sociological question is what determines ethnic mobility. Intermarriage is clearly important. Increased rates of exogamy among Aboriginals over time must account for a growing number of descendants of mixed Aboriginal/non-Aboriginal unions, many of whom identify with an Aboriginal group. Other sociological factors may come into play. There is now a renewed sense of pride in Aboriginality. Undoubtedly, this has likely stimulated a growing number of Canadians, perhaps even those with distant Aboriginal roots, to declare an Aboriginal identity in the census. Legalistic changes affecting First Nations persons have also contributed to the growth of the Aboriginal population. In particular, the passage of Bill C-31 in 1985 has allowed the reinstatement of First Nations women who had lost their Registered Indian status as a result of marriage to a non-Aboriginal man.

Some of the works in this volume consider the total Aboriginal population as the focus of analysis while others are based on one or more specific Aboriginal subgroup. In this context, throughout the chapters, the reader will come across the term "Aboriginal peoples," "indigenous peoples," and "First Peoples" as descriptors of this population. While desirable, the authors could not always separate the Aboriginal population into its component subgroups because of lack of access to the appropriate data at a lower level of aggregation.

The Aboriginal population of Canada comprises three major subgroups: North American Indians, Métis, and Inuit. The North American Indians (also referred to as First Nations) consist of "Registered Indians," or Status Indians (legally recognized under the Indian Act) and "non-Registered Indians," or non-Status Indians. Members of the latter subgroup are not entitled to be registered under the Indian Act but do self-identify as North

American Indian. The Métis are descendants of mixed couples formed when European explorers had children with Aboriginal women. A significant proportion of those descendants integrated neither in the Indian group nor in the non-Aboriginal group and instead developed their own cultural identity. The Inuit includes populations originating from the Arctic region and thus remains highly isolated from mainstream Canada.

ANALYTICAL APPROACH

Of concerns to this volume are the dichotomies of macro versus micro and quantitative versus qualitative in regard to level and type of analysis. Some social science disciplines give preference to the micro and qualitative approaches (for instance, anthropologists mostly study small groups and make inferences about larger universes—cultural areas, ethnicity, nation). In many of the other social sciences—more notably economics and demography—analytical emphasis is often on the macro level (i.e., population level). To a large extent, this orientation is facilitated by the availability of huge amounts of statistical data on populations (e.g., census, large sample surveys). The predominant approach of this book is macro; therefore, most of the studies are confined to major subdivisions, such as provinces, rural versus urban, and ethnic categories (e.g., Amerindian, Status and non-Status, Métis and Inuit, etc.) We do not see this as a weakness. The authors are very clear in their specification of the underlying social demographic *processes* and *mechanisms* that are assumed responsible for observed phenomena reflected in the statistical findings. Consequently, inferences are grounded in theory consistent with the established literature, thus helping to minimize the ecological fallacy—i.e., the drawing of false inferences about lower level (e.g., individual) processes from aggregate level correlations. This potential problem is non-existent in those works in this volume that are based on individual-level data (taken from either surveys or censuses) and properly aggregated to the population or group level. (This is a common approach in the sciences, which is also adopted by major statistical organizations such as Statistics Canada and Indian and Northern Affairs Canada before their publications are released in the public domain.)

In a number of cases, authors present evidence based on small groups and communities. For example, the chapter on counting Aboriginals through censuses by Goldmann and Delic discusses historical cases of small area Aboriginal populations; Chandler's study on Aboriginal suicide reveals interesting insights owing to the stratification of Aboriginal groups (reserves) according to the degree to which they preserve traditional values; Romaniuk reports on the fertility increase during the early stage of modernization among the James Bay Indians based on a 1968 survey of this group.

DEMOGRAPHIC PERSPECTIVES

After a long period of depopulation that lasted almost three centuries following the arrival of Europeans, the Aboriginal population of Canada reached its nadir of about 100,000 inhabitants by the turn of the twentieth century, at which time a slow journey toward demographic recovery began. But it was only after the end of World War II, and especially as of the 1970s, that Canadian Aboriginals witnessed major population growth and significant improvements in the area of medical services and education in a context of rapid economic growth in the country. Aboriginal people underwent what demographers call a demographic transition, that is, a shift in reproductive patterns and mortality from a traditional high regime to an eventual modern situation characterized by reduced fertility and mortality rates. Even though the Aboriginal population is still trailing in both these demographic dimensions in comparison to the nation, eventual completion of the demographic transition is well underway.

Declines in birth and death rates are by no means the only changes of wide importance. Contemporary Aboriginal people are witnessing changes in other aspects of their demography. These include later age at entry into sexual unions for women; increased rates of cohabitation and single parenting; steady growth of the elderly population notwithstanding a high percentage of Aboriginal youth (due to high fertility in the past); increased rates of internal migration, often of a circular nature between reserves and cities; and the growth of urban Aboriginal populations. All of these trends signal challenges and opportunities for the Aboriginal peoples of Canada.

Anatole Romaniuk's chapter, "Canada's Aboriginal Population: From Encounter of Civilizations to Revival and Growth," examines the long-term demographic history of the Aboriginal peoples. In early history, prior to and during the initial stages of contact with the Europeans, this population experienced a "regime of precarious stationary population," primarily caused by the Europeans having introduced infections to which Aboriginals lacked immunity and thereby raising mortality to very high levels, leading to a protracted period of depopulation. This was followed by demographic recovery starting at around 1900 as the epidemics receded due to antivirus inoculations and reduced death rates, the rise in fertility associated with early modernization as traditional fertility-inhibiting factors (e.g., breast-feeding) weakened before large-scale adoption of birth control. Romaniuk embarks on an elaborate exploration of the anthropological, medical, economic, social, and political contexts underlying these historical changes. In doing so, he presents a version of demographic transition theory that is more in tune with Aboriginal historical experience, departing in several respects from the classical version of transition theory. While taking stock of the past, Romaniuk's analysis also delves into the possible future and speculates on the kinds of demographically driven policy issues regarding Canadian Aboriginal population over the twenty-first century. The author sees significant room for improving the "demographic quality" of the Aboriginal population through the enhancement of "human capital"— namely, investments in education, job skills, and health promotion.

Romaniuk concludes that, over the long run, the future of Aboriginal people as an ethnic entity will depend on their fertility rate. For the time being, their childbearing performance is high enough to ensure their sustained growth in numbers. And that is going to last for a while. But in the longer term, Romaniuk sees the prospect of Aboriginal peoples entering a stage of demographic maturity and thus joining the growing number of nations that no longer reproduce themselves as very likely. This raises some important questions for policy analysts to ponder: What will be the place of the First Peoples in twenty-first century Canadian society? How will an expanding and increasingly ethnically diverse population (due to increased immigration) ultimately impact the Aboriginal settlement patterns and treaty rights? Will the emerging new Canada remain fully committed to the special status the First Peoples have enjoyed historically as a distinct society?

The application of concepts of descent and racial/ethnic classification in the census has evolved quite substantially since the early pre- and post-Confederation censuses in the face of changes in immigration and corresponding shifts in the ethnic distribution of the nation. In "Counting Aboriginal Peoples in Canada," Gustave Goldmann and Senada Delic delve into an informative account of the treatment of the Aboriginal question dating as far back as the first census of New France in 1666 by Jean Talon. A variety of terms has been applied when counting the Aboriginal population over the censuses. Witness, for example, the designations of "American

Indian" and "Native Indian." The Métis population was at one time referred to as "Half-breeds," and the Inuit as "Eskimo." As well, the classifications of subgroups and the application of descent rules in the censuses have not been uniform. As a case in point, although the ethnic origin of the European population was determined along patrilineal lines for most censuses between 1871 and 1971, the rules for descent for the Aboriginal population have varied among tribes between matrilineal and patrilinial affiliation.

To arrive at some understanding of the possible demographic future of a population, demographers often rely on population projections. Demographer Ravi Verma, in his "Population Projections for the Aboriginal Population in Canada: A Review of Past, Present, and Future Prospects, 1991 to 2017," undertakes a careful review of several population projections of the Aboriginal population and its main subgroups—Registered Indians, Métis, and Inuit. As Verma explains, usually, evaluation of projection results is done by *ex-post facto* examination, whereby the analyst checks the accuracy of projected population numbers against the numbers observed by age and sex in the census taken at a later date in relation to the base year of the projection. Verma applies this approach in his investigation. Verma concludes that there is much uncertainty in the projected population figures for the total Aboriginal population because some of this growth may have resulted from changes in reporting patterns of Aboriginal identity—namely, ethnic mobility. This remains the most difficult and elusive factor in forecasting the future Aboriginal population, according to Verma.

To what extent the inaccuracy in projections may have affected the programs that these projections were purported to serve is difficult to say. Although not necessarily precise, population projections, in combination with other variables, may be useful in planning for the future in a constantly changing world. Stated differently, population forecasts and projections may be viewed as part of the "anticipatory management" toolbox of government bureaucracy. That it is not to say that any projection is acceptable. The methodology, and, even more importantly, the assumptions that form the base of the projections, must be sound in order to enhance the credibility of the results.

According to Eric Guimond, Norbert Robitaille, and Sacha Senécal in their "Another Look at Definitions and Growth of Aboriginal Populations in Canada," Aboriginal affiliation is not necessarily permanent and is not automatically transferred to the next generation. As a consequence, group

boundaries are becoming increasingly fuzzy, and statistical definitions of
Aboriginal populations in Canada are increasingly divergent with respect to
the related population counts. Ethnic mobility is the main component of the
recent demographic explosion of North American Indian and Métis populations. Therefore, excluding ethnic mobility from the analytical framework
of the demography of Aboriginal populations prevents an accurate understanding of Aboriginality.

Stewart Clatworthy and Mary Jane Norris examine another important
social demographic topic concerning Canadian Aboriginal population. In
their chapter on "Aboriginal Mobility and Migration in Canada: Patterns,
Trends, and Implications, 1971 to 2006," it is noted that a commonly held
view in the literature is that there has been a mass exodus by First Nations
people away from reserves in favour of cities. A movement of this nature
did take place shortly after World War II that continued through the 1960s
and the 1970s; however, this type of movement has leveled off considerably since the 1980s. Recent statistical evidence, including the data from
the 2006 Census is consistent with this (see also Taylor & Bell, 2004, for a
similar situation for Australia, New Zealand, and the United States). When
Clatworthy and Norris compared different combinations of origin and destination settlement areas for the Registered Indians (i.e., reserves, rural,
urban non-Census Metropolitan Areas, urban Census Metropolitan Areas)
with respect to in-, out- and net migration flows, they found that the settlement area of major growth was not urban centres but reserve communities.

Unlike other Aboriginal groups, those registered under the Indian Act
have certain rights and benefits, especially if they live on reserves, including taxation exemptions, access to funding for housing and post-secondary
education, as well as land and treaty rights. Aboriginal populations living
off-reserve, including those in Métis and Inuit communities, do not have
legal access to these rights and benefits. Therefore, the varying landscape
of rights and benefits that exists between on- and off-reserve communities
and between those Registered and non-Registered is important to understanding the recent pattern of migration among the different Aboriginal
groups in Canada.

Clatworthy and Norris also find that there is a high level of circular
migration among First Nations to and from reserves. Often, this is dictated
by the variable nature of seasonal labour outside the reserve areas, as well
as by the proximity of many reserve communities to cities, which reduces

the costs of relocation for migrants. Social networks play a part in this by facilitating movement and resettlement of migrants; the presence of family and friends in the city and on reserve promotes the intensification of circular migration between the reserve and the city (Denton, 1972).

As well, there is an unusually strong tendency among Aboriginals to move residentially within the city. This phenomenon is often associated with poor housing, substandard and unsafe neighbourhood conditions, and poverty. An unfortunate outcome of this type of frequent mobility for Aboriginals is that, for the children, this often results in an unstable education experience, poor grades, and high dropout rates.

Many social programs that provide services to urban Aboriginals, such as health care, family support and counselling, and education, are designed on a neighbourhood basis to ensure a co-ordinated response to multi-faceted family and individual needs. Frequent moves result in the disruption of services provision to families. High needs families would be particularly disadvantaged by this, most especially lone female parents with children. These types of families are among the most mobile and yet often in the most need for assistance. The frequent movement of Aboriginals may serve to limit opportunities for individuals and their families to establish meaningful and lasting social relationships within both the Aboriginal and broader communities. In this sense, high frequency of moving may translate into high levels of social isolation and a barrier to social cohesion in the urban Aboriginal communities and neighbourhoods.

EPIDEMIOLOGICAL PERSPECTIVES

We can identify four important features pertaining to Aboriginals health and mortality conditions. First, the Aboriginal peoples find themselves in the midst of an epidemiological transition, a situation opposite to that of advanced societies, which have long completed this transition (Omran, 1971; Olshansky & Ault, 1986). Second, infectious and parasitic diseases associated with poverty maintain a pernicious grip on Aboriginal populations; all the while, a new wave of diseases associated with socio-economic progress—i.e., the degenerative diseases, including cancer and cardiovascular ailments—is growing in prominence. Third, Aboriginal death rates exceed those of non-Aboriginal Canadians by a notable margin. Consequently, Aboriginal life expectancy lags well behind that of others in Canada. A fourth feature is the relatively high incidence of premature death by traumatic causes to Aboriginal Canadians (injuries and poisonings), these being of two types: intended (i.e., suicide and homicide) and unintended (i.e., motor vehicle accidents and other forms of injuries).

The root causes of high death rates among Aboriginals are social, which means that many of the deaths (especially to infants and children) are preventable (Gracey & King, 2009; King, Smith, & Gracey, 2009; Waldram, Herring, & Young, 2006; Adelson, 2005; Wilkinson, 2005; Marmot & Wilkinson, 2003). Public programs and policies must be tailored specifically to eliminate the social conditions that promote high death rates. Much personal suffering could be eliminated through programs tailored at reducing—and hopefully eliminating—personal conflict and aggression within communities. This would have the desirable effect of reducing personal trauma and the incidence of suicide, homicide, and injuries. Programs must also be directed at lifestyle modification to reduce the incidence of morbidities closely connected with health eroding behaviours (e.g., alcoholism, tobacco use, physical inactivity, poor diet, etc.).

In "Alcoholism and Other Social Problems in Canadian Aboriginal Communities: Policy Alternatives and Implications for Social Action," Paul Whitehead and Brenda Kobayashi delve specifically into the problem of alcohol in First Nations communities, which these authors consider to be the leading epidemiological problem for this population. Much of their focus is on what types of interventions are necessary to combat this long-standing problem. In developing their argument, the authors contrast the dominant view exemplified in the *Report of the Royal Commission on Aboriginal Peoples* with a more action-oriented perspective that emphasizes proximate causes of the problem rather than distant determinants such as colonialism and racism (which they see as embodying more of a rhetorical approach that doesn't present real solutions). Their "proximate causes model" places emphasis on the implementation of solutions that, on the whole, would have a more immediate effect in engendering positive change. The key intervention is to reduce access to alcohol, to reduce consumption as much as possible. According to the research cited by Whitehead and Kobayashi, there is now sufficient empirical proof for the efficacy of this proximate approach as validated by the experiences of many international settings and also across some Aboriginal communities. The alternative of doing nothing is clearly unacceptable.

The problem of suicide among Aboriginals is addressed by Michael Chandler in his chapter, "Cultural Continuity and the Social-Emotional Well-Being of First Nations Youth." Suicide is a pernicious problem that has plagued Aboriginal communities in Canada and in other parts of the world, such as in Australia and the United States (Trovato, 2001). The suicide problem is particularly pronounced among the youth. In Canada, First Nations youth suicide rates are five to seven times higher than among non-Aboriginal youth. Among Inuit youth, suicide rates are among the highest in the world, at 11 times the national average (Health Canada, 2008).

From a collectivist perspective, the incidence of suicide can be viewed as a mirror of the socio-emotional health of a community. This is a central assumption of Chandler's chapter. Grounded on the idea of "cultural continuity," Chandler's conceptualization of the problem allows for a clear understanding of the "why" aspect of the suicide problem. On the basis of his observations of British Columbia First Nations communities, Chandler determined that variations in communities' degree of cultural continuity—that is, a community's ability to maintain sameness (i.e., Aboriginal culture rooted in established traditions) all the while embracing positive change—explains community differences in suicide incidence. In settlements with higher levels of cultural continuity, individuals are firmly connected to others and the community at large. In such contexts, the youth are less likely to experience confusion about who they are, and they are sheltered from psycho-emotional conflict that can often lead to suicide.

The challenge to overcome this social calamity is to find and then implement suitable interventions. The usual top-down approach, of outsiders telling Aboriginals what to do, will most certainly not prove successful, according to Chandler, as most Aboriginals would find this approach demeaning. A "lateral transfer" approach is advocated, whereby Aboriginals from successful communities that have high levels of cultural continuity would pass on their knowledge to those communities in need of help.

Malcolm King approaches the broader question of Aboriginal health. In his chapter, "Addressing the Disparities in Aboriginal Health through Social Determinants Research," King reiterates the point that, for the most part, health problems in a population emanate from conditions in the social environment of the individual and the community. This perspective to the investigation of health inequities is often referred to as the "social determinants of health" approach. King opines that increased government spending on health care would do little to eliminate health disparities by race, ethnicity, or social class. He advocates the importance of reducing unemployment and poverty and improving access to higher education to help improve the health of disadvantaged groups such as Aboriginals. The epidemiological literature has firmly established that persons with higher levels of education enjoy lower risk of premature mortality as compared to those who have low education, and that the more socio-economically privileged do better in terms of physical and mental health (Kunitz, 2007; Wilkinson, 2005; Marmot & Wilkinson, 2003; Berkman & Kawachi, 2000).

If the health deficit associated with being Aboriginal were to be eliminated, there would be approximately 20,000 fewer deaths annually in the Aboriginal population, according to King. Health researchers should be more actively involved in promoting this message to government officials and to the public at large. In particular, education underachievement is an important issue in matters of health and longevity. Why then, asks King, should we not spend more resources with the goal of reducing educational disparities?

Regions that comprise the circumpolar North are predominantly inhabited by indigenous peoples. Given the paucity of data on this part of the world, T. Kue Young's chapter on "North-North and North-South Disparities: A Circumpolar Perspective" is a welcome addition to the literature. His study helps to fill our knowledge gap concerning the health of Aboriginal peoples of the circumpolar North and health disparities therein. The circumpolar North encompasses several countries, including Canada, United States (Alaska), Denmark, Iceland, Norway, Sweden, Finland, and the Russian Federation. Young examines 27 such regions of the circumpolar North in regard to various population health indicators, including infant mortality, perinatal mortality, life expectancy, incidence of tuberculosis, and cause-specific mortality rate. His main objective is to ascertain whether the people of "the North" have worse or better health than people in "the South," and whether there are significant health disparities among Nordic Peoples themselves. Statistical comparisons are made between northern regions and the nation-states these regions are part of (e.g., northern territories of Canada vs. Canada; Alaska vs. USA, etc.), and among the northern regions themselves. Young's main conclusion is that substantial disparities do exist. With regard to differences between the populations of the North and the larger populations to which they belong (e.g., Inuit in the Arctic vs. Canada as a whole), two extreme situations are identified. In Scandinavia, the northern regions are almost indistinguishable from the country-at-large in terms of most health indicators. At the opposite end are the cases of Greenland and the northern territories of Canada, especially Nunavut, where the disparities with Denmark and Canada, respectively, are substantial. Inequalities in health are correlated with regional differences in education levels and other social factors, whereas variables such as health care expenditures per capita are found to be relatively unimportant. Thus, Young's results reinforce the idea that social determinants are substantially important in the explanation of health disparities across the populations of the circumpolar North.

SOCIOLOGICAL PERSPECTIVES

Scholars are divided on the question of what causes social change. Some social scientists affirm that major transformations in society often result from the effects of long-term demographic change; others assert that social change emanates from technological developments that have the effect of altering how people lead their lives. One body of research in this area of sociological study concerns itself with the relationship of long-term mortality declines in society and their impacts on the family institution. On this theme, Uhlenberg (1980: 313) has written that many of the most significant changes in the American family over the course of the twentieth century (e.g., the changing status of children, the increasing independence of the nuclear family, the virtual disappearance of orphanages and foundling homes, the rise in societal support of the elderly, the decline in fertility, and the rise in divorce) cannot be adequately understood without clear recognition of the profound changes (i.e., declines) that have occurred in death rates. Since the family is one of the most important social groups in which an individual has membership and in which close relationships exist, it is precisely in the family sphere that we should expect death to have its greatest impact. The loss of a parent, a child, a sibling, or a spouse disrupts established family patterns and requires readjustment. As the experience of losing intimate family members recedes from being a pervasive aspect of life for individuals (in the past) to a rare event (in the present), there develops changes in family structure and relationships (Uhlenberg, 1980).

For Canada's Aboriginal peoples the transition from a high to a low mortality regime should imply that on average parents and their children live longer, and, as compared to earlier generations, the family should be a more enduring entity because, in the lower mortality regime of the present, the frequency with which a person witnesses the premature death of a loved one is greatly diminished. Children would therefore have access to a larger pool of immediate and extended family members. In a low mortality context, most fathers and mothers would see their progeny reach adulthood, and there would be greater overlap in the amount of years lived across the generations. Under a high mortality regime, however, family life is frequently disrupted by death, a large proportion of children are orphaned, and many parents experience the loss of their infants.

These ideas serve the basis of Frank Trovato's study of "Death and the Family: A Half Century of Mortality Change in the Registered Indian Population of Canada as Reflected in Periodic Life Tables." Through a life table analysis covering roughly the second half of the twentieth century, Trovato outlines how survival probabilities for this population have improved and explores the interconnectedness of mortality decline with various types of family dynamics involving children and parents. For instance, since the early 1950s, the probability of a Registered Indian child becoming orphaned has dropped significantly; a greater number of First Nations children today live to celebrate their twentieth birthday in the presence of both his/her parents; and more First Nations children have all four grandparents alive. Trovato's analysis gives cautious optimism for the future of First Nations children and their families, as increased survival probabilities set the stage for a more enduring family context. However, more research is clearly needed if we are to gain a more complete understanding of the psycho-emotional correlates of mortality decline and other demographic changes.

As already noted in regard to the Aboriginal population of Canada, ethnic mobility is now recognized as a real phenomenon and not just the consequence of data errors. Notwithstanding the growing number of demographic investigations in this area, few scholars have looked at this concept critically. Chris Andersen, in his study "Ethnic or Categorical Mobility? Challenging Conventional Demographic Explanations of Métis Population Growth," presents a critical interpretation of this concept with special reference to the case of the Métis population. He distinguishes between population change due to ethnic mobility, as understood in the demographic sense, and change due to what he calls "categorical mobility." The former refers to changes in respondents' perceptions of census classification boundaries while the latter has to do with the dichotomy of "primordialism" versus "constructivism." Primordialism is consistent with a more traditional (historical) conception of ethnicity, one based on biological rules of descent (i.e., tracing one's ethnic origin through one's male ancestor). Constructivism is diametrically opposed to this view. It is the postmodernist alternative of the conceptualization of identity, presented as a constantly modifiable (i.e., ahistorical) perception of belongingness that the individual negotiates through life depending on his/her changing circumstances.

For Andersen, sustaining an argument in favour of a primordialist notion of ethnic mobility requires a rigidly positivistic understanding of indigenous identities, which is wholly at odds with what we know about how these identities have been shaped in the heat of social and political developments in Canada. The very idea of ethnic mobility in the primordialist sense requires a philosophical commitment to the categorical stability of the census category of ethnicity (e.g., Métis) that it neither possesses nor deserves. According to Andersen, it is not necessarily peoples' ethnicity that is changing in Canadian society, but their perception of categorical boundaries and where they might fit themselves into them.

Clearly, the occurrence of ethnic mobility from census to census makes it difficult to assess real trends in the Aboriginal population because "ethnic drifters" may not be at all representative of the Aboriginal population in regard to socio-economic characteristics. They may have higher levels of education and income and thus artificially inflate the quality of life indicators observed for the Aboriginal peoples as a whole. This could potentially lead to incorrect conclusions on the state of socio-economic improvements in the Aboriginal populations, and possibly lead to wrong policies (e.g., less assistance needed). This raises an important question for further research: Are the social economic characteristics of ethnic drifters different than those of the Aboriginal population in general?

Evelyn Peters, Roger Maaka, and Ron Laliberté explore the variegated nature of Aboriginal identity in their study, "'I'm Sweating with Cree Culture not Saulteaux Culture': Urban Aboriginal Cultural Identities," by examining the concept of identity from the perspective of three dimensions: (1) the theoretica/conceptual; (2) the administrative (i.e., census practices); and (3) the empirical (how the Aboriginal person actually defines him or herself in relation to the larger ethnic or cultural subgroup). At the theoretical level, the distinction is made between the essentialist and the social constructionist perspectives. The former implies there is a stable core of the self with respect to common origin on the one hand and identity on the other. The latter perspective considers identity as a social construction (constructivist perspective). For these authors, this distinction proved useful in sorting out responses obtained in their survey of Aboriginals in the city of Saskatoon, Saskatchewan. A substantial proportion of respondents identify themselves not in the generic sense of Aboriginal identity (e.g., "Indian" or "First Nations") but rather as being part of a specific subgroup (e.g., Cree, Ojibwey, Dene, etc.). This suggests that the average person on the street is more likely to identify himself with a specific tribal or ethnic affiliation that has evolved historically (i.e., primordially) rather than with artificial, socially constructed categories (by census administrators or politicians) of Aboriginalness.

Language is an important component of ethnicity and ethnic identity. The extent to which a population maintains and promotes its language will largely determine continuity of the group. Jim Frideres in "Continuity or Disappearance: Aboriginal Languages in Canada," concerns himself with the relationship of linguistic continuity and structural factors (employment, mobility, education, community size, income, intermarriage) across Aboriginal communities. The broad picture that emerges from his analysis indicates a general regression in the use of Aboriginal language in general, though less so on reserves than off reserve areas. It appears that some tribal Aboriginal languages are slowly disappearing. What is to be done about this problem remains an important question. Some First Nations communities are dealing with this problem by implementing classes to teach their Native mother tongues (e.g., Cree, Inuktitut). In some provinces (e.g., Alberta) Native language classes are being offered at the primary and secondary school levels. Sustained promotion of Native languages in the schools would seem especially important for linguistic continuity and Aboriginalness.

Much of the Aboriginal studies literature emphasizes the problematic features of Aboriginal life and precarious socio-economic conditions. Under this "deficit paradigm" more often than not Aboriginals are characterized as victims besieged by numerous problems and challenges. Over recent years, some scholars have challenged this perspective in light of new evidence concerning the Aboriginal population. They point to the achievement of significant progress by Aboriginals toward self-government and that at the same time there has been a notable expansion of organizational capacity and socio-economic opportunities among Aboriginals, such that we are now seeing a more assertive and resilient Aboriginal community, with an increasing number of Aboriginals extricating themselves out of poverty and a marginal status (Ponting & Voyageur, 2001; Redding, 2003; Townsend & Wernick, 2008; Castellano, 2008; Jamieson, 2008).

The chapter by Cora J. Voyageur, "The Eagle Has Landed: Optimism among Canada's First Nations Community," exemplifies this new perspective. According to Voyageur, important gains have been made by First Nations, especially in the areas of communal solidarity, mutual trust, co-operative endeavours, collective interests, voluntary help associations, and social and extended family networks. These are important ingredients of "social capital," all of which are based on a deeply ingrained sense of Aboriginal culture and psychology. The First Nations population may be moving away from its "deficit" situation toward gradual socio-economic integration with the rest of Canadian society, at the same time striving to maintain its own cultural identity and traditions. First Nations may be at the cusp of a new stage of social and economic evolution, moving toward a more hopeful future.

All this optimism must be tempered by the reality that there is still a long way to go before socio-economic parity with the general Canadian population is achieved. According to the 2006 Census, there exists a wide post-secondary education deficit for First Nations adults. Only 42% of First Nations people aged 25 to 64 had completed a post-secondary education as compared with 61% of the non-Aboriginal population. In 2006, about 60% of First Nations people in the prime working ages of 25 to 54 were employed, whereas for non-Aboriginals this figure stood at almost 82%. The median income of First Nations people was $14,517, which was about $11,000 lower than the figure for non-Aboriginal Canadians. Again, according to the 2006 Census, among First Nations people living off-reserve, only about 45% owned their homes as compared to 75% among the non-Aboriginal population. Furthermore, First Nations people are more likely to live in crowded homes in need of major repairs.

In considering these statistics it is important to mention that there are important socio-economic variations within the First Nations population based on whether one lives on-reserve or off-reserve, and whether one is Status or non-Status Indian (Gionet, 2008a, 2008b). Undoubtedly, the elimination of gross disparities in socio-economic conditions between Aboriginal peoples and the rest of Canada remains one of the most important challenges for policy analysts, but just as importantly we must also examine in greater detail disparities *within* the Aboriginal population.

INTERNATIONAL PERSPECTIVES

The international studies included in this volume pertain to three categories of Aboriginals peoples. The first concerns American Indians, Australian Aborigines, and New Zealand Māoris. These are all indigenous peoples in English-speaking countries that share the common historical experience of colonization and similar (though not identical) socio-economic, demographic, and epidemiological patterns as the Canadian Aboriginals. The second category is the indigenous populations of the circumpolar North, encompassing the Scandinavian countries (i.e., Sami in Norway, Sweden, and Finland) and the Palio/Eskimo of Greenland. The third category is the Aboriginal populations of the Russian North and Siberia.

As is the case with the Registered Indians of Canada, American Indians (and Alaska Natives) have a special relationship with their federal government. The United States Congress has the duty to manage relations with the American Indians, and as such there are standing Senate committees in the Bureau of Indian Affairs and numerous special offices within most federal agencies. C. Matthew Snipp's chapter, "American Indian Education," is a synthetic history of education policies and their effects on the American Indians. American Indians display disadvantages in education attainment. Ironically, the goals embraced by the early assimilationists, which was to spread knowledge about Anglo-American culture through education, was best realized by giving American Indians and Alaska Natives more control over their schooling. According to Snipp, this control has been a significant factor for improved levels of socio-economic success for American Indians.

Similar to First Nations Peoples in Canada, the Australian Aborigines are often viewed as having strong mobility proneness for making frequent temporary moves, that is, movements between locales that are not of a permanent nature that usually involve durations of a few days to several months. According to Sarah Prout in "Interrogating the Image of the 'Wandering Nomad': Indigenous Temporary Mobility Practices in Australia," this type of movement by indigenous people differs radically from the common forms of movement in the general Australian population. For example, it often involves continual returns to a "home-base" after frequent journeys away. The home-base may be a particular community, town, or settlement. And often, there are two or more home-bases, which are viewed by the individual as an extension of one another. For many indigenous people, short-term mobility in Australia is a perpetual movement between a series of locales within which an individual has family. Thus, this type of mobility involves no particular physical home-base, and "home" for the individual is embedded within a social network of "relatedness" rather than in a specific geographic region or locale. Therefore, the commonly held perception that indigenous people are naturally inclined toward frequent mobility because of an essentially nomadic history and culture is a simplification of reality. In fact, the most pervasive theme that emerges from Prout's analysis is the highly adaptive nature of indigenous mobility practices that is not simply the product of a nomadic predisposition to wander. Many factors drive and shape their movements (not often recorded in the official statistics). These include seasonal variations in availability of bush foods, cultivation of and contestation within familial networks, the advent of various sporting and cultural festivals, the need and/or desire to access social, retail, and recreational services and opportunities, market opportunities, and ceremonial activities.

Nicholas Biddle, John Taylor, and Mandy Yap in "Closing Which Gap? Demographic and Geographic Dilemmas for Indigenous Policy in Australia" address the problem of socio-economic gaps between indigenous and non-indigenous populations in Australia. In his apology to the stolen generations in early 2008, Australian Prime Minister Kevin Rudd outlined a "new partnership on closing the gap." These targets set for the Australian Aborigines by the prime minister focus on outcomes relative to the non-indigenous Australians in the areas of health, employment, housing, and education—to halve, within a decade, the gaps in literacy, numeracy, employment outcomes and opportunities, and infant mortality rate; and within a generation, to close the large gap in life expectancy between indigenous and non-indigenous people. According to Biddle and colleagues, the full actualization of these targets is hampered by a number of demographic factors, including the geographic isolation of indigenous people in remote Australia, their high fertility rates, and their exceptionally young age structure.

In "From Common Colonization to Internal Segmentation: Rethinking Indigenous Demography in New Zealand," Tahu Kukutai and Ian Pool identify two conventions in the demography of indigenous populations. First, there is the tendency to focus on the routinized and unreflexive use of identity categories and labels in demographic research on indigenous populations. Second, many studies in this area are focused on patterns at the population (i.e., aggregate group) level. This, according to Kukutai and Pool, may actually obscure the complexity of the indigenous reality at a lower level of analysis (e.g., at the subgroup level). These authors find that there is in fact emerging evidence of significant socio-economic differentiation *within* indigenous populations. The evidence uncovered by these authors for the New Zealand Māori, Australian Aborigines, and North American (Canadian and American Aboriginals) is consistent with this assertion. Thus, we are seeing, in the new millennium, across these Aboriginal populations an emerging form of indigenous socio-economic differentiation. While this in no way implies having to abandon investigations of inter-ethnic differentials, the growing internal diversity within Aboriginal populations challenges researchers to pay greater attention to within-group demographic and socio-economic processes among Aboriginal peoples.

The chapter by Andrey Petrov looks at the indigenous peoples of the Russian North, "Indigenous Minorities and Post-Socialist Transition: A Review of Aboriginal Population Trends in the Russian North." Petrov describes the atypical demographic transition of these populations. Instead of having a fertility rate that decreases over time toward a low mortality level, mortality actually increases toward the level of fertility. Petrov also finds that there is a notable disequilibrium in the numbers of young adult males and females in the age composition of these populations (i.e., substantially fewer males than females). Although higher male mortality and emigration could account for much of this, Petrov asks whether this situation may not reflect negative ethnic mobility among young male adults in this region. By "negative ethnic mobility" Petrov means the tendency for Aboriginals to declare themselves as non-Aboriginal in the census. The extent of negative ethnic mobility in the Russian North radically distinguishes the Rusian North Aboriginals from Australian, New Zealand, Canadian, and American Aboriginal peoples.

FUTURE OUTLOOK AND CHALLENGES

In this closing section, we identify a number of research challenges and policy concerns that we see as especially important for the future of the

Aboriginal peoples over the course of the twenty-first century. The second half of the twentieth century was an eventful period in the history of Canadian Aboriginal peoples. A number of longed-for developments have occurred in unison. Along with exceptional population growth (now over one million), there has been a revival of Aboriginal culture and pride. There have been important gains in education, health, and human capital, and significant strides have been made in the struggle for recognition. These developments herald for the First Peoples a new era of promise for the future.

Social change often arises from complex interconnections across different spheres of the social world. In the demographic sphere, we may mention the near completion of demographic transition for the Aboriginal peoples. Declining fertility and increased longevity now account for unprecedented increases in population aging. The current age structure still comprises a significant proportion of children and youth, but over the course of the twenty-first century there will be a growing proportion of seniors, who will face very different needs than their youthful counterparts. For example, a growing senior population will require not only pension security but also more health care and assistance with disabilities. These eventualities will necessitate proper planning and reassessment of how resources are allocated.

Population renewal in the long term is rooted in the success with which a society promotes adequate rates of childbearing. For the Aboriginal population this is an important aspect of their future. With increased levels of urbanization and socio-economic modernization, societies shift their fertility toward what appears to be a universal norm of smaller families. Unless the Aboriginal peoples are an exception to this apparent societal tendency, their fertility rate will at some point fall to around replacement level or possibly even below replacement (i.e., less than 2.1 children per woman on average). Over the long term, this situation could translate into population decline due to negative natural increase. Unlike the rest of Canada, the Aboriginal population cannot count on immigration as a source of growth. But what may be lost in demographic quantity can be compensated to some extent with gains in demographic quality. Investing in human capital, that is, education, professional training and health, and at the same time strengthening social capital premised on the already existing ethos of co-operation and mutuality among Aboriginals, stand out as effective ways of ensuring long-term viability of First Nations in the face of a rapidly changing Canadian society.

As noted in several chapters in this volume, ethnic mobility (or ethnic drift) has been responsible for significant population growth among Aboriginals Peoples in Canada over recent years. Demographers and other social scientists interested in the quantification of Aboriginal conditions are faced with the challenge of having to find appropriate means to adequately separate the components of population growth—i.e., fertility, mortality, and migration—from the contribution to population growth due to shifts in self-identification. Proper accounting of population growth into these separate components is especially important for government policies and programs, as well as for the preparation of realistic population forecasts and projections of Aboriginal populations in Canada.

Although the future is always difficult to predict, to some extent the future can be *made* through careful planning and action. This can only be achieved through a solid understanding of the demographic, social, epidemiological, and socio-political processes already underway in the Aboriginal population of Canada. A full understanding and appreciation of the past as well as current conditions is imperative for the formulation of positive change. We have already stated that one of the most important challenges is to improve the socio-economic status of Aboriginal peoples. Perhaps the increasing urbanization of Aboriginal will open up new socio-economic opportunities not readily available on reserves. More than half of the Aboriginal population are residents of urban centres (e.g., 60% of First Nations). Their numbers in urban areas are expected to rise steadily over the course of the twenty-first century. A policy response is needed that looks at the situation of urban Aboriginals and helps make urban areas more welcoming and prosperous for Aboriginals (D'Alesio, 2011). Although historically urban living has not been a panacea for, and may have contributed to, the development of an urban underclass, the time has come to place Aboriginal urbanization at the forefront of the research and policy agenda: How can urbanization help to maximize the socio-economic opportunities of the Aboriginal peoples?

At the same time, an ongoing challenge is how to improve the status of reserves. It is doubtful that the First Peoples can survive for long as a political and cultural distinct entity without reference to a territory (even though a micro-territory). The reserve is the land base where geography, biology, and culture meet to preserve and perpetuate the Aboriginal ethnos. It is here that Aboriginals can best preserve their traditional identity, customs, and languages. It is from this base that Aboriginals, even those living in urban areas, stand to receive their cultural sustenance.

An issue of some importance concerns the growing diversity of Canada's population and the possible impact this might have on the Aboriginal population. Over the course of the next century, Canada's population will continue to be heavily driven by immigration policies. In the light of the immigration trends of the past half century, this will mean increasing population diversity along racial, ethnic, and linguistic lines. How will this play out in regard to the special status of the Aboriginal peoples as a distinct society?

We are struck by the many similarities among the indigenous populations of Canada, United States, Australia, New Zealand, and circumpolar regions. More cross-national comparative studies are needed to gain a more complete understanding of these similarities and to uncover the differences that may prevail among these different indigenous populations.

REFERENCES

Adelson, N. (2005). The embodiment of inequity: health disparities in Aboriginal Canada. *Canadian Journal of Public Health*, 96, S45–S61.

Berkman, L.F., & Kawachi, I. (Eds.). (2000). *Social epidemiology*. Oxford, UK: Oxford University Press.

Castellano, M.B. (2008). Reflections on identity and empowerment: Recurring themes in the discourse on and with Aboriginal youth. *Horizons*, 10(1), 7–12.

D'Alesio, R. (2011, April 14). Improving the urban Aboriginal experience. *The Globe and Mail*, p. A17.

Denton, T. (1972). Migration from a Canadian Indian reserve. *Journal of Canadian Studies*, 7, 54–62.

Gionet, L. (2008a). *First Nations people: Selected findings of the 2006 Census* (Catalogue No. 11-008: 52–58). Ottawa, ON: Statistics Canada.

————. (2008b). Inuit in Canada: Selected findings from the 2006 Census. *Canadian Social Trends*, 86, 59–64.

Gracey, M. & King, M. (2009). Indigenous health part 1: Determinants and disease patterns. *Lancet*, 374, 65–75.

Health Canada. (2005). *A statistical profile on the health of First Nations in Canada for the year 2000* (Catalogue No. H35-4/30-2000). Ottawa, ON: First Nations and Inuit Health Branch, Health Canada.

————. (2008). *Acting on what we know: Preventing youth suicide in First Nations*. The Report of the Advisory Group on Suicide Prevention. Retrieved from http://www.hc-sc.gc.ca/fniah-spnia/pubs/promotion/_suicide/prev_youth-jeunes/index-eng.php

Jamieson, R. (2008). The national Aboriginal achievement foundation: Aboriginal success stories. *Horizons, 10*(1), 38–39.

King, M.A. Smith, A., & Gracey, M. (2009). Indigenous health part 2: the underlying causes of the health gap. *Lancet, 374*, 76–85.

Kunitz, S.J. (2007). *The health of populations: General theories and particular realities.* Oxford, UK: Oxford University Press.

Marmot, M.G., & Wilkinson, G. (2003). *Social determinants of health: the solid facts* (2nd ed). Copenhagen: World Health Organization.

O'Donnell, V. (2008). Selected findings of the Aboriginal Children's Survey 2006: Family and community. *Canadian Social Trends, 86*, 65–72.

Olshansky, S.J., & Ault, A.B. (1986). The fourth stage of the epidemiologic transition: The age of delayed degenerative diseases. *The Milbank Quarterly, 64*(3), 355–391.

Omran, A.R. (1971). The epidemiologic transition: A theory of the epidemiology of population change. *Milbank Memorial Fund Quarterly, 49*(4), 509–538.

Ponting, R.J., & Voyageur, C.J. (2001). Challenging the deficit paradigm: Grounds for optimism among First Nations in Canada. *The Canadian Journal of Native Studies, 21*(2), 275–307.

Redding, J. (2003, August 4). Most Aboriginal children are healthy and well-adjusted. *Maclean's*, 41.

Taylor, J., & Bell, M. (2004). Continuity and change in Indigenous Australian population mobility. In J. Taylor & M. Bell (Eds.), *Population mobility and Indigenous peoples in Australasia and North America* (pp. 13–42). London, UK: Routledge.

Townsend, T., & Wernick, M. (2008). Hope or heartbreak: Aboriginal youth and Canada's future. *Horizons, 10*(1), 4–6.

Trovato F. (2001). Aboriginal mortality in Canada, the United States and New Zealand. *Journal of Biosocial Science, 33*, 67–86.

Uhlenberg, P. (1980). Death and the family. *Journal of Family History, 5*(3), 313–320.

Waldram, J.B., Herring, A., & Young, T.K. (2006). *Aboriginal health in Canada.* Toronto, ON: University of Toronto Press.

Wilkinson, R.G. (2005). *The impact of inequality: How to make sick societies healthier.* New York, NY: The New Press.

Young, K.T., & Bjerregaard, P. (Eds.). (2008). *Health transitions in Arctic populations.* Toronto, ON: University of Toronto Press.

PART I
DEMOGRAPHIC PERSPECTIVES

1

CANADA'S ABORIGINAL POPULATION

FROM ENCOUNTER OF CIVILIZATIONS TO REVIVAL AND GROWTH

Anatole Romaniuk

INTRODUCTION

The demographic literature on Canada's Aboriginal peoples is fairly extensive, but studies that take a long historical view are few and by now somewhat dated.[1] This study endeavours to capture the broad configuration of the Aboriginal peoples' demographic evolution from early contact with Europeans to the present. The main stages thereof are identified, and the underlying historical context explored. While taking stock of the past and present, the study will also address the demographically driven policy challenges that emerge for Canada's First Nations in the twenty-first century.

In the four centuries since the Europeans first set foot in this country, the demography of the Aboriginal peoples has taken dramatic twists, from near extinction to impressive recovery. However, their resilience against superior forces, vitality, and ability to recover under the most adverse of conditions should not blind us from recognizing the inherent vulnerability of a minority numerically weaker, fragmented, and widely dispersed that is still contending with many attributes of an underprivileged class of people.

As we proceed with the review of Aboriginal peoples' major demographic shifts over time, we will come to recognize, in its variegated manifestations, the potency of culture in shaping reproductive behaviours. We shall also take cognizance of the fact that, unlike immigrant minorities, this population represents a sui generis entity in Canada, struggling for the recognition and preservation of its identity and special political status. Canada's Aboriginal minority may be looked upon as part of a wider family of indigenous minorities across North America, Siberia (Bobrick, 1992; Forsyth, 1994) and the world, including the Aborigines of Australia (Grey, 1990) and the Māori of New Zealand (Pool, 1991). They are part of what some call the "Fourth World."

The Native peoples' demographic evolution can best be comprehended when examined against the historical background of the encounter between the Aboriginal and European civilizations. This encounter is to be understood as a dynamic process that is still unfolding, and not as a dated event. A brief sketch of this historical encounter is in order.

The European colonization of the vast territory that is today's Canada was piecemeal, spanning over three centuries or so. As late as 1793, on his northeast exploratory voyage along the river that bears his name, Alexander Mackenzie reports that the Indians he met on his way "had heard, indeed, of white men, but this was the first time that they had ever seen a human being of a complexion different from their own" (1911, Vol. II: 89). The two civilizations at that time of the encounter were at vastly different technological and economic stages of development. The ultimate takeover of Canada by the Europeans was the consecration of "[the] superiority of the gun over the bow and arrow, of the steel axe over the stone axe, of the steel plough over the stone hoe or digging-stick" (Sametz, 1964: 33).

Historically, the relations between Natives and newcomers have taken various turns. Economically, from the outset and well into the nineteenth century, the fur trade (Ray, 1998) dominated the encounter. Eventually, the fur trade led to the depletion of game, which further upset the precarious balance between nature and population. Capitalism largely transformed the country's economics and demographics as European immigration reached new heights. However, unlike the long period of partnership that characterized the fur trade, the Natives hardly played a role in the emerging new Canadian (European) society. They were relegated to passive, helpless, and often troubled onlookers of what was happening around them. By contrast, the advent of the welfare economy in the aftermath of the Second World War had a salutary effect on their demographic fortune.

Politically, too, this encounter underwent significant shifts over time. In the earlier days, the relation between the two communities, though occasionally marred by armed conflict, was one of coexistence and accommodation, in many ways symbiotic (in the instance of the fur trade). However, as the colonial powers took hold, the lot of the indigenous inhabitants turned into one of political and economic dependence—the government tightened its control over their destiny and aimed for their ultimate assimilation. After World War II, the Canadian government pursued integration, and, as of the late twentieth century, self-government is on the policy agenda. We shall see how these and similar economic and political factors played out to influence the demographic behaviour of Canada's Native peoples.

Taking a historical perspective, the main demographic stages of the Aboriginal peoples can be stated concisely. After what was likely in the long run a quasi-stationary demographic state, punctuated by ups and downs due to natural disasters and inter-tribal warfare, Aboriginal peoples underwent almost three centuries of depopulation with the coming of the Europeans. Stabilization and a slow recovery followed at the turn of the twentieth century. After World War II, a notable dynamic growth followed a rapid decline in mortality, on the one hand, and an increase in natural fertility, on the other. One of the remarkable features of the Aboriginals' postwar demographic experience was the advent of a cycle of natural fertility increase associated with the early modernization processes. Eventually, by around 1970, they entered a demographic transition from a traditional high to a modern low fertility, almost a century after Canadians of European stock. Today, at the beginning of the twenty-first century, the transition is well underway, but they still have some way to go before reaching parity with the latter.

With these preliminary remarks in mind as to the overall historical setting in which Aboriginal peoples have evolved demographically, we shall take a closer look, chronologically, at each of the demographic stages just identified, starting with early contact—a subject upon which the knowledge marshalled remains scant and dubious, and which has stirred the most controversy. To give substance to the description of each demographic stage, I have endeavoured to elaborate on the underlying social, political, medical, and economic contexts of each stage.

DEMOGRAPHIC REGIME OF THE PRE- AND EARLY CONTACT ERA: A PRECARIOUS DEMOGRAPHIC EQUILIBRIUM

The size of Canada's Native population upon the arrival of the Europeans has been and still is a hotly disputed subject. Emotions, ideologies, and self-serving interests sometimes colour the discussion. In the words of the historian Olive Dickason (1992), "The earliest European accounts of the New World all spoke of the 'great multitudes of people'; it was later, when coloni-zation was gaining momentum, that the large stretches of territories were found unoccupied, and the notion of 'empty continent' gained currency" (27). There has been no shortage of attempts, through a variety of tech-niques, to come up with some figures for Canada's Aboriginal population prior to or upon early days of contact with Europeans. Thus, Thornton (1987) has estimated a population in excess of two million "north of the United States" (242). To arrive at this figure, he applied the so-called "standard hemispheric depopulation ratio," that is, the ratio of the presumed pre-contact population to the lowest population revealed by modern censuses, which he assumed to be 20 to 1 or 25 to 1 (1987: 31). Others have produced much lower figures. Mooney (1928) estimated the Aboriginal population of America north of the Rio Grande to be 1.2 million, and that of Canada to be close to 200,000. His calculation relied on historical material of individual tribes, by adding the tribe-by-tribe estimates. Similar figures were advanced by Kroeber (1939), who resorted to a technique that combined historical records and approximations of the carrying capacity of the relatively homo-geneous natural areas that he had established for that purpose. Later, the Canadian demographer, Hubert Charbonneau, put forth a ballpark figure of 300,000 for Canada's Aboriginal population in the early contact years. He derived this figure from the estimates available from different tribal sources, which survived to the twentieth century, by upwardly adjusting the figures by 40% to make allowances for assumed omissions and understatements (Charbonneau, 1984: 31).

A review of the estimation (and underlying methodology) of the Aboriginal population in the western hemisphere has been provided by Henry F. Dobyns (1966). The "standard hemispheric depopulation ratio" used in these estimates, in particular, has been the subject of devastating critiques by Peter Kunstadter (1966) and such well-known demographers as Keyfitz and Carmagnani (1966). Though methodologically more sound, even Charbonneau's estimate is not problem-free. Charbonneau had to make arbitrary assumptions about the upward adjustments for presumed undercounting. Nor can we be sure that all the tribes that no longer exist have been accounted for.

This said, I do not wish to give the impression of being dismissive of the, I would say, almost heroic attempts to arrive at least at some guess estimates, not the least out of intellectual curiosity. How can we not avoid asking a question such as, what might have been America's population before Columbus set foot thereon? But, "Estimating the Unknown," the title of William Denevan's (1992) introductory chapter in his edited collection *The Native Population of the Americas in 1492*, is in itself evocative of the hazards of such an enterprise. As for myself, other than reporting these various population figures as a matter of record, I do not feel I can add anything constructive to the already long and frustrating debates.

Uncertain as we are of the population numbers, we can nevertheless, in very broad terms, piece together a picture of what most likely was the demographic regime in those earlier days of contact. To recreate that time's demographic regime, we combine two approaches. One is inferential, based on the analysis of the fundamental factors known to have governed the life of Aboriginal inhabitants. There are four sets of such factors—biotic environment, technology, living or subsistence conditions, and political organization. The second approach, which we may call observational, makes use of the earlier explorers' and administrators' accounts. Although fleeting and space-confined by necessity, and admittedly sometimes biased, explorers' accounts are highly edifying as to the Aboriginal settlement patterns, living conditions, family, marriage customs, and sexual mores.

In what follows, we shall deal first with those factors that affected mortality, survival, on the one hand, and procreation, fertility, on the other, and then see how they coalesce to produce the sought-for demographic regime at the pre- and early contact era.

Mortality And Survival

Aboriginal inhabitants of Canada contended with harsh climatic conditions for most of the year. They had to hunt, trap, fish, and gather for sustenance, which, in the words of Dickason, is "land-intensive" (1992). The state of technology was that of the late Stone Age. Stone axes, digging sticks, or hoes with blades made from shells were the tools used in agriculture and housekeeping. There was no practical application of the wheel for transportation or manufacturing. The only domestic animal was the dog, which was useful for transportation and hunting but of little value for either food or clothing (Jenness, 1977). Horses came into play in Canada later in time.

Clearly, under such biotic and technological conditions, the carrying capacity of the land and the productivity of work must have been exceedingly low. Widely dispersed nomadic or semi-nomadic settlements reported by the early explorers, missionaries, and pioneers stand out as the dominant landscape in those early days of contact. In his exploration of the St. Lawrence and the Great Lakes, Chevalier de La Salle speaks of the "unbroken wilderness" and "dreadful conditions of savages" (Abbott, 1898: 92). Alexander Mackenzie (1911) makes similar remarks on the whole region north of the St. Lawrence and far into Hudson's Bay: it was "a vast area inhabited only by a few savages, whose numbers are proportionate to the scantiness of the soil" (Vol. II: 343).

Contrasting with this picture of a widely predominant demographic void are two better-populated regions: one is in the west, on the Pacific shore with its abundant sea resources and relatively advanced storage and preservation technology; the other region coincides with the semi-agricultural land along the St. Lawrence River.

But even in the latter region the numbers were not large. The allegedly "very populous" sedentary Huron nation, which, as Father Paul le Jeune reports, presented "attractive prospects for missionary work to spread the word of Gospel," turned out to be 12,000 when the census was taken in 1639 (Mealing, 1963: viii). The mighty Iroquois nations that occupied relatively large and fertile lands overarching the present day US–Canada border were estimated at 38,000, according to Kroeber (1939), and 56,000, according to Price (1979: 44). And, the Seneca nation, "the most numerous of all Iroquois counted about a thousand or twelve hundred men capable of bearing arms" (Kellogg, 1917: 180). The strength of the invading armies, as described in many early reports, were in the hundreds, rarely in the thousands and never in the tens of thousands—an indication of a rather limited demographic capacity to raise armies of a certain size even among such powerful, warlike nations as the Iroquois.

As one moves southward, deeper into today's United States, to climatically more hospitable lands, the landscape of settlements appears to be more hospitable. Samuel de Champlain remarks, "Pour ce qui est de midi de la grande revière [Saint Laurent] elle est fort peuplée, et beaucoup plus

que le coté du nord" (Dumont, 1962: 190).[2] The impression conveyed by
the explorers' reports is that of a settlement pattern of clusters of ethnocultural communities that were separated by considerable stretches of
Niemandsland, as it were, to ensure a safe distance in case of unexpected
attacks by feuding tribes.

Reports by pioneers also abound with references to exceedingly poor
living conditions and the lack of the most elementary notions of hygiene
and sanitation. Thus, Father Marquette, a member of Chevalier de La Salle's
expedition, was struck by the habitat of a cluster of Indian wigwams several
leagues from the mouth of the Chicago River: "The savages were poor, but
few in numbers, and their abodes comfortless" (Abbott, 1898: 62). Likewise
for the Miami tribe; it was reported that "a few wretched wigwams were
scattered over snow-white plains, where poverty, destitution, and repulsive
social habits reigned, such as perhaps never witnessed in civilised life" (63).
The depressingly poor state of the housing shocked many explorers and led
them to lament the suffering they had to endure while lodging with their
indigenous hosts. Father Marquette remarked, "You cannot stand upright
in this house, as much on the account of the low roof as of the suffocating
smoke" (Abbott, 1898: 62–63). "It was a martyrdom. It almost killed me,"
bewailed Father Paul le Jeune in *The Jesuit Relations* (Mealing, 1963: 32–33).
Blindness and coughing, for example, were often observed. Note, in passing,
that poor housing conditions continue to be a reality for many Aboriginal
peoples today.

As much as these and similar observations may shock the sensibility of
modern man—Aboriginal and non-Aboriginal alike—those were the conditions of the Neolithic man generally and not just of the Canadian Natives.
The Neolithic population was living in a precarious, volatile equilibrium
with its natural environment. Under such conditions one would expect
the subsistence and environment-related causes of deaths to be widely
prevalent. Reports by explorers, missionaries, and early administrators
frequently mention famine and death from starvation. Hunting accidents,
drowning, exposure to frost, and food poisoning to name but a few environmental and occupational hazards, as well as the dangers associated with
the nomadic mode of life, were significant causes of mortality. Note that
some of these causes, like poisoning and violent accidents, are still prevalent today. Infanticide and the abandonment of the old and impaired (which
to some extent have survived to more recent times) are known to have been

practised to varying degrees as a survival strategy under continuous eco-logical stress (Balikci, 1972; Jenness, 1977; Thwaites, 1899, Vol. 1: 257).

We hardly know anything about specific diseases prior to the coming of the Europeans. The only sources from which some inferences can be drawn about possible diseases are the preserved and mummified skeletons and dentures found in different parts of the two Americas, which may be relevant to one climatic area but not to the others. The single most important disease that has been suggested from such remains is that of parasitic infections and various types of worms, like hookworm and roundworm in the diges-tive system, which caused anaemia and compromised the immune system. However, the incidences of parasitic infection tend to decrease as we move from warm tropical areas up north to cold areas. On the other hand, animal food consumption, predominant in the north, increased the risk of meat-born parasitic contaminations. The other disease that might have been present in some strains is what is known as tuberculosis. (For a good sum-mary of pre-contact diseases see Waldram, Herring, & Young, 2006.)

On the other hand, no evidence has been found of the epidemics that re-currently swept over the Old World and took a heavy toll on its populations. This perceived absence of a wide range of Old World epidemics—which as we will see later brought so much devastation to the Natives in the wake of the encounter with Europeans—has led some students to question whether mortality among western hemisphere inhabitants was that high in pre-contact times.

While compelling, the subsistence thesis—the scarcity of resources and recurrent famines that kept population growth in check—might not in itself be sufficient to explain the underpopulation of early North America. At best it may attest to the truth of the precarious living conditions in the northern regions. But how then does one explain the underpopulation of the regions south of the border with all their natural beauty, exuberance, and abundance, which caught the eye and admiration of explorers? As Father Membré, one of La Salle's companions on his 1679 journey along the majestic Mississippi River remarked, "These prairies are capable of sustain-ing immense population....These fields are full of all kinds of game....Peach trees are so loaded in the gardens of the Indians, that they have to prop up the branches" (Abbott, 1898: 264–265).

It follows that none of the three population-depressing factors—biotic environment, technology, and subsistence or living conditions—offers a sufficient explanation of the demographic regime of underpopulation, which in all likelihood prevailed in Canada in the pre-or early contact era. We are left with the one remaining population-related factor: the weakness of the socio-political structure and organization. The prevalent political organization was the band or tribe, more rarely chiefdom. As such it was ill-equipped to secure internal peace and to protect the tribe from outside predators. In their writings, missionaries and administrators frequently mentioned blood revenges and feuds. Public justice was either non-existent or ineffective. Inter-tribal war was endemic, typical of most prehistoric stateless communities, a kind of Hobbesian state of "war of all against all." Mackenzie remarks, "There is no regular government among them...no sufficient communication to defend themselves against an invading enemy, to whom they fall an easy prey" (1911, Vol. II: 322). The narratives of explorers and missionaries abound with warfare horror stories: "Around the lovely shores of Lake Peoria there had been seventeen flourishing Indian villages. These were all destroyed, in awful scenes of conflagration and massacre. The survivors fled beyond the Mississippi, six hundred miles from their desolated homes. And even to these regions the ferocious Iroquois pursued them, thirsting for blood and scalps" (Abbott, 1898: 219).

Needless to say, the history of humankind is full of horrors of warfare, and no one should point the finger at Aboriginal peoples as the culprits of such abominations. But what sets the Neolithic society apart is its narrow-based political organization, if any, and the nature of the warfare it waged. Because of the lack of larger stable state structures, the victorious parties were unable to integrate the vanquished tribes and thus increase their population and extend their territory. Such practices as the adoption of war prisoners or their integration into the tribe, even in an inferior social status as slaves, were apparently limited. The nature of the warfare itself had its peculiarities. Rather than a means for territorial and demographic aggrandisement, war seems to have been an end in itself, a kind of self-perpetuating culture (Kroeber, 1939; Farb, 1972). Preventive strife was a self-preservation strategy, according to Kroeber, the well-known American anthropologist: "The group that tried to shift its value from war to peace was almost certainly doomed to early extinction" (148). He makes the case, whereby the main cause of the underpopulation of North America is to be found in the culture, meaning the warfare culture, rather than in its subsistence resources. Speaking of eastern American agriculturists, Kroeber argues that any surplus in wealth only increased the potential for war, but that "war kept the population down to the point where more agriculture was not needed" (149), so the process became a vicious circle.

We have dealt so far with what in Malthusian parlance is called the "positive checks" on the population, i.e., mortality, whether natural or man-made. Let's turn now to fertility, the other component of natural population growth.

Procreation and Fertility

Explorers and early pioneers were unimpressed by the prolificity of Native families. They were struck by the small number of offspring and the frequency of barrenness among women. Father Gabriel Sagard (1969), in his voyage in 1623 through the Huron lands, offers enlightening observations on the state of both mores and childbearing. He observed that though women seemed to desire many children for their old age, they were not as prolific as one would expect: "les femmes n'y sont pas si fécondes que par deçà: peut-être tant à cause de leur lubricité, que du choix de tant d'hommes" (111).[3] Samuel de Champlain, the "Father of New France," made similar observations about tribes inhabiting the St. Lawrence. While some of these explorers may no doubt have confused high child mortality, i.e., the small numbers of surviving offspring, with low fertility, some of their explanations are nevertheless plausible.

First and foremost, due to the absence of animal milk or equivalent natural substitutes, mothers breastfed their children over a long duration, and this in turn tended to depress fecundability and space pregnancies further apart. The delaying effects of breastfeeding on the resumption of ovulation, and hence of pregnancy, is well documented in the demographic literature (Romaniuk, 1981a; 1981b).

Second, there were impediments to pregnancy that could best be subsumed under the label ecological hardship. Malnutrition, not to speak of outright sporadic starvation, poor hygiene, and accidents due to the nomadic life in a harsh long winter habitat may have delayed conception and caused pregnant women to miscarry or abort. Jean Talon, the first intendant of New France, its first official statistician and a keen observer of indigenous lives, in an apparent comparison to French colonists in his *Mémoires*, refers to Native women's barrenness, protracted nursing, and hard work: "Il n'en est pas de même des sauvages dont les femmes sont assez stériles, soit que le grand travail auquel elles sont obligées retard leur portée, soit qu'elles nourrissent trop longtemps leurs enfants à leur lait" (Talon, 1976: 355).[4] Similar views were later echoed by Alexander Mackenzie in his voyage through northwestern Canada in 1792–1793: "The women are not very prolific: a circumstance which may be attributed in great measure, to the hardships that they suffer, for except a few small dogs, they alone perform that labour which is allotted to beasts in other countries" (1911, Vol. II: 23–24). Similar observations have been made regarding some tribes south of the border: "It is evident to anyone acquainted with this race that the birth rate is abnormally low"; "Bareness is common among Chinooks tribe." Among the Nootka tribe, "women rarely have two or three children" (Aberle, 1931: 63). These and similar observations led A.M. Carr-Saunders (1922), the well-known demographer of earlier generations, to conclude that fecundity does increase with civilization.

Third, there are those factors that can be categorized under conjugal instability and promiscuity, both of which may delay pregnancy. Father Gabriel Sagard, like many other observers of the early and later contact period, makes the case for a rather fluid notion of marriage among some Native tribes. Regarding the Hurons, he observed, "Plusieurs jeunes hommes, au lieu de se marier, ont souvent les filles à pot et feu, qu'ils appellent non-femmes, ekenhona, parce que la cérémonie du mariage n'en a point été faite, mais asqua, c'est-à-dire compagne ou plutôt concubine. Et ils vivent ensemble pour autant de temps qu'il leur plait, sans que cela empeche le jeune homme et la fille d'aller voir parfois leurs autres amis et amies librement et sans craindre de reproche ni blame" (Sagard, 1969: 106). He goes on to point out the promiscuity in the Huron society. "et les jeunes hommes de Canada et particulièrement du pays de nos Hurons, sont toujours en licence de s'adonner au mal sitôt qu'ils peuvent, et les jeunes filles de se prostituer sitôt qu'elles sont capables" (105–106).[5] In his *Voyage*, Mackenzie also mentions the rather lax attitudes toward extramarital relations, notwithstanding the severe penalties women may have had to endure for their infidelity at the hand of jealous men: "Chastity is not considered as a necessary virtue"; "it seldom happens that a woman is without her favourite, who, in the absence of the husband, exacts the same submission, and practices the same tyranny" (1898, Vol. 2: 310). Here again, I have no way to attest to how universal those sexual and marital mores were among Amerindians of those days. One undisputable factor remains, and a decisive one in childbearing—prolonged breastfeeding.

On the other hand, I have found no specific references to sexually transmitted diseases in the earlier explorers' reports. But this does not mean there were none, given the rather lax sexual mores reported for some tribes. The quote above from Sagard (1969: 111)—"Les femmes n'y sont pas si fécondes...peut-être tant à cause de leur lubricité, que du choix de tant d'hommes"—points out the cause of the problem. Note that syphilis among some tribes, namely on the west coast, was reported later, though suspected to have been imported by European sailors.

The other factor to be considered about procreative behaviours is abortion. Was it practised, and if so, how prevalent was this, the oldest practice of birth control? According to some observers, Native women seemed to have reverted to abortion. "Abortions were frequent," according to *The Jesuit Relations and Allied Documents* (Thwaites, 1899, Vol. 1: 257). The willingness to artificially terminate the pregnancy and/or to put an infant daughter to death immediately after birth can be attributed to harsh economic conditions and women's low status. "They often sought to escape the added burdens of maternity, especially in seasons of want, by the twin practice of pre-natal abortion and infanticide," notes Diamond Jenness (1977: 52). As many primitive populations of the world, the Aboriginal peoples may have known and actually practised some forms of contraception (Vogel, 1970), but more likely occasionally rather than systematically as a means of birth control. Nor is the effectiveness of these practices borne out conclusively by various studies on this continent as well as elsewhere in the world, in pre-modern times.

Demographic Regime

I have drawn a rather grim picture, some would say unkind, of Aboriginal peoples' lives in those bygone days. But those were more than likely conditions of the Neolithic man wherever he has lived, in America, Europe, or elsewhere. The demographic regime was that of a population in precarious equilibrium with its natural environment. Mortality fluctuated widely due to the hazards of nature and arguably frequent inter-tribal warfare.

Fertility, on the other hand, might not have been high enough to offset the excess of deaths to ensure a sustained population growth. Our analysis of reproductive conditions in those days—presumed high pregnancy waste due to a nomadic mode of life and poor sexual hygiene, marital instability observed among some tribes, and most importantly prolonged breastfeeding causing delays in the resumption of ovulation and longer lactational amenorrhea—has led us to conclude that the prevailing reproductive regime may best be qualified as suboptimal, that is, one that falls far short of the reproductive potential of women under normal reproductive conditions.

For brevity's sake, the demographic regime of pre- and early contact among Aboriginal peoples may best be termed the regime of precarious demographic equilibrium of a stationary population over the long run.

COLLAPSE OF DEMOGRAPHIC EQUILIBRIUM AND DEPOPULATION

The conquest of Canada by the French, followed by the British, upset the existing precarious demographic equilibrium. A number of events combined to set off the spiral of depopulation as the conquest took hold and expanded. There are those that affected health and mortality directly, those that adversely altered the Aboriginals' relation to the natural environment, those that caused inter-tribal warfare, and those that were liable for social disorganization.

The single most important factor in the Native peoples' demographic demise was the introduction of new contagious diseases by European colonists. Measles, scarlet fever, diphtheria, chicken pox, smallpox, typhus, typhoid fever, malaria, yellow fever, and possibly tuberculosis were some of the diseases brought in by the Europeans. These diseases were all the more lethal to the host population as it lacked natural immunity. Nor did these diseases strike out at a single point in time; rather, they reoccurred over a protracted time—probably over three centuries—with the opening of Canada to European colonization. The spread took epidemic proportions and decimated entire tribes. Nor were these diseases limited to the contact areas; they often travelled faster, well ahead of the white man's advances. Noble David Cook (1998) may have somewhat overstated the case when he attributes the conquest of the Americas to the epidemics of infectious diseases imported by Europeans—"[these] diseases conquered the Americas before the sword could be unsheathed"—but he is not very far off the mark. The destructive processes across the American continent were more complex and varied. As the author of a highly enlightening study, *Conquest: The Destruction of the American Indios*, M. Livi-Bacci puts it, "the Conquest delivered a shock to the entire indigenous demographic system: survivorship, unions, reproduction, mobility and migration. The greatest impact was naturally that of new diseases...so we have to assign them major 'responsibility' for the losses of human life in the initial phases" of the conquest (2008: 231).

In Canada, smallpox was by far the greatest killer until immunization was introduced late in the nineteeth century. According to John Heagerty in his *Four Centuries of Medical History in Canada* (1928), "there is little doubt that smallpox was one of the chief factors in the extermination of the red man" (65). It has even been alleged that smallpox might have been used as germ warfare against the Indians. At least one case was documented, which involved a stratagem offered by Sir Jeffery Amherst to Col. Henry Bouquet in his 1763 campaign against the Indians: "Could it not be contrived to send the smallpox among these disaffected tribes of Indians? We must on this occasion use every stratagem in our power to reduce them" (Heagerty, 1928: 43). The scourge was so feared that the menace alone of letting it loose could bring certain tribes into submission. "The most dreadful epidemic of small-pox in the history of Canada was that of the years 1755 to 1757," when "all activities, even war which was being constantly waged, ceased" (Heagerty, 1928: 39).

Epidemics, and again most conspicuously smallpox epidemics, impacted Aboriginal tribes, not only in terms of their demographics but also in terms of the politics vis-à-vis the advancing European power and inter-tribal power struggles. Clark Wissler (1936) goes as far as to argue that epidemics played a role in redrawing the ethnic map: "it is possible...that the small-pox broke the power of the Gros Ventre in 1780, giving the Assiniboine a chance to dominate and that when the latter fell victims to the disease in 1838, the Cree profited thereby reaching their peak in numbers about 1860" (19). In turn, "the extinction of the buffalo around 1880 should have effectively checked Cree expansion" (19).

The introduction of firearms and horses (that predated guns) to the Canadian Prairies, coupled with the expansion of the fur trade, significantly modified the relationship between the Natives and their natural habitat (see, among others, Roe, 1951, 1955; Ewers, 1969; Ray, 1998). At first, these technological novelties had beneficial results in that they enhanced humankind's control over the natural resources and made it easier to acquire food. Through the fur trade, new commodities, particularly household items, made their way into the Native lifestyle, adding a modicum of comfort. It has even been argued that the arrival of the horse helped to alleviate the hardships of women, on whose shoulders traditionally befell the heavy task of carriers in the frequent wanderings of a people prone to nomadism.

But the victory over the natural environment and the benefits derived from the fur trade were short-lived. It was a Pyrrhic victory. It did not take long for the acquired marginal improvements in material well-being (and to some extent political independence) to evolve into economic hardship and in some places outright disaster. With the introduction of the gun and the horse and the ever-growing commercialization of fur and the wasteful slaughter of large animals, by indigenous peoples and later by the European settlers, the land was virtually stripped of its food and fur-bearing game. The caribou in the east and the sea otter on the northwest coast almost vanished. Commercial overkill of whales and walruses led to widespread starvation in the Arctic and sub-Arctic in the 1870s. Buffalo were particularly affected. The saga of their indiscriminate mass slaughter is well known (Roe, 1951; Sandoz, 1978). The buffalo, which inhabited the vast regions of the plains in America west of the Mississippi River and in western Canada, estimated in the millions, was the Plain Indians' mainstay: "To the Plain Indians, the animal [buffalo] furnished a preponderantly large proportion of their daily necessities in food, together with clothing, housing, fuel, tools, weapons" (Roe, 1951: 197). After 1830, the era of systematic destruction, which was triggered and sustained by the fur trade, culminated in "the shocking holocausts [of the buffalo] of 1870–74 in the south and in the final one of 1880–93 in the northern habitat" (Roe, 1951: 191). As if these calamities were not enough, Natives' economic base, their hunting and food gathering grounds, were severely curtailed by land expropriation and settlers' land grabbing. All this led to the pauperization of the Natives and ultimately to their economic and political dependence, their confinement to reserves and to handouts by the state.

Warfare did not subside. On the contrary, caught up in the French and British colonial power rivalries, inter-tribal conflicts grew in scope and, due to firearms, in destructiveness. The expansion of the fur trade and the depletion of game led to frequent battles over hunting grounds. Horses enabled warfare to be carried further afield where foot soldiers could not have ventured.

To this catalogue of the destructive forces surrounding Aboriginal life, there is yet one left: alcohol. Alcohol addiction spread rapidly through the trading companies. Alcohol was used to reward the Aboriginals for their services. Aboriginal people, unlike some European populations with relatively high consumption levels of alcoholic beverages, lacked the moderating mechanism of alcohol consumption. Binge drinking was the typical pattern of alcohol enjoyment. Rampant alcoholism was and still is probably the chief culprit destructive to both family and community cohesion and to the individuals themselves.

The foregoing aimed primarily at exposing the state of Aboriginal health and mortality. Yet, we don't know how these calamities may have affected procreative behaviour; in fact, no such question has been asked as far as I know. But there can be little doubt that, while causing so many deaths, the epidemics also had some direct or indirect debilitating effects on procreation. It has been medically documented that certain contagious diseases such as measles may cause permanent sterility in men and women (McFalls & McFalls, 1984). All we can say with a reasonable degree of supposition is that the birth rate, already relatively low in the pre- and early contact times, may have fallen even lower as a result of widespread disease. Hence, fertility was a factor, albeit far less so than mortality, in the depopulation of Aboriginal peoples that accompanied the conquest and early colonization. Note, for this long-drawn period of depopulation I put forth somewhat arbitrarily a figure of an average rate of 35 births per 1,000 population. (For a fertility history reconstructed, see Figure 1.1.)

In sum, the Aboriginal peoples of Canada, in post-contact times and way into the second half of the nineteenth century, were plagued by distractive forces of human lives with increasing intensity as they came more and more into contact with and under the influence of the newcomers. There is general agreement among demographers that since the opening of Canada to the Europeans and until almost 1900, the excess of deaths over births has been the rule rather than the exception. Charbonneau, in his historical study (1984), speaks of three centuries of Amerindian depopulation.

DEMOGRAPHIC STABILIZATION AND RECOVERY

The process of depopulation reached its nadir at about 100,000 inhabitants by the turn of the twentieth century, and a slow journey toward demographic recovery began thereafter. Underlying this at first sluggish but predictable recovery was the progressive control over, and elimination of, the very same causes that were responsible for the depopulation.

First and foremost, the fight against the epidemics took a turn for the better. Inoculation against smallpox was intermittently and locally applied early and routinely late in the nineteenth century. It is also likely that with time the Indians acquired some natural immunity against imported contagious diseases. Interbreeding with Europeans probably contributed to this natural resistance as well, according to Charbonneau (1984). But many other infectious diseases, particularly influenza, continued to wreak havoc on their health. Tuberculosis remained pervasive, often fatal, until the advent of penicillin and antibiotics shortly after World War II. The disease thrived, particularly on the reserves with its crowded housing and proximities, and even more so in the residential schools. The Inuit population remained the last hotbed of tuberculosis well into the 1960s, when the disease declined steeply.

Then Pax-Canadiana brought an end to inter-tribal warfare, which was one of the major causes of the underpopulation of North America. The last inter-tribal battle of importance was fought in 1870 at the Oldman River between the Blackfoot and the Cree. Owing to the government relief policy, famines and starvation subsided.

These changes for the better caused a moderate but steady population increase. According to statistics that the government began collecting in the second half of the nineteenth century, the Aboriginal population, estimated at 107,000 in 1901, rose to 133,000 in 1931 and to 166,000 in 1951, representing an average annual increase of 0.73% and 1.11% over the two periods, respectively. One cannot be certain whether this increase reflected demographic gains, better enumeration or both. Inferentially, however, one can well argue that Native peoples were at long last climbing out of their long-drawn demographic demise. Though epidemics subsided, mortality was still high. The question may be asked whether indigenous peoples have recovered their traditional pre-contact and early contact childbearing habits. It is possible—to the tune of 40 births per 1,000 population. In other words, fertility has probably recovered its traditional moderately high level, sufficient to offset mortality, still relatively high, and even to generate a modest rate of natural population growth.

As Amerindians took the road of demographic recovery, the second half of the nineteenth century saw a string of events that were bound to determine their fate as a distinct cultural and political entity in the long run.

The jurisdictional transfer in 1867 of Rupert's Land and the North-Western Territories—a huge mass of land that was home to numerous indigenous tribes—was a watershed not only in Canada's history but also in Native peoples' history. Native people, who up to that point in time enjoyed a practically uninhibited freedom to pursue their traditional activities and way of governance, were brought under the rule of the Canadian government. The construction of the Canadian Pacific Railway, linking eastern and western Canada, was a powerful impetus to the unity of the country and to its economic expansion and massive westward European settlement. Yet, at the same time, the encroachments on Native lands by white settlers and the intervention by Canadian authorities in matters of local governance unleashed recurrent political tensions. The uprisings led by the Métis Louis Riel in 1867 to 1870 and in 1885 can be seen as the last stand of a nascent nation that was committed to preserving its traditional ways of life against the advancing frontiers of an "alien civilisation" (Stanley, 1960: 49).

Of historical importance was the adoption of the Indian Act in 1876. Indians acquired a special political status in Confederation, which was bound to have far-reaching political, social, and economic consequences. The policy concerning reservations, whereby tracts of land were set aside for Amerindians' exclusive use, was pressed forward with greater vigour. The Crown treaties, which compensated Natives in cash and in kind in exchange for the renunciation of their ancestral lands, were also pushed forward. Segregation in the form of reservations, along with many other restrictive measures, went hand-in-hand with attempts to assimilate them into the dominant society. Banning certain rituals and traditions, replacing traditional chiefs with elected chiefs who reported directly to the dominion administration, and removing children from their parents for the duration of their education (the so-called residential schools) are instances of interference in the lives of the Native peoples, with assimilation as the ultimate goal. Amerindians, in the words of Dickason, became "the most regulated peoples in Canada...Their lives would be interfered with at every turn, down to the personal level" (1992: 283). The offshoot of these increasingly controlling colonial policies was their growing dependence on the government for sustenance. In the parlance of the time, they became "wards" of the government. Thus, the dependency mentality that was to develop into a long-standing trait was born and, as we shall see, was bound to affect their procreative behaviour, and even, to some extent, their health. Then again, government-assisted projects to steer Amerindians away from traditional activities were deemed expedient as a matter of policy. With the depletion of game and the encroachment by white settlers on their hunting grounds, they could no longer rely on nature for sustenance.

To summarize, the second half of the nineteenth and the first half of the twentieth century have been marked by two opposing tendencies as far as demographics of Aboriginal peoples goes: on the one hand, there was slow but predictable demographic recovery due to the progressive elimination of epidemics, but, on the other, policies of assimilation and disenfranchisement tended to undercut their numbers. Some Amerindians moved out of reserves, while others were disenfranchised by choice or force for one reason or another. According to the historian Miller (1989) the government moved to deliberately keep the size of the Indian population under its jurisdiction as small as possible.

History is replete with unexpected and unintended twists and ironies. Not infrequently actions taken with a particular purpose in mind unwittingly defeat their own purpose. Such was the case with the reservation and treaty policies. Although intended as a means of political and economic control over the Aboriginal peoples, and with the ultimate goal of total assimilation, these policies turned into a means of securing their survival as a distinct society Such policies helped the First Nations to assert their political identity, and in conjunction with other developments that we shall probe next, they also helped to bring about a remarkable demographic growth.

POSTWAR DEMOGRAPHIC ACCELERATION: UPSURGE IN NATURAL FERTILITY AND DECLINE IN MORTALITY

In the aftermath of the Second World War important changes have taken place in the Aboriginal way of life. The shift from a subsistence and trade-based economy to a wage and welfare economy led Amerindians to relinquish much of their nomadic way of life. The policy of resettlement was aimed at consolidating small settlements into ones that were larger, more stable, with better-equipped housing and on-site, albeit small, employment opportunities. Great strides were made in public education, at the primary and, to a lesser extent, at the secondary levels. Post-secondary education continued, however, to remain largely off-limits to Aboriginal youth, notwithstanding its wide democratization in Canada. It is, however, in the public health and general welfare that the greatest headways were made.

To put it succinctly, for both Canada as a whole and for Aboriginal peoples within it, the years since the end of World War II saw the mercantile-turned-capitalist economy give way to a more generous, socially conscious welfare economy with a wide assortment of social assistance programs. The advent of the welfare economy and the broad societal changes just mentioned had two major demographic consequences, one expected and another unexpected.

It is in the area of health that the expected consequences stand out most prominently. Prior to World War II, one can speak of minimalist public health intervention: it was sporadic and reactive to crisis situations like epidemics and famines. According to Young (1988), the emphasis was on medical relief rather than on the provision of comprehensive health services. After the war, however, one can speak of massive government intervention in public health. The Aboriginal peoples entered the epidemiological transition that combined both preventive and curative medicine. The most important postwar event in the history of medicine was the successful use of antibiotics against infectious diseases. Tuberculosis, the last of the many deadly epidemics that plagued the Aboriginal communities, took a dramatic turn. In the 1950s, it was nearly eradicated, thanks to antibiotics, except in the far North, as mentioned earlier.

Predictably, from then on there was an impressive reduction in mortality and commensurate gains in longevity. The pre-war rate of infant mortality in the range of 200 to 250 infant deaths under the age of one year per 1,000 births, dropped to between 80 and 90 by 1960 and to 12 by 1990. Correspondingly, the expectation of life at birth rose from approximately 38 to 56 and at last to 71 years, respectively (Romaniuk, 1981a).

The unexpected by-product of such economic and health progress was an increase in reproductive performance. I say "unexpected" because, generally, modernization brings about a reduction in fertility. Modernization, as measured by such indicators as education, health care, and urbanization, on the one side, and a decline in fertility rate, on the other, go hand-in-hand. So what caused the Aboriginal peoples to depart from the predictable path?

The mere fact that almost all births were henceforth taking place in the maternity wards of hospitals or local health units, under the supervision of qualified medical personnel, coupled with many mothers undergoing pre- and post-natal check-ups, was bound to result in at least some reduction in miscarriages and stillbirths, primary and secondary sterility, and maternal deaths. Furthermore, as Native peoples gave up their nomadic mode of life for a sedentary and more comfortable one, complications in pregnancy may have decreased as well. But the major factor in the fertility increase was the massive switch from traditional, protracted breastfeeding to bottle-feeding (Romaniuk, 1981a). Younger mothers either gave up breastfeeding completely or drastically reduced its duration. As a result, fecundity increased and birth intervals shortened (Romaniuc, 2003). The increase in natural, meaning uncontrolled, fertility at the early stage of modernization has been observed elsewhere as well in the world prior to the onset of the demographic transition, so it is not unique to Aboriginal people (Romaniuk, 1981b). In traditional, pre-modern society, a host of biological and cultural factors, such as protracted lactation, prolonged postpartum sexual abstinence, and sterility due to malnutrition and infections, particularly venereal, kept fertility well below the potential. With modernization these fertility-depressing features were either removed or weakened. Yet, birth control had not reached the critical level so as to counter these modernization-associated factors, causing childbearing to increase.

The Aboriginal peoples, despite their opening up to modern influences, were apparently not yet prepared psychologically to embrace birth control practices within marriage on a significant scale. Nor did they have easy access to birth control like contraception or abortion until about the 1970s. The birth rate jumped from a pre-war time range of 40 to 42 to a range of 47 to 49 births per 1,000 population over the postwar period up to the mid-1960s. During the same period, the death rate dropped from about 20 deaths per 1,000 in 1945 to about 8 per 1,000 in the 1970s. The two rates combined to produce an impressive average rate of natural growth, slightly in excess of 3 % per annum, a growth never experienced before, nor likely to be matched in the future. The population rose from 166,000 in 1951 to 220,000 in 1961, representing an average net annual increase of 2.9%.

CONTEMPORARY REGIME: DEMOGRAPHIC TRANSITION

In the 1970s, Aboriginal demographics started to depart in some major ways from the past. In order to set the stage for the discussion of what happened, I have chosen to preface it with preliminary remarks of two kinds: those concerning legalistic and/or structural changes, and those concerning behavioural changes.

In earlier days, culture and biology coincided, so there were no problems identifying an Indian or an Inuit. As Europeans and indigenous peoples came together and intermingled over time, they gave birth to a new category of people, the Métis, or what was called in the earlier days in the census, the "half-breed." In the past Amerindians were confined to their traditional habitats, which later were to become reserves. By virtue of the Indian Act—a kind of constitutional pact between the original inhabitants and the newcomers (with all its amendments since the middle of the nineteenth century when it was first adopted)—the concept of Status Indians was consecrated (refer to Appendix A for more detail on this aspect and other definitional aspects of Canadian Aboriginals).

But this relative insulation of Aboriginal people has been upset, as they have been caught in the spiral of the country's economic and social developments that gathered speed in the post-World War II years, and more so as of the 1960s. More Aboriginal people moved out of reserves, an increasing number found their way into urban centres, and many were disenfranchised by choice or force for one reason or another. Nor were the Aboriginal chiefs eager to share the benefits accrued to reserves from the government and other sources with those who severed ties with their kin and no longer participated in communal life. So what took hold was the legal distinction between the Status Indians, meaning those registered under the Indian Act, living on reserves or outside but preserving their status as Indians, on the one hand, and the non-Status Indians, on the other. Whereas the former fall under the jurisdiction of the Indian Act and are administered by Aboriginal Affairs and Northern Development Canada (AANDC), the latter are regarded as any other ethnic group in Canada. Further differentiations, as we shall see later, came about with changes in the statistical (census) determination of Aboriginals via their origin and their identity.

Thus, the study of Aboriginal demography grew in complexity. Statistically, changes in the status and in the ethnic identification introduced discontinuity in the statistical time series. Analytically, the matter became more demanding too. Whereas in the earlier periods we dealt globally with the population, making only passing references to its growth components, fertility and mortality, we have had to take a closer look at each of these factors. And that is not all. We ought henceforth to also make explicit accounts for ethnic mobility (or ethnic transfer), which have been largely ignored in the past. Finally, substantively, anyone trying to deconstruct the complex notion of Aboriginality will find that there is no unique and simple way of saying who is Aboriginal in Canada (Guimond, 2003; Goldmann & Siggner, 1992).

As for socio-demographic behavioural changes, Aboriginal people have entered what is known in demographers' parlance as the demographic transition—the shift from traditional high vital rates to modern low rates. The fast pace of modernization under its variegated manifestations—economic growth, welfare, education, and urbanization—has set into motion a string of new attitudinal and behavioural expressions in matters of procreation, which are more typical of modern times. Childbearing became more selective, and the fertility rate declined sharply, as the chance of infant survival, in particular, improved dramatically. The advent of social and economic differentials in fertility has been yet another distinctive feature of the demographic transition. All the while Aboriginals have become increasingly migratory, with the urban centres being the main attraction. (See Clatworthy and Norris chapter in this volume.)

With these remarks in mind, we shall next take a closer look first at each of the growth variables—fertility, mortality, and ethnic mobility—and then see how they merge to produce novel demographic configurations and population numbers.

Fertility: Transition from Traditional High to Modern Low Levels

As spectacular as the rise in fertility associated with early modernization was, it happened to be a short-lived—it lasted about one and a half decades. Almost suddenly, without any perceived warning sign, the birth rate took a nosedive from its high point of about 46 to 48 around 1965, to about 28 births per 1,000 population by 1980. For Status Indians, the total fertility declined, first rapidly then slowly, from almost six births per woman in 1966–1971 to 2.6 in 2003. How did this happen? All one can say is that much of the period during which the fertility sharp decline took place coincided with an acceleration of socio-economic development—education, health, housing, labour force participation, income. Regrettably, we are in no position to establish analytically meaningful linkages and mechanisms underlying the decline in fertility against the background of these socio-economic developments.

Table 1.1 Total Fertility Rate (TFR) per Woman for Status Indians Only, Canada, 1966–2006

Year	TFR	Year	TFR	Year	TFR
1966–71	5.86	1985	3.24	1996	2.73
1975	4.16	1986	3.18	1997	
1976	3.95	1987	3.03	1998	
1977	3.74	1988	2.92	1999	
1978	3.62	1989	2.86	2000	
1979	3.52	1990	2.83	2001	2.86
1980	3.41	1991	2.85	2002	
1981	3.33	1992	2.87	2003	
1982	3.33	1993	2.86	2004*	2.63
1983	3.29	1994	2.80	2005	
1984	3.27	1995	2.76	2006	

Rates are calculated from the Indian Register and are adjusted for the late reporting and under-reporting of births and deaths. Rate for the period 1966–71 is not adjusted for under and late reporting. For methodological problems see George & Loh, 2003.

* Estimate from Clatworthy, 2006.

Source: Statistics Canada, Demography Division.

However, this much might be said at this point: this striking downturn in fertility occurred spontaneously—spontaneously in the sense that it was not brought about by large-scale family planning masterminded and directed by the government or any central agency, as might have happened in some developing countries. No grand scale family planning program ever took place in Canada, generally or specifically targeted at Aboriginal populations. To be sure, unlike populations of some developing countries, they have benefited from the "spill over" effects of various public health amenities, including some limited family planning services, available to the Canadian population at large. The collapse of the Aboriginal birth rate coincided with the contraceptive revolution in Canada—birth control pills and IUDs in the 1960s and sterilization in the 1970s—which most likely spilled over into Aboriginal communities.

When studying the Aboriginal peoples' transition to low fertility we cannot help but be stricken by two idiosyncrasies. One is the tardiness thereof—by about a century—as compared to that of Canada as a whole. Why so late? After all the two populations lived side-by-side, albeit at some considerable social distance, for almost four centuries. Second, the transition to low fertility has not yet run its course. Aboriginal fertility is still higher than Canada's, the total fertility rate in recent years standing at about 2.5 and 1.5, respectively. It is possible that the transformations in Aboriginal society have not yet gone far enough to bring about a full cycle of demographic transition. On all the key developmental scores—health, education, and income—the Aboriginal population falls short of Canada's at large, and this by a significant margin.

One of the hallmarks of early fertility transition to modernity is the emergence of social, economic, and residential differentials in childbearing behaviours. As with many other populations, the process of transition did not start off simultaneously across all social boundaries; rather, it occurred sequentially. It set off with groups in the vanguard of social change, the most educated and urbanized. Education, while delaying family formation, tends to further non-family roles (work, profession) and receptivity to modern birth control technology. Urbanization, while promoting aspirations that are more work and consumption-oriented, entails a whole array of disincentives for having large families. Thus, kinship support for raising children is more difficult to come by in cities than in traditional communities, and the cost of housing is higher as well. Higher incomes, earned as a result of economic growth, make the choice more meaningful between family and non-family investments (consumption of luxury goods and leisure), with this choice tilting toward the latter. Quality of children takes precedence over quantity as wealth rises. Finally, for women, the taking up of wage employment poses a difficult dilemma in terms of both the "opportunity cost" of childbearing and the incompatibility of the dual role of working and parenting. The advent of highly efficient modern contraceptive technologies, along with greater job opportunities brought about by economic growth, has opened up alternatives to parenthood. Significant differentials in childbearing performance by education and habitat have emerged, as revealed in Table 1.2.

Table 1.2 Total Fertility Rate by Rural–Urban Habitat and Level
of Education, Registered Indians, 1981–1986

Habitat		Education			All Registered Indians
Rural	Urban	Less than grade 9	Grades 9–13	Higher than grade 13	
3.49	2.34	3.70	2.95	2.29	2.78

Source: Ram, 1991.

There are differentials in fertility by Aboriginal subgroups as well: the Inuit retain the highest edge on the fertility scale, and the Métis the lowest (see Table 1.3). A more detailed geography of Aboriginal fertility would reveal the progression of higher fertility from south to north, from settlements more exposed to modern influences by the simple fact of their vicinity to urban agglomerations and the availability of wage employment, to those still largely insulated in the north (Bone, 1992).

In attempting to offer an explanation for the late onset of the Aboriginal fertility transition and the persistence of its still high rate compared to the rest of Canada's, it is tempting to go beyond the purely developmental indicators. There must be something else that keeps Aboriginal fertility relatively high. I offer three explanations thereof.

The first is what may be called the ideational outlook, the way Aboriginal peoples see themselves and the world surrounding them. Some scholars have indeed argued (see Frideres, 1988) that Aboriginal peoples have a holistic and cosmo-centric, rather than Western homo-centric, view of the universe. The emphasis, so the argument goes, is on group interests rather than on individual or self-interests; on co-operation rather than competition; present rather than future; extended family rather than immediate family. How much of these sentiments, aspirations, and views of the world are actually internalized by individuals and couples in their childbearing decision making remains debatable. It could be plausibly argued, however, that if co-operation rather than competition is indeed this society's organizational principle, then the spirit of "social capillarity"—the process by which parents, moved by the desire to boost their children on the social ladder, have fewer offspring (Dumont, 1890)—may not have been embraced by Aboriginal peoples at large.

Table 1.3 Total Fertility Rate per Woman for Aboriginal Groups for Specified Periods*

Period	All Aboriginals	All Indians	Status Indians	Indians On-Reserve	Indians Off-Reserve	Non-Status Indians	Métis	Inuit
1966–1971	5.52	5.31	N/A	7.05	4.20	N/A	N/A	N/A
1971–1976	4.09	4.02	4.18	5.27	3.53	3.03	4.06	5.39
1976–1981	3.20	3.12	3.23	3.97	2.77	2.42	3.07	4.87
1981–1986	2.85	2.78	N/A	3.76	2.58	N/A	2.54	4.45
1986–1991	2.86	3.00	2.91				2.46	4.54
1991–1996	2.86	2.98	2.86				2.48	3.99
1996–2001	2.60	2.81	2.68				2.15	3.21

* Derived by "own-children" method from the census data on children by age in "census family" and their presumed mothers. N/A means data not available.

Source: Ram, 2000.

Second, there is what Trovato (1987) calls the "survival" strategy. He argues that Aboriginal subculture still embraces strong pro-natalist norms as a survival strategy. Many of the social norms and values that have taken hold by the fiat of the evolutionary process of adaptation, and which have sustained a high fertility in the past, are still present in Aboriginal communities in various degrees. The menace faced from the European invasion, annihilation, or assimilation, may have reinforced such survivalist instincts. The concept of survival strategy in relation to childbearing, however, requires clarification. What does it really mean?

What Trovato probably meant by the survivalist strategy is not so much that individuals decided to have children for the sake of community survival, but rather that they held onto a set of collectively fostered values, rules, and opinions that ultimately led to their either having more children or to their opposing external influences that tended to undermine pro-family standards. Contraception and particularly abortion was and still is met with public disapproval. At the height of the wave of sterilization practices that swept Canada in the 1970s, Aboriginal newspapers routinely denounced these practices in their communities, claiming ethnic genocide. Public opinion and peer pressure may have indeed acted as impediments in a diffused way to the small family norms to permeate Aboriginal society. Instances of deep-seated customs that countervail the adoption of small family norms are many throughout the world. In India the longing for a son, who alone is entitled to perform various ceremonial rites and ensure kin continuity, is one such example. Among populations of tropical Africa, the strongly felt cult of ancestry and the importance of an extended kinship network is another.

The third explanation of continued relatively high Aboriginal fertility is what may be called existential conditions, a combination of social, cultural, and economic factors that are not the same as economic or social developments, though they share qualities with these developments. Under the concept of existential conditions one could identify, for example, the culture of poverty. The latter can coexist with average or relatively high developmental indicators. The heavy reliance on the national welfare system, which in Native communities is closely associated with poverty, could be seen as a factor inhibiting the emergence of prudential attitudes in the matters of procreation. The prevalence of female single-parent families is twice as high among Status Indians as compared to other Canadians, respectively about 20% and 10%, and it has even slightly increased over the period of 1981 to 1996, according to Hull (2004). The propensity toward extramarital childbearing is also revealed by the high rate of adolescent fertility among 15 to 19 years old, with an upward tendency, from 100 in 1986 to 150 per 1,000 by 1999. The rates are four to six times higher compared to other Canadian women of the same age (Robitaille, Kouaouci, & Guimond, 2004). Children still remain an asset to their parents as helpers, and they count on them for support in their old age in rural areas and among poorly integrated urban dwellers.

Health, Morbidity, Mortality

The epidemiologists identify three stages in the dynamics of epidemiological evolution from pre-modern to modern times. The first stage, "the age of pestilence and famine," is followed by "the age of receding pandemics," and the third, "the age of human made and degenerative causes of death." History calls for yet another intermediate stage specific to Aboriginal peoples, immediately after the first stage, which we shall call the stage of "diseases of European origin." We have already dealt with the first stage in the section on the demographic regime in pre- and early contact eras, a stage where mortality fluctuated widely due primarily to the hazards of nature and inter-tribal warfare. The section on demographic collapse dealt with the epidemics brought by the Europeans, while the section on demographic recovery took care of "the age of receding pandemics" in a

Table 1.4 Life Expectancy at Birth and Infant Mortality Rate,
Status Indians and Total Canadian Population, 1975–2001

| Year | Expectancy of life at birth in years | | | | Infant mortality rate per 1,000 births | |
| | Status Indians | | Total Canadian | | Status Indians | Total Canadian |
	Male	Female	Male	Female		
1975	59.2	65.9	70.3	77.6	39.0	14.3
1980	60.9	68.0	71.8	79.0	24.4	10.4
1985	63.9	71.0	73.1	80.0	17.9	8.0
1990	66.9	74.0	74.3	80.8	14.7	6.8
1995	68.0	75.7	75.2	81.4	15.0	6.0
2000*	70.2	75.2	76.3	81.8	9.4	5.4
2001*	71.4	75.5	77.0	82.0	8.0	5.5

* Statistics Canada, 2005.

Source for Status (Registered) Indians: Verma, Michalowski, & Gauvin, 2004.

Canadian Aboriginal context. The last stage, "the age of human made and degenerative causes of death," is still underway for the Aboriginal peoples. In the epidemiologists' words, they are still only midway in the epidemiological transition from predominantly infectious and parasitic diseases to degenerative and man-made causes of death (Young, 1988; Trovato & Werner-Leonard, 1991). While infectious and parasitic diseases associated with poverty still maintain their grips, a new wave of diseases associated with "civilization," that of degenerative diseases, is taking hold.

The two most significant mortality parameters are the life expectancy at birth, (that is, the number of years newborns can expect to live under the observed age-specific mortality rates) and the infant mortality rate (the ratio of deaths of infants under the age of one year to the total births during the year). For Status Indians, the expectation of life at birth rose from approximately 59 years for males and 66 years for females in the 1970s, to 70 and 76 years, respectively, for the period 1995 to 2001. For the same periods, the infant mortality fell approximately from 80 to 39 and to 9 infant deaths per 1,000 births.

Table 1.5 identifies the causes of death. For comparability between the Native population and the broader Canadian population, the rates of deaths are standardized for age distribution. Generally speaking, the relatively high

Table 1.5 Age Standardized Mortality Rates for Status Indian Population
and Total Canadian Population, Average for 1978–1981 and
1982–1985, and 1999

Disease category	1978–1981		1982–1985		1999	
	Indian	Canadian	Indian	Canadian	Indian	Canadian
Circulatory	313.8	344.2	315.0	301.2	213.6	231.8
Injury/Poisoning	278.1	64.3	218.2	55.0	123.9	42.2
Neoplasm	118.5	168.0	120.0	171.0	141.5	186.5
Respiratory	102.7	46.5	90.6	49.9	63.6	64.4
Digestive System	70.8	74.2	49.2	26.1	33.0	23.8
Other causes	201.3	74.2	174.4	73.9	33.0	22.0
All Causes	1,085.1	726.0	967.9	677.1	N/A	N/A

Sources: 1978–1981 and 1982–1985 data: Harris & McCullough, 1988; 1999 data: Health Canada, 2003.

level of prevalent morbidity among Native people mirrors ecological and
socio-economic conditions as well as culturally determined attitudes and
behaviours. A significant component of mortality is made up of traumatic
deaths due to accidents, violence, and poisoning. These deaths are partly
environmental, and partly poor men's afflictions—substandard housing,
alcoholism, and other ills that reflect the underprivileged status of many
Natives. Traumatic deaths, we have already seen, are not new phenomena.
They have always been more or less prevalent throughout history, epitomiz-
ing a kind of socio-cultural heritage and reflective of ecological conditions.

Particularly striking is the high incidence of death from injuries, four
times that of non-Aboriginals during the period 1978–1981 and three times
in 1999—the latter an apparent improvement, but still troublesomely
high. There are two components to injury: one intentional—suicide and
homicide, as such sociologically and psychologically determined; the other
unintentional—vehicle accidents, burns, drowning, and poisoning, as such
primarily environment and activity determined. For example, motorcar
injuries occupy the first place among all causes of death, followed closely by
suicide at 23% and 20%, respectively, for the province of Manitoba from 1989
to 1993 (Manitoba Injury Prevention Newsletter, 2004).

Table 1.6 Smoking Status of First Nations On-Reserve (2002–2003) and Canada (2003), by Age Group, Aged 18 Years and Over, in Percentage

	First Nations on-reserve						Canada					
	18+	18–29	30–39	40–49	50–59	60+	18+	18–29	30–39	40–49	50–59	60+
Non smoker	41.2	30.3	36.3	39.2	55.2	71.9	75.8	68.5	73.4	72.1	76.9	87.7
Daily smoker	46.0	53.9	49.1	49.6	33.6	23.5	19.0	21.6	20.8	22.9	19.9	10.6
Occasional smoker	12.8	15.9	14.6	11.2	11.2	4.6	5.2	9.9	5.9	5.0	3.2	1.8

Source: Health Canada, 2009.

As for lifestyle related morbidities, we shall examine: smoking, alcohol, and body mass index as expression of eating habits and physical exercise.

Table 1.6, taken from a report by Health Canada (2009), shows the prevalence of smoking among First Nations on the reserves by age and among Canadians at large. What is most revealing is that the overall prevalence of smoking is much higher among Aboriginals than among non-Aboriginals, at 46% and 19%, respectively, with all ages over 18 in the former category having reported smoking on a daily basis. The anti-smoking campaign conducted in recent years in Canada has apparently been much less effective among Aboriginal folks.

According to the 2009 Health Canada report, the proportion of those reporting alcohol consumption in the 12 months preceding the survey is lower for the First Nations on-reserve population compared to the general Canadian population, with 65.6% of the former group (69.3% for males and 61.7% for females) as against the latter 79.3% (82.0% for males and 76.8% for females). This seems to dispel the reputation Aboriginal people have for being given to alcoholism. However, where the root problem seems to reside is in the prevalence of heavy or binge drinking. The proportion of First Nations who reported heavy drinking (defined as having five or more drinks on one occasion) on a weekly basis for both sexes combined was 16.0%, or double that of those in the general Canadian population at 7.9%. For males over 18 years the percentages stand at 20.9% and 12.4%, for Aboriginals and all Canadians, respectively. The largest difference is among females, with 10.2% of Aboriginal females reporting heavy drinking on a weekly basis compared to 3.3% in the general Canadian female population.

Finally, in the category of morbidity causes, let's look at the body mass index (BMI). The BMI is the ratio of a person's weight and height. There is a correlation between diet, or the way we eat and what we eat, physical activities, and our weight. According to Health Canada (2009), "First Nations adults (18 years and over) living on-reserve are generally less likely than adults in the general Canadian population (20 to 64 years) to be of normal weight. More First Nations adults than their Canadian counterparts are considered obese. Thus, 73.0% of First Nations adults are heavier than normal weight, compared to the already high figure of 48.0% among other Canadians. The First Nations and Regional Longitudinal Health Survey also reported that almost one-third (31.2%) are in obese classes I and II (Body Mass Index 30.0 to 39.9) and 4.8% are deemed morbidly obese (obese class III, Body Mass Index 40.0 and greater)" (Health Canada, 2009: 6).

Turning now to suicide as an example of the problem of intended injuries, Table 1.7 speaks for itself. When matched against all Canada, the high rates of suicide, and to a lesser extent homicides, prevalent among Aboriginal peoples are an expression of a broader social and psychological malaise from which they suffer. Youth is particularly affected. A more refined infranational investigation would reveal that the phenomenon is by no means uniform across the ethnic and geographical dimensions. According to the report issued in 1995 by the Royal Commission on Aboriginal Peoples, communities that remained partly isolated from the government's acculturation processes tend to have lower suicide rates. In other words, Native communities that have retained some of their historical traditions have lower suicide rates. This is the point elaborated by Chandler in this volume.

There are other theories as well. Kunitz (1990) has argued that the relatively high incidence of Aboriginal deaths due to violence may be related to the pattern of socialization on reserves: "Among band-level peoples a primary method of conflict resolution was spatial dispersion rather than formal institutional controls of internalized self-control. When tribes are forced onto reservations, this mechanism can not operate adequately" (660). The incidence of suicides and homicides, well in excess of the levels prevalent in mainstream society, may indeed reflect the claustrophobia of life on reserves and the general malaise, tensions, and stresses of a community

Table 1.7 Suicide Rates by Age Group, Males and Females, Status Indian and Total Canadian Population (per 100,000), 1989–1993

Age	Indians		Canada	
	Male	Female	Male	Female
0–14	3.6	4.1	0	0
15–24	125.7	35.0	24.1	4.5
25–34	93.3	28.1	26.7	6.2
35–44	50.3	18.8	26.0	7.8
45–54	30.9	11.1	24.5	8.2
55–64	24.7	9.1	23.9	6.5
65+	25.2	2.4	24.3	5.4

Source: Bobet, 1996.

facing the challenges of social change. The high incidence of smoking, over-consumption of alcohol, a growing use of substance abuse among youngsters, and the traumatic effects of these behaviours—suicide, homi-cide, family violence, and child abuse—poignantly depicted by Anastasia Shkilnyk in her remarkable book *A Poison Stronger Than Love: The Destruction of an Ojibwa Community* (1985), remain a serious interrelated multi-faceted health, social, and political problem.

It has been claimed that the Native suicide rate is much worse than the statistics indicate because typically the numbers, in most of the cases, do not include non-Status Indians, Métis, and Natives living off reserva-tions (Health Canada, 2009). An interesting bit of information: 60% of all Aboriginals who commit suicide are acutely intoxicated at the time. This compares to 24% for non-Aboriginal suicides.

In brief, what really sets Aboriginal people apart from the rest of Cana-dian society is not so much their general morbidity or mortality. There are three areas where they are clearly at a disadvantage and require special attention by public health policy holders: (1) morbidities related to environ-mental conditions; (2) morbidities related to lifestyle (such as eating habits and diet, and acquired behaviours that endanger rather than enhance health that are transmitted from generation to generation); and (3) social pathologies. Remarkably, the very similar ills are to be found among many indigenous peoples across the world, as studies by M. Gracey and M. King have revealed (2009). Everywhere they share a similar historical fate of colonization, oppression, marginalization, and socio-cultural disruption (King, Smith, & Gracey, 2009).

These findings have implications for public health policy concerning Aboriginal people. What can be done to improve their health, to bring it at par with mainstream Canadian society? In searching for ways to accomplish this, we shall separate the general causes of death prevalent among Canadians, mostly degenerative associated with old age, from the causes of death prevalent in the Aboriginal population, specifically traumatic, both unintended and intended, as well as those causes associated with lifestyle. While general public health policy is expected to take care of the former, the latter requires public programs and government action to be tailored specifically to Aboriginal conditions. The expected pay-off is double-fold. One is direct—the alleviation of suffering and the reduction of the risk of death from traumatic causes; the other is indirect. The abuse of alcohol can cause liver and brain damage and other negative effects, including vehicle accidents, while smoking can cause lung cancer and cardiovascular diseases. Obesity is a health problem in many respects. The prevalence of diabetes among Aboriginal peoples may have genetic causes as well as those associated with lifestyle (Young, 1987). Furthermore, any health policy has to take a life course approach: "It is increasingly recognized that many diseases in adulthood have their origin in early childhood and prenatal life, probably mediated through fetal and infant nutrition. Substantial evidence has been accumulated relating to the early life origins of diabetes, cardiovascular diseases, cancer, mental health, and neurocognitive development" (Waldram, Herring, & Young, 2006: 122). It follows that pregnant mothers and infants should be the prime target of any public health policy. For solutions to alcohol and related social problems, the reader is referred to the Whitehead and Kobayashi chapter in this volume.

Ethnic Mobility, Miscegenation, Definitional changes

The question of ethnic mobility has hardly received serious attention in the past. Not that it didn't exist. In fact, it probably was quite a potent factor in inter-ethnic and interracial transfer dynamics. The admixture of Europeans and Amerindians has occurred since the early contact period through intermarriage and sexual encounters, and many on both sides can claim having origins of the other. The clearest case of the inter-ethnic admixture in

Table 1.8 Aboriginal Population (in 1,000) by Origin (Ancestry) and by Identity (Self-identification), 1981–2006

Census year	Origin (O) (Single and multiple responses)	Identity (I)	I/O x100	Annual average increase for specified periods (%)			
				Origin	Identity	Natural increase*	Ethnic mobility identity-based (col. 6 – col. 7)
(1)	(2)	(3)	(4)	(5)	(6)	(7)	(8)
1981	491.5	–				2.4	
1986	711.7	464.6	65.3	9.0		2.7	
1991	1,002.7	614.0	55.7	8.2	6.4	2.4	4.0
1996	1,102.0	799.0	72.5	2.0	6.0	2.0	4.0
2001	1,332.0	976.3	73.3	4.2	4.4	1.6	2.8
2006	1,678.0	1,172.8	69.9	5.2	4.0	1.5	2.5

* There are no 2001 and 2006 estimates of the natural growth for the census Aboriginal population; therefore, the natural growth for the Status Indians was used as an approximation thereof. This approximation is probably in excess of real natural growth of the Aboriginal census population, fertility being higher among reserve than urban Aboriginals.

Sources: For the censuses of 1981 to 2001, Statistics Canada, Aboriginal Peoples of Canada: A Demographic Profile, Catalogue No. 96F0030XIE2001007; for the 2006 Census, Statistics Canada, 2006 Census: Aboriginal Peoples in Canada in 2006: Inuit, Métis and First Nations, 2006 Census, Table 1, Catalogue No. 97-558-XIE.

Canada is the Métis group, which as such enjoys constitutional status. But we have no way to determine how exactly the inter-ethnic encounter played out demographically, or to provide any quantification thereof. One could only presume that over the centuries the losses have outweighed the gains, as miscegenation and acculturation generally benefit the dominant society. In Canada, government policies, particularly in the nineteenth and first half of the twentieth centuries, deliberately aimed precisely at that end through enfranchisement and assimilation.

With the rise of multicultural ideology, there has been a change of view regarding the question of ethnic mobility, particularly in relation to Aboriginal peoples. Changes in census content have been made to reflect policies of multiculturalism. The question as to how to define and measure ethnicity statistically has garnered considerable interest (see Guimond and his colleagues in this volume). Suffice it to say that the criteria for identification of Aboriginality have become progressively broader. In a bid to reproduce as fine a picture as possible of the country's ethnic and cultural mosaic, the 1986 Census added the possibility of multiple responses to determine respondents' ancestral background. Furthermore, as of the 1986 Census, respondents have two ways to mark their ethnic affiliation—origin and identity (see Appendix A).

Populations based on the census ethnicity concepts indentified above, and related growth rates are posted in Table 1.8.

The approach used to estimate the numbers subjected to ethnic mobility (ethnic transfer) has been the residual method, which is the difference between intercensal change in population size and natural growth over the corresponding intercensal period. The residual method has obvious weaknesses. To generate reliable data, this method would require the population to be closed to migration (this is the case at the national but not the sub-national levels). It would also require no changes in the census definitions, and population coverage of the consecutive censuses would have to stay almost the same, as would the invariability of ethnic structure between consecutive censuses. None of these conditions are fully met. Hence, discontinuities in the time series are difficult to interpret. How do we explain, for example, that ancestry "multiple responses" rose from 49.2% 1986 to 62.4% in the 2006 Census? One possible explanation is growing ethnic diversity and inter-ethnic marriages. To determine gains and loses for a given ethnic group between censuses, one would need to examine individual census records, so as to distinguish between intergenerational and intragenerational ethnic mobility.

Clearly, both sets of census population data—origin and identity—are problematic. But if one had to choose between the two, the identity-based, in the opinion of this author, is a more meaningful entity, sociologically, politically, and demographically. (For a critique of the census origin-based population see Krotki, 1995.)

Notwithstanding the definitional problems we singled out, trends toward Aboriginality mirror the reality of Canadian politics to a large extent. The reported shifts in identity in favour of Aboriginality coincide with political events and confrontations triggered, in particular, by the White Paper put forward in 1969 by the federal government, which the Aboriginal leadership rallied against, calling it a ploy to assimilate them and rob them of their identity and special status in Confederation. These events served as a catalyst for the introduction of provisions in the censuses that ultimately accommodated the Aboriginal aspiration as sui generis entity in Canada.

By the same token, these events led them to take advantage of the new identity options offered in the census. (For a more in-depth discussion of Aboriginal identity, see Chris Andersen and Evelyn Peters and colleagues in this volume.)

Population Growth, Size, Regional Settlement Patterns: Contemporary Period

Having dealt with the components of population growth in the previous sections—fertility, mortality, and ethnic mobility—we can now turn our attention to the numbers they generated in terms of population growth and size. In doing this we shall focus on two specific groups: first, the identity-based Aboriginal populations, because, as already mentioned, of its greater meaningfulness socially and politically; second, the Status (Registered) Indian population because of its special standing under the Indian Act. By virtue of this act, Status Indians enjoy entitlements specific to them, including the right to keep a residence on a reserve and to elect their own representatives to negotiate with the federal government over land claim settlements and other rights under treaties with the Crown. They are the core and the mainstay of the Amerindian ethnos. Consequently, their demographic profile is of particular interest to the public generally and to policy makers in particular.

Table 1.9 reveals the growth dynamics of the three major identity-based Aboriginal groups—First Nations that is Indians, Métis, and Inuit—for the period of 1986 to 2006. As one can see, in the twenty year time frame, numbers have risen by a factor of 2.1 for the First Nations, 3.8 for Métis, and 1.7 for Inuit. Put differently, the annual net growth stood at 5.6%, 13.9%, and 3.4%, respectively, thus exceeding by far, save for the Inuit, their respective annual rates of natural growth of about 2% to 3%, a clear indication of the substantial number of First Nations, and even more so of Métis, identifying themselves as such. Lumped together, their number has multiplied in 20 years by a factor of 5.2. For the same period, all of Canada's population had multiplied by a factor of only 1.2, about half of which was due to net international migration. (As time passes, the latter may be all that keeps Canada's population from declining.)

More recently, a comparison between the growth dynamics of the Aboriginal population and non-Aboriginal population reveals two fundamental differences, which demonstrates that the two are still at different stages of demographic transition, particularly in two respects. First, in

Table 1.9 Aboriginal Population: Indians, Métis and Inuit, Identity-based (in 1,000s), 1986–2006

Census year	Indians	Métis	Inuit	Undetermined	Total*
1986	329.7	103.1	30.1	1.5	464.5
1991	460.7	135.0	36.2	0	632.2
1996	529.0	204.1	40.2	25.6	799.0
2001	608.9	292.3	45.1	30.1	976.3
2006	698.0	389.8	50.5	34.5	1,172.8
Increase 1986 to 2006	112%	278%	68%		152%

* Figures are rounded and may not add up exactly to the totals shown in table's last column.

Sources: Statistics Canada, 2008, Aboriginal Peoples in Canada in 2006: Inuit, Métis and First Nations, 2006 Census: Aboriginal Peoples, Table 1, Catalogue No. 97-558-XIE.

regard to childbearing performance: whereas the Canadian population at large no longer has enough children to replace their parent generations, its total fertility being close to 1.5 births per woman, the Aboriginal population's fertility is well above the generational replacement level, about 2.5 births per woman. Second, in regard to mortality or its antipode—survival or lon-gevity—the picture is revealing as well. With all the health improvements in the twentieth century, Aboriginal people still lag behind Canada at large in life expectancy, by about five years. Their mortality regime is still a mixture of the past dominated by infectious, parasitic, and traumatic diseases, and the advanced, dominated by degenerative and chronic diseases.

Table 1.10 brings together relevant basic demographic parameters for Status Indians. Over the period under review, 1966 to 2006, their number increased by 241% or by a factor of 3.41. Both the on-reserve and off-reserve populations grew substantially, though an increasing numbers of Status Indians take residence outside of the reserves. In 1966, 85.5% lived on reserves as compared to only 56.1% in 2006. (For a more detailed account, see the Clatworthy and Norris chapter in this volume.)

An important comment is in order at this point. Inflating the numbers and at the same time introducing distortions in the continuity of the Aboriginal population statistics are not the action of the census officials alone. Legislators have done their part. Thus, a significant increase (and discontinuity) in population time series has originated with the introduction

Table 1.10 Status Indians On and Off Reserves, Proportion On-Reserve as Percentage of Total Status Indians, Average Inter-Period Annual Rate of Increase (ARI), Birth Rate (BR), Death Rate (DR), Rate of Natural Increase (RNI), 1966–2006

Year	On-reserve		Off-reserve	On- & Off-reserve		BR per thousand	DR per thousand	RNI %
	Total (000)	%	Total per thousand	Total per thousand	ARI %			
1966	180.4	80.5	43.7	224.2				
1971	188.5	73.2	69.1	257.6	2.82	34.78*	7.90*	2.69*
1976	209.6	72.6	79.3	288.9	2.32	30.50	7.47	2.30
1981	227.5	70.3	96.3	323.8	2.30	29.81	6.27	2.35
1986†	264.2	68.1	123.6	387.8	3.68	31.95	5.12	2.68
1991	304.8	59.6	207.0	511.8	5.71	28.30	4.31	2.40
1996	354.4	58.0	256.5	610.9	3.60	24.83	5.09	1.97
2001	396.7	57.5	293.4	690.1	2.60	20.20	5.50	1.47
2006	428.4	56.1	335.1	763.6	2.10	20.50	5.12	1.54

* Data are for 1972.

† Population figures from 1986 on are inflated due to the reinstatement, following the enactment of the 1985 Bill C-31, of those who have lost their Indian status (generally Indian women married to non-Indians and their children), altogether about 120,000 between 1985 and 1996.

Sources: Population data on and off reserves to 1986 are taken from Basic Department Data, 1989, Indian and Northern Affairs Canada; Population data for 1991 to 1996 and data on vital statistics for the specified period are from Statistics Canada, Demography Division, Birth and death rates are adjusted for underreporting and late reporting.

of the 1985 Bill C-31, which removed the earlier gender discrimination and reinstated Indian status to Indian women married to Canadians (including non-Status Indians), as well as to their children. Between 1986 and 1999 some 218,000 individuals (women and their children) were thrown in the Status Indian pool by virtue of Bill C-31. About 80% of these women chose off-reserve residence, and only 20% on-reserve residence. Additional re-instatements can be expected in the years to come, although at a slower pace (Clatworthy, 2003).

So far we have dealt with the overall increase in the size of the Status Indians, which was prompted, largely as we have seen, by the ethnic transfers. But what about natural growth, that is growth based on the balance between births and deaths? The relevant birth and death rates and natural rate of increase are presented in the three right-hand columns of Table 1.10. Accordingly, the crude birth rate has declined from 35 births per

1,000 population in the 1970s to 25 by the mid-1990s and to about 20 most recently, still twice that of Canada. Although Aboriginal mortality by age is still relatively high compared to the non-Aboriginal population, their crude death rate, because of a much younger age structure, is lower than that of Canada's population—about 5.0 against 7.1 per 1,000, in recent years. The rate of natural increase fell from 2.7% early in the 1960s to 2.0% per annum in the 1990s and to 1.5% most recently. By 2006, the natural increase for all-Canada population had reached its nadir, almost nil (0.04%), and stands to decline further if the fertility persists at its generational sub-replacement rate.

This hurried sketch of the most recent demographic profile of Aboriginal peoples calls for two additional general observations. First, on the all-Canada scale, the Aboriginal population numbers cited above are small in relative terms, but by no means trivial. The total Aboriginal population, by whatever definition, exceeds the population of any Maritime province taken individually, and it is more or less equivalent to that of either Manitoba or Saskatchewan. Still, its numerical weight in relation to the total Canadian population is weak. Canadians who identify with any Native groups represent only 4% of the entire Canadian population, according to the 2006 Census. However, there are significant regional variations: only about 1% to 3% resides in the Atlantic provinces, Quebec, and Ontario; slightly over 5% in British Columbia; 6% in Alberta; slightly over 15% in Manitoba and Saskatchewan; and 25% in the Yukon. In the Northwest Territories, Native groups constitute half of the total population and 85% in Nunavut.

Second, the demographic surge notwithstanding, the First Nations of this country continue to suffer from three historically fundamental demographic weaknesses. One is their ethnic fragmentation, small size, and loss of their language. According to the 2006 Census, among Aboriginal ethnicities reporting their mother tongue, the largest group, the Algonquian family, weighs in at 140,000, followed at a distance by the Inuktitut family at 32,000, and the Athapaskan family at 19,000. All other groups count in the thousands and hundreds only (see Frideres on languages in this volume). The related weakness resides in their wide territorial dispersion. Generally, they are isolated, in single groups or clusters of tribal settlements, spread over the vastness of this country. Given this dispersion, the population lacked, and perhaps is still lacking, strong political links and a cohesive institutional superstructure. This type of settlement pattern goes back deep into history. Colonization did not do much to alter it, except that new dimensions were added by writ of the legislation—that of political and administrative fragmentation—making this their third weakness. The legal divide between Status and non-Status Indians, the on-reserve and off-reserve dichotomy, the Treaty and non-Treaty Indians, and Status Indians with band membership and those lacking it, are cases in point. The significant feature of this fragmentation is that the basic entities, like reserves, are small in size and weak in organization and economic viability.

We have sketched out the broad contours of what we have called the contemporary demographic regime of the Aboriginal population, primarily in terms of vital rates—fertility and mortality. But these variables were by no means the only change of a sweeping magnitude. Changes often occur not in isolation but in unison. We are witnessing shifts in matrimonial behaviours, including delayed and informal marriages; a rise in single motherhood; a steady aging of the population concomitant with a still high proportion of youth competing with the elderly for public resources; heightened migration, often circular between reserves and cities; and finally, a significant rise in the urban Aboriginal population, which signals both challenges and opportunities. Changes that are taking place amount to nothing less than a demographic revolution. Some bode well for the future of Aboriginal peoples, while others underscore inherent structural weaknesses as we shall see later.

In the meanwhile we shall try to make a general assessment of the demographic evolution in its historical perspective, as reported in this chapter.

OVERALL ASSESSMENT OF ABORIGINAL POPULATION EVOLUTION IN HISTORICAL PERSPECTIVE

In the second half of the twentieth century, Aboriginal peoples made a quantum jump in their growth. By the turn of that century, they hit their first million, due in part to a surge in census identification and also because of natural growth, that is, the positive gain of births over deaths. The second half of the twentieth century was indeed an eventful period, a golden age of sorts, in the history of Canadian Aboriginal people, for during that period a number of longed-for developments occurred in unison. With the exceptional population growth, we have also witnessed the revival of Aboriginal cultural and political identity, along with significant headways in the struggle for recognition, heralding for the first inhabitants of this land, if not a paradigm shift then at least a new, hopefully more promising era in their history. (See Voyageur's chapter for more on this theme.)

Yet, as much as we like, and should, celebrate the Aboriginal people's demographic revival at this particular point in their history, our view ought to be a much more subdued, to say the least, when we mull over their demographic fortune since the inception of European colonization about four centuries ago. The demographic growth of Aboriginal people over that long-drawn-out historical period pales in comparison with the growth of the European population. Acutely revealing in this regard is the demographic experience of the French Canadians. From an initial *souche* of just 10,000 or so French colonists, who landed during the seventieth century and made Nouvelle-France their permanent home (Charbonneau et al., 1987), they grew into a nation of some six million. This feat is all the more remarkable given their long isolation from the metropolis and losses through out-migration and assimilation. However, unlike the French Canadians, for whom "La revanche des berceaux" ("the revenge of the cradle") lasted from the inception of colonization to about 1965, the Aboriginal peoples' baby boom started only in the post–World War II years and was histori-cally short-lived, and an excessive mortality held down the population growth well into the twentieth century. Even more impressive growths have occurred in some recent immigrant groups from Third World countries. The so-called visible minority population, estimated at 1,130,000 in 1981 grew to 5,068,000, according to the 2006 Census, or from 4.7% of the total popula-tion to 16.8%. So, when measured against the background of the growth experiences of non-Aboriginal populations, the Aboriginal peoples' growth in its historical perspective should give us pause. They have not been on the receiving end of history, from whatever angle the matters are seen, a fact that becomes plain as one reads the historian J.R. Miller and his insightful reflection on the Native–newcomer relations (2004), or any author who has written about the Aboriginal fate in a spirit I like to call "sympathetic objectivity." All things considered, the idea behind this statement is that the Aboriginals, and more to the point, First Nations' demographic success of the second half of the twentieth century should not be taken for granted as forerunner of things to come. Many more challenges lay ahead, for both Canada as a whole and the First Nations in particular, as they step farther into the twenty-first century with all the uncertainties of the emerging era of globalization. It is precisely some of these challenges that we will try to address in the final section.

In interpreting the demographic events concerning the First Nations we need to be mindful of their very status in the broader context of Canadian society, that is, of the historical context of the encounter between the two civilizations, Aboriginal and European, and the complex relationships between the indigenous inhabitants and the newcomers. While these relations have changed throughout the course of history—from partnership to outright subordination, and to affirmative emancipation—the fundamentals that marked them can be encapsulated in two words: ethnocentricity and dependence. Ethnocentricity has given rise to a string of upshots—the First Nations struggle for recognition and special political status with reserves as their territorial mainstay; solidarity and co-operation rather than competition as a principle of social organization. All these factors may positively influence procreative behaviours by reinforcing family values. By contrast, the dependency has created a string of problems, such as a culture of poverty, pervasive welfare dependence, and excessive levels of pathologies (alcoholism, suicide, homicide, accidents, and violence) on the reserves, all of which intrude on the demographic domain, particularly health but also reproductive behaviours (Romaniuk, 2008).

Some authors (e.g., Spady, 1982), quite rightly it seems to me, have described the Aboriginal person as a person alternating between two cultural poles—the relatively confined Aboriginal culture on the one side, and the assertive Western culture on the other. The lure of the latter may prove to be irresistible; hence assimilation into mainstream society.

A GLIMPSE INTO THE FUTURE: PROSPECTS AND CHALLENGES

As we step further into this century, we can expect the growth momentum of the Aboriginal populations to continue for a good while. By 2017, they may reach anywhere from 1,390,000 to 1,442,000 as per identity, up from 1,173,000 in 2006, according to projections compiled by Ravi Verma in this volume. These projections are conditional projections—that is, they are predicated upon the fulfillment of the underlying assumptions about population growth components. Yet, as history has time and again demonstrated, forecasts more often than not miss their targets. Mortality and *a fortiori* fertility are difficult to predict. Inter-ethnic mobility (i.e., ethnic transfer) makes any forecast highly problematic. The legalistic and definitional determinations of one's ethnicity elude any prognostication, as they are often taken at the whim of legislators or census officials. "Identity" in general poses problems in analysis and interpretation because of its ubiquitous character allied with a changing historical context, as Philip Kreager (1997) has aptly demonstrated.

Rather than agonizing about future numbers, I have chosen to devote the remainder of this chapter to thoughts on the demographic and political environment in which Canada's First Nations are likely to evolve. As much as we can rejoice in their recovery from the long-lasting demographic depression, in the long run, their survival as a distinct ethnic entity with historical rights is not a foregone conclusion. In their struggle to assert their pre-eminence as the first inhabitants of this land, they will have to contend with and overcome a score of obstacles. Some are rooted in history, others in geography and demography; still others stem from federal government policies and political forces operating nationally and even internationally. I shall confine myself to the challenges ahead that are demographically driven.

To begin, the historic demographic weaknesses of the Aboriginal population—their territorial dispersal and political fragmentation along with their relatively modest numbers—present many challenges. In an age of electronic communication, it is possible to overcome distance and bring communities closer. The greatest challenge, however, is political. How to overcome not only geographic barriers but more importantly cultural diversity and political factionalism are questions best left to the politicians to ponder, who in fact have been doing so since the idea of Aboriginal self-government was brought to the fore of national political debate. The revival of historical entities—individual groups or families thereof (Cree, Ojibway, Dene, Inuktitut, Athapaskan, etc.)—that share common cultural affinities may be one of the policy options. This would infuse historical and cultural content back into the unification process, a process that the policies of assimilation and fragmentation tend to pre-empt. Yet, at the same time, such a policy could revive historical rivalries and undermine the unifying principle of the First Nations' concept. As Peters and her colleagues (in this volume) demonstrate, most Amerindians identify themselves with their ethnic group rather than with the generic "First Nations."

The dilemma that Aboriginal peoples have faced throughout history, and will likely face with even greater acuity in the future, is the dilemma of integration and assimilation into mainstream society versus the preservation of their "Aboriginality." The latter stands out as the Aboriginal leadership's undisputable option: "Common to all tribal groups was the desire to retain their distinctive traditions, culture and languages; treaties rights and benefits; and other inherent rights accruing to them as Aboriginal peoples," writes John Leslie (2004: 16). To the extent that we can grasp the forces operating in Canadian society at large and what we may be able to read on the forward-looking radar as to how these forces may be shaping the country's destiny, the question about the future of Aboriginal peoples within Confederation remains unsettled, notwithstanding real breakthroughs and successes won in the last three or four decades. Again, as Leslie (2004) writes, "Whether contemporary Canadian society, still imbued with the liberal democracy principles espoused by the White Paper, can accommodate collectivist Native aspirations and notion of asymmetrical citizenship is a moot point. Until this fundamental issue is resolved, Indian policy will remain a highly contentious and problematic field of Canadian public policy" (23). I would go one step further by asking this question: While surviving, though not unscathed by the colonial trauma, will Aboriginal peoples within Canada (and elsewhere in the world), as they press forward into the depth of the twenty-first century, withstand, as a *distinct* society, the onslaught of globalization?

Central to the future of the Aboriginal peoples is the status of the reserves. It is doubtful that Indians can survive for long as a political and cultural distinct entity without reference to a territory, be it only a micro-territory. The reservation is the land base where geography, biology, and culture meet to preserve and perpetuate the First Nations ethos. It is here that they best preserve their identity, their native customs, and, to some extent, their languages. It is from this base that their urbanized counterparts stand to receive their cultural sustenance and demographic reinforcement.

Yet the reservation's very existence in the long run stands to be challenged by the forces of modernity. Economists generally agree that vital to the sustainable development and self-government of the reserves is a healthy economy, and so, generally, does the First Nations' elite: "Most of the Indian leaders consider that a reserve-based economy is an essential constituent of self-government" (Boldt, 1994: 230). But can such an economy take root given the geographic isolation and the small size of the reserves and as such their inability to create meaningful economies of scale? Can reserves generate enough local employment opportunities to meet the needs of a growing number of youths and adults, and thus avert a mounting reservations' proletariat from fading away into the urban and industrial centres of the south? Can it deter its educated youth from being assimilated into the dominant society? The alternative—having to cope with a sizeable body of unemployed driven to despair on the reserves—is not an option one wishes to contemplate. Creation of a reserve-based sustainable modern economy that would supersede the traditional tribal economy and government benefits in ways charted and articulated, for example, by Menno Boldt in his *Surviving as Indians* (1993, ch. 5) remain an enormous challenge. Some relief may come by way of building up the effective land base or economic zone through treaty or purchase (M. King, personal communication, 2008), thus making room for a growing reserves' population. Legal settlements of treaty claims, current and prospective, could generate additional resources in dollars, land, mineral reserves, and so on and to bring more wealth and prosperity to communities (White, Spence, & Maxim, 2007).

There is yet another important question, purely demographic. Will reserves be able in the long run to maintain a birth rate high enough to offset the outflow toward urban centres of its inhabitants? For, if anything, reserves are the only places one should expect to have the capacity, in the foreseeable future at least, to produce a surplus of births required to maintain the demographic strength of its own population and that of its urban counterparts. It is more likely than not that the latter will adopt small family norms prevailing generally in the urban milieu, and that that will occur sooner than later.

The antidotes to this, in ways a circumspect picture of the reserves' future, are developments that transcend the relatively narrow base of the reserves and take on a broader significance at the societal level of the whole of Canada. Cora Voyageur, in her chapter in this volume, identifies a variety of opportunities opening up to Aboriginal professionals, in education and health sectors, in culture and in community support networks, in business and finance, and in banking activities targeting Aboriginal clientele, individuals and corporations, on reserves and beyond. The devolution of the administrative responsibilities from the federal government to First Nations, assuming the self-government project gains further ground, will carry with it many more opportunities for the Aboriginal peoples' mounting generations.

Any policy that is directed at strengthening the Aboriginal peoples' position in Confederation ought to recognize the uniqueness of the North. The preponderance of Aboriginals in the remote north, namely in the Northwest

Territories (and their sizeable proportion in the Yukon), has potentially important political ramifications. It is here that they stand the best chance of forming a politico-administrative territorial body and enjoying a broad power structure of self-government on par with other provinces. The special status recently acquired by the territory Nunavut in the Arctic may be a step in that direction (Légaré, 1998). Will the Aboriginal peoples of the north succeed where Louis Riel failed more than a century ago in his bid for an autonomous Aboriginal territory? The reference is made to Louis Riel's abortive rebellion in 1870 and 1885, which was an attempt to create a semi-autonomous territorial entity in lieu of the defunct Hudson's Bay Company's Northwest Territory (Stanley, 1960). The future will tell. For all intents and purposes, the North remains for the Aboriginal people a strategically important bastion of power in the body politic of Canadian Confederation.

When demographers speak of growth, they have numbers, quantity, in mind. And that is fittingly so. Numbers matter a great deal, particularly in a democratic political setting. But there is also quality. In this respect Native peoples stand to gain much. Healthier, better-educated, and more productive individuals can make up, to some extent, for their shortfalls in numbers. As Malcolm King's chapter in this volume demonstrates, there is a significant correlation between health, education, and employment, the latter two being strong determinants of the former. In this long, drawn-out encounter of European and Aboriginal civilizations, the importance of demographic quality, of human capital, cannot be overstated for the First Nations to assume the pre-eminent place they are entitled to by the sheer weight of history. And there is much catching up to be done in this regard, not only on the reserves but also in the urban communities, so as to avoid situations, where, in Boldt's words, "Indians who have migrated to the city have moved from reserve unemployment, destitution and despair to urban unemployment, destitution and despair" (1993: 245). So there is a lot of room for building up the human capital. Moreover, while investing in human capital, the Aboriginal leadership should be mindful of strengthening the social capital premised on the already existing ethos of co-operation and mutuality in Aboriginal communities. (For an interesting discussion of social capital, its conceptualization and its measurement, in regards to First Nations communities, see Mignone et al., 2004).

I am now going to delve into the issue that is absolutely central to the survival of the Canada's First Nations and of Aboriginal peoples in general as a distinct ethnocultural entity with special status. It is fertility. Society's demographic renewal is clearly rooted in childbearing. Oddly enough, its importance is often overlooked in discussions of the future of Aboriginal peoples. Nor is there any ground for optimism on this score. Unless the Aboriginal peoples are an exception to what appears to be a universal tendency toward ever-lower reproductive norms as societies undergo modernization, their fertility rate will settle somewhere below the replacement level, probably sooner than later. This is all the more so because the government and the entire Canadian political establishment are not prepared to give any serious consideration to an effective pro-family policy that would boost the flagging birth rate, at least to the generational replacement level of two babies per woman. Such a policy, to be effective, would require a significant reallocation of national resources from production to reproduction, and that is not in the cards for Canada's body politic, preoccupied by mercantile motifs, adhering to a short-sighted policy of importing cheap labour (see Romaniuk, 2012). Given this state of affairs, Aboriginal peoples are most likely to enter sooner or later the stage of demographic maturity, that is, the advanced stage in human demographic evolution whereby people live longer and healthier, but reproduce themselves less and less (generally with a fertility rate under generational replacement level). Thus, Aboriginal people will join the growing number of nations that no longer reproduce themselves. This is where Canada is now. However, Canada has leverage, unavailable to them, for better or worse—immigration.

And this leads me to another important point. The future of Aboriginal peoples cannot be divorced from what appears to be in store for Canada as a whole. The commitment of Canada's federal government to the policies of steady population growth by way of ever-increasing immigration favouring diversity is bound to have consequences of historical proportions for Canada and its Aboriginal peoples alike. Two questions follow from the premises of these policies that are worthy of being weighed by the Aboriginal elite.

What will be the place of the First Nations in this rapidly emerging multicultural society, which is assertively supplanting the order that has prevailed historically, the Canada of "the three founding nations French, British and First Nations"? Over the four centuries of coexistence between the latter and the two former, institutional and political accommodations have been worked out between them, by no means fully satisfactory, but which have so far ensured First Nations a unique place in Confederation. With the radical about-face in Canadian immigration policy, there is for them a quantum leap from a historically established political setting of mutual accommodation to the uncharted waters of an emerging new society, some calling it trans-national, as such divorced from this land's history.

The second question is how the policy of immigration-sustained growth of Canada's population is likely to affect the First Nations settlement pat-terns and treaty rights over land in the long run. The encroachment on Natives' land, or lands they can claim on historical grounds, is expected to continue and even worsen as a result of mounting non-Aboriginal popula-tion pressure. The stakes for eventual land compensation stand to increase, while the space available for modern and traditional Native activities (hunt-ing, fishing) may shrink, as will the landmass available for their potential demographic expansion in the future. Parenthetically, one may caution against readily accepting Canada's supposed empty landmass as justifica-tion for resettlement from overpopulated regions of the globe. It is this author's view that this "empty" space is empty only in a relative sense; it ought to be preserved for the wealth of ecological life not just for Canada but for the world.

As mentioned at the outset of this section, the Aboriginal population is expected to grow for a while. But it is unlikely to sustain itself for long enough to keep pace with Canada's population growth. The Aboriginal population will be dwarfed in relation to the Canadian population, the latter of which is ever-growing in size and diversity, and in the long run stands to be marginalized to the point of becoming irrelevant as a political player. Inescapably, then, immigration policy presents itself to the First Nations' politicians as an issue of paramount importance. Yet there are no indica-tions so far that they are in any perceptible way part of the decision-making process in formulating policies on migration, nor does it seem that they have actively sought any participation in an area that matters so much for their peoples' future. Once again, it seems that they remain, in Leslie's words, "on the periphery of power and decision making" (2004: 16).

Such seems to be the broad spectrum of demographically driven policy issues that Canada's First Nations are most likely to confront in this century. If the future cannot be predicted, the future can be made. This sounds paradoxical only if we discount the role of human volition in social processes. The First Nations, by virtue of history and their special status in Confederation, could well, and should, become significant players in shaping Canada's destiny. It may be helpful at this point to recall the history of the Aboriginal peoples' relationship with the European newcomers. Historians J.R. Miller (2004) and Olive Dickason (1992, 2002) identify three historically distinctive phases in this relationship. The first phase was one of mutually beneficial co-operation—characterized by partnerships in trade, and military and political alliance against revolutionary America. The second phase, for most of the nineteenth and first half of the twentieth centuries, was that of colonial power attempting to subvert their identity and assimilate them. The third, the most recent in the second half of the twentieth century, was dominated by First Nations' struggle for recognition, which turned out to be in many ways successful. During that latter phase, preoccupied with their own survival, they were looking inwardly rather than outwardly to Canadian society at large. A fourth phase is in the making, I would dare to argue: one of healing and reconciliation, the Aboriginal elite admittedly opening up to Canadian society at large, and putting into motion processes that could possibly produce a new partnership of mutually beneficial co-operation in shaping the destiny of Canada. While reaping the economic benefits of globalization, they may stand up in partnership to fend off the potentially detrimental influences of globalization to the country's nationhood.

POST SCRIPTUM

I have tried to retrace the broad strides of Canada's Aboriginal peoples' demographic history from a *Janus*-like position—with one eye turned to the past, the other to the future. To be life-giving, history must be forward-looking. No one can turn back the clock and retrieve what has been lost in the mazes of history, however great the nostalgia may be for the days gone by. It is fitting to conclude with words borrowed from Thomas Sowell, the author of *Conquests and Cultures*, the third book of his monumental trilogy, who delves into the past of the Indians of the western hemisphere and other great world cultures: "What is clear is that their [Indians'] world was irretrievably shattered—biologically, militarily, socially, and politically—and that their fate would henceforth be determined by how well they evolved new ways of dealing with a radically different and ever-changing reality around them" (1999: 328).

Figure 1.1 Birth Rates for Canadian Aboriginals (First Nations) and Quebec/Canada, 1651–60 to 2008

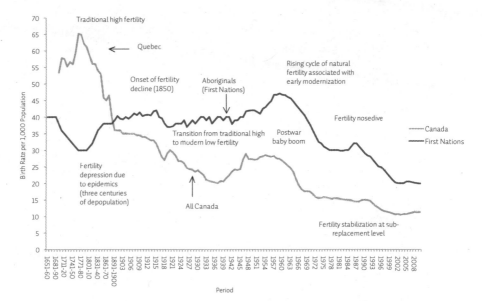

Sources: For the First Nations, birth rates for the periods prior to 1900 are constructs based on the contextual analysis of fertility in this chapter's sections, "Demographic Regime of the Pre- and Early Contact Era" and "Collapse of Demographic Equilibrium and Depopulation." For the years 1900 to 1973, birth rates are estimates derived from the proportion of children under age the age of five, as per A. Romaniuk, 1981, "Increase in Natural Fertility during the Early Stages of Modernization: Canadian Indians Case Study," Demography, 18(2): 157–172. For a few missing years, the values of birth rates have been derived by interpolation. For the quinquennial census years from 1976 on, the birth rates are those shown in the Table 1.10 of this chapter, for Status Indians, on- and off-reserves. For the intercensal years, birth rates have been derived by interpolation. For all Canada, birth rates are from J. Henripin's 1961 Census Monograph, Trends and Factors of Fertility in Canada; Table 1.1 for the period 1681 through 1880 refers to New France and Catholics of the province of Quebec, and Table B.6 for the periods 1840 to 1921 refers to all Canada. From 1921 through 1982, the birth rates are as reported in Statistics Canada Vital Statistics publications, as per A. Romaniuc, Fertility in Canada: From Baby-boom to Baby-bust (Statistics Canada, Catalogue No. 91-524E). From 1982 onwards, birth rates are from Vital Statistics, posted at Index Mundi (http://www.indexmundi.com/facts/canada/birth-rate).

The purpose of Figure 1.1 is to show the trends of birth rates of the First Nations against the background of the all-Canada trends and to highlight their respective distinctive features at various historical stages.

For the First Nations, the figure shows three centuries of demographic collapse, recovery by the turn of the nineteenth century, rising fertility at earlier stages of modernization, one-century lag in the onset of transition from traditional high to modern lower fertility, sharp downturn, and stabilization of fertility.

For all Canada, the figure shows traditional high fertility, transition to modern low fertility, postwar baby boom followed by the baby bust, and the emergence of sub-replacement fertility regime.

The time scale in the figure is in ten-year periods prior to 1900, and three-year periods from 1900 onward.

NOTES

1. Much of the material in this chapter has been first published in the article "Aboriginal Population of Canada: Growth Dynamics under Conditions of Encounter of Civilisations," 2000, *The Canadian Journal of Native Studies*, 20(1).
2. As to the south of the big river [Saint Lawrence] the region is well inhabited, and more so than on its northern side.
3. The women are not as fertile as one would expect, maybe as much because of their promiscuity as because of the choice of so many men.
4. It is not the same for the savages whose women are rather sterile either because of the hard work they have to endure or because of the prolonged breastfeeding of their babies.
5. Several young men, instead of getting married, entertain relations with girls "pot et feu," whom they call not-wives, ekenhona, because no marriage ceremony took place, but asqua, that is, companions or rather concubines. And they live together as long as it pleases them, and they may go with other men without fearing any reproach or blame....And the young men of Canada, particularly in the country of our Hurons, are always free to indulge in free sex as soon as they can, and the girls prostitute themselves as soon as they are capable.

REFERENCES

Abbott, J.S.C. (1898). *Chevalier de La Salle and his companions*. New York, NY: Dodd, Mead.

Aberle, S.B.D. (1931). Frequency of pregnancies and birth interval among Pueblo Indians. *American Journal of Physical Anthropology*, 16(1), 63–80.

Balikci, A. (1972). Female infanticide on the Arctic Coast. In M. Nagler (Ed.), *Perspectives on the North American Indians* (pp. 176–189). Toronto, ON: McClelland & Stewart.

Barsh, R.L. (1994). Canada's Aboriginal peoples: Social integration or disintegration? *The Canadian Journal of Native Studies*, 14(1), 1–46.

Bobet, E. (1996). Inequality in health: A comparison of Indian and Canadian mortality trends. Medical Service Branch Report. Ottawa, ON: Health and Welfare Canada.

Bobrick, B. (1992). *East of the sun: The epic conquest and tragic history of Siberia*. New York, NY: Henry Holt.

Boldt, M. (1994). *Surviving as Indians: The challenge of self-government*. Toronto, ON: University of Toronto Press.

Bone, R.M. (1992). *The geography of the Canadian North: Issues and challenges*. Toronto, ON: Oxford University Press.

Burpee, L. (Ed.). (1927). *La Vérendrye, journals and letters of Pierre Gaultier de Varennes Sieur de la Vérendrye and his sons*. Toronto, ON: The Champlain Society.

Carr-Saunders, A.M. (1922). *The population problem: A study in human evolution*. London, UK: Oxford University Press.

Charbonneau, H. (1984). Trois siècles de dépopulation amérindienne. In L. Normandeau & V. Piché (Eds.), *Les populations amérindienne et Inuit du Canada* (pp. 28–48). Montréal, QC: Les presses de l'Université de Montréal.

Charbonneau, H., Bates, R., Boleda, M., et al. (1987). *Naissance d'une population—Les Français établis au Canada au XVIIe siècle*. Montréal, QC: Presses de l'Université de Montréal.

Clatworthy, S. (2003). Impact of the 1985 Amendments to the Indian Act on First Nations populations. In J.P. White, P. Maxim, & D. Beavon (Eds.), *Aboriginal conditions* (pp. 63–90). Vancouver, BC: University of British Columbia Press.

———. (2006). *Registered Indian population projections for Canada and regions, 2004–2029*. Ottawa, ON: Indian and Northern Affairs Canada.

Cook, N.D. (1998). *Born to die: Disease and New World conquest, 1492–1650*. Cambridge, UK: Cambridge University Press.

Denevan, M.W. (1992). *The native population of the Americas in 1492*. Madison, WI: University of Wisconsin Press.

Dickason, O.P. (1992/1994). *Canada's First Nations: A history of founding peoples from earliest times*. Toronto, ON: McClelland & Stewart.

Dobyns, H.F. (1966). Estimating Aboriginal American population: An appraisal of techniques with a hemispheric estimate. *Current Anthropology*, 7(4), 395–416.

Douville, R., & Casanova, J.-D. (1964). *La vie autochtone à l'époque de la colonisation française*. Paris: Hachette.

Driver, H.E., & Massy, W.C. (1957). *Comparative studies in North America Indians*. Philadelphia, PA: The American Philosophical Society.

Dumont, A. (1990/1890). *Dépopulation et civilisation*. Paris: Economica.

Dumont, J. (Ed.). (1962). *Les voyages de Samuel de Champlain*. Montréal, QC: Les amis de l'histoire.

Ewers, J.C. (1969). *The Hors in Blackfoot Indian culture, with comparative material from other Western tribes*. Washington, DC: Smithsonian Institution Press.

Farb, P. (1972). *Les Indiens: Essai sur l'évolution des sociétés humaines*. Paris: Éditions du Seuil.

Forsyth, J. (1994). *A history of peoples of Siberia, Russia's North Asian colonies, 1581–1990*. Cambridge, UK: Cambridge University Press.

Frideres, J.S. (1988). *Native peoples in Canada: Contemporary conflicts*. Scarborough, ON: Prentice Hall.

George, M.V., & Loh, S. (2003). Estimating the fertility level of Registered Indians in Canada: A challenging endeavour. *Canadian Studies in Population, 30*(1), 117–135.

Gibbins, R., & Ponting, R.J. (1986). *Arduous journey: Canadian Indians and decolonization.* Toronto, ON: McClelland & Stewart.

Goldmann, G., & Siggner, A. (1992). Statistical concepts of Aboriginal people and factors affecting the counts in the census and the Aboriginal peoples survey. In *Towards the XXIst century: Emerging socio-demographic trends and policy issues in Canada* (pp. 265–281). Ottawa, ON: Federation of Canadian Demographers.

Gracey, M., & King, M. (2009). Indigenous health part 1: Determinants and disease patterns. *Lancet, 374,* 65–75.

Grey, A. (1990). *A matter of life and death: Contemporary Aboriginal mortality.* Canberra: Aboriginal Study Press.

Guimond, E. (2003). Définitions floues et explosion démographique: identité mouvante des groupes autochtones au Canada. In D. Newhouse & E. Peters (Eds.), *Des gens d'ici: Les autochtones en milieu urbain* (pp. 39–85). Ottawa, ON: Policy Research Initiative, Government of Canada.

Harris, J. & McCullough, R. (1988). *Health Status Indicator derived from vital statistics, for the Status Indians and Canadian population, 1978–1986.* Ottawa, ON: Health and Welfare Canada.

Heagerty, J.J. (1928). *Four centuries of medical history in Canada* (Vol. I). Toronto, ON: Macmillan.

Health Canada. (2003, March). Closing the gaps in Aboriginal health. *Health Policy Research Bulletin 5.* Retrieved from http://www.hc-sc.gc.ca/sr-sr/pubs/hpr-rpms/bull/2003-5-aboriginal-autochtone/index-eng.php

———. (2009). *A statistical profile on the health of First Nations in Canada: Determinants of health, 1999 to 2003* (Catalogue No. H34-193/1-2008E-PDF). Retrieved from http://www.hc-sc.gc.ca/fniah-spnia/pubs/aborig-autoch/2009-stats-profil/index-eng.php

Henripin, J. (1972). *Trends and factors of fertility in Canada.* 1961 Census Monograph. Ottawa, ON: Statistics Canada.

Henry, A., Sr. (1809). *Travels and adventures in Canada and the Indian Territories between the years 1760 and 1776.* New York, NY: I. Riley.

Hull, J. (2004). Aboriginal single mothers in Canada, 1996: A statistical profile. In J.P. White, P. Maxim, & D. Beavon (Eds.), *Aboriginal policy research: Setting the agenda for change,* Vol. II (pp. 183–200). Toronto, ON: Thompson.

Innis, A.H. (1910). *The fur trade in Canada.* New Haven, CT: Yale University Press.

Jenness, D. (1977). *The Indians of Canada.* Toronto, ON: University of Toronto Press.

Kellogg, L.P. (Ed.). (1917). *Early narratives of the Northwest 1634–1699.* New York, NY: Charles Scribner.

Keyfitz, N., & Carmagnani, A. (1966). Commentary—Estimating Aboriginal American population: An appraisal of techniques with a hemispheric estimate. *Current Anthropology, 7*(4), 435–436.

King, M., Smith, A., & Gracey, M. (2009). Indigenous health part 2: The underlying causes of the health gap. *Lancet, 374,* 76–85.

Kreager, P. (1997). Population and identity. In D.I. Kertzen & T. Fricke (Eds.), *Anthropological demography* (pp. 139–174). Chicago, IL: University of Chicago Press.

Kroeber, A.L. (1939). *Cultural and natural area of Native America.* Berkeley, CA: University of California Press.

Krotki, K.J. (1995). The eight million artificial Canadians, their future and related policies. In *Towards the XXIst century: emerging socio-demographic trends and policy issues in Canada* (pp. 173–187). Ottawa, ON: Federation of Canadian Demographers.

Kunitz, J.S. (1990). Public policy and mortality among Indigenous populations of North America and Australasia. *Population and Development Review, 6*(4), 647–672.

Kunstadter, P. (1966). Commentary—Estimating Aboriginal American population: An appraisal of techniques with a hemispheric estimate. *Current Anthropology, 7*(4), 436–437.

Légaré, A. (1998). An assessment of recent political development in Nunavut: The challenges and dilemmas of Inuit self-government. *The Canadian Journal of Native Studies, 23*(2), 271–300.

Leslie, F.J. (2004). The policy agenda of native peoples from World War II to the 1969 White Paper. In J.P. White, P. Maxim, & D. Beavon (Eds.), *Aboriginal policy research: Setting the agenda for change,* Vol. I (pp. 15–23). Toronto, ON: Thompson.

Livi-Bacci, M. (2008). *Conquest: The destruction of the American Indios.* Cambridge, UK: Polity Press.

Mackenzie, A. (1911). *Voyages from Montreal through the continent of North America to the frozen and Pacific Oceans in 1789 and 1793.* Two volumes. Toronto, ON: The Courier Press.

Manitoba Injury Prevention Newsletter. (2004, Spring). Summary. Retrieved from http://www.hsc.mb.ca/impact/publications.htm

McFalls, J.A. Jr., & McFalls, M.H. (1984). *Disease and fertility.* Orlando, FL: Academic Press.

Mealing, S.R. (Ed.). (1963). *The Jesuit relations and allied documents.* Toronto, ON: McClelland & Stewart.

Mignone, J., Longclaws, J., O'Neil, J., & Mustard, C. (2004). Social capital in First Nations communities: Concept and measurement. In J.P. White, P. Maxim, & D. Beavon (Eds:), *Aboriginal policy research: Setting the agenda for change,* Vol. II (pp. 125–140), Toronto, ON: Thompson.

Miller, J.R. (1989). *Skyscrapers hide the heavens: A history of Indian-White relations in Canada.* Toronto, ON: University of Toronto Press.

———. (2004). *Reflections on native-newcomer relations.* Toronto, ON: University of Toronto Press.

Mooney, J. (1928). *The Aboriginal population of America North of Mexico.* Washington, DC: The Smithsonian Institution.

Morrison, B.R., & Wilson, C.R. (1995). *Native peoples: The Canadian experience.* Toronto, ON: McClelland & Stewart.

Pool, I. (1991). *Te Iwi Maori: New Zealand population past, present and projected.* Auckland, NZ: Auckland University Press.

Price, J.A. (1979). *Indians of Canada: Cultural dynamics.* Scarborough, ON: Prentice Hall.

Ram, B. (1991, June). *Assimilation and fertility of Native Indians: Some new evidence.* Paper presented at the Annual Meeting of the Canadian Population Society, Kingston, Ontario.

————. (2000). New estimates of Aboriginal fertility, 1966–2001. *Canadian Studies in Population, 31*(2), 179–190.

Ray, A.J. (1998). *Indians in the fur trade: Their role as trappers, hunters, and middlemen in the lands Southwest of Hudson Bay, 1660–1870.* Toronto, ON: University of Toronto Press.

Robitaille, N., Kouaouci, A., & Guimond, E. (2004). La fécondité des Indiennes à 15 à 19 ans, de 1986 à1996. In J.P. White, P. Maxim, & D. Beavon (Eds.), *Aboriginal policy research: Setting the agenda for change,* Vol. II (pp. 201–224). Toronto, ON: Thompson.

Roe, F.G. (1951). *The Indian and the Hors.* Norman, OK: University of Oklahoma Press.

————. (1955). *The North American Buffalo: A critical study of the species in its wild state.* Toronto, ON: University of Toronto Press.

Romaniuc, A. (1986). Transition from traditional high to modern low fertility: Canadian Aboriginals. *Canadian Studies in Population, 14*(1), 69–88.

————. (2003). Fertility of a community in transition: The case of James Bay Indians, Canada. *The Canadian Journal of Native Studies, 23*(2), 227–275.

Romaniuk, A. (1981a). Increase in natural fertility during the early stages of modernisation: Canadian Indians case study. *Demography, 18*(2),.157–172.

————. (1981b). Increase in natural fertility during the early stages of modernisation: Evidence from an African case study, Zaire. *Population Studies, 34*(2), 293–331.

————. (2008). History-based exploratory framework for procreative behaviour of Aboriginal people of Canada. *Canadian Studies in Population, 35*(1), 159–186.

————. (2012). Stationary population as policy vision. *Optimum Online: The Journal of Public Sector Management, 42*(1).

Sagard, G. (1969). *Le grand voyage au pays des Hurons.* Montréal, QC: Les amis de l'histoire.

Sametz, Z.W. (1964). The progressive integration of man with the environment. In P. Camu, E.P. Weks, & Z.W. Sametz (Eds.), *Economic geography of Canada* (pp. 33–51). Toronto, ON: Macmillan.

Sandoz, M. (1978). *The Buffalo hunters.* Lincoln, NE: University of Nebraska Press.

Shkilnyk, A.M. (1985). *A poison stronger than love: The destruction of an Ojibwa community.* New Haven, CT: Yale University Press.

Sowell, T. (1999). *Conquests and cultures: A world view.* New York, NY: Basic Books.

Spady, D.W. (1982). *Between two worlds.* Edmonton, AB: Boreal Institute for Northern Studies.

Stanley, F.G. (1960). *The birth of Western Canada: A history of the Riel rebellions.* Toronto, ON: University of Toronto Press.

Statistics Canada. (2005). *Projections of the Aboriginal populations, Canada, provinces and territories, 2001 to 2017* (Catalogue No. 91-547-XIE). Ottawa, ON: Stastistics Canada.

Talon, J. (1676). *Archives coloniales Canada*, corr. gén. 2, 1663–1706.

Thornton, R. (1987). *American Indian holocaust and survival: A population history since 1492*. Norman, OK: University of Oklahoma Press.

Thwaites, R.G. (1899). *The Jesuit relations and allied documents*. Vol. 1. Cleveland, OH: Burrows Brothers.

Trovato, F. (1987). A macrosociological analysis of Native Indian fertility in Canada: 1961, 1971, and 1981. *Social Forces, 66*(2), 463–485.

Trovato, F., & Werner-Leonard, A. (1991). Analysis of Native mortality. *Journal of Indigenous Studies, 2*(1), 1–15.

Verma, R., Michalowski, M., & Gauvin, R.P. (2004). Abridged life tables for Registered Indians in Canada, 1976–1980 to 1996–2000. *Canadian Studies in Population, 31*(2), 197–235.

Vogel, V.J. (1970). *American Indian Medicine*. Norman, OK: University of Oklahoma Press.

Waldram, J.B., Herring, A., & Young, T.K. (2006). *Aboriginal health in Canada*. Toronto, ON: University of Toronto Press.

White, J., Spence, N., & Maxim, P. (2007). Assessing the net effects of specific claim settlements in First Nations communities in the context of community well-being. In J.W. White, D. Beavon, & N. Spence (Eds.), *Aboriginal well-being, Canada's continuing challenge* (pp. 185–208). Toronto, ON: Thompson.

Wissler, C. (1936). *Population changes among the Northern Plains Indians*. New Haven, CT: Yale University Press.

Young, T.K. (Ed.). (1987). *Diabetes in the Canadian Native population: Biocultural perspectives*. Toronto, ON: Canadian Diabetes Association.

———. (1988). *Health care and cultural change: The Indian experience*. Toronto, ON: University of Toronto Press.

2

COUNTING ABORIGINAL PEOPLES IN CANADA

Gustave J. Goldmann and Senada Delic

INTRODUCTION

Census data and concepts can be compared to a mirror that reflects the values of the society at the time that the census is conducted. The content of the questionnaire, the wording of the questions, and the concepts that underlie the classifications used in the data are consistent with society's perceptions of the issues. Census counts of Canada's Aboriginal peoples serve as an excellent illustration of the impact of the changes in social conditions over time on published data. For instance, the application of concepts of descent and racial/ethnic classification of Canadian society has evolved substantially since the early pre- and post-Confederation censuses. Furthermore, the classification of subgroups and the application of descent rules were not uniform for all groups in society. For example, although the ethnic origin of the European population was determined along patrilineal lines for most censuses between 1871 and 1971, the rules for descent for the Aboriginal population varied from tribal to matrilineal to patrilineal. The impact of these differences on the reported counts has been the source of debate and discussion among Aboriginal communities, federal departments and agencies, and social scientists. This chapter will attempt to shed some light on the debate and to explore the impact of population flows of the Aboriginal peoples on socio-demographic analyses.

This chapter begins with a brief history of census taking as it applies to the Aboriginal peoples, followed by an introduction of the concepts and definitions that will be used in the analysis and discussion. The terminology used in this chapter reflects the terms used in the official documents on which the analysis is based. A historical context analysis of the census collection instruments from 1871, the first census conducted after Confederation, to 2006 provides a context for understanding the counts of the Aboriginal population used in this chapter. The chapter continues with an empirical analysis of census counts, highlighting variations that cannot be explained by "natural" population processes. The chapter concludes with a discussion of ethnic mobility as a partial explanation for some of the more recent trends in population growth among the Aboriginal peoples.

THE HISTORICAL CONTEXT

The history of census taking in Canada began in 1666 when Jean Talon conducted the first full enumeration of the colony of New France. However, long before Jean Talon's census, the indigenous population of the territory we presently refer to as Canada maintained approximate counts of their communities through oral tradition. The earliest recorded count of the Aboriginal population conducted by the Jesuit missionaries in 1611 also predates the first census. The Jesuits prepared the statement for the territory that largely corresponds to Nova Scotia, New Brunswick, Maine, parts of New England, and the lower Saint Lawrence (Statistics of Canada, 1876). The language used by the enumerators indicates that the counts were concerned only with "warriors" and "souls," terms that clearly indicate the concerns of the authorities of the day. It is also interesting to note that they counted all Indians without taking into consideration their tribal affiliation.

In 1639, the Jesuits prepared another count of the population. In this instance, the counts were limited to the "confederation of Hurons" (Statistics of Canada, 1876). This enumeration included information on the dwellings and communal groupings. Estimates were made of the number of villages (32), the number of lodges (700), the number of fires (2,000), and the number of persons (12,000). The rounding of the numbers to the nearest hundred is a clear indication that they are estimates.

The two successive enumerations of the Aboriginal population, which were taken after the Huron-Iroquois war of 1648–1649, were conducted in 1665 by Jesuit missionaries and in 1677 by Wentworth Greenhalgh (Statistics of Canada, 1876). The 1665 enumeration provided the first recorded count of the Indian population by tribe, listing a total of 2,040 warriors that included Mohawks (400), Oneidas (140), Onondagas (300), Cayugas (300), and Senecas (1,200). As with the count of 1611, the enumerators were concerned with both the numbers of warriors and souls; hence, the total for this enumeration was given as 11,700 souls. However, no clear definitions of either term were published with the numbers. It is not obvious from the records we consulted exactly who was considered to be a warrior, nor whether the number of souls represents the total population or only that proportion considered to be eligible for conversion to Christianity (i.e., excluding Shamans, the elderly, and others who were deemed to not be suitable "Christians").

In 1677, Wentworth Greenhalgh published counts of the same population for the British government. Although his numbers differed somewhat from those published by the French Jesuit missionaries (the total population according to Greenhalgh was only 10,750 souls), the terminology and classification were the same. He did, however, also count the number of villages and lodges.

Numerous attempts were made to collect data on the Aboriginal peoples between 1677 and 1851. Many of these enumerations were conducted by the Hudson's Bay Company in the territories that it administered and were published as counts, simple lists, and memoirs of the administrators of the local area.

The context for classifying Aboriginal origins and for counting the Aboriginal population in early Canadian censuses was shaped during the period between the first recorded count and the first Census of the Canadas in 1851. Some form of census of population has been the primary survey instrument used to collect information about the Aboriginal Peoples living in Canada for most of the period covered in this chapter, with five notable exceptions—the Report of the Special Committee of the House of Commons in 1857, the Special Statement of the Aboriginal Population in Canada in 1871, and the three post-censal surveys of Aboriginal peoples conducted in 1991, 2001, and 2006. Therefore, the empirical analyses presented later in this chapter are based on published census counts.

DEFINITIONS

As of 2013, in Canada, the decennial census is conducted during the first full year of every decade (i.e., the year 1951, 1961, 1971, etc.). Prior to the repatriation of the Constitution, the decennial census was conducted under the authority of the British North America Act, 1867. More recently, it has been conducted under the authority of the Constitution Act, 1982. National quinquennial censuses began in 1956 and have been collected every 10 years from that time (i.e., 1966, 1976, 1986, etc.) under the authority of the Statistics Act.[1] The content of the quinquennial censuses consisted of basic demographic counts until 1986. At that time, more extensive content was introduced by Statistics Canada.

Until 1971, census data were collected by a trained census representative who directly interviewed at least one person in every household and solicited proxy information for the others. Self-enumeration was introduced in the census for most of the population in Canada in 1971. This collection methodology relies on the respondents completing the questionnaires for themselves. It is acknowledged that in many instances one person responded on behalf of the other members of the household, which may be similar to the situation when data were collected by an interviewer. Since consistency, completeness, and accuracy are important in a census, the introduction of self-enumeration brought with it a requirement for thorough testing of the collection vehicles as well as the methods for distributing and retrieving the census forms.

Early censuses covered a full range of social, demographic, agricultural, and economic themes. They generally included a range of questionnaires (referred to as schedules before 1951) that contained hundreds of questions in total. In fact, the 1941 Census had eight schedules with a total of 1,128 questions (Dominion Bureau of Statistics, 1941: 13). Dividing the census into two components, a sample survey and a full population survey, was introduced in 1941 when the housing questionnaire was administered to 10% of the population. The goal was to reduce respondent burden and collection and processing costs. Weights were calculated that allowed total population estimates to be produced from the sample counts. This methodology has been applied in some fashion in the census from that point in time.

The collection and processing of census data are extremely complex operations that are very well documented in the administrative reports produced for each census. Therefore, they will not be described here. However, reference will be made to the instructions given to the census collection staff and, for the more recent censuses, to the respondents. These directions are particularly relevant in the discussion of the rules that govern how descent was to be derived for different groups in the population, and in particular for the Aboriginal peoples.

Information derived from census data serves a broad spectrum of researchers, analysts, educators, and administrators from the public and private sectors of Canadian society. "Their needs are as varied as their interests" (Goldmann, 1992). What they have in common is a requirement for information that is geographically detailed and that identifies small population groups that might be missed in a sample survey (i.e , small area data) and that cross-classifies a number of key characteristics, such as age, sex, marital status, and ethnic origin. Census data are used in a variety of applications including determining trends in the socio demographic, economic, and social development of the population, assessing the effect of government policies, planning for the needs of communities, and locating potential markets for goods and services. To some extent, the requirements for the information influence how the data are presented and, in some instances, what data are collected. This is particularly true for data on the Aboriginal population living in Canada. The requirements of the original Indian Act, 1876 and all its subsequent revisions and the Constitution Act have had considerable impact of the classifications of Aboriginal people in the census. Extensive consultations with Aboriginal leaders have been conducted prior to every census since 1981 to ensure that the data that are collected are relevant to the needs of their communities.

Officials used a variety of terms in counting the Aboriginal population that reflect the legislation and common understanding at the time of the particular census. Indians have been referred to as North American Indian and Native Indian (North American). They have been further classified by band membership (or lack thereof), tribal affiliation, treaty status, whether they lived on- and off-reserve and, in more recent censuses, by their status with respect to the Indian Act. The Métis population was referred to as Half-breeds, Breeds, and Indian. The Inuit people were referred to either as Inuit or Eskimo. These changes in terminology and their impact on the counts are traced in the discussion on the individual censuses that appears later in this chapter.

In all censuses, except 1891, which did not include questions dealing with the ethnic or racial origins of the population, the Aboriginal population was counted through the question on ethnic origin/ancestry/race. The ambiguities of the concept of ethnicity have been addressed by a number of social scientists (see Cohen, 1992; Goldmann, 1998; Goldscheider, 1992; Isajiw, 1992; Pryor, Goldmann, Sheridan, & White, 1992; Ryder, 1956). This issue is further complicated by the tension that exists between the concepts of ancestry and identity. Ancestry refers to the ethnic or cultural group or groups to which the person's ancestors belong. Identity in this context refers to persons who reported identifying with at least one Aboriginal group. Evidence during the testing of the questions for the 1991 Census suggested that respondents did not necessarily distinguish between the two concepts. The results of the 1991 Census show that some people may have been drawn to respond based on their identity, in spite of the caveats and explanatory notes included with the question (Pryor, Goldmann, Sheridan, & White, 1992). Consequently, data are collected on both identity and ancestry for the Aboriginal population since the 1996 Census.

Another factor that complicates how the ethnic identity of an individual is determined is the rate of intermarriage between ethnic and racial groups in Canadian society. In the case of marriages between members of the North American Indian population and non-Indian population, the situation is somewhat more complex since "the distinction between Indian and non-Indian is strictly a legal one" (Frideres, 1988). Before the passage of Bill C-31 (An Act to Amend the Indian Act) in 1985 any Indian woman who married a non-Indian man lost status with respect to the Indian Act for herself and for her offspring. Conversely, if a non-Indian woman married an Indian man, she gained Indian status, as did the couple's offspring (Frideres, 1988: 4). With the passage of Bill C-31 many of these Indian women and their children were eligible to apply to regain their status. The analysis presented later in this chapter shows the impact of this legislation.

FROM 1871 TO 2006[2]

In this section, we present a brief summary of the principal features and instructions given to census collection staff and respondents that apply specifically to the collection of data and presentation of results on Aboriginal peoples of Canada. While we have examined collections recorded as early as 1611, we focus on presenting the results from the collection period between

1871, when the ethnic origin question was first formally introduced to census questionnaire, and 2006.[3] Appendix A contains detailed information for the 1961 to 2006 census years. The information included in the following summary relates only to selected years, particularly those from 1961 and onward, and it centres primarily on those factors that may serve to explain some of the differences and peculiarities in the data presented in the next section, and particularly the descent paradigms shown in Table 2.4.[4]

Although the enumerators of the first post-Confederation census, the 1871 census, as well as the 1881 census, were explicitly asked to make a clear distinction between the origin and the place of birth of the respondents when using these terms as indicators of ethnicity, no specific instructions were given to enumerators as to how to ascertain and record the Aboriginal ethnicity in these two censuses. The 1886 Census of Manitoba and the 1885 North West Census did, however, include detailed instructions to enumerators, particularly with regards to how to count Métis. Their records were meticulously recorded and reported in these two censuses.

The 1901 Census was the first decennial post-Confederation census that made explicit reference to the Aboriginal population in the instructions to the census representative. Enumerators in this census were instructed to record the names of the tribes in the case of the Indians and to clearly note various combinations of "persons of mixed white and red blood—commonly known as half-breeds." The observed rules for descent in this census were patrilineal for the white population. Any mixture including some Aboriginal origin was classified as "other breed," regardless of which parent was an Indian. The matrilineal descent for Aboriginal people was first recognized in the 1911 Census. Hence, in the following two decennial censuses, the 1921 Census and the 1931 Census, the enumerators were instructed to derive ancestry along matrilineal side for Indians and patrilineal side for others. Children from mixed-race marriages were classified as non-white, regardless of which parent was an Indian.

The 1961 Census introduced the long and short form questionnaires, in which ancestry question referred specifically to ethnic and cultural origin and in which instructions to enumerators stated that the decent was to be determined along patrilineal side for all. In the case of Aboriginal populations, the enumerators were instructed to determine whether or not Indians were band members and to code Treaty Indians as band members. Furthermore, the enumerators were instructed to code respondents of mixed white and Indian parentage as Indians only if they lived on a reserve. If they lived off-reserve, they were to be coded according to patrilineal lines.

Self-enumeration for most of the population of Canada, except for the on-reserve residents and those living in remote northern areas, was first introduced in the 1971 Census. The 1986 Census introduced a separate question on Aboriginal identity, in addition to the Aboriginal origin question. No specific rules were imposed on how ancestry was to be established, and an accommodation was made to allow multiple origin responses. The 2006 Census entailed the same enumeration rules, which were presented to the respondents filling in either electronic or paper questionnaires and to the enumerators interviewing the on-reserve and northern residents.

ANALYSIS AND DISCUSSION

The way in which Aboriginal peoples were counted varied over time. First, the criteria that determined how descent was to be established for the Aboriginal population ran the gamut from "not specified" to "ambilineal" (see Table 2.6). Second, the 1986 Census introduced self-identity as well as ancestral origins as a means of classifying the Aboriginal population by including two questions—one focusing on ethnic origin (ancestry) and a second asking with which group the individual identified. Third, some Aboriginal communities refused to participate in the census.[5] Finally, the capturing of responses to the question on ethnic origin underwent a fundamental transformation in the 1981 Census. From that point in time, the question and the data began to reflect more precisely the multicultural nature of Canadian society by including multiple responses for ethnic origin.

The following charts and tables present the counts of the Aboriginal population from three different perspectives. We begin with an overview of the growth of the Aboriginal population classified by ancestry (origin) and of the total population of Canada between 1871 and 2006. Figure 2.1 shows that the growth of the Aboriginal population approximates an exponential curve and that of the total population of Canada follows a geometric pattern.[6]

Table 2.1 shows that growth of the Aboriginal population when measured by ancestry was somewhat erratic between 1871 and 2006. Much of the volatility between 1951 and 1971 can be attributed to changes in definitions, methods by which Aboriginal people were classified (as described earlier) and methods of determining descent (see Table 2.6).[7]

Figure 2.1 Total Population Declaring Aboriginal Ancestry, 1871–2006

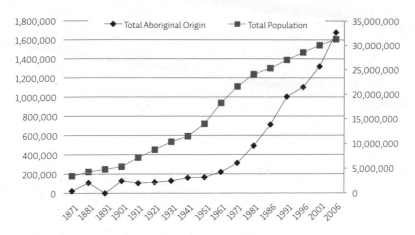

Source: Statistics Canada, Censuses of Canada, 1871 to 2006.

Table 2.1 Aboriginal Ancestry Population and Total Population of Canada, 1871–2006, Including Average Annual Growth Rates

Year	Total Aboriginal Origin	Total Population	AAGR Aboriginal (%)	AAGR Canada (%)
1871	23,037	3,485,761		
1881	108,547	4,324,810		
1891	0	4,833,239		
1901	127,941	5,371,315		
1911	105,611	7,206,643		
1921	114,083	8,788,483		
1931	128,890	10,376,786		
1941	160,937	11,506,655		
1951	165,607	14,009,429	0.29	1.99
1961	220,121	18,238,247	2.85	2.67
1971	312,765	21,568,310	3.51	1.69
1981	491,465	24,083,495	0	1.11
1986	711,725	25,309,330	7.41	0
1991	1,002,675	26,994,045	6.85	1.30
1996	1,101,960	28,528,125	1.89	1.11
2001	1,319,890	30,007,095	3.61	1.02
2006	1,678,235	31,241,030	4.80	0.81

Source: Statistics Canada, Censuses of Canada, 1871 to 2006.

Natural population increase is defined as the difference between the crude birth rate (CBR) and the crude death rate (CDR) (Pressat, 1983). The highest natural population increase will occur when the CBR is at its highest and the CDR is at its lowest. Examining CBR and CDR indicators for all countries from 1955 to 2000, it was found that the maximum natural population growth ranged from 55.8 per 1,000 for the period between 1950 and 1955 to 52.2 per 1,000 for the period between 1995 and 2000 (United Nations, 2006b). In other words, one can say that a theoretical maximum for population growth can range from 5.2% to 5.6% over the period between 1950 and 2000.

According to the *Demographic Yearbook* published by the United Nations Statistical Division, the highest rate of increase (including migration) between 2000 and 2005 is 2.6%, recorded for Central Africa (United Nations, 2006a). We can see from the results in Table 2.1 that the growth for the Aboriginal population defined by ancestry has exceeded this value for most years since 1961, and it has also exceeded the theoretical maximum in at least two cases—from 1981 to 1986 and from 1986 to 1991. The dramatic increase in the Aboriginal population between 1981 and 1986 can be attributed in part to the number of people who were able to reclaim their ancestry after the passage of amendments to the Indian Act in 1985. This event resulted in a phenomenon that has been labelled "ethnic mobility" (Goldmann, 1998; Robitaille & Guimond, 2003). Ethnic mobility is defined as the increase or decrease in a population group defined by ethnocultural characteristics that cannot be explained by natural processes or by migration. There are two types of ethnic mobility—self-ascribed and imposed. If an individual changes the population group with which he or she identifies, it is referred to as self-ascribed ethnic mobility. Imposed ethnic mobility occurs when the definition of the group is changed over time. This is often reflected in the collection instruments. Ethnic mobility is the only plausible explanation for these increases given that we are analyzing a closed population in which there is virtually no immigration (Guimond, 1999).[8]

A comparison of growth rates for the Aboriginal population defined by self-identification with those for the total Canadian population shows similar results.

In fact, the growth rates for the Aboriginal population are consistently close to the theoretical maximum described earlier. This result is logical

Table 2.2 Population Declaring Aboriginal Identity and Total Population of Canada, Including Average Annual Growth Rates, 1986–2006

Year	Total Aboriginal Identity	Total Canada	AAGR Aboriginal (%)	AAGR Canada (%)
1986	464,455	25,309,330		1
1991	613,820	26,994,045	5.58	1.3
1996	799,010	28,528,125	5.27	1.11
2001	976,305	30,007,095	3.38	1.02
2006	1,172,790	31,241,030	4.29	0.81

Source: Statistics Canada, Censuses of Canada, 1986 to 2006. Calculations by the authors.

Table 2.3 North American Indian, Métis, and Inuit populations of Canada (1871–2006) by Ancestry and Identity

Year	North American Indian		Métis		Inuit	
	Ancestry	Identity	Ancestry	Identity	Ancestry	Identity
1871	23,035		2			
1881	108,547					
1891						
1901	93,460		34,481			
1911	105,611					
1921	110,814				3,269	
1931	122,911				5,979	
1941	118,316		35,416		7,205	
1951	165,607					
1961	208,286				11,835	
1971	295,215				17,550	
1981	313,655		76,520		23,200	
1986		286,230		59,745		27,290
1991		443,285		128,700		35,495
1996		535,075		210,055		41,085
2001		608,850		292,310		45,070
2006		698,025		389,785		50,485

Source: Censuses of population, 1871 to 2006.

when one considers that it is often easier, and more meaningful, to change the group with which one identifies since this is a subjective measure.

The effect of changes in concepts and definitions become more apparent once we unpack the counts for the Aboriginal population (Table 2.3). While it is difficult to quantify the impact of any of the following factors, it is clear that the counts reflect changes in the formulation of the questions that dealt with ethnic/racial origins, changes in the instructions given to the census collection staff (and/or respondents), differences in the socio-political climate at the time the census was conducted, and the number of incompletely enumerated reserves. For instance, the no counts shown for the Métis between 1911 and 1931 and between 1951 and 1971 are due to the lack of specific instructions to the census collection staff on how to classify this segment of the population. The fact that no counts of Inuit are available before 1921 can be attributed to changes in the spatial coverage of the census and to instructions (or lack thereof) given to census collection staff. Finally, the addition of a question on self-identification (in addition to ancestry) introduces an important conceptual discontinuity in the counts of Aboriginal Peoples.

Table 2.4 provides a summary of the descent rules that were applied to the ancestry data for each of the census years considered in this chapter.

The descent rules that were de rigueur up to 1941 appear to have been influenced by evolutionary theory. According to the nineteenth-century evolutionary paradigms, societies were classified on a scale that, based on Lewis Henry Morgan's interpretation, spanned a continuum from "savagery" to "barbarism" to "civilization." It was commonly believed by evolutionists that descent among civilized societies was promulgated along patrilineal lines. They also believed that, among less civilized societies, descent was matrilineally based, and among the Aboriginal populations (referred to as savages by Morgan) it was based on tribal affiliation (Zeitlin, 1990: 119). It is possible that the pattern seen in Table 2.4 reflects the conceptual thinking at the time the earlier censuses were conducted. Contemporary sociological theory certainly supports the ambilineal determination of ancestral origins used since 1981. In fact, the most recent censuses included questions on the birthplace of the mother and the father.

The rules also reflect legislative and policy imperatives of the government of the day. For example, the revisions of the Indian Act in 1924 and 1951 had an impact on how the Aboriginal people were classified in the census. The current Indian Act and the Constitution Act, 1982 provide

Table 2.4 Descent Rules by Census Year by Ethnic/Racial/Tribal Origins

Census	White / European	Indian	Métis	Eskimo	Other non-white	Other mixed
1871	Not specified	Not specified	Not specified	Not specified	Not specified	Not specified
1881	Not specified	Not specified	Not specified	Not specified	Not specified	Not specified
1891	N/A	N/A	N/A	N/A	N/A	N/A
1901	Patrilineal	Tribal	Complex	Not specified	Not specified	Not specified
1911	Patrilineal	Matrilineal	Not specified	Not specified	Not specified	Non-white
1921	Patrilineal	Matrilineal	Not specified	Not specified	Not specified	Non-white
1931	Patrilineal	Matrilineal	Not specified	Not specified	Coloured	Non-white
1941	Patrilineal	Indian	Half-breed	Eskimo	Coloured	Non-white
1951	Patrilineal	Patrilineal	Place of residence	Not specified	Patrilineal	Patrilineal
1961	Patrilineal	Patrilineal	Place of residence	Not specified	Patrilineal	Patrilineal
1971	Patrilineal	Patrilineal	Patrilineal	Patrilineal	Patrilineal	Patrilineal
1981	Ambilineal	Ambilineal	Ambilineal	Ambilineal	Ambilineal	Ambilineal
1986	Ambilineal	Ambilineal	Ambilineal	Ambilineal	Ambilineal	Ambilineal
1991	Ambilineal	Ambilineal	Ambilineal	Ambilineal	Ambilineal	Ambilineal
1996	Ambilineal	Ambilineal	Ambilineal	Ambilineal	Ambilineal	Ambilineal
2001	Ambilineal	Ambilineal	Ambilineal	Ambilineal	Ambilineal	Ambilineal
2006	Ambilineal	Ambilineal	Ambilineal	Ambilineal	Ambilineal	Ambilineal

the fundamental impetus for the definition of the Aboriginal peoples to be included in the censuses since 1986. However, it is beyond the scope of this study to discuss these changes and their impact.

BEYOND THE COUNTS

Earlier in this chapter we defined ethnic mobility as the change in the size of a population group described by ethnocultural characteristics that cannot be explained by natural processes or by migration. This definition can be applied within a generation or across generations. In either case, it is not clear at this stage to what extent the characteristics of the "ethnically mobile" population differ from those of the "non-mobile" population. Current data sources do not allow us to measure these effects directly since it would require an extensive qualitative study of both sub-populations— those who changed their identity and those who did not.[9]

Nevertheless, it is possible to pursue the first stages of such an analysis by examining one of the factors that can contribute substantially to

Table 2.5 Distribution of Census Families Declaring Aboriginal Identity
by Intermarriage (2001)

	Number	%
Endogamous	48,137	60.7
Exogamous	31,117	39.3
Total	79,254	100.0

Source: 2001 Census, Public Use Census Microdata File (families). Calculations by the authors.

intergenerational ethnic mobility—exogamy. Exogamous unions are defined
as the marriage or common-law union of two people who declare different
ethnic identities. In this chapter, we are concerned only with those who
declare an Aboriginal identity. Therefore, an exogamous couple would have
one partner who is Aboriginal by identity and one who is not. Furthermore,
since we are interested in the effect on the next generation, that is, the children of these couples, the analysis that follows examines only two-parent
families with at least one child present in the household. This stage of the
analysis was conducted on the 2001 census public use microdata family file.

In 2001, there were slightly fewer than 80,000 census families with
children present in the household and in which at least one of the parents
declared an Aboriginal identity. It must be noted that these counts do not
include data for the population in the reserves who did not participate in
the census. Of those families, 60% were in endogamous unions.

The literature on acculturation and contact theory suggests that people
who live in ethnically heterogeneous areas have greater opportunities to
associate with members of other groups in a social setting, thereby increasing the possibility of intermarriage (Alba, 1990; Fong & Wilkes, 2003; Gans,
1997). Reserves can be considered to be somewhat homogenous when
we look at the population that declares North American Indian identity.
Similarly, it can be assumed that Inuit communities are equally homogenous. Métis communities are more difficult to classify in this way. While
the 2001 census public use microdata files do not contain specific identifiers
for Aboriginal communities, it is possible to examine the population living
in Census Metropolitan Areas (CMA) and those living outside these areas.
This provides us with a rough proxy of a stratification of the population living within and outside Aboriginal communities since all reserves and Inuit
settlements are outside of CMAs.

Table 2.6 Distribution of Aboriginal Families with Children by Type of Residence (CMA or non-CMA) and by Intermarriage (2001)

		non-CMA		CMA		Total
		n	%	n	%	n
Endogamous	n	42,328	67.9	5,809	34.3	48,137
	%	87.9		12.1		100
Exogamous	n	19,980	32.1	11,137	65.7	31,117
	%	64.2		35.8		100
Total	n	62,308	100	16,946	100	79,254

Source: 2001 Census, Public Use Census Microdata File (families). Calculations by the authors.

The majority of Aboriginal couples with children living in a metropolitan area (65%) are in exogamous unions (either married or common-law). We also see from the results shown in Table 2.6 that over two-thirds of the couples who are in endogamous unions are living in non-CMA areas. It can be seen that an association exists between the two variables shown in the table above. In fact, a simple calculation of the odds ratio shows that endogamous couples with children are approximately four times more likely to be living in non-CMA areas. The significance of this association is shown in the results of a simple logistic model in which intermarriage is the dependent variable and whether the couples are living in a CMA is the independent variable. The full specification of the model is not shown given that it is a simple bivariate regression. The resulting likelihood coefficient is 1.396, and it is statistically significant to the 0.05 level. Therefore, it can be concluded that exogamous Aboriginal couples with children are more likely to live in CMAs (the complement of the odds-ratio test). While these results confirm that living in heterogeneous areas significantly increases the likelihood of exogamy, they do not necessarily confirm that Aboriginal couples with children living on reserves or Inuit communities are more likely to be endogamous, since the data in the public use samples do not include the necessary community identifiers. Additional analyses are required to determine the specific effects of living in Aboriginal communities and the effect of exogamy on the next generation. This analysis will be conducted on the full census files in the next phase of this project.

CONCLUSION

This chapter documented the changes in concepts, questions, collection instruments, and collection methods used to conduct the censuses between 1871 and 2006, with a particular focus on the contemporary period (from 1961 to 2006; see Appendix A). The possible impact of changes in collection methods and instruments on population counts was shown in two ways: through a historical analysis of published census data over this period of time and by comparing actual population growth and decline against theoretical models. Given that the Aboriginal peoples in Canada form an essentially "closed" population from a demographic perspective (i.e., there is negligible growth or decline due to immigration and emigration), it is possible to compare growth and decline of these groups against theoretical models of population growth. In fact, these comparisons showed differences that cannot be attributed to traditional demographic flows.

The conclusion drawn in the last paragraph leads naturally to a discussion on the appropriateness of the standard population equation to measure flows in the Aboriginal population of Canada. It has been shown in previous studies that ethnic mobility serves to explain in part the composition of the error term in the standard population equation (see Goldmann, 1992; Goldmann, 1998; Robitaille & Guimond, 2003). It was argued in this chapter that ethnic mobility is an additional component of flow that should be included in the traditional population equation, especially when analyzing the growth and decline of the Aboriginal population. The differences between the models of growth for the Aboriginal population and the theoretical models provide empirical evidence of ethnic mobility.

This study has shown that it is possible to analyze the impact of ethnic mobility on the characteristics of the Aboriginal populations (First Nations, Métis, and Inuit) by isolating factors that are clearly associated with changes in identity. That avenue of analysis needs to be explored further by comparing the characteristics of the population that has experienced some form of ethnic transfer with those who did not, both within generations and across generations. It is clear to the authors, and hopefully to the readers, that this is the start of a larger research agenda into the socio-demographic theories of population growth and decline.

NOTES

1. Quinquennial censuses of the three Prairie provinces have been conducted since these provinces joined Confederation. This requirement is included in their terms of union.

2. The Government of Canada decided to eliminate the mandatory long-form census in 2011. It has been replaced by a voluntary survey of the population. The change in collection methodology is likely to introduce inconsistencies between the data produced through the survey and previous data collected through the census. Therefore, no comparable analysis will be possible with the data collected in 2011.

3. The first official nominal census, conducted in 1666 by Jean Talon, presented no
   · records of Aboriginal population because no inquiries were made into the origins of the population at that time. An ethnic origin question first appeared in the 1871 Census (Department of Agriculture, 1873), though no specific instructions were given to the enumerators with respect to the collection or coding of Aboriginal origin until the early 1900s (Department of Agriculture, 1871; Department of Agriculture and Statistics, 1901). We have provided brief descriptions of these censuses and the recorded counts to illustrate the evolution of the census instruments and regional differences in the approaches used.

4. All direct quotations are taken either from the administrative manual, the general report or the publication containing the tabulations for the respective censuses or surveys. Therefore, they are not directly referenced. However, all relevant documentation is included in the list of references and the endnotes at the end of this document, and the authors can provide further information upon request.

5. No attempt is made in this chapter to assess the impact of the refusals.

6. Exponential growth rates are calculated with the following formula:

$$r = \frac{ln\left(\frac{P_n}{P_0}\right)}{n}$$

Geometric growth rates are calculated with the following formula:

$$r = \sqrt[n]{\frac{P_n}{P_0}} - 1$$

7. No growth rates were calculated before for the period before 1951 since the geographic definition of Canada was still in flux—i.e., provinces were still being added.

8. The rates of net migration of Aboriginal peoples from the United States are not sufficient to influence the results.

9. In fact, the characteristics of the ethnically mobile population will be the focus of further research by one of the authors of this chapter.

REFERENCES

Alba, R. (1990). *Ethnic identity: The transformation of white America*. New Haven, CT: Yale University Press.

Cohen, R. (1993). Ethnicity, the state and moral order. In G.J. Goldmann & N. McKenney (Eds.), *Challenges of measuring an ethnic world: Science, politics and reality* (pp. 365–390). The Joint Canada–United States Conference on the Measurement of Ethnicity, Washington, DC: Bureau of the Census; Ottawa, ON: Statistics Canada.

Department of Agriculture. (1871). *The 1871 Census: Manual containing the census act and the instructions to officers employed in the taking of the first census of Canada—1871*. Ottawa, ON: I.B. Taylor.

Department of Agriculture and Statistics. (1901). *The fourth census of Canada, 1901: Instructions to officers*. Ottawa, ON: S.E. Dawson.

Dominion Bureau of Statistics. (1941). *The eighth census of Canada, 1941: Instructions to commissioners and enumerators*. Ottawa, ON: Edmond Cloutier.

Fong, E., & Wilkes, R. (2003). Racial and ethnic residential patterns in Canada. *Sociological Forum, 18*(4), 577–602.

Frideres, J.S. (1988). *Native peoples in Canada: Contemporary conflicts*. Scarborough, ON: Prentice Hall.

Gans, H.J. (1997). Towards a reconciliation of "assimilation" and "pluralism": The interplay of acculturation and ethnic retention. *International Migration Review, 31*(4), 875–892.

Goldmann, G.J. (1993). Canadian data on ethnic origin: Who needs it and why? In G.J. Goldmann & N. McKenney (Eds.), *Challenges of measuring an ethnic world: Science, politics and reality* (pp. 431–446). The Joint Canada–United States Conference on the Measurement of Ethnicity, Washington, DC: Bureau of the Census; Ottawa, ON: Statistics Canada.

———. (1998). Shifts in ethnic origins among the offspring of immigrants: Is ethnic mobility a measurable phenomenon? *Canadian Ethnic Studies, 30*(3), 121–148.

Goldscheider, C. (1993). What does ethnic/racial differentiation mean? Implications for measurement and analyses. In G.J. Goldmann & N. McKenney (Eds.), *Challenges of measuring an ethnic world: Science, politics and reality* (pp. 391–406). The Joint Canada–United States Conference on the Measurement of Ethnicity, Washington, DC: Bureau of the Census; Ottawa, ON: Statistics Canada.

Guimond, E. (1999). Ethnic mobility and the demographic growth of Canada's Aboriginal populations from 1986 to 1996. In A. Bélanger, *Report on the demographic situation in Canada, 1998–1999* (pp. 187–200). Ottawa, ON: Statistics Canada.

Isajiw, W.W. (1993). Definition and dimensions of ethnicity: A theoretical framework. In G.J. Goldmann & N. McKenney (Eds.), *Challenges of measuring an ethnic world: Science, politics and reality* (pp. 407–430). The Joint Canada–United States Conference on the Measurement of Ethnicity, Washington, DC: Bureau of the Census; Ottawa, ON: Statistics Canada.

Pressat, R. (1983). *L'Analyse démographique: Concepts, méthodes, résultats*. Paris: Presse Universitaires de France.

Pryor, E.T., Goldmann, G.J., Sheridan, M.J., & White, P.M. (1992). Measuring ethnicity: Is "Canadian" an evolving indigenous category? *Ethnic and Racial Studies*, 15(2), 214–235.

Robitaille, N., & Guimond, É. (2003). La reproduction des populations autochtones au Canada: Exogamie, fécondité et mobilité ethnique. *Cahiers Québécois de Démographie*, 32(2), 295–314.

Ryder, N.B. (1956). The interpretation of origin statistics. *Estadistica: The Journal of the International American Statistical Institute*, 53, 651–665.

Statistics Canada. (1973). *The 1971 Census of Canada: Population—ethnic groups* (Catalogue No. 92-723, Vol. 1, Part 3). Ottawa, ON: Statistics Canada.

———. (1976). *The 1971 Census of Canada, general review: Administrative report of the 1971 Census* (Catalogue No. 99-740, Vol. VI, Part 1). Ottawa, ON: Statistics Canada.

———. (1984). *The 1981 Census of Canada: Population—ethnic origin* (Catalogue No. 92-911). Ottawa, ON: Statistics Canada.

———. (1989). *The 1986 Census: Ethnicity, immigration and citizenship—the nation* (Catalogue No. 93-109). Ottawa, ON: Statistics Canada.

———. (1989). *Profile of ethnic groups* (Catalogue No. 93-154). Ottawa, ON: Statistics Canada.

———. (1991). *The 1991 Census of Canada: Aboriginal peoples procedures manual for canvasser reserve areas and Indian settlements* (Catalogue No. 92N0011E c.1). Ottawa, ON: Statistics Canada.

———. (1993). *The 1991 Census: Ethnic origin* (Catalogue No. 93-315). Ottawa, ON: Industry, Science and Technology Canada.

———. (1996). *The 1996 Census of Canada: Ethnic origin procedures manual—automated coding* (Catalogue No. 92-N0037-XPE c.3). Ottawa, ON: Statistics Canada.

———. (1996). *The 1996 Census of Canada: Indian Band/First Nation procedures manual—automated coding* (Catalogue No. 92-N0084-XPE c.3). Ottawa, ON: Statistics Canada.

———. (1997). *The 1996 Census: The 1996 census handbook* (Catalogue No. 92-352-XPE). Ottawa, ON: Statistics Canada.

———. (1998). *The 1996 Census profile of federal electoral districts (1996 representation): Aboriginal, ethnic origin and visible minorities* (Catalogue No. 95-F0180-XDB Part 1). Ottawa, ON: Statistics Canada.

———. (2001). *The 2001 Census profile of federal electoral districts: Citizenship, immigration, birthplace, generation status, ethnic origin, visible minorities and Aboriginal peoples* (Catalogue No. 95-F0309-XPB c.2). Ottawa, ON: Statistics Canada.

———. (2002). *The 2001 Census handbook* (Catalogue No. 92-379-XPB). Ottawa, ON: Statistics Canada.

———. (2003). *The 2006 Census content consultation report* (Catalogue No. 92-130-XPE). Ottawa, ON: Statistics Canada.

———. (2007). *The 2006 Census: A national overview—population and dwelling counts, 2006 Census* (Catalogue No. 92-200-XPB). Ottawa, ON: Statistics Canada.

Statistics of Canada. (1876). *Census of Canada 1665 to 1871, Volume IV*. Ottawa, ON: I.B. Taylor.

United Nations. (2006a). *Demographic yearbook (2003)*. Retrieved from http://unstats. un.org/unsd/demographic/products/dyb/DYB2003/table01.xls

———. (2006b). *World population prospects: The 2006 revision*. Retrieved from http://unstats.un.org/unsd/databases.htm

Zeitlin, I.M. (1990). *Ideology and the development of sociological theory*. Englewood Cliffs, NJ: Prentice Hall.

3

POPULATION PROJECTIONS FOR THE ABORIGINAL POPULATION IN CANADA
A REVIEW OF PAST, PRESENT, AND FUTURE PROSPECTS, 1991 TO 2017

Ravi B.P. Verma

INTRODUCTION

Data on the Aboriginal identity population have been available in Canada since the 1991 Census. The numbers increased from 632,160 in 1991 to 1,172,800 in 2006 (Norris, Kerr, & Nault, 1995; Statistics Canada, 2003, 2008), meaning that, over 15 years, this population has increased at an average annual growth rate of 4.2%. This high rate of growth could be due to higher fertility, declining mortality, and non-demographic factors such as declining reinstatements under Bill C-31, and changes in reporting patterns over time, including increasing tendency to self-identify as Aboriginal. However, the observed growth rate of the Aboriginal population has been affected by the revisions done to take account of fewer incompletely enumerated reserves and the net census undercoverage during this period. As the estimates of the adjusted census counts of the Aboriginal population are available since 1991, we will update the estimates of the growth rate for the periods 1991 to 1996 and 1996 to 2001 and use these updated estimates to compare with the projected growth rates. Then we will address the question, what is the projected demographic future of the Aboriginal population into the new millennium?

The objectives of this chapter are threefold. First, accuracy of the projections prepared by Norris, Kerr, and Nault (1995) for the Royal Commission on Aboriginal Peoples (RCAP) based on the 1991 Aboriginal Peoples Survey (APS) will be assessed by comparing the projected figures with the adjusted census counts obtained in 1996 and 2001. The details of adjustments are presented later in the chapter. Second, I will examine the prospects for future growth of the Aboriginal population. For this purpose, I use the set of projections prepared for the Heritage Canada by Statistics Canada (2005) by identity group. Finally, the consistency of the projected figures in the two sets of projections based on the 2001 census—one, prepared by Statistics Canada (2005) and the second, published in 2007 by Indian and Northern Affairs Canada (INAC) and Canada Mortgage and Housing Corporation (CMHC)—will be examined. The chapter focuses on these topics, specifically on projections that are based on the cohort-component method.

REVIEW OF CONCEPTS, BASE POPULATION, METHODOLOGY, AND COMPONENT ASSUMPTIONS
Concept of Aboriginal Population

The Aboriginal identity population used in the projection series by Statistics Canada is based on the Aboriginal identity questions in the 1991 Aboriginal Peoples Survey (APS) and 2001 census. The APS asked, "with which Aboriginal group do you identify?" The identity was based on the basis of ancestry/ ethnicity questions. The 2001 census question referred to "those persons who reported identifying with at least one Aboriginal group, i.e., North American Indian, Métis or Inuit (Eskimo), and/or those who reported being a Treaty Indian or a Registered Indian as defined by the Indian Act of Canada and/or who were members of an Indian Band or First Nation" (Statistics Canada, 2002). However, the 1993 National Census Test showed that the two questions in the 1991 APS and 1996 census yielded comparable results despite the differences in wording (Statistics Canada, 2002). The Aboriginal population was counted the same way in 2006, 2001, and 1996, providing comparable data for three census years (Statistics Canada, 2008). So, the data on the Aboriginal population by identity groups are comparable over the period of 1991 to 2006.

Base Population

For the 1995 projections, the base population was the Aboriginal ancestry population, which was derived from the 1991 post-censal APS based on responses to the ancestor/ethnic origin question. In contrast, the 2005 projections of the Aboriginal population used the Aboriginal identity population, which is based on the Aboriginal identity questions in the 2001 census. The adjusted Aboriginal identity population was 727,900 in 1991 and 1,066,500 in 2001, showing an increase of 46.5%.

The adjustments of the 2001 Census data on the Aboriginal identity population for the projections by Statistics Canada (2005) were done in four steps:

1. In the 2001 Census, the number of people who had indicated multiple identities (about 6,655) was allocated equally to the groups they identified with.
2. Also, 23,460 people did not identify themselves as an Aboriginal person, but indicated being either a Registered Indian or a member of an Indian Band. They were added to the North American Indian group.
3. In 2001, there were only 30 incompletely enumerated reserves with an estimated total population of 31,020; this was a significant decrease when compared to the 78 and 77 reserves not enumerated in 1991 and 1996 (for an estimated total population of 37,623 in 1991 and 43,566 in 1996). The estimates of population not enumerated on these reserves were for the total population, not just for the Aboriginal population; however, the large majority of the population living on reserves had Aboriginal identity, and so about 95% of them were added to the enumerated population living on all reserves.
4. Lastly, the national net undercoverage rate of 10.35% for Indians living on reserves estimated by the Reverse Record Check study was used to adjust the Aboriginal population by identity group for each province. The net undercoverage rates for the total Canadian population by province were used for the Aboriginal identity population residing off-reserve.

The adjusted base population for the projections of the Aboriginal identity population (Statistics Canada, 2005b) was 1,066,500. This is slightly higher than the adjusted base population used by INAC and CMHC (2007) for their projections, which was 1,064,300, showing a small difference of 2,200 persons. While this difference may explain a small part of the total differences in the projected size for 2016 or 2017, the other factors affecting the size of the population seem more important. These are the assumptions on the components of population change (fertility, mortality, migration, Bill C-31 legislation, and changes in reporting patterns overtime).

Projection Methodology

The 2005 series of projections on the Aboriginal identity population were developed using the cohort–component method starting with a census base population. The base population used in the projection model is adjusted as described in the previous section. The projected demographic components of population change (births, deaths, and migration) and the non-demographic factors such as reinstatements and inheritance under Bill C-31 and identity transfer (ethnic transfer) through intergenerational trans-fer were then applied to the adjusted base population.

In a special scenario, the birth component based on an inflated total fer-tility rate to take account of ethnic/identity transfer (i.e., mothers assigning an Aboriginal identity to their children) has been used.[1]

Methods used in developing the components of the population change are discussed elsewhere in detail (Statistics Canada, 1995, 2005b). However, the assumptions of fertility rates and expectation of life at birth are shown in Appendix Tables 3.5 and 3.6, respectively.

ACCURACY OF THE PROJECTED POPULATIONS BASED ON THE 1991 APS

The accuracy of the 1991-based projections could be assessed by comparing the projected population to the adjusted census counts of 2001. The accu-racy of the 2001-based projections could not be assessed as the estimates of the adjusted census counts of 2006 for Aboriginal population due to the net census undercount and incompletely enumerated Indian reserves and settlements were not available at the time that this chapter was prepared.

Caution should be exercised when comparing projected results with the adjusted census counts because of the following outstanding issues. First, the data obtained from the APS are statistical estimates based on a probability survey. The target population of the APS involved all persons living in Canada at the time of the 1991 Census who reported Aboriginal origins and/or reported being registered under the Indian Act. The results from the survey were adjusted initially by Statistics Canada to compensate for non-response and selected characteristics of the sample and the target population. Although the data were collected directly through personal interviews, both sampling and non-sampling errors are inevitable in all such surveys to a greater or lesser degree (Norris, Kerr, & Nault, 1995).

Second, Aboriginal self-identification is not an ascribed characteristic. Patterns in Aboriginal self-identification can change over time. Between 1996 and 2001, a growing number of people who had not previously identified with an Aboriginal group are now doing so. Changes in Aboriginal participation from one census to another can also have an impact on the comparison.

The projected counts of total Aboriginal populations, North American Indians, and Métis under all scenarios were less than the adjusted census counts (Table 3.1). For Inuits, however, the differences were small. An explanation for the underestimation of the future population may be more due to non-demographic than demographic factors. The projected population grew at a fairly rapid pace under the high growth scenario as mortality is assumed to decrease, while fertility remains constant at the level estimated for 1991 throughout the projection period.

It may be pointed out that the 1991 set of projections were based solely on the demographic factors of change. Other factors affecting the change in self-identification were not considered. The differences of about -10% in 1996 and -17% in 2001 for the total Aboriginal population based on continuation of current trends in fertility, mortality, and migration may be attributable to the other factors. The under-projection was largest among the Métis, -29% in 1996 and -46% in 2001, and around -4% for North American Indians in both 1996 and 2001. The differences are comparatively low for the Inuit, 1% in 1996 and -2% in 2001.

A comparison by age was also examined and revealed that an under-projection was evident at all ages for the Métis. For North American Indians, the under-projection occurred among children and the age groups of the middle-aged population. In an analysis of the error of closure for the 2001 Census adjusted counts based on the 1996 adjusted figures, Verma (2005) found that the differences were extremely high for Métis. This has been due to the exclusion of the identity transfer assumption in the projection model. That conclusion still holds, and now the conceptual refinement about intergenerational identity transfer can be added to the mix.

Table 3.1 Comparison of the Projected Counts of the Aboriginal Population
(in 000s) by Identity Group Based on the 1991 Census with the
1996 and 2001 Adjusted Census Counts, Canada

		1991-based projections		
	Adjusted Census	High	Current Trends	Low
Total Aboriginal Population				
1991	720.6	720.6	720.6	720.6
1996	904.3	818.4	811.4	810.9
2001	1066.5	914.4	890.5	887.9
North American Indian				
1991	550.6	550.6	550.6	550.6
1996	648	629.3	624	623.6
2001	713.1	705.8	687.4	685.3
Métis				
1991	139.4	139.4	139.4	139.4
1996	214.2	154.1	152.8	152.8
2001	305.8	169.2	165.0	164.6
Inuit				
1991	37.8	37.8	37.8	37.8
1996	42.1	43	42.5	42.5
2001	47.6	48.1	46.6	46.4

Statistics Canada (2011) has published the new projections of Aboriginal identity in Canada from 2006 to 2031. This is based on 1,279,000 as a base population (adjusted for net undercoverage and partially enumerated reserves) using the microsimulation approach. This base population in 2006 is higher than the projected numbers in 2006 based on the adjusted base population from the 2001 census.

Sources: Adjusted Census Population: for 1991: Norris, Kerr, & Nault, 1995; for 1996: Verma, 2005; for 2001: Statistics Canada, Catalogue No. 91-547. For Aboriginal Population Projections, 1991–2001; Norris, Kerr, & Nault, 1995.

A COMPARISON OF STATISTICS CANADA AND INAC/CMHC PROJECTIONS

Table 3.2 shows a comparison of the projected Aboriginal population by identity group produced by Statistics Canada for the period 2001 to 2017 and those by INAC and CMHC for the period 2001 to 2026. According to both sets of projections under the medium scenario, the projected Aboriginal population in 2016 at the Canada level would be about 1.4 million. The estimated base populations for North American Indians and Métis for 2001 have some differences due to the fact that the INAC/CMHC series use the adjusted 2001 figure for Métis that does not include any individuals who have also identified themselves as a "Registered or Treaty Indian" according to the Indian

Table 3.2 Comparison of Projections of the Aboriginal Population
By Identity Group Based on Adjusted 2001 Census Counts,
Prepared by Statistics Canada (2005b) and INAC/CMHC
(2007) Canada, 2006, 2011, and 2016

Year	North American Indian		Métis		Inuit		Total Aboriginal Population	
	Statcan	INAC and CMHC	Statcan	INAC and CMHC	Statcan	INAC and CMHC	Statcan	INAC and CMHC
	(Medium Growth Scenario, Population in 000s)							
Adjusted Census*								
2001	713.1	743.9	305.8	274.2	47.6	46.2	1,066.5	1,064.3
Projected								
2006	786.0	820.4	329.2	294.3	53.4	51.4	1,168.6	1,166.1
2011	865.5	896.9	353.0	316.1	59.9	57.0	1,2/8.4	1,270.0
2016	953.1	974.3	376.1	338.0	68.4	63.1	1,397.6	1,375.4
Average Annual Rate of Growth (%), 2001–2016								
	2.0	1.8	1.4	1.4	2.4	2.1	1.8	1.7

Statistics Canada (2011) has published the new projections of Aboriginal identity in Canada from 2006 to 2031. This is based on 1,279,000 as a base population (adjusted for net undercoverage and partially enumerated reserves) using the microsimulation approach. This base population in 2006 is higher than the projected numbers in 2006 based on the adjusted base population from the 2001 census.

* Base year population is adjusted for multiple responses and those who reported being a Registered Indian and/or band member and without reporting an Aboriginal identity; census net undercount and incompletely enumerated reserves.

Sources: For Statistics Canada Projection: Statistics Canada, Projections of the Aboriginal Populations, Canada, Provinces and Territories Detailed Statistical Tables 2001 to 2017, Catalogue No. 91-547, Scenario B01. For INAC and CMHC Projections: Indian and Northern Affairs Canada and CMHC, 2007, Aboriginal Demography: Population, Household and Family Projections, 2001–2026.

Act (INAC and CMHC, 2007: Footnote 12). Consequently, the projected population in 2016 for North American Indians and Métis prepared by these two departments are slightly different. According to Statistics Canada (2005b), under the medium scenario, the North American Indian population increases from 713,100 in 2001 to 953,100 by 2016, an increase of 33.7%. The Métis population from 305,800 to 376,100, an increase of 23.1%, and the Inuit population will grow from 47,600 to 68,400, an increase of 43.7%. In 2016, while INAC and CMHC (2007) projections show slightly higher total for the North American Indians, they show slightly lower total for the Métis, Inuit, and the total Aboriginal population. As the assumptions about the components of population change used in these two sets of projections vary only slightly,[2] for North American Indians and the Métis, the projected populations and the corresponding annual rates of growth tend to be similar for these two groups.

However, for the Inuit, the mortality assumption was different under the two series. While Statistics Canada series (2005b) assumed an increase in life expectancy at birth from 62.6 years in 2001 to 63.90 years for males, and 69.8 years in 2001 to 72.90 for females by 2017, INAC and CMHC (2007) assumed a constant trend. This assumption was based on a recent study on the historical trends in life expectancy at birth in the Inuit-inhabited areas of Canada, which revealed no significant improvements during 1991 to 2001 period (Wilkins et al., 2008). According to this study, the estimated life expectancy at birth for Inuit males was 66 years in 1991, 64.8 in 1996, and 64.4 in 2001. For females, these figures were higher at 69.6 in 1991, 71.3 in 1996, and 69.8 in 2001. Also, the INAC and CMHC (2007) series were produced for the Registered Indians and non-Status Indians separately using their component assumptions, whereas the Statistics Canada series (2005b) of projections are produced for the North American Indians.

In general, a part of the differences in the projected populations are due to differences in the base populations. For the total Aboriginal group, there is a shortfall of 2,300 in the INAC and CMHC series, while it is understood that the Aboriginal groups overlap, it becomes a subjective matter decision as to which pattern of demographic growth applies to individuals who belong to more than one group. Given the importance of overlap and divergence in growth patterns, this decision can lead to substantial differences between the series. This only highlights the importance of clearly defining the base population and assumptions about future course in components of change.

AN ANALYSIS OF PROJECTED NUMBERS AND RATES OF GROWTH

In this section, we will discuss the population changes based on Statistics Canada projections (2005b).

Table 3.3 shows the adjusted population of Aboriginal identity groups for the years 1996 and 2001, and the projected totals under five scenarios for the years 2006, 2011, and 2017. The corresponding average annual growth rates for the five periods, 1996–2001, 2001–2006, 2006–2011, 2011–2017, and 2001–2017 at the Canada level are presented in Table 3.4. The assumptions on five growth scenarios regarding fertility, mortality, migration, and ethnic transfer are summarized below:

- High Population Growth (A): Constant fertility rate estimated for 2001, declining mortality, internal migration from the 1996–2001 mobility pattern, and no ethnic transfer;
- Medium Population Growth (B): Slow decline in fertility rate over the period 2001–2017, and declining mortality, internal migration from the 1996–2001 mobility pattern, and no ethnic transfer;
- Moderate Population Growth (C): Moderate decline in fertility rate based on the average of the slow and rapid decline in fertility levels, declining mortality, internal migration from the 1996–2001 mobility pattern, and no ethnic transfer;
- Slow Population Growth (D): Rapid decline in fertility rate converging to the replacement level of 1.8 in 2017, declining mortality, and internal migration from the 1991–1996 mobility pattern, and no ethnic transfer; and
- Very High Population Growth (S; special): Constant fertility rate estimated for 2001 inflated due to ethnic transfer, declining mortality, internal migration from the 1996–2001 mobility patterns.

In 2001, the size of the Aboriginal population in Canada was about 3.4% of the total Canadian population. This was higher than the proportion of the Aboriginal population in Australia (2.2%) and the United States (1.5%), but much less than the proportion of the Aboriginal population (Māori population) in New Zealand (14%) (Statistics Canada, 2003).

Between 1996 and 2001, the Aboriginal population in Canada grew from 904,300 to 1,066,500 with an average annual rate of growth of 3.4%. During the earlier period of 1991 to 1996, the average annual rate of growth was higher at 4.6%. However, both of these growth rates were much higher than the total Canadian population growth rates of 1.0% and 0.9%. By 2017, the Aboriginal population at the Canada level is projected to vary from 1,390,200 under low growth scenario to as high as 1,475,000 under special scenario of high growth taking into account ethnic transfers.

Table 3.4 demonstrates that, for all Aboriginal identity groups except North American Indian, and under all scenarios, the projected average annual growth rates are considerably less than those observed for 1996 to 2001. In particular, the disparity is highest for the Métis group, the group most affected by non-demographic factors of population change such as

Table 3.3 Observed and Projected Aboriginal Population by Identity Group and, by Growth Scenarios and Projected Canadian Population (Scenario P5), Canada, 1996–2017

	Notes	Aboriginal Population Projections by Scenarios					Canadian Population
		A	B	C	D	S	
Total Aboriginal Population		Population (in 000s)					
1996	*	904.3	904.3	904.3	904.3	904.3	29,610.8
2001	*	1,066.5	1,066.5	1,066.5	1,066.5	1,066.5	31,021.3
2006	†	1,169.5	1,168.6	1,168.9	1,166.6	1,182.3	32,270.5
2011	†	1,282.8	1,278.4	1,280.8	1,268.5	1,308.9	33,640.3
2017	†	1,431.8	1,420.0	1,427.9	1,390.2	1,475.0	35,271.4
North American Indian							
1996	*	648.0	648.0	648.0	648.0	648.0	
2001	*	713.1	713.1	713.1	713.1	713.1	
2006	†	786.7	786.0	786.4	784.2	794.6	
2011	†	868.6	865.5	867.9	856.8	885.0	
2017	†	979.7	971.2	978.7	945.2	1006.6	
Métis							
1996	*	214.2	214.2	214.2	214.2	214.2	
2001	*	305.8	305.8	305.8	305.8	305.8	
2006	†	329.4	329.2	329.1	329.1	333.9	
2011	†	354.0	353.0	353.0	352.6	363.4	
2017	†	383.1	380.5	380.9	379.3	398.5	
Inuit							
1996	*	42.1	42.1	42.1	42.1	42.1	
2001	*	47.6	47.6	47.6	47.6	47.6	
2006	†	53.5	53.4	53.4	53.3	53.7	
2011	†	60.2	59.9	59.9	59.0	60.6	
2017	†	69.1	68.4	68.4	65.6	69.8	

* Adjusted Census counts.

† Projected population. (A) High Population Growth; (B) Medium Population Growth; (C) Moderate Population Growth; (D) Slow Population Growth; and (S) Special, Very High Population Growth.

Sources: Adjusted Census Counts for 1996: Verma, 2005; and for 2001: For Aboriginal Population Projections, Statistics Canada, Catalogue No. 91-547. For Canadian Population Projections, Statistics Canada, Catalogue No. 91-520-SCB.

Table 3.4 Average Annual Growth Rates of the Observed and Projected Aboriginal Population by Identity Group and by Growth Scenarios, and Canadian Population Projection (Scenario P5), Canada, 1996–2017

Aboriginal Identity Groups	Notes	High Population Growth	Medium Population Growth	Moderate Population Growth	Slow Population Growth	Special, Very High Population Growth	Canadian Population Medium
		Average Annual Growth Rates (%) of Projected Aboriginal Population in Canada by Scenarios					
Total Aboriginal Population							
1996–2001	*	3.4	3.4	3.4	3.4	3.4	0.9
2001–2006	†	1.9	1.8	1.9	1.8	2.1	0.8
2006–2011	†	1.9	1.8	1.8	1.7	2.1	0.8
2011–2017	†	1.8	1.8	1.8	1.5	2.0	0.8
2001–2017	†	1.9	1.8	1.8	1.7	2.0	0.8
North American Indian							
1996–2001	*	1.9	1.9	1.9	1.9	1.9	
2001–2006	†	2.0	2.0	2.0	1.9	2.2	
2006–2011	†	2.0	1.9	2.0	1.8	2.2	
2011–2017	†	2.0	1.9	2.0	1.7	2.2	
2001–2017	†	2.0	1.9	2.0	1.8	2.2	
Métis							
1996–2001	*	7.4	7.4	7.4	7.4	7.4	
2001–2006	†	1.5	1.5	1.5	1.5	1.8	
2006–2011	†	1.4	1.4	1.4	1.4	1.7	
2011–2017	†	1.3	1.3	1.3	1.2	1.6	
2001–2017	†	1.4	1.4	1.4	1.4	1.7	
Inuit							
1996–2001	*	2.5	2.5	2.5	2.5	2.5	
2001–2006	†	2.4	2.3	2.3	2.3	2.4	
2006–2011	†	2.4	2.3	2.3	2.1	2.5	
2011–2017	†	2.3	2.2	2.2	1.8	2.4	
2001–2017	†	2.4	2.3	2.3	2.0	2.4	

* Adjusted Census counts.

† Projected population.

Source: Computed from previous table, Table 3.3.

ethnic transfers and legislative changes (Siggner & Haget, 2004; Siggner & Costa, 2005). For the other two groups, North American Indians and Inuit, the disparity was relatively very small.

A moderate decline/increase in the projected growth rate in comparison with that observed during 1996 to 2001 is expected due to the net effect of a decline in fertility and declining mortality. However, the large deviation between the past and future growth rates among Aboriginal groups, particularly for the Métis, may be a result of the unpredictability of how the effects of changes in reporting patterns over time will impact their numbers in the future. This aspect of change in reporting patterns is not considered in the current projection model, as reliable information on identity transfer was not available to develop a realistic assumption on this component of change. Currently, we have relatively more comparable data on the Aboriginal population by identity groups since the 1996 Census, and by estimating the number of births and deaths for these groups we can explore developing some estimates of identity transfer through the residual method.[3]

CONCLUSION

The census Aboriginal identity population in Canada—after adjusting for multiple responses, including those who reported being a Registered Indian and/or band member without reporting an Aboriginal identity, incompletely enumerated reserves, and net census undercounts—increased from 904,300 in 1996 to 1,066,500 by 2001, which resulted in an average annual growth rate of 3.4%.

Under various assumptions regarding future courses in fertility, mortality, and ethnic transfers, the Aboriginal identity population is projected to vary between 1,390,200 and 1,431,800 in 2017.

Under the medium growth scenario (B), the average annual growth rate of the Aboriginal population could be expected to be about 1.8% during the period 2001 to 2017, as compared with 0.8% for the Canadian population. Thus, the Aboriginal population may grow twice as fast as the total Canadian population. However, as identity transfer is not featured prominently in the projection model, the growth of identity groups may be different in the future than those presented in this study. This will have the largest impact on the Métis population. The questions that remain are:

How do we incorporate identity transfer into the projection model? How do we measure its impact on the growth rate in the past?

Establishing a historical trend is difficult as people self-identify with an Aboriginal group, and this self-interpretation can change over time (identity transfer). This is reflected in the large increase of the Aboriginal population between 1991 and 2001. Development of indices of components of population growth is still not an easy task and has to rely on indirect methods. As such, future scenarios of growth for the Aboriginal population by identity group will remain uncertain to a large extent until we can generate historical estimates of identity transfers so as to arrive at more realistic assumptions to be incorporated in the projection methodology.[4]

While discussing the various possible scenarios for projected Aboriginal population, the most likely scenario was not indicated. It is difficult to single out one particular scenario as the most likely growth scenario due to certain limitations and constraints with demographic projections. These are conditional projections, based on the assumptions and rationale of components of population change, and are not predictions. Also, they are not based on any statistical modelling, so the percent level of uncertainty associated with a particular series of projections cannot be calculated. Therefore, the approach generally followed is to select a range of scenarios, most often three, that are likely to encompass plausible future trends. This enables the user to make his/her own judicious choice among the selected series. Statistics Canada is to not favour any particular series and stipulates, "no single set of estimates should be labeled as most probable" (Romaniuc, 1990; and George, 2001). The high and low growth scenario of projections can be considered a kind of confidence interval. In the case of three scenarios with labels as "high," "medium," and "low," the user generally picks the medium, treating the others as outside possibilities.

The detailed analysis of the future growth of population and other trends such as age structure, growth of elderly population, etc. is generally done using the medium projection scenario that would reflect a continuation of currents trends. The medium is also taken as a reference scenario for making the detailed analysis of demographic trends in future. The results based on the medium scenarios are expected to fall between the high and low growth scenarios. The alternative scenarios are usually discussed to examine a possible range of growth possibilities.

Table 3.5 Projected Total Fertility Rates (Children per Woman Aged 15–49) for the Aboriginal Population by Identity Group, Canada for Horizon Years, 2016, 2017, and 2026

Aboriginal Identity Projections*, 2001–2017	Horizon Year 2017				
	Constant 2001	Slow Decline	Moderate Decline	Rapid Decline	Ethnic Transfer
North American Indian	2.86	2.71	2.56	2.18	3.12
Métis	2.17	2.06	1.95	1.93	2.48
Inuit	3.37	3.19	3.02	2.36	3.47

Aboriginal Identity Projections†, 1991–2016	Horizon Year 2016		
	High Constant 1991	Medium Slow Decline	Low Rapid Decline
Registered Indian	2.9		2.2
Non-Status Indian	2.1		1.6
Métis	2.5		1.8
Inuit	3.4		2.5

Aboriginal Identity Projections‡, 2001–2026		Horizon Year 2026		
	2001	High	Medium	Low
Registered Indian	2.8		Declining	
Non-Status Indian	2.1		Declining	
Métis	2.1		Declining	
Inuit	3.4		Declining	

Sources: * Statistics Canada, Catalogue No. 91-547, Text Table 2.2.
        † Norris, Kerr, & Nault, 1995, Table 19.
        ‡ INAC with CMHC, 2007.

Table 3.6 Estimated and Projected Life Expectancy (in years) at Birth by Sex for Aboriginal Population by Identity Group, Canada, for Selected Years, 1991, 2001, and 2017

Aboriginal Identity Projections[†], 2001–2017	Estimated* 2001		Horizon Year 2017 2017 (Declining)	
	Male	Female	Males	Females
North American Indian	71.10	76.70	73.30	78.40
Métis	71.90	77.70	74.10	79.70
Inuit	62.60	71.70	63.90	72.90
Inuit (Wilkins et al., 2008)	64.40	69.80	No-change[§]	

Aboriginal Identity Projections[‡], 1991–2016	1991 (Constant)		2016 (Declining)	
	Males	Females	Males	Females
Registered Indian	66.9	74	72.9	80.1
Non-Status Indian	71.4	77.9	76.2	82.3
Métis	70.4	76.9	75.5	81.3
Inuit	57.6	68.8	63.6	76.3

Sources: * Statistics Canada, Catalogue No. 91-547, Text Table 2.3.

  † Catalogue No. 91-547, Text table 2.3.

  ‡ Norris, Kerr, & Nault, 1995, Table 19.

  § No-change assumption of Inuit mortality under the projections of Aboriginal Population Projections by INAC with CMHC, 2007.

AUTHOR'S NOTE

The author appreciates the feedback received from André Cyr, Cathy Cannors, Réjean Lachapelle, Johanne Denis, Russell Wilkins, and Nancy Zukerwich, including Ian Kisbee for editorial assistance, Statistics Canada, and two external reviewers, M.V. George (Emory University and University of Alberta), and Frank Trovato (University of Alberta) in preparing earlier version of this chapter. He thanks the reviewer of the University of Alberta Press for providing some comments. Lastly, he is also indebted to K.G. Basavarajappa for reviewing and copy editing the final version of this chapter.

NOTES

1. Under the special scenario, the total fertility rates for each Aboriginal identity group were inflated based on the continuity index, which is defined as the total number of children with a given identity related to the number of children born to mothers with the same identity. For 2001, the value of the continuity index was observed to be 109 for the North American Indians, 114 for the Métis, and 103 for the Inuit, indicating gains in the number of births for each particular Aboriginality.

The modified total fertility rate would stay constant over the projection period and equal to 3.12 for the North American Indians, 2.48 for the Métis, and 3.47 for the Inuit.

2. Assumptions developed under the "Medium Growth Scenario" by INAC and CMHC (2007) are "Moderate decline in fertility, moderate decline in the volume of migration at a pace observed for the decade of the 1990s, gradual improvement in average life expectancy at birth, except for the Inuit (life expectancy for the Inuit is assumed to remain constant), parenting patterns and distribution of transfer of Aboriginal identity to children remain at their current levels; and declining rate of reinstatement of status under provisions in the Indian Act as amended in 1985." Assumptions developed under the medium population growth scenario of Statistics Canada (2005b) are "slow decline in fertility rate over the period 2001–2017, and declining mortality, internal migration from the 1996–2001 mobility pattern, and no ethnic transfer."

3. Guimond (1999) has used the residual approach to estimate the ethnic mobility for Aboriginal identity groups for the periods 1986–1991 and 1991–1996. The natural increase (births minus deaths) is subtracted from the growth of Aboriginal population by identity groups adjusted due to net census undercounts for the years t and $t+5$ to estimate the ethnic mobility. Verma (2005) also proposed some ideas for using the residual approach for the indirect estimation of the intra-generational ethnic mobility for the period 1996–2001. Statistics Canada (2011) has published the new projections of Aboriginal identity in Canada, using the micro-simulation approach, providing two assumptions of intragenerational ethnic mobility. For details, see Statistics Canada (2011).

4. Some initiatives have recently been undertaken by Statistics Canada and its partners to improve the flexibility of the projections of the Aboriginal population in Canada. In 2008, the Demography Division in Statistics Canada studied the feasibility of doing projections of the Aboriginal population using micro-simulation. Another ongoing project at Statistics Canada is the analysis of the 1991 Canadian census mortality follow-up study. The age standardized mortality rates (ASMR) per 100,000 person-years at risk for any aboriginal origins and non-Aboriginal origins aged 25 years and over were 797.7 for Aboriginal origin men and 566.7 for non-Aboriginal origin men. For females, these rates were lower at 559.8 and 318.9 (Wilkins, Tjepkema, Mustard, & Choinière, 2008).

REFERENCES

George, M.V. (2001). Population forecasting in Canada: Conceptual and methodological developments. *Canadian Studies in Population, 28*(1), 111–154.

Guimond, E. (1999). *Ethnic mobility and the demographic growth of Canada's Aboriginal populations from 1986 to 1996* (Catalogue No. 91-209-XPE). Ottawa, ON: Statistics Canada.

Indian and Northern Affairs Canada (INAC) and Canada Mortgage and Housing Corporation (CMHC). (2007). *Aboriginal demography, population household, and* family projections, 2001–2026. Ottawa, ON: Aboriginal Affairs and Northern Development Canada.

Norris, M.J., Kerr, D., & Nault, F. (1995). *Projections of the population with Aboriginal identity in Canada, 1991–2016.* Ottawa, ON: Statistics Canada.

Romaniuc, A. (1990). Population projection as prediction, simulation and prospective analysis. *Population Bulletin of the United Nations, 29,* 16–31.

Siggner, A.J., & Costa, R. (2005). *Aboriginal conditions in census metropolitan areas, 1981–2001* (Catalogue No. 89-613-MIE-N.008, p.13). Ottawa, ON: Statistics Canada.

Siggner, A.J., & Hagey, J. (2004, June). *Measuring demographic and non-demographic change in the Aboriginal population residing in urban areas of Canada.* Paper presented at the annual meetings of the Canadian Population Society, Manitoba.

Statistics Canada. (2002). *2001 Census dictionary* (Catalogue No. 92-378-XPE). Ottawa, ON: Statistics Canada.

————. (2003). *Aboriginal peoples of Canada: A demographic profile, 2001 census analysis series* (Catalogue No. 96F0030XIE2001007). Ottawa, ON: Statistics Canada.

————. (2005a). *Population projections for Canada, provinces and territories 2005–2056* (Catalogue No. 91-520 Occasional). Ottawa, ON: Statistics Canada.

————. (2005b). *Projections of the Aboriginal populations, Canada, provinces and territories, 2001 to 2017* (Catalogue No. 91-547-XIE). Ottawa, ON: Statistics Canada.

————. (2008). *Aboriginal peoples in Canada in 2006: Inuit, Métis and First Nations, 2006 Census* (Catalogue No. 97-558-XIE). Ottawa, ON: Statistics Canada.

————. (2011). *Population Projections by Aboriginal Identity in Canada, 2006 to 2031* (Catalogue No. 91-552-X). Ottawa, ON: Statistics Canada.

Verma, R.B.P. (2005). Evaluation of projections of populations for the Aboriginal identity groups in Canada, 1996–2001. *Canadian Studies in Population, 32*(2), 229–255.

Wilkins, R., Tjepkema, M., Mustard, C., & Choinière, R. (2008). *The Canadian census mortality follow-up study, 1991 through 2001* (Catalogue No. 82-003-X). *Statistics Canada Health Reports,* 19(3), 25–43.

Wilkins, R., Uppal, S., Finès, P., Senécal, S., Guimond, E., & Dion, R. (2008). *Life expectancy in the Inuit-inhabited areas of Canada, 1989 to 2003* (Catalogue No. 82-003-XPE). *Statistics Canada Health Reports,* 19(1), 7–20.

4

ANOTHER LOOK AT DEFINITIONS AND GROWTH OF ABORIGINAL POPULATIONS IN CANADA[1]

Eric Guimond, Norbert Robitaille, and Sacha Senécal

INTRODUCTION

Why are there so many definitions of Aboriginal populations in Canada? What is the explanation behind the recent Aboriginal population explosion? The answers to these questions are critical because of their implications for the enumeration of Aboriginal populations (which definition to use), the monitoring of socio-economic characteristics (interpretation of trends), and the development of policy and programs to improve the quality of life of Aboriginal populations. The purpose of this chapter is to examine these fundamental questions using a demographic perspective. The chapter focuses on the demographic explosion of Aboriginal populations between 1986 and 2006, especially in large Canadian cities, and shows that the classic components of growth (i.e., fertility, mortality, and migration) cannot account for all the observed growth. Finally, we introduce ethnic mobility, the phenomenon by which individuals and families experience changes in their ethnic affiliation, as an explanation of the fuzzy group boundaries and the demographic explosion of Aboriginal populations.

ABORIGINAL GROUP BOUNDARIES: FUZZY AND VARIABLE

At first glance, coming up with a population count for Aboriginal groups would seem an easy task. Unfortunately, such is not the case. There is no universal statistical definition of Aboriginality (refer to Appendix A). The history of the Canadian census, for example, indicates that changes to the enumeration procedures of Aboriginal groups have been almost as regular as the census itself. In most cases, these changes involved modifications to the terminology that describes Aboriginal groups and/or to the criteria used for determining Aboriginality (Guimond, 2009; Goldmann, 1993; White, Badet, & Renaud, 1993). With respect to terminology, the census of Canada has in the past used expressions such as Indians, Half-breeds, Eskimo, Métis, Native Indians, Status or Non-Status Indians, and North American Indians. Since the first census of Canada in 1871, skin colour, race, language, place of residence, ancestry of mother, ancestry of father, and ancestry of mother or father have all been used to define Aboriginality at one time or another.

The 2006 Census of Canada, still the only source of demographic and socio-economic data that covers all Aboriginal groups in Canada, gathered information on four concepts: ethnic origin, self-identification as an Aboriginal person, Registered Indian,[2] and membership in a First Nation. Such data serves to estimate the size and characteristics of Aboriginal populations in Canada, in whole or in part.

Intuitively, one could think that there is a hierarchical structure to these concepts of Aboriginality. For example, the Registered Indian population could be part of the population with Aboriginal identity, which in turn could be part of the population with Aboriginal origin. However practical or logical this world view may appear, the actual 2006 Census data shows a much more complex reality. Indeed, the populations as defined by these three concepts partially overlap each other (Figure 4.1). Together, the concepts of Aboriginal origin, Aboriginal identity, and Registered Indian define seven subsets of different sizes, the total of which comes to 1.8 million persons. The two largest subsets are composed of people reporting Aboriginal origin only (632,760; 35.2%) and people self-reporting Aboriginal origin, Aboriginal identity, and Indian legal status (572,140; 31.8%). The other two "one-dimensional" subsets—Aboriginal identity only and Registered Indian only—respectively include 80,735 (4.5%) and 9,810 (0.5%) persons.

Figure 4.1 Three Dimensions of Aboriginality, Canada, 2006

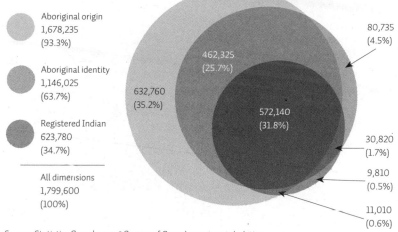

Aboriginal origin
1,678,235
(93.3%)

Aboriginal identity
1,146,025
(63.7%)

Registered Indian
623,780
(34.7%)

All dimensions
1,799,600
(100%)

462,325
(25.7%)

632,760
(35.2%)

572,140
(31.8%)

80,735
(4.5%)

30,820
(1.7%)

9,810
(0.5%)

11,010
(0.6%)

Source: Statistics Canada, 2006 Census of Canada, custom tabulation.

Furthering this analysis of Aboriginality beyond the pan-Canadian perspective reveals significant spatial variations of the relationship between the concepts of Aboriginal origin, Aboriginal identity, and Indian registration, as reported by the 2006 Census. On reserve, these three concepts are almost perfectly overlapping, meaning that nearly all reserve residents have an Aboriginal origin and identity, and are Registered Indians (95.4%; 296,165). With respect to defining Aboriginality, it can therefore be said that group boundaries within a reserve context are clearly identifiable and that the choice of a particular concept has very little implication in terms of population count. Off-reserve, the relationship between origin, identity, and registration is quite different. In 2006, less than one out of five person living off-reserve declared an Aboriginal origin, an Aboriginal identity, and being a Registered Indian (14.9% in rural areas; 19.9% in urban areas[3]). Group boundaries outside a reserve context are not as easily identifiable as those for the population living on-reserve. The concepts utilized for this illustration of Aboriginality off-reserve provide a range of population estimates rather than a unique count. For example, in urban settings (Figure 4.2), depending on which single concept is used to define Aboriginality, the 2006 Census population count varies from 253,080 to 1,002,630 persons. If all three concepts are combined, the population count reaches 1,090,025 persons.

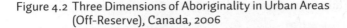

Figure 4.2 Three Dimensions of Aboriginality in Urban Areas (Off-Reserve), Canada, 2006

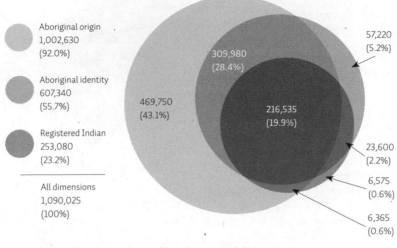

Aboriginal origin
1,002,630
(92.0%)

Aboriginal identity
607,340
(55.7%)

Registered Indian
253,080
(23.2%)

All dimensions
1,090,025
(100%)

309,980
(28.4%)

469,750
(43.1%)

216,535
(19.9%)

57,220
(5.2%)

23,600
(2.2%)

6,575
(0.6%)

6,365
(0.6%)

Source: Statistics Canada, 2006 Census of Canada, custom tabulation.

Admittedly complex, these illustrations of Aboriginal group boundaries still hugely simplify the reality by not distinguishing the three Aboriginal groups recognized in the Constitution Act, i.e., First Nations, Métis, and Inuit peoples. To further illustrate the difficulty of accurately representing Aboriginal group boundaries for statistical purposes, we have in Table 4.1 the 2006 Census population by distinct Aboriginal origins and Aboriginal identities. This table shows 15 different possible responses related to origin, covering single (e.g., North American Indian) and multiple (e.g., North American Indian and non-Aboriginal) responses. For Aboriginal identity, the census provides eight possibilities: North American Indian, Métis, Inuit, non-Aboriginal, and four multiple Aboriginal responses (e.g., North American Indian and Métis). According to this two-dimensional representation of Aboriginality, there are 119 different ways to be an Aboriginal person in Canada, seventeen times more than in the previous illustration of Aboriginal group boundaries. If we try to further improve this representation by reintroducing the concept of Indian registration (Yes, No) and by adding the concept of membership to a First Nation (Yes, No), we now arrive at a definition that would include 479 "types" of Aboriginal peoples.

Table 4.1 Population by Aboriginal Origin and Aboriginal Identity, Canada, 2006

Aboriginal origin	Total	Aboriginal identity					Non-Aboriginal identity
		Total	North American Indian	Métis	Inuit	Multiple Aboriginal identities*	
Total	31,241,030	1,146,025	698,020	389,780	50,480	7,740	30,095,005
Aboriginal / Total	1,678,235	1,034,470	647,020	330,735	49,635	7,080	643,760
Aboriginal / Total single responses	630,425	563,895	443,785	80,345	38,855	905	66,530
North American Indian	512,150	456,775	441,490	14,595	125	565	55,370
Métis	77,295	67,910	2,005	65,595	10	300	9,385
Inuit	40,975	39,205	290	155	38,720	35	1,770
Aboriginal / Total multiple responses	1,047,810	470,580	203,235	250,385	10,780	6,175	577,235
North American Indian and non-Aboriginal	693,355	258,065	188,545	67,385	60	2,070	435,290
Métis and non-Aboriginal	285,755	161,725	3,045	157,740	10	940	124,020
Inuit and non-Aboriginal	18,610	10,070	135	680	9,175	75	8,540
Multiple Aboriginal / Total	50,090	40,715	11,510	24,580	1,535	3,090	9,375
North American Indian and Métis	12,505	11,510	5,485	5,105	0	915	995
North American Indian and Inuit	1,570	1,430	695	25	610	100	140
Métis and Inuit	535	475	10	205	165	105	55
North American Indian, Métis and Inuit	80	70	10	25	15	25	0
North American Indian, Métis and non-Aboriginal	31,290	24,370	4,745	18,195	0	1,430	6,915
North American Indian, Inuit and non-Aboriginal	2,505	1,770	555	325	570	325	730
Métis, Inuit and non-Aboriginal	1,450	945	0	615	160	170	505
North American Indian, Métis, Inuit and non-Aboriginal	165	140	10	85	25	20	20
Non-Aboriginal / Total	29,562,795	111,555	51,005	59,045	845	660	29,451,240

* Includes the following multiple identities: North American Indian and Métis; North American Indian and Inuit; Métis and Inuit; North American Indian, Métis and Inuit.

Source: Statistics Canada, 2006 Census of Canada, custom tabulation.

From this brief discussion of concepts and definitions, it is clear that there is no simple and single answer to the question of who is an Aboriginal person in Canada. First, the concept of Aboriginality in Canada is multi-dimensional, with each dimension yielding a different population count and its own level of complexity. Second, from our spatial analysis of the 2006 Census data, it appears that the notion of Aboriginality varies across the country, indicating again that there is no unique answer. Why are Aboriginal group boundaries fuzzy and in flux? The answer lies with the concept of ethnic mobility, which we will develop further on.

DEMOGRAPHIC GROWTH

Another interesting observation resulting from the analysis of census data is that, independent of the concept used to define Aboriginality, Aboriginal populations have experienced a demographic explosion over the course of the last two decades. From 1986 to 2006, the size of the population with Aboriginal origin went from about 712,000 to 1.678 million people, an overall relative increase of 136%, which is more than five times the relative increase observed for the population with non-Aboriginal origin (24%). In comparison, the Aboriginal identity population[4] increased by 98% and the Registered Indian population by 137%.[5]

For the detailed analysis of population growth between 1986 and 2006, we require a definition of Aboriginal groups based on identity *and* origin. This definition results from an analysis of the comparability of census concepts, wording of question and terminology used to designate Aboriginal groups (Guimond, 2009; Guimond, 1999). Together, Aboriginal identity and origin define Aboriginality in broad and inclusive manner, as opposed to a strictly legal definition. A definition of Aboriginality based on these two dimensions represents the best available operational definition of Aboriginal populations for the detailed analysis of population growth based on 1986 to 2006 Canadian census data.[6]

In the analysis that follows, North American Indian, Métis, or Inuit people are those who have declared at least one Aboriginal origin *and* self-identify as North American Indian, Métis, or Inuit. Persons of Aboriginal origin who do not self-identify with an Aboriginal group are designated as descendants of Aboriginal people. Non-Aboriginal people are defined as all persons of non-Aboriginal origin. Comparable data are available for all of

Table 4.2 Size and Growth Rate* for the Aboriginal Origin Population by Aboriginal Identity, Canada, 1986–2006

Aboriginal origin– Aboriginal identity	Size					Average annual growth rate* (%)			
	1986	1991†	1996	2001	2006	1986– 1991	1991– 1996	1996– 2001	2001– 2006
Aboriginal origin / Total	711,720	973,710	1,101,960	1,319,890	1,678,235	7.0	1.9	3.6	4.9
Aboriginal identity / Total	464,455	613,870	718,950	867,415	1,034,470	6.6	2.3	3.7	3.6
North American Indian	329,730	443,285	494,835	566,555	647,020	7.1	0.9	2.3	2.7
Métis	103,085	128,700	178,525	250,140	330,735	5.1	6.7	7.0	5.7
Inuit	30,105	35,495	39,705	44,625	49,635	3.4	2.3	2.4	2.2
Multiple Aboriginal	1,540	6,385	5,880	6,095	7,080	33.4	1.5	0.7	3.0
Non-Aboriginal Identity	247,265	359,890	383,005	457,485	643,760	7.8	1.2	3.4	7.3
Non-Aboriginal origin (in thousands)	24,310.3	25,991.4	27,426.2	28,319.1	29,562.8	1.2	1.1	0.8	0.9

* Adjusted Rates for partially enumerated Indian reserves and settlements. The rates shown differ from those calculated directly from population counts.

† The question on Aboriginal identity was dropped from the 1991 Census of Canada. Information on Aboriginal identity was collected by the 1991 Aboriginal Peoples post-censal Survey (APS). The 1991 Census count for the Aboriginal origin population is 1,002,675.

Sources: Statistics Canada, 1986 to 2006 Censuses of Canada, custom tabulations. Statistics Canada, 1991 Aboriginal Peoples Survey, custom tabulation.

these groups in the 1986, 1996, 2001, and 2006 Censuses of Canada, and in the 1991 Aboriginal People Survey (APS).

The population growth rate varies significantly from one Aboriginal group to another (Table 4.2). First, the North American Indian population, which accounts for more than 60% of the population with Aboriginal identity, almost doubled between 1986 and 2006 (from 329,730 to 647,020). More than for any other Aboriginal group, the explosive growth of this population during the first intercensal period (7.1%) contrasts with the low growth in the second period (0.9%). The Métis, for whom the population size has tripled over the course of the last two decades (from 103,085 to 330,735), has consistently displayed growth rates in excess of 5%. The Inuit, with a population of 49,635 persons in 2006, is not increasing as fast as the other two Aboriginal groups, but their growth rate is still two to three times higher than that of the non-Aboriginal population. Finally, for the population reporting an Aboriginal origin but no Aboriginal identity, i.e., descendants of Aboriginal

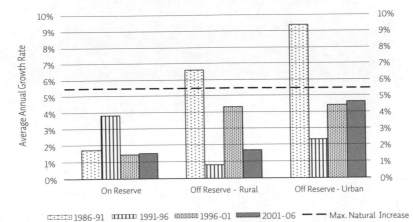

Figure 4.3 Average Annual Growth Rate of the Aboriginal Population by Place of Residence, Canada, 1986–2006

Sources: Statistics Canada, 1986, 1996, 2001, and 2006 Censuses of Canada, custom tabulations; Statistics Canada, 1991 Aboriginal Peoples Survey, custom tabulation.

people, from whom we initially expected growth patterns somewhere between that of Aboriginal and non-Aboriginal people, given the mixed origins of a great majority of them (see Table 4.1), the rates posted between 1986 and 2001 are comparable to those of the North American Indians but have since accelerated to their 1986–1991 level. Looking at the last intercensal period (2001–2006), the descendants of Aboriginal people are the fastest growing segment of the population with Aboriginal origin (7.3%).

Growth of the Aboriginal population varies greatly by place of residence and, again, intercensal period (Figure 4.3). In the period 1986 to 1991, for example, the off-reserve urban Aboriginal population (9.4%) grew five times faster than the on-reserve population (1.7%). From one intercensal period to the next, growth in rural areas first fell sharply to a level comparable to the non-Aboriginal population (from 6.6% to 0.8%), then rose markedly (4.3%), only to drop again during the last period (1.7%).

These population growth rates approach and sometimes largely exceed a theoretical maximum of 5.5% per year for a population that is only subject to the natural movement of births and deaths, which, in practice, should be the case for these populations on the national scale. Such a theoretical maximum is obtained from the highest crude birth rate (60 per 1,000 persons)

Figure 4.4 Migration Flows of Aboriginal Populations* Between Indian Reserves, Rural and Urban Areas, Canada, 2001–2006

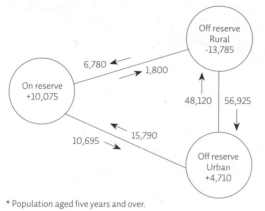

* Population aged five years and over.
Source: Statistics Canada, 2006 Census of Canada, custom tabulation.

observable in exceptional conditions—young population, marrying young, and practising no form of contraception—from which is subtracted the lowest crude death rate (five per 1,000 persons).[7] Such a combination of a high birth rate and a low death rate has probably never been observed. According to the United Nations' *Demographic Yearbook* (1997), the highest national rates of natural increase in the world are approximately 3.5% per year. A population maintaining a growth rate of 5.5% per year doubles every 13 years. After a hundred years, that population would be more than 200 times larger than at the outset.

Migration is clearly not a factor of growth at the national level but is often alluded to in explanations of urban Aboriginal population growth. Contrary to popular belief, there is no mass exodus from Indian reserves and settlements. Multiple analysis of census data on migration and mobility have revealed that, overall, there has been a net inflow to Indian reserves since 1966 (Norris et al., 2004; Clatworthy & Norris, 2003; Clatworthy, 1996; Siggner, 1977). For the most recent intercensal period (Figure 4.4), the resulting impact of movement to and from Indian reserves is a positive net migration of +10,075 persons for these communities. There are three times more people moving between rural and urban areas (105,045 = 48,120 + 56,925) than there are moving to and from Indian reserves (35,065 = 6,780 + 1,800 + 15,790 + 10,695).

More informed users of census data on Aboriginal populations sometimes raise the issue of data quality as an explanation of the observed
spectacular growth patterns. In every census, a certain number of individuals are missed (undercoverage), while others are counted by mistake or
more than once (overcoverage). The difference between these two quantities is called net undercoverage. If the quality of (under)coverage varies,
the relative growth (i.e., rate) derived from the comparison of a population's
size in two successive censuses is distorted: a deterioration of coverage
results in an underestimate of growth, while an improvement in coverage
triggers an overestimate of growth. If the quality of coverage is constant,
we then have a "true" measure of relative growth. On the basis of information available on the population living on fully enumerated Indian reserves
and settlements,[8] there is no spectacular variation in count quality from
1991 to 2006 (Lebel, Caron-Malenfant, & Guimond, 2011; Guimond, 2009,
Table III.6). It may therefore be asserted that the demographic explosion
of Aboriginal populations is not a statistical artefact.

In addition to the undercoverage of the population, there is another
type of data quality issue that affects our capacity to track the Aboriginal
population growth over time. Since 1981, enumeration is not authorized,
is interrupted, or is simply incomplete in some Indian reserves and settlements. No census data is available for these reserves and settlements. From
one census to the next, the number of such reserves and settlements varies,
resulting in a problem of data comparability over time: eight communities
during the 1981 census, 136 in 1986, 78 in 1991, 77 in 1996, 30 in 2001, and 22 in
2006. This issue specifically affects data comparability for populations living
on reserves and settlements. In this analysis, the relative growth measures
shown here (average annual growth rate) are adjusted to take this data
quality issue into account.[9] Clearly, the observed growth of Aboriginal populations is not limited to fertility, mortality, and migration, and is not simply
a statistical artefact caused by variations in data quality. What is the cause
of such extraordinary growth?

ETHNIC MOBILITY

Ethnic mobility is the phenomenon by which changes in ethnic affiliation
happen among individuals and families. From the perspective a specific
group, this phenomenon involves additions and/or deletions to the group.
Such additions and deletions affect the size and characteristics of ethnic

groups. Different terms are used in the literature to designate this phenomenon: ethnic switching, passing, changing identities and changes in self-reporting of ethnic identity. Robitaille and Choinière (1987) have established that there are two types of ethnic mobility: intergenerational and intragenerational.

INTERGENERATIONAL ETHNIC MOBILITY

Intergenerational ethnic mobility, which occurs within families, may happen when a child's ethnocultural affiliation is reported for the first time. Parents and children do not necessarily have the same affiliation, especially when the parents themselves do not belong to the same ethnocultural group. This type of ethnic mobility does not entail any ethnic transfer on the part of the child per se. Instead, it reflects a shift in ethnocultural affiliation across generations, i.e., between parents and children. Practically speaking, intergenerational ethnic mobility is measured through the comparison of the ethnic identity of children to their parent's identity.

Intergenerational ethnic mobility has long been a component of the demographic growth of Aboriginal groups in Canada. The Métis, the second largest Aboriginal group, were "born" from this type of ethnic mobility. Historical, geopolitical, commercial, and cultural circumstances related to the colonization of western Canada led to the genesis of this third Aboriginal cultural group, originally uniting descendants of North American Indian women and French men, most often fur traders. By fostering the emergence of "new types" of Aboriginal people, intergenerational ethnic mobility contributes to the increasing fuzziness and variability of Aboriginal group boundaries previously noted (Figure 4.1; Table 4.1).

If intergenerational ethnic mobility was impossible in Canada, there would be no Métis. The Aboriginal origin–Aboriginal identity matrix shown earlier (Table 4.1) would be drastically smaller and far less complex. The number of "types" of Aboriginal people would drop from 119 to only two: (1) people with North American Indian origin and identity; and (2) people with Inuit origin and identity. But again, the reality is far more complex and the "types" of Aboriginal people more numerous. In essence, this origin-identity matrix is the cumulative result of several generations of intergenerational ethnic mobility, from the initial contact to this day.

On the basis of an analysis of 2001 Census data on the cultural identity of children under the age of five living in a census family,[10] Robitaille, Boucher,

Figure 4.5 Distribution of Children Under the Age of Five According to the Type Union of Parents, by Aboriginal Identity of the Child, Canada, 2001

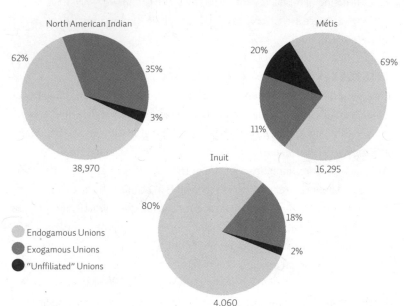

Source: Robitaille, Boucher, & Guimond, 2005.

and Guimond (2005) further exemplified the importance of intermarriage and intergenerational ethnic mobility for Aboriginal groups in two respects (Figure 4.5). First, they observed that children of Métis identity are still in 2001 mainly (69%) from exogamous unions (i.e., only one parent belonging to the group) whereas North American Indian and Inuit children are mostly from endogamous unions (i.e., both parents belonging to the group). Secondly, they also noted that one Métis child in nine (11%) is from a union where no parent has Métis identity ("unaffiliated" union), and a majority (59%, not shown on Figure 4.5) of these Métis children originate from an Indian/non-Aboriginal union.

Adding a geographic dimension to this analysis, we observe that about six out of ten North American Indian children under the age of five that are living in urban areas (off-reserve) in 2001 came from an exogamous union. On-reserve, this proportion drops to one in nine (11%), while the remainder have two Indian parents, which reflects the cultural homogeneity of reserves. Likewise, Inuit children living in rural areas (i.e., for the most part northern Inuit communities) are more likely to have two Inuit parents (91%). Finally, a large majority of Métis children have only one Métis parent (i.e., in exogamous union), regardless of place of residence (>65%). In urban areas, one out of eight Métis children (12%) has no Métis parent ("unaffiliated" unions). Again most often (61%), these Métis children originate from an Indian/non-Aboriginal union.

These observations provide ample evidence that intermarriage and intergenerational ethnic mobility are an integral component of the population growth of Aboriginal groups in Canada. These observations also reveal that the demographic dynamics that contributed to the genesis of the Métis in Canada during the nineteenth century are still at play at the start of the twenty-first century. The Métis population continues to benefit considerably from intergenerational ethnic mobility and to be shaped by exogamous unions between Aboriginal and non-Aboriginal individuals.

INTRAGENERATIONAL ETHNIC MOBILITY

Intragenerational ethnic mobility results from a change in the ethnic affiliation of a person over time. This type of ethnic mobility is responsible for the exceptional growth of Aboriginal populations from 1986 to 2006. According to estimates produced by Guimond (2009) for the 1986–2001 period based on the residual method,[11] nearly 42,000 Indians living off-reserve in 2001 did not self-identify as Indian in 1986 (excluding births), which amounts to one in eight Indian living off-reserve (13%). Over 101,000 Métis in 2001 did not self-identify as Métis in 1986 (excluding births), or four Métis in ten (39%). Among the Inuit, whose growth is rapid but far less spectacular, the contribution of intragenerational ethnic mobility appears to be negligible. Moreover, this analysis also revealed that urban centres are the nexus of intragenerational ethnic mobility among Canada's Aboriginal populations: over 90% of net ethnic transfers estimated nationally for the 1986–2001 period as a whole took place in urban centres. Preliminary analysis of the 2006 Census data indicate that intragenerational ethnic mobility is still the primary component of growth for the Métis population, especially in cities (Lebel, Caron-Malenfant, & Guimond, 2011; Guimond & Robitaille, 2008).

The phenomenon of intragenerational ethnic mobility was also documented among Aboriginal populations in the United States and Australia. In the United States, several researchers became interested in the exceptional demographic growth of the American Indian population observed

Table 4.3 Proportion and Increase in the Number of University
Graduates Among Aboriginal and Non-Aboriginal
Populations, Canada, 1996–2006

	Proportion (%) of the number of university graduates		Increase (%) in the number of university graduates
	1996	2006	1996–2006
Population aged 15 and over			
Aboriginal people	3.3%	5.8%	177.1%
Non-Aboriginal people	13.5%	18.5%	54.4%
Cohort of people aged 35 and over in 1996			
Aboriginal people	4.4%	7.0%	76.7%
Non-Aboriginal people	13.5%	18.8%	1.3%

Source: Guimond, 2003.

between 1960 and 1990.[12] The overall consensus is that changes in self-reporting of ethnic and racial affiliations are a significant component, sometimes the most significant, of the unexplained demographic growth observed in the American Indian population of the United States during this period (Passel, 1996). In Australia, Ross (1996), using a similar approach, estimated that over half of the Aboriginal population growth during the 1991–1996 period can be explained by variations in data quality (i.e., under-coverage and refusal to participate) and by changes in self-reporting of ethnic affiliation.

The effect of intragenerational ethnic mobility extends beyond population size and growth. To fully understand trends in living conditions of Aboriginal populations in Canada, one must consider the possibility that intragenerational ethnic mobility is also in part responsible for observed improvements. To illustrate this point, Guimond (2003) relied on statistics pertaining to the highest level of education taken from the Canadian census. From 1996 to 2006, the number of Aboriginals aged 15 or over with a university degree increased by 177%, from 17,325 to 48,015 people. As a result, the proportion of university graduates among the Aboriginal population went from 3.3% to 5.8%. By comparison, the number of non-Aboriginal graduates increased by 54% during this period, while the proportion of university graduates (18.5% in 2006) was three to four times greater than that observed among Aboriginals. These census statistics seem to indicate that more and more Aboriginal people successfully reach the upper levels of Canada's educational system.

Few people would question the beneficial effect of post-secondary education policies and programs on the overall educational attainment and well-being of Aboriginal people and communities. However, the explanation for the increase observed in the number and proportion of university graduates is not limited to those policies and programs alone. Intragenerational ethnic mobility also contributed to this increase. In this regard, let us focus the analysis solely on cohorts who are at an age where, for all practical purposes, schooling is completed for the large majority, i.e., people aged 35 or over in 1996 (45 or over in 2006): in 1996, 7.8% of Aboriginal adults aged 35 or over were attending school, a sligthly higher proportion than that observed among the non-Aboriginal population (5.8%). If intragenerational ethnic mobility has no effect on the educational level of an ethnic group, then the number of university graduates within that cohort would show small variations, if any. That was the case for the non-Aboriginal population between 1996 and 2006 (Table 4.3): the number of non-Aboriginal university graduates among the cohort aged 35 and over in 1996 increased by only 6.8%. Among Aboriginal populations, the number of university graduates jumped by 76.7% during this period, from 10,535 to 18,615 graduates, an increase far superior to what could be expected from observed school attendance rates at this stage of life. On the basis of this brief analysis, it appears that people experiencing ethnic mobility toward Aboriginal populations in 2006 were more educated than people reporting an Aboriginal affiliation in 1996 and in 2006. A similar effect of intragenerational ethnic mobility was observed among American Indians in the United States (Eschbach, Supple, & Snipp, 1998).

FACTORS OF ETHNIC MOBILITY

Though there is no definitive explanation for ethnic mobility among North American Indian, Métis, Inuit, and non-Aboriginal populations in Canada, three types of factors may be considered (Guimond, 2009). First, there are predisposing demographic factors. In Canada's large urban centres, people of various ethnocultural backgrounds meet, form couples, and have children. Given their mixed ethnocultural origins, once they are adults, those children may "choose" their ethnic affiliation, and such a choice may vary depending on the circumstances. In a nutshell, mixed origins could facilitate

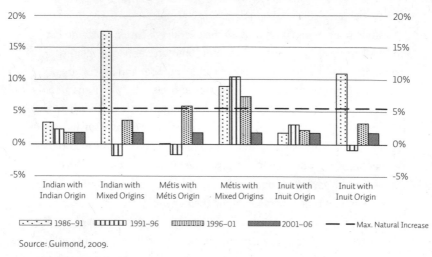

Figure 4.6 Average Annual Growth Rate of the Aboriginal Identity
Groups by Origins, Canada, 1986–2006

Legend: 1986–91   1991–96   1996–01   2001–06   — Max. Natural Increase

Source: Guimond, 2009.

intragenerational ethnic mobility. Prior analysis of the demographic growth
of different segments of Aboriginal groups defined on the basis of origins
has revealed (Figure 4.6) that growth patterns of Aboriginals with mixed
origins, including all Métis, indicate a greater propensity to shifts in self-
reporting of ethnocultural affiliation than individuals who self-report the
same identity and origin (Guimond, 2009). Specifically, this analysis yields
the following insights:

1. The moderate demographic growth of Indians of Indian origin only
    and Inuit of Inuit origin only between 1986 and 2001 does not involve
    a significant contribution from intragenerational ethnic mobility;
2. The erratic nature of the growth of Métis of Métis origin only, Indians,
    and Inuit of mixed origins most likely results from fluctuations in
    intragenerational ethnic mobility, alternating between positive
    and negative;
3. The explosive growth of Métis of mixed origins is attributable to
    very strong net intragenerational ethnic mobility.

Social factors could also foster intragenerational ethnic mobility toward
Aboriginal populations. Different socio-political events—spontaneous,

like the Oka crisis in the summer of 1990, or organized, like the Royal Commission on Aboriginal Peoples from 1991 to 1996—as well as their media coverage raised public awareness and contributed to restoring Aboriginal people's pride. Increased public attention and an improved over-all perception Aboriginal people have of themselves could therefore have encouraged some people to self-report as Aboriginal.

Finally, legal and policy decisions could also further foster ethnic mobility toward Aboriginal populations, especially if such decisions lead to benefits and entitlements. For example, the 1985 amendments to the Indian Act had a considerable demographic impact on the size and growth of the Registered Indian population: on December 31, 2005, 115,551 people had acquired (or re-acquired) Indian status under the 1985 amendments (INAC, 2002). In addition to those amendments to the Indian Act, territorial claim settle-ments and employment equity policies are also likely to generate some level of ethnic mobility.

CONCLUSION

Aboriginal affiliation is not necessarily permanent and is not automatically transferred to the next generation. As a consequence, group boundaries are becoming increasingly fuzzy, and statistical definitions of Aboriginal populations in Canada are increasingly divergent with respect to the related population counts (Siggner et al., 2001). This ethnic mobility is also the main component of the recent demographic explosion of North American Indian and Métis populations. Excluding ethnic mobility from the analytical framework of the demography of Aboriginal populations prevents an accur-ate understanding of the imprecision of definitions, the recent population explosion, and improvements to living conditions. The very existence of the Métis, born of the contact between North American Indians and European colonizers, justifies a four-component analysis of the demographic change of Aboriginal populations in Canada: (1) natural increase, (2) migration, (3) variation in the quality of population counts, and (4) ethnic mobility.

Could we experience another episode of spectacular growth among Aboriginal populations triggered by ethnic mobility? Because of the limited knowledge of this phenomenon, that likelihood is impossible to predict. Nobody foresaw the demographic boom of the 1980s and 1990s. With hind-sight, it seems that large-scale events with much media coverage unfolded at the same time as these booms. If such events triggered the demographic explosion, then future events, especially legal decisions that would grant special rights to certain people, may generate new waves of ethnic transfers within the population. In this regard, it will be interesting to see how the Métis, an Aboriginal group born of intergenerational ethnic mobility, whose growth continues to amply benefit from this phenomenon, will evolve demographically over the coming years. If the experience of the American Indians of the United States is a sign of what is yet to come—positive contribution of intragenerational ethnic mobility to population growth between 1960 and 1990—then ethnic mobility could contribute significantly to the growth of Aboriginal populations in Canada long into the new millennium. More generally, the multicultural composition of Canadian cities will without a doubt be fertile ground for future ethnic mobility and for the increasing fuzziness of group boundaries. In all likelihood, a growing number of urbanites with different ethnocultural affiliations, including Aboriginal people, will form couples and raise children in a multicultural family setting. How children from "mixed" families consider their ethnic affiliation once they enter adulthood will have a considerable impact on the ethnic makeup of our cities, Aboriginal populations, and Canadian society in general.

NOTES

1. The views expressed in this chapter are solely those of the authors and do not necessarily represent those of any other person, agency, organization, or institution.

2. Including Treaty Indians. See Statistics Canada, 2010, 2006 Census dictionary, http://www12.statcan.ca/english/census06/reference/dictionary/pop116.cfm.

3. "An urban area has a minimum population concentration of 1,000 persons and a population density of at least 400 persons per square kilometre, based on the current census population count. All territories outside urban areas are classified as rural. Taken together, urban and rural areas cover all of Canada" (Statistics Canada, 2003: 262).

4. Excluding individuals who do not report an Aboriginal origin. For a discussion of the comparability of census data on Aboriginal identity, see Guimond, 2009.

5. According to the Indian Register, the percentage increase of the Registered Indian population between 1986 and 2006 was 95%. Data from Indian Register and the Census of Canada are not directly comparable due to differences in data collection methodologies and issues surrounding coverage.

6. Since 1996, Statistics Canada has maintained the comparability of the concepts, the wording of questions and the terminology used to designate

Aboriginal groups in the census. This allows the use of a definition that better reflects cultural, legal, and political delineations of Aboriginal groups. See Guimond, 2006.

7. These were in effect highest fertility and lowest mortality rates observed when first discussed by Guimond (1999).

8. "Fully enumerated" refers to Indian reserves and settlements where enumeration was completed (Statistics Canada, 2008b).

9. Incompletely enumerated Indian reserves and settlements at any census year are excluded from our calculations of growth rates in order to ensure comparability of populations and geographies over time.

10. A census family "refers to a married couple (with or without children of either or both spouses), a couple living common-law (with or without children of either or both partners) or a lone parent of any marital status, with at least one child living in the same dwelling. A couple living common-law may be of opposite or same sex. Children in a census family include grandchildren living with their grandparent(s) but with no parents present" (Statistics Canada, 2003: 146). Same sex common-law couples have been excluded from this analysis.

11. The estimate of ethnic mobility is obtained by the method of estimation by residual. This method consists of: (1) calculating the population expected in year $t+n$ (P_e^{t+n}) by taking the population observed in t (P_o^t) and subtracting an estimate of deaths ($D^{t,t+n}$), adding net migration ($M^{t,t+n}$) and all other known factors (net undercoverage of the population) ($V^{t,t+n}$) for the observation period ($t, t+n$), assuming that ethnic mobility is nil; and (2) subtracting the population expected in year $t+n$ (P_e^{t+n}) from the population observed in that year (P_o^{t+n}). The result of this subtraction represents the estimate of net ethnic mobility ($ß^{t,t+n}$) during the observation period ($t, t+n$). This method may be applied to a population as a whole or by age group. In the past it has been used to estimate changes in the ethnic identification of Aboriginal populations in the United States (Passel, 1996; Eschbach, 1993) and ethnic minorities in the former USSR (Anderson & Silver, 1983).

12. See Eschbach, Supple, & Snipp, 1998; Passel, 1996; Eschbach, 1993.

REFERENCES

Anderson, B.A., & Silver, B.D. (1983). Estimating Russification of ethnic identity among non-Russians in the USSR. *Demography, 20*(4), 461–489.

Clatworthy, S. (1996). *The migration and mobility patterns of Canada's Aboriginal population.* Ottawa, ON: Canada Mortgage and Housing Corporation, and the Royal Commission on Aboriginal Peoples.

———. (2003). Impacts of the 1985 amendments to the Indian Act on First Nations populations. In J. White, P. Maxim, & D. Beavon (Eds.), *Aboriginal conditions: Research foundations for public policy* (pp. 63–90). Vancouver, BC: University of British Columbia Press.

Clatworthy, S., & Norris, M.J. (2003). *Aboriginal mobility and migration: Recent patterns and implications.* Ottawa, ON: Indian and Northern Affairs Canada, Strategic Research and Analysis Directorate.

Crégheur, A. (1988). *Assessment of data on Aboriginal identity: 1986 Census of Canada.* Ottawa, ON: Statistics Canada, Housing, Family and Social Statistics Division.

Dickason, O.P. (1996). *Les premières nations du Canada. Depuis les temps les plus lointains jusqu'à nos jours.* Quebec, QC: Les Éditions du Septentrion.

Eschbach, K. (1993). Changing identification among American Indians and Alaska Natives. *Demography, 30*(4), 635–652.

Eschbach, K., Supple, K., & Snipp, C.M. (1998). Changès in racial identification and the educational attainment of American Indians, 1970–1990. *Demography, 35*(1), 35–43.

Goldmann, G. (1993). *The Aboriginal population and the census: 120 years of information—1871 to 1991.* Paper presented at the 22nd General Population Conference of the International Union for the Scientific Study of Population (IUSSP), Montreal, Canada.

Guimond, E. (1999). Ethnic mobility and the demographic growth of Canada's Aboriginal populations from 1986 to 1996. In A. Bélanger (Ed.), *Report on the demographic situation in Canada, 1998–1999* (Catalogue No. 91-209-XPE, 187–200). Ottawa, ON: Industry Canada.

———. (2003). Changing ethnicity: The concept of ethnic drifters. In J. White, P. Maxim, & D. Beavon (Eds.), *Aboriginal conditions: Research foundations for public policy* (pp. 91–107). Vancouver, BC: University of British Columbia Press.

———. (2006, May 10). Aboriginal demographics: Population size, growth and well-being. Presentation to the House of Commons Standing Committee on Aboriginal Affairs and Northern Development, Ottawa.

———. (2009). *L'explosion démographique des populations autochtones du Canada de 1986 à 2001* (Unpublished doctoral dissertation). Université de Montréal, Département de démographie, Montréal, QC. Available at https://papyrus.bib.umontreal.ca/jspui/handle/1866/6827

Guimond, E., & Robitaille, N. (2008). *Aboriginal populations in Canadian cities: What's behind the spectacular growth?* Paper presented at the Strength in Number Series, co-organized by Statistics Canada and Indian and Northern Affairs Canada, Vancouver.

Indian and Northern Affairs Canada (INAC). (2005). *Basic departmental data 2000.* Ottawa, ON: Information Management Branch, Corporate Information Management Directorate, First Nations and Northern Statistics Section.

———. (2010). *Estimates of demographic implications from Indian registration amendment,* Ottawa, ON: Minister of Public Works and Government Services Canada. Retrieved from http://www.ainc-inac.gc.ca/br/is/bll/exp/est-eng.pdf

Isajiw, W.W. (1993). Definition and dimensions of ethnicity: A theoretical framework. In G.J. Goldmann & N. McKenney (Eds.), *Challenges of measuring an ethnic world: Science, politics and reality* (pp. 407–430). The Joint Canada–United States

Conference on the Measurement of Ethnicity, Washington, DC: Bureau of the Census; Ottawa, ON: Statistics Canada.

Lebel, A., Caron-Malenfant, É., & Guimond, E. (2011). *Mobilité ethnique des Autochtones dans le modèle de projection Demosim*. Paper presented at Colloque de l'Association des démographes du Québec et du Centre interuniversitaire québécois de statistiques sociales, Sherbrooke.

Norris, M.J., Cooke, M., Beavon, D., Guimond, E., & Clatworthy, S. (2004). Registered Indian mobility and migration in Canada: Patterns and implications. In J. Taylor & M. Bell (Eds.), *Population mobility and indigenous peoples in Australasia and North America* (pp. 136–160). London and New York, NY: Routledge.

Norris, M.J., Kerr, D., & Nault, F. (1995). *Projections of the population with Aboriginal identity, Canada, 1991–2016*. Ottawa, ON: The Population Projections Section, Demography Division, Statistics Canada.

Passel, J.S. (1996). The growing American Indian population, 1960–1990: Beyond demography. In G.D. Sandefur, R.R. Rindfuss, & B. Cohen (Eds.), *Changing numbers, changing needs: American Indian demography and public health* (pp. 79–102). Washington, DC: National Academy Press.

Pressat, R. (1985). *The dictionary of demography*. New York, NY: Blackwell.

Robitaille, N., Boucher, A., & Guimond, E. (2005). *Mobilité ethnique intergénérationnelle chez les populations autochtones du Canada 1996–2001*. Paper presented at the 25th General Population Conference of the International Union for the Scientific Study of Population (IUSSP), Tours, France.

Robitaille, N., & Choinière, R. (1987). L'accroissement démographique des groupes autochtones du Canada au XXe siècle. *Cahiers québécois de démographie, 16*(1), 3–35.

Robitaille, N., & Guimond, E. (2003). La reproduction des populations autochtones du Canada: Exogamie, fécondité et mobilité ethnique. *Cahiers québécois de démographie, 32*(2), 295–314.

Ross, K. (1996). *Population issues, Indigenous Australians* (Occasional Paper No. 4708.0). Canberra: Australian Bureau of Statistics.

Savard, R., & Proulx, J.R. (1982). *Canada: Derrière l'épopée, les autochtones*. Montréal, QC: l'Hexagone.

Siggner, A.J. (1977). *Preliminary results from a study of 1966–1971 migration patterns among Status Indians in Canada*. Ottawa, ON: Demography Section, Program Statistics Division, Indian and Eskimo Affairs Program.

Siggner, A.J., Hull, J., Vermaeten, A., Guimond, E., & Jantzen, L. (2001). *New developments in Aboriginal definitions and measures*. Paper presented at the Annual Meeting of the Canadian Population Society, Université Laval, Quebec City.

Statistics Canada. (1989). *General review of the 1986 Census* (Catalogue No. 99-137E). Ottawa, ON: Department of Supply and Services Canada.

———. (2003). *2001 Census dictionary* (Catalogue No. 92-378-XIE). Ottawa, ON: Industry Canada.

———. (2005). *Coverage: 2001 Census technical report* (Catalogue No. 92-394-XIE). Ottawa, ON: Industry Canada.

————. (2008a). *2006 Census dictionary* (Catalogue No. 92-566-XWE). Ottawa, ON: Industry Canada. Retrieved from http://www12.statcan.ca/english/census06/reference/dictionary/index.cfm

————. (2008b, January 15). *The daily* (Catalogue No. 11-001-XIE). Ottawa, ON: Industry Canada.

Tapinos, G. (1985). *Éléments de démographie: Analyse, déterminants socioéconomiques et histoire des populations.* Paris: Armand Colin.

United Nations. (1997). *Demographic yearbook 1995* (Table 4, 140–151). New York, NY: UN.

White, P.M., Badets, J., & Renaud, V. (1993). Measuring ethnicity in Canadian censuses. In G. J. Goldmann & N. McKenney (Eds.), *Challenges of measuring an ethnic world: Science, politics and reality* (pp. 223–269). The Joint Canada–United States Conference on the Measurement of Ethnicity, Washington, DC: Bureau of the Census; Ottawa, ON: Statistics Canada.

5

ABORIGINAL MOBILITY AND MIGRATION IN CANADA

TRENDS, PATTERNS, AND IMPLICATIONS, 1971 TO 2006

Stewart Clatworthy and Mary Jane Norris

INTRODUCTION

Census-based research on patterns of geographic mobility and migration in Canada reveals significant group variations within the Aboriginal population, as well as Aboriginal–non-Aboriginal differentials; yet, this research also demonstrates some demographic similarities. This chapter builds upon previous census-based analyses, exploring the latest patterns and trends in Aboriginal mobility and migration with data from the 2006 Census—the most recent available at the time of writing (refer to Appendix A for a detailed definition of the migration variable used in this study based on the Canadian census). As such, the findings presented here provide an update of the authors' earlier article on Aboriginal mobility and migration, based on censuses spanning the period from 1971 to 2001 (Clatworthy & Norris, 2007). In addition, 2006 Census data are also used to update earlier demographic research on age–gender specific analyses of Aboriginal and Registered Indian mobility and migration patterns (Norris, 1985; 1990; 1996; 2000; Norris, Cooke, & Clatworthy, 2003; Norris, Cooke, Beavon, Guimond, & Clatworthy, 2004).

This study explores whether the trends and patterns observed in Aboriginal mobility and migration in previous censuses have continued or changed in relation to several aspects, such as reserve and rural–urban migration, the role of migration in the growth of urban Aboriginal populations, residential mobility and population turnover, and age–gender patterns. Specific issues examined in this regard include six key areas: (1) an overview of the measures and patterns of Aboriginal migration, comprising migration flows by origin and destination and net migration flows and rates by location; (2) the contribution of migration to population change, especially in relation to growth of the Aboriginal population in urban areas; (3) measures, patterns, and effects of residential mobility particularly within urban areas; (4) reasons for moving, in relation to migration to and from reserves, and reasons for residential moves; (5) age–gender patterns of Aboriginal mobility and migration in urban areas and of Registered Indian migration on- and off-reserve; and (6) implications of migration and residential mobility.

Data from the 2006 Census are used to examine the mobility and migration patterns of four Aboriginal population groups: Registered Indians, non-Registered Indians (First Nation populations), Métis, and Inuit. Migration patterns over the five-year period 2001–2006 are considered for the different Aboriginal groups within the context of previous trends from earlier five-year intercensal periods, especially 1996–2001, and to some extent, 1991–1996 and 1986–1991. In the case of Registered Indians, long-term trends in migration span 35 years, covering intercensal periods over a succession of censuses, starting from the 1971 Census, with the 1966–1971 five-year period, through to the 2006 Census with the 2001–2006 period. The study also examines the 2005–2006 patterns of residential mobility for Aboriginal populations in major urban areas. (Refer to Appendix A for a more detailed definition of the Aboriginal population.)

As with our previous analysis, we assess the contribution of net migration to Aboriginal population change, especially in relation to growth in urban areas. We ask the following key question in relation to the 2001–2006 intercensal period: To what extent has migration contributed to the rapid increase in the Aboriginal population living off-reserve, especially in large urban areas? This approach helps to address and clarify some of the misinterpretations surrounding migration, including the impression that the demographic explosion of urban Aboriginal populations observed in recent censuses is the result of an exodus from Aboriginal communities.

In order to assess some of the policy implications and considerations concerning Aboriginal mobility and migration, we consider reasons for migration and residential moves. Policy implications and considerations address a number of areas, including the compositional effects on urban populations—their demographic and socio-economic characteristics; education—program delivery and high mobility and student performance; housing—on- and off-reserve; and social isolation and social cohesion. It should be emphasized that the intention of this chapter is to basically highlight the implications of mobility/migration patterns in various areas, such as housing and education; however, these areas are not the focus of this study but rather ones for which mobility and migration patterns and trends can have implications. A more detailed focus on aspects of housing and education is beyond the scope of this study.

CENSUS MIGRATION DATA

The Census of Canada collects mobility and migration data using two questions: (1) Where did you live five years ago? (2) Where did you live one year ago? The migration analyses presented in this chapter use data from the five-year mobility question. Both questions provide residential and migration data, and in the case of migration flows, at the same level of geographic detail, at the sub-provincial period. Data from either question can be configured to distinguish among three subgroups, which include the following groups: *Non-movers*, who lived at the same residence at the outset of the reference period (i.e., either five years ago or one year ago); *Migrants*, who lived in a different community at the outset of the reference period; and *Residential movers*, who lived at a different residence in the same community at the outset of the reference period. Combined, these latter two groups comprise the total population of movers during the reference period.

Two population subgroups are excluded from the analysis, including individuals who migrated to Canada from abroad and individuals who migrated from an Indian reserve that was not enumerated by the census.[1] Migration rates are presented both as five-year and average annual rates computed for the five-year period.

The analysis of residential moves uses data from the one-year mobility question. Residential mobility rates presented in this study are calculated for the non-migrant population and generally reflect the annual rates for the 12-month period preceding census day.

While the census provides the most complete and consistent set of data concerning the mobility and migration patterns of Aboriginal peoples, census data are limited in several respects. First, the census is administered to a sample of the population and excludes individuals living in various institutions including prisons, chronic care facilities, and rooming houses. Second, a significant portion of the population living on-reserve is not captured by the census due to undercoverage (i.e., individuals missed by the census) and incomplete or non-enumeration. Although undercoverage occurs both on- and off-reserve, levels of undercoverage (including non-enumeration) are known to be substantially higher on-reserve. As a consequence, the geographic distribution of the Aboriginal population captured by the census is biased. The proportion of the population residing on reserves is underestimated while that off-reserve is overestimated. As Registered Indians form the vast majority of the population residing on-reserve, this population is most under-represented in the census data. Third, the census migration and mobility data also present some conceptual limitations, which tend to be more pronounced for the five-year than the one-year question given the longer time period. For example, many characteristics of migrants (e.g., education, marital and family status, and socio-economic attributes) are known only at the end of migration reference period (i.e., at the time of the census). Migrant characteristics at the time of migration may differ. The census also does not capture multiple moves, migrants who leave and return to the same location, or those who die during the time interval.

ABORIGINAL POPULATION DEFINITIONS

For purposes of this study, the Aboriginal identity population has been configured into four subgroups: 623,780 Registered Indians (regardless of Aboriginal group(s) identity), 133,160 non-Registered Indians, 355,500 Métis (non-Registered,) and 49,110 Inuit (non-Registered). Distinguishing the population on the basis of Indian registration status is important to any analysis of Aboriginal mobility or migration. Unlike other Aboriginal groups, those registered under the Indian Act have certain rights and benefits, especially if they live on-reserve. Among other things, these include taxation exemptions, access to funding for housing and post-secondary education, as well as land and treaty rights. Aboriginal populations living off-reserve, including those in Métis and Inuit communities, do not have legal access to the same rights and benefits as Registered Indians living on-reserve.

Differences in rights and benefits between on- and off-reserve, registered and non-Registered can contribute to different patterns of migration among Aboriginal groups.

Geographic Distribution of the Population

As noted previously, this study's scope is restricted to internal migration. In this regard, mobility and migration are examined within the context of four mutually exclusive geographic areas: Indian reserves and settlements, rural areas, urban non-census metropolitan areas (urban non-CMAs), and census metropolitan areas (CMAs). CMAs are defined as urban areas with a minimum core population of 100,000. Urban non-CMAs include all other urban areas, including census agglomerations (CAs) with a core population of at least 10,000, and smaller urban areas. As defined for this study, both of these urban geographies exclude Indian reserves and rural fringe areas located within the broader boundaries of the urban areas. Rural areas comprise all remaining areas, including the undeveloped fringes of urban areas, but excluding lands defined as Indian reserves and settlements[2] (Clatworthy & Norris, 2007).

In other words, for purposes of this study, the "reserves and settlements" geography is distinct from urban or rural areas, regardless of their rural/urban geography. Nevertheless, it is worth noting that reserves can differ in their degree of urbanization: while many are "rural," others are classified as "urban." As well, it is also the case that individual First Nations vary in the proportions of their band populations (mainly Registered Indians) residing off-reserve. Thus, while there can be some band populations that are "predominantly urban," there are also others that are mainly rural or very remote. However, it is not the intention of this study to focus on either specific reserves or individual First Nations/Aboriginal communities but rather to provide an overall analysis of mobility based on reserve geography and First Nation populations at the national level.

According to the 2006 Census, about 26% of the total Aboriginal population resided on Indian reserves or settlements; 21% resided in rural areas; 22% lived in small urban centres (urban non-CMAs); and 31% lived in the larger urban CMA areas. The geographic distribution of the Aboriginal population contrasted sharply with that of the non-Aboriginal population, which was heavily concentrated in urban areas (81%), especially large urban areas (65%)[3] (Figure 5.1).

Figure 5.1 Distribution of Aboriginal and Non-Aboriginal Population by Geographic Location, Canada, 2006

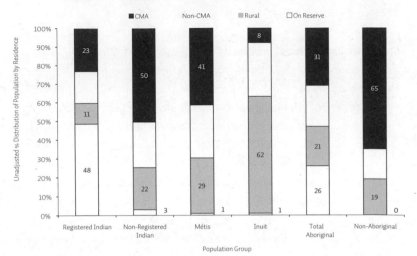

Source: Statistics Canada, 2006 Census of Canada.

Pronounced differences in geographic distributions also exist among the four Aboriginal groups: the non-Registered Indian and Métis populations being most heavily concentrated in urban areas, 74% and 69%, respectively; while a majority of the Inuit population lived in rural areas (62%). The Registered Indian population differed from other Aboriginal groups in that almost one-half (48% of the population enumerated in the census) lived on-reserve (probably understated due to incomplete enumeration of reserves and settlements); and considerably less urbanized at 40% (similarly, probably overstated) than the non-Registered Indian and Métis populations (Figure 5.1).

OVERVIEW OF RECENT MOBILITY RATES OF ABORIGINAL POPULATIONS

Aboriginal groups differ in their propensity to move, and it would appear the more urbanized the population the greater the mobility. As both 2001 and 2006 Census data show, mobility rates vary widely among Aboriginal groups, being highest among non-Registered Indians and Métis. Mobility rates among Aboriginal peoples (with the exception of Inuit) continue to exceed the non-Aboriginal.

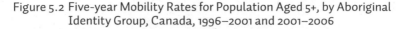

Figure 5.2 Five-year Mobility Rates for Population Aged 5+, by Aboriginal Identity Group, Canada, 1996–2001 and 2001–2006

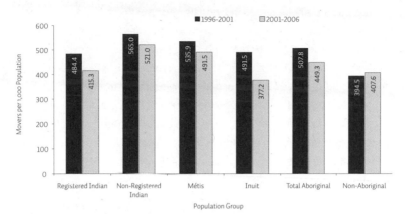

Source: Statistics Canada, 2001 and 2006 Censuses of Canada.

While variations in mobility rates across Aboriginal groups were similar over the past two and earlier censuses, rates among all Aboriginal sub-groups declined between 2001 and 2006. These declines were largest among Inuit (23% lower) and Registered Indians (14% lower). Mobility among non-Registered Indians and Métis fell by about 8% (Figure 5.2).

Recent Patterns of Population Growth

The rapid growth of the Aboriginal population, especially in major urban areas has been the subject of a number of demographic studies (Clatworthy, Hull, & Loughren, 1997; Guimond, 1999, 2003; Siggner & Costa, 2005; Guimond, Robitaille, & Senécal, 2009). Measuring the extent of Aboriginal population change with census data is complicated owing to intercensal variations in: concept(s) and definitions (e.g., population); wording of census questions; incomplete enumeration and undercoverage; and the popula-tion's propensity to identify their Aboriginal heritage and affiliation.

Notwithstanding these difficulties, census estimates can provide a rough measure of the scale of recent population changes (Clatworthy & Norris, 2007). Unadjusted census estimates of growth for the total Ab-original identity population during the 2001–2006 period indicate the Aboriginal population enumerated by the censuses increased by about 196,500 individuals between 2001 and 2006 (a 20% increase) (Figure 5.3).

Substantial increases to the Aboriginal identity population occurred both on-reserve and in rural and urban areas off-reserve. The on-reserve population increased by about 22,000 individuals, representing an annual growth rate of about 1.5% during the period. Some portion of the reported growth on-reserve is associated with fewer non-enumerated reserves experienced by the 2006 Census. Most growth (about 89%) occurred off-reserve, where annual average growth rates exceeded the overall total growth of 3.7%. The population increase of about 45,000 individuals in rural areas represents an annual growth rate of about 4.1%. Growth in the urban Aboriginal population totalled about 129,000 individuals. Most urban growth occurred in large cities, where the average annual rate of growth approached 5.3% for the period. Growth in areas off-reserve appeared higher between 2001 and 2006, compared to the previous 1996–2001 intercensal period. However, it should be noted that the two periods are not directly comparable given that data across the three censuses have not been adjusted for differentials in undercoverage and incomplete enumeration.

The pattern and scale of population growth reported for the time period are similar to those identified for the earlier 1996–2001 and 1986–1996 time periods (Clatworthy & Norris, 2007). The very high rates of growth of the urban Aboriginal population, which characterize the 1986–2001 15-year period, cannot be explained by natural increase (i.e., the excess of births over deaths). This situation raises a key question: To what extent has migration contributed to growth in the Aboriginal populations living on-reserve and in rural and urban areas?

Crude Migration Rates by Aboriginal Groups and Place of Residence

Both 2001 and 2006 Census data illustrate significant variations in five-year crude migration rates among Aboriginal groups. Over the 2001–2006 period, 203,450 Aboriginal people changed their community of residence (representing about 191 migrants per 1,000 population). The pattern of five-year migration rates among Aboriginal groups is generally similar to that observed for mobility. In 2006, as in 2001, migration rates were highest among non-Registered Indians (221 migrants per 1,000) and Métis (210 per 1,000), and lowest among Inuit (125 per 1,000), whose rates were lower than the non-Aboriginal rate of 189. In the case of Registered Indians, migration rates were also lower than non-Aboriginal in 2006, with a rate of 179, although not in 2001 (Figure 5.4).

Figure 5.3 Growth in the Population Reporting Aboriginal Identity
by Location of Residence, Canada, 2001–2006

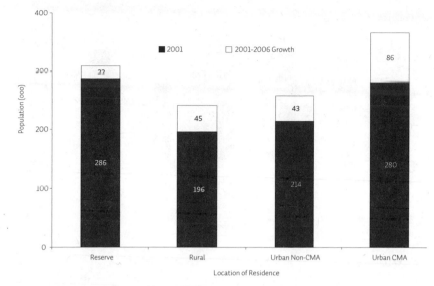

Source: Statistics Canada, 2001 and 2006 Censuses of Canada.

Decline in Aboriginal Migration Rates Between 2001 and 2006 Censuses

Over both censuses, migration rates among non-Registered Indians and
Métis remained considerably higher than that of the non-Aboriginal population. However, migration rates also declined during the 2001–2006 period
among all Aboriginal subgroups. These declines were largest among Inuit
(13% lower) and ranged between 5% and 7% among other Aboriginal groups.

In relation to the earlier 1996–2001 period, then, the volume of both
Aboriginal mobility and migration between 2001 and 2006 was lower. Aboriginal populations though, with the exception of the Inuit, were still more
likely to move between 2001 and 2006 than the non-Aboriginal population.
With respect to migration between 2001 and 2006, a smaller portion of the
Aboriginal population changed communities than in the previous 1996–2001
period, and five-year migration rates for both Registered Indians and Inuit
fell below the level of the non-Aboriginal population. This recent lessening
of high mobility of Aboriginal populations could suggest eventual convergence toward non-Aboriginal rates, perhaps owing to greater residential
stability of Aboriginal populations in urban areas over time (Norris &
Clatworthy, 2011).

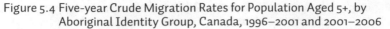

Figure 5.4 Five-year Crude Migration Rates for Population Aged 5+, by Aboriginal Identity Group, Canada, 1996–2001 and 2001–2006

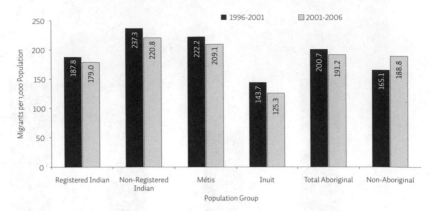

Source: Statistics Canada, 2001 and 2006 Censuses of Canada.

Variations in Aboriginal Migration Rates by Place of Residence

Volume and rates of migration vary not only across Aboriginal groups but also by their place of residence. Five-year crude migration rates over the 2001 to 2006 period in Table 5.1, for each Aboriginal group by geographic location, show that the overall rate of migration among Registered Indians (179 per 1,000) is lower than that of non-Registered Indians (221) and Métis (209). The lower Registered Indian rates reflect the relatively low rates of migration to (as well as from) reserves. The crude migration rate among the 52% of Registered Indians who live on-reserve is only 94 migrants per 1,000 population, in contrast to much higher crude migration rates among Registered Indians living in off-reserve locations, with a rate of 294 in urban non-CMA areas. Furthermore, in locations off-reserve, Registered Indian rates are significantly higher than those reported for the non-Registered Indian and Métis populations (with urban non-CMA rates of 254 and 250, respectively). Similarly, the overall low rate of migration recorded for the total Inuit population (125) reflects quite low levels of migration to and from rural areas,[4] with the exception of major urban areas of CMAs, where the Inuit migration rate of 323 migrants per 1,000 exceeds that of all other Aboriginal groups and that of the non-Aboriginal population.

While overall Aboriginal residents of reserves display much lower levels of migration (98 per 1,000) than the non-Aboriginal population in general, (189 per 1,000), rates of Aboriginal migration off-reserve are considerably

Table 5.1 Five-Year Crude Migration Rates (per 1,000 population)
by Aboriginal Identity Group and Place of Residence,
Canada, 2001–2006

Location	Crude Migration Rates by Population Group 2001–2006					
	Registered Indian	Non-Registered Indian	Métis	Inuit	Total Aboriginal	Non-Aboriginal
Reserve	94.1	N/A	N/A	N/A	97.6	N/A
Rural	223.0	218.4	192.2	76.3	190.4	174.6
Non-CMA	294.1	254.0	250.0	174.0	264.9	196.9
CMA	243.6	207.7	192.7	323.4	217.3	190.6
Total Residence	179.1	220.8	209.1	125.4	191.3	188.8

N/A means not applicable due to small population counts.
Source: Statistics Canada, 2006 Census of Canada.

higher than those of the non-Aboriginal population in both rural areas
(about 10% higher) and urban areas (35% higher).

Migrant Origin and Destination Flows

Table 5.2 provides a summary of the migration flows over the 2001–2006
period between reserves and off-reserve locations for each of the four Aboriginal groups. Inter-area origin-destination flows are based on the four
types of locations: residence on-reserve; rural areas; urban non-CMAs; and
urban CMAs. It should be noted that flows within the same area, such as
within CMAs, are not shown for specific areas due to a lack of the required
data at the time of writing. However, intra-area migration accounts for a
significant share of flows (18% of Registered Indian migrants, 38% of non-
Registered Indians, 13% of Métis, and 12% of Inuit). Much of this intra-area
flow (with the exception of the Inuit) is most likely attributable to within
urban same area flows based on analyses of previous censuses (Clatworthy
& Norris, 2007).

In the case of migration between different locations, flows between the
two urban areas combined—from non-CMA to CMAs, and from CMAs to
non-CMAs—represented a major component of migration among each
of the groups, accounting for the largest share of moves among both non-
Registered Indian (19%) and Métis (21%) migrants, and significant shares of

Registered Indians (14%) and Inuit (11%) migrants. Some other dimensions of the migration flows of the four groups, however, do differ. These differences relate, in part, to variations among subgroups with respect to geographic distribution and degree of urbanization. For example, moves to and from Indian reserves and settlements are common only among the Registered Indian population. Migrants originating from or relocating to reserves formed close to a third (32%) of all Registered Indian migrants during the period. Practically two-thirds (65%) of Registered Indian moves between on- and off-reserve locations in 2006 involved moves to reserves, similar to patterns observed over the 1996–2001 and earlier census periods. As well, 70% of moves to reserves involved migrants from urban areas (Table 5.2). Reciprocal moves between reserves and urban areas have tended to constitute an important dimension of the migration patterns of Registered Indians.

Apart from the flows between urban CMAs and urban non-CMAs, two other migration streams combined—from large (urban CMA) and small (urban non-CMA) cities to rural destinations—account for a significant share, close to a third, of non-Registered Indian and Métis migrants, at 31% and 32%, respectively, and, to a lesser extent, 27% of Inuit migrants; with even less, 16% of Registered Indians. In the opposite direction, flows of migrants from rural origins to city (urban CMA and non-CMA) destinations are most notably significant among Inuit migrants, accounting for 43%, followed by 31% of Métis, 24% of Registered Indians, but only 7% of non-Registered Indians (Table 5.2). Unlike other Aboriginal groups, non-Registered Indian migrants are most likely to move within the same type of area, most likely urban. In the case of Inuit, previous analysis of 2001 Census data suggests that intra-area migration tends to be much more characterized by significant flows between rural areas, a dimension that constitutes a minor component of migration for all other Aboriginal populations.

Net Migration Flows and Rates

The redistribution of population arising from net losses or gains of migrants appears to be generally minimal, such that at the national level migration has not been a major net contributor to Aboriginal population growth in urban areas overall. Findings from the 2006 Census, along with those from previous censuses since 1986 continue to debunk the "myth" of large net outflows of Aboriginal populations from reserves to cities as direct contributors to urban growth.

Table 5.2 Distribution of Aboriginal Migrants by Inter-Area Origin / Destination Flow and Aboriginal Identity Group, Canada, 2001–2006

Inter-Area Origin/ Destination Flows	Registered Indian		Non-Registered Indian		Métis		Inuit	
	Number	%	Number	%	Number	%	Number	%
Urban Non-CMA to On-Reserve	7,855	7.8	250	1.0	290	0.4	20	0.4
Urban Non-CMA to Rural	9,940	9.9	3,955	15.1	12,030	17.5	1,010	18.6
Urban Non-CMA to Urban CMA	7,875	7.8	2,630	10.0	7,670	11.2	265	4.9
Urban CMA to On-Reserve	6,860	6.8	235	0.9	265	0.4	10	0.2
Urban CMA to Rural	6,505	6.5	4,070	15.5	9,795	14.3	485	8.9
Urban CMA to Urban Non-CMA	6,205	6.2	2,460	9.4	6,950	10.1	330	6.1
Rural to On-Reserve	6,345	6.3	70	0.3	210	0.3	40	0.7
Rural to Urban Non-CMA	14,240	14.1	915	3.5	12,090	17.6	1,695	31.2
Rural to Urban CMA	10,045	10.0	795	3.0	9,155	13.3	615	11.3
Reserve to Rural	1,430	1.4	65	0.2	220	0.3	175	3.2
Reserve to Urban Non-CMA	5,340	5.3	80	0.3	175	0.3	35	0.6
Reserve to Urban CMA	4,645	4.6	35	0.1	240	0.3	35	0.6
Total Inter-Area Flows	79,430	78.9	15,310	58.3	58,800	85.6	4,695	86.5
Incompletely Enumerated Reserves 5 years ago	900	0.9	15	0.1	30	0.0	10	0.2
Outside Canada	1,805	1.8	980	3.7	1,130	1.6	65	1.2
Intra-Area Flows (e.g., urban CMA to urban CMA)	18,555	18.4	9,950	37.9	8,760	12.7	660	12.2
Total Migrants	100,690	100.0	26,255	100.0	68,720	100.0	5,430	100.0

Source: Statistics Canada, 2006 Census of Canada.

Although some 19% of the Aboriginal population changed their community of residence between 2001 and 2006, the net effects of the relocations on the geographic distribution of the population were considerably less. About 199,450 Aboriginal people (or 18.8% of the total population), aged five or more years, relocated to a different community within Canada between 2001 and 2006 (excluding external migrants living outside Canada five years ago). Net moves during the period among the four geographic areas, including reserves and off-reserve rural and urban areas (as shown in the boxes in Figure 5.5), totalled only 27,330 or about 2.6% of the population aged five or more years, considerably less in relation to the 19% of the population

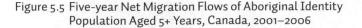

Figure 5.5 Five-year Net Migration Flows of Aboriginal Identity
Population Aged 5+ Years, Canada, 2001–2006

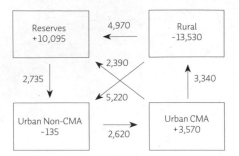

Source: Statistics Canada, 2006 Census of Canada.

that changed communities. Both reserves and large urban areas reported net inflows of Aboriginal migrants, largely at the expense of rural areas. As shown in Figure 5.5, the Aboriginal population living on reserves gained about 10,095 migrants as a consequence of net inflows from both rural and urban areas (similar to net inflow in previous census period of 1996–2001). All off-reserve geographic areas reported net outflows of migrants for the period. Rural areas lost 13,530 individuals through net outflows to all other areas (twice the net size of the net outflow of some 6,400 over 1996–2001.) Although small urban centres (urban non-CMAs) experienced a net inflow of migrants from rural areas, which practically offset the net outflows to both large cities (CMAs) and to reserves, such that Aboriginal population losses for smaller cities through migration was only 135, a much smaller loss than that was sustained over the previous 1996–2001 period with a net outflow of some 4,100 migrants. As in the previous 1996–2001 period, large urban centres recorded net inflows of Aboriginal migrants from both rural areas and smaller urban centres. However, while the direction of net flows between reserves, rural areas, urban non-CMAs, and CMAs did not change between 1996–2001 and 2001–2006, urban CMAs did experience a reversal of net migration from -430 in 1996–2001 to +3,570 in 2001–2006. Compared to the net inflows of migrants from both rural areas and smaller urban centres to CMAs, net outflows of migrants from CMAs to reserves were smaller over 2001–2006, resulting in an overall net gain of migrants, while over 1996–2001 net outflows from CMAs to reserves were larger than the net gains of migrants from rural and smaller urban areas.

Table 5.3 Volume of Net Migration Flows by Aboriginal Identity Group and Location, Canada, 2001–2006

Location	Registered Indian	Non-Registered Indian	Métis	Inuit
Reserves	9,645	305	130	-10
Rural Areas	-12,755	-760	590	-820
Urban Non-CMAs	115	60	-775	765
CMAs	2,995	395	55	65
Net Migration Flows	25,510	1,520	1,550	1660
Percentage of Population Aged 5+	4.6%	1.3%	0.5%	3.6%

Source: Statistics Canada, 2006 Census of Canada.

Aggregate data for the total Aboriginal identity population mask some important differences in the net migration patterns among the different Aboriginal populations. The volume of net migration by geographic area is presented in Table 5.3 for each of the four Aboriginal groups.

The geographic pattern of net migration changes for Registered Indians is similar to that presented previously for the total Aboriginal population. Reserves gained about 9,650 Registered Indians through migration during the period, while all off-reserve geographic areas recorded net migration losses. Net migration losses of Registered Indians occurred only for rural areas and were significant, with a net loss of 12,755, whereas both large and small urban areas, as well as reserves, recorded net inflows between 2001–2006, at the expense of rural areas. Increased inflows from rural areas combined with reduced outflows to reserves resulted in a reversal of Registered Indian net migration for non-CMAs and CMAs. Among Registered Indians, overall net moves between reserves and off-reserve rural and urban areas totalled 25,510, or about 4.6% of the population aged five or more years (Table 5.3).

Compared to the Registered Indian population, the contribution of migration to changes in the geographic distribution of other Aboriginal groups during the 2001–2006 period was much smaller. In the case of non-Registered Indians, net moves between reserves and off-reserve rural and urban areas among non-Registered Indians totalled only 1,520, or about 1.3% of the population aged five or more years. Reserves and urban areas recorded net inflows between 2001 and 2006, at the expense of rural areas.

Net outflows from rural areas increased sharply between 1996–2001 and 2001–2006, resulting in a reversal of net migration for rural areas. Increased inflows from rural areas combined with reduced outflows to CMAs resulted in a reversal of non-Registered Indian net migration for non-CMAs.

Net moves between reserves and off-reserve rural and urban areas among Métis totalled only 1,550, or about 0.5% of the population aged five or more years. Reserves, rural areas, and CMAs recorded net inflows between 2001 and 2006, at the expense of non-CMAs. In contrast with the previous five-year period, reserves recorded a small net gain of Métis migrants between 2001 and 2006, as a result of net inflows from urban areas. Although several changes in the direction of net flows between types of geographic areas occurred between 1996–2001 and 2001–2006, the overall volume of net moves between all geographies was greatly reduced.

Net moves among Inuit totalled 1,660 or about 3.6% of the population aged five or more years. As in the case of the previous five-year period, urban areas (especially non-CMAs) recorded net inflows between 2001 and 2006. Moves away from rural areas to urban areas represented the main dimension of Inuit migration during the period.

Contribution of Migration to Population Change

Net migration rates can be used to measure the impact of migration on changes in the size of the population in each geographic area. As illustrated in Figure 5.6, for most Aboriginal subgroups net migration rates tend to be quite small for most geographic areas. Population size impacts were most significant for the Registered Indian populations residing in rural areas and on-reserve, and for Inuit residing in small urban areas. In rural areas, the net outflow of Registered Indian migrants averaged 35.8 per 1,000 population annually. Net inflows of Registered Indians to reserves averaged 7.4 per 1,000 population annually. In small urban areas, the net inflow of Inuit migrants averaged 12.5 per 1,000 population. For the other remaining specific Aboriginal groups and locations, average annual rates of net migration ranged between 7.4 and -6.0 per 1,000 population, implying that migration between 2001 and 2006 generally contributed to only minor changes in the geographic distribution of Aboriginal populations.

In many respects, the patterns of Aboriginal migration identified for the 2001–2006 period are similar to those reported for the previous five-year periods of 1996–2001 (Clatworthy & Norris, 2007), 1991–1996, and 1986–1991

Figure 5.6 Average Annual Rate of Net Migration (per 1,000 Population) by Aboriginal Identity Group and Location, Canada, 2001–2006

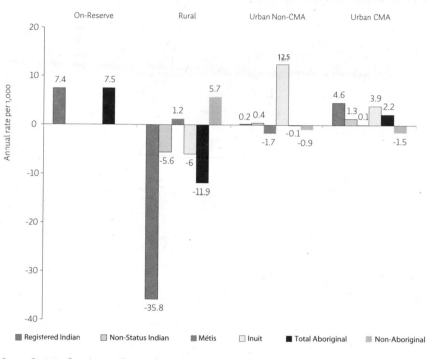

Source: Statistics Canada, 2006 Census of Canada.

(Clatworthy & Cooke, 2001; Norris, Cooke, Guimond, Beavon, & Clatworthy. 2004). Reserves continued to experience relatively small net inflows of migrants, almost exclusively Registered Indians. Rural areas experienced small net inflows of Métis and non-Registered Indian migrants, but much larger outflows of Registered Indian migrants. Urban areas also continued to record net outflows of migrants, most notably Registered Indians, although the impact of migration on the size of the urban Aboriginal population remained quite small. Rural areas and smaller urban centres (non-CMAs) continued to experience net out-migration. Net outflows were large only in the case of rural areas. In addition to reserves, large urban areas recorded net inflows, with net rates of 4.6 and 3.9 among Registered Indians and Inuit, respectively, which, while not large, were nevertheless greater than their rates of less than 0.5 in the 1996–2001 period.

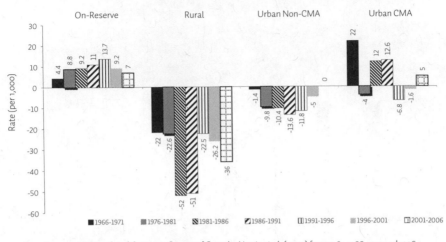

Figure 5.7 Average Annual Rate of Registered Indian Net Migration by Location and Five-Year Period, Canada, 1966–1971 to 2001–2006

Sources: Siggner (1977) from 1971 Census of Canada; Norris et al. (2004) from 1981, 1986, 1991 and 1996 Censuses of Canada; Clatworthy & Norris (2007) from 2001 Census of Canada.

Due to changes in census population definitions, long-term migration trends are available only for the Registered Indian population. As revealed in Figure 5.7, net inflows of Registered Indian migrants to reserves, first reported for the 1966–1971 time period by Siggner (1977), have continued throughout the past 35-year period. The net impact of the population inflow has remained more or less relatively stable over the past three decades, although more recently showing signs of slight decreases, with a net in-migration rate of around 50 per 1,000 Registered Indians on-reserve, over a five-year period, or, on an annual basis, of about 10 in-migrants per 1,000.

Net out-migration of Registered Indians from rural areas and smaller urban areas has also occurred consistently throughout this period. With the exception of rural areas, which continued to experience high net outflows of migrants, the net effects of migration on the geographic distribution of the Registered Indian population continued to be small during the 2001–2006 period.

A more complex pattern of net migration exists for large urban areas. Large urban centres recorded net inflows of the Registered Indian migrants throughout most of the 1966–1991 period. The net outflows of the Registered Indian migrants from major urban centres reported for both the 1991–1996 and 1996–2001 periods reflect a reversal of the longer-term migration trend. However, over the most recent 2001–2006 period, it appears that migration has contributed slightly to growth of the Registered Indian populations in urban CMAs, although not to the same extent as observed in previous censuses. In the case of the smaller urban areas, the impact of migration on the Registered Indian population is practically nil, with a small net in-migration rate of 0.2 per 1,000. It appears that while the long-term migration patterns of Registered Indians have tended to slow population growth in both rural and small urban areas, migration has contributed to population growth in large cities and urban CMAs, for four of the seven intercensal periods observed, as well as consistently contributing to growth on reserves.

As in previous censuses of the past two decades, although high rates of migration characterize all Aboriginal populations, especially those off-reserve, data for the 2001 to 2006 time period clearly suggest that overall migration has not played a major role in altering the geographic distribution of the Aboriginal population. Nor has it served as a significant component of recent population growth in any of the geographic areas considered in this study, apart from rural areas. These findings clearly imply that the recent high rates of Aboriginal population growth must result from other factors. As noted by Clatworthy, Hull, and Loughren (1997) and Guimond (1999), these other factors are both numerous and complex and include natural increase (i.e., the excess of births over deaths), changes in levels of census coverage, legislative changes (e.g., the 1985 amendments to the Indian Act), and changes in self-reporting of Aboriginal identity (ethnic mobility or ethnic drift).

The factor of ethnic mobility appears to account for much of the reported recent population growth reported for the Registered Indian, non-Registered Indian, and Métis populations, especially in off-reserve areas. In terms of its contribution to the growth of Aboriginal populations, ethnic mobility represents the residual component of growth that cannot be accounted for by demographic (natural increase, migration) and legislative factors, and net undercoverage (Clatworthy, 2006; Siggner & Costa, 2005; Guimond, 2003). A 2009 article, "Aboriginal Populations in Canadian Cities: Why are They Growing so Fast?" (Guimond, Robitaille, & Senécal) demonstrates the significant impact of ethnic mobility among different Aboriginal groups over the 1996–2001 and 2001–2006 periods, especially among Métis, and in urban areas.

Sub-National Variations in Components of Growth

The national level data presented in this report are generally indicative of the patterns identified for all regions across Canada. However, the impacts and significance of ethnic mobility, migration, and natural increase in contributing to urban Aboriginal growth can vary by cities and regions (Clatworthy & Norris, 2007; Norris & Clatworthy, 2011). Results from an analysis of the components of urban growth for the 1996–2001 intercensal period (the most recent period analyzed at the time of writing), identifies the role of migration in urban growth vis-à-vis other factors, and clearly demonstrates the diversity of factors contributing to growth and how these factors vary in importance regionally and across cities. Migration has been more of a significant factor in the growth of some urban areas, although generally not at the expense of reserves (Norris & Clatworthy, 2011).

Major Urban Areas

While movement to and from urban areas, especially involving large cities, accounts for a significant share of the volume of Aboriginal migration, it tends not to be a significant component of growth in urban areas overall. However, the 2001 Census analysis of the 1996–2001 period shows that the impact of net migration on Aboriginal population growth in urban areas does vary across cities (Clatworthy & Norris, 2007). Even though some cities recorded high growth rates, and experienced high gross migration rates—that is, high rates of in- and out-migration to the cities—effects of net migration did not tend to contribute significantly to population growth. In fact, some cities that recorded net outflows of migrants during the period nevertheless also reported high rates of Aboriginal population growth— often due to the effects of ethnic mobility. Annual net migration rates, which varied widely across cities, accounted for only a small component of the total growth rates for several cities recording net inflows of migrants, with the exception of a few.

While ethnic mobility and to some extent natural increase account for much of urban growth overall, individual cities can vary in their categories of growth factors. For some cities, natural increase is as major component of growth as natural increase, such as the Prairie cities of Winnipeg, Saskatoon, and Regina. In other cities, such as Vancouver, Toronto, and Montreal, ethnic mobility accounts for practically all, at least 80%, of growth over the 1996–2001 period. And for several cities, such as Edmonton,

Calgary, Ottawa–Hull/Gatineau, Thunder Bay, and Hamilton, both natural increase and net migration are major contributors to their Aboriginal populations. Furthermore, even in those cities where the net migration effects are small, the age–gender compositional effects of migration, of Aboriginal youth and young adults migrating to cities, could indirectly contribute to population growth through natural increase (Norris & Clatworthy, 2011).

Residential Mobility

Residential mobility refers to changing one's place of residence within the same community. This aspect of mobility is important as it represents the major process though which households and individuals adjust their housing consumption to reflect changes in needs and resources. High levels of residential mobility may result from family instability and difficulties in acquiring adequate and affordable housing. While the mainstream literature (e.g., Rossi, 1955) tends to view a residential move as a voluntary response to changing household or individual circumstances (e.g., family formation, development or dissolution; changes in income or place of work) moving may also occur involuntarily as a consequence of events such as eviction or dwelling loss to fire or condemnation.

Residential mobility rates presented in this study are defined as the proportion of the non-migrant population that changed residence in the previous 12-month period. The rates reflect moves made during the year preceding the 2001 census and are presented as the number of residential movers per 1,000 non-migrant population aged one or more years.

Residential Mobility Rates by Aboriginal Groups and Place of Residence: Declines Between 2001 and 2006 Censuses

Residential mobility rates among all Aboriginal groups continued to exceed that of the non-Aboriginal population in 2005–2006. For the 2005–2006 period, the overall rate of residential mobility among the non-migrant Aboriginal population was 127.7 per 1,000 non-migrant population, a rate about one and a half times that reported for the non-Aboriginal population of 86.3 (Figure 5.8).

However, as noted earlier, mobility in general has declined overall between the 2001 and 2006 Censuses, including migration rates, and it would appear to the case for one-year residential mobility rates, which reinforces the suggestion that this recent lessening of high mobility may owe

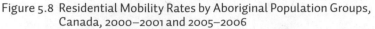

Figure 5.8 Residential Mobility Rates by Aboriginal Population Groups, Canada, 2000–2001 and 2005–2006

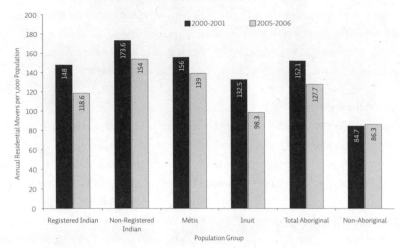

Source: Statistics Canada, 2001 and 2006 Censuses of Canada.

to greater residential stability of Aboriginal populations in urban areas over time (Norris & Clatworthy, 2011). Residential mobility rates of all Aboriginal groups in 2005–2006 were lower than their rates in 2000–2001, with declines of 26% for Inuit, 20% for Registered Indians, and 11% for non-Registered Indians and Métis. Similarly, declines in overall rates of Aboriginal residential mobility were also observed by residence, with decreases of 40% on-reserve, 23% in rural areas, 17% in urban non-CMAs, and 10% in urban CMAs.

As with mobility in general, residential mobility rates differ not only across Aboriginal populations but also according to location of residence. Aboriginal residential mobility rates remained much higher in urban areas than reserve and rural areas and continued to exceed those of the non-Aboriginal population in all off-reserve areas. In urban areas, Aboriginal populations moved at a rate of 192.5 per 1,000, roughly twice the rate of non-Aboriginals, at 97.7, in 2005–2006. Among the Aboriginal population, the rates of mobility on-reserve (50.7 per 1,000 non-migrant population) and in rural areas (66.3 per 1,000 non-migrant population) were of similar magnitude, but sharply lower than those reported in urban non-CMA and CMA areas (177.0 and 202.2 per 1,000 populations, respectively); these rates were similar to, but lower than, residential rates observed over the 2000–2001 period (Figure 5.9).

Figure 5.9 Aboriginal Residential Mobility Rates by Place of Residence, Canada, 2000–2001 and 2005–2006

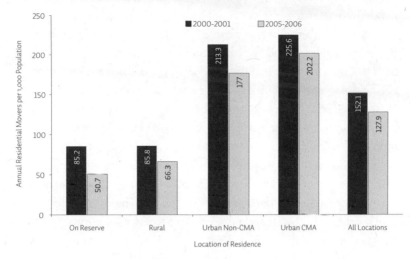

Source: Statistics Canada, 2001 and 2006 Censuses of Canada.

Figure 5.10 One-Year Residential Mobility Rates for Selected Cities, Aboriginal and Non-Aboriginal, Canada, 2005–2006

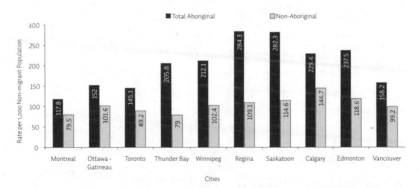

Source: Statistics Canada, 2006 Census of Canada.

The significantly higher rates of residential mobility of Aboriginal people in urban areas compared to non-Aboriginal urban residents can also be observed in specific major urban centres, as shown in Figure 5.10. Aboriginal populations in Thunder Bay, Regina, and Saskatoon are about 2.5 times more likely to move residentially than their non-Aboriginal counterparts.

Reasons for Migration

Migration reflects the interplay among personal characteristics of potential movers, characteristics of communities of residence, and those of potential destinations. The propensity to move is influenced by age, gender, and stages in the life cycle and personal attributes of individuals (e.g., education level, attachment to traditional culture). The decision to move is the outcome of competing "pushes" or reasons for leaving one's current place of residence, while the "pulls" are the benefits to be gained by moving to a potential destination. For example, reserves contribute to a unique set of push–pull factors that affect migration patterns related to the rights and benefits associated with Registered Indian status and residence on-reserve. Aboriginal communities and reserves can also serve as potential destinations for city dwellers, in the preservation of ties with home community and maintenance of cultural traditions and language. For example, communities have been cited by some migrants as their preferred choice to raise children and to retire (Cooke, 1999). Also, reserve communities and cities do differ widely in their economic, socio-cultural, and geographic characteristics, such that migration flows between individual communities and cities are outcomes of particular sets of circumstances (Norris & Clatworthy, 2007); for example, community characteristics such as location are also known to affect migration (Clatworthy & Cooke, 2001).

An analysis of 1991 Aboriginal Peoples Survey (APS) data on the reasons for migration among Registered Indians to and from reserves cited family and housing as the major reasons regardless of destination, while education was a major reason for leaving reserves, and employment a major reason for moves between urban communities; with respect to gender differences, women were more likely to move for family and community-related reasons (Clatworthy & Cooke, 2001).

Reasons for Residential Moves

For populations in general, many of the events that can trigger residential moves (e.g., marriage, family development, buying a new home) occur at the young adult ages, As illustrated in Figure 5.11, the general pattern of residential mobility over age groups is quite similar for both Aboriginal and non-Aboriginal populations, with mobility highest among cohorts aged 20 to 34 years (rates ranging from 200 to 355 residential movers per 1,000 urban residents), and among children aged 1 to 6 years (rates ranging from 200 to

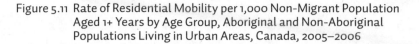

Figure 5.11 Rate of Residential Mobility per 1,000 Non-Migrant Population Aged 1+ Years by Age Group, Aboriginal and Non-Aboriginal Populations Living in Urban Areas, Canada, 2005–2006

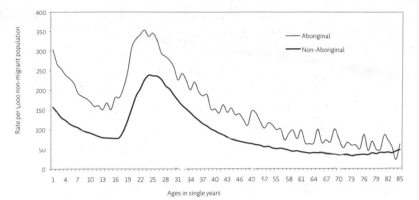

Source: Statistics Canada, 2006 Census of Canada.

305). This pattern most likely reflects higher levels of mobility associated with younger families in the early stages of family development that are attempting to bring their housing consumption in line with the larger space needs of a growing family.

Given that the age structure of the Aboriginal population is much younger than that of the non-Aboriginal population, one might reasonably expect Aboriginal populations to experience higher residential mobility due to age alone. However, Figure 5.11 also reveals for all age groups, including older cohorts, sharply (at least 50%) higher rates of residential mobility for the Aboriginal population than those of the non-Aboriginal population. This suggests that overall Aboriginal–non-Aboriginal differences in urban rates of residential mobility cannot be explained by differences in age structure alone. Factors other than age, including inadequate housing, low rates of homeownership, discrimination, low incomes, and poverty are likely to be more important in explaining the high rates of residential mobility of the urban Aboriginal population.

The analysis of 1991 APS data concerning the reasons for residential moves among Aboriginal peoples clearly identify efforts to improve housing situations as the primary motivation for residential moves, with housing accounting for the largest number of reasons given by APS respondents (57%). Family-related reasons were cited by 16% of respondents; factors related to neighbourhood circumstances (e.g., crime and safety) and accessibility (e.g., to schools or employment) were also cited by 16% of respondents; while involuntary moves were noted by 8% of all respondents. Most of these involuntary moves were linked to substandard housing circumstances (Clatworthy & Cooke, 2001).

The inadequate housing situations both on- and off-reserve that underlie the high levels of residential mobility among urban Aboriginal populations have been well documented (e.g., Clatworthy & Stevens, 1987; Clatworthy, 1980; 1983; 1995; Spector, 1996). Research conducted for the Royal Commission on Aboriginal Peoples by Clatworthy (1995) found that recent Aboriginal movers were considerably more likely than non-movers to experience one or more housing consumption deficiencies (most commonly affordability and quality). A substantial majority of urban Aboriginal movers did not acquire housing that met Canada's standards for affordability (cost in relation to income), quality (condition), or suitability (adequate space). The process of residential mobility does not appear to result in acceptable levels of housing consumption for a significant segment of the urban Aboriginal population. Given this situation, the high levels of residential mobility that continue to characterize the urban Aboriginal population are cause for concern and may constitute an additional dimension of the housing difficulties experienced by the population.

Age–Gender Patterns of Registered Indian Mobility and Migration, On- and Off-Reserve

Analysis of mobility and migration by age and gender provides insight into the associations between mobility and various stages in the life cycle, such as education, labour force transitions (employment, job loss, and retirement) and household and family formation and dissolution (marriage, divorce, widowhood). For example, gender differences among youth and young adults are attributable to younger ages of females at marriage and earlier entry into the labour force. Here, the focus is on the Registered Indian age-gender patterns and differentials of residential mobility, migration, and origin-destination flows to and from reserves.

Mobility rates among Registered Indians have consistently followed the same standard age pattern as that observed for all Canadians, as well as most populations in general: low over the school-age years, peaking during the young adult years of 20 to 29, and then declining fairly steadily thereafter, with young women in the 15 to 29 age group displaying higher mobility than their male counterparts (Clatworthy & Norris, 2007; Norris, Cooke, Guimond, Beavon, & Clatworthy, 2004; Norris, 1985; 1990; 1996). This pattern has continued to the present. For example, with respect to young adults aged 25 to 29, among the Registered Indian population residing off-reserve, women had moved to a greater extent between 2001 and 2006, with a mobility rate of 825 movers per 1,000 population, compared to a corresponding rate of 767 for men. Similar comparisons are observed for non-Aboriginal populations in the same age group, the female rate was higher than that for males (760 versus 702).

Age–Gender Patterns of In-, Out-, and Net Migration by Place of Residence On- and Off-Reserve: Trend toward Gender-Balanced Migration Patterns

The movement to and from reserves is characterized by strong gender differentials. Registered Indian females experience higher rates of migration to and from reserves and, most especially, higher rates of out-migration from reserves. While younger ages at marriage and entry into the labour force of females are contributing factors, major sources of these gender differentials in out-migration can be linked to some extent to the pre-1985 provisions of the Indian Act concerning intermarriage and effects of "Matrimonial Real Property" concerning the divisions of matrimonial real property resulting from marriage breakdown in First Nation communities/reserves (Norris, 2009). For example, prior to the 1985 revisions to the Indian Act, more women characterized the outflow of Registered Indian migrants from reserves to cities, leading to gender imbalance and bias both on reserve and in urban areas.[5]

Among Registered Indians living on reserves, previous censuses have consistently shown that women move from reserves at higher rates than men, especially among youth and young adults. And this is again true for the 2001–2006 period, with average annual out-migration rates among the most mobile age group, 20 to 24, of 16.5 per 1,000 for women, about one and a half times the rate of 11.2 for men (Figure 5.12a). Overall, the out-migration rate for females is 10.3 and 8.2 for males.

However, findings based on the 2006 Census and those from published analyses of earlier censuses (Norris 1985; 1990; 1996; 2000; Norris, Cooke, Guimond, Beavon, & Clatworthy, 2004) suggest trends toward more gender-balanced patterns of out-migration, particularly among youth. Fifteen years earlier, the 1991 Census showed that, among Registered Indian youth aged 15 to 24, rates of five-year out-migration rate from reserves over the 1986–1991 period were significantly higher—1.72 times—for females (86 per 1,000) than for males (50 per 1,000) (Norris, 1996: 210). Five years later, the 1996 Census results also indicated higher female rates but to a lesser degree over the 1991–1996 period: for Registered Indian aged 20 to 24, five-year out-migration rates of females (70 per 1,000) were 1.55 times higher than males (45 per 1,000); while for the 15 to 19 age group, female rates (50 per 1,000) were 1.66 times higher than males (30 per 1,000) (Norris Cooke, Guimond, Beavon, & Clatworthy, 2004: Figure 7.6, 147). By 2006, the ratio of female to male out-migration rates from reserves had declined, based on average annual rates, to 1.47 times for the 20 to 24 age group (16.5 versus 11.2) and 1.31 times for the 15 to 19 age group (11.4 versus 8.7). The results from these past censuses would suggest a trend toward more balanced gender patterns of out-migration from reserves among youth and young adults.

Gender Differentials On-Reserve Less Pronounced for In-migration than Out-migration Rates

Among Registered Indians living on reserves, across all ages for male and females, higher rates of in-migration than out-migration result in net inflows at all ages. Rates of in- and out-migration are highest for young adults (ages 20 to 34), while net in-migration appears to be highest among labour forced-aged adults ranging from 25–29 to 45–49 years. Again, as with out-migration, although not to the same extent, women tend to have higher rates of in-migration to reserves than men, again especially among youth and young adults (Figure 5.12a). Overall, the in-migration rate for females is 17.4 and 15.9 for males, with corresponding net in-migration rates of 7.1 and 7.7, respectively.

In-migration Rates to Off-Reserve Locations: Gender Differentials Appear to be Greatest Among Youth and Young Adults

Off-reserve, patterns of in-, out- and net migration rates of Registered Indians are the opposite to those on-reserve, with higher rates of out-migration than in-migration resulting in net outflows of migrants to reserves across all ages, for both males and females (Figure 5.12b). Gender differentials appear to be greatest among youth and young adults, with higher rates of in-migration among women.

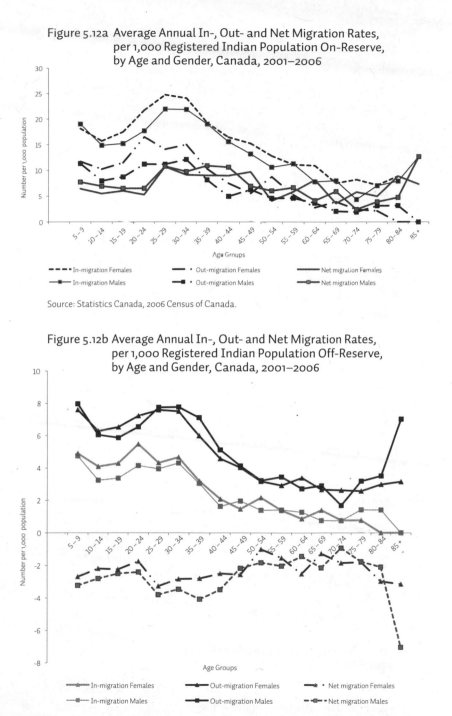

Figure 5.12a Average Annual In-, Out- and Net Migration Rates, per 1,000 Registered Indian Population On-Reserve, by Age and Gender, Canada, 2001–2006

Number per 1,000 population

Age Groups

- - - In-migration Females
—•— Out-migration Females
——— Net migration Females
—■— In-migration Males
—■•— Out-migration Males
—□— Net migration Males

Source: Statistics Canada, 2006 Census of Canada.

Figure 5.12b Average Annual In-, Out- and Net Migration Rates, per 1,000 Registered Indian Population Off-Reserve, by Age and Gender, Canada, 2001–2006

Number per 1,000 population

Age Groups

——— In-migration Females
——— Out-migration Females
—•— Net migration Females
—■— In-migration Males
—■— Out-migration Males
—◆— Net migration Males

Source: Statistics Canada, 2006 Census of Canada.

For Registered Indians of all ages, males and females, the impact of migration appears to be less pronounced for populations residing outside reserves than on reserves. Overall, average annual rates of in-migration among males and females are considerably lower, off-reserve at only 3.0 and 3.4 in-migrants per 1,000, respectively, less than a fifth of the corresponding in-migration rates to reserves of 15.9 and 17.4. Similarly, male and female rates of out-migration from off-reserve locations are also lower, at 5.8 and 5.7, respectively, more so for females, compared to corresponding out-migration from reserves of 8.2 and 10.3. And, finally, the overall net effect of migration on Registered Indian population growth off-reserve is smaller off reserves, with male and female net outflows of 2.8 and 2.3 migrants per 1,000, respectively, compared to corresponding net inflows of 7.7 and 7.1 migrants per 1,000 population on-reserve.

Differentials in Registered Indian Mobility and Migration Between On- and Off-Reserve: Rates Highest Off-Reserve at All Ages, and Both Males and Females

In general, Aboriginal people who live outside their Native communities and settlements tend to move to a greater extent than both those living in Aboriginal communities and the general population (Norris, 1985; 1990; 1996). As was observed for Registered Indians overall, rates of mobility and migration rates are much higher in locations outside reserves at all ages, and for both males and females. Higher rates off-reserve are only partly attributable to movement from reserves and settlements since they also reflect significant residential movement within the same community, as well as between communities. Overall, for Registered Indian females between 2001 and 2006, for every 1,000 residing off-reserve, 581 had moved, compared to a rate of 243 movers (per 1,000 population) among reserve residents. Rates for non-Aboriginal females, although lower at 410 movers per 1,000, were closer to those of Registered Indian women living off-reserve. Rates are highest among young adult Registered Indian women, aged 25 to 29 living off-reserve at about 825, with a corresponding rate of 389 movers per 1,000 among those living on-reserve, and 760 for non-Aboriginal women.

Age-Gender Contrasts in Mobility between Registered Indian and Non-Aboriginal

Contrasts in mobility between the Registered Indian population and the non-Aboriginal population, which appear to be greatest among youth and young adults, tend to be more pronounced among residential movers than

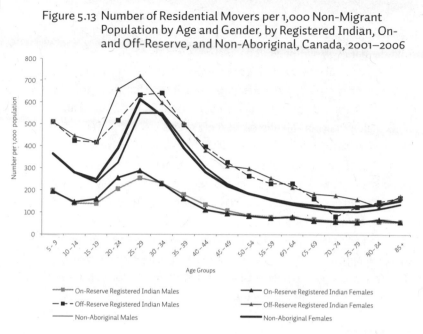

Figure 5.13 Number of Residential Movers per 1,000 Non-Migrant Population by Age and Gender, by Registered Indian, On- and Off-Reserve, and Non-Aboriginal, Canada, 2001–2006

Source: Statistics Canada, 2006 Census of Canada.

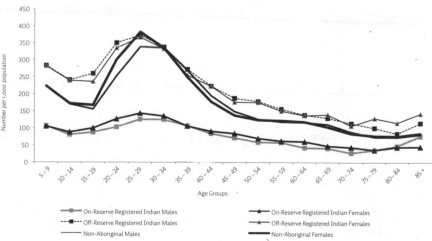

Figure 5.14 Number of Migrant Movers per 1,000 Population by Age and Gender, by Registered Indian, On- and Off-Reserve, and Non-Aboriginal, Canada, 2001–2006

Source: Statistics Canada, 2006 Census of Canada.

migrants. Overall, for the 2001–2006 period among Registered Indians living off-reserve, male and female rates of residential mobility, each at about 430 movers per 1,000 non-migrant population, were about 1.6 times higher than non-Aboriginal rates of around 270 per 1,000. Differentials are less pronounced for migration, with corresponding male and female Registered Indian rates of 256 and 250 migrants per 1,000 population—about 1.4 and 1.3 times higher than non-Aboriginal rates of 189 each per 1,000. Age–gender rates in residential mobility are highest among Registered Indian women aged 25 to 29 off-reserve—with practically 720 residential movers per 1,000, compared to a rate on 612 among non-Aboriginal women and only 287 per 1,000 Registered Indian women on-reserve (Figure 5.13). Registered Indian youth living off-reserve tend to be more similar to non-Aboriginal youth in their rates of migration than in their rates of residential mobility. In some ages, non-Aboriginal rates are slightly higher, such as for women aged 25 to 29, with a rate of 382, compared to a rate of 367 per 1,000 for Registered Indian women of the same age (Figure 5.14).

IMPLICATIONS

The rest of this chapter explores some of the implications of the findings presented here with respect to urban population turnover and instability; migration and components of growth in relation to population growth and composition; policy development; and impact of policy and program delivery on mobility. While the 2006 Census-based findings suggest some lessening of Aboriginal mobility, results also suggest a continuation of previous patterns of Aboriginal mobility and migration observed in previous analyses of earlier censuses. As such, much of the discussion on implications in Clatworthy and Norris (2007) still remains relevant and is incorporated in the following sections.

Implications of Urban Population Turnover and Instability

Findings from the 2006 Census support the previous conclusions by the authors' in their earlier 2001 Census study (Clatworthy & Norris, 2007) that the most important aspects of recent Aboriginal mobility and migration patterns continue to be related to the high levels of population turnover off-reserve, especially in urban areas, rather than population redistribution (as migration has played only a minor role in this regard). In urban areas, high levels of residential mobility in conjunction with high levels of in- and

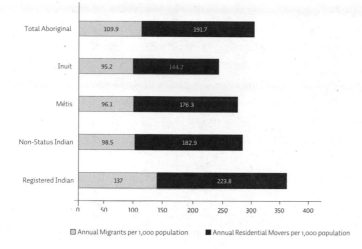

Figure 5.15 Annual Rate of Turnover among Urban Population by Aboriginal Identity Group, Canada, 2005–2006

Total Aboriginal	109.9	191.7
Inuit	95.2	144.2
Métis	96.1	176.3
Non-Status Indian	98.5	182.9
Registered Indian	137	223.8

□ Annual Migrants per 1,000 population   ■ Annual Residential Movers per 1,000 population

Source: Statistics Canada, 2006 Census of Canada.

out-migration result in Aboriginal populations that are in a high state of flux or "churn."[6] As illustrated in Figure 5.15, about 30% of urban Aboriginal residents either migrate in or out of the city or change residence within the city annually, a level of population turnover roughly twice that of the non-Aboriginal population; these findings are similar to those observed over the 1996–2001 period. Among urban Aboriginal residents, population turnover is most pronounced for Registered Indians, with both higher levels of migration to and from cities associated with high levels of movement between cities and reserves and higher rates of residential mobility. Higher levels of residential mobility may reflect more severe socio-economic difficulties, including a higher incidence of inadequate housing conditions among Registered Indians (Clatworthy, 1980; Clatworthy & Stevens, 1987) compared to other Aboriginal populations (Clatworthy & Norris, 2007: 228).

Even though the net impact of migration is relatively minimal in terms of population gain or loss, high rates of in- and out-migration to and from cities, "churn" and high residential mobility among Aboriginal peoples in urban areas can have disruptive effects on individuals, families, communities, and service providers. Neighbourhood-based social programs that provide services to urban Aboriginal populations, such as health, family support and counselling, and education, are designed to ensure a co-ordinated response to multi-faceted family and individual needs. Frequent mobility among Aboriginal families can result in discontinuity or disruption of service provision with negative consequences for the family and service provision agencies.[7] Discontinuity in service delivery can be especially pronounced among high-need families, such as those of lone female parents who are among the most mobile, yet often in the most need.

The provision of education services illustrates the challenges and implications associated with high levels of mobility. In a study of schools in central Winnipeg neighbourhoods, Clatworthy (2000) found a strong relationship between the Aboriginal share of the population and student turnover rates in central city schools. High rates of residential mobility appear to translate into an unstable education environment for many Aboriginal children. Other studies exploring the link between mobility and student performance indicates that frequent mobility by a family is a key contributing factor to student academic underachievement (Astone & McLanahan, 1994; US General Accounting Office, 1994). From another perspective, a study on school change of Aboriginal students in British Columbia public schools suggests that "disruptive school change, or student mobility, is a significant factor in both student-level and school-level school completion for Aboriginal students" (Aman, 2009: 186).

Frequent moves may limit opportunities for individuals and families to establish meaningful and lasting social relationships within both the Aboriginal and broader urban community. If so, mobility may promote social isolation and act as barrier to the development of social cohesion in the urban context. Greater social problems, such as poorer educational attainment could be the consequence of high mobility (Beavon & Norris, 1999). More recent studies on migration and educational attainment suggest that those who move frequently, whether between neighbourhoods or between communities, do not fare as well as those who experience greater residential stability, perhaps associated with factors of social capital, networks, and supports (Beavon, Wingert, & White, 2009).

Implications of Migration on Population Growth and Composition

As a component of growth, migration can also affect population growth indirectly. Even though the net effects of migration on population loss or gain migration may be small, the flows of migrants among reserves, rural

and urban areas can affect the age–gender composition of Aboriginal population. For example, the higher out-migration of women in the outflow of
Registered Indian migrants from reserves to cities prior to 1985 lead to gender imbalance and bias both on-reserve and in urban areas. Also, the influx
of youth and young adult migrants to cities could lead to population growth
through natural increase, and consequently, increased needs and services of
young families, such as housing (Norris & Clatworthy, 2011). As Clatworthy
has previously reported,

> Significant net outflows of younger age cohorts can be expected to
> have effect of lowering the rate of natural increase in rural areas.
> The reverse situation appears to be occurring in urban areas which
> experienced net inflows of young cohorts. Migration appears to be
> accelerating the shift of the age structure of Aboriginal populations
> to older age cohorts in rural areas, while maintaining a more youth-
> ful age structure among urban Aboriginal populations. (Clatworthy,
> 2009: 50)

In addition to demographic impacts on Aboriginal populations, migration can also affect Aboriginal group composition and socio-economic
characteristics.

Implications for Policy Development

High population turnover and the compositional effects of migration have
considerable implications for policy and program development in service
areas, such as education (program delivery, high mobility, and student
performance); and housing (levels of adequacy and affordability). The
compositional effects of high turnover on the urban population can present
challeges of recognizing different needs and services for different groups and
adapting services to the needs of a "changing" population. The myth that
urban growth is largely due to migration from reserves leads to the belief
that characteristics of urban Aboriginal populations are those largely associated with migrants. This is significant since non-movers and movers can
represent different socio-economic, demographic, and cultural characteristics, origins, and needs. Misunderstandings concerning Aboriginal migration,
mobility, and ethnic mobility could adversely affect policy development.
In this respect, the impact of high rates of growth due to ethnic mobility,

especially among the Métis, can have implications for the interpretation of socio-economic and demographic characteristics. It has been suggested that the misinterpretation of trends could lead to an "over-emphasis on migration from Indian reserve to cities...and a policy shift away from First Nations and Inuit communities (Guimond, Robitaille, & Senécal 2009, 16).

The analyses presented here suggest important implications for policy in many areas, not the least of which pertain to family and housing, which are cited as major reasons for moving. For example, findings from APS data clearly identify efforts to improve housing situations as the primary motivation for residential moves; yet, for a substantial majority of urban Aboriginal movers, these moves do not appear to result in acceptable levels of housing consumption. Furthermore, a significant portion of moves, nearly a quarter, could be considered as "forced" rather than voluntary moves, due to reasons associated with neighbourhood circumstances (e.g., crime and safety) and involuntary moves, mostly linked to substandard housing circumstances.

Research on migration and educational attainment also points to a distinction between forced moves as a consequence of events (e.g., eviction; loss of dwelling to fire or condemnation; violence, abusive situations) and those by choice (e.g., to pursue employment or educational opportunites) (Beavon, Wingert, & White, 2009: 222). From this viewpoint, policy could address some of the causes that underlie forced moves, in the areas of affordable housing, safety, and protection. At the school level, policies and programs could be developed to address the factor of mobility in the educational outcomes of Aboriginal students, as part of the schools responsibility to students (Aman, 2009: 192).

IMPACT OF POLICY AND PROGRAM DELIVERY ON MIGRATION

It has been argued that while mobility and migration may affect program delivery, it is also the case that policies and program delivery may affect migration, whether or not this effect is intended. For example, according to some observers (Reeves & Frideres, 1981; Bostrom, 1984), through the 1970s the federal government actively curtailed programs available on reserves as a way to encourage migration off of reserves and reduce its fiscal obligations. It was also suggested that the decreasing effectiveness of public service delivery to a growing urban Aboriginal population may have led to less effective acculturation into urban communities, resulting in return migration to reserves (Norris Cooke, Guimond, Beavon, & Clatworthy, 2004).

However, no real evidence has yet been presented to suggest the implementation of a policy to promote out-migration from reserves, or that better service delivery in urban areas would reduce return migration (Clatworthy & Norris, 2007).

The impact of policy and program delivery has been previously explored using the example of the provision of housing on and off reserves as a related policy challenge in the area of migration (Clatworthy & Norris, 2007). Housing-related commitments were contained in the federal government's response to the recommendations of the 1996 Royal Commission on Aboriginal Peoples (in Indian and Northern Affairs Canada's "Gathering Strength" [1997]). Housing responsibilities differ by government levels: the federal government is traditionally responsible for housing on reserves, while provinces and territories have been accountable for social housing off reserves since the late 1990s. The federal government's role in Aboriginal housing off reserve has been mainly one of cost sharing with the provinces, not actual policy development or administration. Since no urban Aboriginal housing policy exists at the national level, policy and administration tends to be decentralized at provincial and municipal levels, a reflection of the diversity of regional and local housing needs off reserve. As such, policies and programs are not developed in a consistent fashion across cities. Municipal governments often deal directly with housing in the delivery of ad hoc programs and services, frequently in the absence of a policy framework (Hanselmann 2001; Phil Deacon, Research Division, Canada Mortgage and Housing Corporation, personal correspondence, 2001). Such institutional arrangements could possibly affect population and might thereby reduce the level of population turnover and churn, whether or not this effect is intended (Clatworthy & Norris, 2007: 230–231).

One example of the impact of policy and legislation on migration pertains to the Indian Act. Perhaps to some extent the trend observed toward more balanced gender patterns of migration from reserves could be reflective of the 1985 changes to the Indian Act concerning intermarriage provisions, such that Registered Indian women would no longer lose their status and be required to leave their reserve if they married a non-Registered Indian.

CONCLUSION

Many of the patterns, trends, and characteristics of Aboriginal mobility and migration observed with previous censuses continue to hold steady, including differentials and demographic similarities across Aboriginal groups, as well as with the non-Aboriginal population. The net impact of the population inflow of Registered Indian migrants to reserves has remained more or less relatively stable since the 1980s, although more recently showing signs of slight decreases, while rural areas continue to post relatively large net outflows. Net migration does not appear to be a major contributor to the recent growth of Aboriginal populations in urban areas. Also, within urban areas, most Aboriginal populations continue to remain significantly more mobile than the non-Aboriginal population, especially in the case of "residential" mobility. And so, the same implications of mobility and migration continue to remain important given the links between high mobility, "churn" in urban areas, and the social and economic concerns of Aboriginal peoples, such as housing and education.

Yet these more recent signs from the 2006 Census would also suggest that to some extent the high mobility of Aboriginal populations may in fact be starting to lessen. With respect to migration, over the 2001–2006 period, a smaller portion of the Aboriginal population changed communities than in the previous five-year period; and overall migration rates for both Registered Indians and Inuit were below the level of the non-Aboriginal population. However, in the case of total mobility, Aboriginal populations (with the exception of the Inuit) remained more likely to move between 2001 and 2006 than the non-Aboriginal population.

Many of the same considerations identified in previous analyses regarding the outlook for mobility and migration trends among Aboriginal populations and communities apply to this current study. Factors that could serve to increase out-migration from reserve are those associated with employment and housing situations within communities, especially with the growth of the young adult population, labour force participation, and family formation. Alternatively, effects of an aging Aboriginal population could contribute to declining migration, given the association of lower mobility among older adults in general. An additional consideration in the recent lessening of high Aboriginal mobility rates is the greater residential stability of Aboriginal populations in urban areas, and one that could signify eventual convergence to non-Aboriginal rates. However, even if current rates of migration continue, and the net migration effects remain small, the demographic impact of Aboriginal youth and young adults migrating to cities could eventually be expected to indirectly contribute to population growth through natural increase.

As for the present, though, it appears that it is still the high mobility of Aboriginal populations to and from, and within urban areas, and not an exodus of migrants from reserves, that continues to have the greatest implications for the well-being of Aboriginal people.

NOTES

1. As the census collected data for only residents of Canada, it is not possible to fully examine international movement patterns of Aboriginal peoples. Data on Aboriginal migrants moving to Canada suggest that this component of Aboriginal migration is quite small and of little consequence to changes in the national Aboriginal population. For the 2001–2006 period, Aboriginal migrants from abroad numbered 3,930 individuals and represented 1.9% of all migrants aged five or more years. Although the census captures migrants from non-enumerated reserves, migrants into these reserves are not captured. To avoid bias in the estimation of origin-destination flows and rates, all migrants originating from non-enumerated reserves have been excluded from the study.

2. Settlements include Crown land and other communities with Aboriginal populations as defined by Aboriginal Affairs and Northern Development Canada. This category, which is grouped with Indian reserves in this study, includes some, but not all, Métis and Inuit communities.

3. The extent of differences in the geographic distribution of the Aboriginal and non-Aboriginal populations is actually greater than that depicted by the census data, due to higher levels of non-enumeration and undercoverage on reserve.

4. To some extent, the low rate of migration reported among Inuit in rural areas may result from the configuration of census geography in northern rural areas. The census sub-divisions (CSDs), which are used to define rural Inuit communities, may be much larger geographically than those of the communities of other Aboriginal populations. The possibility exists that some Inuit moves within the same rural CSD may in fact involve quite distant relocations. Such moves would not be recorded by the census as migration.

5. Prior to 1985, Registered Indian status could be lost or gained through marriage, and, more specifically, women could lose status if they married a non-Registered Indian husband, whereas for men, non-Registered wives could gain status.

6. The concept of "churning" or "turbulence" is borrowed from analyses of mobility in the context of the developing world, in which the pattern often involves movement between rural and urban areas.

7. One example of this situation involves the experience of the Abinotci Mino-Ayawin program in Winnipeg, a child and family support program aimed at

Aboriginal families with children at high risk. The program was designed and initially staffed on a neighbourhood basis to co-ordinate and focus the resources of several agencies on the needs of families. High levels of mobility among client families resulted in frequent loss of contact with parents and children and the need to abandon the neighbourhood-based staffing approach. In order to maintain service continuity, program staff was required to serve families throughout the city, resulting increased service costs and difficulties arranging and co-ordinating other agency involvement.

REFERENCES

Aman, C. (2009). Exploring the influence of school and community relationships on the performance of Aboriginal students in British Columbia public schools. In J.P. White, D. Beavon, J. Peters & N. Spence (Eds.), *Aboriginal education: Current crisis and future alternatives* (pp. 175–196). Toronto, ON: Thompson.

Astone, N.M., & McLanahan, S.S. (1994). Family structure, residential mobility, and school dropout: A research note. *Demography, 31*(4), 575–584.

Beavon, D., & Norris, M.J. (1999). *Dimensions of geographic mobility and churn in social cohesion: The case of Aboriginal peoples.* Ottawa, ON: Research and Analysis Directorate, Indian and Northern Affairs Canada.

Beavon, D., Wingert, S., & White, J.P. (2009). Churn migration and educational attainment among Aboriginal adolescents and young adults. In J.P. White, D. Beavon, J. Peters & N. Spence (Eds.), *Aboriginal education: Current crisis and future alternatives* (pp. 197–222). Toronto, ON: Thompson.

Bostrom, H. (1984). Government policies and programs relating to people of Indian ancestry in Manitoba. In R. Breton & G. Grant (Eds.), *Dynamics of government programs for urban Indians in Prairie Provinces.* Montreal, QC: Institute for Research on Public Policy.

Clatworthy, S.J. (1980). *The demographic composition and economic circumstances of Winnipeg's Native population.* Winnipeg, MB: Institute of Urban Studies.

———. (1983). *Native housing conditions in Winnipeg.* Winnipeg, MB: Institute of Urban Studies.

———. (1995). *The migration and mobility patterns of Canada's Aboriginal population.* Ottawa, ON: Royal Commission on Aboriginal Peoples.

———. (2000, May). *Patterns of residential mobility among Aboriginal peoples in Canada.* Regina, SK: Urban Aboriginal Strategy Federal Workshop.

———. (2006). *A profile of Aboriginal children, youth, and young adults living off-reserve.* Report prepared for Aboriginal Affairs Branch, Canadian Heritage, Ottawa.

———. (2009). Mobility and migration patterns of Aboriginal populations in Canada, 2001–2006. *Canadian Diversity: Quarterly Journal of the Association for Canadian Studies, 7*(3), 43–51.

Clatworthy, S.J., & Cooke, M. (2001). *Patterns of registered Indian migration between on- and off-reserve locations.* Ottawa, ON: Research and Analysis Directorate, Indian and Northern Affairs Canada.

Clatworthy, S.J., Hull, J., & Loughren, N. (1997). *Implications of First Nations demography.* Ottawa, ON: Research and Analysis Directorate, Indian and Northern Affairs Canada.

Clatworthy, S.J., & Norris, M.J. (2007). Aboriginal mobility and migration in Canada: Trends, recent patterns and implications, 1971 to 2001. In J.P. White, S. Wingert, D. Beavon, & P. Maxim (Eds.), *Aboriginal policy research: Moving forward, making a difference,* Vol. IV (pp. 207–234). Toronto, ON: Thompson.

Clatworthy, S.J., & Stevens, H. (1987). An overview of the housing conditions of registered Indians in Canada. Ottawa, ON: Indian and Northern Affairs Canada.

Cooke, M.J. (1999). *On leaving home: Return and circular migration between First Nations and Prairie Cities* (Unpublished master's thesis). University of Western Ontario, London, ON.

Cooke, M.J., & Belanger, D. (2006). Migration theories and First Nations mobility: Towards a systems perspective. *Canadian Review of Sociology and Anthropology,* 24(2), 141–164.

Department of Indian Affairs and Northern Development Canada. (1997). *Gathering strength: Canada's Aboriginal action plan.* Ottawa, ON: Indian and Northern Affairs Canada.

Guimond, E. (1999). *Ethnic mobility and the demographic growth of Canada's Aboriginal population from 1986–1996.* Ottawa, ON: Report on the Demographic Situation in Canada, 1998–1999, Statistics Canada.

————. (2003). Changing ethnicity: The concept of ethnic drifters. In J. White, P. Maxim, & D. Beavon (Eds.), *Aboriginal conditions: Research as a foundation for public policy* (pp. 91–107). Vancouver, BC: University of British Columbia Press.

Guimond, E., Robitaille, N., & Senécal, S. (2009). Aboriginal populations in Canadian cities: Why are they growing so fast? *Canadian Issues,* (Winter), 11–17.

Hanselmann, C. (2001). *Urban Aboriginal people in Western Canada: Realities and policies.* Calgary, AB: Canada West Foundation.

Norris, M.J. (1985). *Migration patterns of status Indians in Canada, 1976–1981.* Paper prepared for the Demography of Northern and Native Peoples in Canada, Canadian Population Society session, Statistics Canada.

————. (1990). The demography of Aboriginal people in Canada. In S.S. Halli, F. Trovato, & L. Driedger (Eds.), *Ethnic demography: Canadian immigrant, racial and cultural variations* (pp. 33–59). Ottawa, ON: Carleton University Press.

————. (1996). Contemporary demography of Aboriginal peoples in Canada. In D.A. Long & O.P. Dickason (Eds.), *Visions of the heart: Canadian Aboriginal issues* (pp. 179–237). Toronto, ON: Harcourt Brace.

————. (2000). Aboriginal peoples in Canada: Demographic and linguistic perspectives. In D.A. Long & O.P. Dickason (Eds.), *Visions of the heart: Canadian Aboriginal issues* (2nd ed., pp. 167–236). Toronto, ON: Harcourt Brace.

————. (2009). The role of First Nations women in language continuity and transition. In G.G. Valaskakis, M.D. Stout, & E. Guimond (Eds.), *Restoring the* balance: First Nations women, community and culture. Winnipeg, MB: University of Manitoba Press.

Norris, M.J., & Clatworthy, S.J. (2003). Aboriginal mobility and migration within urban Canada: Outcomes, factors and implications. In D. Newhouse & E. Peters (Eds.), Not strangers in these parts: Urban Aboriginal peoples (pp. 51–78). Ottawa, ON: Policy Research Initiative.

———. (2011). Urbanization and migration patterns of Aboriginal populations in Canada: A half century in review (1951 to 2006). Aboriginal Policy Studies, 1(1), 13–77.

Norris, M.J., Cooke, M., & Clatworthy, S.J. (2003). Aboriginal mobility and migration patterns and the policy implications. In J. White, P. Maxim, & D. Beavon (Eds.), Aboriginal conditions: Research as a foundation for public policy (pp. 108–129). Vancouver, BC: University of British Columbia Press.

Norris, M.J., Cooke, M., Guimond, E., Beavon, D., & Clatworthy, S.J. (2004). Registered Indian mobility and migration in Canada: Patterns and implications. In J. Taylor & M. Bell (Eds.), Population mobility and Indigenous peoples in Australasia and North America (pp. 136–160). London, UK: Routledge.

Norris, D.A., & Pryor, E.T. (1984, May). Demographic change in Canada's North. Proceedings of International Workshop on Population Issues in Arctic Societies. Gilbjerghoved, Gilleleje, Denmark.

Reeves, W., & Frideres, J. (1981). Government policy and Indian urbanization: The Alberta case. Canadian Public Policy, 7(4), 584–595.

Rossi, P.H. (1955). Why families move: A study in the social psychology of urban residential mobility. Glencoe, IL: Free Press.

Siggner, A.J. (1977). Preliminary results from a study of 1966–1971 migration patterns among Status Indians in Canada. Ottawa, ON: Indian and Northern Affairs Canada.

Siggner, A.J., & Costa, R. (2005). Aboriginal conditions in census metropolitan areas, 1981–2001. Statistics Canada (Catalogue No. 89-613-MIE, No. 008). Retrieved from http://www.statcan.gc.ca/pub/89-613-m/89-613-m2005008-eng.pdf

Spector, A. (1996). The housing conditions of Aboriginal peoples in Canada. Ottawa, ON: Canada Mortgage and Housing Corporation.

Trovato, F., Romaniuc, A., & Addai, I. (1994). On- and off-reserve migration of Aboriginal peoples in Canada: A review of the literature. Ottawa, ON: Indian and Northern Affairs Canada.

US General Accounting Office. (1994). Elementary school children: Many change schools frequently, harming their education. Report to Honorable Marcy Kaptur, House of Representatives, GAO/HEH-S94-95. Washington, DC: (ED369 526). Retrieved from http://archive.gao.gov./t2pbat4/150724.pdf

PART II
EPIDEMIOLOGICAL PERSPEC

6

ALCOHOLISM AND OTHER SOCIAL PROBLEMS IN CANADIAN ABORIGINAL COMMUNITIES
POLICY ALTERNATIVES AND IMPLICATIONS FOR SOCIAL ACTION

Paul C. Whitehead and Brenda Kobayashi

INTRODUCTION

Since the late 1990s there have been two highly divergent views as to the most effective ways of dealing with the high rates of social problems in Canadian Aboriginal communities. The first view, expressed in the *Report of the Royal Commission on Aboriginal Peoples* (RCAP, 1996), proposes that many social problems within Aboriginal communities can be addressed once broader social changes have taken place both within the larger Canadian society as well as within Aboriginal communities. The second view is articulated by Whitehead and Hayes (1998) in *The Insanity of Alcohol*. Whitehead and Hayes do not disagree with the Royal Commission. However, they take a different approach and argue that the focus should be directed toward the more proximate or immediate problems within Aboriginal communities as this approach can have a more immediate impact on reducing the social problems within these communities. This chapter summarizes the fundamentals on which these views are based and points out the considerably different implications for public policy that are offered by each perspective. It concludes that there is little in the way of common ground in the two perspectives, but suggests ways in which both viewpoints can inform public policy and social action.

The existence of disproportionately high rates of adverse health conditions and social problems, such as shorter life expectancy, higher rates of crime, recidivism, and incarceration, as well as the higher incidence of child abuse and neglect among First Nations, Inuit, and Métis communities (hereinafter referred to as "Aboriginal peoples" and "Aboriginal communities"), in particular among First Nations, is well documented.

The life expectancy of Aboriginal males is 68.9 years, which is seven years shorter than that of non-Aboriginal males in Canada. The life expectancy for Aboriginal females is 76.6 years, which is 5.2 years fewer than the average for non-Aboriginal females in Canada (Health Canada, 2000). The most common cause of death for First Nations people between the ages of 1 and 44 years is injury and poisoning, with suicide and other forms of self-injury noted as the leading causes of death for youths and adults (Health Canada, 2000). Suicide among First Nations and Inuit youth, in particular, is considered an urgent social problem in Canada. The incidence of suicide is five to seven times higher for First Nations youth than for non-Aboriginal youth. In addition, the incidence of suicide among Inuit youth is 11 times the national average, so high that it has been identified as the highest in the world by Health Canada (2006).

Aboriginal peoples are consistently overrepresented in the Canadian prison system (Statistics Canada, 2005). In 1996, Aboriginal persons accounted for 17% of the prison population, while Aboriginal peoples constitute less than 4% of the Canadian population (Statistics Canada, 2008). Moreover, Aboriginal inmates are younger on average than the non-Aboriginal inmates, have less education, are more likely to be unemployed, and are considered to be at a higher risk for re-offending. The rates of re-offending during the first 12 months after release among Aboriginal persons is 29% compared to 13% of non-Aboriginal persons. The proportion of those who return after four years of release is 57% for Aboriginal persons compared to 28% for non-Aboriginal persons (Statistics Canada, 2005). Not only are Aboriginal persons more likely to re-offend, but they are also considered to be at higher risk for such things as substance abuse, unemployment, and personal and family/marital needs—factors that are considered to increase the likelihood of an initial criminal offence (Statistics Canada, 2005).

The problems that face Aboriginal adults also have negative impacts on Aboriginal children. Aboriginal children are much more likely than non-Aboriginal children to live with a lone parent, a grandparent (with no parent being present), or with another relative (Statistics Canada, 2011). For instance, in 2006, it was reported that 29% of Aboriginal children, aged 14 and under, lived with a lone mother, 6% lived with a lone father, 3% of Aboriginal children lived with a grandparent (with no parent being present), and 4% lived with another relative. Furthermore, First Nations children (31%) aged 14 and under, are twice as likely as non-Aboriginal children (14%) to live with a lone mother. Similarly, 6% of First Nations children lived with a lone father as compared to 3% of non-Aboriginal children. Violence against children is also a problem in many First Nations and other Aboriginal communities in Canada. Aboriginal children are more likely to experience abuse by their parents. Half of all the deaths of First Nations children are the result of physical abuse due to parental maltreatment (Health Canada, 2005).

ROYAL COMMISSION ON ABORIGINAL PEOPLES: THE "ROOT CAUSES" MODEL

The Royal Commission on Aboriginal Peoples (hereafter referred to as the Royal Commission) was established on August 26, 1991 to improve the quality of life and standard of living for Aboriginal peoples and their communities. The final report, composed of five volumes, was issued in October 1996. The Royal Commission was given a comprehensive mandate to investigate and provide a historical overview of how the relationship developed and evolved among Aboriginal peoples (Indian, Inuit, and Métis), the Canadian government, and Canadian society as a whole (RCAP, 1996, Vol. 1, Ch. 1: 2).

The Royal Commission charges that Canada assaulted and destroyed the cultural identity of indigenous peoples while it was in the process of building a modern liberal democratic state (RCAP, 1996, Vol. 1, Part 3, Ch. 14: 1). Thus, the "true" image of Canada is blighted by the invasion of Aboriginal peoples by the Europeans, the loss of Aboriginal land and traditional ways of living, as well as the horrible experiences in residential schools—including the attempts at cultural genocide—poverty, inadequate housing, poor sanitation, and the oppressive Indian Act. The image of Canada as a country that holds the highest ideals of freedom and respect for human rights should therefore include the "unfortunate reality" that truly exists for Aboriginal peoples (RCAP, 1996, Vol. 1, Part 3, Ch. 14: 1).

The Royal Commission asserts that the damage to Aboriginal peoples' cultures, languages, identities, and self-respect have resulted in their suffering from higher rates of some diseases, increases in social problems and a "depression of spirit" (RCAP, 1996, Vol. 3, Ch. 3: 3). Moreover, the Royal Commission sees many of the current social problems among Aboriginal peoples as "symptomatic" of the legacy of historical policies of displacement and assimilation forced on them (RCAP, 1996, Vol. 3, Ch. 1: 7). Thus, the Royal Commission sees the high rates of social problems in Aboriginal communities as consequences of the negative experiences to which First Nations and other Aboriginal peoples have been subjected.

The Royal Commission has not only unveiled what it considers to be the "true picture" of the relationship that exists between Aboriginal and non-Aboriginal peoples, but it also claims to provide specific "solutions" to the problems that continue to confront Aboriginal peoples (RCAP, 1996, Vol. 1, Ch. 1: 2). For instance, the Royal Commission points to the higher rates of social problems in Aboriginal communities, such as interpersonal violence, abuse and neglect of children, alcoholism, poverty, and suicide as posing a substantial challenge to policy makers. These conditions, the Royal Commission states, are not only chronic, but are seen as a clear representation of the assault that has taken place on the self-esteem of all Aboriginal peoples (RCAP, 1996, Vol. 3, Ch. 1: 6). The Royal Commission's report, however, does not have a volume, or even a chapter, specifically devoted to social problems. This chapter, therefore, includes our deconstruction of the Royal Commission's report. With a focus on social problems, we construct a model that portrays the Royal Commission's view of what it takes to address many social problems in Aboriginal communities.

RCAP: STEPS TOWARD REDUCING SOCIAL PROBLEMS

What, according to the Royal Commission, is the path that needs to be followed for Aboriginal communities to experience reduced rates of social problems? The Royal Commission suggests that many, if not the majority, of social problems are symptomatic manifestations of the level of "ill health" that is felt by Aboriginal persons. This level of ill health is experienced in ways that are individual, social, psychological, and cultural; it results from deep and complicated "root causes." The root causes, according to the Royal Commission, can and need to be addressed by restructuring Canadian society, such that historic dysfunction can be addressed and the symptoms (social problems) will ease.

This section attempts to provide a faithful representation of the policy direction and social action that the Royal Commission recommends if a reduction in the incidence and prevalence of social problems is to occur. The overall scope of the recommendations, as proposed by the Royal Commission, focuses on ameliorating the lives of Aboriginal peoples and reducing the oppressive burden of social and other conditions that plague many communities. There are two underlying themes: the need to "renew" the relationship between Aboriginal and non-Aboriginal peoples, and the establishment of self-government for Aboriginal peoples.

THEME 1: NEW RELATIONSHIP BETWEEN ABORIGINAL AND NON-ABORIGINAL PEOPLES

The Royal Commission sees the relationship between Aboriginal and non-Aboriginal peoples as being based on the notions of wardship, assimilation, and subordination. The first theme identifies the first step toward change; the creation of a new relationship between Aboriginal and non-Aboriginal peoples.[1] This new relationship is to be based on four principles: mutual recognition, mutual respect, sharing, and mutual responsibility (RCAP, 1996, Vol. 1, Part 3, Ch. 16: 2).

The Royal Commission asserts that there are four stages in the evolution of relationship between Aboriginal and non-Aboriginal peoples: Stage 1: Separate Worlds (before 1500); Stage 2: Nation-to-Nation Relations (1500–1800); Stage 3: Respect Gives Way to Domination (1800–mid-1900s); and Stage 4: Renewal and Renegotiation (mid-1900s to present). Canada, according to the Royal Commission, is now in Stage 4, a stage that is described as a time of "recovery" for both Aboriginal and non-Aboriginal peoples.

To restructure and create a new relationship, both Aboriginal and non-Aboriginal peoples must critically review and understand how the quality of life for Aboriginal peoples has been allowed to deteriorate over the past two centuries. Most importantly, non-Aboriginals must accept responsibility for the policies that they have created because it is these policies that allowed for the abuse of power that persist today (RCAP, 1996, Vol. 1, Part 1, Ch. 7: 15). There are four policy areas or "directions" that are identified by the Royal Commission as being the "most unjust" policies imposed on Aboriginal peoples: the Indian Act, residential schools, community relocation, and treatment of Aboriginal veterans.

Many of the policies on Aboriginal matters are said to be founded on a set of false assumptions, four of which are identified by the Royal Commission: (1) Aboriginal peoples are inherently inferior and incapable of governing themselves; (2) treaties and other agreements were not covenants of trust and obligations; rather, they were devices of statecraft that were less expensive and more acceptable than armed conflict; (3) wardship was considered appropriate for Aboriginal peoples, thereby justifying the actions taken and deemed to be done for their benefit without their consent or involvement in design or implementation; and (4) concepts of development, whether for individuals or communities, could be defined in terms of non-Aboriginal values alone (RCAP, 1996, Vol. 1, Part 2, Ch. 8: 1). These four assumptions, the Royal Commission contends, have not only shaped and developed the first government policies, but they have continued to significantly underpin the institutions that drive and constrain the federal process that develops policy on Aboriginal matters.

The Royal Commission further asserts that the relationship between Aboriginal and non-Aboriginal peoples, as well as the social policies, were based on these set of false assumptions (RCAP, 1996, Vol. 1, Part 2, Ch. 8: 2). As a result, a legacy of dependency, powerlessness, and distrust was created that seriously influenced the thinking and actions of Aboriginal peoples (RCAP, 1996, Vol. 1, Ch. 3: 6). It is this framework of false assumptions that has permitted an abuse of power that continues to have an impact on the incidence of social problems, such as poverty, unemployment, crime, abuse, violence, child neglect, alcoholism, suicide, unequal access to health care, and substandard housing within Aboriginal communities (RCAP, 1996, Vol. 3, Ch. 3: 2).

THEME 2: ABORIGINAL SELF-GOVERNMENT

The second underlying theme of the Royal Commission is the importance of Aboriginal peoples achieving self-government. For self-government to be achieved, the relationship between Aboriginal and non-Aboriginal peoples is to be transformed from one that permits the domination of Aboriginal peoples to one where the "Canadian federation" recognizes the authority of Aboriginal peoples to chart their own futures within Canadian society (RCAP, 1996, Vol. 3, Ch. 1: 7). The Royal Commission makes four recommendations that constitute a foundation for the new relationship: (1) old treaties must be honoured and new treaties must be created; (2) Aboriginal people must be provided with the means and access to implement self-determination and self-government, specifically, land and resources must be equally distributed and/or redistributed; (3) wealth that is generated from the land must be equally distributed; and (4) economic policies must be developed to revitalize Aboriginal nations and communities so that they can foster self-reliance (RCAP, 1996, Vol. 3, Ch. 1: 6).

Aboriginal peoples contend that they have the inherent right to determine their own future and govern themselves under institutions of their own choice and design (RCAP, 1996, Vol. 2, Ch. 3-1.3: 1). Self-government is, therefore, crucial because it provides Aboriginal peoples with a "vehicle" to negotiate adaptations in mainstream Canadian institutions that help to serve Aboriginal peoples, such as health services, housing, and community services (RCAP, 1996, Vol. 3, Ch. 7: 3). An Aboriginal government, as envisioned by the Royal Commission, is one that has the power to create a new set of public policies to handle Aboriginal affairs. Further, it is expected that as the number of policies that serve the social needs of Aboriginal peoples increases, the ability of the Canadian government to use its power to abuse Aboriginal peoples will decrease. In essence, Aboriginal governments would be able to reverse the abuses of power through the development of new public policies on Aboriginal affairs (RCAP, 1996, Vol. 3, Ch. 7: 3).

The Royal Commission recognizes that the gross disparities that have persisted over generations between the quality of life of Aboriginal peoples and most Canadians, along with the pain of deprivation and disorder in the lives of Aboriginal peoples, is intimately bound up with their identity and experience. Thus, self-government is just one step toward providing Aboriginal peoples with the means to create their own distinct institutions to serve the social needs of Aboriginal peoples, as well as to reflect the cultural priorities of each community being served (RCAP, 1996, Vol. 3, Ch. 7).

The creation of new relationships and self-government are the longer-term goals proposed by the Royal Commission. In addition to these longer-term goals, the Royal Commission has identified a number of "immediate actions" that can be taken. These actions comprise four "major dimensions" along which social, economic, and cultural initiatives need to be addressed in order to reduce social problems. The four dimensions are as follows: (1) health and healing of individuals, families, communities, and nations; (2) economic opportunity and living conditions in urban and rural Aboriginal communities; (3) human resources; and (4) Aboriginal institutions adapting Western mainstream institutions (RCAP, 1996, Vol. 5, Ch. 1: 7).

These "short-term" actions are supposed to address both the social issues such as poverty, health, housing, and family violence as well as the cultural issues such as language, spirituality, child care, traditional ways of life, and educational issues that impact Aboriginal peoples. Moreover, issues that affect family, health and healing, housing, education, and cultural policy are seen to be especially important as they have a direct impact on the life, welfare, culture, and identity of Aboriginal peoples (RCAP, 1996, Vol. 3, Ch. 1: 7).

The Royal Commission recommends that policy making should begin with four immediate actions. The first dimension, health and healing, is a key component and objective for social policy and an "essential first step" toward changing the relationship between Aboriginal and non-Aboriginal peoples and developing Aboriginal self-governments. Healing, in particular, aims at restoring the physical, social, emotional, and spiritual vitality in individual and community social systems (RCAP, 1996, Vol. 5, Ch. 1: 7). Healing applies to both Aboriginals and non-Aboriginals because it is said to encompass learning about and acknowledging the errors of the past, making restitutions where possible, and correcting the distortions of history. In essence, healing, as proposed by the Royal Commission, requires two things: (1) Aboriginal peoples and communities need to recover from the pain and suffering that resulted from the loss of culture, paternalism, and systematic racism that set in motion a cycle wherein false assumptions were used to establish social policies aimed at maintaining the domination and assimilation of Aboriginal people; and (2) that the pre-condition of non-Aboriginal "healing" will already have occurred (RCAP, 1996, Vol. 5, Ch. 1: 7).

The second dimension proposed by the Royal Commission identifies the recommendations aimed at encouraging and improving the implementation of economic development, housing, and community (RCAP, 1996, Vol. 5, Ch. 1: 12). Changes, for instance, should be made in the way that social assistance funds flow into Aboriginal communities. Such changes can stimulate greater self-reliance by making it possible for these funds to be used to sustain traditional harvesting activities and improving the social and physical infrastructure (RCAP, 1996, Vol. 5, Ch. 1: 12). Another aspect of this dimension comes from initiatives that upgrade housing and community infrastructure (e.g., bring housing, water supplies, and sanitation facilities up to Canadian standards). These initiatives would support the transition to self-government as well as enhance economic development while countering the significant threats to health and well-being. The Royal Commission also states that if the nature of ownership over one's residence on Aboriginal territory is clarified, then the incentives to maintain dwellings and to invest in their improvement will increase. The Royal Commission recommends that a housing initiative be pursued immediately. Further, as Aboriginal nation governments are recognized, they can take over the institutions that manage and finance housing programs, provide technical skills in system design, regulate standards, as well as maintain housing stock (RCAP, 1996, Vol. 5, Ch. 1: 13).

The third dimension proposed by the Royal Commission is the development of human resources. A 10-year initiative is proposed that aims at overcoming the barriers faced by Aboriginal peoples when they seek to participate in the labour force (RCAP, 1996, Vol. 5, Ch. 1: 14). The Royal Commission also sees the need to build on the experience gained from current strategies for training and employment development. Accordingly, private companies, training institutions, and government programs should be encouraged to develop skills training in a full range of technical, commercial, and professional fields (RCAP, 1996, Vol. 5, Ch. 1: 14).

The fourth dimension proposed by the Royal Commission is aimed at "institution development" (RCAP, 1996, Vol. 5, Ch. 1: 14). It is time to make way for Aboriginal institutions. These institutions need to exist before self-governing nations emerge. Their design needs to complement structures in the Aboriginal nations. Having Aboriginal peoples use their own authority and be in charge of family service institutions, for example, is imperative because it is these institutions that emphasize the rebuilding of mutual aid networks within communities and seek to protect vulnerable people from violence (RCAP, 1996, Vol. 3, Ch. 1: 7).

RCAP: SUMMARY

Throughout its report, the Royal Commission emphasizes how important it is for Canadians, both Aboriginal and non-Aboriginal, to understand, acknowledge, and admit to the unfortunate reality that has existed for Aboriginal peoples in Canada over the past 200 years. In this chapter, we have discussed two underlying themes in the report: first, the need to

Figure 6.1 Policy Logic Model of the Royal Commission on Aboriginal Peoples (RCAP)

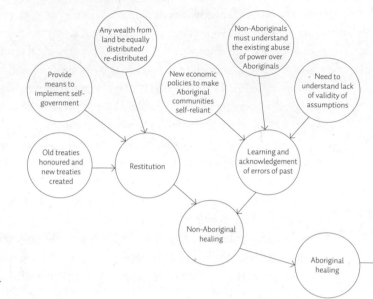

transform and create a new relationship between Aboriginal and non-Aboriginal peoples; and second, the need for Aboriginal peoples to achieve self-government. Before a new relationship between Aboriginal and non-Aboriginal peoples can be created, the old relationship must first be understood. Furthermore, if the relationship is to be transformed, and if this relationship is to move forward in a different direction, then the authority of Aboriginal peoples to chart their own futures within the Canadian federation must be recognized (RCAP, 1996, Vol. 3, Ch. 1: 7).

In brief, the Royal Commission sees the high rates of social problems in Aboriginal communities as indicative of—a symptom of—the level of ill health that is felt by Aboriginal peoples. This ill health is seen as just one of the consequences that arose from non-Aboriginal peoples' subscription to false assumptions that led to an abuse of power. These false assumptions are what constitute some of the "root causes" of social problems. Social problems are viewed as symptoms of historical, cultural, and structural arrangements in Canadian society, and it is the view of the Royal Commission that these root causes need to be addressed before one can expect the incidence of social problems to be reduced. Furthermore, only

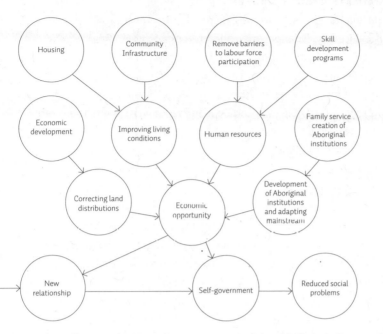

when Aboriginal nations have a strong and durable foundation, made up of people who are healthy, educated, and of "strong body, soul, mind, and spirit," can the likelihood of viable self-government exist to address the many social and cultural issues with the overall goal of reducing the broad array of social problems (RCAP, 1996, Vol. 3, Ch. 3: 3).

The Royal Commission focuses on healing as a prerequisite for the transformation and creation of a new relationship between Aboriginal and non-Aboriginal peoples. Healing encompasses and makes possible personal and societal recovery from the long-term effects of oppression and system-atic racism (RCAP, 1996, Vol. 3, Ch. 3: 3). Healing is identified as an essential first step for achieving change and progress with regards to self-government and economic self-reliance. In fact, the Royal Commission asserts that "in a sense our entire report is about restoring and maintaining whole health among Aboriginal people" (RCAP, 1996, Vol. 3, Ch. 3: 1). The reasoning and logic of the Royal Commission is summarized in Figure 6.1. It is a policy logic model that identifies and provides an overview of the steps required to achieve certain outcomes; it focuses on what the Royal Commission states must be done if there is to be a reduction in social problems in Aboriginal communities.

THE PROXIMATE CAUSES MODEL

Whitehead and Hayes (1998) provide a distinctly different approach to reducing the incidence of social problems in First Nations communities in Canada. They do not disagree with the Royal Commission's assertion that Aboriginal peoples have been subjected to a great many adverse conditions, poor treatment, and suffering. Nonetheless, they propose that when the emphasis is placed on "root causes" (e.g., the European influence on Aboriginal culture and society, the residential school system, the loss of meaning and spiritual decay, and the loss of traditional values and lifestyles), the interest and confidence in the use of preventative interventions to bring about social change are lessened (Whitehead & Hayes, 1998: 88–89). They propose that the higher rates of social problems among Aboriginal peoples, in particular First Nations people, can be reduced if the proximate causes, rather than the underlying, more complicated root causes, are the target of intervention.

Whitehead and Hayes pay particular attention to the role that alcoholism plays in the generation of social problems in First Nations communities. They see the very high rates of alcoholism in many First Nations communities as a social problem that has a considerable amount of what Scarpetti and Andersen (1989: 9) call "primacy." That is, alcoholism not only causes havoc for individuals, families, and communities in its own right, but it is also implicated in a variety of other social problems, such as interpersonal violence, family discord, suicide, abuse and neglect of children, and lost productivity of all kinds.[2]

Whitehead and Hayes (1989: xv) propose that, all other things being equal, the First Nations communities that not only reduce, but are also able to maintain their lower rates of alcoholism, tend to have lower rates of other social problems. Whitehead and Hayes do not contend that simply eliminating alcoholism will cure all social problems within Aboriginal communities. Rather, they posit that reducing the level of alcoholism is an essential first step toward reducing the incidence of a broad range of social problems. It is this reduction in alcoholism that leads to a reduction in alcohol-related problems, which can then lead to subsequent reductions in other social problems (1998: 116). This argument is the key difference from the Royal Commission propositions.

The basis of the Whitehead and Hayes approach to the prevention of certain social problems was not developed until the 1970s. While it owes its intellectual debt to the work of Sully Ledermann (1956), a French mathematician, it is the seminal work of a small group of scientists at what was then the Addiction Research Foundation of Ontario (now, the Centre for Addictions and Mental Health) that translated the theoretical formulations into practical implications for public policy. Jan De Lint, Wolfgang Schmidt, and Robert Popham published several articles (e.g., De Lint, 1968; 1973; De Lint & Schmidt, 1968; 1971a; 1971b; Popham, 1975; Schmidt & De Lint, 1970; Schmidt & Popham, 1975; 1978) wherein they demonstrated that the distribution of alcohol consumption, as Ledermann (1956) theoretically postulated, can be best described by a distribution characterized by a single variable—the average level of consumption in a population—and that dispersion maintains a constant relationship to the mean level of consumption such that the distribution of consumption takes the form of a logarithmic normal curve. The evidence from this research demonstrates that the rates of various forms of alcohol-related damage (e.g., cirrhosis of the liver, certain cancers, and suicide) are a function of the average level of consumption in a population.

The basis of this work and the implications for public policy were examined by an internationally respected team of researchers in the field of alcohol studies (Bruun et al., 1975); it concluded that this framework had considerable validity. In addition, Frankel and Whitehead (1981) tested this model and compared its explanatory value to the principal competing hypothesis of the day. Frankel and Whitehead concluded that what has come to be called the "single distribution theory" is the better predictor of rates of alcohol-related damage in populations. The primary prediction of this perspective is that as the average consumption of alcohol increases so does the proportion of the population that drink at a level that is associated with an increased risk of alcohol-related damage (Whitehead & Hayes, 1998: 66). Other tests of the model (e.g., Whitehead, 1977) offer further validation.

As previously indicated, Whitehead and Hayes do not disagree with the Royal Commission's assertions about the events and circumstances to which Aboriginal peoples have been subject; rather, they contend that there are proximate causes that affect the level of alcohol consumption that, if addressed, can result in lower rates of alcohol-related damage, some of which are often manifested in an array of other social problems. Some of these more proximate causes are cultural and social. As such, according to Whitehead and Hayes, the target for the prevention of alcohol-related damage is directed at the average level of consumption in the population. Moreover, strategies need to be aimed at the factors (cultural, structural, economic, and legal) that contribute to drinking in order to reduce the level of consumption as well as the rates of alcohol-related damage. In essence, effective strategies can not only reduce alcohol consumption and the alcohol-related damages that are likely to occur, but, most importantly, if alcoholism is reduced, the rate of other social problems has a greater chance of being reduced.

CULTURAL ISSUES

Whitehead and Hayes assert that the culture of many First Nations communities contain definitions about alcohol that are favourable to drinking, heavy drinking, intoxication, and the use of alcoholic beverages as a means of coping with situations, events, or moods. They also cite other cultural traits (e.g., the ethic of non-interference and the idea that alcoholism is best seen as a developmental stage, that is, part of the natural order of things) that result in alcohol prevention getting little attention as a means of dealing with alcohol-related damage (1998: 88–93).

SOCIAL ISSUES

Whitehead and Hayes contend that not only does the cultural "wetness" of First Nations communities need to change, but so does its social wetness. That is, the availability of alcoholic beverages and the occasions when they can be consumed need to be reduced if there is to be a reduction in alcohol-related damage. Among the factors that come into play are increasing the cost of alcoholic beverages and passing and enforcing laws and bylaws that restrict the distribution/sale, possession, and consumption of alcoholic beverages. Figure 6.2 is the policy logic model that expresses the approach espoused by Whitehead and Hayes.

The types of social and cultural changes mentioned above can be implemented where Aboriginal communities exist, such as on First Nations reserves. It is required that there be social structures, a sense of community, and sufficient leadership and followership for positive changes to happen. Geographical isolation can be helpful, but it is not an absolute necessity. Among the first things that need to prevail is the acceptance of the idea that alcoholism is not inevitable and that, for the good of the community, actions

Figure 6.2 Whitehead and Hayes's Policy Logic Model

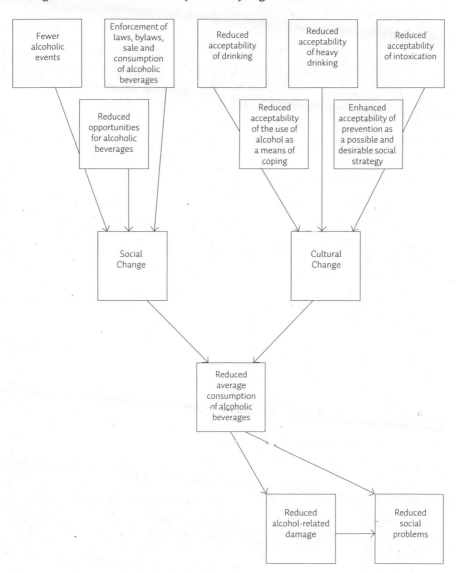

need to focus on the prevention of alcohol-related damage. Experience with the National Alcohol and Drug Abuse Program (NNADAP), as evaluated by Murray et al. (1989) and Whitehead and Hayes (1998), has shown that interventions need to be targeted and strategically planned. This means that the criteria for funding and other support(s) must be established and applied such that there is no expectation that whatever a community considers is within its best interest will be funded.

The resources for this process need to be, at least in part, indigenous; this applies particularly to leadership. Some of the resources that are not immediately available can be imported, and it behooves the federal, provincial, and territorial governments to actively promote and financially support such endeavours. Thus, the process needs to be a collaborative one in order to gain real participation and understanding. In addition, there need to be criteria and processes for screening proposals that are open and transparent, as well as facilitative services made available to communities to improve the quality of their requests and plans for implementation. The following section provides two examples where a reduction in social problems has taken place. These examples illustrate how addressing consumption of alcoholic beverages can affect the rates of many social problems that impact Aboriginal communities.

TWO EXAMPLES

A question that is often asked is whether there are real life examples of communities that illustrate the applicability of the proximate cause model. The answer is that there are, but the caveat that must be included, as with so many other social phenomena that are observed in naturalistic settings rather than in experimental situations, is that they never occur in pure form. Two examples are offered here: Alkali Lake in British Columbia, and La Romaine in Quebec. What the two examples have in common, and what they illustrate, is a direct focus on drinking and reducing/keeping down the rate of alcoholism as a means of addressing other harmful social problems.

Alkali Lake

Lambert, in his article "Trails of Tears and Hope," describes the extent of alcohol-related problems that affected the Indian community of Alkali Lake (population 400), which is situated about 160 kilometres north of

Vancouver. He claims that its history "resembles that of many other indigenous peoples" (Lambert, 2008: 1).

Lambert tells the story of a husband and wife (Andy and Phyllis Chelsea) who found sobriety. After a year of sobriety and campaigning on an anti-alcohol platform, the Alkali Lake band elected Andy Chelsea its chief. By the 1960s, the community was experiencing the unraveling of the tribe's social and cultural fabric (Lambert, 2008: 1). For instance, the community was experiencing unemployment rates that were so high that the vast majority of residents subsisted on government payments. Other problems such as child abuse and neglect, suicide, domestic violence, and hunger were epidemic. More importantly, drinking binges had become the dominant social activity such that tribal members would sometimes find the corpses of their fellow Indians frozen on their doorsteps after they had collapsed in an overnight drunken stupor. Drinking binges could also be seen among the Alkali Lake children, who often quaffed alongside their parents during the weekend parties that spilled into the following week. Not drinking was considered a means of exiling oneself from community life. One researcher had estimated that, in 1972, 93% of the Alkali Lake population over the age of 16 were considered heavy drinkers. Locally, the community was known as "the Indians of Alcohol Lake." A lone couple, the Chelseas, set about change among the Alkali Lake community when they not only gave up alcohol but maintained their own sobriety for the best interests of their family. At one time they were isolated within the community because of their sobriety. The Chelseas started a grassroots movement that eventually turned Alkali Lake into an officially—and for the most part practically—dry community. New social norms were established within this community, and as a result of the growing number of adults becoming sober, sobriety by the mid-1980s had become the rule (Lambert, 2008: 1).

This story of Alkali Lake illustrates what a community is capable of doing to address alcohol-related damage when the right conditions are put in place and shows the benefits for the community when anti-alcohol campaigns are implemented. It also demonstrates how improvements can be lost and regained and that there is no certainty that the future will resemble yesterday. Persisting as a dry community proved to be an even greater challenge than getting there in the first place.

La Romaine

La Romaine is a Montagnais community on the Lower North Shore of the St. Lawrence River. It is a fly-in community with a smaller white community a brief walk away. La Romaine is officially dry, and there is much community sentiment that it should remain that way. The community is by no means free of problems; for example, there is a high rate of poverty, the average level of education is low, and the rate unemployment is high. The community does, however, have lower rates of interpersonal violence, homicide, suicide, as well as lower rates of abuse and neglect of children. This is in marked contrast to the situation in other Montagnais communities in the area that have more availability of alcohol, higher rates of alcoholism, higher rates of violence of all types, and serious problems with child abuse and neglect.

It is true that, on occasion, in the middle of winter when the river is frozen, some of the men from La Romaine will set out, by snow machine, on an "alcohol run" to a distant community. Some have perished in the process. It is important to note, however, that these outings are rare and do not result in large quantities of alcohol finding their way onto the reserve.

The neighbouring white community has a small hotel with a bar. Some Indians from La Romaine have been known to go to the hotel and drink. It is not a common practice, however, because the hotel bar is not a very welcoming place for Indians, and such drinking is frowned upon by many members of the La Romaine community.

In the early 1990s, the white community applied for a licence to offer the sale of alcoholic beverages for off-premise consumption. The reserve community formally opposed the application on the grounds that it would increase the availability of alcoholic beverages in their community and lead to higher rates of alcohol-related damage and other social problems. The reserve used some of its NNADAP prevention funds to support this effort, which, by the way, was successful.

Remarkably, when this effort came to the attention of the Quebec Regional Office of the Medical Services Branch of Health Canada, which funds the NNADAP program, La Romaine was told that such lobbying was an inappropriate use of NNADAP prevention funds. Even worse, the La Romaine reserve was told that the money they spent would have to be repaid. Leaders of the community were justifiably astounded and they appealed to the good sense of the Quebec Regional Office. The issue was taken up by the Steering Committee of the NNADAP program, which is made up of representatives of tribal organizations and some regional office personnel. The discussion of the issue was by no means brief, but in the end, the decision was that La Romaine had not used funds for an inappropriate purpose. Indeed, what the community had done was entirely consistent with the initiatives aimed at the prevention of higher rates of consumption and the resultant alcohol-related damage (Paul C. Whitehead participated in the process).

CONCLUSION: IMPLICATIONS FOR SOCIAL ACTION

This chapter has summarized two divergent models for addressing the elevated rates of social problems in many Aboriginal communities. The two perspectives are markedly different and suggest quite different directions for social action. The first view, reflected in the Royal Commission's report, proposes that many social problems can only be meaningfully addressed after deep and comprehensive social changes have taken place both within the larger Canadian society as well as within Aboriginal communities. The second view, proposed by Whitehead and Hayes, takes a different approach to reducing the incidence of social problems among Aboriginal people. Their focus is more on the proximate causes of social problems that, if successfully addressed, can result in a reduction in the incidence of other social problems without requiring large-scale changes in the broader society.

The model of change articulated by the Royal Commission resonates with many Aboriginal leaders, and we do not suggest nor do we expect that it will be abandoned by them. It is an important model for many reasons, including that it is aspirational with respect to a variety of goals that include self-determination and self-government. Some may argue that the 2008 apology by Prime Minister Harper for the indignities visited on Aboriginal people by residential schools, as well as the financial settlement of many of these claims, can be taken as a sign of progress and healing. Whether it signals greater movement on the part of non-Aboriginals toward their own healing in order to foster healing among Aboriginals, however, is doubtful. Simply agreeing that abuse and cultural genocide in residential schools was an evil does not necessarily make "white society" more sympathetic to the aggressive pursuit of land claims in Ontario, British Columbia, or other provinces in Canada. Furthermore, these goals, in our opinion, may be achievable, at least in large part, without requiring broad social, cultural, and political change in the non-Aboriginal community.

There is no indication that the broader Canadian society is prepared to subscribe to a number of changes, such as equal distribution of land and income. In 2006, 10 years after the release of the Royal Commission report, the Assembly of First Nations (AFN) assessed the responses and actions undertaken by the federal government. The AFN concluded that the key elements recommended by the Royal Commission, which were to successfully transform and create a new relationship between Aboriginal and non-Aboriginal peoples, had not been implemented by the federal government: "Canada has failed in terms of its action to date" (AFN, 2006: 2).

Whitehead and Hayes are of the view that the responsibility for addressing certain social problems, in particular, alcohol-related damage, should fall more squarely on Aboriginal communities, as is illustrated in the Alkali Lake and La Romaine examples. Their perspective is quite different from those who hold the point of view that these problems are but a manifestation or symptom of the assaults that have been visited on Aboriginal peoples. Proponents of the latter view, such as the Royal Commission, may argue that the Whitehead and Hayes approach is an instance of blaming the victim.

The Royal Commission's position, while ideologically and politically attractive to some, will not likely be wholly embraced by any provincial, territorial, or federal government, irrespective of political stripe. Moreover, progress on the Royal Commission's agenda will be, at best, slow and piecemeal. This would violate one of the key requirements for change articulated by the Royal Commission, which is that the response needs to be comprehensive. Waiting for comprehensive actions to take place will delay improvements that could otherwise be realistically achieved in the near term. Take, for example, conditions such as poor housing, inadequate sanitation, and toxic water. They involve fundamental community needs that ought to be addressed directly and promptly. The Whitehead and Hayes approach, however, not only receives superior empirical support but can be helpful to governments and to Aboriginal communities in at least three ways. First, it holds out promise that addressing proximate causes can reduce some social problems. Second, it focuses attention on a social problem that has primacy, such that, if addressed, will aid in the reduction of related problems. Third, it is a counterforce to the idea that problems are so complex that little or nothing can be done about them in the near or medium term.

Some may reject one or both models on empirical, ideological, or political grounds. What, then, are the governments and Aboriginal communities to do if the two most prominent approaches for reducing the rates of social problems within Aboriginal communities have very little common ground? The alternative of doing nothing is all that is left. Doing nothing, until everything can be done should be seen as unacceptable. Waiting for a reduction in the incidence of social problems that are deeply hurtful to the mind, spirit, and body until large-scale social and political change takes place is in our view fatalistic, flawed, and unfortunate. The human and social toll to individuals, families, and communities in the form of alcoholism, interpersonal violence, crime, abuse and neglect of children, and lost productivity is simply too severe to tolerate. Furthermore, asking Aboriginal people to wait for the promise of monumental social and political changes that, as of 2013, are not on the horizon can only mean that little or no improvement or a worsening of conditions will result in another generation of Aboriginal peoples facing unnecessary suffering.

NOTES

1. The RCAP consistently uses the expression "renewed relationship," which is based on the assertion that between the years 1500 and 1800 the relations between Aboriginals and non-Aboriginals were "nation-to-nation relations" (Vol. 1, Part 3, Ch. 16: 2).
2. Another social problem that has considerable primacy is poverty. Poverty is seriously implicated in a variety of social and health problems. Its place in the past, present, and future of Aboriginal communities warrants a chapter of its own.

REFERENCES

Assembly of First Nations. (2006). *Royal Commission on Aboriginal Peoples at 10 years: A report card.* Retrieved from http://www.afn.ca/cmslib/general/afn_rcap.pdf

Bruun, K., Edwards, G., Lumino, M., Makela, K., Pan, L., Popham, R.E., et al. (1975). *Alcohol control policies in public health perspective.* Helsinki: Finnish Foundation for Alcohol Studies.

De Lint, J. (1968). Alcohol use in Canadian society. *Addictions, 17,* 14–28.

———. (1973). The validity for the theory that the distribution of alcohol consumption in a population approximates a logarithmic normal curve of the type proposed by Sully Ledermann: A brief note. *Drinking and Drug Practices Surveyor, 7,* 15–17.

De Lint, J., & Schmidt, W. (1968). The distribution of alcohol consumption in Ontario. *Quarterly Journal of Studies on Alcohol, 29,* 968–973.

————. (1971a). Consumption averages and alcoholism prevalence: A brief review of epidemiological investigations. *British Journal of Addictions, 66,* 97–107.

————. (1971b). The epidemiology of alcoholism. In Y. Israel & J. Mardones (Eds.), *Biological basis of alcoholism* (pp. 423–442). New York, NY: Wiley.

Frankel, B.G., & Whitehead, P.C. (1981). Drinking and damage: *Theoretical advances and implications for prevention*. New Brunswick, NJ: Rutgers Center of Alcohol Studies.

Health Canada. (2000). *Statistical profile on the health of First Nations in Canada.* Retrieved from http://www.hc-sc.gc.ca/fniah-spnia/pubs/aborig-autoch/stats_ profil-eng.php

————. (2001). *Unintentional and intentional injury profile for Aboriginal people in Canada* 1990–1999. Retrieved from http://publications.gc.ca/collections/collection_2012/ sc-hc/H35-4-8-1999-eng.pdf

————. (2006). First Nations and Inuit health. Retrieved from http://www.hc-sc. gc.ca/fniah-spnia/promotion/suicide/index-eng.php

Lambert, C. (2008). Trails of tears and hope. *Harvard Magazine.* Retrieved from http:// harvardmagazine.com/2008/03/trails-of-tears-and-hope.html

Ledermann, S. (1956). Alcool, alcoolisme, et alcoolisation. Vol. 1. *Données scientifiques de caractère physiologique, économique et social* (Institut National d'Études Démographiques, Travaux et Documents, Cahier No. 29). Paris: Presses Universitaires de France.

Murray, G.G., Douglas, R., Gliksman, L., Rosenbaum, P.D., Burstes, J.S., Whitehead, P.C., & Klap, R.S. (1989). *Final report of the evaluation of selected NNADAP projects.* Toronto, ON: Addiction Research Foundation.

Popham, R.E., & Schmidt, W. (1975). The prevention of alcoholism: Epidemiological studies on the effects of government control measures. *British Journal of Addictions, 70,* 125–144.

Royal Commission on Aboriginal Peoples (RCAP). (1996). *Report of the Royal Commission on Aboriginal Peoples.* Retrieved from http://www.ainc-inac.gc.ca/ch/rcap/sg/ sgmm_e.html

Scarpetti, F.R., & Andersen, M.L. (1989). *Social problems.* New York, NY: Harper and Row.

Schmidt, W., & De Lint, J. (1970). Estimating the prevalence of alcoholism from alcohol consumption and mortality data. *Quarterly Journal of Studies on Alcohol, 31,* 957–964.

Schmidt, W., & Popham, R.E. (1975). Heavy alcohol consumption and physical health problems: A review of the epidemiological evidence. *Journal of Alcohol and Drug Dependency, 1,* 27–50.

————. (1978). The single distribution theory of alcohol consumption: A rejoinder to the critique of Parker and Harmon. *Journal of Studies on Alcohol, 39,* 400–419.

Statistics Canada. (2005). Returning to correctional services after release: A profile of Aboriginal and non-Aboriginal adults involved in Saskatchewan corrections from 1999/00 to 2003/04 (Catalogue No. 85-002-XPE20050028411). *Juristat*, 25(2). Retrieved from http://www.statcan.gc.ca/pub/85-002-x/85-002-x2005002-eng.pdf

————. (2006a). Aboriginal Peoples in Canada in 2006: Inuit, Métis and First Nations, 2006 Census. *The daily*. Retrieved from http://www.statcan.gc.ca/daily-quotidien/080115/dq080115a-eng.htm

————. (2006b). Aboriginal peoples in Canada in 2006: Inuit, Métis and First Nations, 2006 Census: First Nations people. Retrieved from http://www12.statcan.ca/census-recensement/2006/as-sa/97-558/p19-eng.cfm

————. (2008). *2006 Census: Aboriginal peoples in Canada in 2006: Inuit, Métis and First Nations, 2006 Census*. Retrieved from http://www12.statcan.ca/census-recensement/2006/as-sa/97-558/pdf/97-558-XIE2006001.pdf

Whitehead, P.C. (1977). *Alcohol and young drivers: Impact and implications of lowering the drinking age* (Non-medical use of drugs directorate monograph series No. 1). Ottawa, ON: Health and Welfare Canada.

Whitehead, P.C., & Hayes, M. (1998). *The insanity of alcohol: Social problems in Canadian First Nations communities*. Toronto, ON: Canadian Scholars' Press.

7

CULTURAL CONTINUITY AND THE SOCIAL-EMOTIONAL WELL-BEING OF FIRST NATIONS YOUTH

Michael J. Chandler

INTRODUCTION: THREE EASY PIECES

In a slavish application of the classic "rule of thirds," this chapter is divided into three talking points. The first of these has to do with working out how to best aggregate or disaggregate information concerning the health and well-being of indigenous communities. The second concerns what I will go on to describe as cultural continuity—a concept that I hope to demonstrate is useful in sorting out possible socio-cultural determinants of indigenous community well-being. Finally, I plan to finish by commenting on what I take to be some of the possible action or policy implications of evidence that show that the well-being of Canada's diverse First Nations population varies as a direct function of cultural health.

In a volume such as this, primarily given over to the work of demographers, epidemiologists, and other "compilers" of various stripes, there is every reason for caution, less what is said proves to be true of no one in particular. That is, social scientists, who are regularly paid for adding things up, need to be especially vigilant about getting the business of aggregating and disaggregating just right, and about the special dangers inherent in indiscriminately tarring all indigenous peoples with the same broad and defamatory brush. As it is, the social science literature in general, and the literature concerned with indigenous populations in particular, continues to get much of this picture badly wrong. That is, despite the fact that more than half of North America's cultural richness is owed directly to the remarkable diversity of its remaining indigenous peoples (Chandler, 2001), and despite the fact that this small nubbin of the total population hosts at least 20 mutually uninterpretable languages, a welter of unique cultural and spiritual practices, and has suffered a patchwork history of different colonial regimes, the woods continue to be full of badly mistaken claims concerning what is supposedly true about the whole of the loosely federated Aboriginal world. For ease of reporting, or of streamlining government practices, or owing to simple ignorance or sloth, far too many contributors to the literature on indigenous well-being continue issuing claims that indiscriminately bracket together, and then batch-process all of Canada's First Nations, Inuit, and Métis communities, communities that are united, as far as I can see, by little more than their "otherness" and a shared history of abuse.

SUICIDE AS A "COALMINER'S CANARY" OF CULTURAL DISTRESS

My own working case in point, that is, the particular matter to which I will largely confine my comments in this chapter, is suicide, especially youth suicide, as it is suffered in British Columbia's 200-plus First Nation communities. Given additional time, much the same story could potentially be told about other provinces and about a whole raft of other social and health-related problems facing other of Canada's indigenous groups—problems such as elevated "accident" and diabetes and alcoholism and HIV infection and school dropout rates. For present purposes, however, I will confine myself to talk of suicide, not just because of its heartbreaking finality, but because it is, arguably, a "coalminer's canary" of cultural distress. When, in certain especially bleak quarters, whole swaths of people, especially young people, no longer judge life to be worth living, then more is signaled than the isolated fact that the rate suicide among First Nation youth is somewhere between five and twenty times that of the general population.

I. Youth Suicide among Canada's Indigenous Peoples—The Generic Story

The generic version of this sad story is that, riding roughshod over the obvious differences that divide them, Canada's several hundred First Nations, when considered as a group, are often said to suffer from the highest rate

Figure 7.1 Youth Suicide Rate by Band (1987–1992)

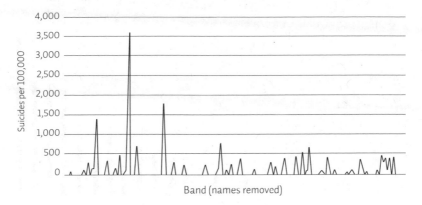

Band (names removed)

of suicide of any culturally identifiable group in the world (Kirmayer, 1994)—rates at least three to five times higher than that of the general Canadian population. Tragic as this obviously is, the prospects for First Nation youth are more tragic still. One in four youth suicides in Canada are completed by First Nation youth, and over half of all First Nation suicides are youth suicides. However disgraceful, and true after a fashion, such generic summary figures may be, they also—and this will be my point—tend to be deeply misleading.

Aboriginal Suicide Rates as "Actuarial Fictions":
Tarring all Indigenous Peoples with the Same Broad, Defamatory Brush

My point is not that Kirmayer (1994), or British Columbia's various statisticians (e.g., British Columbia Vital Statistics Agency, 2001), have somehow gotten their sums wrong. Rather, the problem with all such broad-brush, generic claims is that they are, at best, actuarial fictions that, by aggregating data across a whole country, or a whole province, fail to capture the lived experience of any of Canada's unique indigenous communities. Consequently, spectacularly high rates of suicide—particularly youth suicide—are often mistakenly imagined to be a uniform or endemic feature, common to all contemporary indigenous communities. The actual truth of the matter, however, is quite different.

Figures 7.1 and 7.2 detail the rate of youth suicide in BC, first by more culturally appropriate means: first by band of origin, and then by tribal council.

Figure 7.2 Youth Suicide Rate by Tribal Council (1987–2000)

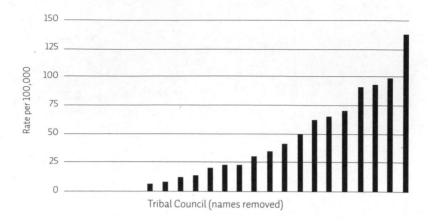

What all of this better-differentiated evidence obviously amounts to is a clear demonstration that youth suicide rates vary dramatically from one band or tribal council to the next. More particularly, these same data also show that close to half of all BC First Nations communities suffered no youth suicides; that no such suicides have occurred in one in five of the province's 27 tribal councils, and that almost 90% of BC's youth suicides occurred in only 10% of its 200-plus bands. The evident conclusion to be drawn from all of these data is that being suicidal is not, as is often wrongly imagined, some defining attribute of BC's indigenous peoples, but instead constitutes a problem that occurs in epidemic proportions in some few First Nation communities and not at all in others.

II. "Cultural Continuity" as a Possible Protective Factor Against Suicide in First Nations Communities

Having demonstrated that indigenous youth suicides are not uniformly distributed across BC's First Nations bands—but exist instead in epidemic proportion in the occasional community, and not at all in many other communities—the glaring questions that demands to be answered are: What especially characterizes those communities in which youth suicide rates are alarmingly high? And what distinguishes them from others in which the rates of youth suicide are actually lower than that characteristic of typical non-indigenous communities?

What my research collaborators and I (e.g., Chandler, 2000; 2001; Chandler & Lalonde, 1998; 2008; Chandler, Lalonde, Sokol, & Hallett, 2003) have judged to be an especially promising candidate "hunch" about what might prompt disproportionate numbers of First Nation youth to take steps to end their own lives is the unhappy prospect of having grown up in communities that have suffered the collapse of what we have termed cultural continuity, defined here as a "rooted-ness" in one's cultural past, matched with a sense of "ownership"of those collective means necessary to insure the persistence of one's cultural into the future.

Having introduced the concept of cultural continuity awkwardly obliges me to try to build a case for having ventured so much of my available research capital in the high-risk exploration of what some would judge to be an unnecessarily narrow-gauged and esoterically theory-guided search for a specific class of possible socio-cultural determinants of indigenous health and well-being. Why not, instead, play it safe and simply include every possible factor previously shown to correlate with community level success—why not, in short, throw in the kitchen sink?

I want to begin what amounts to a defence of such a theory-driven research strategy by first rehearsing the classic philosophical claim that, if they are to remain somehow recognizable as instances of what selves and cultures are ordinarily taken to be, then both individuals and whole cultural communities must satisfy at least two constitutive conditions. That is, selves and whole cultural groups are both: (a) forced by their temporally vectored nature to constantly change; and (b) all such inevitable change notwithstanding, selves and whole cultural groups must also be understood to somehow remain recognizably the same. According to William James (1891), who said all of this best, "Life is like a skiff moving through time with a bow as well as a stern" (110). This double-ended metaphor was intended by James to help capture the fact that enduring identities, if they are to somehow count as belonging timelessly to one and the same "continuant," must necessarily be both quintessentially historical or backwards referring, and, at the same time, forward anticipating, and so all about securing some stake in their own as yet unrealized futures. As such, personal and cultural continuity (which embed both sameness and change simultaneously) are not elective "features" of persons, or whole cultural groups, but constitutive conditions of their coming into being.

From Collapse of Cultural Continuity to Youth Suicide

Simply put, the logic that has driven this program of research requires that, if, owing to some train of collective assaults, the temporal course of the identity of whole cultural groups has been fractured or disabled—as continues to be the case with certain of Canada's First Nation communities—then life is likely to seem no longer worth the trouble it costs, and, paradoxically, suicide becomes a live prospect. On these grounds, it was anticipated that First Nations communities that have met with greater success in preserving backward referring ties to their own cultural past, and forward anticipating practices that provide them with some community control over their collective futures, should be the same communities that actually experience few if any youth suicides. By contrast, communities with none or few of these continuity-preserving practices should routinely suffer youth suicide rates many times greater than those found in the general population.

Measuring Cultural Continuity

While it would have been at least technically possible to more or less aimlessly troll through an all but limitless sea of arbitrarily chosen socio-demographic variables, all in the hope of snagging something, anything, that happened to correlate with the variable rates of youth suicide evident in BC's almost 200 bands, the whole point in having a theory is to avoid such random searches. My research colleagues and I (Chandler & Lalonde, 1998; Chandler, Lalonde, Sokol, & Hallett, 2003) did bother to determine whether community level rates of youth suicide varied with band-level measures of socio-economic standing, or with how urban or rural these communities were. They did not. Instead, utilizing group data from Statistics Canada, the Department of Indian Affairs and Northern Development, and the Office of the Chief Coroner of BC, we were able to construct an index of cultural continuity initially made up (in the first instance) of six marker variables expressive of the degree to which each of BC's individual bands have already secured some measure of cultural continuity, as indexed by markers of self-government; of having gained some control over the delivery of health, education, policing services, and cultural resources; and of otherwise litigating for Aboriginal title to traditional lands.

Utilizing these proxy measures made it possible to "score" each First Nations community along a six-point scale ranging from low to high levels of cultural continuity. For the years 1987 to 1992, and again 1993 to 2000,

Figure 7.3 Youth Suicide Rate by Number of Factors Present (1987–1992)

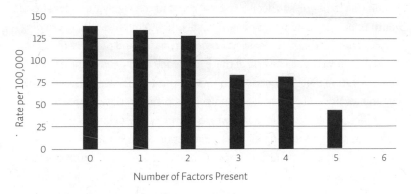

Figure 7.4 Total Suicide Rate by Number of Factors Present (1993–2000)

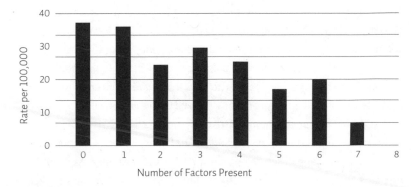

results indicate a strong negative correlation between the number of cultural continuity factors present in each communities and its suicide rate (See Figure 7.3).

In a second follow-up (replication) study, covering the period 1993 to 2000, three more predictor variables were added, including band-level knowledge of indigenous languages, a majority of women in band government, and control of child protection service. Results from this follow-up study (see Figure 7.4) again showed a strong negative correlation between cultural continuity and band-level suicide rates. Taken together, these data show, not only where in the province First Nations suicides occur and re-occur, and where they are absent, but also what community level risk and protective factors especially distinguish such "have" and "have-not" bands.

III. Potential Action and Policy Implications

In addition to offering a theory-based account of the highly variable rates of youth suicide evident in BC's diverse First Nations communities, the findings just reported also carry at least two potential action and policy implications. The meaning of the first of these is already contained in the earlier demonstration that all generic claims about the suicide rates calculated by summing across all of the diverse indigenous communities that make up a province's (and by implication a whole country's) First Nations population amounts to a meaningless "actuarial fiction." The second turns on the live prospect that First Nations communities that are free of youth suicides actually possess indigenous knowledge about how to create a world in which their children judge life to be worth living.

Action and Policy Implications: Part A

The evidence already presented suggests that if, in light of the radical diversity in the rates of youth suicide evident across BC's First Nations communities, there really is no "monolithic Indigene," no "other," and no such thing as the suicidal Aboriginal, then any totalizing, blanket statement created by arithmetically averaging across all of the real cultural diversity that does exist—all attempts to tar everyone with the same broad brush—automatically amounts to some actuarial fiction—some myth that, in addition to being seriously misleading and defamatory, tends to sponsor the misappropriation of scarce human and financial resources. As such, no one-size-fits-all solution strategy to the problem of Aboriginal suicide in BC could possibly be made to work. Rather, any serious attempt to address this health problem must necessarily begin with concerted efforts to determine how such problems are actually distributed across existing indigenous communities.

Action and Policy Implications: Part B—Indigenous Knowledge, Knowledge Transfer, and the Exchange of Best Practices

Second, what the research reported above also makes plain is the existence of a large but poorly appreciated source of real cultural knowledge about how the problem of First Nations youth suicide might be addressed. That is, clearly contained in the finding that almost half of BC's indigenous communities have youth suicide rates lower than the general population is the evident fact that real indigenous knowledge about how to address this problem must already be well-sedimented within these communities. If proper attention and weight were given to this fact, then it would become necessary to radically rethink two of government's most cherished catch phrases of the day: knowledge transfer and the exchange of best practices.

Knowledge transfer, as commonly understood, is a top-down process by means of which scientific knowledge generated within the academy is made to trickle down until it eventually reaches community-level workers. In addition to being suspect on other grounds, such "made in Washington or Ottawa" solutions are broadly seen as disrespectful by "served" communities, and openly confirmatory of the positional inferiority commonly accorded to indigenous cultures. The research that I have summarized suggests, as an alternative, that *if* indigenous knowledge is recognized as real knowledge, *then*, in the place of more traditional top-down approaches, what needs to be seriously explored is the possibility of a community-to-community lateral transfer of indigenous knowledge and best practices between groups that have enjoyed greater and lesser levels of success in meeting the needs of their own children.

In short summary, then, at least two obvious action or policy implications flow from this research. The first of these turns upon exposing as false what I have called the myth of the monolithic indigene—the actuarial fiction that it is possible to capture the diversity of a whole province's or country's Aboriginal life in a single, totalizing (often statistical) gaze. The second implication is that, in light of the rich fund of indigenous knowledge that evidently insulates so many First Nation youth from suicide, usual top-down strategies of knowledge transfer should be retired in favour of a more lateral transfer between more and less successful communities.

CONCLUSION

The research summarized here supports four summary conclusions. First, recourse to some means of preserving a sense of cultural persistence is a recurrent parameter of self-understanding, perhaps common to all human cultures. Second, those communities that fail to successfully sustain a sense of cultural continuity suffer a loss of connectedness to their own future and are thereby placed at special risk for suicide. Third, First Nations communities that succeed in taking steps to preserve their heritage culture and work to control their own destinies are dramatically more successful in insulating their youth against the risks of suicide. Fourth, among the obvious action or policy implications that flow from this research are included both: (a) the importance of abandoning any one-size-fits-all approaches to the problem of youth suicide; and (b) the need for a new approach to knowledge transfer that abandons traditional top-down strategies in favour of a more lateral transfer of knowledge that draws upon indigenous knowledge already demonstrated to be present in more successful First Nations communities.

REFERENCES

British Columbia Vital Statistics Agency. (2001). *Analysis of health statistics for Status Indians in British Columbia: 1991–1999.* Vancouver, BC: Author.

Chandler, M.J. (2000). Surviving time: The persistence of identity in this culture and that. *Culture and Psychology, 6*(2), 209–231.

———. (2001). The time of our lives: Self-continuity in Native and non-Native youth. In H.W. Reese (Ed.), *Advances in child development and behavior.* Vol. 28 (pp. 175–221). New York, NY: Academic Press.

Chandler, M.J., & Lalonde, C.E. (1998). Cultural continuity as a hedge against suicide in Canada's First Nations. *Transcultural Psychiatry, 35*(2), 191–219.

———. (2008). Cultural continuity as a protective factor against suicide in First Nations Youth. *Horizons—A Special Issue on Aboriginal Youth, Hope or Heartbreak: Aboriginal Youth and Canada's Future, 10*(1), 68–72.

Chandler, M.J., Lalonde, C.E., Sokol, B.W., & Hallett, D. (2003). Personal persistence, identity development, and suicide: A study of native and non-native North American adolescents. *Monographs of the Society for Research in Child Development, 68*(2, serial No. 273). Malden, MA: Blackwell.

Health Canada. (1991). Statistical profile on native mental health (Background Report of the Statistical and Technical Working Group, Mental Health Advisory Services, Indian and Northern Health Services). Ottawa, ON: Medical Services Branch Steering Committee on Native Mental Health, Medical Services Branch Health & Welfare Canada.

James, W. (1891). *The principles of psychology.* London, UK: Macmillan and Company.

Kirmayer, L. (1994). Suicide among Canadian Aboriginal people. *Transcultural Psychiatric Research Review, 31,* 3–57.

Statistics Canada. (2001). *Canada year book.* Ottawa, ON: Government of Canada.

8

ADDRESSING THE DISPARITIES IN ABORIGINAL HEALTH THROUGH SOCIAL DETERMINANTS RESEARCH

Malcolm King

I've spent most of my research career, more than 30 years by now, in the study of respiratory diseases, particularly cystic fibrosis and chronic bronchitis, where I've worked at developing new treatments to deal with the difficulties such patients experience with clearing their lungs of excess mucus. I always enjoy attending the major international conference in this specialty area, namely the American Thoracic Society meeting. In May 2007, the meeting was held in San Francisco, attended by some 16,000 delegates, with about 3,000 scientific presentations. As I wandered through the vast array of posters, I came across one such poster dealing with pulmonary arterial hypertension (PAH) that was manned by a young medical resident, who was being generally ignored by the hundreds of people viewing other posters in the area. I struck up a conversation with the presenter; to me, his presentation was more interesting than all the others in the grouping. Most of the other presentations involved new drug treatments for this very serious medical condition, where typically a success would be an improvement in 20% or 30% in this or the other statistic. However, the poster I was looking at showed something completely different; it showed the effect of a major risk factor associated with dying from pulmonary arterial

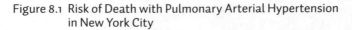

Figure 8.1 Risk of Death with Pulmonary Arterial Hypertension
in New York City

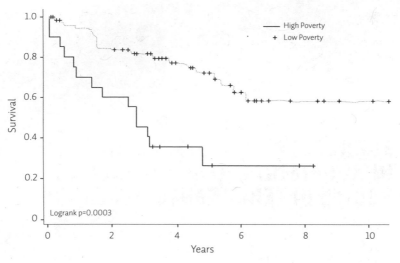

Source: Okun et al., 2007.

hypertension—namely, poverty. It turns out that in New York City, where this trainee worked (Columbia University), one's chance of dying in the first year after the initial consultation for PAH was four times greater if one lived in a poor neighbourhood than in an affluent neighbourhood (Okun et al., 2007). Furthermore, this dramatic gap in survival persisted out beyond eight years (Figure 8.1). Nearly 30% of the patients from the bottom income quartile neighbourhoods were dead after one year, while only 7% of those in the upper quartile neighbourhoods had passed away in this same time. No solution to the problem was offered, other than the obvious implication that if one could fix poverty, or at least reduce the disparity in income, there could be a huge effect on a medical condition, a much greater effect than any drug treatment could promise.

Of course, one might be tempted to dismiss this study as being irrelevant to Canada, since it was carried out in New York City, a city of huge disparities in personal wealth, and in a country where nearly 30% of the population has no medical insurance. However, not long before the 2007 ATS conference, an article appeared in the *American Journal of Medicine* (*AJM*) (Chang, Kaul, Westerhout, Graham, & Armstrong, 2007) showing that in fact significant poverty-related disparities in mortality do occur in Canada. The *AJM* article was written by a team of cardiology researchers, led by Dr. Paul Armstrong of the University of Alberta. The team did a similar analysis, looking at the risk of dying during the year following a heart attack in Edmonton, Alberta. Those from the lowest income quartile, based on residence, had a 30% risk of dying during this critical first year, while those in the upper quartile of income had a 15% risk of dying (Figure 8.2). This is a doubling of risk associated with economic status, and this within one of the wealthiest and best-served regions of Canada, with our universal access to health care. So perhaps the disparities are less in Canada than the United States, but they're still there. Even in Edmonton, Alberta, with universal health care access and one of the best health care systems in the world, there's still twice the chance of dying in the year following your heart attack if you come from a poor neighbourhood. It makes one question whether we really have universal access.

The comforting thing about this Edmonton study is that low income doesn't have to be a death sentence. When low-income patients received the ideal therapy—revascularization—the disparity in survival disappeared. The risk of dying after one year was down to about 5%, regardless of income status. The problem is not that simple, however. Although some patients undoubtedly experienced access issues due to poverty and/or geographical factors, many of those from the lower-income groups had additional risk factors that kept them from receiving the optimal therapy (Chang, Kaul, Westerhout, Graham, & Armstrong, 2007).

If we could fix income, would we fix these health disparities? Let's look at another example, this one coming from a Canadian study involving First Nations people, where the disparities in health are well known. Dr. Sonia Anand of McMaster University, the lead author of this study, worked with the First Nations community of Six Nations of the Grand near Brantford, Ontario. They collected blood samples from residents of the reserve, as well as from people of European descent in the neighbouring communities. These samples were analyzed for cardiovascular disease (CVD) risk, using measures such as cholesterol level, as well as other biomedical risk factors. The researchers also asked people socio-economic questions, such as "what is your family income?" The resulting findings are a classical example of the effect of income on health, in this case cardiovascular disease risk versus family income (Figure 8.3). For each group, Aboriginal people and those of

Figure 8.2 Income and Risk of Death after a Heart Attack in Edmonton, Alberta, Canada

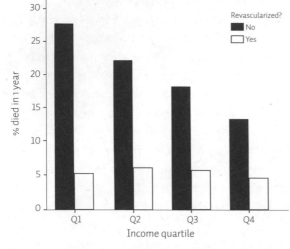

One-year mortality rate by socio-economic status and revascularization status at one year.
Source: Chang, Kaul, Westerhout, Graham, & Armstrong, 2007.

European descent, the highest risk was found for the people with the lowest income. However, what was most interesting was the fact that for the Aboriginal people, although this gradient of disease risk versus income still held, at each income level the risk of developing cardiovascular disease was significantly higher (Anand et al., 2001). In other words, income couldn't explain all the excess disease risk. There were other factors that contributed to the health-risk disparity seen in the Aboriginal group. The study didn't explain these additional risk factors, but other studies involving indigenous peoples suggest that social factors such as loss of language and culture, lack of self-determination, and the loss of the connection to the land may play a role (King, Smith, & Gracey, 2009). These are factors that don't fit within the conventional socio-economic triad of income, employment, and education.

Chandler and Lalonde (1998) further delved into factors that relate to health in indigenous peoples in their exploration of suicide rates in the First Nations peoples of British Columbia. It is well known that suicide rates in First Nations people in Canada are greatly elevated over the general population, particularly among youth. What Chandler and Lalonde found, however, was that there was a wide variation in suicide rates. On some reserves in

Figure 8.3 Income and CVD Risk Factors among People of Aboriginal and European Ancestry, Canada

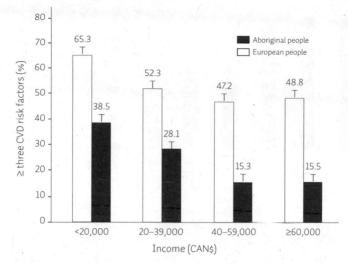

Study based on individuals between 35 and 75 years who were Six Nations Band Members (Reserve in Brant County, Ontario, Canada) who had lived on the Six Nations reserve for at least five years, and who had no history of cancer or other serious chronic disease such as renal or liver failure; and individuals of European ancestry (randomly sampled, ages between 35 and 75 years from three cities in Canada: Hamilton, Toronto, and Edmonton).

Source: Anand et al., 2001.

British Columbia, the rate was sky-high, more than 100 times the national average, but on other reserves, the suicide rate was zero—no suicides in more than a decade. Why the difference? It turns out that the suicide rate was related community factors, or measures of self-determination, in the communities. For each of six factors identified, such as taking control of education, social services and housing, establishing their own police force or fire department, and having women in council, the suicide rate was higher than if these factors were not in place. And when one looked at the cumulative effect of all of these measures of self-determination, the suicide rate went progressively down, from an out-of-control high rate to zero, when all six factors were present (Figure 8.4). Yet none of these First Nations set out to reduce their suicide rate, or indeed to fix any other health problems, by taking steps toward self-determination. In some ways, this is an indigenous parallel to the Whitehall study of some 30 years ago, led by Sir Michael Marmot, which found that civil servants who had a sense of control in

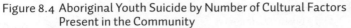
Figure 8.4 Aboriginal Youth Suicide by Number of Cultural Factors Present in the Community

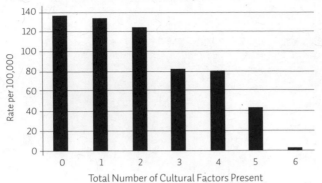

Cultural factors (self-government, land claims participation); community control factors (health services, education, cultural facilities, police/fire services).

Source: Chandler & Lalonde, 1998.

their lives lived longer and healthier lives than those who had less control (Marmot & Wilkinson, 2006).

There have been many studies since the 1970s that look at the general indicators of health and well-being related to socio-economic status. In a now classic study carried out in the 1980s in the United States, J.S. House, R.C. Kessler, and A.R. Herzog (1990) explored an overall index of socio-economic status, based primarily on income and education. They examined the effect of aging on two important variables, namely the number of chronic conditions that we face as we age, and their effect on our functional status. As we age, the number of chronic conditions increases, and our functional status decreases. House, Kessler, and Herzog (1990) found that socio-economic indicators predicted the variation at any given age in the number of chronic conditions, with those in the lowest bracket of socio-economic status having the most chronic conditions, and vice versa. The opposite was true for functional limitations: those worse off socio-economically had lower functional status than those who were better off in every age grouping.

In Canada, we don't have such an extensive data set around health, education, and income, but there is one study I would point to—namely, one carried out in Manitoba by Mustard and colleagues (1997). This study shows that both income and education are predictors of age-adjusted mortality. Those with the higher income levels and higher levels of educational attainment have a lower risk of dying.

To bring in an Aboriginal example, we can look to the 2002–2003 First Nations Regional Health Survey (NAHO, First Nations Centre, 2005), a health survey of people living on reserves across Canada, carried out by the Assembly of First Nations. This regional health survey looked at the effect of education (whether respondents graduated from high school or not) and employment (currently working for pay) on perceived general health. The results were very clear: those with better education and paid employment were more likely to be in good health, and vice versa.

Perhaps an even more powerful example of the effects of socio-economic factors on Aboriginal health is to be found in the recent mortality study conducted by Statistics Canada (Tjepkema, Wilkins, Senécal, Guimond, & Penney, 2009). These authors examined mortality hazard ratios in Registered Indians (First Nations) and Métis Canadians. In First Nations men, 62% of the excess mortality was explainable by adjusting for socio-economic factors such as education, income, and employment. In Métis men, the figure was 68%. Among females, the effects of socio-economic factors on mortality were significantly less—29% explainable for First Nations females and 28% for Métis females. This lower dependence on socio-economic factors for females is consistent with the American data of Backlund, Sorlie, and Johnson (1999). Apparently a relatively greater health gain can be achieved by addressing socio-economic disparities in males.

These studies fit with the general concept of the social determinants of health (Figure 8.5), as developed by the Ottawa Charter under Marc Lalonde and subsequently Monique Bégin, cabinet ministers in the governments of the 1970s and 1980s. How important are these social determinants of health? Shockingly important, it turns out. Here's a striking statement made by Sir Michael Marmot, head of the WHO Commission on the Social Determinants of Health at the June 2007 International Meeting on Health Promotion and Education in Vancouver: "In the US, 886,202 deaths would have been averted between 1991 and 2000 if mortality rates between Whites and African Americans were equalized. This contrasts to only 176,633 lives saved by medical advances" (Woolf as cited in Marmot, 2007).

The statement was attributed to Steven Woolf (Woolf, Johnson, Fryer, Rust, & Satcher, 2004), an American public health researcher in Virginia. Here's what the statement is based on: the rate of decline of age-adjusted

Figure 8.5 Determinants of Health: Conceptual Model

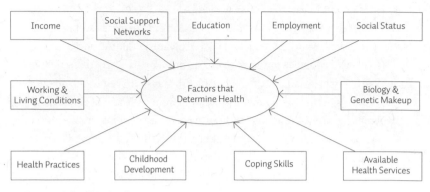

Source: Adapted from Reading, 2001.

mortality in Western society is fairly small but steady, except for the occa-sional blip, such as the 1918 influenza epidemic. People are living longer, and so their chance of dying in any given year of life is lower. Now assum-ing every bit of this increase in longevity can be attributed to biomedical advances, including advances in diagnostic techniques, improvements in medical and surgical interventions, and new drugs—and this is a very big assumption, indeed—then the number of extra lives saved per year can be calculated from the decline in age-adjusted mortality over the whole US population. This is represented by the small black bars in the graph (Figure 8.6a), and added up over a decade, the estimate comes to 176,000. Now, here's where race comes in: African Americans live shorter lives, significantly shorter than white people, and if that "problem" could somehow be fixed, bringing the life expectancy of African Americans up to the level of white people, then the numbers of lives that could be saved each year is repre-sented by the black bars in the companion graph (Figure 8.6b). Over the decade of the 1990s, that number would have added up to 886,000 deaths averted due to health deficits associated with race (Woolf Johnson, Fryer, Rust, & Satcher, 2004).

Comprehensive Canadian Aboriginal mortality data are difficult to access due to identification issues, but applying Woolf's logic to Aboriginal people in Canada—in this case, First Nations for whom there is data, indicating an ongoing life expectancy gap of about six to eight years (Wilkins, Tjepkema, Mustard, & Choinière, 2008)—this would lead to the conclusion that proportionately similar numbers of lives could be saved if

Figure 8.6a Potential Number of Lives Saved by Improvements in Age-
Adjusted Mortality Rates in the United States, 1991–2000

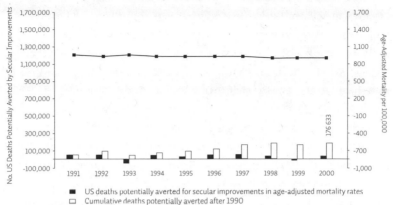

US deaths potentially averted for secular improvements in age-adjusted mortality rates
Cumulative deaths potentially averted after 1990
US age-adjusted mortality rate

Figure 8.6b Difference in Age-Adjusted Mortality Rates of Whites and
African Americans, 1991–2000, and Potential Number
of Lives Saved if the Rates Had Been Comparable

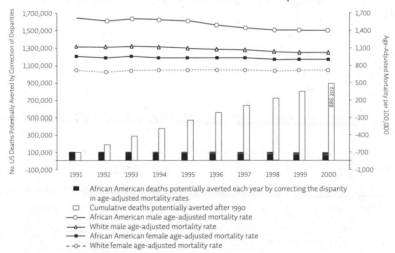

African American deaths potentially averted each year by correcting the disparity
in age-adjusted mortality rates
Cumulative deaths potentially averted after 1990
—○— African American male age-adjusted mortality rate
—△— White male age-adjusted mortality rate
—■— African American female age-adjusted mortality rate
- -○- - White female age-adjusted mortality rate

Source: Woolf, Johnson, Phillips, & Philipsen, 2007.

the health deficit associated with being Aboriginal could be fixed; this can
be estimated at about 20,000 deaths averted per decade, according to the
relative population.

Ridiculous, one might say; you can't fix someone's race. You can't fix
being Aboriginal in the Canadian context. And further, race isn't actually a

social determinant of health. Perhaps not directly, but race or indigeneity is nevertheless there through an interaction of factors such as education, income, employment, social networks, access to health care, alienation from society, and the effects of colonization (King, Smith, & Gracey, 2009). So, while we're not actually talking about fixing race, we are talking about changing conditions so all racial and ethnic and cultural groups enjoy the same health status and the chance of living long and healthy lives.

Woolf and colleagues (2007) continued their studies in an area that is less politically and socially charged—namely, the interrelation between education and health, which crosses racial and cultural lines. These researchers used the well-known data on the influence of education on life expectancy in a similar analysis. Taking American statistical data from a very large sample (Backlund, Sorlie, & Johnson, 1999), people who complete high school, but not college, live shorter lives than college graduates. The reasons for this are complex, and open to interpretation; factors such as increased income, better employment, improved health understanding, and better social networks all come into play. Nevertheless, the overall effect of education is undeniable: on average, there is a lower age-specific mortality, i.e., increased longevity, in those who are better educated. Backlund and colleagues (1999) also studied the effect of income on lifespan. Most of the income effect on mortality is actually one of poverty. Those in the bottom quarter of income are at much greater risk than those above them. There's relatively little benefit, in terms of longevity, in having a high income versus the mid-range. These two factors—education and income—are of course linked, as you can easily imagine, as is employment, at least in men. Having less than a college education means your risk of dying in any given year is 40% higher than the risk associated with having a college education or better. When combined with the other associated socio-economic factors, the elevated education risk is 70% (Backlund, Sorlie, & Johnson, 1999).

Woolf and colleagues (2007) applied the education–health data in the same way they applied the race data, calculating the number of excess deaths per year that could be attributed to lower educational levels. They added up a staggering 1,369,335 excess deaths in the seven-year period from 1996 to 2002. And again, they similarly attributed the total decline in overall mortality to advances in biomedicine, coming up with the figure of 178,193 lives spared during this same seven-year period. Their conclusion was, therefore, that doing whatever was necessary to fix the educational gap, i.e., bringing the health of a college education to those with only high school or less, would achieve more than seven times the effect of all of the achievements in biomedical advances. Addressing educational and other social indicator deficits could potentially lead to a much greater health gain than more conventional biomedical approaches.

Now we need to bring these socio-economic risk factors into perspective. How does the elevated risk of dying associated with lower educational attainment compare with so-called medical risk factors? Here's an example that puts this into perspective: the risk associated with high blood pressure. The following is from the "Seventh Report of the Joint National Committee on Prevention, Detection, Evaluation, and Treatment of High Blood Pressure" (Chobanian et al., 2003): "Between the ages of 40 and 69, each blood pressure increase of 20 mm Hg systolic or 10 mm Hg diastolic was associated with a more than twofold increase in the stroke death rate...or ischemic heart disease mortality down to optimal blood pressure, throughout middle age." The researchers commented that a 10 mm Hg reduction of systolic blood pressure or a 5 mm Hg reduction of diastolic blood pressure could, in the long term, be associated with a 40% lower risk of stroke death and a 30% lower risk of death from ischemic heart disease or other vascular causes throughout middle age.

So, in other words, the 40% increased risk of death associated with having a suboptimal education alone, or the 70% increase when associated income and employment are also factored in, are equivalent to having a 10 or 15 mm mercury increase in blood pressure. Does the health system pay attention to blood pressure as a risk factor? Of course it does. And are health research resources invested in developing treatments and strategies to bring down the excess pressure associated with elevated risk. Of course they are—in a major way. So why aren't we spending health research dollars on improving educational attainment? Is it because we don't see the evidence? It's right there, and it has been there for years. Is it because we think that other dollars should be spent on fixing educational deficits? Of course other dollars should be spent, but health researchers should be stepping up to the plate and taking their rightful part in addressing this important health issue. Education underachievement is a health issue; so is underemployment; so is poverty; and we as health researchers need to be part of the solution.

Let us once again return to the Edmonton heart attack study (Chang, Kaul, Westerhout, Graham, & Armstrong, 2007). As we have seen, in patients who managed to receive the best available therapy, the one-year death rate was reduced to about 5% and the income disparity was eliminated (see Figure 8.2). Reducing the death rate even further would require advances in biomedicine beyond what is currently available—for example, through proteomics or stem-cell research. This is certainly a noble goal, and one that should be pursued. But surely reducing the death rate associated with the income gap is also a noble goal; certainly the potential health gain is greater than what could possibly be achieved by biomedical advances.

We need to define health more broadly, such that initiatives targeting education or poverty are evaluated not only for themselves but also for their potential to improve health (Chandler & Lalonde, 1998; King, Smith, & Gracey, 2009). Further, this very process would result in synergies in funding, since the benefits of improving education, reducing income disparities, and addressing socio-cultural inequities would translate into improved health far beyond what we can currently realize purely through technological advances. We need to commission studies to look at the cost of social interventions to improve health, to examine these costs in terms of potential health gains, and to weigh these costs against the conventional approaches on which we have focused most of our attention. This is not to say that we should totally abandon our support for genetics and molecular biology. These have been valuable and should be continued. However, we need to do the analysis, and weigh all the evidence, before deciding on our future course. We should always be thinking in terms of the potential for health gain of maximizing the benefit of our health research spending to improve the health of all Canadians.

REFERENCES

Anand, S.S., Yusuf, S., Jacobs, R., Davis, A.D., Yi, Q., Gerstein, H., Montague, P.A., et al. (2001). Risk factors, atherosclerosis, and cardiovascular disease among Aboriginal people in Canada: The study of health assessment and risk evaluation in Aboriginal peoples. *Lancet*, 358(9288), 1147–1153.

Backlund, E., Sorlie, P.D., & Johnson, N.J. (1999). A comparison of the relationships of education and income with mortality: The national longitudinal mortality study. *Social Science & Medicine*, 49(10), 1373–1384.

Chandler, M.J., & Lalonde, C.E. (1998). Cultural continuity as a hedge against suicide in Canada's First Nations. *Transcultural Psychiatry*, 35, 193–211.

Chang, W.-C., Kaul, P., Westerhout, C.M., Graham, M.M., & Armstrong, P.W. (2007). Effects of socio-economic status on mortality after acute myocardial infarction. *American Journal of Medicine, 120*(1), 33–39.

Chobanian, A.V., Bakris, G.L., Black, H.R., Cushman, W.C., Green, L.A., Izzo, J.L., Jr., et al. (2003). Seventh report of the joint national committee on prevention, detection, evaluation, and treatment of high blood pressure. *Hypertension, 42*(6), 1206–1252.

House, J.S., Kessler, R.C., & Herzog, A.R. (1990). Age, socio-economic status, and health. *Milbank Quarterly, 68*, 383–411.

King, M., Smith, A., & Gracey, M. (2009). Indigenous perspectives on health: The underlying causes of the health gap. *Lancet, 374*(9683), 65–75.

Marmot, M. (2007). Achieving health equity: From root causes to fair outcomes. *Lancet, 370*(9593), 1153–1163.

———. (2007, June). *Commission on Social Determinants of Health interim statement.* Presentation at the International Union for Health Promotion and Education Conference, Vancouver, BC. Retrieved from http://www.who.int/social_determinants/thecommission/en/

Marmot, M., & Wilkinson, R.G. (Eds.). (2006). *Social determinants of health* (2nd ed.). New York, NY: Oxford University Press.

Mustard, C.A., Derksen, S., Berthelot, J.M., Wolfson, M., & Roos, L.L. (1997). Age-specific education and income gradients in morbidity and mortality in a Canadian province. *Social Science & Medicine, 45*(3), 383–397.

National Aboriginal Health Organization (NAHO), First Nations Centre. (2005). First Nations regional longitudinal survey 2002/03. Ottawa. Retrieved from http://rhs-ers.ca/english/pdf/rhs2002-03reports/rhs2002-03-technicalreport-afn.pdf

Okun, J.M., Lederer, D.J., Horn, E.M., Berekashvili, K.K., Rosenzweig, E.B., Barst, R.J., et al. (2007). Poverty predicts worse outcome in pulmonary arterial hypertension (PAH). *American Journal of Respiratory Critical Care Medicine, 173*, A714.

Reading, J. (2001). *Healthy public policy and the health of Aboriginal peoples.* Unpublished manuscript, Canadian Institutes of Health Research, Institute of Aboriginal Peoples' Health.

Tjepkema, M., Wilkins, R., Senécal, S., Guimond, E., & Penney, C. (2009). Mortality of Métis and registered Indian adults in Canada: An 11-year follow-up study. *Health Reports, 20*(4), 31–51.

Wilkins, R., Tjepkema, M., Mustard, C., & Choinière, R. (2008). The Canadian census mortality follow-up study, 1991 through 2001. *Health Reports, 19*(3), 25–43.

Woolf, S.H., Johnson, R.E., Fryer, G.E., Rust, G., & Satcher, D. (2004). The health impact of resolving racial disparities: An analysis of US mortality data. *American Journal of Public Health, 94*(12), 2078–2081.

Woolf, S.H., Johnson, R.E., Phillips, R.L., & Philipsen, M. (2007). Giving everyone the health of the educated: An examination of whether social change would save more lives than medical advances. *American Journal of Public Health, 97*(4), 679–683.

9

NORTH-NORTH AND NORTH-SOUTH HEALTH DISPARITIES
A CIRCUMPOLAR PERSPECTIVE

T. Kue Young

INTRODUCTION

Our Canadian experience suggests that people in the "North" have worse health than those in the "South." Within the "North," Aboriginal people tend to fare worse than non-Aboriginal people (Waldram, Herring, & Young, 2006). Does this hold true in other circumpolar countries? Can anything be learned from other circumpolar countries? We often forget that Canada has a northern border also, and that it is part of a circumpolar community of regions that share certain common features not only in geography and climate, but also in demography and health. This chapter presents an overview of key health indicators of various regions in the circumpolar North and identifies disparities between North and South, and within the North itself.

DEFINING THE CIRCUMPOLAR NORTH

Health statistics, which are most often collected by government agencies, are usually aggregated by administrative divisions. For the purposes of this chapter, the circumpolar North is defined as composed of the administrative divisions shown in Table 9.1.

Table 9.1 Administrative Divisions/Regions in the Circumpolar North

[US] United States	[DK] Denmark	[RU] Russian Federation
[Ak] Alaska	[Gl] Greenland	[Mu] Murmansk Oblast
[CA] Canada	[Fo] Faroe Islands	[Ka] Kareliya Republic
[Yk] Yukon	[IS] Iceland	[Ar] Arkhangelsk Oblast
[Nt] Northwest Territories	[NO] Norway	- [Ne] Nenets AO
[Nu] Nunavut	[Nd] Nordland	[Ko] Komi Republic
	[Tr] Troms	[Yn] Yamalo-Nenets AO
	[Fm] Finnmark	[Km] Khanty-Mansi AO
	[SE] Sweden	[Tm] Taymyr AO
	[Vb] Västerbotten	[Ev] Evenki AO
	[Nb] Norrbotten	[Sk] Sakha Republic
	[FI] Finland	[Ma] Magadan Oblast
	[Ou] Oulu	[Ky] Koryak AO
	[La] Lappi	[Ck] Chukotka AO

AO = autonomous okrug.

The whole of Alaska and Greenland are included. Northern Canada includes only the three northern territories, all located above 60° N latitude. While the Nunavik region in northern Quebec and the Nunatsiavut region in Labrador are often regarded as part of the Canadian Arctic, health data from these regions are generally difficult to obtain.

The northernmost counties in Norway, Sweden, and Finland constitute the northern regions of those countries. ("County" here refers to *fylke* in Norway, *län* in Sweden, and *lääni* in Finland). These regions, plus those of Murmansk Oblast, Kareliya Republic, Arkhangelsk Oblast, Nenets Autonomous Okrug, and Komi Republic in European Russia, are also members of the Barents Euro-Arctic Council.

The situation in Russia is quite complex. The Russian Federation is composed of different types of administrative divisions called federal "subjects" (*subetkty*), including republic, *kray, oblast,* autonomous *okrug,* and federal city, with varying degrees of autonomy, but all sending representatives to the Federal Council (*Sovet Federatsii*), the upper house of the Russian parliament. In this chapter, *kray, oblast,* and *okrug* are used as Anglicized terms (with "s" added to form the plural) rather than their translations as "territory," "region," and "area," which are not consistently used in the literature. (The shorter geographical names are used instead of the more formal Russian versions—for example, Murmansk Oblast instead of Murmanskaya Oblast, and Koryak Autonomous Okrug instead of Koryakskiy Autonomous Okrug).

Autonomous okrugs (hereafter AO), with the exception of Chukotka, are generally part of some higher-level units such as oblasts or krays, and usually represent the traditional territories of some indigenous ethnic groups. Demographic and health data are usually available for these AO separately. Both the Nenets AO and Arkhangelsk Oblast, to which the Nenets AO is subordinate, are included on our list. The Yamalo-Nenets, Khanty-Mansi, Taymyr, Evenki, and Koryak AO are included, but not their "parents" Tyumen Oblast, Krasnoyarsk Kray, and Kamchatka Oblast, which extend far into the southern parts of Siberia. All 13 Russian regions selected here are among those designated as "Far North districts and equivalents" under Decision #1029 of the USSR Council of Ministers adopted in 1967. Part or all of their territory lies above the Arctic Circle. For further information on definitional issues of the Russian North, see Kozlov and Lisitsyn (2008). Note that as of January 1, 2007, the Taymyr, Evenki, and Koryak AO ceased to exist as distinct federal subjects.

INDIGENOUS PEOPLES OF THE NORTH

There is substantial ethnic diversity within the circumpolar North. In North America, the indigenous people of the North belong to the Athapaskan and Eskimo-Aleut language families. In Fennoscandia, the indigenous Sami belong to the Finno-Ugric family (which also comprises Finnish). In the Russian North there is a diversity of language families: the Chukotko-Kamchatkan, Uralic (Finno-Ugric and Samoyedic branches), and Altaic (Turkic and Tungusic branches), as well as several language isolates. The traditional subsistence lifestyles were based on hunting and fishing, to which had been added reindeer herding and trapping of fur-bearing animals a few centuries ago in historical times. All had experienced varying degrees of colonization by external powers and are today incorporated into modern nation-states dominated by cultures of predominantly European origins. (Greenland, with some 90% of its population Inuit, has achieved Home Rule from Denmark, with substantial internal self-government.)

DATA SOURCES

Publicly available data sources from official statistical agencies and health ministries were accessed. Where possible, the five-year mean of 2000–2004 were computed to provide stable rates for regions with small populations. Where appropriate, direct age standardization to the European Standard Population was performed (Eurostat, 2002). The choice of this standard is out of convenience as many published statistical data from the Nordic countries are already standardized to this population.

The choice of health indicators is limited to what is consistently available across the circumpolar North. Some data gaps are closed by making special requests to the relevant statistical or health agency to acquire the data. By and large, the health indicators are derived from population registries and censuses, vital statistics, and disease registries, where data are generally comparable across nations and regions. For basic health indicators, there is overall comparability internationally with identical or similar definitions, or for which standard criteria have been established by international agencies such as the World Health Organization. For a detailed discussion of concepts and definitions, see the monograph *Circumpolar Health Indicators* (Young, 2008), where a list of statistical agencies and their URL addresses can also be found. These statistics are updated periodically in the interactive website of the Circumpolar Health Observatory (http://circhob/circumpolarhealth.org).

MEASURING DISPARITIES

Several types of comparisons can be made. One would be between northern regions and the nation-states of which they are parts—e.g., Northern territories of Canada vs. Canada, Alaska vs. USA, and in the case of Greenland and Faroe Islands, with Denmark. Iceland would be the only "region" that is also a sovereign state and would not be compared with some larger political entity. Another comparison would be among the northern regions themselves.

Within the northern regions, the indigenous population could be compared with the non-indigenous population. However, only Alaska consistently breaks down its health and demographic statistics into "Alaska Native" and other races, while, for Greenland, distinction is made between "Greenland-born" and those born outside Greenland. (Note that "Alaska Natives"—not "Alaskan Natives"—collectively refer to Eskimos, Athabascan Indians, and Aleuts. "Eskimo" is acceptable usage in Alaska and officially used by Native organizations themselves.) The "Greenland-born" has traditionally served as a proxy for Inuit but such practice is expected to be less and less valid. The Canadian and Russian censuses provide substantial information on the indigenous populations. In the Canadian North, some health status indicators are broken down by Inuit and First Nations, and others are collected, but generally not released, by the territorial governments, while other types of health data require additional programming to extract the needed information from the various databases.

Despite their comprehensive population registries, ethnicity information is not recorded in the Nordic countries, so the Sami population can only be estimated imprecisely.

Disparities in health between regions can be illustrated visually by the use of bar graphs and maps, examples of which are presented in this chapter. To quantify disparities there is a choice of difference and ratio measures (Keppel et al., 2005). For example, life expectancy at birth for men in the Koryak AO in Russia (the worst region) during 2000–2004 was 29 years lower than Iceland (the best region), while the tuberculosis incidence rate in Koryak AO (also the worst) was 106 times that of Norrbotten county in Sweden (the best). It should be cautioned that different types of measures tell different stories, offer different slants for interpretation, and suggest different policy implications. Especially when used in demonstrating temporal trends, totally opposite conclusions can sometimes be made (i.e., Are things getting "worse" or "better"?).[1]

COMPARATIVE HEALTH INDICATORS

Appendix Tables 9 3, 9 4, and 9 5 compare the circumpolar regions and countries in terms of certain geographical, demographic, health status, socio-economic, and health care characteristics.

Demographic Characteristics

Appendix Table 9.3 shows the absolute population sizes of the various circumpolar regions. In North America, Alaska and the three northern Canadian territories constitute less than 0.5% of the total population of the United States and Canada, respectively. Both Greenland's and Faroe Islands' population is only 1% that of Denmark. In contrast, a much higher proportion of the national population of Norway (10%), Sweden (6%), and Finland (12%) reside in their northern counties. In Russia, it is about 5%.

From a policy perspective, it is to be expected that the extent to which northern regional issues and needs occupy the attention of national governments would reflect their share of the population.

Within the North, indigenous people account for only 4.5% of the total population. However, they are a substantial minority in regions such as Alaska (19%), Yukon (25%), and Finnmark (31%); they also comprise about half of the population of the Northwest Territories and constitute the overwhelming majority in Nunavut (86%) and Greenland (88%). In Arctic Russia, in none of the autonomous okrugs (AO), where the traditional homelands of indigenous people are located, do indigenous people form the majority, ranging from 2% in the Khanty-Mansi AO to 41% in the Koryak AO.

In terms of age distribution, 31% of Alaska Natives and 27% of Greenland-born Greenlanders are under the age of 15; similarly, the proportion in the Northwest Territories and Nunavut, with their high proportion of indigenous people, is 25% and 35%, respectively. The proportion of those 65 and over in these populations is correspondingly low (Alaska Natives 6%, NWT 4%, Nunavut 2%, Greenland 6%). The northern regions of Fennoscandia generally do not differ from their national patterns: for example, 18% of the population of northern Sweden is under 15 years of age and a similar proportion (also 18%) is aged 65 and over.

Alaska Natives, Greenlanders, and the population of Nunavut have very high teen pregnancy rates (reflected in the age-specific fertility rate for ages 15 to 19). There is a direct linear relationship between the proportion of indigenous people in the region's total population and that region's age-specific fertility rate for ages 15 to 19 (Figure 9.1).

Life Expectancy and Infant Mortality

In North America, life expectancy at birth (LE_o) for Alaska is the same as that of the United States all races combined. For Alaska Natives, there is a drop of about five years. In Canada, the territorial values decline as the proportion of indigenous people increases, such that there is a difference of 11 years between the Nunavut and the Canadian national value. In Fennoscandia, there is essentially no difference between the northern and the national life expectancies. Russia as a country is suffering from an unprecedented health crisis, with the male LE_o less than 60 years. Among the northern regions, the difference between the best region (Iceland) and the worst (Koryak AO) is 29 years in men and 21 years in women.

Figure 9.1 Relationship Between Percentage of Population that is
Indigenous and Age-Specific Fertility Rate for Ages 15–19

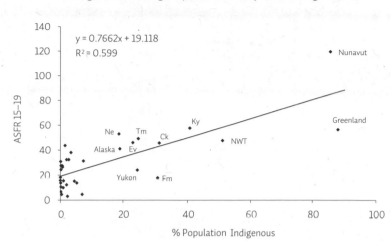

A similar pattern is observed for infant mortality rate. The lowest rates
(below 5 per 1,000 live births) are observed in the Nordic countries (with
little difference between North and South), an intermediate group consist-
ing of northern Canada, Alaska, and Greenland, and worst of all the Russian
regions. There are substantial disparities between the Alaska Native and
Alaska all-state rates, and Nunavut's is almost three times the Canadian
national rate. The highest northern regional rate, reported from the Evenki
AO in Russia, is 13 times that of the Faroe Islands.

Determinants of Health Outcomes

The relationship between life expectancy and per capita health expenditures
and with GDP per capita is curvilinear (Figure 9.2): life expectancy improves
with resource inputs only up to a certain level, beyond which life expectancy
actually declines with additional resource inputs. The relationship between
macroeconomics and health is complex and there is a vast literature (see,
for example, the review by Subramanian, Belli, & Kawachi, 2002). The use
of GDP as a measure of economic well-being of a region is itself problematic,
particularly in the northern context, where natural resource extractions by
external corporations and the importation of labour create wealth that is
not necessarily distributed to the inhabitants, especially indigenous people
(Glomsrød & Aslaksen, 2006).

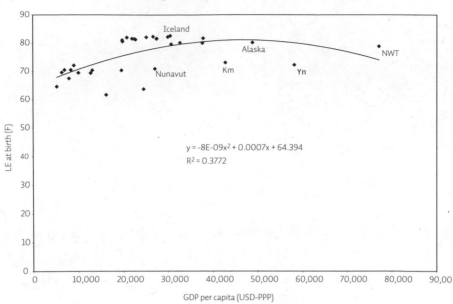

Figure 9.2 Relationship Between GDP per Capita and Life Expectancy at Birth Among Females

The relationship between tuberculosis incidence and the attainment of tertiary education is exponential: the disease rate rapidly declines with increases in education, and then tapers off with further rises in education levels (Figure 9.3). Such a relationship typifies the role of the social determinants of health: there is nothing unique about tuberculosis, as its substitution with other health problems will also show some association with some other measure of socio-economic status such as income or employment. Here tertiary education is chosen purely out of convenience, as it is relatively comparable across countries and educational systems, compared to, say, primary or secondary education, which affect a much larger proportion of the population and thus is a more appropriate measure, but is harder to compare internationally. Nevertheless, the state of higher education of a population/region does reflect the general state of education.

MULTIVARIATE MODELLING

To determine what factors are independently responsible for differences in health outcomes, a series of stepwise multiple linear regression models were run. Each model's independent variables list consists of the following

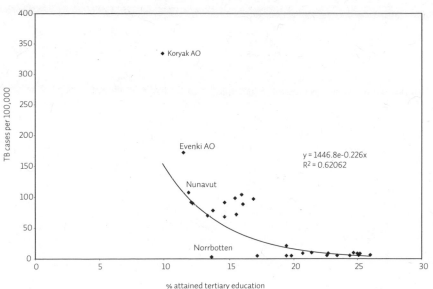

variables: mean January temperature, mean July temperature, percentage
urban, percentage indigenous, percentage population under age 15, per
capita health expenditures, GDP per capita, and percentage of adults who
attained tertiary education. The independent variable list represents a mix
of geographical/environmental, demographic, socioeconomic, and health
care variables. These are summarized in Table 9.2.

Rather than examining each model or the specific health outcome
separately, it is worth remarking that education, here representing socio-
economic status, is most frequently associated with health outcomes.
Health expenditures also appear in some models as an independent predictor. The proportion of indigenous people in the population has an impact
on fertility and mortality from certain causes (respiratory diseases and
injuries), independent of socio-economic status, which as a group tend to
be lower in than non-indigenous people in the same region. An independent
role for mean temperature (winter or summer) in health status can also be
observed—the colder the climate, the higher the infant mortality and the
lower the life expectancy. This corroborates other studies on the effect of
cold on health status (see the review by Mäkinen & Rytkönen, 2008) and

Table 9.2 Summary of Multiple Regression Models Identifying Independent Determinants of Health Outcomes

Dependent variable	Independent variables	Standardized coefficient [beta]	P value	Model R²
Infant mortality rate	January temperature	-0.893	0.000	0.768
	July temperature	-0.439	0.001	
	GDP	-0.280	0.013	
Life expectancy (M)	Education	0.488	0.017	0.723
	January temperature	0.328	0.002	
	Health expenditures	0.291	0.033	
Life expectancy (F)	Education	0.681	0.000	0.722
	January temperature	0.287	0.029	
ASMR – all causes	Education	-0.676	0.000	0.457
ASMR – circulatory	Education	-0.606	0.001	0.367
ASMR – respiratory	Indigenous	0.557	0.003	0.310
ASMR – injuries	Education	-0.768	0.000	0.589
ASMR – cancer	Indigenous	0.618	0.000	0.693
	Education	-0.396	0.003	0.693
Perinatal mortality rate	Education	-0.502	0.003	0.577
	January temperature	-0.387	0.018	
TB incidence	Education	-0.683	0.000	0.647
	Urban	-0.311	0.022	
Total fertility rate	Health expenditures	0.452	0.022	0.530
	Indigenous	0.396	0.023	
Fertility age 15–19	Indigenous	0.706	0.000	0.739
	January temperature	-0.346	0.005	

deserves further research as climate change in the Arctic has become an emerging public health issue. It is discussed in further detail elsewhere (Young & Mäkinen, 2010).

CONCLUSION

Substantial disparities exist across different circumpolar regions. In terms of disparities between the North and the nation-states to which they belong, two extremes can be identified. In Scandinavia, the northern regions are almost indistinguishable from the country-at-large in terms of most health indicators. At the other extreme are Greenland and the northern territories of Canada, especially Nunavut, where the disparities compared with Denmark and Canada are substantial. Alaska as a state tends not to differ much from the all-race US rates, but Alaska Natives within Alaska generally fare much worse than the state average. The health (and demographic) crisis in Russia is evident—with some indicators, such as incidence of tuberculosis, certain northern regions are at particularly high risk, within a country that is itself also at substantially elevated risk relative to other circumpolar countries.

In multivariate analyses, to identify factors that are most important in predicting health outcomes, social factors (usually education) consistently appear as independent determinants. Health care variables (such as expenditures per capita) are less important in the presence of other factors.

This study represents a first step in compiling and comparing health indicators across different northern regions in the circumpolar world, regions that have very different demographic makeup, political structures, and health care systems but share similar climate and geographic isolation and remoteness. There are still many gaps. Health status needs to be measured beyond the routinely available and time-honoured mortality-based indicators, for example, to include data on health-related behaviours and self-reported health status from surveys. However, expanding the scope of such measures requires additional work on the comparability of these measures internationally. Although the health of indigenous people is of major concern, it can only be indirectly addressed due to the lack of ethnic-specific health data in many jurisdictions.

Ultimately researchers and policy makers are interested in the answer to this question: Why are some northern regions healthier than others? International comparative studies of health and demography represent one potentially productive approach.

NOTE

1. For example, in comparing black and white infant mortality rates in the United States during the twentieth century, both rates have declined substantially. In terms of the black/white ratio, it has increased from about 1.5 to 2.5 by the end of the century, whereas, in terms of the black/white difference, it has declined from about 170 deaths/1,000 live births to 15 deaths/1,000 live births. So are things getting better or worse?

Table 9.3 Summary of Selected Geographic and Demographic Indicators of Circumpolar Countries and Regions

	Geographic Indicators				
	Main city	Latitude N	Avg. July temp.	Avg. Jan. temp.	Total population (2004)
United States					293,191,500
Alaska	Anchorage	61	15	-9	661,700
- Alaska Natives					109,500
Canada					31,995,200
Yukon	Whitehorse	62	13	-14	30,900
Northwest Territories	Yellowknife	62	16	-25	42,800
Nunavut	Iqaluit	64	7	-25	29,600
Denmark					5,401,200
Greenland	Nuuk	64	7	-8	56,900
- Born in GL					50,200
Faroe Islands	Torshavn	62	10	3	48,300
Iceland	Reykjavik	64	11	-2	292,600
Norway					4,591,900
Nordland	Bodø	67	12	-1	236,900
Troms	Tromsø	70	11	-3	152,700
Finnmark	Alta	70	12	-16	73,100
Sweden					8,993,500
Västerbotten	Umeå	64	15	-8	256,400
Norrbotten	Luleå	66	15	-10	252,700
Finland					5,228,200
Oulu	Oulu	65	16	-10	459,700
Lappi	Rovaniemi	67	14	-13	186,700
Russian Federation					143,821,200
Murmansk Oblast	Murmansk	69	12	-11	876,400
Kareliya Republic	Petrozavodsk	62	15	-12	705,900
Arkhangelsk Oblast	Arkhangelsk	65	15	-13	1,311,200
- Nenets AO	Naryan-Mar	68	12	-16	41,900
Komi Republic	Syktyvkar	62	17	-15	1,001,100
Yamalo-Nenets AO	Novy Urengoy	66	14	-23	519,200
Khanty-Mansi AO	Surgut	61	18	-18	1,462,800
Taymyr AO	Dudinka	69	13	-26	39,400
Evenki AO	Tura	64	17	-34	17,500
Sakha Republic	Yakutsk	62	18	-39	949,800
Magadan Oblast	Magadan	60	11	-16	176,500
Koryak AO	Palana	59	11	-15	24,100
Chukotka AO	Anadyr	65	11	-20	51,100

Density	% indigenous	% <15	% 65+	CBR	TFR	ASFR 15–19
32	2	21.1	12.4	14.1	2.03	43.7
0.40	18	24.0	6.1	15.7	2.27	44.6
-	-	30.6	6.0	23.2	3.14	81.9
3.50	5	18.6	12.7	10.6	1.52	15.2
0.07	26	20.1	6.1	11.5	1.58	23.8
0.04	51	25.9	4.2	16.0	1.96	47.8
0.02	86	36.0	2.3	25.6	3.04	119.7
125	0.20	18.7	14.9	12.1	1.76	6.7
0.03	89	26.2	5.3	16.1	2.39	56.6
-	-	28.4	5.6	16.5	2.42	58.4
35	0	23.6	13.4	14.6	2.51	15.9
3	0	22.9	11.7	14.5	2.00	18.3
15	1	20.0	14.9	12.5	1.81	10.0
7	1	20.1	16.1	11.3	1.82	15.5
6	5	20.4	13.6	12.4	1.80	13.8
2	31	21.2	13.1	13.2	1.91	17.9
20	0.40	18.1	17.2	10.7	1.64	4.6
5	2	18.0	17.4	9.8	1.56	3.1
3	7	17.4	18.3	9.3	1.67	4.6
17	0.20	17.9	15.3	10.9	1.74	10.6
8	0.10	20.4	13.9	12.9	2.15	13.8
2	2	17.9	15.7	9.6	1.84	12.3
8	0.20	16.4	13.0	9.6	1.27	26.7
6	0.20	16.2	7.1	9.5	1.20	24.4
4	0.70	16.1	12.2	9.8	1.25	26.4
2	0.60	16.8	11.5	10.1	1.31	27.5
0.20	19	23.1	6.5	14.5	1.95	53.0
20	0.10	17.7	8.1	10.6	1.30	30.9
0.70	7	22.6	1.6	13.1	1.61	31.3
3	2	20.6	3.0	13.0	1.56	32.4
0.05	25	23.4	2.9	14.8	1.91	49.3
0.02	23	24.3	4.2	14.9	2.01	46.1
0.30	3	24.3	5.3	14.5	1.82	38.1
0.40	3	17.1	4.6	10.6	1.27	32.4
0.10	41	22.3	4.2	11.9	1.81	57.8
0.10	31	21.1	1.9	12.9	1.63	45.8

Table 9.4 Summary of Selected Mortality and Morbidity Indicators of Circumpolar Countries and Regions

	Mortality and Morbidity Indicators			
	CDR	LE(M)	LE(F)	IMR
United States	8.4	74.6	80.0	6.9
Alaska	4.7	74.5	80.1	6.8
- Alaska Natives	6.3	68.1	75.4	10.8
Canada	7.1	77.2	82.2	5.3
Yukon	4.8	74.9	80.1	7.4
Northwest Territories	4.1	74.6	78.8	6.0
Nunavut	4.4	66.6	70.9	15.3
Denmark	10.7	74.9	79.6	4.7
Greenland	7.8	64.6	70.4	12.7
- Born in Greenland	8.4	63.7	77.0	12.1
Faroe Islands	8.0	77.0	81.3	1.7
Iceland	6.3	79.0	82.6	2.6
Norway	9.5	76.6	81.7	3.6
Nordland	10.3	76.7	82.0	3.9
Troms	8.9	76.5	81.5	4.0
Finnmark	9.2	74.6	80.6	4.7
Sweden	10.4	77.8	82.3	3.3
Västerbotten	10.3	77.6	82.1	3.8
Norrbotten	11.0	76.6	81.6	4.6
Finland	9.4	74.8	81.6	3.3
Oulu	8.5	74.3	81.6	2.7
Lappi	9.5	73.7	81.1	3.8
Russian Federation	15.8	58.8	72.1	13.3
Murmansk Oblast	12.8	57.6	70.5	11.0
Kareliya Republic	18.2	55.1	69.6	9.7
Arkhangelsk Oblast	17.1	55.9	70.5	10.1
- Nenets AO	13.2	53.8	69.0	10.1
Komi Republic	14.4	56.6	69.5	8.6
Yamalo-Nenets AO	5.8	61.8	72.2	13.4
Khanty-Mansi AO	6.9	61.3	73.0	6.9
Taymyr AO	10.3	54.2	67.5	17.3
Evenki AO	12.6	53.6	64.6	22.5
Sakha Republic	10.1	57.9	70.4	13.4
Magadan Oblast	12.5	56.6	69.4	11.8
Koryak AO	16.5	49.9	61.7	14.7
Chukotka AO	11.2	53.6	63.7	20.3

		Mortality and Morbidity Indicators			
ASMR all causes	ASMR circ.	ASMR resp.	ASMR injuries	Perinatal mortality	TB incidence
698.9	247.8	63.3	53.1	6.9	5.3
683.3	208.5	60.2	86.0	4.9	9.7
939.0	226.0	95.3	160.4	5.5	35.3
585.6	186.2	44.8	39.5	6.3	5.4
732.4	212.6	56.3	93.2	8.5	5.3
809.9	229.5	97.1	83.9	8.7	21.2
1,090.1	244.3	203.8	149.9	9.5	107.6
751.3	248.9	66.0	47.6	6.8	8.4
1,433.8	421.5	143.8	197.9	15.6	137.5
1,482.9	421.0	153.2	217.9	-	-
608.8	237.2	48.7	31.8	3.4	3.4
559.6	214.4	43.1	40.0	4.0	3.6
624.8	226.0	53.8	42.6	5.3	6.3
632.8	242.4	49.7	44.5	6.2	4.9
648.6	257.2	57.3	39.7	4.4	5.7
743.8	287.0	63.6	52.7	4.1	9.8
590.5	239.9	36.3	40.1	5.2	4.9
604.2	252.1	32.1	39.5	6.2	5.0
642.5	265.3	41.3	46.2	5.3	3.1
670.2	270.9	47.7	69.8	5.4	8.6
698.0	301.3	52.6	66.4	5.4	8.8
714.2	288.9	49.7	82.1	5.9	8.9
1,453.9	793.2	65.1	213.0	11.9	88.8
1,924.4	1,116.3	62.0	207.2	9.7	72.1
1,991.8	1,096.1	73.7	293.4	11.3	78.5
1,908.3	1,071.0	67.2	305.7	13.5	91.9
1,688.7	1,031.1	25.4	295.5	16.8	49.8
2,021.1	1,046.3	91.4	306.8	8.1	90.5
1,364.7	687.2	58.0	173.0	9.7	97.1
1,451.1	810.4	48.0	165.2	7.8	104.1
1,714.2	959.0	59.0	350.5	12.0	70.1
2,119.8	846.6	84.8	400.4	12.1	172.2
1,660.7	787.6	53.4	243.3	15.2	91.4
2,134.9	1,140.8	174.5	261.7	13.1	98.4
2,924.2	1,581.7	146.4	442.3	9.3	333.9
3,305.5	2,114.1	309.3	348.0	15.0	68.4

Table 9.5 Summary of Selected Socio-economic and Health Care Indicators of Circumpolar Countries and Regions

	SES		Health Care	
	GDP per capita [USD-PPP]	% attained tertiary education	Rate hosp. beds	Rate physicians
United States	37,750	24.4	275	214
Alaska	48,905	24.7	220	217
- Alaska Natives		7.1		
Canada	30,040	22.6	198	213
Yukon	32,740	23.4	191	197
Northwest Territories	77,212	19.4	586	119
Nunavut	27,102	11.9	115	24
Denmark	30,774	25.2	358	304
Greenland	19,552	-	713	153
- Born in Greenland		11.3		
Faroe Islands	22,738	-	547	186
Iceland	30,570	-	248	361
Norway	37,910	26	372	381
Nordland	20,775	19.8	333	335
Troms	22,478	25.1	401	587
Finnmark	19,803	21.4	220	368
Sweden	26,710	17.1	250	317
Västerbotten	25,159	19.4	351	381
Norrbotten	27,578	13.6	264	215
Finland	27,460	25	222	315
Oulu	21,938	22.7	214	349
Lappi	19,725	20.7	256	187
Russian Federation	8,950	16	969	436
Murmansk Oblast	8,288	15.5	1,004	447
Kareliya Republic	6,294	13.7	1,003	478
Arkhangelsk Oblast	6,891	12.1	1,106	454
- Nenets AO	43,542	9.9	1,373	432
Komi Republic	9,941	12.2	977	398
Yamalo-Nenets AO	58,175	16.8	1,058	460
Khanty-Mansi AO	42,824	15.9	909	434
Taymyr AO	7,874	13.3	2,063	457
Evenki AO	5,184	11.5	2,732	538
Sakha Republic	12,985	14.6	1,277	465
Magadan Oblast	12,629	15.4	1,409	526
Koryak AO	16,112	9.9	3,420	369
Chukotka AO	24,531	14.6	2,315	711

REFERENCES

Eurostat. (2002). *Health statistics: Atlas on mortality in the European Union*. Annex I: Standard European Population. Luxembourg: Eurostat.

Glomsrød, S., & Aslaksen, I. (Eds.). (2006). *The economy of the North*. Oslo: Statistics Norway.

Keppel, K., Pamuk, E., Lynch, J., Carter-Pokras, O., Kim, I., Mays, V., Pearcy, J., Schoenbach, V., & Weissman, J.S. (2005). Methodological issues in measuring health disparities. National Center for Health Statistics. *Vital and Health Statistics Series 2*(141), 1–16.

Kozlov, A., & Lisitsyn, D. (2008). Arctic Russia. In T.K. Young & P. Bjerregaard (Eds.), *Health transitions in Arctic populations* (pp. 71–102). Toronto, ON: University of Toronto Press.

Mäkinen, T., & Rytkönen, M. (2008). Cold exposure, adaptation and performance. In T.K. Young & P. Bjerregaard (Eds.), *Health transitions in Arctic populations* (pp. 245–264). Toronto, ON: University of Toronto Press.

Subramanian, S.V., Belli, P., & Kawachi, I. (2002). The macroeconomic determinants of health. *Annual Review of Public Health, 23*, 287–302.

Waldram, J.B., Herring, A., & Young, T.K. (2006). *Aboriginal health in Canada: Historical, cultural, and epidemiological perspectives* (2nd ed.). Toronto, ON: University of Toronto Press.

Young, T.K. (2008). *Circumpolar health indicators: Sources, data, and maps*. Oulu, Finland: Circumpolar Health Supplements No.3. Retrieved from http://www.ijch.fi/CHS/CHS%202008(3).pdf

Young, T.K., & Bjerregaard, P. (Eds.). (2008). *Health transitions in Arctic populations*. Toronto, ON: University of Toronto Press.

Young, T.K., & Mäkinen, T. (2010). The health of Arctic populations: Does cold matter? *American Journal of Human Biology, 22*, 129–133.

PART III
SOCIOLOGICAL PERSPECTIVES

10

DEATH AND THE FAMILY
A HALF CENTURY OF MORTALITY CHANGE IN THE REGISTERED INDIAN POPULATION OF CANADA AS REFLECTED IN PERIOD LIFE TABLES

Frank Trovato

INTRODUCTION

Though gradual and often imperceptible to the individual, the reduced appearance of death in society generates profound changes across virtually all spheres of the social world.[1] In the realm of the family institution, for instance, the transition from a high to a low mortality regime implies, among other things, that parents and their children live longer; and in comparison to earlier generations, the family unit becomes a potentially more enduring entity: children would have access to a larger pool of immediate and extended family members alive. In low mortality settings, the frequency with which a person witnesses the premature death of a loved one is diminished to such an extent that death becomes almost unnoticed (Aries, 1974). Orphanage is rare in a low mortality society, and the vast majority of fathers and mothers see their progeny reach adulthood. The majority of parents would enjoy the experience and excitement of witnessing their children's most memorable life events, including graduation from school, first job, marriage, and the arrival of grandchildren.[2] This picture contrasts sharply with the family situation in a high mortality regime, where life is frequently disrupted by the omnipresence of death. In this type of mortality regime, many children are orphaned early in life while a large percentage of parents would see some of their infants and young children snatched away them by the clutches of death. Maternal mortality rates would be high, as would be the incidence of widowhood and widowerhood (Dupaquier, Helin, Laslett, Livi-Bacci, & Sogner, 1981; De Rosas & Oris, 2002; Uhlenberg, 1980).

In this study, I examine a number of ideas about the interrelationship of mortality and the family with specific reference to one of Canada's Aboriginal subgroups, the Registered Indian population.[3] The analysis is grounded on various life table measures covering three distinct periods over approximately a half century: 1950–1952, 1976–1980, and 1996–2000. Over this 50-year period, this population has seen significant demographic growth as well as gradual improvements in socio-economic conditions (Romaniuc, 1980; 1984; 1987; Waldram, Herring, & Young, 2006). Through this investigation, I attempt to achieve two principal objectives: (1) to demonstrate that there have been significant survival improvements in the Registered Indian population in the latter half of the twentieth century; (2) to examine change in relative survival chances for Registered Indians in relation to the larger Canadian population, so as to determine whether the survival disadvantage of the Indians has either increased or decreased over time.[4] More broadly, through this analysis I hope to stimulate further research into the life course of Aboriginal children and their families.

In the proceeding section, I develop a theoretical framework concerning the association of mortality change and family change, building in part on selected historical evidence based on the Western European setting and then on impressionistic evidence concerning the First Peoples family in the pre-contact regime, followed by an account of the long-term effects of colonization (i.e., the post-contact regime) on the First Peoples' children and their families. The ensuing sections concern themselves with the analytical approach to the empirical analysis and related data issues. The study closes with the presentation of findings and some directions for further research.

THEORETICAL FRAMEWORK: MORTALITY DECLINE AND FAMILY CHANGE

The profound differences between Western and First Peoples family histories must be acknowledged at the outset. Of great significance in the case of First

Peoples are their experience of conquest, colonization, and the enduring effects of these historical developments on their lives (Lieberson, 1961; Livi-Bacci, 1997; Cunningham, 2003; Tait, 2003; Wesley-Esquimaux & Smolewski, 2004). There are no such parallels in the family history of non-Aboriginal peoples in the Western world. My reliance on aspects of the family history of the West is intended to serve as a conceptual backdrop against which family change, and more specifically, change in the societal conception of childhood relates to long-term mortality declines in society.

The Western Case

That there is a connection between long-term mortality declines and widespread change in the social conception of childhood has been the subject of intense interest among family historians. Space restrictions prevent me from delving extensively into this literature; therefore, I restrict myself to a brief sketch of an argument formulated by the history of mentalities scholar Philippe Aries (1962) in his groundbreaking work, *Centuries of Childhood*. Aries (1962) recognized that the history of the family is intimately connected to the history of childhood. He posed the idea that in ancien régime Europe the social psychological environment toward children was in general one of indifference. Through a deep analysis of indirect evidence (e.g., artworks, literature), Aries argued that until the late seventeenth century Western European society had no real conception of childhood: "In medieval society the idea of childhood did not exist...this awareness was lacking" (125).

Shorter (1975), in his *The History of the Modern Family*, presented an even more forceful argument, adding that in preindustrial Europe there prevailed a generalized atmosphere of neglect and "lovelessness" toward infants and young children. "Small children were seen...as creatures apart from people...They came at the Will of God, departed at His behest, and in their brief mortal sojourn deserved little adult sympathy or compassion" (169).[5] This type of orientation toward the child is thought to have persisted into the eighteenth century, and it was not until late in the nineteenth century that a definite change in mentality had taken hold. As the demographic transition unfolded in Europe, infant and childhood death rates dropped precipitously, eventually reaching modern low levels by the middle of the twentieth century. Eventually, birth rates declined as well, reaching unprecedented low levels in most Western countries by the third decade of the twentieth century. Against this demographic backdrop, there occurred massive displacement of population, away from the rural areas to the cities, a phenomenon fuelled by the industrial revolution.

In this context of rapid social change, a new view of the child emerged, a profound change in mentality, thought to have originated with the nobility and the privileged urban classes as far back as the sixteenth century, which then gradually diffused to the urban middle and lower classes, and finally much later in the nineteenth and early twentieth centuries, to the country-side (Shorter, 1975). Thus, according to Stone (1977), the key features of the modern family "were all well established by 1750 in the...middle and upper sectors of English society. The nineteenth and twentieth centuries merely saw their much wider social diffusion" (8–9).[6] The orientation of indiffer-ence in the ancien régime ultimately gave way to a new mentality based on caring, love, and affection toward the child. Increasingly, the private and public life of the child would become the subject of concern and attention to society (Becker, 1960; van de Walle & van de Walle, 1990). Formal mea-sures, from universal education to child protection laws, were instituted to promote children's well-being and healthy development. Within the realm of the family institution, parents began to invest more time and resources to their children as to enhance their future success in life. The era of the "child king" had begun (Aries, 1962, 1980).[7]

As to the causes of family change and shift in mentality toward the child, historians have posed varying explanations, ranging from ideologi-cal and religious to political, economic, and demographic factors (see e.g., Macfarlane, 1978; Macfarlane 1986; Stone, 1977; Shorter, 1995; Goode, 1970), but it would seem clear that, as Aries (1962) maintained, long-term mortality declines cannot be dismissed as a prime cause, most especially in regard to the societal conception of childhood. As infant and childhood death rates fell during the demographic transition parents eventually perceived large families as being no longer be necessary as a means of guaranteeing the survival of some of their progeny to adulthood (Davis, 1963). A small family size meant more attention and care could be devoted to fewer children. With this shift in thinking the extended family system typical of traditional folk society would gradually be supplanted by the nuclear conjugal form, characterized by Goode (1970) as being disposed "toward fewer kinship ties with distant relatives and a greater emphasis on the 'nuclear'...unit of couple and children" (1).[8] At its core, the new family form would be grounded in sentiment, which is a central feature of the modern psyche—the idea that we as individuals are willing to rearrange our lives, if necessary, so that emotional considerations toward those who are most meaningful to us gain the highest priority. This is perhaps most clearly evident in the high priority we place on romantic love as the basis for spouse/partner selection, or the extreme care and importance parents devote to their infants and children such that their welfare is the highest priority, and the reservation of our most intimate attention to immediate family members (Aries, 1972; 1980; Goode, 1970; 1959; Shorter, 1975; Stone, 1977; Macfarlane, 1986).

First Nations Peoples

At the risk of overgeneralization, from Jaffe's (1992) extensive exploration of the Amerindian family of the distant past, we learn that, depending on the geographic setting, the dominant modes of production would have been a combination of agriculture, pastoralism, and hunting and gathering. Health conditions are thought to have been poor and death rates excessively high, with life expectancy at birth in the range of between 30 and 35 years. This means that infant and childhood mortality rates must have been exceptionally high and conjugal unions frequently broken by the premature death of a partner, the consequent result being a high rate of orphanage of children (Jaffe, 1992). Such demographic conditions might promote very high birth rates in a population, as high death rates coupled with low fertility would ultimately lead to the population's extinction. By modern standards birth rates must have been quite high for the Amerindians.[9]

As to the structure of the family, Jaffe (1992) concluded the nuclear family could not have been viable and that therefore polygamy must have been widespread among the prehistoric Amerindians because "very high death rates would have led in many instances, to a lack of marriage partners and the necessity to 'double up'" (68). Furthermore, under the high mortality regime of the time, "extensive community or group support was needed" to raise the children: "both parents, or proxy parents, or some other parenting system, were needed to sustain the child both physically and emotionally and to pass on the cultural heritage" (70). Given that orphanage was very high, few children under the age of 15 would have both parents living; "therefore it follows that others in the tribe must have had to take on the parents' job or the group would soon disappear. There would be no new generation to replace the previous one" (70).

Concerning the Amerindians' mentality toward children, we lack concrete evidence, and all we can do is to rely on impressionistic accounts by missionaries during the early years after culture contact (e.g., *The Jesuit Relations*, 1906). From the writings of Father Joseph Francois Lafitau, most notably in his *Customs of the American Indians Compared with the Customs of Primitive Times* (1974/1724), we get the inescapable feeling that the Amerindian child occupied a focal point in his or her community, and would not have been treated with indifference or neglect:

> The Indian women are careful not to give their children to others to be nursed. They would think that they were cheating themselves out of the affection due a mother...The Indian women love their children extremely passionately and...their tenderness is...real, solid and lasting. (356)

More recent accounts are consistent with the view that in traditional Aboriginal culture, children have always been afforded a high place. The Royal Commission on Aboriginal Peoples (1996) wrote,

> [Aboriginal] children hold a special place in Aboriginal cultures. According to tradition, they are gifts from the spirit world and have to be treated very gently lest they become disillusioned with this world and return to a more congenial place. They must be protected from harm because there are spirits that would wish to entice them back to that other realm. They bring a purity of vision to the world that can teach their elders. They carry within them the gifts that manifest themselves as they become teachers, mothers, hunters, councilors, artisans and visionaries. They renew the strength of the family, clan and village and make the elders young again with their joyful presence. (23)

In the contemporary context, the many difficulties often reported in the media about Aboriginal families would seem to indicate a less tranquil situation concerning conditions faced by children. To a significant degree, the precarious conditions in which many First Nations people find themselves today are manifestation of the long-term effects of colonization, a point emphatically expressed by Armstrong (1996):

We are all very much aware of the history of the colonization process, which has systematically achieved, through various well-known measures, a breakdown in the structures upon which the well-being and health of our peoples depended. Our present social conditions bear this out. What is not well-known is that the influences of a patriarchal and imperialistic culture upon a people whose systems were fundamentally co-operative units has been not only devastating, but also dehumanizing to a degree that is unimaginable. I speak in particular of the damage to the family-clan systems as the base units of social order in Aboriginal societies in North America. I speak in specific of the severe and irreversible effects on Aboriginal women, and the resultant effect on our nations. In traditional Aboriginal society, it was woman who shaped the thinking of all its members in a loving, nurturing atmosphere within the base family unit. In such societies, the earliest instruments of governance and law to ensure social order came from quality mothering of children. (ix)

These wrongs continue to have serious negative effects on the lives of Aboriginal people in a variety of ways (see, for example, De Wit, De Wit, & Embree, 2000; La Prairie, 1994; LaRoque, 1994; Pfeiff, 2003; Royal Commission on Aboriginal Peoples, 1996; 1995; Shkilnyk, 1985; York, 1989; Smith, 2003; Tait, 2003; Wesley-Esquimaux & Smolewski, 2004; Annett, 2005; Anderssen, 1998). One of the most pernicious features of the colonial experience relates to the residential school system. Aboriginal communities have yet to recover fully from this experience (Royal Commission on Aboriginal Peoples, 1995, 1996; Tait, 2003; Wesley-Esquimaux & Smolewski, 2004; Barman, 2003; McGillivray, 1997).[10] In the days of the residential schools, children were separated from their families and communities. The colonial authorities felt that through education the children would be spared a brutish life on reserves and that they would benefit from learning the ways of the dominant culture. In reality, as Olive Dickason (2009) points out, the residential schools failed to provide the minimum standard of education to the children. Indeed, First Nations children were often treated as free labourers at the service of the school authorities (Barman, 2003; McGillivray, 1997). Worse, many of them endured horrendous psychological and physical abuse: "Children were controlled through abasement, cultural devaluation, humiliation and corporal punishment....[The experience can be summarized] as one marked by emotional, physical and sexual abuse, social and spiritual deprivation, and substandard education" (McGillivray, 1997: 158). It is no surprise that, given this experience, later, many of the individuals who had been abused as children would turn into abusers themselves. For many such individuals, violence has become a normative way of dealing with frustration and despair, consequently, a legacy of abuse (toward children especially) has permeated many of Canada's Native communities (La Prairie, 1994).

These problems acknowledged, it would be incorrect to assume complete uniformity in severity of conditions across all First Nations families in Canada. It would seem reasonable to assume that some families today are faring better than expected, while others may not be faring so well. An early study by Dosman (1972) provides some insight on this point. He identified three family types: the affluent Indian family; the anomic Indian family; and the welfare Indian family. The core characteristic of the affluent family is the attainment of middle-class status and lifestyles. In this type of family, traditional extended family relationships remain important as reflected in the frequent presence of non-nuclear family members in the home; marital and family relationships are generally stable; and individuals experience little overt discrimination from non-Aboriginals. The anomic families are economically marginal with low incomes, though respectable. They manage to maintain a stable family life and to provide for their children, but are handicapped by limited education and lack of training; consequently, they experience high degrees of job instability. The welfare family represents the largest group of Aboriginals (Larson, Goltz, & Hobart, 1994), distinguished by very high levels of personal disorganization, alcoholism, violence, the breakdown of normal family life, and high rates of teen pregnancies (Garner, Guimond, & Senécal, 2009; Smith, 2003; Guimond & Robitaille; 2008; Moffat & Herring, 1999; Chandler & Lalonde, 2008; Whitehead & Hayes, 1998). Many of the children in this family context are taken into care by the welfare authorities.

A CONJECTURAL THESIS

From this brief and admittedly incomplete overview of the First Nations family experience, I have suggested that in the pre-contact regime the Amerindian family may have been in a state of equilibrium with its environment, marked by high mortality and high fertility rates. Although one cannot be absolutely certain, it would also seem that Amerindian children were afforded a high place in their society and treated with much care and affection. With colonization the First Nations family began to suffer greatly, manifested to this day in a host of social pathologies across many Aboriginal communities.

Notwithstanding these facts, it is also true that during the historical period for which this study is concerned—early 1950s to the end of the twentieth century—First Nations Peoples in Canada have seen some socio-economic improvements and mortality declines. This leads me to surmise that the overall well-being of the average First Nations child and his family has been improving, and the family of the average child should now be a more enduring unit as compared to earlier times, when families were frequently broken by the early appearance of death. Fewer Aboriginal parents at the beginning of the twenty-first century face the wrenching experience of losing an infant or a child, even though there remains ample room for improvement in this area. The typical child would be expected to enjoy access to a larger constellation of family and kin most especially siblings, parents, and grandparents, and fewer children would experience orphanhood or the loss of a brother or sister. This conjecture may seem overly optimistic, but one should not lose sight of the fact that real progress is being noted across various aspects of Aboriginal life (see Ponting & Voyageur, 2001; Turcotte & Zhao, 2004a; 2004b; Jamieson, 2008).[11]

ANALYTICAL APPROACH

A question of interest in this investigation is whether the product of a sexual union would experience appreciably different survival probabilities if that union involved a Registered Indian couple as opposed to a man and woman from the mainstream Canadian society.[12] One may also ask whether a child born to the Aboriginal parents would experience the same chance of surviving past childhood as would a non-Aboriginal child. A number of such types of questions are examined, including: (1) the probability that a baby would survive his/her childhood; (2) the probability of a child experiencing the death of a sibling; (3) the probability that a mother would experience the death of at least one child; (4) the probability of a child being orphaned; (5) the probability of a child having four grandparents alive; (6) the probability that a child and his or her parents will celebrate the child's twentieth birthday; (7) the probability of a woman becoming widowed at different points in her conjugal union; (8) the probability of a middle-aged daughter having parents still alive; and (9) the average number of years of life remaining in old age for conjugal partners.

To illustrate the analytical approach, I use a hypothetical example from Keyfitz (1968: 16–17) involving a married couple where the husband is five years older than the wife, and at the time of marriage the groom was aged 25 and the bride 20 (see also the Appendix at the end of this chapter). For this couple, what is the joint probability that both partners will both be alive to celebrate their fortieth wedding anniversary? Using appropriate values in the life tables corresponding to ages x and $x + 40$ for men and women we compute

$$\left[\frac{l^f 60}{l^f 20} \right] \left[\frac{l^m 65}{l^m 25} \right]$$

where l corresponds to the survivorship function in the life table (the number of survivors to age x conditional on being alive at age x-1). The indexed values of x in this example are 20 and 60 for the woman, and 25 and 65 for the man. The symbols m and f represent the corresponding life table functions for males and females, respectively. Keyftiz's (1968: 17) calculation derives the following probability based on 1964 US life tables:

$$\left[\frac{84,572}{96,955} \right] \left[\frac{64,132}{94,854} \right] = 0.5898$$

Thus, under 1964 mortality conditions, the chance that a bride of 20 and a groom of 25 would be living 40 years later was almost 59%.

Other probabilities can be computed. For example, using the same data source, Keyfitz (1968: 17) found the conditional probability that the wife is alive and the husband dead 40 years after their wedding as being approximately 28%. That is,

$$\left[\frac{l^f 60}{l^f 20} \right] \left[1 - \frac{l^m 65}{l^m 25} \right] = \left[\frac{84,572}{96,955} \right] \left[1 - \frac{64,132}{94,854} \right] = 0.2825.$$

And the probability that the husband is alive and the wife dead, is nearly 9%:

$$\left[1-\frac{l^f60}{l^f20}\right]\left[\frac{l^m65}{l^m25}\right] = \left[1-\frac{84,572}{96,955}\right]\left[\frac{64,132}{94,854}\right] = 0.0864.$$

These types of conditional probabilities can be computed for different periods with appropriate life tables. The change in probabilities for a specific scenario can then be interpreted for possible improvements or deterioration in survival chances over time. Though clearly conjectural, this approach affords an indirect way of looking at some interesting interrelationships of mortality with aspects of the family life course and childhood in particular in the absence of complex longitudinal micro data. It is hoped that this analysis will help stimulate further study in this aspect of Aboriginal family life.[13]

DATA LIMITATIONS

The abridged life tables for Registered Indians are for the periods of 1950–1952, 1976–1980, and 1996–2000. Henceforth, these periods are referenced in relation to their respective central years, i.e. 1951, 1978, and 1998. The life tables for 1951 were computed with data from the Mortality Database (Statistics Canada Health Division) and appropriate population denominators listed in the published tabulations from the 1951 Census of Canada (Dominion Bureau of Statistics, 1953b). Unfortunately, from the 1951 census tables it is impossible to distinguish between Aboriginal subgroups; therefore, mortality and population data for the 1951 period are for all Aboriginal peoples (defined in the census as "Indians, Eskimos, and Métis"). The Registered Indian tables for 1978 and 1998 are from Verma, Michalowski, & Gauvin (2004). The deaths and population counts that were used to derive these tables were adjusted by these authors for late reporting of deaths and births to the Indian Register. For the total Canadian population the life tables used are single years of age tables for 1950–1952, 1975–1977, and 1995–1997, respectively (Dominion Bureau of Statistics, 1953b; Statistics Canada, 1979; 2002).

Some potential biases may exist in the Registered Indian data. This might be especially so for the post-1985 period (i.e., the 1998 tables). Specifically, the 1998 Registered Indian life tables are likely to have been greatly influenced by Bill C-31 registrations (Bill C-31 registrants are individuals who regained their Registered Indian status in accordance with legislative changes introduced in 1985). This population, which numbers about 110,000, resides largely off-reserve (more than 80%) and is believed to have quite different (better) health and mortality attributes than the pre-Bill C-31 (i.e., "regular" Status Indian) population, most of which resides on reserves (Clatworthy, personal communication, July 7, 2009). This gives rise to the possibility that any measured changes (i.e., improvements) over time in Registered Indian mortality (post Bill C-31) may be due at least in part to the addition of Bill C-31 registrants to the Registered Indian population. The impact of Bill C-31 registrants on mortality may be especially important among adult cohorts. Although Bill C-31 registrants form only about 18% of the total Registered Indian population, they account for close to 30% of the population aged 25 and over (Clatworthy, personal communication, July 7, 2009). If their mortality characteristics more closely approximate those of the general Canadian population, then the life tables prepared by Verma and colleagues (2004) for the post-1985 period (1998 tables) are likely to show an upward trend in survival among older age cohorts. Mortality changes among the non-C-31 population may be quite different and improvements among these cohorts less pronounced. Unfortunately, in the present investigation it is not possible to control for this possible source of biases.

Furthermore, as the life tables are based on the Indian Register death event data, mortality improvements associated with Bill C-31 registrants may also be overstated. This situation results from the fact that those who were entitled to registration under Bill C-31, but who died prior to application or approval, did not get recorded in the death records of the Indian Register. In other words, the register does not contain complete mortality records for the entitled Bill C-31 population (i.e., the Bill C-31 population on the register may be biased toward survivors). As a consequence, the 1998 survival probabilities for adult cohorts may be biased upwards. However, this bias, if it exists at all, would be expected to be small. Similarly, the impacts of Bill C-31 registrations on the mortality of cohorts under 20 years should be quite small. This is due to the fact that (in 1998) nearly all Bill C-31 registrants were over this age, and most of the children born to the Bill C-31 population (since 1985) do not qualify for registration (due to inter-marriage) and are not on the register or in the register's death event files. For younger cohorts, the survival probabilities of the 1998 series would appear to largely reflect the circumstances of children born to the pre-Bill

C-31 population. The effects of Bill C-31 registrations on Registered Indian mortality will be much more pronounced off-reserve due to the concentration of Bill C-31's in this location. (For most cohorts 25 and over, Bill C-31 registrants in 1999 accounted for more than 50% of the off-reserve population). This raises the possibility that improvement in survival probabilities for the Registered Indians after 1985 (i.e., in the 1998 life table in this analysis) may be largely associated with the off-reserve population. Since life tables for the on- and off-reserve populations are not available, it is not possible to test this proposition in the present investigation.

Finally, it must be acknowledged that there are vast differences between Aboriginal and non-Aboriginal peoples in Canada with respect to demography, health, and socio-economic and cultural conditions; therefore, family life must also differ in important ways. First Nations families are more likely to be poor and headed by a single parent; they have more than twice the rate of marital breakdown than the general population; many women never marry formally; and there is a high incidence of out-of-wedlock births (Garner, Guimond, & Senécal, 2009; De Wit, De Wit, & Embree, 2000; Larson, Goltz & Hobart, 1994).[14] Clearly, in view of these important differences one must interpret with caution the results of this analysis.

ANALYSIS

Table 10.1 looks at the demographic profiles of Registered Indians and the Canadian population at three points in time: 1951, 1978 (1976 for Canada), and 1998 (1996 for Canada). A quick inspection of this table reveals the very different demography of the Registered Indians. In 1951, Registered Indians had an estimated total fertility rate (TFR) of 6.22 children per woman, nearly twice that of the nation as a whole (3.50). In that year, the average length of life was about 55 and 59 years for First Nations males and females, respectively. In the larger society men and women enjoyed substantially longer life expectancies at birth (66 and 71 years, respectively). Under demographic conditions prevailing in the mid-to-late 1990s, Registered Indian women had an average of 2.90 children as compared to only 1.55 for Canadian women.

Both populations have witnessed important improvements in longevity since the early 1950s. By 1998, life expectancy for the Registered Indians had risen to 68.3 years for a baby boy and 74.5 years for a baby girl. For Canadian boys and girls these figures were considerably higher, at 75.7 and 81.5 years, respectively. Though clearly lagging in relation to the nation as a whole, the

Table 10.1 Demographic Dynamics of Registered Indians and Canada, 1951, 1978, and 1998

Demographic variable	1951		1978		1998	
	RI	Canada	RI	Canada	RI	Canada
CDR per 1,000	18.47	9.0	15.76	7.3	10.83	7.1
CBR per 1,000	43.66	27.2	30.20	15.7	22.40	12.2
Crude RNI (%)	2.52	1.82	1.45	0.84	1.16	0.51
e0 male	54.75	66.4	59.99	70.3	68.28	75.7
e0 female	59.00	70.9	66.61	77.5	74.49	81.5
TFR	6.22	3.50	3.59	1.82	2.90	1.55
GRR	3.04	1.71	1.75	0.89	1.41	0.76
NRR	2.51	1.61	1.63	0.87	1.37	0.75
Mean length of a generation (α)	27.23	28.08	25.58	26.80	24.35	28.64
% women surviving to (α)	83.4	94.7	94.0	97.8	98.0	99.0
Intrinsic birth rate per 1,000	43.26	25.16	2.73	10.34	2.09	7.74
Intrinsic death rate per 1,000	9.6	8.21	8.3	15.57	8.0	17.89
Intrinsic RNI (%)	3.37	1.70	1.90	-0.52	1.29	-1.01
% population <15	48.1	32.43	35.6	16.8	29.1	13.1
% population 15–64	49.6	60.26	57.8	62.7	60.1	58.9
% population 65+	2.3	7.31	6.7	20.5	10.9	28.0

Registered Indians have been progressing steadily through the demographic transition and are approaching the end of this process, as evidenced by their long-term declines in birth and death rates, rising life expectancy at birth, and declines in intrinsic rates of growth (from 3.37% in 1951 to 1.29% in 1998).

In this and subsequent tables: "RI" means Registered Indians; the periods for the general Canadian population correspond to 1951, 1976, and 1996, and for Canada 1951, 1976, and 1996. The symbol (α) denotes the average age of mothers at which they give birth to their daughters in the stable equivalent population. The age distributions pertain to the stable equivalent populations under the demographic conditions for a given period. Age-specific fertility rates for the Registered Indians are not available for 1951 (earliest period for which data are available is 1968). Age-specific fertility rates (per 1,000 women) for 1951 were estimated: 15–19 = 155.88;

Table 10.2 Probability of Child Survival to Age 15, Canadian Indians
and Others in Canada, 1951, 1978, 1998

Period	RI		Canada		RI/Canada	
	Boy	Girl	Boy	Girl	Boy	Girl
1951	0.8969	0.9079	0.9418	0.9542	0.953	0.951
1978	0.9466	0.9582	0.9805	0.9833	0.965	0.974
1998	0.9791	0.9815	0.9912	0.9926	0.988	0.989

20–24 = 315.31; 25–29 = 276.01; 30–34 = 225.00; 35–39 = 166.61; 40–44 = 74.61;
45–49 = 31.48. These rates were derived by assuming the same average rate
of annual change between 1951 and 1968 as between 1968 and 1985.

Probability of an Infant Surviving to Age 15

Table 10.2 shows differential probabilities of an infant surviving to age 15 for
boys and girls. A boy born into the Registered Indian group in 1951 had nearly
a 90% chance of surviving childhood, whereas a baby girl in this population had a probability of 91%. By the latter part of the 1990s, these survival
probabilities had risen to almost 98% for both boys and girls. The chances
surviving childhood for Canadian boys and girls have been notably better
across each of the three study periods, reaching over 99% by the late 1990s.
From a comparative point of view, it is of particular interest to note that the
relative survival gap between Registered Indians and Canadians in general
have been narrowing over time and, by the end of the observation period,
had virtually converged.

In this and subsequent tables, "RI/Canada" means the ratio of Registered Indians probability to that of Canada.

Probability of a First-born Child Experiencing the Death of a Sibling

Table 10.3 looks at another aspect of a child's possible encounter with death.
It looks at the probability of a first-born child (i.e., the index child; see this
chapter's Appendix) experiencing the death of at least one sibling under the
mortality conditions of 1951, 1978, and 1998. The probabilities are based on
the assumption that this event takes place before the index child reaches
age 15. From the results, it appears that the chance of a child seeing at
least one sibling perish in childhood has reduced substantially over time.
In 1951, there was a 17% probability of this event for the Registered Indians,

Table 10.3 Probability of the Index Child Experiencing the Death
of at Least One of His Siblings (Out of Two Siblings)
Before Reaching Age 15

Period	RI	Canada	RI/Canada
1951	0.1742	0.0506	3.44
1978	0.0835	0.0183	4.56
1998	0.0341	0.0077	4.43

whereas for Canadian children this would have happened for only 5% of cases. By the middle of the 1970s, the probability had declined to just over 8% for Registered Indians. The decline in probabilities for Canadian children was also significant: from just over 5% in 1951 to less than 2% in 1976. During the late 1990s, about three out of 100 Registered Indian children would experience the death of a younger sibling. For other Canadian children, this event would occur on the average to less than one out of every 100 children. Notwithstanding these important declines in probabilities, in a relative sense, as of late 1990s, a Registered Indian child had a fourfold greater chance of experiencing the death of a younger sibling as compared to the average Canadian child.

Probability of Orphanhood

Table 10.4 presents the probabilities that a child would be orphaned before he/she reaches age 15. Fortunately, both populations have seen improvements in this measure over time. In 1951, the chance of a Registered Indian child losing his father was about 10%, falling to 7% in 1978, and to 3% by 1998. The chances corresponding to the death of a child's mother follow a similar trend, though the corresponding levels are lower. In 1998, out of 10,000 Indian children, 10 would experience the death of the parents. Although the chances of this event happening have reduced significantly over time, in relative terms the risk of losing both parents remains substantial higher for the Registered Indian child (about 10 times greater in 1998).

Probability of a Child Having all Four Grandparents Alive

For many children, grandparents represent an important source of socialization and emotional support. As shown in Table 10.5, under 1951 conditions the likelihood of a newborn Registered Indian child having all

Table 10.4 Probability of a Child Being Orphaned Before Reaching Age 15 Under Varying Conditions

Condition	RI			Canada			RI/Canada		
	1951	1978	1998	1951	1978	1998	1951	1978	1998
Father dies	0.1041	0.0733	0.0339	0.0317	0.0256	0.0190	3.28	2.86	1.78
Mother dies	0.0885	0.0434	0.0188	0.0177	0.0066	0.0061	5.00	6.58	3.08
Both parents die	0.0092	0.0032	0.0010	0.0006	0.0002	0.0001	15.33	16.00	10.00
Number of children out of 10,000 experiencing the death of both parents	92	32	10	6	2	1			

Table 10.5 Probability of a Child Having all Four Grandparents Alive at Age 0 and 15

Period	Age 0			Age 15		
	RI	Canada	RI/Canada	RI	Canada	RI/Canada
1951	0.4700	0.6281	0.75	0.1365	0.3447	0.40
1978	0.4870	0.7644	0.62	0.1829	0.4679	0.39
1998	0.7832	0.8562	0.91	0.3561	0.6341	0.56

four grandparents alive was 47%. This was about 63% for newborns in the general population. By 1998, the likelihood of this condition occurring had improved to just over 78% for a Registered Indian infant and to about 85% for other infants in Canada. At age 15, the probability of an Indian child having four grandparents alive was just under 14% in 1951, increasing to almost 36% by 1998. For Canadian children aged 15 the corresponding probabilities were 34% and 63%, respectively. It is important to note that over time the relative differences in the two probabilities between Indians and others have been narrowing.

Probability of a Child and His/Her Parents Experiencing His/Her Twentieth Birthday

Under conditions of falling mortality parents are more likely to witness major life transitions among their adult children. On such significant transition is the celebration of a child's twentieth birthday. One way to look at the effects of changing mortality conditions on this type of situation is through a hypothetical scenario. Suppose a child has just been born to a mother aged

Table 10.6 Probability that a Child Just Born to a Mother Aged 22 and a Father Aged 27 Will Be Alive 20 Years Later and that Both Parents Are Also Alive at the Twentieth Birthday of Their Child

Male child	RI	Canada	RI/Canada
1951	0.6100	0.7459	0.82
1978	0.7058	0.8647	0.82
1998	0.8491	0.9164	0.93
Female child			
1951	0.6215	0.7584	0.82
1978	0.7255	0.8734	0.83
1998	0.8649	0.9198	0.94

22 and a father aged 27. What is the probability that in 20 years' time the child and both parents are alive to celebrate the child's twentieth birthday? Table 10.6 addresses this question for both male and female children. With respect to a male Registered Indian child, the chance of this joint probability increased from 61% in 1951 to almost 85% in 1998; and for an Indian female child, the chance rose from 62% to 86%, respectively. Improvements in these probabilities have been somewhat more substantial for the average Canadian boy and girl. It is important to note, however, that the relative survival disadvantage for the Registered Indians has been declining over time.

Probability of a Conjugal Union Being Broken by Death

As death rates decline the likelihood of a marriage being broken by death before a couple reaches old age should reduce significantly. If a man and a woman marry at ages 25 and 20, respectively, the risk of either spouse dying at any point in time will depend largely on the amount of time elapsed since the union took place. Table 10.7 considers three duration scenarios in the life of a conjugal union at 20, 40, and 50 years. In 1951, there was a 15% chance of a Registered Indian woman becoming widowed within 20 years of her union. The probability increases to 44% 40 years into the union and to 68% in the case of 50 years elapsed. For a Canadian couple the corresponding risks are much lower: 5% at 20 years; 29% at 40 years; and 55% at 50 years. Moving closer to the present, one notes major declines in the risk of widowhood for both populations. In 1998, an Indian woman had a 7% risk of becoming widowed within 20 years of her marriage, and 29% and 52% probabilities,

Table 10.7 Probability of a Female Spouse Becoming Widowed within 20, 40, and 50 Years of Union

Period	RI			Canada			RI/Canada		
	20 yrs.	40 yrs.	50 yrs.	20 yrs.	40 yrs.	50 yrs.	20 yrs.	40 yrs.	50 yrs.
1951	0.1462	0.4353	0.6751	0.0509	0.2891	0.5482	2.87	1.51	1.23
1978	0.1404	0.4048	0.6023	0.0416	0.2578	0.5163	4.78	1.57	1.17
1998	0.0701	0.2854	0.5187	0.0294	0.1657	0.3827	2.38	1.72	1.36

respectively, into the 40th and 50th year of the union. The corresponding values for a Canadian woman follow a similar declining trend but are
comparative lower. This means that the relative risk of widowhood is greater
among Registered Indian women.

Probability of a Middle-Aged Daughter Having Elderly Parents Alive

All other things being equal, increased longevity in a society should imply
that the lives of middle-aged children and the lives of their aging parents
will overlap for a longer number of years. However, one of the consequences
of increased longevity is that middle-aged daughters are often the principal caregivers for the aging parents, while at the same time also tending
to the responsibilities of their own young families (Kobrin, 1976). Table 10.8
considers three conditions: the probability of a 50-year-old daughter having
no parents alive; the chance of this person having only one parent alive;
and the likelihood of having both parents alive. As might be expected, in
both the Registered Indian and Canadian populations the odds of having no
living parents has declined over time due to major improvements in old age
mortality. For the Registered Indians, the drop has been from 42% in 1951
to 15% in 1998. For other Canadians, this fell from 19% to 6% over this time
interval. The likelihood of having one parent alive has increased since 1951
for the Indians but not for Canadians (who actually experienced a decline,
from 53% in 1951 to 43% in 1998, due to the larger survival gains associated
with the condition of having two parents alive among Canadian women.)
Since the sum of the probabilities across the different conditions in the table
must equal 1.0, the noted decline for Canadian women is a function of a
much larger increase in the odds of having two parents alive. Thus, in 1998,
the chance of a Registered Indian daughter having two aging parents alive
was only 34% and almost 51% for other women in Canada.

Table 10.8 Probability of a 50-year-old Daughter Having
0, 1, or 2 Elderly Parents Alive

Period	RI: parents alive			Canada: parents alive			RI/Canada		
	0	1	2	0	1	2	0	1	2
1951	0.4248	0.4695	0.1058	0.1944	0.5270	0.2785	2.19	0.89	0.38
1978	0.2894	0.5225	0.1881	0.1191	0.5192	0.3617	2.43	1.01	0.52
1998	0.1450	0.5199	0.3351	0.0637	0.4281	0.5081	2.28	1.21	0.66

Average Years of Life Remaining In Youth and In Old Age For Men and Women

In virtually all human populations female life expectancy exceeds male life expectancy. As shown in Table 10.9, the gap in life expectancy between the sexes has tended to widen in both Registered Indian and non-Aboriginal populations. For a hypothetical young couple forming a union at ages 25 (male) and 20 (female) the woman would have more years to live than her male partner. For instance, for the Registered Indians, the female advantage has been widening, from 7.2 years in 1951 to just over 10 years in 1998, while for Canadians this has changed from 8.2 to 10.3 years, respectively. Near the end of life, for a male partner aged 65 and his female partner aged 60, the evidence suggests that in both populations the differential has been widening in favour of females. In 1951, the advantage for Registered Indian females was 5.4 years and 5.3 years in the general population. By the later part of the 1990s, the gender gap had expanded to 8.1 years for Canadians and to 6.7 years for the Registered Indians. It can be concluded that, in general, women outlive their husbands; consequently, they spend more years in old age as widows.

CONCLUSION

In this investigation, period life tables for the Registered Indian and Canadian populations were examined over three points in time covering more or less a half century of observations between the early 1950s and the year 2000. The principal aim of the study was to demonstrate the importance of survival improvements for the Aboriginal populations over this period in the context of certain aspects of the family life course and to highlight relative differences in survival over time between the Registered Indians and the rest of Canada. It was surmised that increased survival probabilities for children should help promote stronger emotional bonds in the family unit and, in general, more enduring relationships between

Table 10.9 Average Years of Life Remaining at Selected Ages for Men and Women

Population	Average years of life remaining at age 20 Female	Average years of life remaining at age 25 Male	Difference: Female 20 – Male 25	Average years of life remaining at age 60 Female	Average years of life remaining at age 65 Male	Difference: Female 60 – Male 65
RI						
1951	46.0	38.8	7.2	17.4	12.0	5.4
1978	49.99	40.93	9.06	18.18	13.23	4.95
1998	56.20	46.11	10.09	20.63	13.90	6.73
Canada						
1951	54.4	46.2	8.2	18.6	13.3	5.3
1976	59.0	47.6	11.4	22.0	14.0	8.0
1996	61.9	51.6	10.3	24.1	16.0	8.1

parents, children, siblings, and extended kin. In a declining mortality context, the primacy of the child has been shown to rise to centre stage, becoming the focal point of the family unit, the main recipient of love, affection, protection, and caring. The elevation of the child to a centre stage in the family and in the community may be one of the defining features (though clearly not the only one) associated with long-term improvements in mortality. Survival improvements cannot materialize in the absence of important structural changes in society, most importantly health gains accrued from socio-economic modernization. This empirical study shows that the decline in mortality risk since 1951 has been quite pronounced for the Registered Indians. For instance, the probability of an infant surviving to age 15 increased significantly since 1951, such that by the late 1990s, 98% of all Registered Indian infants could be expected to attain age 15, a figure that is roughly comparable to the national population. Improvements were also noted in connection with the probability of a child experiencing the premature death of a sibling; the probability that a mother would see one or more of her children die prematurely; the odds of a child being orphaned; and the likelihood of a child having all four grandparents alive.

These empirical results can only be viewed as suggestive. Major life course events, such as timing of entry into first union, timing and spacing of children, and other family dynamics, may occur on average at different points in the typical life course of Aboriginal and non-Aboriginal persons. For instance, given the relatively high incidence of teen motherhood among

Aboriginals in Canada, it is likely that many more Registered Indian children live with a lone-parent mother as compared to non-Aboriginal children (Garner, Guimond, & Senécal, 2009; O'Donnel, 2008). Consequently, death events are likely to have quite different consequences for Aboriginal and non-Aboriginal families.

An important complexity that must be addressed in subsequent research involves the growing number of mixed Aboriginal unions and the children of such unions. Perhaps as much as one-half of all children born to Registered Indians since 1985 (i.e., after Bill C-31) are the result of mixed parenting arrangements. In off-reserve areas this may be even higher (Clatworthy, personal communication, July 7, 2009). How do the family dynamics of mixed unions differ from unions in which both partners are Aboriginal? To what extent are the family processes hypothesized in the present investigation actually occurring in these different types of unions? Deep analyses are needed if we are to further our understanding of the socio-emotional interior of the Aboriginal family in its varied socio-geographical contexts (urban, rural, north, south, off-reserve, on-reserve, Status, non-Status).

In closing, I have surmised that over the course of the second half of the twentieth century, in a context of significant mortality declines coupled with gradually improving socio-economic conditions, the First Nations family has been changing, becoming a more enduring entity with the child as its central focus of attention. I suspect this process is well underway among the younger generations of First Nations peoples and that further significant improvements in family stability are forthcoming, such that fewer Aboriginal children are placed in the care of welfare authorities. This may sound overly optimistic in the face of the many negative reports in the media on the plight of Canada's First Nations peoples; but one should not lose sight of the improvements that have been taking place. Indeed, scholars have recently challenged the "deficit paradigm" toward Canadian Aboriginals in the light of positive social, cultural, and economic developments in this population over the latter half of the twentieth century and into the new millennium (Ponting & Voyageur, 2001; Redding, 2003; Townsend & Wernick, 2008; Castellano, 2008; Jamieson, 2008).[15]

APPENDIX: ANALYTICAL STRUCTURE
As a way to illustrate the analytical approach taken in this study, Table 10.10 shows a hypothetical three-generation family progressing through its life

Table 10.10 Schematic Structure for the Study of Mortality and the Family Life Course (Husband, Wife, Three Children, and Grandparents) Progressing Through the First 15 Years in the Life of the Index Child (the First-Born Child)

Family member	Age of family member at time of union of index child's parents	Age/time axis (index child as reference)				
		Year (0)	Year (2)	Year (4)	...	Year (14)
Mother	age 20	age 22	age 24	age 26	...	age 36
Father	age 25	age 27	age 29	age 31	...	age 41
Index child— boy/girl		birth of index child	age 2	age 4	...	age 14
Second child— boy/girl			birth of sibling 1	age 2	...	age 12
Third child— boy/girl				birth of sibling 2	...	age 10
Paternal grandfather	age 52	age 54	age 56	age 58	...	age 68
Paternal grandmother	age 47	age 49	age 51	age 53	...	age 63
Maternal grandfather	age 47	age 49	age 51	age 53	...	age 63
Maternal grandmother	age 42	age 44	age 46	age 48	...	age 58

course. The progression of the family members through age and time is indexed on the basis of the first-born child (i.e., the index child) of a couple who had formed a conjugal union when the husband/male partner was aged 25 and the wife/female partner aged 20. This couple has three children, each spaced by two years. Their first progeny is the index child, born when the father was 27 and the mother 22 years old. The index child and the other members of the family (including the paternal and maternal grandparents) are followed 15 years into the life of the family.

AUTHOR'S NOTE

Many thanks to Ravi Verma for allowing me to use the life tables that he and his colleagues developed for the Registered Indian population based on data from the Indian Register. Thanks also to Shirley Loh for providing me with the fertility rates for the Registered Indians. I have benefited from the careful critiques and comments of earlier versions of this chapter by Stewart Clatworthy, Anatole Romaniuk, N. Lalu, Thomas Burch, and Judah Matras. It goes without saying that any errors and omissions are the sole responsibility of the author.

NOTES

1. A variety of explanations of mortality change through history have been formulated under the headings of demographic, epidemiological, and health transitions. See, for example, Omran, 1971; Caldwell, 1990; McKeown, 1976; Preston, 1976; Riley, 2001.

2. According to Uhlenberg (1980), many of the most significant changes in the Western family over approximately the past one and a half centuries cannot be adequately understood without a clear recognition of the profound changes in survival probabilities that have occurred—including, for example, the changing status of children, the increasing independence of the nuclear family, the virtual disappearance of orphanages and foundling homes, the rise in societal support of the elderly, the decline in fertility, and even the rise in divorce. In his study of the American case, Uhlenberg (1980) discovered that around 1900 in the United States, parents had on average 4.2 children, and about 62% of all couples would experience the death of one or more of their progeny before they reached age 15. By 1940, the average family size had fallen to just under three children and the probability of parents seeing one of their offspring perish in childhood declined to 16%. By 1976, this probability had dropped to just 4% (Uhlenberg, 1980). Concerning the role of death in family disruption in Canada, until midway into the twentiteth century the death of a spouse was the principal factor for the breakup of marriages (Basavarajappa, 1978). By 1960, spousal death was still the most important determinant of the dissolution of a marriage, accounting for 90% of all broken marriages. However, by the early 1980s, death became less important in a context of rapidly increasing divorce rates and improved survival probabilities (Larson, Goltz, & Hobart, 1994; Matras, 1989).

3. A Registered Indian is a person who by virtue of the Indian Act is deemed by the Canadian government to be an Indian and therefore entitled to Registered Indian status (sometimes referred to as "Status Indian"). "Non-Registered Indians" are sometimes referred to as "non-Status Indians" in the literature. Throughout this chapter, I shall at times uses terms such as "First Peoples," "First Nations," and "Aboriginal Peoples" when describing the Aboriginal population of Canada in plural terms. The term "Amerindian" is also used in certain places to refer broadly to the North American First Peoples in the context of the pre-contact regime.

4. A complete examination incorporating the other Aboriginal groups (Métis, Inuit, and non-Status Indians) could not be executed as the necessary life tables do not exist.

5. A glimpse of the high mortality context in preindustrial Europe is offered by Levine (1977), based on family reconstitution data from the French village of Colyton. Between 1538 and 1849, the child survival rate fluctuated between 62%

and 70%, which means that death probabilities for children were in the range of 30% and 38%. These probabilities for contemporary children in the industrialized world seldom exceed 10%.

6. For Stone (1977), "affective individualism" (i.e., sentiment) is a core feature of the modern Western family. That is, "intensified affective bonding of the nuclear core at the expense of neighbours and kin; a strong sense of individual autonomy and the right to personal freedom in the pursuit of happiness; a weakening of the association of sexual pleasure with sin and guilt; and a growing desire for physical privacy" (8–9).

7. This theme was adopted by Becker (1960) to develop an economic theory of fertility decline, in which he asserted that children in modern society can no longer be viewed as instrumental utility for parents (e.g., extra hands on the family farm, old age security, etc.), but rather as a source of pride, joy, satisfaction, and self-fulfillment for parents. In modern time, couples are motivated to have children because of their perceived psycho-emotional utility. Others have also relied on this same idea as part of theorizing about the fertility transition of developing societies (see e.g., Caldwell, 1981).

8. For Shorter (1975) and Stone (1977) the precipitating factor for the elevation of the child in society was a change in attitude (mentality) by parents and the community toward the child. "With the surge of sentiment...infant mortality plunged, and maternal tenderness became part of the world we know so well" (Shorter, 1975: 204). What remains unanswered is what caused the change in mentality in the first place. For Aries (1962), the change in mentality was the result of large-scale mortality declines, especially infant and childhood mortality. As infant mortality dropped, parents began to change emotional orientation toward the child.

9. Jaffe (1992) opined that the Amerindian birth rate "was probably at or near the physiological limit" (77). However, the case can be made that fertility levels might in fact have been suboptimal. As noted by Romaniuk (in this volume), a combination of adversities may have accounted for this, including frequent warfare, high levels of sterility, a high frequency of spontaneous abortions and maternal mortality, malnutrition, and cultural practices that worked against the achievement of high birth rates (e.g., prolonged breastfeeding of infants).

10. Although day schools for Aboriginal children set up by the colonial governments go back to the time of New France in the seventeenth century, the establishment of residential schools, in which Aboriginal children were taken to live and study away from their communities, is thought to have first occurred in 1848. The last residential school was closed in 1996. It is believed that during the span of this period some 150,000 Aboriginal children were affected, of which 80,000 are still alive (CBC Newsworld, June 10, 2008). For more coverage on the residential schools and their legacy, the interested reader is referred to various stories in the Globe and Mail (e.g., January 7, 2008; February 25, 2008; June 9, 2008; June 10, 2008a, June 10, 2008b; June 18, 2008; June 28, 2007; April 24, 2007; April 25,

2007; October 27, 2008). On the theme of "healing" from the residential school experience among First Nations people, see also: Cunningham (2003); Young (2003); Anderson & Lawrence (2003); Wesley-Esquimaux & Smolewski (2004); Castellano, Archibald, & DeGagné (2008).

11. See also the special issue of *Horizons* (Winter 2008).

12. The term "sexual union" is used to take into account the possibility that a couple may form either a traditional marital union or a consensual union (i.e., cohabiting).

13. To adequately study the family life course that would include mortality as a family event would require a large cohort of cases followed through at least several decades of observation. With such data various family processes could be investigated: union formation; age at which parents have their first and last child; the spacing of children; age at which children exit the parental household; age at retirement from the labour force by one or both parents; and the timing of death for family members, and so forth.

14. For the situation concerning American Indians see Sandefur, Rindfuss, & Cohen (1996) and Snipp (1989).

15. As a further illustration of this point, Jeff Reading (2003), a former scientific director of the Institute of Aboriginal Peoples' Health of the Canadian Institutes of Health Research, has openly indicated that the vast majority of Canadian Aboriginals are in actual fact quite well: "I would characterize most Aboriginals as being healthier than most non-Natives" (41). With specific reference to media stories of Aboriginal children in Labrador sniffing gasoline, Redding writes that, "Anyone who's never been to a Native community might assume that's endemic. In fact, most of the children are healthy and well-adjusted. Definitely, we have problems, but we really have to balance the message" (41).

REFERENCES

Allard, Y.E., Wilkins, R., & Berthelot, J.M. (2004). Premature mortality in health regions with high Aboriginal populations (Statistics Canada, Catalogue No. 82-003). *Health Reports*, 15(1), 51–60.

Anderssen, E. (1998, October 12). Canada's squalid secret: Life on Native reserves. *The Globe and Mail*, pp. A1, A4.

Anderson, K., & Lawrence, B. (Eds.). (2003). *Strong women stories: Native vision and community survival*. Toronto, ON: Sumach Press.

Annett, K.D. (2005). *Hidden from history: The Canadian holocaust* (2nd ed.). Vancouver, BC: The Truth Commission into Genocide in Canada.

Aries, P. (1962). *Centuries of childhood: A social history of family life* (R. Baldick, Trans.). New York, NY: Vintage.

———. (1974). *Western attitudes toward death: From the middle ages to the present* (P.M. Ranum, Trans.). Baltimore, MD: Johns Hopkins University Press.

———. (1980). Two successive motivations for the declining birthrate in the West. *Population and Development Review*, 6, 645–650.

Armstrong, J. (1996). Invocation: The real power of Aboriginal women. In C. Mille & P. Chuchryk (Eds.), *Women of the First Nations: Power, wisdom, and strength* (pp. ix-xii). Winnipeg, MB: University of Manitoba Press.

Barman, J. (2003). Schooled for inequality: The education of British Columbia Aboriginal children. In N. Janovicek & J. Parr (Eds.), *Histories of Canadian children and youth* (pp. 212–235). Toronto, ON: Oxford University Press.

Basavarajappa, K.G. (1978). *Marital status and nuptiality in Canada. 1971 census of Canada profile studies. Vol. V* (Part 1). Bulletin 5.1-4 (Catalogue No. 8-1200-553). Ottawa, ON: Minister of Supply and Services.

Becker, G. (1960). An economic analysis of fertility. In *Demographic and economic change in developed countries. Universities National Bureau Conference Series No. 11* (pp. 209–240). Princeton, NJ: Princeton University Press.

Caldwell, J. (1981). *A theory of fertility decline.* New York, NY: Academic Press.

————. (1990). Introductory thoughts on health transition. In J.C. Caldwell, S. Findley, P. Caldwell, G. Santow, W. Cosford, J. Braid, & D. Broers-Freeman (Eds.), *What we know about health transition: The cultural, social and behavioural determinants of health* (pp. xi-xii). Canberra: Australian National University.

Castellano, M.B. (2008). Reflections on identity and empowerment: Recurring themes in the discourse on and with Aboriginal youth. *Horizons, 10*(1), 7–12.

Castellano, M.B., Archibald, L., & DeGagné, M. (2008). *From truth to reconciliation: Transforming the legacy of residential schools.* Ottawa, ON: Aboriginal Healing Foundation.

CBC Newsworld. (2008, June 10). Residential schools for Natives. [Television broadcast]. Canadian Broadcasting Corporation.

Chandler, M.J., & Lalonde, C.E. (2008). Cultural continuity as a protective factor against suicide in First Nations youth. *Horizons, 10*(1), 68–72.

Chiang, C.L. (1984). *The life table and its applications.* Malabar, FL: Krieger.

Corrado, R., & Cohen, I. (2008). The over-representation of Aboriginal youth in custody: Policy challenges. *Horizons, 10*(1), 79–82.

Cunningham, C. (2003). Indigenous by definition, experience, or world view. *British Medical Journal, 327*(August 23), 403–404.

Curry, B. (2007, April 25). Pupils' deaths included in panel mandate. *The Globe and Mail*, p. A4l.

————. (2008, June 10). Apology to spare no detail, Strahl says. *The Globe and Mail*, pp. A1, A4.

————. (2008, October 27). Hunt begins for long-missing students: Neglected graves probed in renewed effort to solve mystery of aboriginal children's fates. *The Globe and Mail*, pp. A1, A8.

Curry, B., & Howlett, K. (2007, April 24). Natives died in droves as Ottawa ignored warnings. *The Globe and Mail*, pp. A1, Al4.

Davis, K. (1963). The theory of change and response in modern demographic history. *Population Index, 29*(4), 345–366.

De Rosas, R., & Oris, M. (Eds.). (2002). *When dad died: Individuals and families coping with distress in past societies*. Bern: Peter Lang.

De Wit, M.L., De Wit, D.J., & Embree, B.G. (2000). Natives' and non-Natives relative risk of children's exposure to marital dissolution: The role of family volatility and implications for future nuptiality in Native populations. *Canadian Studies in Population*, 27(1), 107–133.

Dickason, O.P. (with D.T. McNab). (2009). *A concise history of Canada's First Nations: A history of founding peoples from earliest times*. (4th ed.). Toronto, ON: Oxford University Press.

Dominion Bureau of Statistics. (1953a). *Canadian life table 1951*. Ottawa, ON: Minister of Trade and Commerce.

———. (1953b). *Ninth census of Canada, 1951. Volume II: Population*. Cross-classification of characteristics. Ottawa, ON: Minister of Trade and Commerce.

Dosman, E.J. (1972). *Indians: The urban dilemma*. Toronto, ON: McClelland & Stewart.

Dunning, R.W. (1959). *Social and economic change among the Northern Ojibwa*. Toronto, ON: University of Toronto Press.

Dupaquier, J., Helin, E., Laslett, P., Livi-Bacci, M., & Sogner, S. (Eds.). (1981). *Marriage and remarriage in populations of the past*. New York, NY: Academic Press.

Flanagan, T. (2008, June 18). The worst choice, except for all the others. *The Globe and Mail*, p. A13.

Frideres, J.S., & Gadacz, R.R. (2008). *Aboriginal peoples in Canada: Contemporary conflicts* (8th ed.). Toronto, ON: Prentice Hall.

Garner, R., Guimond, E., & Senécal, S. (2009, June 9). Aboriginal teenage mothers: Their socio-economic conditions in early adulthood. Paper presented at the Canadian Public Health Association annual conference, Winnipeg.

Goode, W.J. (1970). (1959). The theoretical importance of love. *American Sociological Review*, 24, 38–47.

———. *World revolutions and family patterns*. New York, NY: The Free Press.

Gottlieb, B. (1993). *The family in the Western world from the black death to the industrial age*. New York, NY: Oxford University Press.

Guimond, E., & Robitaille, N. (2008). When teenage girls have children: Trends and consequences. *Horizons*, 10(1), 49–51.

Hanawalt, B.A. (2001). Childrearing among the lower classes of late Medieval Europe. In R.I. Rotberg (Eds.), *Population history and the family: A journal of interdisciplinary history reader* (pp. 23–44). Cambridge, MA: MIT Press.

Jaffe, A.J. (1992). *The first immigrants from Asia: A population history of the North American Indians*. New York, NY: Plenum Press.

Jamieson, R. (2008). The national Aboriginal Achievement Foundation: Aboriginal success stories. *Horizons*, 10(1), 38–39.

Keyfitz, N. (1968). *Introduction to the mathematics of population*. Reading, MA: Addison-Wesley.

Kobrin, F.E. (1976). The fall in household size and the rise of the primary individual in the United States. *Demography*, 13, 127–138.

Lafitau, Father J.F. (1974/1724). *Customs of the American Indians compared with the customs of primitive times* (Two volumes, W.N. Fenton & E.L. Moore, Ed. and Trans.). Toronto, ON: The Champlain Society.

La Prairie, C. (1994). *Seen but not heard: Native people in the inner city*. Ottawa, ON: Minister of Justice and Attorney General of Canada.

LaRoque, E.D. (1994). *Violence in Aboriginal communities*. Ottawa, ON: Royal Commission on Aboriginal Peoples.

Larson, L.E., Goltz, J.W., & Hobart, C.W. (1994). *Families in Canada: Social context, continuities and change*. Scarborough, ON: Prentice Hall.

Leacock, E. (1986). The Montagnais-Naskapi of the Labrador Peninsula. In R.B. Morrison & C.R. Wilson (Eds.), *Native peoples: The Canadian experience* (pp. 140–171). Toronto, ON: McClelland & Stewart.

Levine, D. (1977). *Family formation in an age of nascent capitalism*. New York, NY: Academic Press.

Lieberson, S. (1961). A societal theory of race relations. *American Sociological Review, 26*(6), 902–910.

Livi-Bacci, M. (1997). *A concise history of human world population* (C. Ipsen, Trans.). Cambridge, MA: Blackwell.

Macfarlane, A. (1978). *The origins of English individualism: The family, property and social transition*. Oxford, UK: Basil Blackwell.

————. (1986). *Marriage and love in England 1300–1840*. Oxford, UK: Basil Blackwell.

MacGregor, R. (2007, June 28). Fontaine walks the line between abuses past and protests present. *The Globe and Mail*, pp. A1, A12.

Marmot, M., & Wilkinson, R.G. (Eds.). (2005). *Social determinants of health* (2nd ed.). Oxford, UK: Oxford University Press.

Matras, J. (1989). Demographic trends, life course, and family cycle—the Canadian example: Part I. Changing longevity, parenting, and kin-availability. *Canadian Studies in Population, 16*(1), 1–24.

McGillivray, A. (1997). Therapies of freedom: The colonization of Aboriginal childhood. In A. McGillivray (Ed.), *Governing childhood* (pp. 135–199). Aldershot, UK: Dartmouth.

McIlroy, A. & Curry, B. (2008, June 9). 97 years later, apology at last. *The Globe and Mail*, pp. A1, A4.

McKeown, T. (1976). *The modern rise of population*. London, UK: Edward Arnold.

Moffat, T., & Herring, A. (1999). The historical roots of high rates of infant death in Aboriginal communities in Canada in the early twentieth century: The case of Fisher River, Manitoba. *Social Science and Medicine, 48*, 1821–1832.

O'Donnell, V. (2008). Selected findings of the Aboriginal Children's Survey 2006: Family and community. *Canadian Social Trends, 86*, 65–72.

Omran, A.R. (1971). The epidemiologic transition: A theory of the epidemiology of population change. *Milbank Memorial Fund Quarterly, 49*(4), 509–538.

O'Neill, K. (2008, January 7). Residential school money hits the north. *The Globe and Mail*, p. A7.

————. (2008, February 25). Graphic list of abuse to settle claims. *The Globe and Mail*, p. A10.

Pfeiff, M. (2003). Out of Davis Inlet. *Canadian Geographic, 123*(1), 42–52.

Pinchbeck, I., & Hewitt, M. (1969). *Children in English society: From Tudor times to the Eighteenth Century*. Volume I. London, UK: Routledge and Kegan Paul.

————. (1973). *Children in English society: From the Eighteenth Century to the Children Act 1948*. Volume II. London, UK: Routledge and Kegan Paul.

Ponting, R.J., & Voyageur, C.J. (2001). Challenging the deficit paradigm: Grounds for optimism among First Nations in Canada. *The Canadian Journal of Native Studies, 21*(2), 275–307.

Preston, S.H. (1976). *Mortality patterns in national populations*. New York, NY: Academic Press.

Reading, J. (2003, August 4). Most Aboriginal children are healthy and well-adjusted. *Maclean's, 41*.

Riley, J.C. (2001). *Rising life expectancy: A global history*. Cambridge, UK: Cambridge University Press.

Rollett-Echalier, C. (1990). *La politique a l'egard de la petite enfance sous la IIIe Republique*. Paris: Institut National d'Études Démographiques.

Romaniuc, A. (1984). *Current demographic analysis. Fertility in Canada: From baby-boom to baby-bust* (Catalogue No. 91-524E). Ottawa, ON: Minister of Supply and Services Canada.

————. (1987). Transition from traditional high to modern low fertility: Canadian Aboriginals. *Canadian Studies in Population, 14*(1), 69–88.

————. (2000). Aboriginal population of Canada: Growth dynamics under conditions of encounter of civilisations. *The Canadian Journal of Native Studies, 20*(1), 95–137.

Royal Commission on Aboriginal Peoples. (1995). *Choosing life: Special report on suicide among Aboriginal people*. Ottawa, ON: Minister of Supply and Services Canada.

————. (1996). *Gathering strength*. Ottawa, ON: Minister of Supply and Services.

Sandefur, G.D., Rindfuss, R.R., & Cohen, B. (Eds.). (1996). *Changing numbers, changing needs: American Indian demography and public health*. Washington, DC: National Academy Press.

Shkilnyk, A.M. (1985). *A poison stronger than love: The destruction of an Ojibwa community*. New Haven, CT: Yale University Press.

Shorter, E. (1975). *The making of the modern family*. New York, NY: Basic Books.

Sinclair, C.M. (1998). Suicide in First Nations people. In A.A. Leenaars, S. Wenckstern, I. Sakinofsky, R.J. Dyck, M.J. Kral, & R.C. Bland (Eds.), *Suicide in Canada* (pp. 165–178). Toronto, ON: University of Toronto Press.

Smith, G. (2003, February 14). Assumptions challenged on wife abuse among natives. *The Globe and Mail*, p. A5.

Snipp, M.C. (1989). *American Indians: The first of this land*. New York, NY: Russell Sage Foundation.

Statistics Canada. (1979). *Life tables, Canada and provinces and territories, 1975–1977* (Catalogue No. 84-532). Ottawa, ON: Minister of Supply and Services.

————. (1981). *Deaths by cause, age, sex, period, and ethnicity.* [Special tabulation by author]. Mortality Database. Vital Statistics and Disease Registry. Ottawa, ON: Statistics Canada.

————. (2002). *Life tables, Canada and provinces and territories, 1995–1997* (Catalogue No. 84-537-XIE). Ottawa, ON: Minister of Supply and Services.

Stone, L. (1977). *Love, sex and marriage in England, 1500–1800.* New York, NY: Harper and Row.

Sweetgrass, F. (2007, June 28). Make Canada see the oppression. *The Globe and Mail,* p. A17.

Tait, C.L. (2003). *Fetal alcohol syndrome among Aboriginal people in Canada: Review and analysis of the intergenerational links to residential schools.* Ottawa, ON: The Aboriginal Healing Foundation.

Thwaites, R.G. (Ed.). (1906). *The Jesuit relations and allied documents* (71 volumes). Cleveland, OH: Burrows Brothers.

Townsend, T., & Wernick, M. (2008). Hope or heartbreak: Aboriginal youth and Canada's future. *Horizons, 10*(1), 4–6.

Turcotte, M., & Zhao, J. (2004a). *A portrait of Aboriginal children living in non-reserve areas: Results from the 2001 Aboriginal Peoples Survey* (Catalogue No. 89-597-XIE). Ottawa, ON: Housing, Family and Social Statistics Division, Statistics Canada.

————. (2004b). Well-being of off-reserve Aboriginal children. *Canadian Social Trends,* Winter, 22–27.

Uhlenberg, P. (1980). Death and the family. *Journal of Family History, 5*(3), 313–320.

van de Walle, E., & van de Walle, F. (1990). The private and the public child. In J.C. Caldwell, S. Findley, P. Caldwell, G. Santow, W. Cosford, J. Braid, & D. Broers-Freeman (Eds.), *What we know about health transition: The cultural, social and behavioural determinants of health* (pp. 150–164). Canberra: Australian National University

Verma, R.B.P., Michalowski, M., & Gauvin, P. (2004). Abridged life tables for Registered Indians in Canada, 1976–1980 to 1996–2000. *Canadian Studies in Population, 31*(2), 197–235.

Waldram, J.B., Herring, D.A., & Young, T.K. (2006). *Aboriginal health in Canada: Historical, cultural, and epidemiological perspectives.* Toronto, ON: University of Toronto Press.

Wesley-Esquimaux, C.C., & Smolewski, M. (2004). *Historic trauma and Aboriginal healing.* Ottawa, ON: Aboriginal Healing Foundation.

Whitehead, P.C., & Hayes, M.J. (1998). *The insanity of alcohol: Social problems in Canadian First Nations communities.* Toronto, ON: Canadian Scholars Press.

Wotherspoon, T., & Satzewich, V. (2000). *First Nations: Race, class, and gender relations.* Regina, SK: Canadian Plains Research Centre.

Wright, J.V. (1995). *A history of the native people of Canada. Volume 1* (10,000–1,000 BC). Hull, QC: Canadian Museum of Civilization.

————. (1999). *A history of the native people of Canada. Volume 2* (1,000–AD 500). Hull, QC: Canadian Museum of Civilization.

York, G. (1989). *The dispossessed.* London, UK: Vintage.

Young, T.K. (1988). *Health care and cultural change: The Indian experience in the Central Subartic.* Toronto, ON: University of Toronto Press.

————. (1994). *The health of Native Americans: Towards a biocultural epidemiology.* New York, NY: Oxford University Press.

————. (2003, August 23). Review of research on Aboriginal populations in Canada: Relevance to their health needs. *British Medical Journal, 327,* 419–422.

ETHNIC OR CATEGORICAL MOBILITY? CHALLENGING CONVENTIONAL DEMOGRAPHIC EXPLANATIONS OF MÉTIS POPULATION GROWTH

Chris Andersen

INTRODUCTION

Between 1996 and 2006, Census Canada recorded an astonishing 91% increase in the "Métis identity population,"[1] from 204,000 in 1996 to about 390,000 in 2006. Aside from standard demographic factors such as fertility and mortality,[2] demographers attribute much of this growth to "ethnic mobility," the phenomenon by which individuals change their ethnic affiliation from one census to the next. Ethnic mobility has become an increasingly popular explanation for tracing both movement *into* and *between* categories of Aboriginal identification. Guimond (2003a) argues, for example, that successive decades of ethnic mobility have produced "fuzzy categories,"[3] which have, in turn, increased the difficulty of measuring contemporary Aboriginal populations.

Logic #1: Ethnic Mobility → Fuzzy Categories

Conversely, this chapter will argue that the logic in this statement overstates the epistemological correlation between census category and ethnic affiliation—that is, it possesses a misplaced confidence in the ability of existing census categories to measure the deep complexity characterizing the measurement of Aboriginal identity—and *understates* the primordiality of what Sawchuk (1998) has elsewhere clunkily termed "ethno-Aboriginality."[4] More specifically, I argue that ethnic mobility cannot be used to explain the recent Métis population change because neither existing census categories nor historical Canadian Aboriginal policy provide the solid foundational boundaries between categories required to assume it. Instead, I argue that it may well be that changing perceptions of census categories, rather than peoples' ethnicity, is fuelling the increase in the so-called "Métis population."

Logic #2: Fuzzy Categories → Categorical Mobility

The chapter's argument is laid out in four parts. The first part briefly takes up a discussion of ethnic mobility: I define it and link it to a particular moment in the ethnicity literature; explain how demographers determine its influence; survey the literature that has harnessed it conceptually; and explain its policy implications. The second section traces the genealogical history of ethnicity in the Canadian census, beginning with an explication of its complex relationship with race, ancestry/origins, and identity. I then sketch the racial and patriarchal logics that underpin the construction of "Indian" ethnicity and that set the stage for the more recent rise in the so-called Métis population. In the third part, I denaturalize the idea of ethnic mobility as a way to explain changes in Métis population. I suggest that such an argument illegitimately transforms administrative/census categories into ethnic ones by assuming that changes in census responses are indicative of changes in self-perceptions of ethnicity, rather than changes in individual perceptions of categorical boundaries. The chapter concludes with a discussion of the nature of ethnicity and the slipperiness of "Métis" within administrative attempts to measure it. I begin, however, with a discussion of ethnic mobility.

ETHNIC MOBILITY

The recent growth in Canada's Aboriginal population as a whole, and the Métis population in particular, we are told, is unlikely the result of natural demographic factors—unlikely, demographers explain, because the change represents annual growths that far outpace any previously recorded in Canada. Despite the tendency of news media to emphasize the relatively high fertility rates in Aboriginal communities (Guimond, Kerr, & Beaujot, 2004: 62; Norris, Beavon, & Guimond, 2004: 1) and the 1996 Royal Commission on Aboriginal Peoples' failure to account for it (Kerr, Guimond, & Norris, 2003), Canadian demographers have recently begun to point to another phenomenon: ethnic mobility. At its most general level, ethnic mobility refers to the "phenomenon by which individuals and families experience changes in their ethnic affiliation" (Guimond, 2003b: 42). In a more specific census/enumeration context, Siggner and Costa (2005) argue that it "refers to people changing, from one census to the next, the reporting of their Aboriginal affiliations from a non-Aboriginal identity to an Aboriginal identity" (11) (or between categories of Aboriginality themselves).

The very plausibility of ethnic mobility is anchored in ethnicity scholarship's recent turn toward constructivism. While academic research on ethnicity initially emphasized a primordialism, and positioned ethnicity as largely immutable and bestowed at birth as a "cultural given," following in the footsteps of Barth's (1969) pioneering work, more recent accounts emphasize ethnicity's fluid, practical, and boundary-making qualities. This research hangs its hat on "the claim that ethnicity is the product of a social process...made and remade rather than taken for granted, chosen depending on circumstances rather than ascribed through birth" (Wimmer, 2008: 971).

Siggner, Guimond, and their co-authors anchor their arguments in elements of these constructivist ideals. Guimond, Kerr, and Beaujot (2004) note, for example, that "efforts to establish time series data on Aboriginal populations will always be hindered by the 'fluid or situational character' of such concepts as ancestry or cultural origins" (60). Likewise, Siggner (2003a: 140) approvingly paraphrases Eschbach, Supple, and Snipp's (1998) earlier position on American Indian ethnicity, stating that "ethnic boundaries are assuming an ambiguity and fluidity, where membership in an ethnic category is the outcome of a social process of identification and no longer a fixed attribute." Finally, Guimond (2003b: 104) suggests that, especially in hyper ethnically mixed environments like Canada's cities, the increased mixed marriages that inevitably result provide the children of these unions with several choices regarding their ethnicity that didn't exist previously.

Not surprisingly, these discussions of ethnicity are tied strongly to discussions of origins/ancestry and identity. This follows official data uses of origins and identity as two of the three axes (along with "race") through which Statistics Canada measures ethnicity. Here, origins are used "to determine the roots or ethnic background of a person" (Statistics Canada, 2011), while identity is tied to self-perception, apparently to allow differentiation between self- and ancestral perception. Conceptually, this is not an unreasonable definition, as it accords with accepted constructivist orthodoxy emphasizing subjective assessment of common culture and ancestry (see Brubaker, 2004; Wimmer, 2008). As I explore below, however, the extent to which census classifications geared toward administrative clarity for governing individuals categorized as "Indians" can substitute for actual self-identification is highly debatable.

In any case, existing Statistics Canada confidentiality standards prevent the direct linkage of individuals across censuses (Guimond, Kerr, & Beaujot, 2004: 76). Thus, ethnic mobility estimates are produced using "estimation by residual" (Guimond, 2003b: 105). This method involves demographers adjusting their computational formulas to account both for technical problems (previous under-enumeration, etc.) and classical demographic factors such as fertility, mortality, and net migration. From these, expectations of population behaviour are derived for specific time periods and then compared to the actual observed population change. Differences between expected and observed change are explained by ethnic mobility. In the United States, researchers suggest that, from about 1971 onward, ethnic mobility can account for unexpected changes in American Indian population growth (Passel, 1976; 1997; Thornton, 1997), education levels (Eschbach, Supple, & Snipp, 1998), and geographical location (Eschbach, 1993). Likewise, ethnic mobility is used in Canada to explain recent unexpected growth in Aboriginal populations (Guimond, 2003a; 2003b; Guimond, Kerr, & Beaujot, 2004; Romaniuc, 2000), educational attainment levels (Guimond, 2003b; Siggner, 2003b; Siggner & Costa, 2005), geographical location (Guimond, 2003b; Norris, Beavon, & Guimond, 2004; Siggner, 2003b; 2003c; Siggner & Costa, 2005), fertility (Guimond, 2003b), and even, possibly, employment levels (Siggner & Costa, 2005).

Guimond (2003b) explains these changes by reference to the increased impact of ethnic drifters, a term employed by Ryder (1955: 473) nearly a half century earlier in his seminal article on the difficulties of measuring ethnicity through the census. Why might someone "drift"? Research on indigenous "ethnic" mobility has emphasized political upheaval over the previous four decades of minority relations with liberal democratic states such as Canada, the United States, New Zealand, and Australia, which has shaped the assimilation/acculturation impulses of those filling out census forms. In Canada, little research has been carried out on the mobility into Aboriginal self-identification or between existing administrative distinctions. However, the constructivist literature's emphasis on subjective assessments of common culture and ancestry and individual choice has shaped discussions of Canadian Aboriginal populations in two contexts.

First, researchers note the numerous legal, social, and political events over the past two decades that have spurred the increase in personal awareness or pride that anchor individuals' choice to change their declaration of ethnic affiliation. In turn, such events have also fostered attempts by Aboriginal organizations to shape the official taxonomies used to collect information on their constituents. Thus, census creation, collection, and interpretation represent a key political site around which subjugated collectivities mobilize and through which they attempt to legitimize their collective selves in colonial nation-states. Thus, increased pride shapes not only individual self-perception but also collective efforts to engage in the earliest stakes of census construction, a process evident in the creation of the 1991 and 2001 Aboriginal Peoples Survey, as well as the more recent 2006 Aboriginal Children's Survey (Statistics Canada, 2008; see Andersen, 2008).

The ethnic mobility apparently underscoring the recent "Métis population" surge has mainly been attributed to increased pride. Though Guimond (2003a: 43) curiously suggests that Métis are particularly susceptible to ethnic mobility, given their origins in the historical ethnic mobility between First Nations women and Euro-Canadian fur traders (as though First Nations in adjacent communities were not involved in this sexual economy), research has also pointed to several recent social and political events exerting a powerful impact on peoples' likelihood of self-identifying as Métis, despite their past failure to do so. Siggner and Costa (2005) argue that, for example, as much as three-quarters of the enormous increase in the Métis population between 1996 and 2001 was influenced by a number of highly publicized events throughout the 1980s and 1990s. For example, Métis received significant recognition in the final report of the Royal Commission on Aboriginal Peoples (1996); Louis Riel was recognized as a "father of Confederation," and his conviction as a traitor due to his involvement in the Métis Rebellion was vigorously debated. Furthermore, discussion of a Métis enumeration process during the Meech Lake constitutional process (1992) was one of the political and jurisdictional issues affecting the Métis. "In recent years, the Métis have won important court hunting rights cases...and greater land rights recognition in provinces such as Saskatchewan" (Siggner & Costa, 2005: 12).

Second, these impacts are hypothesized to exert enormous influence on future population projections and their subsequent policy initiative planning since, presumably, motivations behind changes in census self-identification will carry over into venues such as social service organizations. Thus, increases in identification both with origins and with identity are apparently tied to the incentives for such mobility, particularly with respect to movement by Aboriginal individuals into the Status Indian category first introduced in the 1981 Census questionnaire. Researchers (e.g., Guimond, 2003a; 2003b; Guimond, Kerr, & Beaujot, 2004; Norris, Beavon, & Guimond, 2004; Siggner 2003a; 2003b; 2003c; Siggner & Costa, 2005) point to the impact of broad legislative enactments, particularly Bill C-31,[5] on the non-demographic growth of the Status Indian population during the mid-1980s (also see Romaniuc, 2000: 122). Positioned as an example of ethnic mobility, this growth is explained by reference, for example, to the fact that increases in the status Indian population were motivated in part by eligibility for post-secondary education funding (Siggner, 2003b: 144). This incentive exerted a particularly powerful role during the mid-1980s when the bulk of re-admission took place (also see Kerr, Guimond, & Norris, 2003).

Moreover, although legislative enactments certainly played a role in bolstering the status Indian population, Guimond, Kerr, and Beaujot (2004) suggest that incentives attached to existing legal definitions may play a larger role in the movement into Aboriginal identity in the future, particularly for "mixed ancestry" individuals and their families: "the central element here is the notion of benefits, real or perceived, attached to Aboriginal affiliation" (74). White (2003) states more generally (in a discussion that fits squarely into this more specific one) that "policy mak-ers need to understand that there is a relationship between how people define themselves and their rights and entitlements. As policies or laws are changed to confer rights on groups, individuals will change their identity to take advantage of the perceived benefits" (37).

Thus, ethnic mobility apparently possesses important policy implica-tions. On the one hand, Siggner and Costa (2005) worry that ethnic mobility makes it difficult to assess real trends in the Aboriginal population: ethnic drifters may artificially inflate the quality of life indicators for Aboriginal

people and, in doing so, blur the very real problems faced by specific subsec-
tors of the Aboriginal population. On the other hand, Kerr, Guimond, and
Norris (2003) argue more generally that "demographers produce population
projections to answer the question of how many. The policy and program
analysts rely on these projections to answer the question of how much. If
present demographic models cannot accurately say how many, how can
policy analysts effectively determine program costs?" (58). I will argue below
that, while these are important questions, they have little or nothing to do
with the ethnicity of respondents, since policy analysts attribute relatively
little policy attention to the nature or intensity of Aboriginal clienteles' affili-
ative feelings, nor to their subjective assessments outside their choice of
administrative categories contained in the census.

To this point in the chapter, I have taken for granted demographers' epistemological correlation between respondents' actual self-identification and
their specific choices on census categories that serve as a proxy. Research
has demonstrated, however, that in Canada (as elsewhere) what counts
as ethnicity has changed radically both in terms of its relationship to race
and identity and how Canadian officials have measured it. In this context,
the arbitrariness of Canadian policy about the administrative boundaries
of "Indian" makes it difficult to produce reliable definitions of more recent
census categories like "Métis" since the two are so strongly administratively entwined. In the next section, I detail some of this complexity to
demonstrate the degree to which administrative convenience, rather than
acknowledgement of Indigenous perceptions of cultural ties and ancestry
(i.e., ethnicity), has shaped the construction of census categories. This is
not all bad, obviously (since some correlation exists between ethnicity and
census categories), but it does substantially muddy the relationship.

ABORIGINALITY OR ADMINISTRATIVE CLARITY?
A HISTORY OF CANADIAN CENSUS TAKING

The relationship of ethnicity to its conceptual predecessor, race, has a long
history in Canada, reflected in changing census terminology during the last
four centuries. Certainly, Canadian discourses of multiculturalism have
sought, in presenting ethnicity as an integral component of diversity, to
distinguish it teleologically from the earlier discussions of race that characterized nineteenth- and early twentieth-century Canadian government
classification schemes (see Day, 2000). Indeed, even before race replaced

ethnicity in the mid-1940s, race itself was undergoing a transformation from difference rooted in biology to that rooted in culture. By the 1950s, earnest discussions ensued regarding whether race held any scientific validity at all (see Boyd, Goldman, & White, 2000; Walker, 1997: 12–20). For example, despite the fact that racial origin played a central role only 50 years earlier in the taxonomy of the 1901 Census, by 1951 enumerator instructions on ascertaining ethnic origin declared that it referred "to the cultural group, *sometimes erroneously called 'racial' group*, from which the person is descendant" (Canada, 1951a: 44, emphasis added).

Though conceptually separating race from ethnicity is tempting (see, for example, Morning, 2008), Wimmer (2008: 974) notes that doing so requires ignoring three important historical facts: first, that groups were variously treated as races and ethnicities that moved from one to the other (and back again); second, that phenotypical markers such as skin colour were never sufficient harbingers of categorization and as such were always accompanied by numerous additional criteria (lifestyle, occupation, moral turpitude, etc.); and third, that while race is often thought of as imposed and ethnicity self-ascribed, many "ethnic groups" suffered the kinds of outsider oppression and dispossession normally associated with racial imposition.

In any case, race and ethnicity retain in common, first, their differentiation from white Euro-Canadian normativity (see Andersen, 2008) and, second, the importance of commonality of descent or origins (Morning, 2008: 242). As argued above, origins represent one of the three axes of measurement used by contemporary Census Canada officials to measure ethnicity. However, while ethnic and racial origin information has been collected in nearly every census since Canadian Confederation.[6] Canada's history of enumerating race/ethnicity has been "erratic" at best (Boyd, Goldman, & White, 2000: 33). "Race" was present in various census questions as late as 1824, then replaced by "origins" for 80 years, then reappeared (in various guises) in all the censuses between 1901 and 1941 (see Ryder, 1955: 468). Moreover, the identifying features of "race," particularly with respect to the role of patrilineality, produced statistically dubious estimations of population "mixing" (see Ryder, 1955). In keeping with the growing scientific consensus of the era, by 1951, all references to racial origin were dropped in favour of a new question on ethnic origin. Soon after, ethnicity replaced race as the ubiquitous standard for dividing (Canadian) humanity culturally, spurred on by legislative changes such as Canada's 1970s multicultural policy and the subsequent formulations of various ministries and departments dedicated to producing policy based on a national goal of ethnic diversity. And although Census Canada's 1996 addition of a "visible minority" question is arguably a return to biological-cum-racial designations (see Wargon, 2000), ethnicity remains a crucial cog in the official taxonomy of measuring Canadian diversity.

The investment in the current definitions notwithstanding, census understandings of ethno-Aboriginality (whether based in origin, race, and/or identity) have experienced considerable change over the past four centuries. While rudimentary, Jesuit-produced estimates of local Aboriginal populations began more than four centuries ago (see Goldmann, 1993: 1), a century and a half later, the Nova Scotia Census of 1767 distinguished between ethnicity and race, including the option of "Indian" in the latter based largely on their "colour" (along with "white" and "black"). Less than a century after that, the Censuses of Upper and Lower Canada combined ethnicity with place of birth, and "Indian" was transformed from a "colour" to an ethnic origin, along with 25 different choices for countries of origin (see White, Badet, & Renaud, 1993, Table 1: 225).

In his still indispensable discussion of the evolving census criteria for measuring Aboriginality between 1871 and 1991, Goldmann (1993) notes that the main category in use for most of the twentieth century, "Indian," was of course derived from the 1876 Indian Act and its predecessor legislation.[7] Moreover, enumerator instructions through most of the twentieth century, which required ascertaining the patrilineage of respondents, fit not uncoincidentally into the patriarchal basis of this act; from an ethnicity standpoint, however, this patriarchy wreaked havoc with actual ethno-Aboriginality boundaries tied both to territory and to kinship. That is to say, administrative presuppositions attempted to run roughshod over existing forms of "on the ground" ethnicity in the communities themselves.

For example, Lawrence (2003: 51–52) notes that, although "Indianness" was treated colonially as a state of racial purity, patriarchal considerations of the Indian Act meant that only certain intermixing—namely, a status Indian woman's marriage to a non-Status man—resulted in *legally* consequential "mixedness," whereas the marriage and offspring of non-Status women and Status Indian men maintained its juridical purity.

Such patrilineal trajectories were in direct conflict with many indigenous collectivities' philosophies in which women held equally esteemed positions. Mohawk scholar Audra Simpson (2008) eloquently states that "the Indian Act represented the state's efforts to flatten a competing system of gendered subject formation and social organization, including Indigenous genealogies, philosophical systems, and modes of governance" (254).

While perhaps administratively useful (though even this is debatable), by the middle of the twentieth century, census classification schemes for taxonomizing Aboriginality became almost dizzyingly complex, bordering on a comical mix of patriarchy, geographical location, and ancestral origins. For example, 1951 Census rules of descent differed for those living on- and off-reserve: enumerators were asked to substitute geographical location for the "normal" requirement of patrilineal descent such that "(a) For those living on Indian reserves, the origin will be recorded as 'Native Indian'; (b) for those not on reserves the origin will be determined through the line of the father, that is, by following the usual procedure" (Canada, 1951b: 45). Goldmann (1993:16) shows that this remained the case for the 1961 Census as well, a logic that in fact remained in operation until the 1981 Census.

The impact of these patriarchal logics needs further emphasis. While "Métis" today are hoisted on a petard of racial "mixedness," in reality this mixedness is the result of emphasis rather than actual biological "dilution." Métis are certainly mixed, but the patriarchal emphasis on entry into and exit out of "Indian" status demonstrates that numerous individuals designated administratively as "Indians" were equally mixed, biologically speaking. And yet, Indian status carries with it a presumptive purity that, even today, tends to shape the commonsense differentiation between "Indians" and "Métis." This issue is explored in more detail in the chapter's third part, but suffice it to say for now that the porousness of Indian status, especially prior to 1951, renders the presumed biological differentiation between these two categories logically difficult to sustain.

The census change that arguably exerted the biggest impact on measuring ethno-Aboriginality is not the 1971 Census Canada change from canvasser to self-enumeration (though on-reserve respondents remained and still remain canvassed in person) but rather, the 1981 approach to classifying ethnicity. Question 26 of the 1981 questionnaire asks, "to which ethnic or cultural group did you or your ancestors belong on first coming to this continent?" Responses included, "Inuit; Status or registered Indian;

Non-status Indian; or Métis" (Statistics Canada, 1981: 6). These administrative categories more or less form the basis of today's major census taxonomies of Aboriginality and represent the first use of the categories that have since assumed contemporary ubiquity.

The 1986 Census reproduced these categories with one important exception. For the first time, a self-perception (or identity) question was added: "Do you consider yourself an aboriginal person or a native Indian of North America, that is, Inuit, North American Indian or Métis?" (Statistics Canada, 1986b: 3). If answering affirmatively, respondents were given the options of Inuit, Status or Registered Indian, non-Status Indian, or Métis (1986a: 3). The 1986 Census Dictionary explains the addition of this identity question to account for respondents who might lack "aboriginal" ethnicity but nonetheless possess "legal" Indian status (Statistics Canada, 1986c: 5). Interestingly, the 1986 Census Guide suggests that "Aboriginal children, even if adopted by non-aboriginal families, should also have a 'Yes...' response" (Statistics Canada, 1986a: n.p.). Though the Aboriginal portion of the 1986 Census was deemed valid (see Guimond 2003a), the results were never released to the public, due to broader validity concerns about the dataset as a whole (Boyd, Goldman, & White, 2000: 45).

Five years later, the 1991 Census removed all reference to self-identification for Aboriginality, again asking a question regarding ethnic origin —namely, "To which ethnic or cultural group(s) did this person's ancestors belong?" (question 15)—while offering respondents the option of North American Indian, Métis, and Inuit/Eskimo (Statistics Canada, 1991a: 8) [8] A separate, more specific question asked whether the respondent was a "registered Indian as defined by the Indian Act of Canada." If so, he or she was allowed to specify an Indian Band or First Nation (Statistics Canada, 1991b, question 16, 8), an option that produces a more nuanced proxy for ethnicity. Interestingly, the accompanying census guide suggests that any respondents who regained status under Bill C-31 should answer "yes" while those "whose Indian status has never been regained under Bill C-31 and who are not members of an Indian band, leave the Indian Band or First Nation blank" (Statistics Canada, 1991c: 5–6, emphasis in original). Such instructions appear to have relatively little to do with identifying actual strands of ethnicity and everything to do with administrative clarity, since many people who were not official band members nonetheless retained ties to kin who qualified as band members.

The census for 1996 saw the reintroduction of a self-perception question (and/or the adult perception of their children) for all Aboriginal respondents, through question 18: "Is this person an Aboriginal person, that is, North American Indian, Métis or Inuit (Eskimo)?" If yes, the respondent was directed to question 20, which asked about Indian Band/First Nation membership—if they had membership, they were provided space to specify their Indian Band/First Nation. Regardless, in question 21 the respondent was also asked about Treaty Indian or a Registered Indian status as defined by the Indian Act of Canada (added at the request of western First Nations people, where the term "Treaty Indian" was more common). Both the 2001 and the 2006 censuses carried forward virtually unchanged the categories used in the 1996 census.

As the history of Canadian census taking makes clear, census questions regarding so-called ethno-Aboriginality and their more recent turn into self-identification represent a complex tension between administrative requirements, Aboriginal respondent self-perception and, though to a much lesser extent than is appreciated, ethnicity. More importantly, the "Métis" category, which appears in the 1981 survey instrument, is the result of more than a century of Aboriginal policy making (reflected directly in census questions) through which tens of thousands of Aboriginal individuals lost their status. Thus, while many might suggest that choosing "Métis" constitutes an act of self-perception (one of the two pillars of ethnic identification), the category also contains the detritus of a previous century of Canadian attempts to whittle down responsibility for so-called Status Indians. Given this historical context, how can we be certain about what self-identification as Métis actually means?

In the next section, I explore the logic underlying the ethnic mobility argument used to explain recent growth in the so-called Métis population. I argue that although these categories undoubtedly measure some level of ethnicity, the boundary instability of the attendant groups upon which this "ethnicity" is based make these crude measures at best. Indeed, it makes as much sense to understand these changes as the result of categorical mobility: changes in responders' perceptions of census classification boundaries themselves. I will now examine this issue of categorical mobility in two contexts: the recent growth of the "Métis population" and the growth of the Status Indian population during the mid-1980s.

FROM ETHNIC TO CATEGORICAL MOBILITY

Recall from the first part of the chapter that ethnic mobility is defined as the phenomenon by which respondents change their ethnic classification from one census to the next. As Guimond (2003a: 35) clearly explicates, ethnic mobility has apparently vastly increased the difficulty in defining Aboriginal populations because changing social relations have produced numerous changes in what he terms "Aboriginal groups." The logic of his argument, as presented in the introduction, is thus that increased ethnic mobility produces increasingly fuzzy categories that in turn complicate our contemporary understandings/definitions of Aboriginality. In the context of the Métis population, this has, he argues, produced a veritable explosion. His dataset is restricted to the 1986–1996 period, but this population increase is equally apparent in the latest 2006 Census results. Using data on "mixed" marriages, he appears to demonstrate that, with respect to Métis, only one in two children of mixed Métis–other marriages are identified as Métis. He refers to this as "intergenerational ethnic mobility" (though, interestingly, this form of mobility does not require self-perception, a supposed hallmark of ethnicity). Regarding intragenerational ethnic mobility—in which individuals change their own perceptions over time—Guimond (2003a: 44) attributes as much as 56% of the population growth between 1986 and 1996 to this mobility.

Guimond's (2003a) argument is compelling, but only if one takes for granted the solidity of the category "Métis" upon which his argument rests. As I show, such solidity requires a definition that holds little uniformity (other than vulgar racial overtones) or holds little validity for those who use it. Perhaps more pointedly, its contemporary fuzziness appears to prevent the very process of ethnic mobility that Guimond (2003a) suggests is crucial to its production.

Fuzzy Categories → Categorical Mobility

It is instructive to note that the category "Métis" contained in the Census Canada questionnaires from 1981 to 2006 contains little in the way of definition. And while census categories tend to reflect the three "Aboriginal peoples" laid out in the Constitution Act of 1982 (and thus would appear to hold some broader validity), this observation is not necessarily that helpful in a Métis context, since the courts have only recently fashioned a definition of Métis (see *R. v. Powley*, 2003). In his discussion of the growth of the Métis population, Guimond (2003a) positions "the" Métis as "born from the contact between Indians and European colonizers" (45). (This is a curious definition insofar as all individuals designated administratively as Indians are born out of this contact as well.) Elsewhere, he defines Métis more lengthily both to denote a specific connection or affiliation with a historically rooted socio-political entity (i.e., the Métis Nation) rooted in the territories of what is now western Canada, but also, contrarily, to suggest that "the *Métis* culture cannot be associated with any specific language or ethnic origin—it is rather a cultural, linguistic and territorial mosaic with which a population has identified and developed an original culture. The sense of belonging to this culture has varied over time and in response to political and social events" (Guimond, Kerr, & Beaujot, 2004: 62).

These definitions are problematic not because they are contradictory—though they certainly are—but rather because current census classification for Métis cannot distinguish between the contrasting definitions. Thus, while we acknowledge perceptions of common culture and ancestry (i.e., ethnicity) as an important element of Aboriginal identity, the current census category "Métis" doesn't allow us to gain any specificity about that common culture or origins. In turn, this makes difficult an argument for ethnic mobility, since we cannot know which ethnicity the individual is ascribing to in his or her self-selection as Métis or even what changing responses from census to census is actually indicative of.

Giokas and Chartrand (2001: 85) remind us that the term "Métis" has been applied in at least three different contexts: (1) to refer to all Red River people of "mixed ancestry" (including both French and English speakers); (2) to refer to other mixed ancestry people whose history lies outside not only Red River but also western Canada more generally; and (3) to refer to those of mixed ancestry whose genealogy has floated in and out of Indian Act Indian status since its rules were produced. This latter issue is perhaps particularly pressing given the impact of current "out-marriage" rules associated with the Indian Act.[9] Current census classifications that rely on mixed ancestry as a pillar of Métis identity cannot deal with the issue that those who are Status Indians are also of mixed ancestry. Thus, while mixed ancestry should not retain such differentiating power, the common-sensical adoption of definitions that emphasize this component needlessly reproduces its validity as a distinguishing characteristic and needlessly muddies real political distinctions between Métis and First Nations (Cree, Blackfoot, Dene, Mohawk, etc.) "ethnicities."

An instructive way to understand the futility of explaining contemporary movement between existing census categories as a result of ethnic mobility is to examine the recent impact of the *Powley* decision on the Sault Ste. Marie, Ontario community and the identification of the *Powley* decision's protagonist, Steve Powley. Briefly, the *Powley* decision is a harvesting rights decision that fashioned a broad definition of Métis to include self-identification as Métis and acceptance by a Métis community. Prior to *Powley*, the Supreme Court had yet to produce a decision on the meaning of Métis in section 35 of the 1982 Constitution Act, a major venue through which Aboriginal peoples press their claims juridically.

The *Powley* case involved a father and son ("the Powleys") charged with hunting without a proper licence and illegal possession of a game carcass. In defending against these charges, the Powleys argued, according to existing legal precedent, that they were Métis under section 35 of the Constitution Act, 1982 and that (again, according to an existing line of Canadian Aboriginal rights jurisprudence) the community to which they claimed allegiance was Métis prior to the effective sovereignty of the Canadian state (i.e., when Canadian state institutions actually took control "on the ground"). The case eventually included the Powleys, the Ontario Crown, and numerous interveners from various Aboriginal organizations, hunting and fishing conservation associations, and the various provincial and federal Ministries of Justice. While the case was ostensibly about hunting in the Sault Ste. Marie, Ontario area, the decision was eagerly anticipated for its likelihood to fashion a definition of Métis that was applicable to a broader set of confines than those contained in the case itself (see Andersen, 2005 and 2010 for a more in-depth discussion of the *Powley* case).

The case is interesting not for its eventual findings but, rather, for Steve Powley's own reflection, before his death, on his self-identification. Though the court found a Métis community in the Sault Ste. Marie region, historical evidence reveals a vastly more complicated situation. Neither the category "Métis" nor "Indian" possessed any lived salience during the era in question (before 1850): labels such "voyageur" or "tripper" or "half-breed" held far more currency. And while several residents during this era identified in

certain contexts as "half-breeds," lifestyle rather than mere mixed ancestry distinguished "Indians" from others in the region. Moreover, following
the Robinson-Superior Treaty of 1850, many of the so-called "half-breeds"
took treaty along with the "Indians," gaining their status and becoming full-fledged band members. Indeed, it wasn't just the case that Steve
Powley's direct descendants were Status Indians for several generations
(prior to "marrying out" at the beginning of the twentieth century). In the
original Powley trial, the Powleys sought relief against the charges by argu-
ing for their treaty rights by virtue of their direct descendancy from original
Robinson-Superior treaty signatories.

Clearly, like many in the community of Sault Ste. Marie, the Powleys'
ethnicity—their "subjectively felt sense of belonging based on the belief
in shared culture and common ancestry" (Wimmer, 2008: 973)—contained
the detritus of juridical, legislative, and policy-making attempts to produce
governing structures over the course of the latter half of the nineteenth
century. Little more than a century and a half later during the post-Powley
era, Steve Powley has posthumously become a Métis hero, despite the fact
that he didn't self-identify as Métis until just before the trial. Moreover, in
a rare interview given prior to the Supreme Court ruling on the decision,
Powley explained that he knew little about his Aboriginal ancestry, let alone
self-identification as Métis: "'I was a white man right up until a few years
ago,' Powley, 54, said in an interview. 'My mother would not admit she was
native. I had red hair just like him,' he says, nodding toward his son Roddy,
29. 'She said we had just a tiny bit of native blood'" (MacCharles, 2003: A10).

The point of including this interview is not to "out" Powley, nor to
somehow demonstrate that he was not what or who he pretended to be.
As Guimond (2003a) demonstrates convincingly, thousands if not tens of
thousands of individuals are in exactly the same (admittedly leaky) boat as
Powley. However, Powley's interview should give us pause to think about
what ethnic mobility might actually mean in situations like this one where,
first, the historical roots are so complex and, second, where Powley is so
estranged from them. Presumably, the "social and political events" listed
by Guimond (2003b) and Siggner (2003a) would include the Powley decision among them: however, the question that needs to be asked here is,
did Powley's ethnicity actually change, or, upon being vindicated in the
court room, did Powley merely readjust his perception of what the category
"Métis" entailed to include himself, his children, and his community?

CONCLUSION

The point of this chapter has been to focus on the recent rise of ethnic mobility explanations to analyze apparently otherwise unexplainable trends in Aboriginal population growth. Keying off this recent literature, I fashioned a broad definition of ethnicity to include subjective feelings of attachment based on perceptions of common culture and ancestry (see Wimmer, 2008). I traced historical and contemporary contours of census taxonomies of Aboriginality and demonstrated their emphasis on synoptic, administrative utility rather than ethnic affiliation. Finally, the chapter challenged the notion of ethnic mobility as an adequate explanation for Métis population changes in particular, and instead, using the Powley decision and its protagonist, Steve Powley, I suggested that far from ethnic mobility causing definitional fuzziness, definitional fuzziness was producing categorical mobility.

For two reasons, the policy implications of this argument are, at least at this stage, astoundingly minor. First, unlike Indian status and despite arguments to the contrary, Métis (as opposed to, for example, non-Status Indians) classification provides little in the way of specific incentives not already available under numerous existing social policy categories. It is true that we are long past the days of "a Métis card and a Loonie will get you a Coke," but at the same time census classification and political membership are two entirely different animals, and we are probably a generation away from seeing the political effects of this categorical mobility. Second, the urban Aboriginal policy environment—where a bulk of the Aboriginal population of whatever stripe is located—is becoming increasingly needs-based and status-blind. In this context, most urban Aboriginal social services organizations do not require potential clients to undertake a "cultural means" test or to demonstrate their ethnicity—needs-based means simply that ancestry and self-identification (*whatever* the self-identification) are usually sufficient.

In the end, we simply don't need an ethnic mobility argument to explain the fuzziness of existing categories of Aboriginality as they relate to Métis. A century and a half of irrational, erratic, arbitrary, disjointed, post hoc, inconsistent, misapplied, and misinterpreted Aboriginal policy does a much more thorough job of producing fuzzy categories than changes in individual self-perception ever could. To borrow from Giokas and Chartrand (2001), "since there is no consistent basis for designating persons as falling into the category of Indians, it should not be surprising that little or none is present in the case of those who fall between the categories into the boundary group called Métis" (2001: 106). The term "Métis"—at least as it appears in the census—has no consistent basis of personal affiliation based on culture and belonging. It is not, therefore, simply or straightforwardly a form of ethnicity (though it contains elements of ethnicity within it) and as such, it cannot be used to explain movement "in" or "out" (such as the case may be) of particular census categories.

Moreover, a consequence of this argument is that we cannot un-ring a bell—either contemporary ethnic mobility produces fuzzy categories or a hundred years of Canada's Aboriginal policy does. If the latter is the case, we need to take a closer look at the categories used to establish these claims of ethnicity rather than attempting to put the cart before the horse. As any Métis will tell you, the horse goes first, and if the horse doesn't go, the cart isn't going anywhere.

AUTHOR'S NOTE

In addition to the anonymous reviews, I thank Anatole Romaniuk for his useful comments. I would also like to acknowledge the generous financial assistance of the Social Sciences and Humanities Research Council of Canada, which made this research possible.

NOTES

1. Though I will have more to say about this in the third part of this chapter, a basic division exists in the literature between two uses of the term "Métis." The first denotes a socio-political nation that rose to prominence in the middle and late nineteenth century, whose metropolis was Red River (on the plains of what is now southern Manitoba) and whose ancestors self-identified as such. The second denotes mere mixed ancestry and refers to anyone of mixed ancestry who self-identifies as Métis today.

2. The Aboriginal population in Canada is assumed to be "closed," and, as such, migration, net or otherwise, does not factor into estimates.

3. Categories are, of course, central to our ability to make sense of ourselves and the world around us. They allow us to sort the vast cacophony of sights, sounds, and feelings into discernable "chunks" through which we can efficiently interpret our experiences (Brubaker, 2003: 71). This chapter is based on the premise that a century of haphazard Aboriginal policy has left a sizeable (and unpredictable) "gap" between how Aboriginal people self-categorize and the categories the Canadian state finds administratively useful for governing the Aboriginal population.

4. Sawchuk (1998: 26–27) argues that, although "Canadian" Native leaders legitimately balk at the idea of being understood as "simply part of an ethnic group," the processes of identity reformation that have occurred in the last four decades constitutes a specific instance of larger processes of ethnic identity negotiation. Thus, he coined the term "ethno-Aboriginality" to capture both the distinctiveness of Aboriginality and its conceptual links to the larger processes that shape ethnicity temporally.

5. Bill C-31 was a 1985 amendment to the Indian Act, originally created as an omnibus piece of legislation in 1876 to regulate the lives of those designated "Status Indians" (see Tobias, 1991). Bill C-31 was meant to correct the numerous points of gender discrimination inherent in the act through which only Status Indian *women* could lose their status. One of the manifestations of this patriarchy was that, prior to Bill C-31, *non*-Status women (whether "white," Asian, Métis, or whichever) automatically gained status as Indians upon their marriage to a Status man, while Status women automatically lost theirs upon their marriage to a non-Status man (see Clatworthy, 2003; Jamieson, 1978). In an interesting irony, this patriarchy has produced Census Canada results in which nearly 9,000 individuals self-identified as Status Indians despite their lack of Aboriginal ancestry or self-identification (Guimond et al., 2004: 62). More recently, Bill C-3 was enacted to correct the remaining discrimination in Bill C-31. Whether or not it has actually done so is a matter of debate. (See AANDC, 2011, January 31).

6. The 1891 Census is the exception.

7. Though the most infamous piece of Canadian legislation dealing with Status Indians is the 1876 Indian Act, Canada and its previous governing regimes had been enacting "Indian" legislation to define legal "Indians" and their band status for 26 years prior to the 1876 act, including legislation in 1850, 1857, 1859, and 1869.

8. Note that Eskimo was added to the response category of "Inuit" provided in 1986 "in order to avoid confusion" (Statistics Canada, 1991a: 52).

9. The Indian Act regulates distinctions between s.6(1) and s.6(2) Status Indians. These distinctions are well worn in the literature so I will skip their explanation here. Suffice it to say that, until the 2011 passing into law of Bill C-3 (which amends certain provisions of Bill C-31, the legislation that governed distinctions between different administrative categories of "Indians"), subsequent "out-marriage" over two generations leads to the loss of status. See Clatworthy (2003).

REFERENCES

Aboriginal Affairs and Northern Development Canada (AANDC). (2011, January 31). *Gender equity in Indian Registration Act (Bill C-3) comes into force January 31, 2011.* [News release]. Retrieved from http://www.aadnc-aandc.gc.ca/eng/1305220833814/1305304882371

Andersen, C. (2005). Residual tensions of empire: Contemporary Métis communities and the Canadian judicial imagination. In M. Murphy (Ed.), *Reconfiguring*

Aboriginal–state relations: The state of the federation, 2003 (pp. 295–325). Montreal and Kingston: McGill-Queen's University Press.

———. (2008). From nation to population: The racialization of "Métis" in the Canadian Census. *Nations and Nationalism, 14*(2), 347–368.

———. (2010). Mixed ancestry or Métis. In. B. Hokowhitu et al. (Eds.), *Indigenous identity and resistance: Researching the diversity of knowledge* (pp. 23–36). Dunedin, NZ: University of Otago Press.

Barth, F. (1969). *Ethnic groups and boundaries: The social organization of cultural difference.* Boston, MA: Little, Brown and Company.

Boyd, M., Goldman, G., & White, P. (2000). Race in the Canadian Census. In L. Driedger & S. Halli (Eds.), *Race and racism: Canada's challenge* (pp. 33–54). Montreal and Kingston: McGill-Queen's University Press.

Brubaker, R. (2004). *Ethnicity without groups.* Cambridge, MA: Harvard University Press.

Canada. Dominion Bureau of Statistics. (1951a). *Ninth census of Canada 1951: Instructions to commissioners and enumerators.* Ottawa, ON: Edmond Cloutier.

———. (1951b). *Ninth census of Canada 1951: Questionnaire.* Ottawa, ON: Edmond Cloutier.

Clatworthy, S. (2003). Re-accessing the population impacts of bill C-31 section 6. In J. White, P. Maxim, & D. Beavon (Eds.), *Aboriginal conditions: Research foundations for public policy* (pp. 63–90). Vancouver, BC: University of British Columbia Press.

Day, R. (2000). *Multiculturalism and the history of Canadian diversity.* Toronto, ON: University of Toronto Press.

Eschbach, K. (1993). Changing identification among American Indians and Alaska Natives. *Demography, 30*(4), 635–652.

Eschbach, K., Supple, K., & Snipp, M. (1998). Changes in racial identification and the educational attainment of American Indians, 1970–1990. *Demography, 35*(1), 35–44.

Giokas, J. & Chartrand, P. (2001). Who are the Métis in section 35? A review of the law and policy relating to Métis and "mixed blood" people in Canada. In P. Chartrand (Ed.), *Who are Canada's Aboriginal peoples? Recognition, definition, and jurisdiction* (pp. 83–125). Saskatoon, SK: Purich Publishers.

Goldmann, G. (1993). *The Aboriginal population and the census: 120 years of information—1871 to 1991.* Paper presented at the 22nd General Population Conference of the International Union for the Scientific Study of Population (IUSSP), Montreal, Canada.

Guimond, E. (2003a). Changing ethnicity: The concept of ethnic drifters. In J. White, P. Maxim, & D. Beavon (Eds.), *Aboriginal conditions: Research as a foundation for public policy* (pp. 91–108). Vancouver, BC: University of British Columbia Press.

———. (2003b). Fuzzy definitions and population explosion: Changing identities of Aboriginal groups in Canada. In D. Newhouse & E. Peters (Eds.), *Not strangers in these parts: Urban Aboriginal peoples* (pp. 35–48). Ottawa, ON: Policy Research Initiative.

Guimond, E., Kerr, D., & Beaujot, R. (2004). Charting the growth of Canada's Aboriginal populations: Problems, options and implications. *Canadian Studies in Population*, 31(1): 55–82.

Jamieson, K. (1978). *Indian women and the law in Canada: Citizens minus*. Ottawa, ON: Supply and Services Canada.

Kerr, D., Guimond, E., & Norris, M.J. (2003). Perils and pitfalls of Aboriginal demography: Lessons learned from the Royal Commission on Aboriginal Peoples projections. In J. White, P. Maxim, & D. Beavon (Eds.), *Aboriginal Conditions: The Research Foundations for Public Policy* (pp. 39–62). Vancouver, BC: University of British Columbia Press.

Lawrence, B. (2003). *"Real" Indians and others: Mixed-blood urban Native peoples and indigenous nationhood*. Vancouver, BC: University of British Columbia Press.

MacCharles, T. (2003, March 17). Métis rights on hunting challenged in top court; Ontario man seeks parity with full-status Indians: Opponents cite concerns over conservation. *Toronto Star*, p. A10.

Morning, A. (2008). Ethnic classification in global perspective: A cross-national survey of the 2000 census round. *Population Research and Policy Review* 27, 239–272.

Norris, M.J., Beavon, D., & Guimond, E. (2004). *Registered Indian mobility and migration: An analysis of 1996 Census data*. Strategic Research and Analysis Directorate. Indian and Northern Affairs Canada.

Passel, J. (1976). Provisional evaluation of the 1970 census count of American Indians. *Demography*, 13(3), 397–409.

———. (1997). The growing American Indian population, 1960–1990: Beyond demography. *Population Research and Policy Review* 16, 11–31.

Romaniuc, A. (2000). Aboriginal population of Canada: Growth dynamics under conditions of encounter of civilisations. *The Canadian Journal of Native Studies 20*, 95–137.

Ryder, N. (1955). The interpretation of origin statistics. *Canadian Journal of Economics and Political Science*, 21(4), 466–479.

Sawchuk, J. (1998). *The dynamics of Native politics: The Alberta Métis experience*. Saskatoon, SK: Purich Publishers.

Siggner, A. (2003a). The challenge of measuring the demographic and socio-economic conditions of the urban Aboriginal population. In D. Newhouse & E. Peters (Eds.), *Not strangers in these parts: Urban Aboriginal people* (pp. 119–130). Ottawa, ON: Policy Research Initiative.

———. (2003b). Impact of "ethnic mobility" in socio-economic conditions of Aboriginal peoples. *Canadian Studies in Population*, 30(1), 137–158.

———. (2003c). Urban Aboriginal populations: An update using the 2001 census results. In D. Newhouse & E. Peters (Eds.), *Not strangers in these parts: Urban Aboriginal people* (pp. 15–21). Ottawa, ON: Policy Research Initiative.

Siggner, A.J. & Costa, R. (2005). *Aboriginal conditions in census metropolitan areas, 1981–2006*. Ottawa, ON: Social and Aboriginal Statistics Division, Statistics Canada.

Simpson, A. (2008). From white into red: Captivity narratives as alchemies of race and citizenship. *American Quarterly, 60*(2): 251–257.

Statistics Canada. (1981). *Census questionnaire.* Ottawa, ON: Statistics Canada.

———. (1986a). *Census dictionary.* Ottawa, ON: Statistics Canada.

———. (1986b). *Census questionnaire.* Ottawa, ON: Statistics Canada.

———. (1986c). *Reference guide.* Ottawa, ON: Statistics Canada.

———. (1991a). *Census dictionary.* Ottawa, ON: Statistics Canada.

———. (1991b). *Census questionnaire.* Ottawa, ON: Statistics Canada.

———. (1991c). *Reference guide.* Ottawa, ON: Statistics Canada.

———. (1996). *Census questionnaire.* Ottawa, ON: Statistics Canada.

———. (2008). *Aboriginal children's survey (ACS).* Retrieved from http://www23.statcan.gc.ca/imdb/p2SV.pl?Function=getSurvey&SDDS=5108&Item_Id=22502

———. (2011). *Ethnic origin reference guide, 2006 Census* (Catalogue No. 97-562-GEW2006025). Retrieved from https://www12.statcan.gc.ca/census-recensement/2006/ref/rp-guides/ethnic-ethnique-eng.cfm

Thornton, R. (1997). Tribal membership requirements and the demography of "old" and "new" Native Americans. *Population Research and Policy Review 16,* 33–42.

Tobias, J. (1991). Protection, civilization, assimilation: An outline history of Canada's Indian policy. In. J. Miller (Ed.), *Sweet promises: A reader on Indian–white relations in Canada* (pp. 127–144). Toronto, ON: University of Toronto Press.

Walker, J. (1997). *"Race," rights and the law in the Supreme Court of Canada: Historical case studies.* Toronto, ON: Osgoode Society for Canadian Legal History/ Waterloo, ON: Wilfrid Laurier Press.

White, J. (2003). The limits of our knowledge and the need to refine understandings. In J. White, P. Maxim, and D. Beavon (Eds.), *Aboriginal conditions: Research as a Foundation for Public Policy* (pp. 35–38). Vancouver, BC: University of British Columbia Press.

White, P., Badets, J., & Renaud, V. (1993). Measuring ethnicity in Canadian censuses. In G. Goldmann et al. (Eds.), *Challenges of measuring an ethnic world: Science, politics and reality* (pp. 221–267). The Joint Canada–United States Conference on the Measurement of Ethnicity, Washington, DC: Bureau of the Census; Ottawa, ON: Statistics Canada.

Wimmer, A. (2008). The making and unmaking of ethnic boundaries: A multilevel process theory. *American Journal of Sociology, 113*(4): 970–1022.

12

"I'M SWEATING WITH CREE CULTURE NOT SAULTEAUX CULTURE"
URBAN ABORIGINAL CULTURAL IDENTITIES

Evelyn J. Peters, Roger C.A.Maaka, and Ron F. Laliberté

INTRODUCTION

Questions of identity are a key focus in contemporary society. As Paul Gilroy (1997) notes, "We live in a world where identity matters. It matters both as a concept, theoretically, and as a contested fact of contemporary life. The word itself has acquired a huge contemporary resonance, inside and outside the academic world" (301). Increasingly, views about the nature of identity have moved away from essentialist perspectives that define it as a recognition of common origin or shared characteristics with another person or group, leading to a natural allegiance. Identities are now viewed as socially constructed. Rather than representing a pre-existing "essential self," identities are negotiated and evolving as they are constructed to differentiate between "self" and "other" (Hall, 1996).[1]

If identities are evolving and negotiated, then state definitions of population groups can affect identity formulation, particularly in the contemporary era where modern states are often providers of social and economic benefits. The census is an instrument of government that has similar potential to affect individual's identities. As Scott (1998) argued, census categories do not simply count existing population groups in society. Instead, because census categories are embedded in state institutions, they can structures peoples' daily lives.

This chapter compares the categories defining Aboriginal people available in the Canadian census with the ways that Aboriginal residents of Saskatoon, Saskatchewan, described their own identities.[2] The 2006 and 2011 census categories emphasize the general categories, "North American Indian," "Métis," and "Inuit," rather than specific cultural groups such as "Cree," "Ojibwa," or "Red River Métis." The question of the degree to which census categories map onto the ways Aboriginal people defined themselves is especially interesting in cities because early research found that, in cities, specific cultural origins became less important as pan-tribal or pan-Aboriginal groups emerged. However, more recent research emphasized the growing importance of particular Aboriginal cultural identities in urban life.

The next section explores the role of the census in creating group definitions and describes the enumeration of Aboriginal peoples in the Canadian census. A summary of the literature on the implications of urbanization for Aboriginal identity formation is followed by a methods section. After the data are analyzed, a conclusion summarizes the chapter's main findings.

CENSUS PRACTICES AND ABORIGINAL PEOPLE

Censuses do not simply count existing groups of people. While census categories are often presented as neutral, scientific "facts," they reflect social and political reality. Enumeration in the census can be the result of citizen lobbying (Kertzer & Arel, 2002; Peterson, 1987). Phrasing in the census can reflect broader state objectives, for example, the decision not to use cultural markers to differentiate between citizens in order to promote national unity and cohesion (Blum, 2002; Goldscheider, 2002). Scott noted that a major achievement of modern statecraft was to categorize state populations and places to make them much more amenable to state interventions (1998: 183).

Whatever the sources of census categories, these categories can shape as well as reflect social and political realities. According to Scott (1998), "The builders of the modern nation-state...do not merely describe, observe, and map; they strive to shape a people and landscape that will fit these techniques of observation" (81–83). Population categories "can end up becoming categories that organize people's daily experiences precisely because they are embedded in state-created institutions that structure that experience." Recognition of particular groups in the census can lead to claims for particular services in particular locations. Statistical comparisons of inter-group characteristics can support the demand for remedial measures (e.g. Urla, 1993). Remedial measures can support increased employment for marginalized groups.

The tendency in censuses is to simplify, or aggregate, because the cost of delivering, coding, and publishing detailed questions can be overwhelming. Andersen (2008) suggests that the need in the census for short, simple questions "requires census takers to assume that their categories hold a stable, plain meaning" (360) across population categories and locations. Based on his analysis of Métis enumeration, he argues that the contemporary Canadian census aggregates groups with different cultures, political circumstances, and histories. Aggregation may result in the lack of support for initiatives that address specific needs and values and lead to their social and political marginalization (Peterson, 1987). Indigenous peoples have spoken out against definitions (including census categories) that homogenize indigenous identities (Bose, 1996).

Although terminology and particular practices have varied, the Canadian census has enumerated Aboriginal populations since 1971.[3] As defined by the Canadian Constitution (1982) the Aboriginal people of Canada include three groups: the North American Indians (often called First Nations in Canada); the Métis, who are descendants of Europeans and First Nations people and who created a distinct cultural and political group in western Canada; and the northern Inuit peoples. The census terminology "North American Indian" includes individuals who are registered under Canada's Indian Act as well as individuals who identify with this category but who are not registered.

While the census has historically collected information about individual's ancestry or ethnic origins, the 1996 Census introduced a question that asked individuals who reported Aboriginal ancestry whether they "identified" with their reported ancestry. The "identity population" (those who identified as a North American Indian, Métis, or Inuit person) was considered to more accurately capture the meaning of what had been termed a "core Aboriginal population" (Goldmann & Siggner, 1995). The question was meant to provide an "indicator of an individual's feelings, allegiance or association" with Aboriginal culture (Goldmann, 1993: 11).

The Canadian 2006 and 2011 Censuses include several questions to enumerate Aboriginal populations:

Q 18. Is this person an Aboriginal person, that is, North American Indian, Métis or Inuit (Eskimo)? [The question has check-off boxes for each group.]

Q 20. Is this person a member of an Indian Band / First Nation? [If the answer is "yes," respondents are asked to write in name of band or First Nation.]

Q 21. Is this person a Treaty Indian or a Registered Indian as defined by the Indian Act of Canada? ["Yes" or "No" check-off boxes listed.] (UN Statistics Division, 2006).

Most of the published data on Aboriginal peoples in Canada is based on the categories of North American Indian, Métis, and Inuit. Question 20 allows respondents to indicate membership in a particular First Nation, but this information is not available in Statistics Canada's published materials. While Aboriginal Affairs and Northern Development Canada keeps statistics on Registered Indians in different bands/First Nations, legislation defining entitlement for Registered Indian status means that not all First Nations people who identify themselves with these categories are registered. The question this chapter attempts to address is whether these aggregate census categories match the ways respondents in a Saskatoon study described their identities.

ABORIGINAL IDENTITIES IN URBAN AREAS

Researchers and policy makers have often viewed Aboriginal cultures and identities to be incompatible with success in urban areas (Peters, 2000). In her book "Real" Indians and Others, Bonita Lawrence (2004) describes the racism that Aboriginal people face in many cities: "It is impossible to understand the lives of urban mixed-bloods without an awareness of the extent to which their families have had to struggle to assert a Native identity in a hostile white environment" (133).

In this environment, urban Aboriginal people have resisted pressures to assimilate and have created cultural communities and identities in urban areas. The 2010 Environics Institute study of Aboriginal people in eleven large Canadian cities found that a large majority were proud of their

Aboriginal heritage and culture. US researchers documenting early strategies of resistance noted that individuals worked across tribal identities to create "pan-Indian" organizations that were not based on the specific cultural practices of particular tribal groups (Fixico, 2001; LaGrand, 2002: 254; Weibel-Orlando, 1999: 301). Strauss and Valentino (2001) argue that government policies helped to create pan-Indian organizations and identities by encouraging urban migrants to loosen their ties with tribal communities. However, they found that third and fourth generations were more aware of tribal affiliations, seeking connections with their tribes of origin.

In Canada, the Royal Commission on Aboriginal Peoples (1993) highlighted the challenges posed by heterogeneous Aboriginal populations, reporting that "the diversity of origins and cultures of Aboriginal people living in a particular city often poses difficulty in establishing a sense of community" (4). Proulx's (2003) study of Community Council Project (CCP), an alternative justice program designed for Aboriginal people in Toronto, found that Anishnabe cultural practices predominated but respect for other First Nations also existed. Proulx (2003) argued that cultural inclusiveness was central to Aboriginal community in Toronto, although there was continuing tension in the face of diversity and limited resources and "fears of the erosion of particular Aboriginal identities and practices, as programmatic pan-Aboriginal approaches appear poised to homogenize distinctiveness" (163–164).

Other studies found that urban Aboriginal people used different strategies to cope with particular and more inclusive urban Aboriginal practices. Wilson and Peters (2005) found that Toronto Anishinabe people participated in ceremonies governed by other First Nations customs and practices because they were in a minority and events were infrequently organized following only Anishnabe protocols. When they wished to experience their own language and ceremonies, they travelled to their home reserve. Proulx (2006) argued that some urban Aboriginal peoples utilized culturally specific and pan-Aboriginal resources strategically "during policy and program negotiations with non-Aboriginal stakeholders" (421), which suggests that these options were not mutually exclusive. Researchers note that urban Aboriginal cultural identities are not simply transferred from earlier traditions or from remote Aboriginal communities, but draw instead on cultural traditions and identities that are consciously and systemically being reconstructed differently in cities (Newhouse, 2011; Proulx, 2006).

METHODS OF DATA COLLECTION AND ANALYSIS

This chapter was drawn from a collaborative research project that focused on urban Aboriginal identities in Saskatoon, involving the Saskatoon Indian and Métis Friendship Centre (SIMFC) and researchers in the Departments of Geography and Native Studies at the University of Saskatchewan. Saskatoon is a Canadian prairie city with a population of 21,535 First Nations and Métis people, which represents 9.3% of the Saskatoon population in 2006. In 2006, slightly more than half of the Saskatoon Aboriginal population (54.3%) identified as First Nations, and slightly less than half identified as Métis (Statistics Canada, 2008). Very few Inuit live in Saskatoon. The location of the researchers at the University of Saskatchewan and a previous relationship with the SIMFC were factors in choosing Saskatoon. The SIMFC downtown urban office facilitated the research process. A protocol governing the research and writing process was negotiated with the SIMFC before the grant application was submitted.

The questionnaire was created in a two-day seminar by the researchers (faculty and graduate students, a majority of whom identified as First Nations of Métis). Researchers drew on their own experiences and the results of previous work on urban First Nations and Métis identities in Canadian cities (Belanger, Barron, McKay-Turnbull, & Mills, 2003; Berry, 1999; Lawrence, 2004). The questionnaires were open-ended, inviting participants to share their stories and experiences and the sense they made of these events that shaped their identities (Clandinin & Connelly, 2000). There were also some closed-ended questions that collected specific information about demographics and histories to help provide a context for responses.

The SIMFC helped us to identify participants by disseminating information about the study and referring individuals. To include individuals who are not clients of urban First Nations and Métis organizations, we also put up posters at the University of Saskatchewan and used researchers' own social networks. Participants were asked to call to schedule an interview, and, at that time, they were asked a screening question about whether they considered themselves to be Aboriginal, and if so, did they identify as First Nations or Métis. Qualitative researchers suggest that saturation (themes begin to be repeated) occurs after about 20 interviews. We attempted to obtain interviews from four groups of adults (26 years or older) stratified by gender and by First Nations and Métis identities. In total, 72 interviews form the basis

Table 12.1 Participant Characteristics

	Number	Average Age	% with More Than High School	% Employed
First Nations adult male	18	41.7	47.4	36.8
First Nations adult female	18	38.7	38.9	22.2
Métis adult male	19	43.7	72.2	50.0
Métis adult female	17	47.0	78.9	42.1
Total	72			

of this chapter. The purpose of this study was not to obtain a representative sample but to gain some understanding of the terminology and descriptive elements participants used to construct their identities.

Table 12.1 summarizes some basic characteristics of the participants. Average ages and education levels for First Nations participants were slightly lower than for Métis participants. Unemployment rates were generally low, but they were lower for First Nations than for Métis. It is important to emphasize, though, that this is not a representative sample, and these data are provided primarily as context for the analysis that follows. Interviewers were First Nations or Métis graduate students. The interviews took place between June 1, 2007 and August 31, 2007. Most were conducted at the SIMFC, but a few were carried out at various locations where individuals were comfortable, including restaurants and university classrooms. Interviews were taped and interview times varied from 45 minutes to one and a half hours. After the interview, participants were offered an honorarium in recognition of their contribution. Tapes were transcribed, and *ATLAS.ti*, a software coding program, was used to explore the structure of the responses.

ANALYSIS

The following sections provide a snapshot of participants' responses to questions about their cultural identities. The quotations that are presented were chosen because they showed in detail the kinds of answers that participants gave.[4] There did not appear to be clear differences by gender, education, or employment status for different types of responses for individuals who identified as First Nation or as Métis.

First Nations Participants

Most (75%) of the individuals who indicated they were First Nations when they called to schedule an interview, identified with a particular First Nations cultural group when they defined their identities in the interviews. Seventeen participants who identified with a particular First Nations group had grown up on a reserve or largely First Nations community. They continued to have ties with these communities, and most spoke their language. Three extended quotations summarize the ways that participants talked about these communities in relation to their identities.

A 53-year-old male had this to say:

> I'm Plains Cree….I like to say that my reserve is still, they do the old way of having sun dances, feasts, everything is all traditional. I'm proud to say that we still have our culture identity and that's what, I guess, most of us learned. We learned these things from, from generations—each were passed down. All these, what do you call 'em, rituals, I guess. Yah….Every time I get interviewed I always say that's my first language, Cree, 'cause I started, well I lived and I was raised with my grandfather and mother when I was born. I was born the old way.

This participant identified not only as "Cree," but as "Plains Cree," recognizing the differences in culture, language, and history of different Cree groups in different areas of the country. It was important to him that the "old way" of celebrating Cree culture was still practised on his reserves. In other words, part of his identity came from the resistance of his First Nation to pressure to change their cultural practices. He also identified with other anchors of specific cultural identities: his first language was Cree, he still spoke it, and he was raised on-reserve with members of his extended family.

Similarly, a 42-year-old woman identified the importance of growing up on her reserve:

> I'm an Ojibwa First Nation from the Gulley First Nation in Manitoba and my cultural identity would be as an Ojibwa Aboriginal woman… I was raised on the reserve. My culture was the Ojibwa culture and I was raised in a traditional home and I learned the traditional ways of our people. My father was a medicine man. He was also a band

councilor. My mother was a homemaker. So having, having lived
that type of a life going to sun dances and sweats and feasts and
powwows I grew up like that but there is also the alcoholism in my
home. As I grew older in my teenage years the missionaries came to
our reserves...they taught us the Gospel...and we kind of grew up
with that in our community as we always had our Indian culture so
I had both, both worlds.

Like the previous participant, this woman identified growing up on
the reserve, learning traditional ways, and participating in ceremonies in
explaining why she identified as an Ojibwa woman. She also talked about
her parents' roles in the reserve social system. While Christianity later came
to the reserve, she talked about "having" her Indian culture even though
she experienced "both worlds."

A 39-year-old man emphasized that his ancestry was what anchored his
identity as a "full-blooded Cree":

Me, I never change what I say. I'm proud to be from where I am.
That's where my dad and my mushum are from. If they're from
somewhere else I would be proud to be from somewhere else but
Kawacatose is my home and I always say I'm full-blooded Cree,
because some people will say they're Cree and their grandparents
might still have half and half in them still, something like that....
And I know my, my parents and my grandparents are all Cree so,
as I say, I'm full-blooded Cree.

This ancestry was linked with Kawacatoose, a Cree reserve from which
the man's father and grandmother came and where he spent part of his
youth.

Five participants regained knowledge of their culture, and often family ties and communities of origin in adulthood, once they discovered their
ancestral origins. What is of particular interest is that despite these experiences, the participants identified with a particular cultural group, rather
than using a more aggregate term such as "First Nations." For example, a
43-year-old male who did not grow up with a strong cultural background
identified as Cree. However, this identity was not based on the Cree culture
of his origins, but on the Cree culture he had learned as an adult:

[I consider myself] more Northern Plains Cree than Swampy. What I was introduced to in my culture. I strongly identify with Northern Plains Cree. Both my parents were Swampy Cree. But they didn't have a cultural identity and it was never passed on to us. [This was because of] residential school for my mother. And her parents. My dad, I don't know his history, exact history, but I'm assuming that he wasn't introduced his own culture other than his trapping, fishing, etcetera...I didn't learn [my culture] from my own community. I learned it within an institution [First Nations University].

In the absence of cultural transmission from his parents, this participant was introduced to Plains Cree cultural practices while he was attending the First Nations University in Saskatoon, and he identified himself with that particular group.

Another example concerns a 42-year-old woman who was raised in foster care in another province but came back to Saskatchewan to find her birth family. She stated, "I'm Cree. But I didn't even know I was Cree until I came here and then found [my real family]....I feel that I am Cree. I know I am for a fact." Despite the loss of connections with their ancestry through the child welfare system or through the silence of parents in the face of racism, these participants identified with specific cultural origins.

Even four individuals, who described their ancestry as "mixed," identified their particular First Nations group, rather than referring to themselves as generally "First Nations": "Japanese, Cree, Saulteaux. Little bit black. I'm kind of a Heinz 57" (Female, 36); "Yah well, my late dad's dad was Cree from Ile a la Crosse. My late mom was Dene Inuit...So I got a few particles of whatever culture" (Male, 59); "So I'd be Plains Cree. I know I got some kind of white blood in me but I'm not sure what kind it is" (Female, 32); "My background is Cree. It's half and half. I don't even speak my language. I went to boarding school and foster homes; I just lost it" (Male, 34).

Only nine individuals used the aggregate terminology of "First Nations," "Indian," or "Native" to describe their identity. While they often knew their community of origin, and some even had Registered Indian status, a common theme in their discussion was their lack of a strong link to a reserve community of origin. Some had been in foster care most of their lives. Some were never taught their "Indian ways." Others absorbed the attitudes of urban society, which failed to distinguish between different cultural groups.

A 39-year-old man who had worked in a number of cities saw himself mainly in terms of the identities ascribed to him by non-Aboriginal society. He defined himself as "an urban Indian" because non-Aboriginal people in the city didn't differentiate between different First Nations cultures and saw him only as Aboriginal: "I see myself like an urban Indian living in the white man's society…Because when I left the reserve, you know, when I first moved into the city all they said was 'Urban Indian' you know…I got yelled at. That's what I was called or a bush Indian, you know."

In a second example, a 43-year-old man who grew up in the city had not been taught "Indian ways," but he identified himself as Aboriginal because he "looks like one." He learned to speak Cree, but he did not define his identity as Cree, or even First Nations. As a child he lived on a reserve and he knew his community of origin, but his contact with that community had been mostly negative. As a result, he classified himself more as "Caucasian male":

Well, sorry to say I'm an Aboriginal. And sorry to say I was never taught any Indian ways and sorry to say that I've been brought, I've pretty well brought myself up with no guidelines of to burn sweet grass, no guidelines on how to do whatever it is, ceremonial. I haven't been to what's called a sun dance. I've been to a pow-wow…What I know is that I'm an Aboriginal. I look like one and I also learned to talk like one. I started when I was 18, 20, 'cause I'm, "You gotta teach me that. Me and you we can talk and everybody else don't know what we're talking about." That's the only reason why I've learned to talk Cree. I class myself more a Caucasian male than an Aboriginal.

Métis Participants

While Métis participants did not identify particular Métis cultural sub-groups, there were nuances in their answers that also suggested different meanings of the term "Métis." Andersen (2008) has argued that the use of a single term homogenizes the different histories, cultures, and political origins of Métis in Canada. In particular, he argued that Métis has come to mean "mixed" racial origins rather than the culturally and politically orga-nized Métis Nation in western Canada. While none of the respondents in this study referred to the Métis Nation in their answers, distinctly different groups emerged from the ways that they framed their identities.

Eighteen (50%) of the participants linked their Métis identities to growing up in a particular community, extended family group, or culture identified with the western Métis Nation. For example, one participant described growing up in a community where Métis identities were taken for granted:

My mom was a Lavallee and my dad was Bourassa. And I married a Gardepy. That's a full-blown Métis...Just growing up there was so many Métis that we didn't even know the difference I don't think. Like the Henrys and the Fiddlers and all that, you know, Bissetts and the Barrettes and the Parenteaus and, you know, we didn't know the difference. 'Cause we grew up with the whole bunch. (Female, 76)

A second respondent, a 34-year-old woman, also grew up in a community with a strong Métis culture. What was important for her was the fact that her parents and grandparents were Métis, but so was learning about Métis history in Saskatchewan in a positive way:

I'm Métis. I was really fortunate to grow in a community where a lot of people there were Métis and the culture is pretty strong and there was never an identity issue because, you know, my mom was, my dad was, and so were my grandparents and, and my siblings and but, yah, positive in that way. Also the school is where we were taught about our history so I learned from an early age about Métis history in Saskatchewan and in Canada so I think that's really quite unique and really built a strong identity.

Other respondents connected Métis identities to different aspects of Métis community life. A 56-year-old woman commented, "I didn't think there was any other kind of people than, than us...'cause we all looked the same and we all shared the same type of culture and traditions." A 48-year-old male indicated, "I speak my language very fluently. So in regards to cultural identity I identify myself as a Métis." Finally, a 27-year-old female identified extended family relationships as something she considered as an important attribute of her Métis identity: "[When I was growing up] it was just a fact like we're Métis...In [Métis] culture family is very important... At my house I had aunts and uncles and everybody over all the time." All of these individuals connected their Métis identities with aspects of prairie Métis Nation culture linked to Métis communities. While there is relatively little work available that describes how Métis people in particular anchor their identities in urban settings, these responses echo some of the US research about the importance of communities of origin and the attributes of culture, including language, that are found there.

In contrast, eleven (30.6%) respondents indicated they were Métis because of their "mixed" First Nations and non-Aboriginal ancestry, or because they did not have status as Registered Indians. The first partici-pant quoted below explicitly recognized different ways of identifying as Métis in different parts of the country:

> My father's from New Brunswick. Like his grandfather came to New Brunswick from Gaspé from a reserve area, Mariah, and his grand-mother was born on a reserve on Gaspé across from Hamilton and in Eastern Canada if you are of mixed descent which means Acadian and Migmah, that's considered Métis...In the prairie provinces they don't recognize people as Métis unless you come from Red River or Batoche (Female, 25).

Other participants use terminology that also showed that their Métis identity came from their "mixed" ancestry. These individuals did not identify with the symbols of western Métis culture mentioned in the quotations summarized earlier. They remarked, "I'm Métis...A crazy little breed...A mix-ture" (Female, 40); "I'd say I'm Métis...My mother is Ojibwa and my father is white" (Male, 41); "I myself am Métis. My father is Treaty, my mother isn't" (Female, 33).

Two participants just simply stated that they were Métis without expanding on their statements, while three additional participants knew they were Métis, but did not feel they had any of the cultural attributes associated with their definition of that identity. The following quotation comes from a 48-year-old man who knew that his ancestry was Métis but felt that he had lost his culture because of the long period of time when he was in foster care: "I'm a lost Métis...Just trying to understand myself because I lost myself so much in the white man world."

Finally, two individuals who initially identified as Métis when they called to make the appointment to be interviewed used more aggregate terminology in their interview. These were individuals who did not have experience of Métis community growing up: "My mother raised me to believe I was not native...And that I had relatives that had really dark skin...So then after the DNA tests were done...I'd probably look like an idiot when I would say 'I'm not Aboriginal'" (Female, 34); "I am a Native person, but I'm also this and I'm also that. I don't run my life as a Native person" (Female, 40).

Implications for Census Terminology

The current terminology of "First Nations" and "Métis" available in the census does not capture the specific ways that respondents characterized their Aboriginal identities in our study. Most (75%) of First Nations participants identified with a particular First Nations culture, rather than referring to themselves using more general terminology. An unexpected result was that participants who identify with a particular First Nations culture included individuals who had been fostered or adopted as children but found their birth parents or communities and relearned their cultural practices as adults. It is beyond the scope of this chapter to explore the reasons for this practice, but it may have something to do with the elements found by Strauss and Valentino (2001), including increasing tribal involvement in cities, and increased support for activities by particular tribal groups. The participants who used more general terminology were primarily individuals who had lost, or who had never had, a background that linked them to a community or cultural group. This is an important finding because it suggests that growing up in rural or reserve communities is not the only anchor for identification with particular First Nations cultures. In other words, it suggests that identification with particular First Nations groups may continue even over several generations in the city. The configuration of Métis responses was slightly different, but they still demonstrated different meanings of the term for different people. Almost all respondents (80.6%) defined Métis either in terms of a Métis Nation cultural background or as "mixed." A minority (19.4%) did not qualify the term, or used more general terminology to refer to themselves. These results suggest that similar processes are occurring in the Métis as in the First Nations community in Saskatoon.

The 2006 and 2011 Censuses, though, aggregate both First Nations and Métis identities. This does not reflect the ways participants defined their identities in this study, and it may contribute to homogenization of these identities in the future. The quotation in the title highlights the implications of the lack of services available that reflect particular cultural identities. The lack of Saulteaux activities in largely Cree Saskatoon did not prevent the respondent from practising a First Nations culture, but he was concerned about the emergence of homogenization, which he called "pan-Indianism." Aggregation in the census may have a similar effect.

Identification in the census can have important implications for indigenous peoples. In the era where modern states are often providers of social and economic benefits, group differentiated programs and services might be directed toward particular areas depending on population size and proportion (Kertzer & Arel, 2002; Urla, 1993). Research can identify socio-economic disadvantage leading to demands for remedial policies, highlight stereotypes that need to be combated, or explore unique situations that require differentiated policy responses. Population numbers can lead to claims for political representation and funding. If particular First Nations and Métis groups are not identified, then it is difficult to target programs and services for these groups, or to compare their socio-economic well-being. Aggregate categories in government programs and policies may nudge organizations toward more aggregate approaches and fail to support the particular cultural identities demonstrated by Aboriginal participants in Saskatoon.

CONCLUSION

This chapter compared the ways that First Nations and Métis participants defined their cultural identities to the terminology that enumerates them in the Canadian census. The Canadian census emphasizes the general terminology "First Nations" and "Métis." In contrast, First Nations participants in this study identified with particular First Nations cultures, for example "Cree" or "Dene." Métis identities were also heterogeneous, including individuals who anchored their Métis identities in prairie Métis Nations cultures and communities and those who identified as Métis because of their "mixed" ancestry. While many of these individuals had grown up on-reserve or in Métis communities, others had reclaimed their identities as grown-ups, despite adoption or the silence of their parents about their ancestry. This practice suggests that identification with particular First Nations and Métis groups will continue. The categories available for self-identification of Aboriginal people in the census may need to move to these more specific identities.

AUTHORS' NOTE

We wish to acknowledge the participants in this study who agreed to talk about their experiences in the city. We would like to thank the interviewers who worked on this project: Tyler Fetch, Michelle Hogan, and Jim Tailfeathers. The Saskatoon Indian and Métis Friendship Centre (SIMFC) was a wonderfully supportive partner. The research was supported through in kind funding from the SIMFC and research grant funding from the Social Sciences and Humanities Research Council of Canada (SSHRC).

NOTES

1. We recognize that, in the context of colonial governments' demands for unbroken historic continuity of tradition as a condition for Aboriginal rights, the representation of Aboriginal identities as negotiated and continuously evolving can have dangerous repercussions when Aboriginal people attempt to assert their Aboriginal rights (Clifford, 1988). On the other hand, viewing Aboriginal identities as static and unchanging ignores the devastating effects of colonialism (Churchill, 2004; Lawrence, 2004). Following Dirlik (1996), we view Aboriginal identities as neither self-conscious mobilization and redefinition of tradition, nor as historical and unchanging reflections of Aboriginal culture. Dirlik (1996: 19–21) argued that rather than emphasizing only a pure and persistent Aboriginal history, Aboriginal peoples draw upon the past to create a new future, struggling with colonialism while resisting its effects.

2. Following the Constitution Act (1982 as amended), we use the term "Aboriginal peoples" to refer to the Indian, Métis, and Inuit peoples of Canada. Most contemporary writers use "First Nations" instead of "Indian." When discussing official government policies, we adopt the terms used in colonial and Canadian government policies and statistics (e.g., Registered Indian, Native). Registered Indians are individuals who are registered under the Indian Act. When referring to a specific First Nations community, we use particular names such as Mi'kmaq, Cree, Ojibway. We also recognize that the term "Métis" has different and contested meanings; sometimes it refers to descendants of First Nations and European people, and sometime it refers to descendants of the Métis Nation that emerged in the Prairie provinces. Finally, when we summarize the US literature, we use the terminology authors employ—for example, "tribe," "Native American," and "Indian."

3. A history of Canadian census terminology is beyond the scope of this chapter, but interested readers are referred to Goldmann (1993) and Goldmann & Siggner (1995).

4. Responses are presented in respondents' own words, but for easier reading they were edited to remove repetition, expressions like "like," "um," "uh," and some sentence fragments.

REFERENCES

Andersen, C. (2008). From nation to population: the Racialisation of 'Métis' in the Canadian census. *Nations and Nationalism*, 14(2), 347–368.

Belanger, Y., Barron, L., McKay-Turnbull, C., & Mills, M. (2003). *Urban Aboriginal youth in Winnipeg: Culture and identity formation in cities*. Winnipeg, MB: Canadian Heritage.

Berry, J.W. (1999). Aboriginal cultural identity. *The Canadian Journal of Native Studies*, 19(1), 1–36.

Blum, A. (2002). Resistance to identity categorization in France. In D.I. Kertzer & D. Arel (Eds.), *Census and identity* (pp. 121–147). Cambridge, UK: Cambridge University Press.

Bose, T. (1996). Definition and delimitation of the indigenous peoples of Asia. International Work Group on Indigenous Affairs, 1996. Retrieved from http://www.iwgia.org/SW312.asp

Churchill, W. (2004). A question of identity. In S. Greymorning (Ed.), *Will to survive: Indigenous essays on the politics of culture, language, and identity* (pp. 59–94). New York, NY: McGraw Hill.

Clandinin, J., & Connelly, M. (2000). *Narrative inquiry*. San Francisco, CA: Jossey-Bass.

Clifford, J. (1988). *The predicament of culture*. Cambridge, MA: Harvard University Press.

Dirlik A. (1996). *The past as legacy and project*. American Indian Culture and Research Journal, 20, 1–31.

Environics Institute. (2010). *Urban Aboriginal peoples study: Main report*. Scarborough, ON: The Interprovincial Groups.

Fixico, D. (2001). Foreword. In S. Lobo & K. Peters (Eds.), *American Indians and the urban experience* (pp. ix-x). Walnut Creek, CA: Alta Mira Press.

Gilroy, P. (1997). Diaspora and the detours of identity. In K. Woodward (Ed.), *Identity and difference* (pp. 299–349). London, UK: Sage/Open University.

Goldmann, G. (1993). *The Aboriginal population and the census. 120 years of information—1871 to 1991*. Ottawa, ON: Statistics Canada.

Goldmann, G., & Siggner, A. (1995). *Statistical concepts of Aboriginal people and factors affecting the counts in the census and the Aboriginal peoples survey*. Paper presented to the 1995 Symposium of the Federation of Canadian Demographers, Ottawa.

Goldscheider, C. (2002). Ethnic categorization in censuses: Comparative observations from Israel, Canada, and the United States. In D.I. Kertzer & D. Arel (Eds.), *Census and identity* (pp. 71–91). Cambridge, UK: Cambridge University Press.

Hall, S. (1996). Introduction: Who needs "identity"? In S. Hall & P. du Gay (Eds.), *Questions of cultural identity* (pp. 1–18). London, UK: Sage.

Kertzer, D.I., & Arel, D. (2002). Censuses, identity formation, and the struggle for political power. In D.I. Kertzer & D. Arel (Eds.), *Census and identity* (pp. 1–42). Cambridge, UK: Cambridge University Press.

LaGrand, J.B. (2002). *Indian metropolis: Native Americans in Chicago, 1945–75*. Champaign, IL: University of Illinois Press.

Lawrence, B. (2004). *"Real" Indians and others: Mixed-blood urban Native peoples and indigenous nationhood*. Vancouver, BC: University of British Columbia Press.

Newhouse, D.R. (2011). Urban life: Reflections of a middle-class Indian. From the tribal to the modern: The development of modern aboriginal societies. In H.A. Howard & C. Proulx (Eds.), *Aboriginal peoples in Canadian cities* (pp. 23–38). Waterloo, ON: Wilfrid Laurier University Press.

Peters, E.J. (2000). Aboriginal people in urban areas. In D. Long & O.P. Dickason (Eds.), *Visions of the heart: Canadian Aboriginal issues* (pp. 237–270). Toronto, ON: Harcourt Brace & Company.

Peterson, W. (1987). Politics and the measurement of ethnicity. In W. Alonso & P. Starr (Eds.), *The politics of numbers* (pp. 187–234). New York, NY: Russell Sage Foundation.

Proulx, C. (2003). *Reclaiming Aboriginal justice, identity and community*. Saskatoon, SK: Purich Publishing.

———. (2006). Aboriginal identification in North American cities. *The Canadian Journal of Native Studies, 26*(2), 405–439.

Royal Commission on Aboriginal Peoples. (1993). *Aboriginal peoples in urban centres*. Report of the National Round Table on Aboriginal Urban Issues. Ottawa, ON: Ministry of Supply and Services Canada.

Scott, J.C. (1998). *Seeing like a state*. New Haven, CT: Yale University Press.

Strauss, T., & Valentino, D. (2001). Retribalization in urban Indian communities. In S. Lobo & K. Peters (Eds.), *American Indians and the urban experience* (pp. 85–94). Walnut Creek, CA: Alta Mira Press.

UN Statistics Division. (2006). Demographic and social statistics, Canadian census 2006. Retrieved from http://unstats.un.org/unsd/demographic/sources/census/censusquest.htm#C

Urla, J. (1993). Cultural politics in an age of statistics. *American Ethnologist, 20*(4), 818–843.

Weibel-Orlando, J. (1999). *Indian country, L.A.: Maintaining ethnic community in complex society*. Champaign, IL: University of Illinois Press.

Wilson, K., & Peters E.J. (2005). "You can make a place for it": Remapping urban remapping urban First Nations spaces of identity. *Society and Space, 23*, 395–413.

13

CONTINUITY OR DISAPPEARANCE
ABORIGINAL LANGUAGES IN CANADA

Jim Frideres

INTRODUCTION

Throughout the twentieth century, there seemed to be an acceleration of language disappearance. Some scholars (Marti et al., 2005; Grimes, 2000; Wurm, 2001) suggest the trend of language (both national and tribal) disappearance (sometimes referred to as "language shift") will continue and in fact accelerate. Skutnabb-Kangas (2004), Nettle and Romaine (2000), and Krauss (1992) argue that by the end of the twenty-first century, 90% of all existing languages in the world will have disappeared. Generally, these claims are based on the number of speakers of the language, and the predictions are based on this sole criterion. Table 13.1 reveals the number of speakers of a single language around the world.

Table 13.1 Percentage of Language Speakers by Total Number
of Speakers of a Language*

Number of Speakers of a Single Language	Percentage
100+ million	<1
10–99.9 million	1
1–9.9 million	4
100,000–999,999	13
10,000–99,999	27
1,000–9,999	29
< 1,000	26
Total Number of Languages	6,059

* Figures as approximate and based on previous research by Crystal, 2000; Krauss, 1992;
Hagege, 2000; Marti et al., 2005.

Given that size is the sole (or major) criterion for predicting language
maintenance, one can see the reasonableness of such predictions. We take
this concern for the retention of languages and apply its implications to Aboriginal languages in Canada.[1] This chapter investigates the structural and
community factors that are related to Aboriginal language use and retention
as we proceed into the twenty-first century. We also assess the likelihood of
language survival for the more than 50 Aboriginal languages in Canada.[2]

With a growing interest in language retention, scholars are beginning to
investigate possible causal factors that facilitate or reduce the continuity
of language (Boermann, 2007; Slavik, 2001). Aboriginal communities have
developed language programs to re-establish their linguistic roots (Anonby,
1997; Brandt & Youngman, 1989; Fishman, 1997). Socio-demographic factors
such as fertility, language transmission, age structure, migration, exogamy,
community participation, group vitality, use of language in home/work,
and other factors have been identified as affecting language continuity
(Fishman, 1997; Huss, Grima, & King, 2003). Others have noted that the
number (percentage) of speakers in a community, the level of institutional
support for the language, community loyalty toward the language, external
economic, political and social pressures, and the death/dispersion of a language community will have profound effects on language continuity (Norris
& Snider, 2008). While we are not able to address all of the above factors,
we will utilize existing data to assess the effect of several factors as they
relate to Aboriginal language use and retention.

LANGUAGE AND CULTURE

Why should we be interested in language retention or continuity? What are the implications and consequences for language loss? First of all, we argue that the philosophy and culture of a people are embedded in their language and given expression by it. Others have argued that the key to identity and retention of culture is one's ancestral language. Thus, language is the basis for the transmission of ideas, values, and perceptions of reality that create or influence one's world view. The production of discourses is especially important here because such discourses create and express the belief system, the world view, by which we judge everything (Rahman, 2001). This kind of impact is referred to as "signitive" influence.[3]

In the case of Aboriginal languages, we must begin by noting that their form and structure are quite different than Euro-Canadian languages. As such, language also shapes the relationship between the mind of the speaker and the person, thing, or event being described (Canada, 2005). Aboriginal languages focus on relationships as well as reinforce relationships, rather than on proving points. Language also is used to establish connections and negotiate relationships with the goal of living in balance. The structure of these Aboriginal languages establishes the relationship between the subject and object of a phrase differently than English or French. For example, Anishnabe permits the speaker to emphasize the identities of the objects as well as the relationship between them, while in English the focus is on "awareness of oneself and what that person has to say" (Canada, 2005).

Stories in an Aboriginal language encourage the imagination. Moreover, words carry the content of messages as well as a sense of continuity, history, and linking the past present and future. As such, Aboriginal languages are associated with the themes of infinity and perpetuity. Euro-Canadians tend to see these words as hyperbole in part because of the analytic, objectivistic traditions of Euro-Canadian thought (Einhorn, 2000). Western languages deal with finite movements, with beginnings and ends, with causes and effects. French and English are clear in differentiating between speakers and audience; speakers deliver messages, and audiences serve as receptors. Moreover, Western languages have little tolerance for ambiguity, incompleteness, and inconsistency. Individuals are expected to present complete, consistent messages, and clarity and precision are highly valued. Language in Aboriginal communities is not about a discourse that assumes completion or expects an ending. The language of Aboriginal people allows individuals to contemplate answers. Speakers of the language purposefully avoid being directive to allow their listeners to glean the meaning and implications of the messages being sent out. Aboriginal speakers stress the existence of the "spiritual world" while Westerners generally cut themselves off from such a conceptualization, considering it suspect or unreal (Caduto & Bruchac, 1989).

Finally, official Canadian languages are representational. Words represent reality. However, in Aboriginal languages words are considered presentational. That is, words bring reality into being or present the being of things. Viewing words as presentational may explain why Aboriginal people consider language as standing for reality. Thus, words are intrinsically powerful, magical, and sacred (Einhorn, 2000). In summary, we find that language shapes people's perceptions of the world, their reaction to their environment and responses to issues and problems that confront them. In the end, we find that languages provide their users with a world view that is created, in part, by their language. The loss of a language brings a new world view to the holder and poses adaptive techniques to bridge the change.

PREDICTIONS ABOUT ABORIGINAL PEOPLES

Since the mid-nineteenth century, Canadians believed that Aboriginal people would disappear through assimilation, intermarriage, or disease. Early indicators of birth and death rates and levels of enfranchisement supported this view, as the Aboriginal populations plummeted drastically. However, as Anatole Romaniuk (2008) points out, this prediction has not come to fruition. The growth of the Aboriginal population in Canada has been phenomenal over the past half century. Even within the past decade, the increase has been short of breathtaking. The total Aboriginal population increased by 45% between 1996 and 2006, compared to an 8% increase in the general Canadian population (Trovato, 2008). Métis and Inuit reveal a 91% and 26% increase, respectively, while First Nations increased their population by 29% (Goldmann & Delic, 2008).

Political actions, such as the introduction of Bill C-31 in 1985 and Bill C-3 in 2010, had a major effect on the subsequent numbers and demographic profile of Aboriginal people. For example, these bills brought into the definition of a "Registered Indian" (First Nations) approximately 200,000 people that previously had not been defined as First Nation (Indian). In addition, others have shown that reporting "Aboriginal" as one's ethnicity in the census has become more acceptable (Taylor & Bell, 2004). Finally, there is some "cachet" attached to the label "Aboriginal" and thus people are prepared to self-disclose on the census form, yet remain somewhat invisible in the real world. In the end, the figures above demonstrate a strong population growth and one that is likely to continue for some time with nearly 40% of the Aboriginal population under the age of 25 (Verma, 2008).

Over the past century, there were indicators that First Nations people were becoming more and more urbanized. Again, it was predicted that First Nations communities would be decimated by the increasing exodus from reserves into the urban centres. Data was presented confirming the increasing urbanization of First Nations, and such a prediction seemed validated. However, once again, we find that since 1980, an increasing number of individuals are returning to their "home lands" and fewer and fewer individuals are leaving their First Nations communities. In some cases, there have been net increases of people migrating to the reserves.

Similar predictions have been made about Aboriginal languages. Since the middle of the twentieth century, there has been an assumption that Aboriginal people would becomes so assimilated (through intermarriage, education, integration) that they would lose their languages as they entered the twenty-first century. There was an assumption that by the fourth generation, the assimilation would be so complete that Aboriginal languages would make up an insignificant portion of the non-official languages spoken. However, the data reveals that, while there has been some loss of language over the years, the dire predictions have not come to fruition. One major reason for this not happening is that Aboriginal identity is critical to maintaining "personal relationships" networks (integrative function) for social and community purposes (Morita, 2007). In addition, Aboriginal languages are now offered as a "credit" subject in secondary and post-secondary schools across the country. Enrollment figures reveal these classes have bloomed over the past decade. While these numbers suggests that these students may not have an Aboriginal mother tongue, it demonstrates they are interested in learning and using the language in their communities. The overall trend reveals an increasing interest in Aboriginal languages, although this interest will vary by language family and specific language. Languages such as Algonquin, Dogrib, Carrier, Blackfoot, and Cree in 2006 revealed more than 10% increases over the 2001 figures. On the other hand, languages such as Ojibway and Salish have shown decreases in both the number of individuals with a mother tongue as well as knowledge of an Aboriginal language. However, some languages have not been able to survive and have become extinct or near extinct as we continue into the twenty-first century.

METHODOLOGY

Much of the data for this chapter are derived from information gathered by Statistics Canada. As such, the thrust of the chapter is related to First Nations (Registered Indians) only. Moreover, it is important to point out that our unit of analysis is the community. The variables measured in the core of this chapter were recorded in terms of percentages, although for some variables, appropriate coding was used, e.g., size of reserve measured in total number of people living in the community. Data are not available for areas where the Aboriginal identity population is less than a population of 250 or when the quality of collected data was deemed by Statistics Canada to be inadequate. The chapter also uses information from Aboriginal Affairs and Northern Development Canada. As a result, the following analysis is based upon a sample of 312 community profiles where data was complete on the variables included in the present chapter. The above constraints must be considered when assessing the results.

The research required that several variables be created from the existing database. Language facility is our major dependent variable and is divided into three different dimensions: mother tongue, Aboriginal language spoken at home, and knowledge of an Aboriginal language. The socio-demographic factors (our independent variables) include employment, mobility, education, size of reserve, proportion of speakers in community, geographical area of residence, e.g., urban, rural, remote, special access, median income, intermarriage, and average age in the community. The chapter will assess the influence these factors have on language continuity for a select sample of Canadian Aboriginal communities.

THEORETICAL PERSPECTIVE

The following figure (Figure 13.1) depicts the overall linkages suggested in previous literature. This model is a dynamic model and accepts that the various dimensions may change over time. That is, as fertility rates change over time, the number of speakers may change and the change in these variables will influence directly or indirectly the language use within a community. Furthermore, the relative impact of the specific factors may change over time. For example, in Canada, Aboriginal language use was forbidden for many years in both public and residential schools. However, over time, these attitudes and restrictions have been removed and greater opportunities for Aboriginal people to learn an Aboriginal language have emerged. Today, Aboriginal languages are offered in all levels of primary and secondary schools, post-secondary educational institutions, and through Aboriginal community organizations.

The model in Figure 13.1 first addresses the role of language in the community, e.g., is it integrative or is it instrumental? The instrumental reasons also are called "pragmatic," "rational," "objective," or "utilitarian" (Rahman, 2001) and focus on the ability to obtain a better job, increase one's income, or further participate in mainstream society. On the other hand, the "integrative" or sometimes called "irrational" or "subjective" reasons reflect personal, emotional, or hedonistic bases. These integrative aspects refer to the dimension of our needs that cannot be measured in terms of better jobs or a higher income (Rahman, 2001). On the other hand, it does not mean that these integrative objectives are less valuable than instrumental goals. In fact, they may be more valuable to the individual.

Figure 13.1 Structural Factors Related to Language Use and Retention

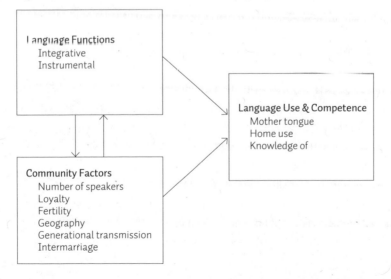

If the language community is marginalized and not fully participating in the larger society, the role of an Aboriginal language can be both instrumental and integrative. It is instrumental in that residents will need the Aboriginal language to function within the community and to carry on interactions, community activities, and various economic transactions (Karan, 2008). At the same time, it provides them with an integrative function in their community. However, there are external pressures on Aboriginal people to enter the mainstream economic and social world. This puts pressure on Aboriginal languages to lose its integrative component (because you can use another language to function in the community and its various political, social, and economic dimensions) and a language shift occurs (to English or French) that is solely instrumental in nature. When the language group is fully participating in the larger "mainstream" society, then the indigenous language has already given to the language loss and the remaining linguistic use is only to be used as an integrative function within the Aboriginal language community (Reyhner & Lockard, 2009).

However, the model also suggests that there are other demographic/structural factors that impinge upon a linguistic community and have an impact on language use/retention. In our model, we have been able to measure a number of community variables that have been identified as possible factors that impact upon language use and maintenance. For example, geographical residence and rate of intermarriage are potential factors acting as facilitators or barriers to language use and sustainability. Nevertheless, the function of language and the structural factors of First Nations communities interrelate with each other and have an impact the accessibility and acceptability of Aboriginal languages (Burnaby & Reyhner, 2002).

LANGUAGE SHIFT, CONTINUITY, AND FLUENCY

Language continuity refers to the extent to which a group of people are able to continue using a language in their everyday life over time. The 2006 Census revealed that nearly 30% of First Nations people in Canada said they could speak one of the over 60 Aboriginal languages well enough to carry on a daily conversation. To identify the language viability of a group, an "index of continuity" has been developed that scholars and politicians alike use to make predictions about how long the language will continue. This index represents the ratio of the number of people who use a language at home relative to the number of people who have that language as their mother

Table 13.2 Number of Aboriginal Speakers and Continuity Index
          for Selected Languages, Canada, 2001

Language	Aboriginal Mother Tongue Population	Continuity Index
Total Aboriginal Language	222,200*	0.64
Algonquian Family	142,090	0.62
Cree	80,075	0.62
Ojibway	23,520	0.45
Attikamek	4,725	0.95
Maliseet	825	0.33
Inuktitut Family	29,675	0.82
Athapaskan Family	18,530	0.63
Dene	9,595	0.81
Dogrib	1,925	0.70
Siouan Family	4,310	0.66
Salish Family	3,210	0.20
Tsimshian Family	2,030	0.26
Wakashan Family	1,445	0.14
Iroquoian Family	670	0.08
Haida Isolate	165	0.06
Kutenai Isolate	170	0.29

* This figure is for 2006. All other figures are for 2001.

Sources: Norris, 2007; 2011; Statistics Canada, 2008; Canada, 2005.

tongue.[1] A ratio of 1.00 represents a complete reproduction of the language and suggests high viability for the language. Anything less than that value suggests that there is language "loss" and that over time the language could be lost. Scholars have used an index value of 0.30 as the threshold for determining the viability of a language (Wurm, 2001; Kinkade, 1991). Table 13.2 provides the reader with a brief profile of some of the major Aboriginal languages in Canada in terms of total numbers as well as the viability of some of the languages.

The data reveal that over a quarter of a million people now report an Aboriginal language as their mother tongue with the three largest language families being Algonquian, Inuktitut, and Athapaskan. Nevertheless, the distribution of Aboriginal mother tongue throughout Canada reveals substantial differences among languages and provinces/territories. For example, the top five most common Aboriginal group languages make up three-quarters of the on-reserve First Nations population that learned an Aboriginal language as their mother tongue. The remaining quarter speak a wide variety of languages. Spatially, Nunavut reveals the highest level of mother tongue retention (81%), while several of the provinces, e.g., Ontario (10%), British Columbia (8%), have some of the lowest percentages.

People with an Aboriginal mother tongue tend to live on a reserve and only 4% of those individuals who have an Aboriginal mother tongue are not Registered Indians. As we enter the twenty-first century, there is general language continuity rate for all Aboriginal languages of 0.64 (home language /mother tongue), a decrease of over 10% since 1981.[5] However, this broad categorization does not take into consideration the differences among the three groups of Aboriginal people—First Nations, Métis, and Inuit.

On the other hand, if we reconceptualize the numerator as "knowledge of an Aboriginal language/mother tongue," there is a continuity rate of 1.20. Norris (2003) refers to this as the "index of ability." The numerator reflects the ability to speak and understand an Aboriginal language in a normal con-versation. This suggests that, overall, while there is some loss of language capacity (e.g., mother tongue), many Aboriginal people are picking up an Aboriginal language as a second language.

Focusing only on First Nations, we find that some communities have flourishing languages. For example, over 10% of First Nations communities have over 80% of the people fluent in the language and are able to read and write the language. An additional 18% have "enduring" languages, which means that over 60% of the population in the community is fluent in their language. On the other hand, we also find that nearly two-thirds of the communities have less than 50% of the population as speakers of their language. Overall, these numbers show that most of the communities have language continuity rates that suggest their languages are viable over time. However, we also know that 11% of the communities in Canada have less than 10 adult speakers, which reveals these are indeed endan-gered languages.

According to the 2001 census, less than one-quarter of the total Aborigi-nal (Indian, Métis,[6] and Inuit) population said they had knowledge of or ability to converse in an Aboriginal language. We also know that one-fifth of the population had learned their Aboriginal language as their first language (mother tongue). When we take into consideration the age of the individual, we find that in the youngest group (0–24 years), the ratio of Aboriginal "home speakers" to the total population is 0.16. For the age group 25–44 the ratio is 0.14 and for those older than 44, the ratio increases to 0.19. These data suggest that younger people are learning an Aboriginal language in school, and it also reflects the loss of language by those in middle age. The data also show that only about 1% of the First Nations population can only speak an Aboriginal language. However, we know that this figure increases with older Aboriginal people.

We also find that about 13 to 18% of the Aboriginal population claim to speak an Aboriginal language most often in their home. These results need to be placed in the context of the work of Norris (2007), who found that the number of young people (0–19) with an Aboriginal mother tongue is decreasing. She also found that in the past two decades, the percentage of Aboriginal people with an Aboriginal mother tongue declined from 41% to just over 30%. Nevertheless, at the same time, the percentage of adults with an Aboriginal mother tongue aged 55 and over increased from 12% to 18%. This overall picture includes First Nations, Métis, and Inuit. If we compare the three different Aboriginal groups, there are major differences in language use and mother tongue. For example, Inuit have a mother tongue rate of 66% while Métis have a 4% mother tongue rate of continuity.

LANGUAGE VIABILITY

Scholars have developed measurements for determining the "viability" or "continuity" of languages, ranging from "viable" to "uncertain" to "endangered" to "extinct." As noted earlier, the main criteria seem to be the size of the population using an Aboriginal language. For example, Cree, with nearly 90,000 speakers is rated "viable," while the language of Tlingit (105 speakers) is rated "endangered." At other times, the basis for determining which category the language will be placed in is based on the ratio of home use to mother tongue speakers. However, we find some small language groups, e.g., Blackfoot (4,000), Maliseet (<700), Dogrib (2,000), have extremely high continuity indexes and are considered "viable" languages in the near future (See Table 13.2). This suggests that there are other structural factors (Barrena et al., 2007) impinging upon the language communities that have an impact on language use and continuity that go well beyond the mere size of a population.

Table 13.3 Percentage of Aboriginals Claiming an Aboriginal Mother Tongue, 1986–2006

Year	All Aboriginal	On-Res.	Off-Res.	Inuit	Métis
1986	28.6	46.6	15.7	62.4	NA
1991	26.9	50.3	18.3	74.3	10.6
2001	21.4	58.2	11.2	70.0	5.4
2006	19.8	62.6	9.2	66.1	4.6

Source: Statistics Canada, 2008. Aboriginal Peoples in Canada in 2006: Inuit, Métis and First Nations, 2006 Census.

The index of continuity for all Aboriginal languages decreased through-out the latter part of the twentieth century, e.g., 0.76 in 1981, 0.65 in 1996. However, as we proceed into the twenty-first century, we find that the index continued its decline but then, for the first time in many years, began to stabilize and perhaps even actually increase slightly. The data show that for on-reserve First Nations, the index is 0.93; off-reserve, 0.73; Métis, 0.76; Inuit 0.99, and other Aboriginal 0.83. Thus, the recent data reveal that, while a steady decrease in the percentage of Aboriginals with a mother tongue is evident, there has been an increase for on-reserve First Nations communities. (See Table 13.3.) We also find that there is a strong linkage between language continuity and where one lives, e.g., reserve vs. city. Only 10% of Aboriginals living in a city have an Aboriginal mother tongue. Four per cent of Aboriginal people in cities have an Aboriginal home language, and only 14% of Aboriginal people in cities reported knowledge of an Aboriginal language. These figures are low compared to the national Aboriginal figures 26% (mother tongue), 18% (home language), and 29% (knowledge of), respectively, with regard to Aboriginal mother tongue.

Another way of assessing the language viability of a group is to assess the extent to which a language is used in the home. The census of 2001 reveals that for the total Aboriginal population, 75% of the people spoke English at home while less than 4% spoke French. The remaining 21% speak an Aboriginal language at home, which is slightly lower than the proportion with an Aboriginal mother tongue. Table 13.4 reveals the home language of the major divisions of the Aboriginal population as well as the ability of an individual to carry on a conversation in that language (Aboriginal knowledge).

Table 13.4 Home Language and Knowledge of Aboriginal Language
         by Aboriginal Identity and Residence, 2006 (percentage)

Language	First Nation			Aboriginal Group	
	On-Reserve	Off-Reserve	Métis	Inuit	Other
English home use	57	84	86	32	85
French home use	2	4	5	<1	7
Aboriginal home use	41	9	3	66	4
Aboriginal knowledge	55	19	6	84	N/A

Sources: Norris, 2011; Statistics Canada, 2008.

These data reveal that there are major differences with regard to residence (on- or off-reserve) and type of Aboriginal. We find, for example, that
for on-reserve First Nations people, just over half have an Aboriginal mother
tongue, 41% use the language at home, and 55% understand an Aboriginal
language (Gionet, 2009). We also know that for on-reserve First Nations
people, 54% of them learned English as their mother tongue and only 44%
learned a non-Aboriginal language only or in combination with English
or French. Just focusing on young children (0–14) living on-reserve, we
find that, in 2006, 39% of them speak an Aboriginal language, up from 36%
in 2001. On the other hand, for off-reserve First Nations people, only 16%
have an Aboriginal mother tongue, 9% use their Aboriginal language at
home, and 19% have a working knowledge of an Aboriginal language.
Those First Nations people living in the city have even less facility with the
language with only 9% with a mother tongue, 3% who use an Aboriginal language in the home, and 12% who have a working knowledge of an Aboriginal
language. For young children (0–14) living in the city, only 6% speak an
Aboriginal language, down from 8% in 2001.

Those who have an Aboriginal mother tongue have a median of 41 years
of age compared to an overall Canadian median age of 35 years. We also
know that age is related to those who claim to have a working knowledge
of their Aboriginal language. For example, while 39% of on-reserve and 6%
of off-reserve children 0–14 have knowledge of an Aboriginal language, this
increases to 56% and 13%, respectively for those in the 25–44 age group.
Moreover, for the 65 and over group, the percentage increases to 81% and
25%, respectively. The data show that overall there has been a growth in

the numbers of speakers who can carry on a conversation in an Aboriginal language, primarily through learning the language in school, e.g., second language acquisition. This suggests that some languages are gaining speakers at a faster rate through second language acquisition than through mother tongue transmission (Norris, 2011).

STRUCTURAL LINKAGES TO LANGUAGE USE

We now move to test our model with regard to factors influencing language sustainability. The results for assessing the impact of structural/demographic community factors are displayed in Table 13.5. On the basis of our literature review, we identified a number of structural variables that were possible correlates of language use and sustainability. Utilizing the "community profiles" presented by Statistics Canada, we assessed the correlations between various structural conditions in First Nation communities and the community's language use and knowledge.

We take each factor in turn. Employment was our first variable and was categorized as "employed" and "unemployed." Results by Biddle, Taylor, and Yap (2008) showed that a correlation between socio-economic status and speaking an indigenous language at home (2005) was –0.62. While we were unable to put together a composite socio-economic status (SES) profile, we do have separate measures with regard to employment, income, and education. Employment also can be used as a proxy for measuring the "integrative/instrumental" aspect of language use. Our reasoning, flawed as it may be, suggests that those communities with high levels of unemployment have no use for non-Aboriginal language because they are unable to integrate into the larger economic system that requires English and/or French and thus would reflect high levels of Aboriginal language use and knowledge and subsequently language continuity. The results do not confirm this reasoning. Although small, the correlations nevertheless reveal that communities with higher levels of unemployment have higher rates of mother tongue, knowledge of, and use of an Aboriginal language at home than those with lower rates of unemployment. Mobility (have you moved in the past five years?) is our second structural variable. We also argue that mobility can be used as a proxy measure of mainstream participation. Those communities that showed high levels of mobility reflect lower levels of Aboriginal language maintenance, which again reveals that the need for knowledge of and use of Aboriginal languages are limited to those communities that have not displayed high levels of mobility. Mobility may mean movement within the First Nations community but more than likely reflects the individual's decision to move out of the community and then back to the First Nations community.

Another proxy measure of participation in the mainstream society focuses on education. Here we note that higher levels of education also are related to language use. We find that the higher the level of education in the community, the lower the level of language use, mother tongue, and use at home. These indicators all suggest that an Aboriginal language plays an important integrative role in a First Nation community that is stable, has a low average education, and has a high rate of unemployment. These communities do not see the need to acquire one of the official languages to participate in the larger social, economic, and political structures of Canadian mainstream society. On the other hand, those communities that have high employment, have high mobility rates as well as high educational achievements, use English as the functional language for integrating into the "mainstream" society, and thus see less need for an Aboriginal language.

We then focused on community size and its relationship to language use. We find there is a small correlation between language use and this factor. However, we then looked at the percentage of people who spoke an Aboriginal language and, not surprisingly, found it highly correlated with mother tongue and use at home. This may suggest that language learning as a second language contributes, in the long run, to the larger number of individuals with an Aboriginal mother tongue. Geographic location of the First Nation community was also thought to have some importance in language maintenance (Slavik, 2001). Using the coding scheme devised by Aboriginal Affairs and Northern Development Canada, (urban, semi-urban, rural, remote), we found a substantial correlation between the location of a First Nations community and language. We find that First Nations in remote/special access regions have a much higher percentage of Aboriginal mother tongue than those in urban or semi-urban First Nation communities. This confirms a strong connection between the geographic residence and the number of people having an Aboriginal mother tongue (Norris, 2003). Those First Nations communities that were classified as urban were much more likely to have low rates of language knowledge, language use, and mother tongue, while isolated First Nations communities tended to have high levels of language use, knowledge of, and mother tongue.

Table 13.5 Correlation Between Selected Community Variables
and Language Facility on First Nation Communities

| | Language Facility | | |
| | Adults | | |
	Mother tongue	Knowledge*	Use at home
Employment	0.07	0.02	0.09
Mobility	−0.41†	−0.36†	−0.41†
Education	−0.33†	−0.29†	−0.46†
Pop. size of comm.	0.09	0.03	0.08
Percent speakers	0.57†	0.51†	0.45†
Geography of reserve	0.56†	0.41†	0.53†
Avg. age on reserve	0.63†	0.39†	0.49†
Median income	−0.12	−0.23†	−0.17
Intermarriage	−0.73†	—	−0.38†

* Knowledge refers to the ability to conduct an everyday conversation with another person
in an Aboriginal language.
† Significant at the 0.05 level.

The age distribution of a First Nations community (as a proxy of "gen-eration") has been suggested as an important factor in language use and continuity (Slavik, 2001). Norris (2007) found that the average age of the mother tongue population was highly correlated to an "index of language continuity," which reveals that the older the age of the mother tongue popu-lation, the higher the index of continuity. However, this has an "expiration" date attached to it as the cohort continues to age; the aging population begins to die off. At that time, if a replacement cohort of younger people is not also obtaining an Aboriginal language, the language will become extinct. However, our results show that the median age of the First Nations community is strongly related to language mother tongue but less so for knowledge and use at home. This suggests that while younger members of the population are not acquiring an Aboriginal mother tongue, they are acquiring an Aboriginal language through second language acquisition.

Our next variable was the income level of the community. We looked at the median income of First Nations communities and its impact on language use. The data show that a modest inverse relationship exists—the higher the median income, the less an Aboriginal language will be used at home, and the less the community will have knowledge of an Aboriginal language and have a low rate of mother tongue. Again these results may reflect the linkage of the community to the "mainstream" society.

We then looked at the correlation between the percentage of individuals in a mixed marriage (one partner speaks an Aboriginal language and the other does not) and language use for 30 languages. Linguistic intermarriage is likely to identify a contemporary instance of group disaffiliation, and the effect of this on the next generation will result in total language loss (Stevens & Schoen, 1988).

This confirms that for communities with high levels of exogamous marriages, there are considerably lower rates of Aboriginal language use. These results also suggest that the non-Aboriginal marriage partners are not interested in learning an Aboriginal language. However, this factor is inextricably intertwined with the issue of whether the individual lives on or off the reserve.

These results reveal that Aboriginal exogamous marriages are associated with diminished continuity of language—demonstrating a strong inverse relationship between language continuity and exogamy. A similar relationship is found when mother tongue is linked to exogamy. However, the correlation is reduced to –0.38 when the dependent variable is use at home. Overall, endogamous families (with both parents speaking an Aboriginal language) result in the highest language continuity in children. This is followed by lone-parent families, and the poorest outcome is for exogamous marriages. The question now is whether the directives of Bill C-31 will have any long-term impact on the rate of "mixed marriages" and thus influence language continuity. This strong correlation supports the contention that language use and continuity is highly related to language facility by both parents.

CONCLUSION

Historical factors such as the discouragement of Aboriginal languages in residential schools and later in public schools have served to rupture the transmission of language from one generation to another. However, First Nations communities are dealing with the lack of mother tongue transmission. For example, we know that in 2006, 12% of Cree speakers have acquired the language through "second language learning," thereby reflecting an interest in the language by the community to retain the language. Language classes are being offered in First Nations communities across the country in both primary and secondary schools; over 2,000 primary and secondary students are currently enrolled in Aboriginal language courses in Alberta alone. In addition, new courses are being developed in First Nations communities for mid-generation adults who were unable to learn or were prevented from learning their language when they grew up. This middle-age cohort finds itself in a peculiar position in the community. The younger members are learning an Aboriginal language in school and the older cohort has continued to use its Aboriginal language. In a sense, this middle cohort is unable to communicate with either the young people or the old. The reader should also be aware that Aboriginal languages such as Cree and Inuktitut are actually dialect chains, meaning they are not sufficiently standardized that a speaker of a dialect at one end would not be able to communicate with another speaker of a dialect of the same language at the far end. Thus, the data needs to be cautiously interpreted until further analysis takes place.

We also find that Aboriginal people, like others, are not homogenous ethnic groups. There is no single set of Aboriginal cultural practices that one can say represent Aboriginalness. The colonial experience, the generational trauma, and the marginalization that Aboriginals have experienced over the past century has resulted in three different types of Aboriginalness: (1) those that emphasize speaking an Aboriginal language, have knowledge of, and participate in Aboriginal ceremonies and rituals, and are linked with other Aboriginal people; (2) those who have both Aboriginal parents who stress the knowledge of ancestral history and are conscious of Aboriginal networks and blood ties. They may speak and understand some Aboriginal language but not at a fluent level; and (3) those who have been raised in Canadian Aboriginal families, and their central indicator of Aboriginalness is having Aboriginal ancestors as well as having some symbolic knowledge and understanding of Aboriginal culture and ceremonies. They are not able to converse in an Aboriginal language but may have some knowledge of words and phrases they can use at appropriate times.

Given these differences in "Aboriginalness," we find that structural factors differentially impact language continuity and use. This leads to the question of the need for language use to sustain Aboriginal identity. The Irish people adopted the "Imperial" English yet retained their identity. The new generation of Jews in North America has lost their ability to speak Yiddish, yet they have retained a sense of community and identity. On the other hand, Ukraine has experienced a similar history of language restriction, yet they retained their language as part of their national identity. All this suggests that language, while important, needs to be interpreted in the historical and cultural context of the group being studied.

We have noted that predictions of precipitous population declines and increasing migration to the cities were a confirmed fact in the 1970s. However, it is clear that these predictions were moderated by values and structural conditions impinging upon Aboriginal people. Out-migration from rural reserves has now been changed to in-migration. Thus, urbanization has stalled. The claims that Aboriginal populations would decrease has changed direction on two fronts. First, legislation was introduced that added thousands of people to the "rolls," although this may be reversed by the year 2050. Second, while death rates for Aboriginal people have decreased substantially, birth rates have not made such a commensurate change. At the present, Aboriginal people have a birth rate twice that of the general population, and today we find that nearly 40% of the Aboriginal population is under the age of 25. The interaction of a young population and language use and continuity remains to be played out.

Laitin (1998) points out that social groups "tip" from one kind of behaviour to another over time. In the present case, we are referring to language use and sustainability. This tipping or cascading occurs because people's choices about their actions are based on what they think others are going to do. It means that people will tip toward learning an Aboriginal language to the extent that they believe that other people are also doing so and that there is some symbolic or functional value in doing so. For example, tipping toward learning an Aboriginal language occurs when a community feels that it would empower the group through the political process. The end result will be the stabilizing of indigenous languages.

Language is a symbol of identity for many Aboriginal people that gives a focal point for mobilization for them for both integrative and instrumental reasons. Those promoting language retention and rediscovery are well-aware of the linkage between language and identity. They resist, rhetorically, by investing in learning their own language hoping that, in the long run, if enough people speak the language, it will be given official recognition by the dominant group. In other cases, people learn an Aboriginal language because it has some symbolic significance. Integrative reasons, such as pride and awareness of Aboriginal identity, are also important issues in language retention. In this respect, resistance language teaching (teaching an Aboriginal language) may be able to resist the domination of a language of power.

AUTHOR'S NOTE

I would like to thank Mary Jane Norris and Anatole Romaniuk for providing a critical review of the document as well as their helpful comments. However, any and all errors remain with the author.

NOTES

1. It is important to understand that the term "Aboriginal" includes "Indians" (First Nations), Métis, Inuit, and "other Aboriginal."
2. Some scholars argue there are 61 different languages.
3. There are two other types of linguistic power: pragmatic and symbolic. Pragmatic power is based on the communicative aspect of language, while symbolic power refers to the association of a language with attributes that have a value, positive or negative in the mind of the perceiver (Rahman, 2001).
4. A language first learned and still understood is referred to as one's "mother tongue."
5. There are two measures of a continuity index. One measure is based on a single response to language, while the other is based on both single and multiple responses. Our measure is based on single responses.
6. Métis have developed a language called Mischif.

REFERENCES

Anonby, S.J. (1997). Reversing language shift: Can Kwak'wala be revived? (Unpublished master's thesis). University of North Dakota, Grand Forks, ND.

Barrena, A., Amoarrortu, E., Ortega, A., Uranga, B., Izagirre, E., & Idiazabal, I. (2007). Does the number of speakers of a language determine its fate? *International Journal of the Sociology of Language, 186*, 125–139.

Biddle, N., Taylor, J., & Yap, M. (2008, October). *Closing which gap? Demographic and geographic dilemmas for indigenous policy in Australia.* Paper presented at Aboriginal Population in Transition—Demographic, Sociological and Epidemiological Dimensions, University of Alberta, Edmonton.

Boermann, M. (2007). Language attitudes among minority youth in Finland and Germany. *International Journal of the Sociology of Language, 187/188*, 129–160.

Brandt, E., & Youngman, V. (1989). Language renewal and language maintenance: A practical guide. *Canadian Journal of Native Education, 16*, 42–77.

Burnaby, B.J., & Reyhner, J.A. (2002). *Indigenous languages across the community.* Flagstaff, AZ: Northern Arizona University, Center for Excellence in Education.

Caduto, M., & Bruchac, J. (1989). *Keepers of the earth: Native American stories and environmental activities for children*. Golden, CO: Fulcrum.

Canada. (2005). *Towards a new beginning: A foundation report for a strategy to revitalize First Nation, Inuit, and Métis cultures*. Ottawa, ON: Task Force on Aboriginal Languages and Cultures, Aboriginal Affairs Branch, Canadian Heritage.

Clatworthy, S., & Norris, M.J. (2007). Aboriginal mobility and migration: Trends, recent patterns, and implications: 1971–2001. In J. White, S. Wingert, D. Beavon, & P. Maxim (Eds.), *Aboriginal policy research: Moving forward, making a difference*, Vol. IV (pp. 123–145). Toronto, ON: Thompson.

Crystal, D. (2000). *Language death*. Cambridge, UK: Cambridge University Press.

Einhorn, L. (2000). *The Native American oral tradition*. Westport, CT: Praeger.

Fishman, J. (1991). *Reversing language shift: Theoretical and empirical foundations of assistance to threatened languages*. Philadelphia, PA: Multilingual Matters.

————. (1997). Maintaining languages: What works? What doesn't? In G. Cantoni (Ed.), *Stabilizing Indigenous languages* (pp. 186–198). Flagstaff, AZ: Northern Arizona University, Center for Excellence in Education.

Gionet, L. (2009). First Nations people: Selected findings of the 2006 Census. *Canadian Social Trends*, Special Edition, 10–18.

Goldmann, G., & Delic, S. (2008, October). *Ethnic mobility—An historical and contemporary outcome for Aboriginal peoples in Canada: Evidence drawn from past trends and current census data*. Paper presented at Aboriginal Population in Transition—Demographic, Sociological and Epidemiological Dimensions, University of Alberta, Edmonton.

Grimes, B. (2000). *Ethnologue*. Dallas, TX: Summer Institute of Linguistics.

Hagege, C. (2000). *Halte a la mort des langues*. Paris: Odile Jacob.

Huss, L., Grima, A., & King, K. (Eds.). (2003). *Transcending monolingualism: Linguistic revitalization in education*. Lisse, The Netherlands: Swets & Zeitlinger.

Karan, M. (2008, July). *The importance of motivations in language revitalization*. Paper presented in Second International Conference on Language Development, Language Revitalization and Multilingual Education in Ethnolinguistic Communities, Bangkok.

Kinkade, M. (1991). The decline of native languages in Canada. In R. Robins & E. Uhlenbeck (Eds.), *Endangered languages* (pp. 143–165). Oxford, UK: Berg.

Krauss, M. (1992). The world's languages in crisis. *Language*, 68, 4–10.

Laitin, D. (1998). *Identity in formation: The Russian-speaking populations in the near abroad*. Ithaca, NY: Cornell University Press.

Malone, D., & Choosri, I. (2002, June 2). *Stabilizing indigenous languages*. Paper presented at the 9th Annual Symposium, Forum for Language Fieldwork, Bozeman, Montana.

Martí, F. et al. (2005). *Words and worlds, world language report*. Clevedon, UK: Multilingual Matters.

Morita, L. (2007). Discussing assimilation and language shift among the Chinese in Thailand. *International Journal of the Sociology of Language*, 186, 43–58.

Nettle, D., & Romaine, S. (2000). *Vanishing voices: The extinction of the world's languages*. Oxford, UK: Oxford University Press.

Norris, M.J. (2003). The diversity and state of Aboriginal languages in Canada. *Proceedings of the conference on Canadian and French Perspectives on Diversity* (pp. 38–55). Ottawa, ON: Canadian Heritage.

————. (2007). Aboriginal languages in Canada: Emerging trends and perspectives on second language acquisition. *Canadian Social Trends, 83,* 20–28.

————. (2011). Aboriginal languages in urban Canada: A decade in review, 1996–2006. *Aboriginal Policy Studies,* 1(2), 4–67.

Norris, M.J., & Snider, M. (2008). Endangered Aboriginal languages in Canada: Trends, patterns and prospects in language learning—Personal correspondence. In C.T. de Graaf, N. Ostler, & R. Salverda (Eds.), *Endangered Languages and Language Learning: Proceedings of the Conference FEL XII.* (pp. 157–185). The Netherlands: Fryske Akademy, Foundation for Endangered Languages.

Rahman, T. (2001). Language-learning and power: A theoretical approach. *International Journal of the Sociology of Language, 152,* 53–74.

Reyhner, J., & Lockard, L. (2009). *Indigenous language revitalization: Encouragement, guidance & lessons learned.* Flagstaff, AZ: Northern Arizona University, Center for Excellence in Education.

Romaniuk, A. (2008, October). *Canada's Aboriginal population: From encounter of civilizations to revival and growth.* Paper presented at Aboriginal Populations in Transition—Demographic Change and Development Conference, University of Alberta, Edmonton.

Skutnabb-Kangas, T. (2004, November 10). Interview with Skutnabb-Kangas by P. Toukomaa. *Berria,* Basque Country.

Slavik, H. (2001). Language maintenance and language shift among Maltese migrants in Ontario and British Columbia. *International Journal of the Sociology of Language,* 152, 131–152.

Statistics Canada. (2008). *Aboriginal peoples in Canada in 2006: Inuit, Métis and First Nations, 2006 Census.* Ottawa, ON: Statistics Canada.

Stevens, G., & Schoen, R. (1988). Linguistic intermarriage in the United States. *Journal of Marriage and the Family,* 50, 267–279.

Taylor, J., & Bell, M. (Eds.). (2004). *Population mobility and indigenous people in Australasia and North America.* London, UK: Routledge.

Trovato, F. (2008, October). *Death and the family: A half century of mortality change (1950–2000) in the Registered Indian population of Canada as reflected by period life tables.* Paper presented at Aboriginal Population in Transition—Demographic, Sociological and Epidemiological Dimensions, University of Alberta, Edmonton.

Verma, R. (2008, October). *Population projections for the Aboriginal population in Canada: A review of past, present and future prospects, 1991–2017.* Paper presented at Aboriginal Population in Transition—Demographic, Sociological and Epidemiological Dimensions, University of Alberta, Edmonton.

Wurm, S. (2001). *Atlas of the world's languages in danger of disappearing.* Paris and Canberra: UNESCO.

14

THE EAGLE HAS LANDED
OPTIMISM AMONG CANADA'S FIRST NATIONS COMMUNITY[1]

Cora J. Voyageur

INTRODUCTION

At 4:18 p.m. on July 20, 1969, American astronaut Neil Armstrong uttered the words, "Houston, Tranquility Base here. The Eagle has landed" ("The Moon," 1969). Those of us who are old enough to remember these famous words were probably glued to our grainy black and white television sets. We marveled at this engineering feat and imagined the possibilities that would derive from those first steps into a new frontier.

The indigenous community also watched the event but interpreted it differently. To them, those famous words meant that a thousand-year-old prophecy had come to fruition.[2] The prediction held that indigenous people of the Americas would suffer at the hands of the European colonizers but that their relationship would change when the "eagle lands on the moon." For example, the First Nation peoples of Canada were placed in a subordinate position vis-à-vis Euro-Canadians and suffered tremendously by the oppressive policies imposed upon them, such as the Indian Act (Voyageur & Calliou, 2007). The Indian Act continues to dictate virtually every aspect of "Indian" life in Canada from cradle to grave. Although its regulations have loosened over time, in the past, it confined First Nations people to reserves (Miller, 2000: 258), rendered them ineligible to vote in provincial and federal elections, prohibited their religious ceremonies, and made it illegal for them to bring lawsuits against the government (Venne, 1981; Voyageur, 2008).

1969 was a significant year for the space program in the United States, but it was also important for the First Nations community in Canada.[3] That year, the federal government proposed its landmark *Statement of Government of Canada on Indian Policy*, 1969 (also referred to as the *White Paper on Indian Policy*). This legislation planned to renege on the treaty promises made to the Indians of Canada that would see the elimination reserve lands and abolish the "special status" given to Indians under those treaties.[4] Essentially, the nation-to-nation agreements through which the First Nations people of Canada agreed to share their land and resources were going to be eliminated by the very government that had negotiated them. It seems that the words used by the treaty commissioners when negotiating the treaties, "as long as the grass grows and the river flows," (Treaty 8) did not mean "forever"—it meant only until the government decided that it would opt out. First Nations people were not going to stand helplessly by while their land and their heritage were unilaterally stripped away from them. The gravity of the impending loss spurred them into action.

The White Paper was countered by the Red Paper—a document produced on behalf of the Indian Association of Alberta under the leadership of then president Harold Cardinal (see Meijer Drees, 2002). While the White Paper intended to eliminate the First Nations people and their rights, it had the opposite effect. It served to galvanize the First Nations peoples' resolve and helped them to organize to fight the proposal. The proposed policy was eventually withdrawn by the federal government in 1970.

The gulf between the societal realities of the First Nations experience in Canada and the awareness of these situations by mainstream Canadian population is substantial. J. Rick Ponting's (2000) study of public opinion and Aboriginal people in Canada reports that they are virtually unknown by Canadian citizens. They are most commonly presented in negative terms in mainstream media where they are portrayed as being in conflict with society by selective reporting of roadblocks and demonstrations (Nancoo & Nancoo, 1997). The steady diet of bad press gives mainstream Canadians the impression that First Nations people are troublesome and one-dimensional (Lambertus, 2004).

Social science research does not help First Nations people improve their collective image outside their community. As common subjects in social sciences research, they are examined through a lens of the atypical or problematic. This attention focuses on the "Indian Problem," or what might be called a "deficit paradigm," and rarely questions the history, discriminatory policies, or context of Aboriginal life in Canada. This type of research fails to recognize and acknowledge strengths and resilience of the First Nations people and their communities.

The First Nations community is a rich, diverse, and vibrant community with positive elements and grounds for optimism. This chapter identifies some of the positive developments for First Nations in Canada in the four decades since the "Eagle landed on the moon." Although the examples cited in this chapter are not exhaustive, they serve as a starting point for a more positive approach to the exploration and discussion of the dynamic aspects of First Nations community. These phenomena include: population growth, human capital development, economic and professional development, politics and policy, legal advances of Aboriginal and treaty rights, and healing and reconciliation.

POPULATION GROWTH

Between 1996 and 2006, First Nations population increased by 29% (Statistics Canada, 2005). The fact that the First Nations population in Canada was almost eliminated makes its recovery a reason for hope. The population shrunk from the estimated two million prior to European contact by disease and epidemics (Thornton, 1987) to a mere 107,000 (Romaniuc, 2000). Over the remainder of the twentieth century, Canada's First Nations population steadily increased to almost 700,000 as of 2006 (Statistics Canada, 2008a). In fact, the First Nations population in Canada increased by 20% between 2001 and 2006.

This population increase is influenced by factors both inside and outside the First Nations community. Inside the community, population increases are caused by a higher fertility, a lower infant mortality rate than witnessed in the past, and a longer lifespan for First Nations people. The fertility rate for First Nations women, 2.9, is almost double that of mainstream women, whose fertility rates sit at 1.5 (Statistics Canada, 2006). Although First Nation females have more children than mainstream females, they are having fewer children than they did in the past. The 2006 First Nations fertility rate of 2.9 is down from the 1986 First Nations women's fertility rate of 3.8 (Barsh, 1994). Bearing fewer children means that First Nation women can expect fewer pregnancy-related health issues. With fewer dependents, they are able to take greater advantage of opportunities for education, training, and employment.

The infant mortality rate serves as an indicator for population health, the effectiveness of health care, and public health initiatives (Human Resources and Skills Development Canada, 2008). The infant mortality rate has been notably higher in the First Nations community than for mainstream Canadians. For example, in 1979, the infant mortality rate for mainstream Canadian society was 10.5 per 1,000 births, while the First Nations community recorded an infant mortality rate of 27.6 (Health Canada, 2011). Mainstream Canada recorded a rate of 5.3 in 2003, and the First Nations community recorded a rate of 6.2 (Government of Canada, 2004). The First Nations community's infant mortality rate decreased from 2.6 times higher than mainstream society in 1979 to a point where it is only 0.9% higher than that of mainstream society (Government of Canada, 2004).

First Nations citizens have a shorter expected lifespan than mainstream Canadians. In 2001, the average lifespan for mainstream Canadians was 79.6 years (77.0 for males and 82.1 for females), while the First Nations' lifespan was shorter by almost six years at 73.9 years (70.4 for men and 75.5 for women). The lifespan for both mainstream Canadians and First Nations Canadians has increased over time. For example, in 1980 the average lifespan for mainstream Canadians was 75.2 years (71.7 for males and 78.9 for females), and the First Nations persons' lifespan was 64.5 years (60.9 for men and 68.0 for women). The gap between mainstream Canadians lifespan and those of First Nation individuals has decreased from 10.7 years in 1980 to 5.7 years in 2001. During that period, mainstream Canada's lifespan increased by 4.4 years, while First Nations peoples' lifespan increased by 9.4 years (Statistics Canada, 2008a).

Outside the community, policy changes, such as Indian Act amendments, particularly the passage of Bill C-31 on April 17, 1985, allowed those who had previously lost their Indian status to reclaim it.[5] This resulted in a significant increase in the number of people with First Nations status. Records show that by 2003, Bill C-31 registrants made up 16% of the Indian registry (Indian and Northern Affairs, 2007).

In addition, numbers have increased as a result of individuals self-declaring as First Nations for the first time. Some people were ashamed of being a First Nations person and saw being "white" as preferable. Many rationalized that passing as white meant an easier life and not having to deal with discrimination and racism experienced by First Nations people. Some who could "pass as white" did so.

The ability for the First Nations to increase its population speaks to the increased accessibility and availability of health care services to that community. There has also been an effort to implement preventative health programming such as nutritional counselling, stop smoking programs, and diabetes awareness.

To recap, the First Nations population has multiplied almost seven-fold in the past century. This was caused by natural increase and a strengthening of the individual First Nation cultural identity, which made people stay true to their heritage despite the low social status associated with First Nations membership and the increased prospects of encountering racism and discrimination. The First Nations population is increasing as a result of increased fertility, a lowered infant mortality rate, and a longer lifespan. These indicators signal an improvement in First Nations living standards.[6] In addition, policy changes allowed those who had lost their status to regain it. Those who had denied their First Nations background in the past are declaring their heritage, thus further increasing the population numbers. The increased population heightens the First Nations' visibility in mainstream society.

HUMAN CAPITAL DEVELOPMENT

First Nations people are joining the wage labour force at numbers never seen before. A Public Works and Government Services Canada report shows 123,345 First Nations people in the paid labour force in 1996 (INAC, 2007). In 2006, this number increased to 236,830 (Statistics Canada, 2008c). These numbers show an increase of 113,485 First Nation workers in the Canadian economy or a 92% increase in a 10-year period.

First Nations people have embraced the notion of meritocracy. Human capital theory states that individuals who invest time, energy, and money in the pursuit of education, training, and other qualities deemed useful will increase their own worth, which in turn makes them more valuable to the

employer (Becker, 1993). Human capital includes innate ability, formal education, vocational education, on-the-job training and on-the-job experience
(Peters & Rosenberg, 1995). Heightened levels of human capital are said to
increase the individual's productive capabilities, thus justifying a higher
salary and increased job security.

Deficiencies in the skills and aptitudes required by advanced industrial
and post-industrial economies contribute to high unemployment rates.
Deficiencies in human capital limit the opportunities available to First
Nations individuals and limit the organizational capacity of First Nations
governments (Calliou, 2008). A variety of indicators demonstrate the
enormous human capital gains in the First Nations population. Emerging
data shows a class of First Nations workers who possess the educational
credentials and skills needed by government and industry. This pool of
human capital is deepening, and First Nations individuals are becoming better equipped to take advantage of job opportunities and positions of power
that arise on or off the reserve.

The majority (61% in 2003–2004 academic year) of First Nations elementary and secondary students are enrolled in band-operated schools (INAC,
2007). Hiring qualified First Nation teachers and incorporating elders into
the formal education of the children has caused the school dropout/push-
out rates to decline. Twenty-nine per cent of on-reserve students remained
in school until graduating from Grade 12 (or 13) for the 2003–2004 academic
year (INAC, 2007).

The participation rate of First Nation individuals in post-secondary
institutions has increased dramatically since the early 1960s, and the gap
between First Nations and the mainstream Canadian population education
attainment levels has narrowed. The post-secondary attainment rate for
First Nation individuals in 2001 was 23%,[7] while for the total Canadian population the rate was 38% (INAC, 2007). This is a remarkable achievement
given the barriers the students face.

First Nations university students commonly say that they want to
put their education to good use by helping their community after completing their studies. Thus, they have a deeper purpose for social justice that
motivates them to succeed. Many First Nations families have at least one
member of an extended family who has attained post-secondary credentials and can now serve as a role model to others interested in college or

university studies. A post-secondary education is not perceived to be as daunting to First Nations people as it once was.

Other heartening educational attainment data includes the fact that the 2006 Census indicated that 42,900 First Nations individuals hold at least one university degree (Statistics Canada, 2008b). This is an increase of 14,055 or 49% in a five-year period. Degree holders from the non-enumerated reserves would be in addition to that number. In 2003 alone, 3,580 First Nations individuals graduated from post-secondary institutions, including 1,163 with baccalaureate degrees and about 200 with post-baccalaureate degrees (INAC, 2007). The distribution of First Nations students across post-secondary disciplines is also improving; there is less clustering in social work and education and more representation across a wide variety of fields such as engineering, law, business, and medicine. These trends bode well for those graduates who want to return to work in the First Nations communities after completing their education. The number of graduating students and the diversity of disciplines also benefit the First Nations community that will be able to employ the graduates in a variety of positions. Many First Nations professionals also work off-reserve in business, government, and academia. This also means that there is less likely to be a glut of qualified band members trained in any particular area.

ECONOMIC AND PROFESSIONAL DEVELOPMENT

Another reason for confidence in the future is that the First Nations communities and individual business owners are increasing their involvement in the economy. The location of some First Nations communities has yielded economic opportunities for them. For example, windfall revenues from natural resources have accrued to a small number of First Nations who have used those revenues to diversify the local economy, upgrade physical infrastructure, improve social and educational services, fund political initiatives, etc. Some others, such as the Mohawks of Kahnawake near Montreal, Muskeg Lake near Saskatoon, Westbank First Nation near Kelowna, Musqueam First Nation in Vancouver, and Tsuu T'ina Nation adjacent to Calgary are located near major urban centres and have capitalized on the retail, real estate, and recreational needs of the large market.

First Nations people are obtaining business skills through organizations such as the Association of Aboriginal Financial Officers and Canadian

Association of Native Development Officers, which operate with the mandate of providing training, regulation, and support for people working in the financial sector in the First Nations community. First Nations people are being recognized for their business acumen. First Nations businessmen David Tuccaro and Doug Goloski, for example, have received national recognition for their business success.

In the past, many First Nations communities had problems obtaining financing for economic ventures because they lacked collateral. First Nations were forbidden from raising revenue through taxation. However, the 1988 Kamloops Amendment to the Indian Act (Bill C-115) helped remedy this situation. This legislative change facilitates non-First Nations partnerships in on-reserve economic development. The Kamloops Amendment clarified the fundamental difference between "designated lands surrenders" and "absolute surrenders." It allows bands the opportunity to lease their lands to non-Natives for commercial, industrial, or residential development, while retaining band jurisdiction over these lands. The statute provides for the leasehold surrender of designated reserve land to non-First Nations entities for economic development under conditions more reasonable than those the Indian Act previously allowed. The leasehold interest can now be seized pursuant to Section 89 (1.1) of the Indian Act and can be used as collateral for loans or mortgages. This allows for the productive use of land without the outright privatization of lands, which would place it risk of being lost. The Kamloops Amendment also allows for bands to tax non-Aboriginal businesses on designated lands with obvious consequent advantage to band governments. The amendment gave the First Nations governments income-generating opportunities and also aimed to increase employment prospects for band members.

The creation of First Nations banking institutions is another positive development that supports the First Nations economy. The oil-rich Samson Cree Nation at Hobbema, Alberta created Peace Hills Trust Company in 1980, and the Saskatchewan Indian Equity Foundation and the Toronto Dominion Bank partnered to form the First Nations Bank of Canada in 1996. These First Nations-controlled institutions offer employment, training, and capital to First Nations members. In theory, the emergence of such financial institutions also increases the likelihood that First Nations businesses will have access to the financial resources they need to get established and to expand their existing operations. Since they were created, each of these financial institutions has thrived and grown. For example, Peace Hills Trust now has nine branches in five provinces and offers a full line of financial services. The First Nations Bank of Canada now operates five branches in four provinces and one territory. It hopes to become completely independent by 2014 (FNBC, 2007). Other First Nations-owned business service and lending institutions include the Alberta Indian Investment Corporation, based in Edmonton, and the National Aboriginal Capital Corporation Association in Ottawa.

Mainstream banks have discovered that First Nations individuals and corporations can be lucrative. First Nations ventures that might not have been funded in the past because they were viewed as too risky, simply because they were First Nations enterprises, are now viewed as viable and attractive by investors and corporations. There is money to be made and partnerships to be struck in the First Nations community. Indeed, mining, forestry, oil and gas, and hydro companies have established Aboriginal relations policies and entered into agreements with First Nations to take advantage of employment and subcontracts for goods and services. First Nations entrepreneurship is burgeoning. Aboriginal Business Canada reports that there were over 20,000 Aboriginal-owned businesses (including Métis and Inuit owners) in 2003.

First Nations professionals are organizing to identify and pursue common interests through professional and industry associations like the Council for the Advancement of Aboriginal Development Officers, Indigenous Bar Association of Canada, Indian and Inuit Nurses Association of Canada, Indigenous Physicians Association of Canada, Aboriginal Investment and Trade Association, and National Aboriginal Forestry Association, to name just a few. Such associations bring a heightened profile for Aboriginal professionals to the mainstream market and offer benefits (e.g., networking and professional development workshops) to their members. Furthermore, members increase their organization's viability by bringing their skills, social and professional networks, and expertise to the group.

Collectively owned economic ventures are also flourishing in various First Nations communities. One spectacular example is Casino Rama, which is owned by the Chippewas of Rama First Nation near Orillia, Ontario. It has become a major player in the off-reserve economy of the district. Other examples of collectively owned First Nations enterprises abound, especially in the tourism/recreation industry. Indeed, cultural tourism and eco-tourism hold considerable promise for expanding opportunities for enterprising First Nations who can tap the eager western European and Japanese markets.

The Enoch Cree Nation, Tsuu T'ina Nation, Paul First Nation, and others have developed golf courses on their land. This economic venture makes productive use of their land and cashes in on golf's popularity. In addition, these courses provide services and employment opportunities for community members as groundskeepers, greenskeepers, and food and beverage workers. Alberta has seen a number of First Nations casinos open since 2007, including the Cree River Casino at Enoch (outside Edmonton), Grey Eagle at Tsuu T'ina (Calgary), Casino Dene (Cold Lake), Stoney Nakoda Resort Casino (Morley), and Alexis Casino (Glenevis). The casinos are seen as a means of providing economic development, programming, and employment in the community.[8] Evidently, the First Nations community is enthusiastic about business as the activities of band-owned businesses, joint ventures with non-First Nations organizations, and individual entrepreneurs demonstrate. However, enthusiasm is not enough to move the First Nations community ahead politically, economically, or socially. Policy changes are needed to enable opportunities to be acted upon, and those changes come as a result of politics.

POLITICS AND POLICY

The politics and policies that rule the First Nations' world have not been easy to live by. Many of these political, economic, and social rules were racist and came from people who knew little about the First Nations' existence. For example, policy held that First Nations people were not given universal suffrage until 1960, which meant that they had little or no political voice. Their rights were also suppressed when they were barred from hiring a lawyer to bring legal actions against the government from 1927 to 1951 (Calliou, 2000). Economically, First Nations were limited in the type of education they could acquire and, thus, the type of employment they could obtain (Voyageur, 1997). Controlled mobility and restrictive commercial policies further hampered First Nations' ability to participate in the mainstream economy (Voyageur, 1997). Socially, the government and the church made concerted efforts to obliterate their culture, religion, and language (Furniss, 1995).

In spite of the repressive rules, First Nations people have still been able to earn spots in mainstream politics. Various First Nations individuals have been elected as members of Parliament (e.g., Ethel Blondin-Andrew,

Elijah Harper, Willie Littlechild, Jeannie Marie Jewel, Nellie Cournoyea, Tina Keeper, and Gary Merasty) or appointed as senators (Len Marchand, the late Walter Twinn, and Lillian Dyck). These individuals have injected Aboriginal interests and perspectives into caucus debates and brought their peoples' insights into policies and the functioning of the larger polity. First Nations governments and political organizations, such as the Assembly of First Nations and tribal councils, negotiate, advocate, and lobby for policy changes that affect their constituents.

Self-government is never far from the minds of First Nations people. The Sechelt Indian Band Self-Government Act (1986), for example, was an early legislative accomplishment for First Nations. An early model of self-government, the act attracted considerable interest from First Nation leaders. No model of self-government is appropriate to all First Nations, but the Sechelt people found this model acceptable as a means of freeing themselves from some of the constraints of the Indian Act. Many other self-government agreements have since been settled, including the Yukon First Nations Claims Settlement Act (1994), the Yukon First Nations Self-Government Act (1994), and the Tlicho Agreement (2002).

Some major policy and legislative victories can be credited to First Nations. The most relevant of these were the comprehensive land claims policy, settlements, and implemention legislation. These have been a major stimulus for self-government and have yielded major benefits for First Nations. For example, the 1998 Nisga'a Treaty provided an estimated $196 million (in 1999 dollars) in compensation,[9] recognized Nisga'a owner-ship of all mineral resources on or under Nisga'a lands; recognized Nisga'a entitlement to a guaranteed share of the harvest of salmon and other marine and wildlife species; guaranteed a specified volume of flow from the Nass River for Nisga'a use; recognized Nisga'a legal jurisdiction over Nisga'a children; repatriated various Nisga'a artefacts from the provincial and federal museums; and protected certain Nisga'a sites under the provincial Heritage and Conservation Act. Also highly significant is the considerable political will of the British Columbia government in proceeding with the treaty despite considerable opposition from many high-profile non-First Nations British Columbians.[10] Similarly, the federal government, led by Jean Chrétien, remained resolute in its determination to pass the enabling legis-lation for the treaty, even in the face of the then Reform Party's attempts to scuttle it by introducing over 450 amendments in the House of Commons.

Considering the extent to which some of these programs and policies seek to combat systemic discrimination, there are particularly noteworthy reasons for optimism. Other policy accomplishments for First Nations are found in the realm of devolution of administrative powers from the federal government to First Nations. Noteworthy examples include the "Indian Control of Indian Education" policy launched in 1974 and the 1998 Nova Scotia tripartite education agreement, which saw the federal, provincial, and First Nations governments participate as equal partners in the education of First Nations students in Nova Scotia (CBC Radio News, 1998, June 19).

More recently, British Columbia's Ministry of Education has entered into Aboriginal Enhancement Agreements with school districts and local Aboriginal communities that aim to increase Aboriginal students' educational achievement though increased emphasis on Aboriginal traditional culture and languages. These agreements involve the partners in decision making and specific goal setting to meet the educational needs of Aboriginal students. As of 2008, 42 agreements have been signed (British Columbia Ministry of Education, 2008).

With self-government agreements comes an enhanced ability to influence the politics and legislation of the larger society to better protect First Nations' interests. The preservation and recognition of Aboriginal and treaty rights is of prime importance to the First Nations' community. Although the federal government had entered into treaties with the First Nations people in most of the country, the government's official view was that it did not have a legal obligation to honour them. According to the government, First Nations rights are contingent upon governmental recognition. The government takes the position that they are morally but not legally bound to uphold Aboriginal and rreaty rights. The First Nations peoples' perseverance and insistence in protecting and enforcing their Aboriginal and treaty rights brought some victories in the courts.

LEGAL ADVANCEMENT OF ABORIGINAL AND TREATY RIGHTS

The Supreme Court of Canada (SCC) has handed down some landmark court decisions that have advanced First Nations' rights. In 1970, the Supreme Court decided the landmark *Drybones* case (*R. v. Drybones*, 1970). That decision recognized that individual Indians had the same human rights as other Canadians. More specifically, the court found that the section (then Section 94[b]) of the Indian Act, which made it an offence for Indians to be intoxicated, was a violation of the Canadian Bill of Rights.[11] The legislation denied Indians "equality before the law" as guaranteed by the Bill of Rights, since the offence applied only to Indians and not to other persons. However, the SCC held that the Bill of Rights did not provide constitutional protection of Indians' rights in the 1974 Lavell and Bedard case, where the Bill of Rights was used to challenge sexual discrimination in the membership provisions of the Indian Act.[12] Because the Bill of Rights was merely a federal statute, the SCC held it could not override another statute such as the Indian Act. In pursuing the same legal issue, Sandra Lovelace eventually won her case before a United Nations tribunal, which was a contributing factor in the Bill C-31 amendment to the Indian Act. The Lovelace case dealt with discrimination against women in the Indian Act, which dictated that women lost Indian status when they married a non Indian. Constitutional protection of Aboriginal and treaty rights would not occur until they were entrenched in 35(1) of the Constitution Act, 1982.

The court's decision in the *Calder* (also known as the Nishga or Nisga'a) case in 1973 was instrumental in making the federal government recognize Aboriginal rights. The SCC ruled that there was a legal notion of Aboriginal rights but only three justices said there were existing rights while the other three justices said such rights were extinguished. Even though the Nisga'a lost the case on a technicality—they neglected to obtain the Crown's permission to sue the Crown—it was the first time the highest court in the land had legally recognized the notion of Aboriginal rights (*Calder v. Attorney General of British Columbia, 1973*). This decision forced the Trudeau government to deal with First Nations' Aboriginal rights claims and led to the federal land claims policy. A quarter-century later, the Nisga'a signed a modern day treaty initialled in 1998, which settled their land claim.

The 1984 *Guerin* (Musqueam) decision was another victory for First Nations because it upheld the federal government's fiduciary (trustee-like) obligation to look out for the best interests of First Nations when dealing with their property (*R. v. Guerin*, 1984). This proved to be a significant incentive for the federal Department of Indian Affairs and Northern Development to curtail its involvement in the day-to-day administration of the affairs of individual First Nations. A corresponding expansion of activities by First Nations governments to take back more control ensued. In 1990, the SCC, in the *Sparrow* decision, expanded the fiduciary duty from only when dealing with First Nations property to a general fiduciary duty to look out for the best interests of First Nations. It also ruled that governments must justify any legislation that has an adverse impact upon Aboriginal rights protected under Section 35 of the Constitution Act, 1982.

The SSC's unanimous decision in another British Columbia case, *Delgamuukw* (also called Gitxsan-Wet'suwet'en) in 1997 proclaimed that, in the absence of treaties, Aboriginal title to the land was not extinguished and that First Nations were entitled to use such ancestral lands almost entirely as they wished. Furthermore, in what must be seen as a cultural victory for First Nation peoples, the court also ruled in the *Delgamuukw* case that the lower courts must take into account Aboriginal oral histories (*Delgamuukw v. British Columbia*, 1997). The *Delgamuukw* decision has been a powerful lever for First Nations in land claims negotiations since it was issued.

Other court decisions on the *Nowegijick* (1983), *Simon* (1985), and *Sioui* (1990) cases gave expansive interpretations to the recognition of "existing Aboriginal and treaty rights" in the Constitution Act, 1982. The court ruled that the treaties must be interpreted in a flexible manner that takes into account changes in technology and practice, but the courts must also construe the treaties in a liberal manner with ambiguities resolved in favour of First Nations people because the honour of the Crown is at stake. The same principles were invoked in the 1999 *R. v. Marshall* decision where the court upheld the Mi'kmaq Treaties of 1760–1761 and said that First Nations people could make a modest living from the sale of fish. Mi'kmaq and Maliseet fishers could fish out of season, without a licence and with nets that violate federal fisheries regulations (*R. v. Marshall*, 1999). The *Sioui* decision stipulated that the treaties cannot be unilaterally altered or extinguished by either side (*R. v. Sioui*, 1990).

Another court decision pertains to justice in criminal trials. In the 1998 Williams case, the court ruled that prospective jurors may be questioned about their racial views to root out those whose prejudices could destroy the fairness of a criminal trial (*R. v. Williams*, 1998).

Since the 1990s, the issue of consultation has taken centre stage in the relationship between First Nations and industry. Government policies require that all provincial, regional, and district staff who are planning industrial management activities must examine whether those actions infringe upon Aboriginal or treaty rights. If they do, the staff must consult with affected Aboriginal communities before proceeding (Government of Alberta, 2005; British Columbia, 1997; Royal Commission on Aboriginal

Peoples, 1996a). The Supreme Court of Canada in *Taku River Tlingit First Nation v. British Columbia* (2004), *Haida Nation v. British Columbia* (2004), and *Mikisew Cree First Nation v. Canada* (2005) decided that the duty to consult with First Nations is necessary when First Nations land, rights, or resources are affected by development.

Much legitimacy and recognition of First Nations' grievances, rights, and perspectives have come from the court decisions and government policies identified above. The fact that First Nations are prepared to bear the enormous expense to bring a case to the Supreme Court of Canada speaks volumes of their determination to protect their inherent rights. First Nations can be heartened that their rights are being upheld by the highest court in Canada.

HEALING AND RECONCILIATION FROM THE EFFECTS OF COLONIALISM

Healing is vital to a healthy community. One of the barriers to healing the horrible legacy of the Indian residential schools was that those responsible for the schools' operation were unwilling to take responsibility for the damage they caused to the students. Since 1990, a number of have helped move First Nations people along the healing journey, including the creation of the Aboriginal Healing Foundation, the federal government's apology, the Churches' acknowledgement of their role, the Indian Residential School Settlement Agreement, and the launch of the Truth and Reconciliation Commission.

The Indian residential school system is a shameful episode in our country's history and few people in the First Nations have been untouched by it.[13] First Nations people have suffered the devastating effects of residential school atrocities either through first-hand experience or by the intergeneration effects.[14] The attendees of these establishments entered what Erving Goffman (1961) called a total institution.[15] They returned to their families and communities forever changed by their experiences. Parents and families were powerless to stop the removal of their children and the changes to their loved ones. While a few former students speak positively about their experiences at residential schools,[16] the majority tell tragic stories of abuse, separation from families, loss of language and culture. The sad legacy of this attempt to assimilate First Nations has contributed to many of the present day social problems that exist in the community. Although this history is grim, the positive news is that there have been major advancements made to acknowledge and rectify this legacy.

Aboriginal Healing Foundation

Since 2000 a number of healing initiatives have been aimed at the First Nations community. The Aboriginal Healing Foundation (AHF) is one such initiative. As part of the federal government's policy, *Gathering Strength: Canada's Aboriginal Action Plan*, the foundation was created on April 1, 1998 and given an 11-year mandate. Its mandate was to "support community-based healing initiatives meant to help those affected by the harsh residential school legacy" (Aboriginal Healing Foundation, 2008). The AHF has funded more than 1,300 projects, such as community wellness programs, traditional healing programs, cultural camps, and one-on-one counselling across the country (Aboriginal Healing Foundation, 2008).

Government: Public Acknowledgements of Responsibility

Prime Minister Stephen Harper's actions toward First Nations people have not been particularly encouraging or supportive since he took office in January 2006. For example, within days of taking office, he scrapped the Kelowna Accord. Struck between the previous federal government and Aboriginal leaders, the Kelowna Accord sought to improve the educational and employment prospects and living conditions for Aboriginal peoples. Harper refused, along with Russia, to sign the United Nation's Declaration of the Rights of Indigenous Peoples in 2007. This document took 11 years to work its way through the UN process to arrive at that historic vote. Canada eventually signed on, however, in November 2010.

The government had been repeatedly asked—and repeatedly refused—to apologize for its role in creating and maintaining the residential school system that undermined First Nations culture and identity. Prime Minister Harper said he would not apologize to the Aboriginal people because he was not responsible for what happened in the residential schools. He had a change of heart and surprised the Aboriginal community when he eventually agreed to offer an apology. On June 11, 2008, Harper apologized to the Aboriginal people of Canada for Canada's role in Indian residential schools. His statement was followed by statements of apology by the leaders of the major political parties.

Churches: Public Acknowledgement of Responsibility

The residential school system was operated by the Roman Catholic, United, Methodist, and Anglican churches. In 1998, the moderator of the United Church of Canada, Reverend Bill Phipps, offered an apology to former residential school students, their families, and communities. Phipps said, "We are in the midst of a long and painful journey as we reflect on the cries that we did not or would not hear, and how we have behaved as a church. As we travel this difficult road of repentance, reconciliation, and healing, we commit ourselves to work toward ensuring that we will never again use our power as a church to hurt others with attitudes of racial and spiritual superiority" (United Church of Canada, 1998: 1).

The Roman Catholic Church negotiated a $25 million settlement for its part in the residential school system, thereby acknowledging its role and compensation for damages caused. The Anglican Church of Canada also acknowledged its liability in their operation of residential schools with a $25 million settlement. This amount was later lowered by 40% to $15.7 million (Sison, 2007: 1). In April 2009, National Chief Phil Fontaine and some residential school survivors were granted an audience with Pope Benedict. At this meeting, the pontiff expressed "sorrow and anguish caused by the deplorable conduct of some members of the church and offered his sympathy and prayerful solidarity" (Delaney, 2009: 1).

Indian Residential Schools Settlement Agreement (IRSSA)

The Indian Residential Schools Settlement Agreement (IRSSA) was negotiated by the Government of Canada, lawyers for former students, the churches, the Assembly of First Nations, and Inuit representatives in September 2007. It is said to be the largest class action settlement in Canadian history at $1.9 billion (IRSSA, 2006). The agreement had a number of components: common experience payment; an independent assessment process; a truth and reconciliation commission; various commemoration activities; an Indian Residential Schools Resolution Health Support Program; and an endowment to the Aboriginal Healing Foundation (IRSSA, 2006). The IRSSA states that any person who can prove they were housed in a residential school for at least one year is eligible for a $10,000 common experience payment. Individuals will also be paid $3,000 for every additional year they were housed in a residential school. Those who suffered particularly harsh physical, psychological, or sexual abuse can have their stories heard by adjudicators in the independent assessment process.

Indian Residential School Truth and Reconciliation Commission

The Indian Residential School Truth and Reconciliation Commission (TRC) was launched in June 2008 with the aim to develop a social memory and to acknowledge the past.[17] It aims to help advance the healing process by former residential school attendees and their families. The selection committee, which chose members of the Truth and Reconciliation Commission, included representatives of the Assembly of First Nations, the United Church, the Métis National Council, and the Inuit Tapiriit Kanatami. The committee had two co-chairs—one appointed by the federal government and one appointed by the Assembly of First Nations. The commissioners were selected by representatives of Aboriginal organizations from more than 300 applications and were appointed by the federal government. The commission consists of three panel members: Chairperson Justice Murray Sinclair, Commissioner Marie Wilson, and Commissioner Wilton Littlechild. The TRC has a five-year mandate and serves as a safe, respectful, and culturally appropriate venue for former residential school students, or anyone affected by Indian residential school experience, to share their personal experiences (Truth and Reconciliation Commission, 2008). The commission will research and examine the conditions that gave rise to Indian residential schools. The TRC commission will travel across Canada and hold public hearing to gather information and hear testimony. From this information, the commissioners will write a final report that will become part of the public record.

As mentioned earlier, few people in the First Nations community have been untouched by the residential school experience. The abuse, the separation from family, the loss of language and culture still haunt some former students and their families. Many say the healing can now begin since those responsible have acknowledged their role in the Indian residential school system. There have been apologies, compensation, and programming put in place to facilitate the healing process.

CONCLUSION

My array of positive changes in the First Nations in the past 40 years has been highly selective but proves progress. I found the examples heartening in many respects. These examples are meant provide a counterweight to those who focus exclusively on the deficit paradigm. Many improvements have occurred in the First Nations community but much remains to be done on these and other fronts. First Nations concerns and interests still dwell on the fringes of Canadian society but their marginalization has diminished substantially and opportunities have opened up for communities and individuals to an extent that would have been unimaginable even 20 years ago.

First Nations people have embraced meritocracy and are gaining educational credentials, starting businesses, and being elected into mainstream politics. They are raising their profiles and are working to shatter the stereotypes held by some mainstream citizens. Their burgeoning population means that they are more visible in the workforce and Canadian society.

First Nations in Canada have every right to feel optimistic about the future. They have made tremendous progress to participate in mainstream society while remaining true to their heritage and culture. They overcame the Trudeau government's failed attempt at assimilation in the 1969 White Paper. Political, legal, and religious authorities have recognized that First Nations' rights, cultures, and claims are viable and supported by Canadian law. Increasing numbers in employment, higher education, and business give First Nations people opportunities for a higher standard of living. The eagle has landed for First Nations people as their economic, social, and political situations continue to improve.

NOTES

1. This chapter is based on J.R. Ponting & C.J. Voyageur, 2005, "Multiple Points of Light: Grounds for Optimism among First Nations in Canada," in D.R. Newhouse, C.J. Voyageur, & D. Beavon (Eds.), *Hidden in Plain Sight: Contributions of Aboriginal Peoples to Canadian Identity and Culture* (pp. 425–454), Toronto, ON: University of Toronto Press.

2. Other indigenous groups around the world have similar prophecies about the eagle landing on the moon, which is said to usher in a new relationship between indigenous peoples and European settlers.

3. I focus exclusively on the First Nations community because of its unique history, its legal relationship with the federal government, and its association with the Indian Act. I make reference to the Aboriginal community periodically in this chapter, which refers to the First Nation, Métis, and Inuit communities as a collective.

4. Treaty making between the indigenous peoples of Canada and the governing powers go back to the mid-1600s. The numbered treaties between the First Nations of Canada and the Crown began with Treaty 1 in 1871. These treaties meant that First Nations people ceded their interest in the land in return for promises such as housing, education, health care, and other commodities. The treaties were deemed to last forever or "as long as the rivers flow and the grass grows" as stated in Treaty 8 signed in 1899.

5. Those who lost their Indian status because they joined the clergy or the military, those who were removed from the band list by the Indian agent, those who obtained a university degree, and women who married non-Indian men, and Indian men who voluntarily enfranchised themselves and their families could apply to regain their Indian status under Bill C-31.

6. This does not mean that First Nations living standards are on par with those of mainstream Canadians. It simply means that the living standards are better than they were.

7. The First Nations educational attainment rate could be higher than 23% but INAC capped funding to the Post-Secondary Education Assistance Program even though tuition costs have increased annually. This means that the number of students able to access education funding has decreased as a result. In addition, the number of First Nations students who have obtained independent funds to obtain educations by scholarships, bursaries, or student loans is unknown.

8. The casinos are not viewed as a panacea, nor have they been welcomed by everyone in the First Nations community. There have been protests against their construction.

9. The compensation formula is extremely complex and contains contingency factors that make it impossible to offer a firm figure here. The inflated figures offered in media reports at the time of the initialling of the treaty probably included other benefits, whereas the reference in my text is only to the compensation component of the settlement.

10. The British Columbia government refused to negotiate unextinguished Aboriginal title for a century.

11. As a mere statute, the Bill of Rights could not override other statutes.

12. Those provisions resulted in only women losing Indian status for marrying a non-Indian.

13. The residential school system began in earnest in 1820, but the federal government became involved in 1874 (Indian Residential Schools Resolution Canada, 2003). Eventually, all of the schools would be funded by the federal government. At their peak in 1931, there were 80 residential schools operating across Canada, with the exception of some of the Maritime provinces (Indian Residential Schools Resolution Canada, 2003). At one time or another, 130 residential schools operated in Canada.

14. Records show that there are approximately 80,000 residential school survivors alive today (Indian Residential Schools Resolution Canada, 2003).

15. Total institutes (hospitals and prisons) have extensive rules and are places where the person's every need is fulfilled, but the person is not given any choices.
16. I do not want to invalidate the experiences of these individuals. I only know that my own experiences in a residential school were not the most pleasant of my life.
17. There have been almost 20 truth commissions held in the last 25 years, including those held in Argentina, Chile, El Salvador, Guatemala, as well as the most well-known one that was held in South Africa.

REFERENCES

Aboriginal Business Canada. (2000). *Aboriginal entrepreneurs in Canada: Progress and prospects* (Catalogue No. 1206-260X). Ottawa, ON: Aboriginal Business Canada.

Aboriginal Healing Foundation. (2008). About us. Retrieved from http://www.ahf.ca/about-us

Attorney General of Canada v. Lavell; Isaac v. Bedard. [1974]. S.C.R. 1349.

Barsh, R.L. (1994). Canada's Aboriginal peoples: Social integration or disintegration? *The Canadian Journal of Native Studies*, 14(1), 1–46.

Becker, G. (1993). *Human capital: A theoretical and empirical analysis with special reference to education* (2nd ed.). New York, NY: Columbia University Press.

Bell, C.E. (1995). Limitations, legislation, and domestic repatriation. *UBC Law Review*, Special Issue, 149–163.

Bourdieu, P. (1986). *Sociology of culture: Theory, culture and society*. Walnut Creek, CA: Sage.

British Columbia (Government of). (1997). *Protection of Aboriginal rights*. Victoria, BC: Ministry of Forests.

British Columbia Ministry of Education. (2008). Aboriginal education homepage. Retrieved from http://www.bced.gov.bc.ca/abed

Calder v. Attorney General of British Columbia. 34 D.L.R. (3d) 145. (1973).

Calliou, B. (2000). *Losing the game: Conservation and the regulation of First Nations hunting, 1890–1930* (Unpublished master's thesis). University of Alberta, Edmonton, AB.

———. (2008). The significance of building leadership and community capacity to implement self government. In Y. Belanger (Ed.), *Aboriginal self government in Canada: Current trends and issues* (3rd ed.) (pp. 332–339). Saskatoon, SK: Purich Publishing.

CBC Radio. (1998, June 16). Newscast.

CBC Radio. (1998, June 19). Newscast.

CBC Television. (2008, June 11). Newscast.

Delaney, S. (2009, April). Benedict apologizes for churches' role in Indian residential schools. *Western Catholic Reporter*, p. 30.

Delgamuukw v. British Columbia. 3 S.C.R. 1010. (1997).

First Nations Bank of Canada (FNBC). (2007). Our history. Retrieved from http://www.firstnationsbank.com

Furniss, E. (1995). *Victims of benevolence: The dark legacy of the Williams Lake Residential School*. Vancouver, BC: Arsenal Pulp Press.

Goffman, E. (1961). *Asylums: Essays on the social situation of mental patients and other inmates*. Chicago, IL: Aldine.

Government of Alberta (2005). *The Government of Alberta's First Nations consultation policy on land management and resource development*. Edmonton, AB: Government of Alberta.

Government of Canada. (2004). The well-being of Canada's young children: Government of Canada report 2003. Retrieved from http://www.socialunion.gc.ca/ecd/2003/report2_e/chapter05_e.html

Haida Nation v. British Columbia (Minister of Forests). [2004]. 3 S.C.R. 511 2004 SCC 73.

Harper, Prime Minister Stephen (2008, June 11). The Apology. [Television special broadcast]. CBC News. Ottawa.

Health Canada. (2002). Healthy Canadians: A federal report on comparable health indicators 2002. Retrieved from http://www.hc-sc.gc.ca/hcs-sss/pubs/system-regime/2002-fed-comp-indicat/2002-health-sante5-eng.php

———. (2011). *A Statistical profile on the health of First Nations in Canada: Vital statistics for Atlantic and Western Canada 2011/2012*. Ottawa, ON: Queen's Printer.

Human Resources and Skills Development Canada. (2008). Indicators of well-being in Canada: Life expectancy at birth. Retrieved from http://www4.hrsdc.gc.ca/.3ndic.1t.4r@-eng.jsp?iid=3

Indian and Northern Affairs Canada (INAC). (2007). *Basic Departmental Data, 2005* (Catalogue No. R12-7/2003E). Ottawa, ON: Departmental Statistics Section, Information Quality and Research Directorate, INAC.

Indian Residential Schools Resolution Canada. (2003). *Indian Residential Schools Resolution Canada*. Treasury Board of Canada Secretariat. Retrieved from http://www.tbs-sct.gc.ca/rpp/2008-2009/inst/ira/iratb-eng.asp

Indian Residential School Settlement Agreement. (2006). Offical court website. Retrieved from http://www.residentialschoolsettlement.ca

Lambertus, S. (2004). *Wartime images, peacetime wounds: The media and the Gustafsen Lake standoff*. Toronto, ON: University of Toronto Press.

Meijer Drees, L. (2002). *The Indian Association of Alberta: A history of political action*. Vancouver, BC: University of British Columbia Press.

Mikisew Cree First Nation v. Canada. [2005]. 3 S.C.R. 388 2005 SCC 69.

Miller, J.R. (2000). *Skyscrapers hide the heavens: History of Indian–white relations in Canada*. Toronto, ON: University of Toronto Press.

The Moon: Miracle in sound. (1969, August). *Time Magazine*. Retrieved from http://www.time.com/time/magazine/article/9171,901168,00.html

Nancoo, S., & Nancoo, R. (1997). *The mass media and Canadian diversity*. Cambridge, MA: Harvard University Press.

Nowegijick v. The Queen. [1983]. 1 S.C.R. 29.

Peters, E., & Rosenberg, M. (1995). Indian attachment to the labour force—Labour force attachment and regional development for Native peoples: Theoretical and methodological issues. *Journal of the Canadian Regional Science Association*, 18(1), 77–105.

Ponting, J.R. (2000). *A cohort analysis of public opinion on Canadian Aboriginal issues, 1976–98*. Calgary, AB: University of Calgary.

Public Works and Government Services Canada. (2008). Aboriginal labour force characteristics from the 1996 Census. Retrieved from http://dsp-psd.pwgsc.gc.ca/Collection/R2-115-2000E.pdf

R. v. Drybones. [1970]. S.C.R. 28.

R. v. Guerin. (1984). 2 S.C.R. 335.

R. v. Marshall. (1999). S.C.R. 26014.

R. v. Sioui. [1990]. 1 S.C.R.1025.

R. v. Sparrow. [1990]. 1 S.C.R. 1075.

R. v. Williams. [1998]. 1 S.C.R. 1128.

Romaniuc, A. (2000). Aboriginal population of Canada. Growth dynamics under conditions of encounter of civilisations. *The Canadian Journal of Native Studies*, 20(1), 95–137.

Royal Commission on Aboriginal Peoples. (1995). *Choosing life: Special report on suicide among Aboriginal people*. Ottawa, ON: Minister of Supply and Services Canada.

———. (1996a). Report of the Royal Commission on Aboriginal Peoples, Vol. 2, *Restructuring the Relationship*. Ottawa, ON: Minister of Supply and Services Canada.

———. (1996b). Report of the Royal Commission on Aboriginal Peoples, Vol. 4, *Perspectives and Realities*. Ottawa, ON: Minister of Supply and Services Canada.

Simon v. The Queen. [1985]. 2 SCC. 387.

Singer, B.D. (Ed.). (1995). *Communications in Canadian society*. Toronto, ON: Nelson.

Sison, M.N. (2007). Church may soon be reimbursed for residential school payouts. *Anglican Journal*, 133(9), 7.

Statistics Canada. (2005). *Projections of the Aboriginal populations, Canada, provinces, and territories* (Catalogue No. 91-547-XIE). Retrieved from http://www5.statcan.gc.ca/bsolc/olc-cel/olc-cel?catno=91-547-XIE

———. (2006). *Infant mortality, 2002 and 2003*. Retrieved from http://www.statcan.gc.ca/pub/82-401-x/2006000/t/4064400-eng.htm

———. (2008a). *Aboriginal peoples in Canada in 2006: Inuit, Métis and First Nations, 2006 Census*. Retrieved from http://www.statcan.ca/Daily/English/050628d050628d.htm

———. (2008b). Canada (Code01) (Table). *Aboriginal population profile, 2006 Census* (Catalogue No. 92-594-XWE). Ottawa, ON: Statistics Canada.

———. (2008c). *Labour Force Activity (8), Aboriginal Identity (8B), Age Groups (13A), Sex (3) and Area of Residence (6A) for the Population 15 Years and Over of Canada, Provinces and Territories, 2001 and 2006 Censuses—20 percent Sample Data*.

Retrieved from http://www12.statcan.ca/english/census06/data/topics/
RetrieveProductTable.cfm?TPL

Taku River Tlingit First Nation v. British Columbia. [2004]. 3 S.C.R. 550 2004 SCC 74.

Thornton, R. (1987). *American Indian holocaust and survival: A population history since
1492*. Norman, OK: University of Oklahoma Press.

Treaty 8 made June 21, 1899 and adhesions, reports, etc. (1966). Reprinted from the 1899
edition by Roger Duhamel, FRSC. Queen's Printer and Controller of Stationery:
Ottawa.

Truth and Reconciliation Commission. (2008). *Schedule "N" mandate for
the Truth and Reconciliation Commission.* Retrieved from http://www.
residentialschoolsettlement.ca/SCHEDULE_N.pdf

United Church of Canada. (1998). *Apology to former students of United Church Indian
residential schools, and to their families and communities.* Retrieved from http://
www.united-church.ca/beliefs/policies/1998/a623

Venne, S. (1981). *Indian Acts and Amendments, 1867–1975: An indexed collection.*
Saskatoon, SK: University of Saskatchewan.

Voyageur, C.J. (1997). *Employment equity and Aboriginal people in Canada* (Unpublished doctoral dissertation). Department of Sociology, University of Alberta,
Edmonton, AB.

———. (2008). *Firekeepers of the 21st century: Women chiefs in Canada.* Montreal
and Kingston: McGill-Queen's University Press.

Voyageur, C.J., & Calliou, B. (2007). Aboriginal economic development and the
struggle for self government. In W. Antony & L. Samuelson (Eds.), *Power and
resistance: Critical thinking about Canadian social issues* (4th ed.) (pp. 135–160).
Halifax, NS: Fernwood.

Weaver, S.M. (1991). A new paradigm in Canadian Indian policy for the 1990s.
Canadian Ethnic Studies, 22(3), 8–18.

PART IV
INTERNATIONAL PERSPECTIVES

15

AMERICAN INDIAN EDUCATION

C. Matthew Snipp

INTRODUCTION

For most Americans, there are few resources more valuable than an education. Educational attainment determines the kind of work individuals will perform, how much they will earn, what kind of home they might occupy, and their health, well-being, and longevity. Most middle-class Americans fare well and live comfortably because of the education they completed as young adults. Poorer groups have lives marked by economic hardship and disadvantage for a variety of reasons, some systematically constructed and others accidental, but especially because they lack the education necessary for participation in the most privileged sectors of the United States economy.

Among these disadvantaged groups, American Indians and Alaska Natives are especially noteworthy. They are one of the least educated and predictably poorest groups in American society. However, education is not an alien experience for them, nor have they been systematically denied access to education in the same way that barriers were erected for African Americans in the Jim Crow South. Nonetheless, the historical as well as the contemporary experiences of American Indians and Alaska Natives with the educational institutions of this nation have often been difficult and fraught with conflict. But the late twentieth century saw important developments that offer hope for the future. This chapter is intended to serve as an overview of the experiences of American Indians and Alaska Natives with the educational institutions of American society.

Beyond the simple matter of reviewing the well-being of a historically disadvantaged group, there are other reasons why Indian education is a matter of considerable importance to the federal government. American Indians and Alaska Natives have a relationship with the federal government that is unlike that of any other group in American society. American Indians occupy a singular position in American society, different from any other racial or ethnic minority group. They possess this status by virtue of being the first people to occupy the land that is now the United States. More directly, they have a unique relationship with the federal government that grows out of a long history of conflict and struggle (Prucha, 1984; Getches, Wilkinson, & Williams, 1998; Wilkins, 2002).

The place of American Indians in American society is rooted within the Constitution and manifest in a variety of special institutions. In particular, Article I, Section 2 segregated American Indians for the purpose of allocating political representation and tax obligations. Article I, Section 8 assigned the duty of managing relations with American Indians to Congress. To carry out this responsibility, there is a standing Senate committee, an agency within the executive branch known as the Bureau of Indian Affairs (BIA), numerous special offices within most federal agencies, an entire volume of the Code of Federal Regulations and a long history of Supreme Court case law, all devoted to issues pertaining to American Indians.[1]

Historically, this unique relationship stems from the fact that initially, in the early history of the United States, American Indians were not considered a part of this nation (Wilkins, 2002). From 1790 to 1871, the federal government dealt with American Indians much as it would with foreign nations, with a mixture of diplomacy, treaty making, and warfare. When the opportunity arose, federal efforts also were devoted to "civilizing" American Indians. This meant persuading them with whatever means necessary to surrender their tribal culture and adopt the habits and lifestyles of Euro-Americans.

By the late nineteenth century, the federal government had successfully overwhelmed the resistance of American Indians and turned to the task of assimilating them into modern society. Adults were expected to become farmers, and later, workers in urban labour markets (Hoxie, 1984; Fixico, 1986). Children were frequently sent to boarding schools distant from their homes. The curriculum of these schools was designed to culturally indoctrinate Indian children with Anglo-American cultural ideals at the same time that it imparted basic academic skills.

The campaign to assimilate American Indians lasted throughout much of the twentieth century. However, the failure of these efforts, combined with increasing American Indian opposition to them, led the federal government to abandon them in the 1960s. In the late 1960s and early 1970s, the federal government gradually replaced the old assimilationist policies with new ones designated by the term "self-determination." These new policies recognized the rights of American Indians to decide their own future and to have the principal responsibility for overseeing the affairs of their communities (Gross, 1989; Castile, 1998).

The balance of this chapter is devoted to presenting an educational profile for American Indians and Alaska Natives living in the United States. The data for this profile are extracted from the 2000 US Census. These data represent the largest and most comprehensive source of information about American Indian education available.

AMERICAN INDIAN AND ALASKA NATIVE EDUCATION IN THE TWENTIETH CENTURY: AN HISTORICAL OVERVIEW

Before presenting data about American Indian and Alaska Native education, some historical background is necessary for placing it in context. As noted above, efforts to educate American Indians in the twentieth century (and earlier) were fuelled by a desire to de-tribalize and assimilate American Indians into Anglo-American society. However, the policies behind these efforts were marked by an abrupt shift in the 1970s when the federal government abandoned its historic assimilation project and allowed American Indians greater control over their education than at any point in history.

Indian Education in the Early Twentieth Century

For the first decades of the twentieth century, the boarding schools represented the cornerstone of the federal government's efforts to educate American Indians. They operated in much the same manner as Richard Henry Pratt and his colleagues originally envisioned, offering a combination of basic academic skills and vocational training, along with an intensive indoctrination in Anglo-American culture. Pratt served as superintendent at Carlisle until 1904 and remained a vigorous advocate for off-reservation boarding schools until his death in 1924.

However, the boarding school system also attracted harsh criticism from opponents who focused on its shortcomings. Advocates for the schools emphasized the successful transitions of Indian students to an Anglo-American lifestyle, often using before and after photographs to demonstrate the civilizing effects of the schools. In response, critics pointed out that many students ran away from these schools, some left prematurely, others returned to their reservation after graduating, while others had trouble adjusting to a non-Indian society (Prucha, 1984). Some of these critics argued that these failures were evidence that it was impossible to educate American Indians. Others argued that the schools were themselves the source of the problems.

In response, the federal government initiated a number of reforms that included building schools closer to the reservations and ending the outing program at some schools. However, major reforms were not set in motion until the publication of a scathing review in a report titled *The Problem of Indian Administration*. This report, also known as the Meriam Report (named for its lead author and study director, Lewis Meriam) was published in 1928 and examined a variety of problems in Indian communities. The authors paid close attention to the boarding schools and faulted them for a number of problems, finding that the boarding school students were poorly fed, overcrowded, in poor health, poorly taught, and unduly regimented (Bolt, 1987).

The publication of the Meriam Report set off a debate inside and out of the government among those concerned with federal policy for American Indians. A change in presidential administrations in 1929 resulted in a new commissioner of Indian Affairs, who in turn appointed W. Carson Ryan to serve as the director of Indian education for the BIA in 1930. Ryan's appointment was notable because he was a well-respected educator and especially because he was responsible for the study of Indian education published in the Meriam Report. Ryan's plans for reforming Indian education consisted of closing down the boarding schools as quickly as was practical, creating a system of day schools to be operated on the most isolated reservations, and, where practical, having American Indian students enroll in local public schools instead of BIA facilities.

Although Ryan's plans were well-founded and well-intended, implementing them proved to be more difficult than he had anticipated. The sheer numbers of American Indian students in boarding schools made it impossible to simply close them down and transfer them to public schools or BIA day schools. The numbers would have overwhelmed the existing resources for educating these children. Instead, the decommissioning of the boarding schools began gradually, but even this met with objections. Bureaucratic stalwarts within the BIA objected to the closing of the boarding schools, and parents also objected to the school closings. Parents of children in public schools raised concerns about an influx of American Indian students and worried that their children would receive a "bi-racial" education, while Indian parents objected to their children being sent to public schools away from the reservation (Bolt, 1987: 237).

Efforts to reform Indian education received an important boost with the appointment of John C. Collier as the commissioner of Indian Affairs in 1933. Collier retained Ryan as the director of education within the Bureau of Indian Affairs and helped introduce several important initiatives for American Indian and Alaska Native education, including two executive orders that reduced the level of missionary activities within the boarding schools. More important, however, was the passage of the Johnson-O'Malley Act, which appropriated funds to support the education of Native children in public schools. Between 1933 and 1943, 16 boarding schools were closed. Funds from the Public Works Administration paid for the construction of 100 day schools on reservations, and in 1943 alone, 37,000 American Indians attended public schools with the support of $1.25 million from the Johnson-O'Malley Act (Bolt, 1987: 240).

The Collier administration also ended the official antipathy in Indian education toward Indian culture and, for the first time, encouraged a limited form of bi-cultural education. In particular, American Indian arts and crafts were encouraged in many schools. The Santa Fe boarding school has become a premiere site for artistically gifted American Indian youths as it has evolved from a boarding school preoccupied with assimilation into what is now known as the Institute of American Indian Arts.

Despite these reforms, the federal government's success in Indian education on the eve of the Second World War was a mixed record at best. In some areas, the advent of community schools was a welcome development that resulted in real improvements in the schooling of Indian children.

In other areas, especially the Plains and the southwest, the results were disappointing. In 1944, by the BIA's reckoning, between 70% and 80% of Navajo and Pueblo Indians in the southwest did not speak or read English (Bolt, 1987: 241).

American Indian and Alaska Native Education Since 1950
Prelude: World War II, the GI Bill, and Indian Education
The onset of World War II diverted both financial support as well as personnel from BIA schools. The reduction in support meant that some schools were closed and special programs such as teacher training were curtailed (Bolt, 1987). Teachers and older students of enlistment age joined the armed services while others left school to work in war-related industries. Compared to World War I, American Indians and Alaska Natives had a significant presence in the combat forces with over 25,000 (mostly) men in the armed services (Bernstein, 1991).

The short-term impact of World War II on Indian education was disruptive at best, and in many respects, it was a substantial setback for many communities. Students who left school early faced a long-term educational disadvantage. School closings and the end of special programs created hardships on a number of reservations (Bolt, 1987). However, World War II also resulted in an unexpected boost for Indian education from the enactment of the GI Bill passed by Congress near the end of the war. Namely, a substantial number of the Indian veterans who served in the war took advantage of GI benefits to further their education after they returned home from military service (Bernstein, 1991).

The GI Bill allowed American Indians and Alaska Natives to return to school and complete their education and especially to pursue an education beyond high school. Looking at the educational attainment of men in this generation, one sees that this is the first group of American Indians and Alaska Natives to advance in higher education in significant numbers. As one study observed, the cohort of American Indian men who were of prime recruitment age during World War II had a very high proportion of educational attainments exceeding high school. These attainments have made this group of men the best educated of any cohort of American Indians and Alaska Natives before or after the war, including cohorts who completed their education as recently as the 1970s (Snipp, 1989).

The GI Bill impressed on many American Indians and Alaska Natives the importance of a college degree and the advantages that accrue to it. However, for students too young to qualify for this assistance in the 1950s, the educational resources available to them were discouraging. For the BIA school programs that served these youths, the postwar environment did not mark a return to the concerns voiced about American Indian education in the 1930s.

American Indian and Alaska Native Education during the Years of Termination and Relocation

After the war, the federal government returned to its efforts to assimilate American Indians and Alaska Natives. In particular, a series of legislative and policy initiatives collectively known as termination and relocation were instituted to settle existing Indian claims against the government and to dissolve the special legal and political status accorded to American Indians. As it was conceived, the Indian Claims Commission was established in 1946 to resolve outstanding legal disputes with the tribes; a few years later, Congress passed legislation to abolish federally recognized reservations; and lastly, starting in the early 1950s, American Indians were assisted in moving to urban areas where they were expected to become part of the mainstream economy. This scheme favoured closing the boarding schools, moving Indian children into public schools as quickly as practical, and emphasizing vocational skills that would quickly lead to urban employment.

The policy makers most concerned with Indian education were convinced that after the war, the educational needs of American Indians and Alaska Natives had fundamentally changed as a result of their wartime experience. For policy makers and many American Indians alike, education was seen as a vehicle for entering the labour market of postwar America. In particular, education was seen less as a vehicle for cultural indoctrination and more as a tool for vocational development. It was no longer feasible to think about focusing on vocations that American Indians could pursue on or near their reservations—that is, farming and farm-related work. To survive in the twentieth century, American Indians needed to acquire skills that would aid them in urban labour markets. For some, this would even mean obtaining a college education (Szasz, 1974).

This type of thinking was entirely consistent with the policies of termination and relocation. In the early 1950s, the Bureau of Indian Affairs instituted programs to encourage American Indians to move to urban areas. Between 1952 and 1972, over 100,000 American Indians had participated in the BIA's relocation programs (Sorkin, 1978). As these programs grew through the 1950s, they caused the BIA to take a greater responsibility for adult vocational training, which strained the agency's resources (Szasz, 1974). At the same time, as a result of the Johnson-O'Malley Act, growing numbers of American Indian children were attending public schools.

While the boarding schools had failed at the task of wholesale assimilation, it was now believed that integrating American Indian students into public schools would hasten this process. As a practical matter, this meant moving students out of BIA boarding and day schools and increasing the attendance of American Indian and Alaska Native children who were not enrolled in school. The latter was viewed as an especially urgent problem; as late as 1953, one report documented that 20,000 American Indian children were not enrolled in school (Bolt, 1987: 44). The closing of reservation boarding and day schools resulted in rising numbers of students in off-reservation public schools and a corresponding rise in the Johnson-O'Malley funds, which were provided to school districts to support the increasing numbers of students. Between 1952 and 1964, the number of American Indian children enrolled in public schools rose from 53,000 to 80,000 (Szasz, 1974: 128).

During the 1950s, the BIA struggled to increase the number of American Indian and Alaska Native children attending school, and while the agency attacked this problem with some success, there were at least two nagging problems that concerned officials and American Indian and Alaska Native leaders. One was a very high rate of school dropouts among children attending public and BIA schools. One study of school dropouts found that about 60% of Indian youths who reached high school left school before receiving their diplomas (Szasz, 1974: 129). It was believed that academic deficiencies were a major factor contributing to this problem. The BIA found that it was not uncommon for American Indian and Alaska Native children to be two grades behind by the age they should have been attending the sixth grade (Szasz, 1974). To address this problem, in 1960, the BIA instituted summer school programs that were designed to improve the academic skills of American Indian children.

The BIA's heavy emphasis on vocational education in an era when record numbers of Americans were attending college was another nagging problem. This was not a new concern. A 1932 study could document only 385 American Indians enrolled in college, and a much smaller number, 52, who had ever completed a program of higher education. Two years later, in 1934, Congress created a loan fund for American Indians who wished to attend college, appropriating $250,000 to establish this program (Szasz, 1974: 135). Nearly three decades later, the need to encourage Indian youth to attend college had taken on a new urgency and the then director of the BIA's Branch of Education, Hildegard Thompson, moved to place more emphasis on post-secondary education. In addition to making more funds available for tuition and related expenses, the BIA replaced the Santa Fe boarding school with the Institute of American Indian Arts in 1962. At the Haskell Institute, a federally operated boarding school for American Indians and Alaska Natives, the last high school class graduated in 1965, and the facility reopened as the Haskell American Indian Junior College (Szasz, 1974).

Although the BIA sought to improve academic deficiencies, stem dropout rates, and encourage Indian students to attend college, the agency's efforts were not sufficient to fully meet the challenges it faced. Indian students were attending school in larger numbers than ever before, but they were also leaving in record numbers. The same was true for American Indians in college. As Szasz (1974) described the situation in the early 1960s,

> increased enrollment did not necessarily mean greater success, for Indian high school graduates continued to be ill-prepared for college. Despite the financial boost given to higher education, it appeared that it would be a long time before these college students could overcome the poor education they had received. Nor could they easily dismiss the cultural barrier maintained by persistent discrimination and the difficulty of adjusting to the lifestyle of non-Indian America. Ironically, the increased enrollment of Indian students in college thus served to demonstrate the weaknesses of Bureau education in the lower grades, and to reiterate the sharp cultural distinctions that separated these students from their counterparts in non-Indian America. (135–136)

INDIAN EDUCATION AND URBANIZATION

One of the most profound developments for Indian America in the years after the Second World War was the experience of rapid urbanization. In 1930, a majority of Americans lived in urban areas. In the same year, barely 10% of the American Indian population resided in cities; the large majority live in rural areas, on or near their reservations. In the span of three decades, nearly half of the American Indian and Alaska Native population resided in urban localities. Events after the Second World War were mainly responsible for this development. Many American Indians did not return to their reservation homes after the war, and the BIA's relocation programs brought many more to urban areas such as Los Angeles, San Francisco, Denver, and Chicago (Fixico, 2000: LaGrand, 2003).

The massive shift in the numbers of American Indians living in urban places presented these urban newcomers with tremendous challenges. American Indian youths in particular found themselves having to adjust to the demands of urban school systems. The adjustment of these youths to non-Indian educational environments was often a difficult process. Urban Indian students were often found falling behind, failing, and dropping out at the same rates of their reservation counterparts (Fuchs & Havighurst, 1983). A "crossover effect" was one theory proposed to explain the lack of success that American Indian students experienced in school. Specifically, American Indian students begin school on par with non-Indian students but lose interest as they reach an age where they become aware of their ethnic heritage; this awareness is manifest in personal alienation and a rejection of non-Indian culture, including academic success (Bryde, 1969). The crossover effect was not exclusively a problem for urban Indian students, but urban schools are presumably more alienating than those located within Indian communities. Although this theory has an intuitive appeal, there is relatively little research or evidence to support it beyond a few limited studies (see Fuchs & Havighurst, 1983; Brown, 1979; Swisher & Deyhle, 1989).

Nonetheless, the lack of success in public schools by American Indian and Alaska Native students precipitated the creation of numerous schools to provide alternatives to traditional public school settings. Many of these schools were established in the 1970s and 1980s in cities where there are large concentrations of American Indians and Alaska Natives. One of the oldest and best-known of these schools is the Indian Community School (ICS) in Milwaukee, Wisconsin. Established in the early 1970s, the school explains its inception and philosophy: "Founded out of the failings and frustrations of the area public schools to address the needs of its native students, ICS succeeds by teaching not only to the students' mind, but to their body and spirit. We believe the role of the Indian Community School is not confined to the world of academics, but must be strongly based in our native cultures and traditions" (ICS, 2004). The school enrolls 361 students in kindergarten through to the eighth grade. Although the Milwaukee school is probably the most successful and best-known example, it is certainly not the only one of its kind.

The number of schools, growing since 1970, that are dedicated to American Indian and Alaska Native students is not limited to urban areas. It should also be noted that many if not most reservations now operate their own school systems. Furthermore, many urban public school systems with sizable numbers of American Indian and Alaska Native students have also instituted programs that acknowledge the cultural heritage of these youths.

SELF-DETERMINATION AND THE INDIAN EDUCATION ACT

The 1960s were a period when there was a growing awareness among American Indians of the importance of education and the need to be directly involved with schools that serve American Indian and Alaska Native students. However, gaining a presence with the governing structure of the BIA, or even a seat on local school boards, was a daunting task for communities with relatively few resources or persons who possess a college degree. A major development that enabled more involvement occurred in 1969. After a lengthy period of study, a Special Senate Subcommittee on Indian Education, led by Senator Edward Kennedy, published a report titled "Indian Education: A National Tragedy—A National Challenge" (also known as the Kennedy Report). This report detailed the singular failings of existing approaches to educating American Indians and identified many of the special needs and circumstances of American Indian and Alaska Native students.

The Kennedy Report was an especially significant document because it led to the eventual passage of the Indian Education Act in 1972. The Indian Education Act was a landmark piece of legislation. Among its undertakings, it established the Office of Indian Education and the National Advisory Council on Indian Education as well as grant programs for adult and youth education. An especially important initiative that was supported by this

legislation was the creation of parent committees. Indian parent committees were formed to provide schools with advice about the educational
needs of their children and projects that would enhance the retention and
academic performance of American Indian students. These projects ranged
from education about tribal culture to after-school tutoring.

The Indian Education Act was directed at students attending public
schools, but it did not have an effect on the oldest existing legislation for
American Indian education: the Johnson-O'Malley Act (Szasz, 1974). The
Johnson-O'Malley programs were supervised by the BIA, and their management was almost unchanged from when they were established in the 1930s.
That is, the Johnson-O'Malley programs were administered with little or
no input from the communities they served. However, in 1975, Congress
passed the Indian Self-Determination and Education Assistance Act (P.L.
93-638), and this law had far-reaching implications for Indian communities and especially tribal governments. Specifically, it mandated the BIA to
contract with the tribes and tribal governments for the services that the
BIA had once provided directly. In the case of Johnson-O'Malley funds, this
legislation enabled many tribal governments to contract with the BIA for
school services. As a result, tribal governments were able to assume greater
control over the schools serving their children (Prucha, 1984).

The Indian Education Act was amended several times in subsequent
years but its scope and major mandates have remained largely unchanged.
A legal and mostly administrative change came in 1994 when the Indian
Education Act was folded into the reauthorizing legislation for the Elementary and Secondary Education Act (ESEA) as Title IX. Title IX-ESEA
programs have continued to support special efforts for American Indians as
well as for Alaska Natives and Native Hawaiians. From 1994 to 2001, Title IX
programs were used, among other things, to encourage schools to incorporate Native cultural knowledge into their curriculums, provide educational
support such as tutoring and summer programs, and solicit the advice of
Native parents.

In 2001, the ESEA was revamped by Congress and re-designated as the
"No Child Left Behind Act" (NCLB). Although the NCLB Act has a substan-
tially different focus than its predecessor legislation, the ESEA, the Indian
Education Act née Title IX appears in the NCLB legislation as Title VII-
Indian, Native Hawaiian, and Alaska Native Education and is substantially
the same as it was passed in 1972. That is, like its predecessors, the NCLB

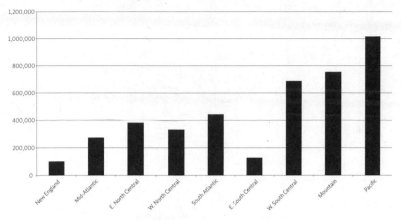

Figure 15.1   Distribution of American Indians and Alaska Natives
Across US Regions

legislation continues to encourage the consultation and involvement of
Native parents and activities that are related to Native culture to improve
the retention and academic achievement of Native students.

A STATISTICAL PROFILE OF AMERICAN INDIAN
AND ALASKA NATIVE EDUCATION

To begin this profile, it will be useful for readers to have a sense of where
American Indians are found in the United States. Figure 15.1 shows the
distribution of American Indians and Alaska Natives across regions of
the United States. There are 4,119,501 persons who identified themselves
as American Indians or Alaska Natives in the 2000 decennial census.[2] As
Figure 15.1 indicates, most of these individuals are living in areas west of the
Mississippi River. The largest populations are found in the states along
the West Coast. The second largest numbers of American Indians and
Alaska Natives are located in the interior states adjacent to the Rocky
Mountains. And the third largest region, the West South Central states,
have a large population of American Indians and Alaska Natives because
this area includes the state of Oklahoma, once designated the "Indian
Territory" (until 1907) because it was the site where tribes from the east
were re-settled in the nineteenth century.

Figure 15.2 and Figure 15.3 show the percentage distribution of American
Indians and Alaska Natives across rural and urban areas in different regions
of the United States. Figure 15.2 shows the rural–urban distribution for all

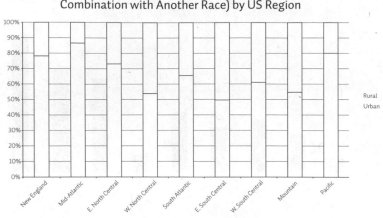

Figure 15.2 Percent Distribution of Rural and Urban Residence for American Indians and Alaska Natives (Alone or in Combination with Another Race) by US Region

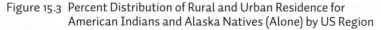

Figure 15.3 Percent Distribution of Rural and Urban Residence for American Indians and Alaska Natives (Alone) by US Region

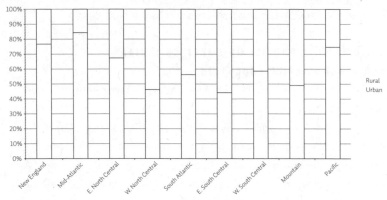

American Indians and Alaska Natives, regardless of whether they reported only one race, or two or more races. Figure 15.3 shows the rural–urban distribution of American Indians and Alaska Natives who reported only one race. Regardless of how they identify, the majority of American Indians lived in urban areas at the time of the 2000 census. Overall, more than two-thirds (67.4%) of the American Indian and Alaska Native population resided in an urban area in 2000. For persons who identified only as American Indian or Alaska Native ("alone"), a smaller share, 61%, were urban dwellers. Similarly, persons for whom two or more races were reported were more common in urban areas—about 78% have an urban residence.

Enrollments

To profile the educational experiences of American Indians and Alaska Natives, this discussion will first review rates of school attendance, i.e., enrollment. School enrollment represents the prevalence of schooling within a given population and measures the exposure of students to educational opportunities. This is especially salient because decades of federal Indian policy were driven simply by the desire to have pupils in school, independent of what they learned, how well they learned, and how they fared in academic work.

Table 15.1 provides some historical statistical data to accompany the foregoing narrative history. This table is based on data obtained from each decennial census taken during the twentieth century. It shows patterns of school enrollments for Americans Indians during the early decades, and later decades include Alaska Natives. The years in the table effectively bookend the twenieth century, capturing the changes in federal policies from forced assimilation and allotment in the early decades of the century (1900–1930), and the current policy of self-determination launched around 1970 (P.L. 93-638, Approved January 4, 1975, 88 Stat. 2203).

Indian education in the early years of the twentieth century involved a large presence of boarding schools. Relatively few reservations had day schools, so being enrolled in school meant being away from family for many, if not most, Indian children. This may partly account for why the majority of Indian children, about 60%, were not enrolled in school at the turn of the century. In 1910, the first year for which comparable data are readily available, the share of Indian children enrolled in school rose sharply from 40.4% to 56.4%—in relative terms, a 40% increase. Nonetheless, Indian school attendance lagged behind the rest of the nation. In 1910, about 64% of all Americans aged 5 to 19 years were enrolled in school (Carter et al., 2006).

In the decades between 1930 and 1970, school enrollments increased steadily, along with the rest of the nation. By 1970, most of the boarding schools had been replaced with reservation day schools or arrangements that allowed Indian children to attend off-reservation schools. A related development is that the American Indian population began moving in large numbers from reservation areas to urban areas after the Second World War. Urban residence almost certainly accounts for the increased enrollment of American Indian youths. Notably, by 2000, the enrollment gap between American Indians and the rest of the nation was nearly closed. At the turn

Table 15.1 School-Age Population and School Enrollments, 1900–2000

Year	School-age population* Number	In school Number	In school Percentage
1900	89,632	36,243	40.4
1910	88,741	50,065	56.4
1930	128,656	78,321	60.9
1970†	220,617	196,091	88.9
1980	500,037	421,532	84.3
1990	564,768	493,477	87.4
2000	696,613	625,303	91.7

* The population covered by this table varies in age: for 1900 and 1930, American Indians ages 5–20; for 1910, American Indians ages 6–19; for 1970, American Indians ages 5–17; and 1980–2000, American Indians and Alaska Natives ages 5–19. In 2000, the population covered is for American Indians and Alaska Natives alone (not in combination with any other race).

† Includes only states with an American Indian or Alaska Native population of 10,000 or more.

Sources: Historical Statistics of the United States, Table Ag915-1097; US Bureau of the Census, 2000 Census, SF-4.

of the twenty-first century, about 92% of American Indians and Alaska Natives ages 5 to 19 were enrolled in school, compared with 93% for the rest of the nation.

A more detailed picture of enrollment patterns for American Indians and Alaska Natives is presented in Table 15.2. This table shows the percentage of American Indians and Alaska Natives enrolled in school for different age groups and compared to other US racial and ethnic groups, specifically African Americans and whites, who represent traditionally disadvantaged and traditionally privileged groups in the United States, respectively. It also represents two categories of American Indian and Alaska Native ethno-racial identity.

In the 2000 Census, for the first time ever, census respondents were allowed to select more than one category to represent their racial heritage. As of 2000, the American Indian and Alaska Native population numbered around 4.1 million and, of this number, about 1.7 million persons were described as having one or more races, in addition to their American Indian or Alaska Native heritage. The vast majority of these persons were either "White and American Indian or Alaska Native" or "African American and American Indian or Alaska Native," and less commonly "African American,

White, and American Indian or Alaska Native." Another 2.4 million persons were identified as being "American Indian or Alaska Native alone," meaning only one race was reported for them in the census. The first column in Table 15.2 shows the age-specific enrollment patterns for persons who reported their race only as American Indian or Alaska Native, and the second column is for persons who reported another race in addition to American Indian or Alaska Native.

The enrollment patterns displayed in Table 15.2 are not especially surprising. In fact, there are some striking similarities. First, American Indians and Alaska Natives who report two or more races are not especially different from those who report only one race. Second, between the ages of 5 and 15, school enrollment is nearly universal and varies little across racial groups, no doubt the result of compulsory schooling laws and access to public schools. Nonetheless, there are some noteworthy differences that appear in this table.

One difference is that compared to African Americans and whites, American Indians are the least likely to have their young preschool-aged children enrolled in school. Slightly over 45% of American Indian and Alaska Native children ages three and four years are enrolled in school. African Americans are the most likely to have their children in preschool, 58%, followed by whites with 51%. Why American Indians are less likely to send their children to preschool is readily apparent. American Indian children are more likely to reside in rural areas where program access and transportation are often serious obstacles. In contrast, African American children are more likely to live in urban areas where preschool programs and transportation are less problematic. No doubt there are factors that also may account for this disparity.

Another notable difference involves American Indians and Alaska Natives aged 18 to 35, typically the years for post-secondary education. The data in Table 15.2 show that, compared to African Americans or whites, American Indians and Alaska Natives are much less likely to be enrolled in post-secondary schooling. For 18- and 19-year-olds, about 55% of American Indians and Alaska Natives are enrolled in school, while 70% of whites and 62% of African Americans are attending school. For 20- to 24-year-olds, these numbers fall off sharply as students graduate or decide to leave school. Nonetheless, there is a large and persistent disparity between

Table 15.2 Percentage Distribution of Persons Aged 3 and Older Enrolled in School for American Indians and Alaska Natives, African Americans, and Whites in 2000

Age	American Indian or Alaska Native alone or in combination	American Indian or Alaska Native alone	African American alone	White alone
3 and 4	45.2	45.6	58.3	50.7
5–9	95.8	95.8	96.6	96.0
10–14	98.6	98.4	98.7	99.1
15–17	92.4	91.7	94.8	96.1
18 and 19	56.3	54.3	62.3	70.4
20–24	27.5	24.9	31.3	38.0
25–34	12.5	11.8	13.4	10.6
35 and over	5.3	5.3	5.2	2.8
Total for all ages	34.6	35.0	34.7	25.5

Source: US Decennial Census, 2000.

American Indians and Alaska Natives and other groups. For this age category, only about 26% of American Indians and Alaska Natives are enrolled in school compared with 31% and 38% for African Americans and whites, respectively. Beyond age 25, there are few differences across these groups because most persons have completed their schooling by this age. However, one small difference is interesting because it shows older American Indians and Alaska Natives (age 35 and over) are more likely than whites to be enrolled in school, 5% versus 3%, respectively. This may reflect participation in remedial education offered through tribal colleges and other vocational and technical training programs.

Table 15.3 presents enrollment rates by showing the percent of American Indians and Alaska Natives enrolled in school in 2000 for a select group of the largest reservation in the United States. The greatest variability in this table can be found by comparing enrollment rates at younger and older ages, where school attendance is most likely to be discretionary, rather than compulsory. For instance, among preschool-aged children, ages three to four years, the Blackfeet reservation has the highest enrollment rates of any of the reservations listed in Table 15.3 with over two-thirds of their children

Table 15.3 Percentage of American Indians or Alaska Natives Aged 3 and Over Enrolled in School, by Age and Reservation, 2000

Reservation	3 years and over	3–4 years	5–9 years	10–14 years	15–17 years	18–19 years	20–24 years	25–34 years	35 years and over
Blackfeet	40.1	66.7	93.8	96.7	90.2	38.2	30.1	10.7	4.5
Fort Apache	43.4	48.8	98.4	98.7	85.8	59.1	13.6	6.8	5.0
Gila River	38.7	28.4	94.6	95.8	66.4	34.3	16.7	8.4	5.7
Navajo	42.0	47.9	96.2	98.3	92.4	59.3	23.4	12.4	5.8
Osage	37.6	56.1	92.2	100.0	95.3	37.8	19.6	15.6	5.7
Pine Ridge	44.5	52.8	93.6	94.6	83.0	58.7	25.8	14.6	5.3
Rosebud	44.7	34.8	94.3	98.6	87.5	51.4	22.7	6.4	4.0
San Carlos	42.1	45.6	97.8	96.6	82.4	47.1	10.3	10.5	4.2
Tohono O'odham	36.8	37.9	94.8	96.9	89.9	58.2	20.6	14.6	6.6
Turtle Mountain	42.7	34.2	100.0	99.0	91.0	65.1	27.7	9.0	3.2
Zuni	37.0	35.2	95.5	97.4	96.7	38.2	30.1	10.7	4.5

Source: US Decennial Census, 2000.

aged three to four in some sort of schooling. In contrast, only 28% of preschool-aged children are enrolled in school on the Gila River reservation.

From age 5 to 17 years, compulsory school attendance laws mean that, with a few exceptions, enrollment is near universal on most of these reservations. Enrollment rates for these ages exceed 90% in almost every instance. The most notable exception is the Gila River reservation where about one-third of teenagers 15 to 17 are not in school. Because in many places, students may leave school at age 16, this low level of enrollment probably signals a serious dropout problem for the Gila River community.

In the post-secondary school ages, 18 and over, there is a great deal of variation among these reservations. The Turtle Mountain reservation in North Dakota appears to have a great deal of success sending students into post-secondary schooling. This reservation has nearly two-thirds of its 18- to 19-year-old population in school and nearly 28% of 20- to 24-year-olds in school. The Blackfeet reservation is also successful in sending students to post-secondary schooling, with 30% of its 20- to 24-year-olds in school. In contrast, the San Carlos reservation has the smallest fraction of 20- to 24-year-olds in school with only 10%.

Educational Attainment

School enrollments are an important measure of educational success. However, an arguably even more important measure of educational success is the number of years of schooling an individual completes. Educational attainment, not enrollment, directly impacts personal qualifications, economic productivity, and success in the labour market.

To begin this discussion, Table 15.4 shows the educational attainment of American Indians and Alaska Natives, African Americans, and whites. This table is limited to persons over the age of 25, commonly an age when many Americans have completed their schooling. Comparing those persons for whom only one race is reported—American Indian or Alaska Native—with the entire Native population that includes persons with two or more races reported highlights some important differences between these groups. For example, American Indians and Alaska Natives for whom only one race is reported are generally less educated than the total population that includes multiracial American Indians and Alaska Natives. For instance, in the total population of American Indians or Alaska Natives, there are relatively fewer persons with educational attainments at high school or below compared to the American Indian or Alaska Native alone population. By the same token, the American Indian or Alaska Native alone population have fewer persons with some college or a degree than the total American Indian or Alaska Native population.

Regardless of how American Indians or Alaska Natives may identify, alone or in combination with another race, they consistently attain less education than white Americans. For example, 29% of the American Indian or Alaska Native alone population has less than a high school education (normally 12 years of school completed). In contrast, only about 15% of white Americans have less than a high school education. At the other extreme, nearly 10% of white Americans have an advanced graduate or professional degree, while barley 4% of the American Indian or Alaska Native alone population possesses a similar degree. In fact, American Indians and Alaska Natives fare no better than African Americans with respect to educational attainment. At any level of educational attainment reflected in Table 15.4, there is barely a percentage point difference between these groups, particularly for the American Indian or Alaska Native alone population. The educational parity that exists for these groups is especially ironic given

Table 15.4 Percentage Distribution of Educational Attainment by Race

Educational attainment	American Indian or Alaska Native alone or in combination	American Indian or Alaska Native alone	African American alone	White alone
Less than 5th grade	3.2	4.2	2.5	0.8
5th–8th grade	6.0	6.9	5.3	3.8
9th–12th grade, no diploma	16.0	18.0	19.8	10.0
High school graduate	28.0	29.2	29.8	30.0
Some college	25.4	23.6	22.5	21.9
Associate degree	7.0	6.6	5.8	6.6
Bachelor's degree	9.2	7.6	9.5	17.2
Graduate or professional degree	5.1	3.9	4.8	9.8
Total	100.0	100.0	100.0	100.0

Source: US Decennial Census, 2000.

the long history where African Americans were denied education in the same years that American Indian children were corralled in boarding schools.

The next table presents a profile of educational attainments for selected reservations. The data in Table 15.5 shows that there are two reservations that stand out with respect to having relatively high levels of education. Nearly three-quarters of the adult population aged 25 and over residing on the Blackfeet and Osage reservations have at least a high school education. The Blackfeet reservation can boast the highest levels of educational attainment with 21% of its adult population having some sort of college degree, in most cases, an associate degree, though 8.7% have baccalaureate or higher degrees. At the other end of the educational spectrum, the Fort Apache and Gila River reservations are profoundly disadvantaged with respect to the human capital that schooling confers. On both of the reservations, over one-third of the adult population aged 25 and over are high school dropouts. Similarly, only one person in 20 has any kind of post-secondary degree and only one or two in 100 has completed four or more years of college. Recalling that over one-fourth of the white population possesses a four-year (or higher) degree, these numbers underscore the deep disparities that exist between these reservations and the rest of the nation.

Table 15.5 Educational Attainment for Persons Aged 25 and Over,
Selected Reservations, 2000

Reservation	25 years and over	Less than 5th grade	5th–8th grade	9th–12th grade, no diploma	High school graduate	Some college	Associate degree	Bachelor's degree	Graduate or Professional degree
Blackfeet	100.0	1.0	5.6	18.7	26.0	27.8	12.2	5.3	3.4
Fort Apache	100.0	1.5	11.3	36.1	31.0	14.7	3.1	2.0	0.3
Gila River	100.0	2.5	10.0	35.9	34.8	11.6	4.2	0.5	0.7
Navajo	100.0	16.1	9.3	20.4	26.9	17.2	5.3	3.5	1.4
Osage	100.0	0.2	3.4	16.5	35.8	26.2	6.4	8.2	3.3
Pine Ridge	100.0	2.0	8.4	23.2	26.9	23.1	7.9	5.6	2.8
Rosebud	100.0	0.2	7.2	23.4	32.0	24.5	5.2	4.7	2.8
San Carlos	100.0	1.4	8.4	33.4	32.6	18.4	4.1	0.9	0.8
Tohono O'odham	100.0	5.6	8.5	24.0	41.0	12.8	4.4	2.0	1.6
Turtle Mountain	100.0	0.8	8.6	21.0	24.3	22.6	13.2	7.4	2.1
Zuni	100.0	1.1	7.7	28.4	32.0	22.8	4.6	2.5	0.8

Source: US Decennial Census, 2000.

Education and Labour Force Participation

Education is, of course, important for many reasons but perhaps none are
more important than its economic value. Education certainly has a role
in helping individuals make wise decisions that affect their well-being.
For example, better-educated persons are less likely to smoke than less
educated individuals. Nonetheless, education also facilitates worker
productivity, and highly educated persons are more highly valued than
workers with less education. Highly valued and well-paid workers typically
enjoy better benefits such as medical insurance, paid vacation time, and
retirement plans. Better-educated workers in most instances also enjoy a
measure of job security and employment stability that is often not in the
work experience of lesser educated workers. That is, better-educated workers are less likely to be unemployed and more likely to be in the labour force
than less educated persons.

The percentages in Table 15.6 reflect the benefits of education for the
labour force participation of American Indians and Alaska Natives ages 18
to 63. Not surprising, American Indians and Alaska Natives with very low
levels of education fare poorly in the labour market. Between 8% and 9% of

Table 15.6 Percentage Distribution of Educational Attainment and Labour Force Participation for Civilian American Indians and Alaska Natives Ages 18 to 63, 2000

Education and labour force status	American Indians or Alaska Natives alone or in combination	American Indians or Alaska Natives alone
Less than high school diploma	100.0	100.0
In labour force, employed	45.0	42.6
In labour force, unemployed	7.8	8.6
Not in labour force	47.2	48.8
High school graduate	100.0	100.0
In labour force, employed	61.9	59.9
In labour force, unemployed	6.9	7.9
Not in labour force	31.2	32.2
Some college	100.0	100.0
In labour force, employed	69.6	69.2
In labour force, unemployed	5.2	5.7
Not in labour force	25.2	25.1
Associate degree	100.0	100.0
In labour force, employed	74.6	73.8
In labour force, unemployed	4.2	5.0
Not in labour force	21.3	21.3
Bachelor's degree	100.0	100.0
In labour force, employed	80.1	79.9
In labour force, unemployed	3.3	3.3
Not in labour force	16.6	16.7
Graduate or professional degree	100.0	100.0
In labour force, employed	81.7	81.5
In labour force, unemployed	2.5	2.5
Not in labour force	15.7	16.2

Source: US Decennial Census, 2000.

American Indians and Alaska Native with less than a high school education are unemployed. However, nearly half of this population is simply not in the labour force. Lacking the most rudimentary educational qualifications, this group represents the so-called "core unemployed"—jobless persons who are not even trying to seek work.

A high school diploma offers some obvious advantages and this is most clearly reflected in labour force participation rates. About 62% of high school graduates participate in the civilian labour force compared to 45% of American Indians and Alaska Natives who have not completed high school, an increase of more than one-third. However, a high school diploma offers little immunity from unemployment. Among American Indians and Alaska Natives in the labour force, the unemployment rate for those with a high school education is only about one percentage point lower than among those persons lacking a high school education, 6.9% and 7.8%, respectively.

Completing high school and attending high school offers some protection against unemployment, but post-secondary credentials provide the most protection and the strongest incentives for labour force participation. Unemployment decreases monotonically by about one percentage point for each successively higher level of post-secondary education to an advanced graduate or professional degree. For example, the unemployment rate for American Indians and Alaska Natives with some college is 5.2% while it is 4.2% for those with a two-year associates degree. Needless to say, American Indians and Alaska Natives with graduate or professional degrees fare best in the labour market. For this group, only 2.5% are unemployed and 82% are employed or actively seeking work.

CONCLUSION

The twentieth century was a period of remarkable change in the education of American Indians and Alaska Natives. The early decades of the century were marked by federal policies that emphasized the use of education as a tool for obliterating the last remnants of American Indians languishing on reservations—"education for extinction" as one author so aptly put it (Adams, 1995). Boarding schools were the principal instruments for accomplishing this aim. These schools were initially located in places distant from the reservation homes of their students. Over time, the numbers of these schools grew and came into closer proximity with the reservations. Distance from their students' reservation homes was considered a virtue, and none of these schools were ever located on reservation land, with the possible exception of Chilloco Indian School, which was built in the Indian Territory.

Perhaps the most significant feature of Indian education in this period was that was an educational curriculum devised by white men to achieve an outcome considered desirable by white men. Never once in the recorded history of this time were Indians ever consulted about whether they considered this a desirable result. Instead, they were solicited and sometimes instructed to send their children to a place where they would be taught how to live in the white man's world. Subordinated in every way by white men, these parents knew that their children needed to know how to fend for themselves in a world made by white men. What many of these parents probably did not fully understand were the lengths that these men would go to destroy the heritage of their children, their concept of themselves, their culture, and their community. But many of these children understood what was at stake, and they rebelled, and they ran away (Lomawaima, 1994).

As successive cohorts of students grew up and left these schools, could it be any surprise that education came to be seen as an instrument of oppression, an institution to be distrusted, and an experience to be endured rather than embraced? Throughout these years, federal officials despaired of their inability to enroll the large numbers of American Indians and Alaska Natives who remained outside the system. However, the federal government began decommissioning the boarding school system in earnest in the 1930s. Concurrently, the percentage of American Indians enrolled in school grew steadily. By 1970, nearly 90% of school-aged American Indians and Alaska Natives were enrolled in school.

The year 1970 coincides with a deeply profound shift in federal policies for American Indians and Alaska Natives. In July of 1970, President Richard M. Nixon addressed Congress with a message that proposed that American Indians should be allowed to set the course of their own destiny and articulated his vision of self-determination for American Indians in federal policy making. Five years later, Congress responded with legislation, the Indian Self-Determination and Education Assistance Act of 1975. Nixon's message and this legislation effectively ended assimilationist policies dating back to the nineteenth century. For American Indian and Alaska Native education, it meant that Native people would determine the content, scope, and purposes of educating their children.

Self-determination as a set of policies shaping education in Native America have been in place for more than a quarter-century, and it is fair to ask, what is the status of American Indian and Alaska Native education in the early twenty-first century? The second half of this chapter was devoted to showing the changes over time and especially the extant American Indian and Alaska Native educational experience—successes or failures—that can derived from the most recent US Census taken in 2000.

In terms of school enrollment, the data from the 2000 Census present a complex picture. In some respects, American Indians and Alaska Natives do not fare as well as African Americans. Blacks, for example, are much more likely to be enrolled in preschool than American Indians and Alaska Natives. Overall, the enrollment patterns of American Indians and Alaska Natives is not too different than the enrollment patterns of African Americans—both groups lag behind whites. Similarly, there is a striking amount of heterogeneity among the large reservations for which data were presented. Some reservations such as the Blackfeet have relatively high levels of enrollment regardless of age, while others, such as the Tohono O'odham, are dramatically lower. One encouraging sign is that, for students of compulsory school age, enrollments are very high regardless of location and vary little from one reservation to another.

Educational attainment is another measure of school success. American Indians and Alaska Natives are more or less on par with African Americans. In fact, whites, American Indians and Alaska Natives, and African Americans have roughly the same shares of persons with high school diplomas. However, they differ in one important respect. These ethnic minorities have more of their people who are high school dropouts, and whites attend and complete college at higher levels than the others. Furthermore, single-race American Indians and Alaska Natives appear to be the most educationally disadvantaged in terms of attainment as well as enrollment. And like enrollment, some reservations are doing well with respect to educational attainment while others have fared poorly.

This profile also examined the impact of disabilities on enrollment and veteran status on attainment. Ostensibly, having some form of disability might prevent a child from being enrolled in school. Although disabilities do limit school attendance for American Indian and Alaska Native children, their impact is not as great as one might expect. Predictably, some disabilities are more limiting than others. A self-care disability slightly impacted the enrollment of children under age 18, and among young adults of college age, a physical disability had the greatest impact on enrollment. In contrast, military service is for some, an avenue to attaining a higher education. Veteran's benefits include financial assistance for attending college and in the past, it has had a visible impact on the American Indian and Alaska Native population (Snipp, 1989). Not surprisingly, military experience is related to higher levels of educational attainment for American Indians and Alaska Natives. Current military requirements stipulate a high school diploma or its equivalent, but this appears to be a springboard for further education. Veterans have relatively high levels of college level education.

Perhaps one of the ultimate values of education is with respect to its impact on material well-being. Without doubt, well-educated persons live longer, healthier, more affluent, and comfortable lives than persons with less education. The profile presented in this chapter focused on labour force participation and poverty in relation to educational attainment. Education, of course, has a tremendous impact on economic well-being and especially in relation to labour force participation and income. Poverty measures incomes above and below an official threshold determined to be a minimum standard of living.

Like most other Americans, education, without question, is an essential resource for the economic well-being of American Indians and Alaska Natives. Labour force participation, a prerequisite for wages and salaries, increases in a near monotonic fashion with higher rates of labour force participation accruing from higher levels of education. Predictably, poverty declines steadily with higher levels of education, with the lowest poverty rates among those with the highest levels of education. However, it also should be said that a high school diploma represents a minimum standard for labour force participation and thereby significantly decreases the risk of living in poverty. American Indians and Alaska Natives who fail to attain this basic credential are deeply at risk for little more than a marginal attachment to the labour force and highly at risk for a life in economic poverty.

In closing, the twentieth century was a time of tremendous change in the education of American Indians and Alaska Natives. Ironically, the goals embraced by the early assimilationists, spreading knowledge about Anglo-American culture through education, were best realized by giving American Indians and Alaska Natives more control over their schooling. Certainly, schooling has been a boon for the material well-being of American Indians. Whether this schooling also results in the overarching aim of the early assimilationists, the destruction of Native culture and traditions, remains to be seen. With American Indians and Alaska Natives in control of their educational institutions, it will be their decision to make.

NOTES

1. The legal status of Alaska Natives and particularly Alaska Native land differs from reservations because the US Supreme Court decision in *Alaska v. Native Village of Venetie Tribal Government*, 522 US 520 (1998) sharply curtailed the sovereign powers of Alaska Native villages.

2. The 2000 Census allowed persons to report more than one race for their heritage. This number includes all persons who reported their race as American Indian or Alaska Native, regardless of whether it was the only race they reported for themselves or in combination with another race. The number of persons who identified one race only ("alone") is substantially smaller—2,475,956 persons were identified as American Indian or Alaska Native in the 2000 Census.

REFERENCES

Adams, D.W. (1995). *Education for extinction: American Indians and the boarding school experience, 1875–1928*. Lawrence, KS: University Press of Kansas.

Bernstein, A. (1991). *American Indians and World War II: Toward a new era in Indian affairs*. Norman, OK: University of Oklahoma Press.

Bolt, C. (1987). *American Indian policy and American reform: Case studies of the campaign to assimilate the American Indians*. London, UK: Allen & Unwin.

Brown, A.D. (1979). The cross-over effect: A legitimate issue in Indian education? In *Multicultural education and the American Indian*. Los Angeles, CA: American Indian Studies Center, UCLA.

Bryde, J.F. (1969). A rationale for Indian education. *Journal of American Indian Education, 8*, 11–14.

Carter, S.B., Gartner, S.S., Haines, M.R., Olmstead, A.L., Sutch, R., & Wright, G. (2006). *Historical statistics of the United States: Millennial edition*. New York, NY: Cambridge University Press.

Castile, G.P. (1998). *To show heart: Native American self-determination and federal Indian policy, 1960–1975*. Tucson, AZ: University of Arizona Press.

Fixico, D.L. (1986). *Termination and relocation: Federal Indian policy, 1945–1960*. Albuquerque, NM: University of New Mexico Press.

———. (2000). *The urban Indian experience in America*. Albuquerque, NM: University of New Mexico Press.

Fuchs, E., & Havighurst, R. (1983). *To live on this earth: American Indian education*. Albuquerque, NM: University of New Mexico Press.

Getches, D.H., Wilkinson, C.F., & Williams, R.A. (1998). *Cases and materials on federal Indian law* (4th ed.). St. Paul, MN: West Group.

Gross, E. (1989). *Contemporary federal policy toward American Indians*. New York, NY: Greenwood Press.

Hoxie, F.E. (1984). *A final promise: The campaign to assimilate the Indians, 1880–1920*. Lincoln, NE: University of Nebraska Press.

Indian Community School of Milwaukee (ICS). (2004). Retrieved from http://www.ics-milw.org

LaGrand, J.B. (2002). *Indian metropolis: Native Americans in Chicago, 1945–1975.* Urbana, IL: University of Illinois Press.

Lomawaima, K.T. (1994). *They called it prairie light: The story of Chilocco Indian School.* Lincoln, NE: University of Nebraska Press.

Prucha, F.P. (1984). *The great father.* Lincoln, NE: University of Nebraska Press.

Snipp, C.M. (1989). *American Indians: The first of this land.* New York, NY: Russell Sage Foundation.

Sorkin, A.L. (1978). *The urban American Indian.* Lexington, MA: Lexington Books.

Swisher, K., & Deyhle, D. (1989). The styles of learning are different, but the teaching is just the same: Suggestions for teachers of American Indian youth. *Journal of American Indian Education, 28,* 1–14.

Szasz, M. (1974). *Education and the American Indian: The road to self-determination since 1928.* Albuquerque, NM: University of New Mexico Press.

Wilkins, D.E. (2002). *Indian politics and the American political system.* Lanham, MD: Rowman & Littlefield.

16

INTERROGATING THE IMAGE
OF THE "WANDERING NOMAD"
INDIGENOUS TEMPORARY MOBILITY PRACTICES IN AUSTRALIA

Sarah Prout

INTRODUCTION

Throughout Australia's colonial history, a fundamental question has lingered uncomfortably over the socio-political landscape: how do two societies with traditionally contrasting "settlement" ideologies coexist? At first contact, the "nomadic" tendencies of Aboriginal and Torres Strait Islander hunter-gatherers (Australia's Indigenous peoples) contrasted sharply with the intrinsic colonial ideals of private ownership, settlement, development, and economic progress. As Young and Doohan (1989) note, Indigenous mobility practices "presented a main obstacle to be overcome if they were to fit into the fledgling society of the new Australia" (1). Governments responded with legislation and administrative practices that attempted to civilize and sedentarize Indigenous populations.

Both societies have experienced significant socio-spatial transformations over the ensuing decades, rendering these early caricatures of contrasting colonial "settlement" and Indigenous nomadism insufficient as illustrations of contemporary Australian population dynamics. The political ideologies driving Indigenous affairs administration have also shifted and oscillated between the principles of guardianship, equality, and choice (Sanders, 2008). However, these divergent settlement traditions continue to underwrite contemporary struggles for an equitable and just spatial coexistence between Indigenous and non-Indigenous Australians (Burns, 2006; Prout & Howitt, 2009).

Indigenous temporary mobility practices remain poorly understood within contemporary mainstream society. They are often explained away as simply the product of a nomadic predisposition to wander (Burns, 2006; Hamilton, 1987; Havemann, 2005; Peterson, 2004; Prout, 2009a; Young & Doohan, 1989). Further, these population dynamics are peripheral to most government policy development processes because of a lack of capture by conventional statistical measures—despite being regularly cited by public servants "on the ground" as a central challenge to service delivery (Prout, 2008; Prout, 2009b; Prout & Howitt, 2009; Taylor, 1998).

Although mobility has been a central feature of Indigenous lived experience for thousands of years, non-Indigenous attempts to understand and conceptualize it through time have been, at best, piecemeal and unsystematic. Consequently, many Indigenous people, for whom frequent movement is integral to lived experience, are marginalized in both public discourse and public policy. Developing more holistic understandings of these population dynamics is therefore fundamental to both the policy agenda of closing the socio-economic gaps, and the broader challenge of redressing Indigenous socio-cultural marginalization.

Building on Taylor and Bell (1994), this chapter seeks to progress scholarly dialogues about Indigenous temporary mobility practices. It draws together the presently disparate and often obscured Australian mobility literature to build a foundational picture of the nature and characteristics of these population dynamics across time and space. It sketches the spatial, temporal, and demographic dimensions of these population dynamics, emphasizing both large-scale patterns and small-scale contingencies. The analysis then turns to an examination of Indigenous temporary mobility in relation to the state and the contextual factors that shape this relationship.[1]

Temporary mobility might be distinguished from migration in that the former involves no permanent population redistribution. Ultimately though, what constitutes "permanence" is subjective (Stillwell & Congdon, 1991). This analysis therefore applies relatively arbitrary parameters to delimit the discussion. Here, temporary mobility includes movements that are anywhere between two days and several months in duration, and take place between (not within) locales. Of course, any discussion that focuses solely on Indigenous temporary mobility practices risks feeding the common and simplistic perception that all Indigenous Australians are highly mobile. On one level, there is clearly a culture of mobility in Indigenous Australia. Collectively, the temporary mobility literature weaves a narrative of frequent, intensive flows of movement through small Indigenous communities, rural towns, regional centres, and major cities. It also suggests, however, that this culture of mobility is diverse and contextual: it cannot be uniformly explained away as the product of an inherently Indigenous predisposition to wander. Further, the narrative of mobility forms only a part of the broader story of Indigenous spatiality. This analysis is situated within a larger body of literature that addresses Indigenous population distribution, migration trends, and immobility (see, for example, Biddle & Hunter, 2006; Biddle, Taylor, & Yap, this volume; Gray, 1989; Smith, 1980; Taylor, 1997; 2006; Taylor & Bell, 1996a; 1996b; 1999; 2004b).

INDIGENOUS TEMPORARY MOBILITY ACROSS TIME AND SPACE

Many small-scale Indigenous mobility studies provide some measure of the frequency and/or volume of movement (Altman, 1987; Birdsall, 1988; Brooks & Kral, 2007; Hamilton, 1987; Marshurbash, 2003; Palmer & Brady, 1988; Smith, 2002, 2004; Taylor, 1988). Taken together, these analyses indicate high levels of temporary mobility. For example, in a year-long population study of a small Central Australian community during the late 1990s, Warchivker, Tjapangati, and Wakerman (2000) estimated that 26% to 58% of the total population comprised highly mobile individuals. That is, while these mobile individuals were present at the community for one or two of four population surveys throughout the year and were in some way associated with the community, they were not defined as part of the "core" resident population. In a 2005 study, Foster et al. made similar observations from their survey of the Alice Springs town camps in Central Australia. They calculated that 36.7% to 39.6% of the total population move frequently in and out of the camps.

A number of complex and policy-relevant questions emerge regarding these mobile individuals and their mobility practices. Who are they? Where do they go? For how long are they temporarily mobile and what factors shape their mobility practices?

The Spatial Dimension

The term "walkabout" is commonly applied to Australian Indigenous mobilities to imply a kind of aimless or erratic wandering off into the unknown. The realities are somewhat less arbitrary. The spatial dimension of Indigenous temporary mobility practices has two chief components: the direction or process of movement, and its spatial scope and shape (Prout, 2007).

The literature identifies three processes of Indigenous temporary mobility. Each might be conceptualized in relation to the notion of a "home-base." The first matches Zelinsky's definition of circulation as "a great variety of movements usually short-term, repetitive, or cyclical in character, but all having in common the lack of any declared intention of a permanent or long lasting change in residence" (1971: 226). This type of mobility involves continual returns to a home-base after frequent journeys away. The home-base may be a particular community, town, or settlement. The second process of Indigenous short-term mobility is known as "bi-local" or "multi-local" residence. This type of mobility involves continual movement between two or more home-bases in more than one community, town, or settlement. These two or more locales may be viewed as extensions of one another: they are places in which an individual might be considered usually resident (see, for example, Burns, 2006). The third process of Indigenous short-term mobility identified in the literature is perpetual movement between a series of locales within which an individual has family. This form of mobility involves no particular physical home-base. "Home" is imbedded within a social network of relatedness rather than a specific geographic region or locale (Taylor, 1992).

Delimiting the spatial scope and shape of Indigenous short-term mobility processes is a fraught task and requires a critical reflection on conventional categories. Some spatial categorizations serve only to entrench misconceptions and further alienate scholars and policy makers from the rationalities that inform Indigenous mobility choices (Prout & Howitt, 2009). Rowley's (1970) "remote/settled" classification is one such example. On one level, it is simply a functional distinction based on calculable differences in population densities and service accessibility (Taylor, 2002; 2006). On another level, it entrenches non-Indigenous interpretations of the socio-spatial landscape where cities (the hubs of modern progress) are central, while the harsh wilderness of the Australian outback is peripheral and—with the exception of profitable mining and pastoral ventures—largely antithetical to progressive economic development. Here, remote living is viewed as problematic not only because it undermines economic productivity, but also because it impedes cost-effective service delivery. Incidentally, much of this vast remote "wilderness" is also often referred to as the "Indigenous domain" (Trigger, 1992). These perspectives run counter to those of many Indigenous people for whom inland Australia has been their home, their sustenance, and their identity for thousands of years.

The divergent conceptual vantage points here are not trivial. With regard to Indigenous spatial practices, these kinds of differences largely explain social policy responses that are incompatible with Indigenous lived experience. Perhaps most importantly though, in the case of temporary mobility, discernable patterns of movement do not readily correlate to conventional remoteness classifications. Similarly, state/territory administrative boundaries have had little bearing on the intentionality of Indigenous temporary mobility practices.[2] By contrast, physical geography, in connection with colonial history, has fundamentally shaped Indigenous socio-spatial organization—and thus mobility practices.

Prior to colonization, climatic considerations and natural resource availability directly affected Indigenous socio-spatial organization and informed cultural and economic practice. Ceremonial activity, hunting, gathering, and trading were inextricably linked to environmental conditions and the seasonal availability of natural resources (Bates, 1985; Burns, 2006; Memmott, Long, & Thompson, 2006; Peterson, 2004; Prout, 2007; Sutton, 1990; Young & Doohan, 1989). In resource-rich and coastal areas that could support dense populations, mobility was more localized (see, for example, Gale, 1981; Smith, 2004). There were seasonal and ceremonial shifts between smaller, more dispersed band formations on various clan estates, and larger population gatherings along the banks of permanent water sources. In general though, these movements were contained within small regions. By contrast, in desert regions smaller, less structured populations ranged more widely—at times temporarily abandoning parts of their country[3] that were experiencing severe drought—to secure and sustain a resource economy and to maintain socio-cultural practices with neighbouring bands (Veth, 2003).

Young and Doohan (1989) provide a detailed analysis of Indigenous mobility practices prior to colonization. They explain that for Indigenous people in Central Australia, mobility was imbedded in cultural practice as people's ceremonial journeys followed dreaming tracks that linked sacred sites. These sites were often water sources or resource-rich places, and thus also important economically. Most journeys were confined to ancestral territories within which particular groups had spiritual knowledge. Travel into the country of neighbouring tribes was less frequent but necessary in order to maintain reciprocal relationships in times of economic need (Young & Doohan, 1989).

Within the context of varied mobility patterns across the continent, spiritual attachment to country was a profound force that firmly and uniformly rooted language groups within their traditional territories (Peterson, 2004). Somewhat paradoxically, these highly mobile hunter-gatherer populations were also highly settled within their regions of socio-cultural belonging (Peterson, 2004). Many remain so. Anthropologist Hugh Brody eloquently captures this spatial reality when he makes a global comparison between hunter-gatherer societies with their agriculturally-based "farmer" counterparts.

> A crucial difference between hunter-gatherers and farmers is that one society is highly mobile, with a strong tendency to both small- and large-scale nomadism, whereas the other is highly settled, tending to stay firmly in one particular area or territory. This difference is established in stereotypes of "nomadic" hunters and "settled" farmers. However, the stereotype has it the wrong way around. It is agricultural societies that tend to be on the move; hunting peoples are far more firmly settled. This fact is evident when we look at these two ways of being in the world over a long time span— when we screen the movie of human history, as it were, rather than relying on the photograph. (Brody, 2000: 7)

However, contemporary correlations between physical geography and mobility practices do not simply reflect continuing pre-colonial forms of movement, but rather, environmental and socio-culturally specific responses and adaptations to the colonial project. As Keesing and Strathern (1998) explain, Indigenous experiences of colonization depended on their physical location (which determined when the colonial frontier reached them); the environmental characteristics of their territories (which determined what kind of economic exploitation, if any, their land was adjudged suitable for); and how each group responded to settler presence (e.g.,

Indigenous peoples whose homelands were located along the coastal
inlet that is now Adelaide, or who occupied the hinterlands surrounding
the Swan River in Western Australia, were devastated by the early colonial
frontier [Gale, 1972; Green, 1984]; by contrast, Indigenous peoples in the
less accessible desert regions remained relatively unaffected by the settling
society until the 1960s [Long, 1989]).

In parts of Australia, attachment to country continues to have a strong
delimiting effect on the spatial dimensions of Indigenous people's mobility
practices. In the resource-rich tropical north, for example, anthropologists describe highly localized patterns of mobility that are based on and
contained within the enduring system of clan estates mapped over the
landscape (Altman, 1987; Morphy, 2008; Smith, 2004). Here, there remains
a deeply interwoven relationship between kinship and country that serves
to consolidate the spatial dimensions of geographically contained and
identifiable "mobility regions." There is intensive movement between
outstations, their surrounding environs, and local townships. There are also
less frequent journeys to larger regional centres or major cities to access
services. Memmott, Long, and Thompson (2006) suggest that "mobility
regions" could be mapped through an understanding of (a) the contemporary expressions of traditional land custodianship and economies; (b) the
spatial arrangement of various language groups, and; (c) the location of
variously sized service centres relative to (a)and (b). In the nation's large
central desert zone and surrounding northern hinterlands, identification
with ancestral homelands, and the largely corresponding distribution of
kin, also plays a significant role in shaping the spatial bound of Indigenous
mobility practices. In the Ngaanyatjarra Lands of the Western Desert, for
example, spiritual attachment to country has a localizing impact on mobility.
Brooks and Kral (2007) argue that because of a relatively short experience of
contact with non-Indigenous society, a history of unbroken contact with the
region, and the fact that no non-Ngaanyatjarra settlements have not been
established on the Lands, connection to country exerts a strong pull to localized living for Ngaanyatjarra people. The Ngaanyatjarra region is socially
"mapped over" by particular kinship groups. Because of these powerful emo-
tive attachments to place, Ngaanyatjarra people feel uncomfortable when
away from their country. This culture of connectedness is established and
cultivated through births, deaths, and ceremonial activities that foster both
a cohesive society and spatial consolidation (Brooks & Kral, 2007).

Young (1990) identified a similar pattern of localized living among the Warlpiri and Anmatyerre peoples of Central Australia. Their country, she explained, is demarcated by spiritual responsibility, common language affiliation, and the location of kin. However, evidence presented by Young and Doohan (1989) suggest that, even by the 1980s, distinct "regions" of movement were not necessarily easily identifiable in Central Australia. They explicitly described the role of colonial policies and practices in altering the socio-spatial systems of organization among the Warlpiri, Anmatyerre, Arrente, Pintupi, and Pitjanjatjarra peoples of Central Australia. Through forced relocations and engagements with the mainstream economy, various groups were moved to distant territories. Some remained and intermarried. Others eventually returned. The overall impact, though, was to expand networks of relatedness (within kinship structures) and spiritual belonging (on country). Young and Doohan (1989) observed that, although their connections lay primarily within Central Australia, many Indigenous people in the region had multiple sets of roots with customary obligations to several regions and expanded kinship networks.

Mobility patterns in the desert were always more spatially expansive than in the tropical north. However, these enlarged spheres of relatedness and belonging that result from responses to colonial impact expand potential mobility trajectories and render particular "mobility regions" in this vast portion of the continent less distinguishable.

In the southern regional hinterlands that border the desert, geographically contained "mobility regions" are perhaps even less distinguishable. Some Indigenous groups within this zone may identify with a particular region and feel a sense of familiarity within it, but their choices of residence and temporary mobility practices are not confined to it. Rather, the location of family is the primary determinant of temporary mobility trajectories (Prout, 2007; 2009a). In these areas, where early administrative policies of separation and forced removal had profound and far-reaching impacts, familial networks may now be dispersed over vast distances.

As early as the 1950s, Beckett (1965) described individual mobility "beats" among "part-Aborigines" in western New South Wales. He explained that these beats were "defined by the situation of kin" and "proximity was only a minor factor" (Beckett, 1988: 131). Over four decades later in the same region, Burns's (2006) observations of the spatial dimensions of mobility in many ways paralleled Beckett's: the towns and communities that a person might regularly visit are not necessarily close together. Rather, the various flows of movement are dictated by the "situation of kin," which have, as Beckett (1965) predicted, greatly expanded. Burns (2006) found that, although there is a definite sense of belonging to the region and a parallel sense of unease beyond it, familiarity with one's country is not the primary consideration that shapes the spatial dimensions of Indigenous mobility. Here, the location of kin no longer mirrors traditional territorial arrangements, and kinship networks are now the primary spatial delimiters of individual mobility trajectories. Further, as a result of both government policies and individual choices regarding engagement with the mainstream economy, these individual kinship networks do not necessarily neatly correspond to a geographical territory. Burns (2006) also noted that the factors that shape temporary movements appear more characteristically "complex, varied and individualistic" (324) than they are in the desert and tropical north.

Similar observations have been made in the Midwest of Western Australia where early administrative policies of forced removal and relocation have profoundly influenced the contemporary spatialities of most Indigenous people (Prout, 2007). While some individuals feel a sense of belonging to the region, many visit towns and communities outside of the region more frequently than those within it. Their familial ties, which have expanded through forced and labour migrations, are stronger in these more distant locales. While much mobility is contained within the Midwest, movements are not necessarily undertaken in a geographical sequence from nearest to farthest town and back. Individuals "stop" only in towns where they have strong and amicable familial ties. In many such cases, it is difficult to distinguish whether a person's sense of belonging to the region is derived from a spiritual attachment to country or the reality that their kinship network lies primarily within the region.

These distinctions were also unclear in Birdsall's (1988) analysis of Nyungar "runs" in the south of Western Australia. She described family "lines" of mobility running up and down the Western Australian coast. However, the towns that formed the line were not geographically sequential or spatially proximate. Rather, they were determined by the specific location of family members. She explains that lines have developed as family members have sought to return from the southern institutions into which they were placed, to the homelands from which they were forcibly removed as children. These journeys have, in some cases, taken more than a generation, and networks of kin have established themselves in various towns along the way (Birdsall, 1988). In these more densely populated, urbanized, and coastal contexts, familial associations seem to have become the primary determinant of the spatial extent of individual mobility trajectories (Birdsall-Jones & Christensen, 2007; Gale, 1972; 1981; 1987). Because familial networks in these parts of the country have, in many cases, been adapted and reconfigured in response to historical administrative practices and policies, individual mobility trajectories no longer necessarily correspond directly to the geographical bounds of ancestral belonging or language group affiliation.

The Temporal Dimension

Indigenous temporary mobilities often mystify health, housing, and education providers because the movements can appear spontaneous and unpredictable in duration. However, the literature suggests that the degree of planning and predictability is largely determined by the factors that shape mobility. For example, temporary ceremonial movement in Australia's central arid lands clearly involves intricate planning, much of which is invisible to non-Indigenous service providers and administrators (Peterson, 2000; Young & Doohan, 1989). In Central Australia, initiation, or *jilkaja*, journeys have become increasingly important mechanisms for reproducing and reinforcing regional Indigenous socialities (Peterson, 2000). They are now more expansive, inclusive, and consequently more logistically complex, than perhaps ever before. Though a *jilkaja* journey centres around an uninitiated boy, they now sometimes extend thousands of kilometres and involve hundreds of participants—an enormous extension of their pre-colonial forms. Peterson (2000) estimates that one long and involved *jilkaja* journey he described would have cost its participants (collectively) at least $120,000. Organizing travel and adequate resourcing, and ensuring proper observation of cultural protocols for those directly involved in and affected by the ceremonial movement, requires significant forward planning and communication.

At larger scales of analysis, temporal patterns of movement can also be distinguished. In Australia's north, for example, there are clear seasonal variations to Indigenous temporary mobility practices. During the dry season (between May and September), when roads and other travelling routes are more accessible and the natural inland environment is most resource-rich, mobility is more frequent and intense (Smith, 2002). During the wet season (October to April), the overall volume of mobility decreases. Despite radical economic and administrative changes since colonization began, these seasonal variations in mobility endure, albeit in many ways transformed. Throughout Australia, there are also planned annual events—large rodeos, sporting carnivals, and festivals—that produce predictable patterns of Indigenous short-term regional movement. These events also generate large population influxes into destination locales and parallel exoduses from source locations.

Other mobilities, however, are neither patterned nor predictable. As Smith (2004) illustrates, such movements are often highly opportunistic: "It is not uncommon for a car or truck-load of people from another settlement to pull up at a relative's house in town, or at an outstation camp and call out to kin trying to persuade them to jump on, these new passengers often leaving without even a bed-roll or a change of clothes, departing to another location and returning weeks or months later" (252).

Although perhaps not patterned, these contingent and opportunistic mobilities are by no means irrational. They are shaped by a very specific set of "knowable" socio-cultural rationalities and conditions that are highly resilient and enduring. These include both the spatial and social bounds of relatedness and the variable and dynamic nature of family circumstances.

Individuals will only embark on an opportunistic, unplanned journey if they are appropriately related to the rest of the travelling party and have family at the proposed destination that will be able to meet their temporary needs (Hamilton, 1987; Peterson, 2004; Smith, 2004; Prout, 2007; 2009a). The expectations and limitations that govern these processes of accessing and providing resources are negotiated differently across time and space. In essence though, collective responsibility and reciprocity within family networks—what Peterson and Taylor (2003) refer to as the Indigenous domestic moral economy—are socio-cultural norms that facilitate much opportunistic mobility. They also command such mobilities.

Travelling from place to place can only be undertaken in this apparently haphazard way precisely because an elaborate network of reciprocal exchanges underpins it, whereby relatives accept unannounced visits from one another and provide the wherewithal for the visitor's survival if necessary. And an important purpose of such journeys, even in the absence of ritual, marital or other commitments, is to maintain this structure of reciprocal interdependence by calling upon it. (Hamilton, 1987: 49)

The literature almost uniformly identifies kinship as a primary driver and/or delimiter of mobility. Amid considerable socio-cultural diversity, and varied post-settlement circumstances, family remains principal social currency for most Indigenous Australians, for as Peterson and Taylor (2003) explain, "personhood is constituted through relatedness" (110). In other words, identity and status is negotiated through each individual's wider sphere of relatedness (Myers, 1986). And, as Hamilton explains above, temporary mobility is often the key mechanism for maintaining and cultivating this relatedness. Further, because family circumstances are dynamic and can change abruptly—a crisis may occur, a feud may erupt, or an illness may suddenly arise—people's mobility practices often reflect these characteristics.

Generally, localized movements are more frequent and therefore shorter (between one day and several weeks), and more expansive movements are longer (between several weeks and several months) (Prout, 2009b; Taylor, 1997; Taylor & Bell, 2004b). However, as the following example illustrates, the duration of much temporary mobility is highly contingent.

A trip may take several forms. A woman, for example, may wish to travel from Perth to DeLand for some purpose but may not be able to find transport past Bayshore. She may wait in Bayshore (for a day, a week or a month) until she can get transport, whereupon she will resume her trip. When she gets back home to Perth, her trip will be over. The separate legs of the trip are not counted as individual trips despite the time spent waiting. However, if while she was waiting for a lift to DeLand she were to avail herself of an opportunity to go to a third town for a visit and then back to Bayhore, that would be a separate trip. If she decides that she will not get transport to DeLand within what she deems as a reasonable period of time, she will give up her objective and return to Perth. This entire period of travel she will refer to as a "wasted trip."[4] (Birdsall, 1988: 147–148)

As subsequent discussion will demonstrate, the ability to be mobile for indeterminate periods of time is clearly associated with structural considerations such as the nature of an individual's relationship with the mainstream economy, a loose emotional and/or fiscal investment in fixed assets such as a house, and the ability to access welfare payments in a broad range of locations. However, these factors are rarely the cause of movement or the determinant of duration. Rather, the way these considerations are navigated reveals alternative emphases that anchor lived experience and ultimately command mobility: the procurement, cultivation, and contestation of relatedness; the fulfillment of socio-cultural obligations; and the independent navigation of relationships with mainstream social and economic institutions. So, whilst many temporary movements may appear impulsive in inception and arbitrary in duration to outsider observers, they are by no means irrational or random. They are highly purposeful and strategic.

The Demographic Dimension

There is wide consensus within the Australian literature that position within the lifecycle has a significant bearing on Indigenous temporary mobility practices. As Taylor (2008a) has compellingly argued, though, Indigenous life cycles do not necessarily correspond to conventional Western categorizations by age. For example, teenage Indigenous boys who go through customary law transition into manhood at a younger age than in Western society. Many Indigenous women also often become mothers at younger ages than their non-Indigenous counterparts, and are grandparents in their early 40s. In relation to mobility, therefore, conventional age/lifecycle categorizations are not sufficient as an explanatory framework (Taylor, 2008a). In addition, Indigenous lifecycle events appear to impact the reasons for and nature of movement more than its frequency. Indeed, the mobility/ age profile is much flatter for the Indigenous population than for the non-Indigenous population.

However, the literature consistently identifies a peak in temporary mobility among Indigenous young adults (roughly 17- to 25-year-olds). Across time and vastly different geographical and socio-cultural regions of Australia, the reasons for this youth mobility appear remarkable consistent. Mobility increases during this phase of the lifecycle as young people begin to independently explore and contest their identities in relation to the state, their cultural contexts, and broader social norms. Here, mobility acts as a metaphorical vehicle through which young adults can explore and establish their own networks of relatedness and belonging.

Anthropologists working on the Cape York Peninsula in northern Queensland have described a "floating" Indigenous youth population (Finlayson, 1991; Martin & Taylor, 1996; Smith, 2004). With kinship ties in two or more locales, and in the absence of notable responsibilities that might anchor them to a particular place, Indigenous youth on the Cape commonly engage in what Smith (2004) and fellow anthropologist Nicolas Peterson refer to as "existential mobility": "Whilst floaters are typically more peripheral [socially], exploiting relatively weak kin ties for shelter and resources, younger people in general are able to exploit opportunities of nebulous social inclusion by 'floating' from place to place, partly in an attempt to redress boredom associated with particularly pronounced exclusion from economic participation and meaningful social roles" (Smith, 2004: 252). Smith (2002) also suggests that such movement among youth is, at least in part, an expression of personal autonomy and resistance to mainstream expectations of economic productivity.

Finlayson (1991) identified a similar group of "young, restless travellers" (216) in Kuranda, Queensland. These "floaters" moved about for excitement and adventure and to seek out partners. And, on northeastern tip of Arnhem Land in the Northern Territory, Morphy (2007a: 42), describes the *dhukarrpuyngu* ("people of the track"), young men and women who are not resident in any one particular locale but who move between the households of more their sedentary relatives.

In the vastly different socio-cultural and environmental context of Western Australia's Midwest, there is a similar trend in youth mobility (Prout, 2007). It was a pronounced feature of young adulthood in generations past, and remains so for the present youth generation. Both groups refer to such practices, then and now, as "just cruising around," "seeing what was happening," and "visiting" (Prout, 2007; 2009a). Burns (2006) also observed a clear pattern of youth mobility in western New South Wales, contrasting it with earlier generations who were fully engaged in employment-related mobility within the pastoral industry. Birdsall (1988) described Nyungar youth mobility as often highly secretive and directed in large part by the formation and disintegration of romantic relationships.

Most case studies of Indigenous temporary mobility specifically identify this pattern of intensive contemporary youth mobility. Such mobilities are widely accepted within Indigenous contexts as a natural part of the lifecycle. Similar patterns of almost perpetual mobility among adults are not as universally tolerated. In some contexts, they are the norm.

> To "stop" is an apt verb to describe this element of Warlpiri residency patterns which are processual. The continuous flow of people is halted each night when people "stop." Warlpiri people move, almost nobody lives in the same place with the same people permanently; rather people follow their own paths, which continually criss-cross those of others forming flows of people through camps. Motion is an integral element of Warlpiri life, and "stopping" aptly characterizes residency patterns in a life where they change on a regular basis, both in terms of *where* one stops and in terms of with *whom* one does so. (Musharbash, 2003: 128–129)

However, in other contexts, individuals who perpetually move are less accepted. They may be described within their socio-cultural networks as drunkards (Birdsall, 1988), troublemakers, and wanderers, or bad parents (Morphy, 2007a). In the latter case, "bad parenting" might be associated with frequent, "troubled" mobilities that affect an individual's children. While many parents with school-aged children deliberately reduce their temporary mobility practices, parenthood is not necessarily a barrier to frequent movement. In some cases, children accompany their itinerant parents, and, in other cases, children are left in the care of their more sedentary grandparents (Prout, 2007; Finlayson, 1991; Martin & Taylor, 1996).

Most mobility studies also identify a "core" group of older Indigenous people who are firmly integrated into a particular community or town (Finlayson, 1991; Finlayson, Daly, & Smith, 2000; Memmott, Long, & Thompson, 2006; Prout, 2007). They are often focal points for younger, mobile family members (Gale, 1981). Middle-aged grandparents who take on childrearing responsibilities with their grandchildren are often part of this core. In northern Australia, the core commonly includes senior men and women who are associated with particular outstations (Morphy, 2008; Smith, 2004). In urban and regional areas, the core often comprises familial matriarchs who bear responsibility for two or more younger generations of kin (Prout, 2007; Birdsall, 1988).

Somewhat paradoxically though, many core individuals engage in temporary movement. While they may be permanently associated with one particular locale, their roles within their families and communities may require considerable temporary mobility (Birdsall, 1988; Morphy, 2007b; Smith, 2002). As Morphy (2007b) notes, focal individuals in northeast Arnhem Land are often also responsible for ceremonial organization and may thus often be away from home. Indeed, the overwhelming frequency of Indigenous funerals throughout Australia means that some senior Indigenous people have become almost perpetual mourners, moving from one funeral or sorry camp to the next (Prout, 2007).

There are also focal men and women whose social status is embedded in the control of vehicle use between larger settlements and smaller outstations (see, for example, Smith, 2002). These individuals are highly mobile as they broker movement of kin and resources between these various locales in order to enhance and expand their sphere of influence. Senior men and women may also be engaged in managerial or advisory roles that require regular short-term travel. In addition, health complications can prompt increased mobility among older people as they frequently travel between medical appointments in larger centres and their hometown or community. Such movements often have flow-on effects as family travel to "keep company'"with them (Coulehan, 1995; Prout, 2007).

Gender differences regarding temporary mobility receive more subtle articulation within the available literature. There are hints that young men are more frequently and expansively mobile than young women. In cities, and to an extent in regional hinterlands, there also appears to be an orientation toward matriarchal socialities that "genders" mobility practices. The only two researchers to have examined aspects Indigenous mobility practices in Australia's urban and coastal zones both describe a "displacement of Aboriginal men" from the city (Gale, 1981; Birdsall, 1988; Birdsall-Jones & Christensen, 2007). They suggest that senior women have become the focal points of Indigenous households while men's roles have become increasingly marginal.[5] It is unclear whether this displacement results in increased mobility among Indigenous men in urban contexts. For women, it has several mobility-related corollaries. Some senior women are highly sedentarized in particular towns and communities, with family maintaining obligations and exercising rights to continually call on them. Others remain firmly associated with a particular town or community but are highly mobile, visiting their children (particularly daughters) to ensure that their safety and parenting are in order (Beckett, 1988; Birdsall, 1988). In some cases, grandmothers' mobilities reflect obligations to both their children and their own mothers who may be frail or in poor health. In these contexts, women appear to be engaged in the majority of socio-culturally oriented mobility, that which is purposed to develop and enrich individual and group Indigenous identities. Such gendered trends are not so clearly articulated in the mobility literature from the desert or the tropical north.

MOBILITY AND THE STATE

The literature conceptualizes the relationship between Indigenous temporary mobility and the governing state in three primary ways. Some scholars describe temporary mobilities that are endosocial. That is, they are unrelated to, unseen, and unaffected by (or simply adapted according to) the practices and policies of the governing state. Other studies focus on the more effectual relationship between temporary mobility and the governing state, noting considerable movement to engage with mainstream markets and access services and facilities. Both of these observations and explanations identify important components of some temporary mobility practices. However, neither is singularly sufficient to explain the totality of the relationship between temporary mobility and the state. The final conceptualization that emerges from the literature is perhaps the most holistic. It describes Indigenous temporary mobilities as physical manifestations of the "enduring and transformed" elements of Indigenous socio-cultural practice and lived experience (Memmott, Long, & Thompson, 2006).

Endosociality

"Endosociality" is an apt term to describe Aboriginal temporary mobility because, as Peterson (2004) suggests,

> much Aboriginal travel does, metaphorically, take place with their backs to the world, turned in on their own domains. This is true of Aboriginal people throughout the continent, although to different degrees. Aboriginal endosociality is partly a product of the same racism that gave rise to the myth of walkabout but it is also a

product of the distinctive culture with its egalitarian ideology, its emphasis on the relational constitution of the person and the importance of place in the constitution of personal identity. Together these factors continue to underwrite frequent mobility in the Aboriginal domain. (235)

In the above quotation, Peterson (2004) offers a stark image of Indigenous temporary mobility in relation to the state. He describes mobility that is characterized by socio-cultural inwardness, a resistantance or imperviousness to external influence. Elements of many Indigenous temporary mobility practices support this assertion. The preceding discussion of the dimensions of temporary mobility clearly established that, above all potential motivations, social and cultural obligations and conflicts are the primary drivers of temporary movement. And, regardless of the underlying rationale for movement, the scope and shape of almost all contemporary Indigenous mobilities are delimited by territories of ancestral belonging and/or networks of relatedness. As Friedman (1997) has argued in the native Hawaiian context, this confinement of movement within networks of familiarity and relatedness is indicative of endosociality. Much ceremonial movement is also endosocial in that it is unrelated to, and often unseen by, mainstream Australia (Peterson, 2000; 2004; Young & Doohan, 1989).

Indigenous temporary mobility can also reflect and engender disinterest in or alienation from the state (Hamilton, 1987; Prout, 2007). Historically, government health, housing, and education services have been symbolic conduits for the expression of colonial rule. Consequently, some Indigenous people have relegated mainstream social and economic institutions to the realm of "whitfella business"—an area of governance in which they have little desire to participate. Frequent Indigenous mobility produces characteristically sporadic interactions with such institutions. This deliberately passive engagement perhaps reflects a defiance or resistance to the perceived social control that such institutions attempt to command over their lives (Prout, 2007).

All of these socio-spatial dynamics indicate a strong association between Indigenous temporary mobility and endosociality. And yet, the concept of endosociality is too limited and simplistic to fully explain Indigenous mobility in relation to the state. It sets up an arguably false dichotomy between Indigenous and non-Indigenous "domains." This dichotomy cannot accommodate Indigenous responses to colonial and globalizing forces or the ongoing selective integration of elements of mainstream society and culture into Indigenous mobility practices (see, for example, Altman & Hinkson, 2007b; Baker, 1990).

Engagement with Mainstream Social and Economic Institutions

A number of studies have identified frequent Indigenous mobility that results from the need or desire to access retail, social, or medical services that are not available in one's home community or town (Memmott, Long, & Thompson, 2006; Prout, 2008; Young & Doohan, 1989). As the subsequent discussion will explain, this kind of mobility is mediated by the size of the settlement in which an individual lives, its proximity to larger regional centres or cities, the types of services available at both source and destination locations, and the needs and desires of the individual.

Scant qualitative evidence also suggests that engagement with the formal economy, either directly or indirectly, can engender Indigenous temporary mobility in several ways. During the first half of the twentieth century, seasonal work, particularly on cattle stations and major transport infrastructure projects, generated considerable temporary mobility for many Indigenous people in different settings right across the country (Burns, 2006; Fink, 1960; Hamilton, 1987; Prout, 2007; Sansom, 1980). While this labour force was made largely redundant in the late 1960s, some seasonal employment related movement still takes place. Short-term contractual jobs in the mining, pastoral, and transport sectors can prompt back and forth movements of workers and/or their families, between the home community and the job site, for the duration of the contract.

A range of additional temporary mobility dynamics that emerge from engagement with the formal economy have received no known scholarship. Examples here include temporary mobility generated by the production and sale of Indigenous art and goods as well as movement associated with responsibilities on various managerial boards and committees (Metta Young, personal communication, 2008). Indigenous men and women are often required to travel to meetings at which they represent their communities, providing expert advice regarding best practice in service delivery, and/or advocating for additional resourcing. If brought into the public consciousness through well-grounded research, these associations would disarm persistent misperceptions that Indigenous temporary mobility is economically counter-productive.

A number of studies have also discussed the effects of Community Development Employment Projects (CDEP)[6] on Indigenous temporary mobility (Brooks & Kral, 2007; Memmott, Long, & Thompson, 2006; Smith, 2002). These studies suggest that the income generated from CDEP work, and the location of projects, can stimulate increased travel. They also contend that the schemes generally serve to entrench localized mobility practices. Brooks and Kral (2007), for example, describe CDEP as the glue that binds Ngaanyatjarra people to the region and enables them to remain on country. If abolished, they predict that travel among the people of the Ngaanyatjarra Lands would increase dramatically. Smith (2002) made parallel observations of the CDEP scheme in Queensland's Coen region. Robust CDEP schemes allowed people to remain on country whilst participating in the formal economy.

Mediation Between the Enduring and the Transformed

Elements of some Indigenous mobility practices seem to be characterized by endosociality, and others are undoubtedly the product of an active engagement with mainstream markets and social institutions. In almost all cases, however, Indigenous temporary mobilities reflect a mediation between the "persistent aspects of cultural production" and the "broader emergent forms of post-colonial life" (Smith, 2004: 239). As Taylor and Bell (2004a) suggest,

> [mobility outcomes] also reflect the subtle interplay with culture
> and tradition that mould spatial behaviour to diverse circumstances
> and geographical settings. As elsewhere, it is this tension between
> the global and the local, between the individual and the group,
> between culture and modernity, and ultimately between space
> and time, that holds the key to understanding of mobility amongst
> Indigenous peoples. (264–265)

Of course, in drawing these distinctions to illuminate tensions and interplays, one risks setting up further false dichotomies, particularly between culture and modernity. Indeed, as Young and Doohan (1989: 25) note, the two components that make up contemporary Indigenous mobility—both traditional functioning and organization, and adaptations to colonialism—are so "interlinked that it is impossible and indeed unrealistic to separate them." There is, however, a sense in which Indigenous temporary mobility practices clearly reflect an iterative negotiation between what Memmott, Long, and Thompson (2006) refer to as the "enduring" and the "transformed" aspects of Indigenous lived experience.

These interplays and negotiations, in some instances, have clear spatial characteristics: individuals and groups move physically between the various places and spaces that affirm their socio-cultural identity and provide opportunities to participate in traditional economic practices and those places that fulfill their needs and desire to access mainstream services and opportunities. The mobility between various outstations in central Cape York and the township of Coen (Smith, 2002; 2004) is one such example. To suggest, however, that smaller settlements are always the sites of enduring socio-cultural practice and larger settlements, the transformed, is too simplistic and risks feeding unproductive discourses about Indigenous authenticity (see, for example, Jacobs, 1996; Morgan, 2006; Sansom, 1982). It could be argued that all socio-cultural practices, regardless of where they are enacted, are in a constant state of transformation. Further, temporary movement to larger settlements, in many cases, fulfills the dual purposes of accessing mainstream markets and institutions and fulfilling enduring socio-cultural obligations of calling upon, and thus maintaining, kinship networks. Regardless of the precise spatial manifestations, Indigenous mobilities are a physical expression of a constant state of negotiation between the endo-social aspects of lived experience, the expectations of the state, and a desire to actively engage with elements of mainstream society and culture.

THE STRUCTURAL SETTING OF MOBILITY

The preceding discussion has identified geography, demography, historical policy, and socio-cultural specificities as central components to the contextual setting of Indigenous temporary mobility practices. Given that Indigenous temporary mobility practices relate to the state in distinctive ways, the contextual setting of movement must also include structural considerations such as settlement size and distribution, and the relative localized penetration of globalizing mainstream economic markets, transport infrastructure, and communication technologies.

Figure 16.1 Temporary Mobility Push–Pull Factors

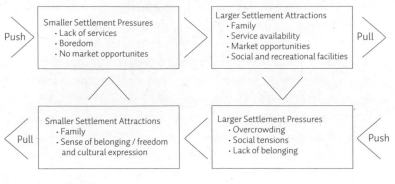

Push
> Smaller Settlement Pressures
> • Lack of services
> • Boredom
> • No market opportunites

Larger Settlement Attractions
> • Family
> • Service availability
> • Market opportunities
> • Social and recreational facilities
> Pull

Pull
> Smaller Settlement Attractions
> • Family
> • Sense of belonging / freedom
>   and cultural expression

Larger Settlement Pressures
> • Overcrowding
> • Social tensions
> • Lack of belonging
> Push

Source: Adapted from Taylor, 1988: 220.

Settlement Size and Location

From census data, Taylor (2006) has identified a trend of increasing Indigenous in-migration to regional services centres with populations between 10,000 and 50,000. He has also highlighted a pattern of growth in smaller Indigenous towns that contrasts with the decline in other small, predominantly non-Indigenous towns throughout rural Australia (Taylor, 2006). Beneath this overarching narrative of in-migration to regional centres, and growth in Indigenous towns, there is a range of temporary mobility practices taking place up and down the settlement hierarchy (see, for example, Young, 1981). These mobilities are shaped by a series of push and pull factors, as summarized in Figure 16.1.

Figure 16.1 illustrates that flows of movement toward larger settlements are often motivated by the need or desire to access services (e.g., banking, retail, and health), alleviate boredom, and visit family. However, the stresses associated with concentrated communal living, such as overcrowding and fighting, combined with a longing for family and freedom of socio-cultural expression available in more intimate and familiar settings, push (and pull) individuals back to smaller settlements. In these smaller settlements, individuals are often more able to fulfill ceremonial obligations, affirm socio-cultural identity, and/or escape conflict that often erupts in larger social settings. However, the lack of services and potential for boredom create a push toward larger settlements, and the cycle continues. As Smith (2004) notes, these push and pull factors demonstrate "the continuity and simultaneous transformation of many factors apparent in pre-colonial mobility practices interwoven with a series of new forms and motivations" (250).

The length of time a person may remain in any one of these settlement types depends upon their original motivation for travel, the distance from origin to destination, and the circumstances they are faced with at their destination. In some cases, individuals who intend to visit only for a short time, or even just to "pass through," remain for 20 to 30 years. In other cases, short-term visits become even more temporary than originally anticipated.

These flows of movement are not restricted to stepwise moves up and down the settlement hierarchy, or movements between small towns and large regional centres. In central Cape York, the small town of Coen is a service centre for the surrounding outstations. Residents of these smaller homelands come to town to get supplies, gamble, and visit with kin. They then return to their respective outstations to fish, hunt, and escape conflict and unhealthy lifestyles "in town" (Smith, 2002; 2004). Coen, however, is a small settlement of approximately 300 residents, with a grocery store, basic amenities, a police station, a primary school, and a primary health care centre. Those who require or desire a level of service and/or retail options beyond the services available in Coen must travel further south to larger regional service centres such as Cairns. These more distant travels are less frequent but may last longer. By contrast, in the Georgina River region, which borders the Northern Territory and Queensland, the large regional service centre of Mount Isa frequently draws Indigenous people from the smaller nearby town of Dajarra and communities on the eastern border of the Northern Territory who come to the town to shop, access the hospital, and visit kin (Memmott, Long, & Thompson, 2006). Mount Isa's proximity to surrounding communities means it exerts a great pull on residents of nearby towns and Indigenous communities for ease of access to services. However, such mobility is often more temporary in nature—perhaps even just one or two days.

Regional services centres clearly play a significant role in the structural geography of Indigenous temporary mobility. Existing research suggests that when Indigenous people require a higher level of service than those available in their towns and communities of residence, their preference is often to travel to a regional service centre rather than a major city (Burns, 2006; Prout, 2007). Regional centres have the full range of services required—hospitals, quality high schools, and a full range of retail and recreational facilities—and are often within the geographical bounds of familiarity for outlying towns and communities. By contrast, major cities are often less familiar and therefore less appealing. While there is clearly a flow of movement toward large regional centres, the literature also emphasizes the temporary nature of much of this movement, noting in particular the counter-forces that draw people back to their communities of origin.

Economic Influences

Economic context is closely linked to settlement size and location and also highly relevant to the setting of Indigenous temporary mobility. As the preceding analysis has demonstrated, a range of economic factors effect Indigenous temporary mobility practices. For example, a thriving informal Indigenous economy may heighten mobility, particularly in the dry season. A strong CDEP program may have a localizing or containing effect on temporary mobility, allowing people to remain more permanently on country. If members of a community have migrated away from their hometowns or communities to pursue employment or education opportunities elsewhere, this may have expanded the mobility trajectories of their relatives who remain (Gale, 1981; 1987; Memmott, Long, & Thompson, 2006; Prout, 2007). All of these possibilities must be considered in attempting to understand and characterize Indigenous temporary mobility practices in any given region at any given scale.

The advent of electronic banking and the proliferation of Centrelink (the federal agency responsible for social welfare and the distribution of welfare payments) offices in smaller settlements have also dramatically changed the landscape of temporary mobility related to the formal economy (Memmott, Long, & Thompson, 2006). In decades past, the administration of welfare payments had a strong structuring effect on Indigenous mobility. Welfare cheques were mailed to individuals, which meant they had to report to, or remain in, particular locales to collect their payment. There was considerable travel to and from particular events and communities, sometimes involving long detours, to collect these cheques (see Young, 1990). Such movements are now unnecessary as payments can be accessed electronically in various locations. However, just as movements related to the collection of payments have diminished, so too has the need to be in a particular locale to collect them. This can have a more freeing impact on individual mobility practices.

Technology and Transport

The accessibility of motor vehicles since the mid-twentieth century, and communications technologies (e.g., mobile phones and the Internet) more recently, have also radically transformed the setting of Indigenous temporary mobility (Altman & Hinkson, 2007b; Cowlishaw, 1999; Hamilton, 1987; Young & Doohan, 1989). Transport, technologies, and improvements to their associated infrastructure bases (e.g., roads and telecommunication networks) have dramatically shrunk both time and space and enabled individuals to more efficiently co-ordinate and undertake movement. They have enhanced Indigenous peoples' capacity to move more rapidly, more often and more distantly than ever before. They have also mitigated many of the climatic obstacles that historically impeded movement. This shrinking of time and space has only intensified over time as cars and phones have become increasingly accessible to more and more Indigenous people.

When Indigenous people first began wage earning in the mid-to-late 1960s, they often pooled their resources to purchase vehicles (Altman & Hinkson, 2007b; Hamilton, 1987). A robust "vehicular culture" has developed over the ensuing decades as evidenced through disproportionate investments in vehicle acquisition and maintenance despite the often prohibitive costs, particularly in isolated contexts (Lawrence, 1991). Such is the value of being able to be mobile, and, in some cases, to regulate the movement of others for social gain (Smith, 2002).

This vehicular culture is one of the common underlying threads that link Australia's many socio-culturally diverse Indigenous peoples. A widespread emphasis on and interest in "the motorcar" exemplifies the central place of mobility in Indigenous lived experience. It is fundamental to their past, their present, and, according to Smith (2002), their future. In describing the aspirations the central Cape York Indigenous population, he identified a common "underlying stress on the continuing importance of mobility, emphasizing garages, petrol and diesel, all aspects of the region's vehicular culture" (Smith, 2002: 3–4). He adds, "Working in the region for the past seven years, it has become obvious to me that Aboriginal understandings of development, alongside most aspects of Aboriginal life, remain fundamentally linked to continuing mobility" (Smith, 2002: 4).

However, the current climate of rapidly rising fuel prices, coupled with persistent Indigenous socio-economic disadvantage, will aggressively test the present union between Indigenous mobility and vehicular cultures. Given that much temporary mobility already maximizes available resources (i.e., cars are almost always full and travel costs are already shared collectively), choices will become increasingly stark. Either many Indigenous people will have to make significant spending cuts in other areas to maintain current vehicle-based mobility practices or vehicular travel will decrease. Either way, global oil prices are likely to radically transform future Indigenous temporary mobility practices.

Since the 1960s, there have also been dramatic changes to human communication practices. Access to telephones and the Internet has certainly increased Indigenous people's capacity to organize logistically complex ceremonial activities (Young & Doohan, 1989). However, there is very little available research that examines the impact of emerging communication technologies (mobile phones, email, web-based virtual networking programs) on Indigenous temporary mobility practices. Anecdotal evidence suggests that these communication technologies rarely alleviate the need or desire for face-to-face interaction. Despite these contextual transformations, certain aspects of Indigenous temporary mobility—such as the principles of reciprocity, collective responsibility, and kin-based networking—endure across the continent.

CONCLUSION

There is, in Australia, a common public perception that Indigenous people are naturally inclined toward frequent mobility because of an essentially nomadic history and culture. In part, this stereotype has persisted because of a lack of accessible mainstream knowledge and understanding that might challenge this simplistic image of the wandering nomad. In drawing together the existing Australian research, this analysis has presented a contrasting image of Indigenous temporary mobility, one characterized by complexity, rationality, and strategic adaptation. Spatially, contemporary mobilities reflect continuing and adapted connectedness to country and/ or kin. Temporally, whilst often spontaneous in inception and unpredictable in duration, these movements are almost always highly purposeful and carefully orchestrated. The nature of, and responses to, such mobilities are also closely related to particular circumstances and stages within the lifecycle. Further, whilst temporary mobilities often bear the markings of endosociality, they are also regularly shaped by various interactions with the encapsulating state and a mediation between these enduring and trans-formed aspects of Indigenous lived experience and structural settings.

Indeed, the most pervasive theme that emerges from the existing Australian Indigenous temporary mobility literature is the highly adaptive nature of Indigenous mobility practices through time. The synthesis clearly demonstrates that Indigenous Australians have not lived in a cultural vacuum for the past 200 years, and contemporary Indigenous short-term mobilities are therefore not simply the product of a nomadic predisposition to wander. Rather, a complex machination of factors drives and shapes con-temporary Indigenous mobility practices. These include seasonal variations (which affect the accessibility of country and the availability of bush foods); cultivation of and contestation within familial networks; the advent of vari-ous sporting and cultural festivals; the need and/or desire to access social, retail, and recreational services and opportunities; market opportunities; and ceremonial activities.

The degree to which any of these considerations shape individual mobil-ity practices is mediated by Indigenous experiences of and responses to government policies, geographical and structural setting, life-stage and aspi-rations, and socio-cultural identity obligations and expressions. Redressing Indigenous marginalization and disadvantage in Australia will therefore require imaginative, regionalized, and sector-specific policy responses that flexibly engage and negotiate with these diverse realities. As more nuanced understandings of Indigenous temporary mobilities grow, so too will the possibilities of framing service delivery policy and practices in ways that more closely match the needs and aspirations of Indigenous peoples.

NOTES

1. "The state" is an admittedly simplistic way of encapsulating all levels of gov-ernment, their administrative practices, and jurisdictional influences. Whilst some may argue that this is a falsely reductionist frame of reference, it is the lens through which many Indigenous people understand and interpret mainstream intervention into their livelihoods and domains.
2. There are perhaps two noteworthy exceptions here. First, divergent policies regarding "native administration" in Queensland and the Northern Territory during the early 1900s altered traditional mobility practices of Aboriginal groups in the Georgina River district (Memmott, Long, & Thompson, 2006). Second, many anecdotal reports suggest that there is currently significant temporary

movement away from the Northern Territory as a result of the administrative restrictions imposed by the 2007 Northern Territory Emergency Response (NTER). For a comprehensive critique of the rationale for, roll-out and implications of the NTER, see Altman and Hinkson, 2007a.

3. The term "country" captures Indigenous Australian's cultural and spiritual connection to their ancestral homelands: the place(s) they identify as being from. It includes not just the physical landscape, but the system of relationships between living things—of which people are a part—in that area.

4. Birdsall (1988) adopted aliases for some of the towns in her fieldwork region in order to preserve the confidentiality of her research participants.

5. Birdsall-Jones and Christensen (2007) suggest that in part, this shift in roles was engendered by socio-economic transitions that occurred most markedly during the assimilation era, when men were increasingly away from their families working on stations, railways, and other unskilled labour roles while women remained in towns with their children to adhere with colonial expectations of regular school attendance. They also describe an enduring gender role dichotomy of women/family, men/country that serves to further alienate Aboriginal men in "settled regions."

6. CDEP is essentially a work-for-welfare scheme administered by particular Indigenous organizations in a range of Indigenous communities. There is an ongoing and hotly contested public debate about whether CDEP schemes actually facilitate meaningful mainstream economic engagement for Indigenous people.

REFERENCES

Altman, J. (1987). *Hunter-gatherers today: An Aboriginal economy in North Australia.* Canberra: Australian Institute of Aboriginal Studies.

Altman, J., & Hinkson, M. (Eds.). (2007a). *Coercive reconciliation: Stabilise, normalise, exit Aboriginal Australia.* Melbourne: Arena Publications.

————. (2007b). Mobility and modernity in Arnhem Land: The social universe of Kuninjku Trucks. *Journal of Material Culture,* 12(2), 181–203.

Baker, R. (1990). Coming in? The Yanyuwa as a case study in the geography of contact history. *Aboriginal History,* 14(1), 25–60.

Bates, D. (1985). *The native tribes of Australia.* Canberra: National Library of Australia.

Beckett, J. (1965). Kinship, mobility and community among part-Aborigines in rural Australia. *International Journal of Comparative Sociology,* 6(6), 7–23.

————. (1988). Kinship, mobility and community in rural New South Wales. In I. Keen (Ed.), *Being black: Aboriginal cultures in 'Settled Australia'* (pp. 117–135). Canberra: Aboriginal Studies Press.

Biddle, N., & Hunter, B. (2006). An analysis of the internal migration of Indigenous and non-Indigenous Australians. *Australian Journal of Labour Economics,* 9(4), 321–341.

Birdsall, C. (1988). All one family. In I. Keen (Ed.), *Being black: Aboriginal cultures in 'Settled Australia'* (pp. 137–158). Canberra: Aboriginal Studies Press.

Birdsall-Jones, C., & Christensen, M. (2007). *Aboriginal housing careers in Western Australian towns and cities.* Perth: Australian Housing and Urban Research Institute.

Brody, H. (2000). *The other side of Eden: Hunters, farmers, and the shaping of the world.* Vancouver, BC: Douglas & McIntyre.

Brooks, D., & Kral, I. (2007). *Ngaanyatjarra lands population survey.* Warburton: Shire of Ngaanyatjarraku.

Burns, J. (2006). *Routes and branches: Residential mobility among Aboriginal people in Western New South Wales* (Unpublished doctoral dissertation). University of New England, Armidale.

Coulehan, K. (1995). 'Keeping company' in sickness and in health: Yolngu from Northeast Arnhem Land and medical related transience and migration to Darwin. In G. Robinson (Ed.), *Aboriginal health: Social and cultural transitions* (pp. 214–222). Darwin: Northern Territory University Press.

Cowlishaw, G. (1999). Black modernity and bureaucratic culture. *Australian Aboriginal Studies, (2)*, 15–24.

Fink, R. (1960). *The changing status and cultural identity of Western Australian Aborigines: A field study of Aborigines in the Murchison District, Western Australia 1955–1957* (Unpublished doctoral dissertation). Columbia University, New York, NY.

Finlayson, J. (1991). *Don't depend on me: Autonomy and dependence in an Aboriginal community in Northern Queensland* (Unpublished doctoral dissertation). Australian National University, Canberra.

Finlayson, J., Daly, A., & Smith, D. (2000). The Kuranda community case study. In D. Smith (Ed.), *Indigenous families and the welfare system: Two community case studies* (pp. 25–52) (CAEPR Research Monograph No. 17). Canberra: Australian National University E Press.

Foster, D., Mitchell, J., Ulrick, J., & Williams, R. (2005). *Population and mobility in the town camps of Alice Springs.* Alice Springs: Tangentyere Council Research Unit, Desert Knowledge Cooperative Research Centre.

Friedman, J. (1997). Simplifying complexity: Assimilating the global in a small paradise. In K. Olwig & K. Hastrup (Eds.), *Siting culture: The shifting anthropological object* (pp. 268–291). London, UK: Routledge.

Gale, F. (1972). *Urban Aborigines.* Canberra: Australian National University Press.

————. (1981). Adjustments of migrants in cities: Aborigines in Adelaide, Australia. In G. Jones & H. Richter (Eds.), *Population mobility and development: Southeast Asia and the Pacific* (Development Studies Centre Monograph No. 27). Canberra: Australian National University.

————. (1987). Patterns of post-European Aboriginal migration. *Proceedings of the Royal Geographical Society of Australasia, South Australia Branch, 67*, 21–38.

Gray, A. (1989). Aboriginal migration to the cities. *Journal of the Australian Population Association, 6*(2), 122–144.

Green, N. (1984). *Broken spears: Aboriginals and Europeans in the Southwest of Australia.* Perth: Focus Education Services.

Hamilton, A. (1987). Coming and going: Aboriginal mobility in north-west South Australia, 1970–71. *Records of the South Australian Museum, 20,* 47–57.

Havemann, P. (2005). Denial, modernity and exclusion: Indigenous placelessness in Australia. *Macquarie Law Journal, 5,* 57–80.

Jacobs, J. (1996). *Edge of empire: Postcolonialism in the city.* London, UK: Routledge.

Keesing, R., & Strathern, A. (1998). *Cultural anthropology: A contemporary perspective.* Toronto, ON: Harcourt Brace.

Lawrence, R. (1991). Motorised transport in Aboriginal Australia. *Australian Aboriginal Studies, 2,* 62–66.

Long, J. (1989). Leaving the desert: Actors and sufferers in the Aboriginal exodus from the Western Desert. *Aboriginal History, 13*(1), 9–43.

Martin, D., & Taylor, J. (1996). Ethnographic perspectives on the enumeration of Aboriginal people in remote Australia. *Journal of the Australian Population Association, 13*(1), 17–31.

Memmott, P., Long, S., & Thompson, L. (2006). *Indigenous mobility in rural and remote Australia: Final report.* Melbourne: Australian Housing and Urban Research Institute.

Morgan, G. (2006). *Unsettled places: Aboriginal people and urbanisation in New South Wales.* Adelaide: Wakefield Press.

Morphy, F. (2007a). Mobility and its consequences: The 2006 enumeration in the North-East Arnhem Land region. In F. Morphy (Ed.), *Agency, contingency and Census Process: Observations of the 2006 Indigenous Enumeration Strategy in Remote Aboriginal Australia* (pp. 33–54). (CAEPR Research Monograph No. 28). Canberra: Australian National University E Press.

———. (2007b). Uncontained subjects: 'Population' and 'household' in remote Aboriginal Australia. *Journal of Population Research, 24*(2), 165–184.

———. (2008, July 3). *(Im)mobility: Regional population structures in North East Arnhem Land.* Paper presented at the Australian Population Association Conference, Alice Springs, Northern Territory.

Musharbash, Y. (2003). *Warlpiri sociality* (Unpublished doctoral dissertation). Australian National University, Canberra.

Myers, F. (1986). *Pintupi country, Pintupi self: Sentiment, place, and politics among Western desert Aborigines.* Canberra: Australian Institute of Aboriginal Studies.

Palmer, K., & Brady, M. (1988). *The diet and lifestyle of Aborigines in the Maralinga region, South Australia.* Adelaide: Maralinga Rehabilitation Studies, Maralinga Tjrutja.

Peterson, N. (2000). An expanding Aboriginal domain: Mobility and the initiation journey. *Oceania, 70*(3), 205–218.

———. (2004). Myth of the walkabout: Movement in the Aboriginal domain. In J. Taylor & M. Bell (Eds.), *Population mobility and Indigenous peoples in Australasia and North America.* (pp. 223–238). London, UK: Routledge.

Peterson, N., & Taylor, J. (2003). The modernising of the Indigenous domestic moral economy. *The Asia Pacific Journal of Anthropology, 4*, 105–122.

Prout, S. (2007). *Security and belonging: Reconceptualising Aboriginal spatial mobilities in Yamatji country, Western Australia* (Unpublished doctoral dissertation). Macquarie University, Sydney.

————. (2008). *The entangled relationship between Indigenous spatiality and government service delivery* (CAEPR Working Paper No. 41). Canberra: Centre for Aboriginal Economic Policy Research, Australian National University.

————. (2009a). Security and belonging: Reconceptualising Aboriginal spatial mobilities in Yamatji country, Western Australia. *Mobilities, 4*(2), 177–202.

————. (2009b). Vacuums and veils: Engaging with statistically 'invisible' Indigenous population dynamics. *Geographical Research, 47*(4), 408–421.

Prout, S., & Howitt, R. (2009). Frontier imaginings and subversive Indigenous spatialities. *Journal of Rural Studies, 25*(4), 396–403.

Rowley, C. (1970). *The destruction of Aboriginal society: Aboriginal policy and practice.* Canberra: Australian National University Press.

Sanders, W. (2008). *Competing principles in the Indigenous policy space.* Lecture presented in the Masters of Applied Anthropology and Participatory Development course, Australian National University, Canberra.

Sansom, B. (1980). *The camp at Wallaby Cross: Aboriginal fringe dwellers in Darwin.* Canberra: Australian Institute of Aboriginal Studies.

————. (1982). The Aboriginal commonality. In R. Berndt (Ed.), *Aboriginal sites, rights and resource development* (pp. 117–138). Perth: University of Western Australia Press.

Smith, B. (2002). *Decentralisation, population mobility and the CDEP scheme in Central Cape York Peninsula* (CAEPR Discussion Paper No. 238). Canberra: Centre for Aboriginal Economic Policy Research, Australian National University.

————. (2004). The social underpinnings of an 'outstation movement' in Cape York Peninsula, Australia. In J. Taylor & M. Bell (Eds.), *Population mobility and Indigenous peoples in Australasia and North America* (pp. 239–261). London, UK: Routledge.

Smith, L. (1980). New Black town or Black new town: The urbanization of Aborigines. In I. Burnley, R. Pryor, & D. Rowland (Eds.), *Mobility and community change in Australia* (pp. 193–208). St. Lucia: University of Queensland Press.

Stern, H., Hoedt, G., & Ernst, J. (2008). *Objective classification of Australian climates.* Canberra: Bureau of Meteorology, Commonwealth of Australia. Retrieved from http://www.bom.gov.au/climate/environ/other/koppen_explain.shtml

Stillwell, J., & Congdon, P. (1991). Migration modelling: Concepts and contents. In J. Stillwell & P. Congdon (Eds.), *Migration models: Macro and micro approaches* (pp. 1–6). London, UK: Belhaven Press.

Sutton, P. (1990). The pulsating heart: Large scale cultural and demographic processes in Aboriginal Australia. In B. Meehan & N. White (Eds.), *Hunter-gatherer demography: Past and present* (pp. 71–80). (Oceania Monograph No. 39). Sydney: Oceania Publications, University of Sydney.

Taylor, J. (1988). Aboriginal population mobility and urban development in the Katherine region. In D. Wade-Marshall & P. Loveday (Eds.), *Contemporary issues in development* (pp. 201–223). Darwin: North Australia Research Unit, Australian National University.

————. (1992). Population mobility: Policy relevance, survey methods and recommendations for data collection. In J. Altman (Ed.), *A national survey of Indigenous Australians: Options and implications* (pp. 86–97). (CAEPR Research Monograph No. 3). Canberra: Centre for Aboriginal Economic Policy Research, Australian National University.

————. (1997). A contemporary demography of Indigenous Australians. *Journal of the Australian Population Association, 14*(1), 77–114.

————. (1998). Measuring short-term population mobility among Indigenous Australians: Options and implications. *Australian Geographer, 29*(1), 125–137.

————. (2002). The context of observation. In D. Martin, F. Morphy, W. Sanders, & J. Taylor (Eds.), *Making sense of the census: Observations of the 2001 enumeration in remote Aboriginal Australia* (pp. 1–11). (CAEPR Research Monograph No. 22). Canberra: Australian National University E Press.

————. (2006). *Population and diversity: Policy implications of emerging Indigenous demographic trends* (CAEPR Discussion Paper No. 283). Canberra: Centre for Aboriginal Economic Policy Research, Australian National University.

————. (2008, July 1–4). *Indigenous demography and public policy: From overcoming Indigenous disadvantage to overcoming disadvantaged indicators*. Paper presented at the 14th Biennial Conference of the Australian Population Association, Alice Springs.

Taylor, J., & Bell, M. (1994). *The relative mobility status of Indigenous Australians: Setting the research agenda* (CAEPR Discussion Paper No. 77). Canberra: Centre for Aboriginal Economic Policy Research, Australian National University.

————. (1996a). Mobility among Indigenous Australians. In P. Newton & M. Bell (Eds.), *Population shift: Mobility and change in Australia*. Canberra: Australian Government Publishing Service.

————. (1996b). Population mobility and Indigenous peoples: The view from Australia. *International Journal of Population Geography, 2*, 153–169.

————. (1999). *Changing places: Indigenous population movement in the 1990s* (CAEPR Discussion Paper No. 189). Canberra: Centre for Aboriginal Economic Policy Research, Australian National University.

————. (2004a). Conclusion. In J. Taylor & M. Bell (Eds.), *Population mobility and Indigenous peoples in Australasia and North America* (pp. 262–267). London, UK: Routledge.

————. (2004b). Continuity and change in Indigenous Australian population mobility. In J. Taylor & M. Bell (Eds.), *Population mobility and Indigenous peoples in Australasia and North America* (pp. 13–43). London, UK: Routledge.

Trigger, D. (1992). *Whitefella comin': Aboriginal responses to colonialism in Northern Australia*. Cambridge, UK: Cambridge University Press.

Veth, P. (2003). "Abandonment" or maintenance of country? A critical examination of mobility patterns and implications for native title. *Land, Rights, Laws: Issues of Native Title*, 2(22), 1–8.

Warchivker, I., Tjapangati, T., & Wakerman, J. (2000). The turmoil of Aboriginal enumeration: Mobility and service population analysis in a Central Australian community. *Australian and New Zealand Journal of Public Health*, 24(4), 444–449.

Young, E. (1981). The medium-sized town in the context of mobility: Rural–urban linkages and decentralization policies. In G. Jones & H. Richter (Eds.), *Population mobility and development: Southeast Asia and the Pacific. Development Studies Centre Monograph No. 27*. Canberra: Australian National University.

———. (1990). Aboriginal population mobility and service provision: A framework for analysis. In B. Meehan & N. White (Eds.), *Hunter-gatherer demography: Past and present* (Oceania Monograph No. 39). Sydney: Oceania Publications, University of Sydney.

Young, E., & Doohan, K. (1989). *Mobility for survival: A process analysis of Aboriginal population movement in Central Australia*. Darwin: Australian National University North Australia Research Unit.

Zelinsky, W. (1971). The hypothesis of the mobility transition. *Geographical Review*, 61(2), 219–249.

17

CLOSING WHICH GAP? DEMOGRAPHIC AND GEOGRAPHIC DILEMMAS FOR INDIGENOUS POLICY IN AUSTRALIA

Nicholas G. Biddle, John Taylor, and Mandy L.M. Yap

INTRODUCTION

In many ways, 2008 was a year of target setting for Indigenous policy in Australia. In his apology to the stolen generations on February 13, 2008, the former Prime Minister Kevin Rudd outlined a "new partnership on closing the gap." More specifically, he set himself and his government a number of "concrete targets" that he hoped to achieve over varying time frames: "within a decade to halve the widening gap in literacy, numeracy and employment outcomes and opportunities for indigenous Australians, within a decade to halve the appalling gap in infant mortality rates between indigenous and non-indigenous children and, within a generation, to close the equally appalling 17-year life gap between indigenous and non-indigenous in overall life expectancy" (Rudd, 2008).

Through the Council of Australian Governments (COAG) processes, the above targets have been made more explicit. Altman, Biddle, and Hunter (2008) used historical data to consider the prospects for this "closing the gaps" agenda and concluded that, although progress had been made in a number of the indicators that are being focused on (or proxies for them), statistical equality is unlikely to occur in the relatively short time frames being considered without substantial policy realignment.

In addition to the difficulties in overcoming a historical legacy of exclusion, there are a number of demographic and geographic dilemmas that will make it difficult for governments to achieve the socio-economic targets that they have set for themselves. The first issue is the distribution of the Indigenous population across Australia. Relative concentration of the Indigenous population in remote Australia, regional towns, and disadvantaged city neighbourhoods mean economic opportunities are less likely to be available at the local level than they are for the non-Indigenous population. The second issue is that both Indigenous and non-Indigenous Australians are highly mobile in different parts of the country, which makes it difficult to target and evaluate policy. The third issue is high Indigenous fertility and a young population, which necessitate additional resources just to keep up with a growing population. The final issue concerns the indicators of socio-economic disadvantage that are being targeted and how appropriate they are in an Indigenous context.

In this chapter, we expand on these demographic and geographic dilemmas using data from the 2001 and 2006 Australian Censuses. We also reflect on the implications for policies that seek to impact on such targets.

RECENT TRENDS IN INDIGENOUS DEMOGRAPHIC AND SOCIO-ECONOMIC OUTCOMES

Collectively, Indigenous Australians are those who identify as descendants of the first human inhabitants of the Australian continent and nearby islands (Flannery, 1994), including Aboriginal and Torres Strait Islanders. According to census estimates, there were 517,200 Indigenous Australians as of July 2006, which represents around 2.5% of the total Australian population (ABS, 2007). This estimated resident population (ERP) was 12.8% higher than the corresponding figure in 2001, a population growth rate that far outstrips that of the non-Indigenous population.

The most recent intercensal period (2001 to 2006) was also a time of rapid economic expansion in Australia. On the back of a resources boom and the most advantageous terms of trade in generations, Australia's gross domestic product (GDP) grew by 17.5% in real terms over the period, and, according to the two census counts, an additional 800,000 jobs were created. The period from 1996 to 2001 was also a time of strong economic growth; however, according to Altman and Hunter (2003) the Indigenous population did not share equally in the benefits.

Table 17.1 Indigenous and Non-Indigenous Outcomes: 2006 and Percentage Change from 2001

	Indigenous		Non-Indigenous		Ratio	
	2006	Change	2006	Change	2006	Change
Employed*	46.1	10.0	61.7	4.7	0.75	5.0
Unemployed (percentage of those in the labour force)	15.5	-21.1	5.0	-29.1	3.08	11.2
Full-time private sector employment*	17.4	13.6	33.4	4.5	0.52	8.7
Employed as managers or professionals (percentage of employed population)	16.3	4.9	29.0	2.6	0.56	2.2
Median weekly income—Not employed[†]	202.0	-2.5	212.0	-1.8	0.95	-0.7
Median weekly income—Employed[†]	521.0	4.1	723.0	5.5	0.72	-1.3
Lives in a dwelling with less than one bedroom per person[‡]	57.5	-6.9	32.4	-8.9	1.78	2.1
Lives in a dwelling owned or being purchased[‡]	27.3	9.3	69.7	-0.4	0.39	9.8
Completed Year 12 (percentage of those 15 years and over not attending high school)	23.9	23.0	49.7	15.9	0.48	6.2
Has a degree or higher*	4.4	50.9	18.3	37.9	0.24	9.4
Attending education institution (percentage of those aged 15 to 24 years)	34.5	-3.2	55.3	0.8	0.60	-3.9

* As a percentage of population 15 years and over.
† Calculated on those aged 15 years and over.
‡ As a percentage of the total population.

The question posed for the last Intercensal period, therefore, is whether the Indigenous population did as well at the end of the cycle as their non-Indigenous counterparts. This question has important implications for a strategy of "closing the gaps"; if significant headway could not be made during such benign circumstances, it is difficult to imagine that such progress would occurr in more uncertain times, or without significant structural adjustment.

The intercensal change in a range of employment, income, and housing outcomes is shown in Table 17.1. Results are given for the population that identified as being Indigenous, the population that identified as being non-Indigenous, and the ratio between the two.[1] Outcomes in 2006 are presented as well as the percentage change from 2001.

Nationally, between 2001 and 2006 the Indigenous employment/population percentage increased from 42% to 46% (a 10% increase). Given the generally favourable economic conditions between 2001 and 2006, perhaps the most telling measures in terms of success in Indigenous employment creation are the Indigenous/non-Indigenous ratios (the last two columns). This shows that employment rates for Indigenous adults moved closer to non-Indigenous rates. This does not reflect a decline in the non-Indigenous employment rate as the change in this variable was also universally positive. Rather, it appears to reflect a faster rate of growth for the Indigenous population.

There was also a decline or improvement in the Indigenous unemployment rate over the period. According to the 2006 Census, 15.5% of the Indigenous labour force was unemployed. While this represented a marked decline from the figure of 19.7% recorded in 2001, it was still three times higher than the figure for the non-Indigenous population in 2006 and almost twice the rate recorded for the non-Indigenous population when it was at its highest during the recession of the early 1990s (Altman, Biddle, & Hunter, 2008). Indeed, because the decline in non-Indigenous unemployment was greater over this same period, the actual gap in unemployment rates widened from a ratio of 2.8 to 3.1. Simply put, according to this particular measure of labour market success, the booming Australian economy has not benefited the Indigenous population as much as it has the non-Indigenous population, except to say that it has drawn more Indigenous adults into the labour force as job-seekers.

Although the future of the program is uncertain, at the time of the 2006 Census, the Community Development and Employment Projects (CDEP) program was an integral part of the Indigenous labour market. CDEP employment peaks among 20- to 24-year-olds; however, 10% to 15% of the adult population were employed in the scheme across the working age population (Biddle, Taylor, & Yap, 2008). In essence, the CDEP scheme allows (primarily) Indigenous Australians within selected communities to forego social security benefits and instead receive a form of wages for employment on projects designed to provide community benefits. However, CDEP jobs are generally part-time with wages usually lower than those received in non-CDEP employment (Biddle & Webster, 2007). In many ways, from a government policy perspective, the corollary of CDEP in terms of planned objectives is full-time private sector employment. Since 1999, the Indigenous Employment Policy (IEP) has placed a focus on facilitating Indigenous participation in the private sector, and much of the subsequent stimulus for Indigenous welfare reform reflects an attempt to articulate what has been the fastest growing part of many regional labour markets in recent years.

Overall, it appears that Indigenous workers more than shared in this expansion of full-time private sector employment. In 2001, 15.4% of Indigenous adults were in such employment and this rose to 17.4% by 2006 (an increase of 13.6%). Comparatively, non-Indigenous full-time private sector employment (population percentage) rose from 31.9% to 33.4% (an increase of 4.5%). As a consequence, the ratio of Indigenous to non-Indigenous employment in full-time private sector jobs rose from 0.48 to 0.52.

In addition to the sector of employment, there are also a number of non-pecuniary benefits of certain occupations, including conditions of employment and standing within the community. In broad terms, managers, administrators, and professionals receive the highest wages and the greatest personal autonomy. In 2006, the Indigenous workforce was found predominantly in low-skilled occupations with the proportion employed as managers, administrators, and professionals only a little over half that of the non-Indigenous share (Table 17.1). However, there was a reasonable amount of growth in this type of employment over the last intercensal period, which led to a small improvement in the ratio between the two populations.

Given this improvement in occupational status between 2001 and 2006, the next question is whether there was an improvement in access to economic resources as measured by median income. Here the situation was more mixed. By looking at median income for those who are employed and those who are not employed separately, it is clear that the difference between the two incomes is much greater for the Indigenous and non-Indigenous populations. This is driven by the substantial differences in Indigenous and non-Indigenous incomes among those employed. This is important in terms of regional labour supply as it argued that the gap between welfare and earned income is sufficiently low for Indigenous people so as to discourage job seeking (Daly & Hunter, 1999). For those not employed, there has been a small decline in median income (keeping in mind that the 2001 figure is adjusted using the CPI). For the employed, on the other hand, large increases in median income are evident for both Indigenous and non-Indigenous workers. However, overall median income for non-Indigenous workers has grown faster than for Indigenous workers, resulting in a widening in the employment income gap.

Overcrowding has significant negative impacts on a number of outcomes. The impacts on health outcomes have been identified historically (Gauldie, 1974; Thomson, Petticrew, & Morrison, 2001) as well as more specifically for the Indigenous population of Australia (Pholeros, Rainow, & Torzillo, 1993; Bailie & Wayte, 2006), while Biddle (2007) showed a significant negative association between overcrowding and education participation after controlling for large household size. Using a fairly crude measure of crowding, we see that between 2001 and 2006 there was a 6.9% fall in the percentage of the Indigenous population who lived in a dwelling with more than one person per bedroom. However, between 2001 and 2006 the percentage of the non-Indigenous population who lived in such households declined at a faster rate than for the Indigenous population, leading to a slight increase in the ratio between the two populations (from 1.74 to 1.78 at the national level).

Clearly, there is a substantial disparity in terms of access to adequate housing for the Indigenous population, which, while improving in absolute terms, worsened relative to the non-Indigenous population in the last intercensal period. The efficacy of any policy responses to this situation will depend heavily on the local housing market and dominant tenure type in a given location. For example, Australian Institute of Health and Welfare (2005: 42) showed that in 2001 there was greater disparity in levels of over-crowding between Indigenous and other households in public or community rental compared to other tenure types.

Between 2001 and 2006 there was a 9.3% increase in the percentage of the Indigenous population who lived in a dwelling that was owned or being purchased by themselves or someone else in the household (from 25.0% to 27.3%). Over the same period, the percentage for the non-Indigenous population stayed roughly the same, leading to a substantial reduction in the disparity between the two populations. However, at 0.39, the national Indigenous/non-Indigenous ratio is still quite low. Despite the positive trend, home ownership still remains the tenure type for only a minority of Indigenous Australians nationally.

The final set of results presented in Table 17.1 refers to education com-pletion. Perhaps more than any policy objective, improving education attainment remains the key to bringing about sustained improvement in Indigenous socio-economic outcomes (Biddle, 2007). In 2006, less than a quarter of the Indigenous population aged 15 years and over (who weren't currently attending high school) had completed Year 12 and only 4.4% had completed at least a bachelor's degree. These figures were 0.48 and 0.24 times the corresponding non-Indigenous rate.

There was improvement in Indigenous education completion in both absolute and relative terms. Although the percentage of the young Indigenous population attending education declined between 2001 and 2006, to a certain extent this reflects a buoyant labour market where the opportunity cost of education is relatively high. However, it also shows that the improvement in completion was more a reflection of the fact that young Indigenous Australians are much more likely to complete education than older cohorts.

There are three main implications from the results presented in Table 17.1 for the likely success of a policy agenda designed to close or at least substantially reduce the gap in outcomes between Indigenous and non-Indigenous Australians. First, there remain large disparities in the key indicators of employment, income, housing, and education. All these areas are likely to be related. For example, post-compulsory education substantially increases a person's prospects of obtaining a high paying job, which is in turn required to obtain access to good quality housing. Intergenerationally, though, poor quality housing leads to low levels of education attendance of young Indigenous Australians (Biddle, 2007).

The second implication is that during a time of rapid economic growth, there were only slight relative gains in most outcomes and deterioration in three key areas (unemployment, income, and overcrowding). This raises the third point: non-Indigenous outcomes also improve and sometimes doing so quite rapidly. So, any goal that has non-Indigenous outcomes as the benchmark is in many ways trying to hit a moving target. Furthermore, it is likely that in a period of economic downturn or below average growth (such as during the subsequent global financial crisis) Indigenous Australians will be the first to lose their jobs—the so-called last-in, first-out principle outlined by Auer and Cazes (2000).

GEOGRAPHIC INFLUENCES ON PROSPECTS FOR CLOSING THE GAPS

The Indigenous population has a far more widespread spatial distribution across the continent and policy needs to be cognizant of the range of specific local conditions that this presents. To illustrate this range, we construct eight categories of "location type" based on the level of urbanization and remoteness in a particular area (Taylor & Biddle, 2008). Table 17.2 labels and defines these and indicates the number of composite statistical regions (Indigenous Areas).[2] The final two columns summarize the distribution of

Table 17.2 Location Type Classification and Population Distribution, 2006

Location type	Description	Number of areas	Percentage of total Indigenous population (%)	Indigenous share (%)
City areas	Urban centres of greater than 100k	141	34.1	1.2
Large regional towns	Urban centres of 10k–100k	94	23.5	3.6
Small regional towns and localities	Urban centres/rural localities of 200–10k	112	16.8	4.0
Regional rural areas	Dispersed locations in regional Australia	22	2.4	2.3
Remote towns	Urban centres in remote Australia	36	7.0	15.4
Indigenous towns	Urban centres/localities in remote Australia with predominantly Indigenous populations	79	11.2	87.6
Town camps	Town camp localities in particular remote towns	3	0.5	97.2
Remote dispersed settlements	Balance of small dispersed settlements in remote Australia	44	4.5	31.4
Australia		531	100	2.4

the Indigenous and non-Indigenous population across this classification, showing first the percentage of the total Australian Indigenous population, and second the share in each location type that identified as Indigenous.

The results in Table 17.2 show that the highest percentage of Indigenous Australians live in city areas or urban centres with population counts greater than 100,000 people. This is followed by large regional towns and small regional towns. When combined with regional rural areas, we can see that more than three-quarters of the Indigenous population live in the more densely settled areas of Australia. However, it is when one focuses on the Indigenous share of each location type that the *relative* concentration in remote Australia becomes apparent. Given the way they are defined, it is no surprise that Indigenous towns and town camps have a large share of the population that identifies as being Indigenous. However, the share is also quite high relative to Australia as a whole in remote towns and remote dispersed settlements.

This distribution of the Indigenous population represents the historical settlement patterns of the non-Indigenous population as well as a

Table 17.3 Indigenous Area Socio-economic Rankings by Location Type, 2006

Location type	Number of areas	Mean	Standard Deviation	Number of areas in lowest:	
				Quartile	Decile
City areas	141	132	109	4	0
Large regional towns	94	226	97	2	0
Small regional towns and localities	112	258	115	12	0
Regional rural areas	22	205	132	4	0
Remote towns	36	318	85	5	0
Indigenous towns	79	447	87	65	38
Town camps	3	522	4	3	3
Remote dispersed settlements	44	448	57	37	12
Australia	531	266	153	132	53

continued preference for living on or close to traditional homelands. However, the distribution of the population also has implications for socio-economic outcomes of the Indigenous population since locational disadvantage (expressed as distance from services and conventional labour markets) has long been argued to be one of the main reasons for continued disparity between the Indigenous and non-Indigenous population (Tesfaghiorghis 1991: 12).

Table 17.3 shows that this is still the case. Using an index constructed across nine socio-economic variables that capture aspects of employment, education income, and housing (Biddle, 2008b), all Indigenous Areas are ranked from 1, being the most advantaged, to 531, being the most disadvantaged. The mean and standard deviation for the ranks within each location type are shown alongside the number of areas that were in the bottom quartile (25%) and decile (10%) of areas.

Indigenous socio-economic outcomes are clearly the most favourable in city areas (based on the nine input variables chosen). The average rank was the lowest of all location types, and there were only four areas in the lowest quartile. All of these were in the outer suburbs of Sydney, Australia's largest city. Large regional towns, small regional towns, and regional rural areas all have a mean rank in the low to mid-200s; however, regional rural areas have

Table 17.4 Employment to Population Ratios and Unemployment Rates by Location Typology, 2006

Location type	Indigenous		Non-Indigenous	
	Employment	Unemployment	Employment	Unemployment
City areas	49.8	14.9	62.5	5.0
Large regional towns	43.5	18.7	59.3	5.7
Small regional towns and localities	43.5	17.9	58.8	5.1
Regional rural areas	48.8	13.3	60.0	4.7
Remote towns	47.9	13.6	73.9	2.9
Indigenous towns	42.3	11.6	83.5	1.8
Town camps	21.1	22.7	80.9	0.0
Remote dispersed settlements	47.3	8.6	74.5	2.8
Australia	46.1	15.5	61.7	5.0

the largest standard deviation of the eight location types, indicating considerable variability depending on location.

Of the four remote location types, remote towns have the most favourable mean ranking, with the other three location types all averaging in the mid-400s or worse. The three areas designated as town camps have a mean ranking of 522 out of a maximum of 531. Clearly, it is in remote Australia and these latter areas in particular where measured outcomes are worse.

However, it is outcomes relative to the non-Indigenous population that targets are being set, and here the picture is more complex. Given conceptual difficulties in calculating a similar index for the non-Indigenous population, we compare employment outcomes only in Table 17.4 (employment to population percentages and unemployment rates).

Table 17.4 shows that while employment rates are generally more favourable in city areas, the gap with the non-Indigenous population is still quite large. Indeed, at almost three times the non-Indigenous rate, the gap in unemployment is very similar to the national average. In addition, Biddle, Taylor, and Yap (2008) estimated that 105,963 new jobs would need to be created between the 2006 and 2016 Censuses to meet the target of halving the employment gap. Importantly, the authors produced separate estimates for 37 Indigenous regions across Australia. Biddle (2008c) also provided an estimate, by Indigenous region, of the number of houses that contain Indigenous Australians that were deemed to be overcrowded. The key finding from both these studies was that the level of need was highest in relative terms in remote parts of Australia, but it was in cities and some regional areas where the greatest total number of jobs or additional houses was required.

Clearly, given the large number of Indigenous Australians and the still large gaps between the non-Indigenous population, urban areas cannot be ignored in any strategy of "closing the gaps." However, as shown in Taylor (2006), Indigenous Australians in urban areas are generally concentrated in disadvantaged neighbourhoods with poor housing and job prospects. As argued in Biddle (2008a) and adapted from Bolt, Burgers, and van Kempen (1998), segregation of the Indigenous population in city and urban areas can be problematic for a number of reasons: the concentration of economic disadvantage; the development of norms and values; school-level interaction or lack thereof; amenities and the absence of political power or voice; and the development of stereotypes.

To demonstrate the level of segregation of the Indigenous population in urban Australia, the urban centre/locality (UCL) classification is used. Those urban centres with both an Indigenous and non-Indigenous population count greater than 2,000 are reported in Table 17.5. For each of the 28 urban centres that fit this criterion,[3] the percentage of the population that identified as being Indigenous in 2006, as well as the change from 2001, are given. The change in the Indigenous and non-Indigenous usual resident count between 2001 and 2006 is also provided.

The measure of segregation presented in the table, the dissimilarity index, measures how evenly the Indigenous population is spread across the neighbourhoods within the city (Massey & Denton, 1988). Using census collector districts (CDs) as a proxy for neighbourhoods, the dissimilarity index measures the degree of departure from a completely even distribution where every CD has the same proportion of Indigenous and non-Indigenous Australians as the city average. The dissimilarity index ranges from 0 to 1 and represents the proportion of Indigenous (or non-Indigenous) Australians who would need to move CDs to result in a perfectly even distribution across the city. The value from the 2001 Census, the 2006 Census, and the change over the five-year period is given. Biddle (2008a) gives results across other dimensions of residential segregation.

Table 17.5 Residential Segregation and Other Characteristics of the Urban Centre, 2001, 2006, and percentage change

Urban centre	Percentage Indigenous		Change in usual resident count (2001 to 2006)		Dissimilarity index		
	2006	Change (2001 to 2006)	Indigenous	Non-Indigenous	2001	2006	Change (2001 to 2006)
Sydney	1.0	6.8	10.5	3.3	0.505	0.528	4.64
Brisbane	1.8	5.9	16.8	10.2	0.386	0.394	2.08
Perth	1.5	1.0	5.7	4.6	0.510	0.510	0.03
Melbourne	0.4	9.7	15.5	5.2	0.591	0.609	3.15
Adelaide	1.2	14.2	16.8	2.1	0.466	0.473	1.38
Cairns	9.4	1.7	14.1	12.0	0.345	0.338	-1.94
Townsville-Thuringowa	6.1	11.0	22.0	9.2	0.312	0.311	-0.40
Newcastle	2.4	25.8	27.9	1.2	0.357	0.336	-5.96
Central Coast	2.3	33.5	45.0	8.0	0.295	0.319	8.26
Darwin	10.4	11.0	13.1	0.7	0.293	0.300	2.26
Wollongong	2.0	14.3	15.3	0.6	0.343	0.342	-0.24
Gold Coast	1.1	8.8	25.4	15.2	0.378	0.402	6.55
Canberra	1.2	4.7	8.5	3.6	0.325	0.340	4.59
Dubbo	13.2	21.7	18.6	-5.1	0.376	0.368	-2.26
Rockhampton	6.4	22.2	28.3	3.7	0.270	0.289	7.02
Alice Springs	18.3	16.8	11.5	-7.5	0.256	0.266	3.77
Hobart	2.7	2.6	3.1	0.5	0.365	0.373	2.35
Mount Isa	18.8	14.1	2.9	-12.3	0.201	0.243	21.13
Toowoomba	3.2	7.2	14.1	6.2	0.352	0.325	-7.65
Mackay	4.8	4.2	18.7	13.7	0.267	0.234	-12.15
Tamworth	9.0	36.6	41.6	1.0	0.318	0.329	3.66
Palmerston	13.3	16.5	26.6	6.3	0.266	0.286	7.71
Broome	24.1	-8.7	-7.1	4.9	0.519	0.543	4.60
Geraldton	9.3	2.9	8.3	5.0	0.442	0.444	0.43
Port Augusta	18.4	13.7	17.2	0.4	0.307	0.277	-9.74
Wagga Wagga	4.8	26.7	36.4	6.5	0.417	0.457	9.49
Kalgoorlie-Boulder	8.1	21.0	21.0	-1.6	0.335	0.333	-0.44
Sunshine Coast	1.2	11.1	29.8	16.8	0.384	0.370	-3.80

The urban centres with the largest Indigenous population are also the five capital cities with the largest non-Indigenous population. Of the more than three million people who were counted as being usually resident in Sydney on census night, 34,279 identified as being Indigenous, with Brisbane, Perth, Melbourne, and Adelaide also having over 10,000 Indigenous usual residents. However, the percentage of the population that identified as being Indigenous in these cities were all below the Australian average (2.43%), which shows once again that, despite having the largest numbers of Indigenous Australians, there was a relative concentration outside these major capital cities.

Outside of these large cities, a number of large urban centres had relatively high Indigenous percentages. These include Cairns, Townsville-Thuringowa, and Darwin, with Indigenous usual resident counts above 5,000. Furthermore, in Dubbo, Alice Springs, Mount Isa, Palmerston, Broome, and Port Augusta, more than 10% of the population identify as being Indigenous.

In terms of the distribution of the population within these cities, as summarized by the dissimilarity index, in 2006 the urban centre with the most uneven distribution of the Indigenous population across neighbourhoods was Melbourne. In Melbourne, around three out of every five Indigenous Australians would have had to change their neighbourhood of usual residence for there to be a completely even distribution of the population. Of the other four large capital cities, Sydney, Perth, and Adelaide all had relatively high levels of segregation based on the dissimilarity index. It would seem, therefore, that Indigenous Australians in large cities tend to have an uneven distribution across neighbourhoods. While segregation was generally highest in large cities, there were also a number of large regional towns that had high values on the dissimilarity index. The most obvious example is Broome, which ranked second out of the 28 urban centres in 2006. However, Wagga Wagga, Geraldton, and the Gold Coast all had values around or above 0.4. It is not only in large cities that residential segregation occurs.

Between 2001 and 2006, 17 of the urban centres experienced an increase in the level of residential segregation, whereas there was a decrease in only 10 (the level of segregation in Perth stayed more or less consistent across the last intercensal period). Of the urban centres where residential segregation increased, by far the greatest increase was in Mount Isa (21.1% increase).

Interestingly, this was the only urban centre that had a sizable decrease in the non-Indigenous population count over the last intercensal period (alongside a moderate Indigenous increase). Although it is not possible to test with the data available, it would appear that the non-Indigenous population who left this urban centre was made up disproportionately of those who lived in similar neighbourhoods to the majority of the Indigenous population.

The other five urban centres with a more than 5% increase in residential segregation (Wagga Wagga, Central Coast, Palmerston, Rockhampton, and the Gold Coast) also had large increases in the percentage of the population who identified as being Indigenous. At least over a five-year period it seems that this is a necessary condition for increases in segregation. It is not a sufficient condition, though, as there were a number of urban centres that had a more than 10% increase in the Indigenous share, yet witnessed a fall in this measure of residential segregation. These urban centres were Newcastle, Dubbo, Kalgoorlie, Wollongong, Port Augusta, the Sunshine Coast, and Townsville. Clearly, it is possible to incorporate a large increase in the Indigenous population without adversely impacting on segregation.

The impact of this segregation is likely to be determined by the type of neighbourhood that Indigenous Australians are concentrated in. If the neighbourhoods have similar socio-economic characteristics to the rest of the city, then it is mainly the social and cultural advantages/disadvantages outlined in Bolt, Burgers, and van Kempen (1998) that need to be considered. However, if Indigenous Australians are concentrated in less well-off neighbourhoods, then the economic and other disadvantages come into play.

To consider whether Indigenous Australians are concentrated in disadvantaged neighbourhoods, we use the Socio-economic Indexes for Areas (SEIFA) advantage/disadvantage index outlined in Australian Bureau of Statistics (2008).[4] The national distribution of Indigenous Australians is summarized in Figure 17.1. Analogous to the Lorenz curves used to study income inequality, all census CDs are ranked based on their SEIFA advantage/disadvantage score, with 1 being the most disadvantaged and 37,457 the most advantaged. The cumulative share of the Indigenous population is then calculated beginning with 0.00007176 for the most disadvantaged CD then continuing through to 1 for the most advantaged.

If the Indigenous population was not concentrated in any particular type of CD, then 10% of the Indigenous population would be in the bottom 10% of CDs, 50% would be in the bottom 50% of CDs and so on. However, if

Figure 17.1 Cumulative Share of Indigenous Population across SEIFA Advantage/Disadvantage Rankings by Cumulative Share of Total Population

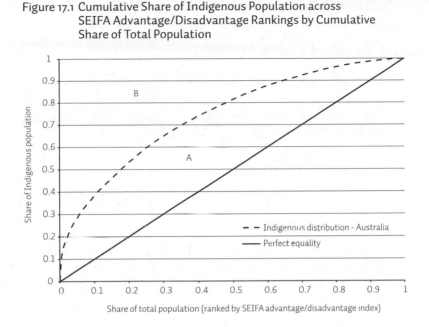

Share of total population (ranked by SEIFA advantage/disadvantage index)

Indigenous Australians are concentrated in disadvantaged CDs, then the cumulative share of the Indigenous population would be greater than the cumulative share of the total population at each point along the curve. On the other hand, if Indigenous Australians were concentrated in advantaged CDs, then the cumulative share of the Indigenous population would actually be less than the cumulative share of the total population.

The distribution of the Indigenous population is given in Figure 17.1 via the broken line. The unbroken line is the hypothetical distribution that would occur if Indigenous Australians were distributed evenly across CDs in Australia.

The dashed line in Figure 17.1 that represents the Indigenous population distribution is quite far away from the line that would represent an even distribution across CDs. It is clear, therefore, that Indigenous Australians are concentrated in relatively disadvantaged CDs based on the SEIFA advantage/disadvantage rank. To give some examples, 38.3% of the Indigenous population are in the most disadvantaged 10% of CDs and nearly 60% are in the bottom 25%. Looking at it from the other end, only 18.5% of Indigenous Australians were in the most advantaged half of CDs.

Much of the locational disadvantage outlined in Figure 17.1 may be an indication of the relative concentration of Indigenous Australians in remote parts of Australia. It is, of course, not feasible to presents graphs similar to Figure 17.1 for each of the urban centres presented in Table 17.5. However, just as the curve in Figure 17.1 is analogous to the Lorenz curves used to study income inequality, it is also possible to summarize using an index related to the Gini coefficient. Relating back to Figure 17.1, the Gini coefficient is equal to the area between the Indigenous distribution and the line of perfect equality (A) divided by the total possible area (A + B). The coefficient ranges from 0 if the Indigenous population is evenly spread across all CDs to 1 if all Indigenous Australians are in the most disadvantaged CD. As can be seen from Table 17.6, the implied Gini coefficient for Australia as a whole is 0.500.

Of course, the urban centres themselves are likely to have quite different levels of disadvantage. To put the Gini coefficient into context, four extra columns are given. These are the average advantage/disadvantage ranking of CDs for the Indigenous and non-Indigenous populations in that urban centre (weighted by population size), as well as the percentage of Indigenous and non-Indigenous Australians from that urban centre that live in the bottom 10% of CDs based on their advantage/disadvantage rank. The rankings in Table 17.6 are normalized to be between 0 and 100.

**Table 17.6 Concentration of Indigenous Australians by Advantage/
Disadvantage Rank of Neighbourhood within Urban
Centres, 2006**

Urban centre	Gini coefficient		Indigenous		Non-Indigenous	
	Value	Urban centre rank	Average rank	Percentage in bottom decile	Average rank	Percentage in bottom decile
Sydney	−0.408	4	41.8	25.1	65.2	5.4
Brisbane	−0.380	7	37.6	21.5	57.3	6.5
Perth	−0.485	2	36.2	13.0	60.2	3.2
Melbourne	−0.294	17	42.6	13.1	57.4	6.0
Adelaide	−0.406	5	24.0	35.3	42.9	13.2
Cairns	−0.366	10	29.8	19.6	48.9	5.8
Townsville-Thuringowa	−0.311	13	34.1	17.6	47.9	5.7
Newcastle	−0.305	15	30.8	22.4	44.8	9.3
Central Coast	−0.213	25	32.7	12.5	42.1	7.5
Darwin	−0.269	19	48.0	7.7	60.5	1.4
Wollongong	−0.303	16	28.9	35.4	42.8	15.9
Gold Coast	−0.205	26	48.8	3.4	57.3	1.6
Canberra	−0.240	20	70.6	1.4	78.1	0.4
Dubbo	−0.346	11	20.7	34.3	35.0	11.9
Rockhampton	−0.232	22	21.3	28.4	32.3	18.4
Alice Springs	−0.219	24	46.9	3.7	58.1	0.0
Hobart	−0.402	6	23.0	45.8	43.5	19.1
Mount Isa	−0.225	23	33.2	17.8	43.0	3.2
Toowoomba	−0.335	12	26.5	21.3	40.9	8.2
Mackay	−0.164	27	40.0	5.1	47.3	2.3
Tamworth	−0.372	8	18.9	41.7	34.3	18.6
Palmerston	−0.306	14	34.1	21.5	51.5	6.6
Broome	−0.366	9	30.7	22.4	58.8	6.6
Geraldton	−0.477	3	15.0	52.1	36.0	18.2
Port Augusta	−0.238	21	11.3	60.1	18.5	39.1
Wagga Wagga	−0.553	1	19.5	53.6	44.7	13.6
Kalgoorlie-Boulder	−0.269	18	37.2	6.8	48.8	2.9
Sunshine Coast	−0.146	28	45.9	3.2	51.8	3.0
Rest of Australia	−0.488	N/A	17.2	51.6	35.6	15.6
Australia total	−0.500	N/A	25.5	38.3	50.6	9.3

The urban centre where Indigenous Australians are most concentrated in disadvantaged neighbourhoods (relative to the distribution of the total population in the urban centre) is Wagga Wagga. With an estimated Gini coefficient of 0.553, there is a greater concentration there than there is for Australia as a whole, and with an average rank of 19.5 out of 100, the neighbourhoods in Wagga Wagga that Indigenous Australians live in are clearly more disadvantaged than the neighbourhoods that non-Indigenous Australian live in (with an average rank of 44.7). Geraldton is another regional town with a high rank; however, the large cities of Perth, Sydney, Adelaide, and to a lesser extent Brisbane all have a high relative concentration of Indigenous Australians in disadvantaged neighbourhoods.

Although on average the Indigenous population lives in more disadvantaged neighbourhoods in every urban centre in the table, the difference is reasonably low in some. For example, although high, the average ranking out of 100 for the neighbourhoods that Indigenous Australians in the Sunshine Coast urban centre live in (45.9) is quite close to that of the non-Indigenous population (51.8). This was also the case for Mackay, the Central Coast, and the Gold Coast. The Gold Coast, along with Melbourne, are interesting cases in that they had high levels of segregation based on the dissimilarity index but a reasonably even spread of the Indigenous population based on the socio-economic characteristics of the area in which they lived.

What this last set of results shows with regards to a strategy of "closing the gaps" is that Indigenous disadvantage is not simply a problem of remoteness. Even in city areas, Indigenous Australians have much lower outcomes than the non-Indigenous population and are concentrated in disadvantaged areas. Encouraging Indigenous Australians to migrate to these areas, as Hughes and Hughes (2008) do, has the potential to simply entrench disadvantage in a different setting.

FERTILITY AND HIGH POPULATION GROWTH: FUTURE JOB AND EDUCATION REQUIREMENTS

A key demographic feature of the Indigenous population that makes it difficult to achieve social policy targets concerning Indigenous Australians is the weight of population momentum derived from a relatively youthful age profile and continued high fertility. Between 2001 and 2006, the Indigenous population was estimated to have grown from around 458,500 to

Figure 17.2 Indigenous and Non-Indigenous Age and Sex Distribution

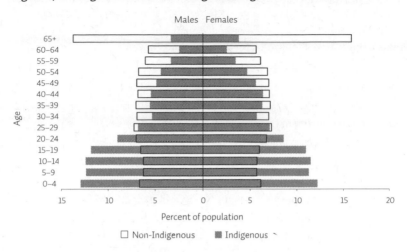

Males   Females

Age

Percent of population

☐ Non-Indigenous   ■ Indigenous

517,000, much faster than the corresponding growth for the non-Indigenous population. There are four main reasons for this growth gap: (1) The age structure of the Indigenous population means that there were more women of childbearing age; (2) For a given age, Indigenous females had higher fertility rates than their non-Indigenous counterparts; (3) Children born to Indigenous fathers and non-Indigenous mothers are invariably identified as being Indigenous; (4) People who were not recorded as Indigenous in an initial census may be captured at a subsequent collection.

The relative contribution of each of these factors to high Indigenous population growth is debatable and has been covered extensively in the past (see Hunter & Dungey, [2006] for a summary). What is important for the purposes of this chapter are the implications for meeting policy targets. To understand why this might be the case, consider the following figure, which has the age profile of the Indigenous and non-Indigenous populations in 2006.

Clearly, Indigenous Australians are much more likely to be of preschool or school age or just starting out in the labour market. Looking forward, this youth bulge will mean that just to maintain the currently low levels of education attendance and employment participation, a large number of schools and educational institutions will be required, and there will need to be a large number of jobs suitable for the Indigenous population.

Consider the number of jobs that will be required to meet the federal government's objective of halving the gap in the employment to population percentage over a 10-year period. For convenience, we can assume that this 10-year period is from 2006 to 2016. After estimating the growth in the working age population (using a cohort–component methodology), 36,091 additional jobs would be required just to maintain the current employment to population percentage. To meet the Rudd government's target of halving the gap in employment to population percentages, however, a total of 71,239 new jobs would be required in net terms over the period. To put these projections into perspective, it is worth revisiting the 49,235 new jobs created over the decade up until 2006. This was during a time of rapid economic expansion—conditions that are not necessarily expected to continue indefinitely into the future. Clearly, to meet the targets the Rudd government has set for itself, employment creation will need to be greater than previously achieved during a time of less certain economic outlook.

Relating this back to the geographic issues presented earlier, in attempting to meet the target of halving the gap in employment outcomes over a decade, there are likely to be regions within Australia that have relatively high need. For example, the Apatula Indigenous region in the Northern Territory had an employment to population percentage in 2006 of 24.8%, well below the national average. If the national target of halving the gap in employment to population percentages was applied locally (that is, all regions should have at least 53.9% of the Indigenous population employed), then, in addition to Apatula, there were four regions that were estimated to require additional jobs greater than or close to equal to the estimated number of people employed in 2006. These were Port Augusta in South Australia and Jabiru, Nhulunbuy, and Tennant Creek in the Northern Territory.

If the policy response to the large relative need for additional jobs in remote Australia is to encourage people to migrate to settled Australia, then this is going to put additional requirements on city and regional labour markets. As shown in the previous section, the Indigenous population in these areas still lags behind that of the non-Indigenous population and is concentrated in disadvantaged neighbourhoods. Furthermore, the four regions with the greatest absolute requirement for additional jobs minimum employment to population percentage were in fact in regional Australia (Coffs Harbour) or in the capital cities (Sydney, Brisbane, and Perth). While the jobs required may be relatively low in proportion to the size of the population, clearly urban and regional Australian job markets cannot be ignored under any policy aim of reducing employment disparities between the Indigenous and non-Indigenous populations.

The other aspect of the age profile presented in Figure 17.2 that will necessitate additional resources just to keep up with population growth is the large cohort of Indigenous Australians passing through school age and onto post-compulsory education. In proportional terms, there are more than twice as many Indigenous Australians in the youngest three age categories as there are non-Indigenous Australians. While the official goal of government is to halve the gap in literacy and numeracy, it is worth considering the requirements to do the same for post-compulsory education attendance.

Focusing on those aged 15 to 24, the results presented earlier in Table 17.1 showed that 34.5% of the Indigenous population of that age was attending education, compared to 55.3% of the non-Indigenous population. Using the same cohort–component calculations as were used for the employment projections, the Indigenous population aged 15 to 24 years is projected to grow by 28% over the 10 years from 2006 to 2016, or 2.5% per annum. To keep the level of education participation at the currently low levels, an additional 9,785 education places will be required by 2016. Given the relatively low access to economic resources of the Indigenous population, it is likely that most of these will need to be funded by the government, including the appropriate income support. However, to halve the gap in education attendance, a total of 23,106 education places will be required. To put this in perspective, this is a little over two-thirds of the total number of Indigenous Australians of that age bracket currently attending education. Once again, a fast growing population will make reducing disparities in socio-economic outcomes difficult.

THE APPROPRIATENESS OF GOVERNMENT INDICATORS

One of the strongest criticisms of socio-economic indices created from census data is that they don't capture all aspects of Indigenous well-being (Taylor, 2008). This applies equally to the targets the governments set for themselves. Usually, these targets reflect mainstream notions of development like private sector employment and completion of formal education. While these are also likely to be important for Indigenous Australians, they miss other aspects that are also valued.

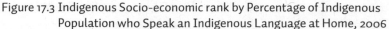

Figure 17.3 Indigenous Socio-economic rank by Percentage of Indigenous Population who Speak an Indigenous Language at Home, 2006

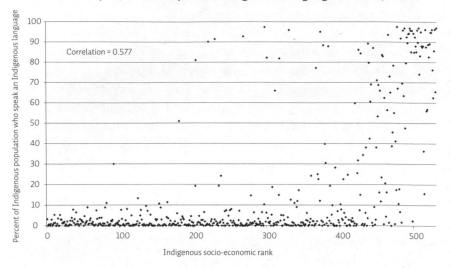

An example of an indicator of well-being that is often argued to be missed in standard socio-economic indices and government targets is cultural preservation. In terms of index creation, this is usually because such concepts are not captured as part of official collections. However, even when they are, they often don't fit easily into the standard methodological approaches. This is demonstrated through the relationship between the socio-economic rank of the Indigenous Areas summarized previously and the percentage of the population who speak an Indigenous language at home (Figure 17.3). While not perfect (for example, there is no indication of how well that person speaks the language), it is still a good proxy for cultural maintenance.

Keeping in mind that a high number along the x-axis indicates high levels of disadvantage, Figure 17.3 shows a high positive correlation between socio-economic disadvantage and the percentage of the population who speak an Indigenous language at home. However, there are a large number of areas where less than 1% of the Indigenous population speaks an Indigenous language (39.7% of all areas), which makes it difficult to see the relationship clearly in the scatter plot. Indeed, when these areas are removed from the correlation analysis, the strength of the association is slightly stronger at 0.618.

While it is not possible to establish the direction of causality, this figure does show that those areas that rank relatively well on the standard socio-economic measures have relatively low levels of Indigenous language retention. Furthermore, although likely to be related to remoteness, this result highlights one of the limitations of an analysis that produces a single index based on census data only. Were they available, it is likely that other variables representing cultural maintenance would also have a similar relationship. This needs to be taken into account in any regionally-based policy designed to improve Indigenous well-being. Ideally, rather than there being a trade-off, development planning should incorporate both Indigenous-specific aspirations and the standard mainstream targets (Calma, 2005).

CONCLUSION

There is little doubt that the Indigenous population of Australia continues to experience high levels of material and social disadvantage. In that sense, the setting of ambitious targets to "close the gap" between Indigenous and non-Indigenous Australians is a welcome move from the new federal government and compares favourably with the more vague notion of "practical reconciliation" followed by the previous Howard government (1996–2007). Furthermore, if monitored accurately and continually, the targets will be useful in holding the government to account.

Altman, Biddle, and Hunter (2008) used previous trends to identify the chance of achieving parity in outcomes in the absence of large-scale structural reform. In most instances, the prospects were not good. In this chapter, we identified a number of geographic and demographic dilemmas that will make it difficult for substantial reductions in disparities to be achieved. These were the relative concentration of the Indigenous population in remote Australia, regional towns, and disadvantaged city neighbourhoods; the migration patterns of both Indigenous and non-Indigenous Australians; high Indigenous fertility and a young population; and the appropriateness of the indicators of socio-economic disadvantage that are being targeted.

This is not an exhaustive list, but it should be kept in mind that none of these issues are insurmountable. However, they do highlight the continual need for evidence-based policy settings that take into account the unique circumstances of the Indigenous population nationally and the variation in local and regional circumstances and aspirations.

NOTES

1. Indigenous Australians include those who identify as being Aboriginal, Torres Strait Islander, or both on the relevant census question. Those who did not state their Indigenous status are excluded from this table and the remainder of the analysis.

2. It should be noted that the town camp category is included here with some reservation. While it is important to separately identify these communities that are generally on the fringe of urban centres and have little or no infrastructure, even at the Indigenous Area level the identification of town camp communities in the Australian Indigenous Geographic Classification (AIGC) is problematic. Only three sets are included (town camps in Alice Springs, Tennant Creek, and Katherine); however, none of the many town camps in the Darwin region are identified, nor are any of the separate living areas in towns like Kununurra, Halls Creek, Fitzroy Crossing, Port Hedland, Kalgoorlie, and Mount Isa. Options for establishing approximate population numbers associated with these locations are, however, limited.

3. There were, of course, many urban centres that had a non-Indigenous population count greater than 2,000, according to the 2006 Census, but an Indigenous population count less than 2,000. However, there was only one urban centre that had a high Indigenous population but low non-Indigenous population—Yarrabah near Cairns, Queensland. As there were only 49 non-Indigenous Australians counted in Yarrabah, this figure was not included separately in Table 17.1 or any other tables in this chapter.

4. Although the SEIFA disadvantage index is more commonly used for such analysis, it is not suitable for Indigenous Australians. This is because the proportion of the population who are Indigenous is used as an indicator of disadvantage, meaning that it is biased toward neighbourhoods with high Indigenous populations.

REFERENCES

ABS (Australian Bureau of Statistics). (2007). *Population distribution, Aboriginal and Torres Strait Islander Australians, 2006* (ABS Catalogue No. 4705.0). Canberra: Australian Bureau of Statistics.

————. (2008). *Socio-economic indexes for areas (SEIFA)—technical paper, 2006* (ABS Catalogue No. 2039.0.55.001). Canberra: Australian Bureau of Statistics.

AIHW (Australian Institute of Health and Welfare). (2005). *Indigenous housing needs 2005: A multi-measure needs model* (AIHW Catalogue No. HOU 129). Canberra: Australian Institute of Health and Welfare.

Altman, J.C., Biddle, N., & Hunter, B.H. (2008). *How realistic are the prospects for 'closing the gaps' in socio-economic outcomes for Indigenous Australians?* (CAEPR Discussion Paper No. 287). Canberra: Centre for Aboriginal Economic Policy Research, Australian National University.

Altman, J.C., & Hunter, B.H. (2003). *Monitoring "practical" reconciliation: Evidence from the reconciliation decade, 1991–2001* (CAEPR Discussion Paper No. 254). Canberra: Centre for Aboriginal Economic Policy Research, Australian National University.

Auer, P., & Cazes, S. (2000). The resilience of the long-term employment relationship: Evidence from the industrialized countries. *International Labour Review, A139*(4), 379–408.

Bailie, R.S., & Wayte, K.J. (2006). Housing and health in indigenous communities: Key issues for housing and health improvement in remote Aboriginal and Torres Strait Islander Communities. *Australian Journal of Rural Health, 14,* 178–183.

Biddle, N. (2007). *Does it pay to go to school? The benefits of and participation in education of Indigenous Australians* (Unpublished doctoral dissertation). Australian National University, Canberra. Retrieved from http://thesis.anu.edu.au/public/adt-ANU20071008.152249/index.html

————. (2008a). *Location and segregation: The distribution of the indigenous population across Australia's major cities.* (CAEPR Working Paper No. 53). Canberra: Centre for Aboriginal Economic Policy Research, Australian National University.

————. (2008b). *Ranking regions: Revisiting an index of relative indigenous socio-economic outcomes* (CAEPR Working Paper No. 50). Canberra: Centre for Aboriginal Economic Policy Research, Australian National University.

————. (2008c). *The scale and composition of indigenous housing need, 2001–06* (CAEPR Working Paper No. 47). Canberra: Australian National University.

Biddle, N., Taylor, J., & Yap, M. (2008). *Indigenous participation in regional labour markets, 2001–06* (CAEPR Discussion Paper No. 288). Canberra: Centre for Aboriginal Economic Policy Research, Australian National University.

Biddle, N., & Webster, A. (2007, February). *The labour force status of Aboriginal and Torres Strait Islander Australians.* Paper presented at the Australian Labour Market Research (ALMR) Workshop, Melbourne.

Bull, G., Burgers, J., & van Kempen, R. (1998). On the social significance of spatial location: Spatial segregation and social inclusion. *Netherlands Journal of Housing and the Built Environment, 13*(1), 83–95.

Calma, T. (2005, September 16). *Overcoming Indigenous disadvantage key indicators report 2005: A human rights perspective.* Paper presented to a workshop on the Overcoming Indigenous Disadvantage Report, Australian Human Rights and Equal Opportunity Commission, Sydney.

Daly, A.E., & Hunter, B.H. (1999). Incentives to work: Replacement ratios and the cost of job loss among unemployed Indigenous Australians. *Australian Economic Review, 32*(3), 219–236.

Gauldie, E. (1974). *Cruel habitations: A history of working class housing, 1780–1918.* London, UK: Allen & Unwin.

Flannery, T. (1994). *The future eaters: An ecological history of the Australasian lands and people.* Chatswood, NSW: Reed Books.

Hughes, H., & Hughes, M. (2008, September 3). Gap worse for remote Indigenous. *The Australian*. Retrieved from http://www.theaustralian.news.com.au/story/0,,24284441-5014047,00.html

Hunter, B.H., & Dungey, M.H. (2006). Creating a sense of "CLOSURE": Providing confidence intervals on some recent estimates of indigenous populations. *Canadian Studies in Population, 33*(1), 1–23.

Massey, D.S., & Denton, N.A. (1988). The dimensions of residential segregation. *Social Forces, 67*, 281–315.

Pholeros P., Rainow, S., & Torzillo, P. (1993). *Housing for health: Towards a healthy living environment for Aboriginal Australia.* Newport Beach: Healthabitat.

Rudd, K. (2008). *Apology to Australia's Indigenous peoples. Speech to the House of Representatives.* Canberra: Parliament House. Retrieved from http://www.pm.gov.au/media/speech/2008/speech_0073.cfm

Taylor, J. (2006). *Population and diversity: Policy implications of emerging indigenous demographic trends* (CAEPR Discussion Paper No. 283). Canberra: Centre for Aboriginal Economic Policy Research, Australian National University.

————. (2008). Indigenous peoples and indicators of well-being: An Australian perspective on united nations global frameworks. *Social Indicators Research, 87*, 111–126.

Taylor, J., & Biddle, N. (2008). *Locations of indigenous population change: What can we say?* (CAEPR Working Paper No. 43). Canberra: Centre for Aboriginal Economic Policy Research, Australian National University.

Tesfaghiorghis, H. (1991). *Geographic variations in the economic status of Aboriginal people: A preliminary investigation* (CAEPR Discussion Paper No. 2). Canberra: Centre for Aboriginal Economic Policy Research, Australian National University.

Thomson, H., Petticrew, M., & Morrison, D. (2001). Health effects of housing improvement: Systematic review of intervention studies. *British Medical Journal, 323*, 187–190.

18

FROM COMMON COLONIZATION TO INTERNAL SEGMENTATION
RETHINKING INDIGENOUS DEMOGRAPHY IN NEW ZEALAND

Tahu H. Kukutai and Ian Pool

INTRODUCTION

Like all niche disciplines, the demography of indigenous populations is bound by particular assumptions and practices. In this chapter, we identify two such conventions and critique their usefulness in the context of New Zealand. First, we consider the routine use of singular identity categories to define the parameters of indigenous populations. In the case of New Zealand, our critique is directed at the ways in which official classifications and data dissemination practices have promoted a unidimensional approach to analyzing Māori. This is a problem the authors are well acquainted with, having explored questions such as "Who is Māori?" from different theoretical perspectives, and at different times (Kukutai, 2004; 2010; 2012; Pool, 1963; 1991). The second convention we examine is the use of inter-ethnic comparisons, to the virtual exclusion of comparisons *within* indigenous communities. In the Anglo settler states of North America and Australasia,[1] policy and research involving indigenous populations often has a comparative focus, with indigenous outcomes assessed in relation to the "mainstream." In New Zealand and Australia, policies known as "closing the gaps" were explicitly constructed on the premise of "helping" Māori and

Aboriginal peoples achieve statistical equality with their non-indigenous counterparts on standard biomedical and socio-economic indicators of well-being (Te Puni Kōkiri, 2000; 2002; Steering Committee for the Review of Government Service Provision, 2009). Comparative approaches in this vein have often been criticized for encouraging a deficit-based view of indigenous peoples, while overlooking the categories and concepts that matter to them (Humpage & Fleras, 2001; Pholi, Black, & Richards, 2009; Taylor, 2008; 2009). In this chapter, we elaborate an additional criticism—that a focus on population-level differences obscures important dimensions of cultural and socio-economic heterogeneity within indigenous populations. Settler state indigenes have consistently been among the most economically and socially marginalized of citizens across a broad range of socio-economic and health outcomes (Altman, Biddle, & Hunter, 2004; Pool, 1991; Snipp, 1988; 1997). However, just as indigenous peoples fare poorly overall in the stratification systems of their homelands, so too are relations within indigenous communities hierarchically organized. This feature of indigenous demography has hitherto received little attention.

We draw on empirical examples from New Zealand to illustrate some of the shortcomings of treating indigenous peoples as internally undifferentiated, using the concept of segmentation as a heuristic device. Segmentation and the related concepts on the core and periphery are well known in the social sciences (Tolbert, Horan, & Beck, 1980). Drawing on Kukutai (2010), we describe the segmentation of Māori with respect to two key dimensions: socio-economic position and ethnocultural attachment. Using analysis of data from the New Zealand Census of Population and Dwellings, we show that those in the core—with strong ideational attachments to Māori identity—are more likely to be materially disadvantaged than those with peripheral attachments. We do not attempt to provide causal explanations, nor do we engage dominant theories of ethnic relations and inequality. The aim is more modest: to identify if intra-Māori segmentation exists across the dimensions of ethnic attachment and socio-economic position, and to explore the potential associations. In so doing, we advocate for approaches that attempt to better reconcile the complexities of indigenous realities with the constraints of official data such as the census. This is important because, despite the various shortcomings, official statistical data are a vital source of information about indigenous peoples and continue to provide the "evidence" base upon which consequential decisions are made.

New Zealand is a fitting context within which to explore patterns of segmentation. A former British colony, New Zealand's history of ethnic relations has largely been one of two peoples: Māori and European. The latter are white New Zealanders of mostly British descent who are also referred to colloquially as Pākehā.[2] Though indigene–settler relations in New Zealand have often been trumpeted as progressive by comparison with the other settler states, Māori have been economically and politically marginalized for much of the nation's history. Recent transformations in economic arrangements—including the labour market and welfare system—and an increased emphasis on human capital investments have provided structural supports for growing economic inequality. At the same time, mercurial state policies toward Māori, generations of intermarriage with Europeans, and Māori political activism have produced complex constraints and incentives associated with Māori identity. Though New Zealand's ethnic terrain has some unique aspects—for example, it is the only settler state where indigenes are the largest ethnic minority—there are sufficient parallels for the Māori example to have implications beyond New Zealand.

CONSTRUCTING INDIGENOUS POPULATIONS

We begin our conceptual critique by emphasizing the disconnection between social scientific theories and demographic practice. In the social sciences generally, there is a consensus that identities—whether conceived as racial, ethnic, or indigenous—are multi-faceted, socially and politically constructed, and historically contingent. At the individual level, indigeneity is understood as a process of identification and engagement with a complex set of symbols, networks, and practices, rather than a fixed quality or way of being. At the group level, what makes a people or group indigenous has been the topic of ongoing, and often vociferous, debate (Barnard, 2006; McIntosh, Colchester, Bowen, & Rosengren, 2002).[3] For the most part, demographers have shown little interest in complex theoretical arguments about indigeniety and *indigenous peoples*, focusing instead on the analysis of statistically or administratively defined *indigenous populations* (Andersen, 2008; Taylor, 2009). Thus, in the literature, indigenes are often treated, theoretically and analytically, as one of many ethnic or racial minorities in a nation's ethnic stratification system.

Despite the lack of scholarly consensus about what makes a "people" indigenous (Maaka & Fleras, 2005), it is nevertheless possible to identify four criteria that are commonly invoked: historical precedence, non-dominance, cultural distinctiveness, and self-ascription (Barnard, 2006). The historical dimension of indigeneity denotes a group's prior occupation of a geographic area that is partly or wholly subsumed, but not necessarily aligned with, the boundaries of the nation-state. The Māori term *tangata whenua*, literally meaning "people of the land," and Canadian "first nations" speak directly to the historicity of the respective groups. Non-dominance is typically understood in the political rather than demographic sense, though the two are synonymous in the settler states. Colonialization and the attendant diminution of indigenous sovereignty are central features of non-dominance, usually underpinned by contemporary political claims for some form of self-determination (Fleras & Elliott, 1992; Maaka & Fleras, 2005).[4] Cultural distinctiveness has historical dimensions, referencing the persistence and/or recovery of traditional lifeways, beliefs, and customs among the descendants of the original inhabitants. For some, this is embodied in the idea of a unique indigenous world view emanating from the integration of humankind with nature (Royal, 2003). Finally, self-identification denotes the power for groups to define their own parameters using criteria that are meaningful to them, in contrast to the historical legacy of imposed legal and bureaucratic classifications.

That demographers have been more amenable to the study of indigenous populations than indigenous peoples is unsurprising. Key historical experiences such as colonialization are difficult to operationalize in ways that are amenable to conventional demographic techniques. Rather than explicitly incorporate indigenous experiences into demographic analysis, the discipline has tended to focus on demographic staples—migration, fertility, and mortality—and how these impact the size and characteristics of indigenous populations. Theoretical and or empirical justifications include the need to advance valued knowledge about an important population group; to assist policy formulation and program delivery; and to clarify the scope conditions of conventional demographic explanations by examining indigenous convergence or divergence from established models (Bedford & Pool, 2004; Jackson, Pool, & Cheung, 1994). Though greater efforts have been made to take account of the self-definition elements, the incorporation of concepts relevant to indigenous peoples are still notably absent (for some exceptions in the New Zealand context, see Douglas, 1977; Stokes, 1987).

This does not mean the demography of indigenous populations has been stagnant or insensitive to change. Scholars have demonstrated a considerable appreciation of the ways in which official classifications and administrative categories have delimited the boundaries of indigenous populations, often in quite arbitrary ways (see, for example, Eschbach, 1993; Kukutai, 2004; Pool, 1967; Snipp, 1988; 1997; Thornton, 1997). The phenomenal growth of indigenous populations in North America has encouraged researchers to look beyond conventional demographic explanations to consider the role of political protest, identity politics, and processes of boundary construction (Cornell, 1988; Eschbach, 1993; Nagel, 1995). Studies of inter- and intra-generational forms of "ethnic mobility" within indigenous populations have challenged primordial notions of identity as immutable and inherited and contributed to a more complex understanding of how shifts in identification at the micro-level can shift boundaries at the statistical level (Guimond, 1999; Eschbach, 1993; Eschbach, Supple, & Snipp, 1998; Pool, 1991). Others have challenged statistics agencies, and those who use statistical data about indigenous peoples, to transform their practices to better align with indigenous values, social structures, and aspirations (see, for example, Andersen, 2008; Kukutai, 2012; Taylor, 2008; 2009).

Yet, despite these significant advances in the field, both the theoretical and analytical treatment of indigenous populations still tends toward the monolith. This is partially due to the tools of the trade. Researchers who view their subjects through the lens of official data are constrained by the legal and bureaucratic categorizations upon which indigenous populations are constructed. Unlike ethnographic or psychological work, which allow for more nuanced explorations of the meaning of identity, demographers are limited to patterns of responses to ethnic, racial, or indigenous identifiers.[5] Despite increased awareness of how the state constructs such categories, there is little reflection on what those categories mean, especially when used as independent variables in multivariate analysis (for critiques on the validity of using ethnic and racial categories, see Rallu, Piché, & Simon, 2006; Zuberi, 2000).

In the case of indigenous peoples, official data may be disseminated on one or several indigenous identifiers but rarely across varying combinations. New Zealand is a case in point. Data on Māori ethnicity, ancestry and tribal affiliation are collected in the quinquennial census, but the most comprehensive data is only available is for the Māori ethnic group (MEG hereafter). In the following sections, we try to show how the multi-dimensionality of indigenous identity at the individual level might be better captured within the constraints of official data such as the census. We argue that this not only brings analytical strategies closer to theories of social identities within the social sciences, but also permits insights into the con-tours of intra-indigenous segmentation. First, we contextualize our analysis by identifying and discussing some of the historical factors that have con-tributed to the segmentation of contemporary Māori society.

THE STRUCTURAL BASIS OF CONTEMPORARY MĀORI SEGMENTATION
Economic Differentiation

Like all Polynesian societies (Kirch, 1989), pre-colonial Māori society was segmented into classes with differentially endowed political authority, pres-tige, and influence. High-ranking positions were almost uniformly obtained through ascriptive processes (e.g., being the first-born son of a high-ranking family), though status could also be achieved for those with exceptional abilities. From the early twentieth century, a small but politically important educated elite emerged that exercised considerable influence in Māori and mainstream spheres. The most notable elites came from the Young Māori Party—a group of prominent, university-educated politicians who used their considerable skills and connections to improve collective Māori health and well-being.

The economic roots of modern Māori segmentation have their basis in factors that have contributed to the broadening of inequality within New Zealand generally—notably, urbanization and the transformation of the labour force. These processes occurred as the nation shifted from a fledgling social democracy into an entrenched welfare state, achieving, among other things, a radical decline in Māori mortality and universal improvements in health.

The urbanization of Māori, described as one of the most dramatic of any developed population on record (Gibson, 1973), has been written about extensively elsewhere (Barcham, 1998; Bedford & Pool, 2004; Gibson, 1973; Pool, 1991). Before World War II, the vast majority of Māori lived a semi-subsistence existence in isolated rural areas in the north and east of the country, and within the social structure of whānau (immediate and extended family), *hapū* (clans), and *iwi* (clan confederations) (Barcham, 1998). New Zealand lacked de jure segregation or native reserves in the North American sense, but de facto ethnic separation predominated, in part because of the way the nation developed socially and economically (Pool, 1991). With urbanization, social and economic relations changed dramatically. In 1945, three-quarters of Māori lived rurally—two decades later, this had dwindled to just over one-third. Today, the vast majority of Māori—more than 80%—are urbanized, with almost half of urban dwellers living in New Zealand's six metropolitan areas, which reflects the pattern for New Zealand generally (Pool, Baxendine, Cochrane, & Lindop, 2005b).

Urbanization was driven by broader economic changes—notably, the postwar boom in manufacturing and attendant labour force demands. Māori migrant workers and their families were assisted into urban areas through training, employment, and housing schemes that explicitly sought to disperse Māori throughout urban areas. The industrialization of the Māori labour force mirrored trends occurring within other developed countries. In 1945, just over half of the Māori male industrial labour force (twice the European share) was concentrated in the primary sector, with most of the remainder in the secondary sector. Over the intervening decades, a number of sectoral shifts occurred. The first involved a movement from the primary to secondary sector. By 1966, the proportion of the Māori work-force in the secondary sector exceeded that of European, for both men and women. Māori continued to be overrepresented in the primary sector, but the inter-ethnic difference was much less marked than in previous decades (Pool, 1991: Table 7.11). Over the next two decades through to 1986, there was a significant movement of Māori into the tertiary sector, though the Māori share continued to be well below that of European. A third shift occurred between 1986 and 2001, a period of major economic restructuring in New Zealand in which manufacturing was severely contracted and the financial services sector greatly expanded. Māori men in particular were vulnerable to the broad sweep of economic rationalization as they continued to be overrepresented in manual jobs that were expendable, even if often well-remunerated. The late 1980s and early 1990s were especially turbulent years. The jobs in which Māori were disproportionately concentrated were either eliminated or workforces downsized dramatically. Economic restructuring was accompanied by the introduction of targeted and more parsimonious benefit regimes. For Māori, benefit usage at the working ages (15–59 years) increased between 1986 and 2001, peaking around 1991, coterminous with high levels of unemployment.

Paradoxically, during the same period in which the inherent vulnerability of the Māori labour force became starkly apparent, there was also increased professionalization among Māori men and women. The service sectors, once the key domain of clerical workers, became increasingly oriented toward management, IT, and/or analytical skills. By 2001, nearly one-quarter of Māori workers were managers or professionals, compared to just over a third of European workers. The difference in production workers had narrowed to 11 percentage points (32% and 21% for Māori and European, respectively). As was true for the population generally, the increasing professionalization of the Māori workforce had distinct spatial features, with a concentration in metropolitan areas, and, in particular, the nation's capital, Wellington (Pool, Baxendine, Cochrane, & Lindop, 2005a).

Since the 1990s, a significant body of research has amassed, tracking the absolute and relative improvements or decline in Māori outcomes in health, housing, education, incomes, and labour force distribution (e.g., Blakely et al., 2005; Sporle, Pearce, & Davis, 2002; Te Puni Kōkiri, 2000; 2002). A good deal of research has either focused on comparisons between Māori and European, or on differences between Māori and non-Māori. Since the 1970s, there have been significant flows of migrants from the Pacific Islands (e.g., Samoa, Tonga), and, more recently, from Asia (e.g., Chinese, Indian), providing for an expanded set of ethnic group comparisons. The patterns are complex but the general consensus is that significant gaps between the average outcomes of Māori and European persist because improvements in Māori outcomes have either not kept pace with gains for European or have been insufficient to diminish inter-group differences.

CULTURAL DIFFERENTIATION

The spatial and labour force transformations described above also impacted patterns of social and cultural organization. The practice of dispersing Māori families in European neighbourhoods, for example, had some benefits in terms of averting inner city slums, but also made it difficult for Māori migrants to retain customary cultural patterns and networks. Two decades into the urban migration, Metge's pioneering study of urban Māori found the traditional tribal unit was "largely an abstract concept" that carried few advantages or obligations (1964: 58). Hopa (1996) used the analogy of a "torn whariki" (woven mat) to describe the untangling of strands that once bound together traditional units of Māori social and economic organization. Nevertheless, as traditional forms were attenuated in urban spaces, new forms of association were forged. These included pan-tribal voluntary organizations (e.g., churches and cultural performance groups); political councils such as the Māori Women's Welfare League and New Zealand Māori Council; and urban *marae* (customary meeting places that were the symbolic focus of traditional Māori culture).

Urbanization not only increased the opportunities for interactions across traditional tribal boundaries but also across ethnic boundaries. Sexual liaisons, and, to a lesser extent, marital relations between Māori and European had long been a feature of New Zealand's ethnic relations. With urbanization, many of the geographic, if not social, barriers were removed. A study using 1960 marriage registration data for Auckland, the country's largest metropolitan area, showed that 42% of Māori were married to a European (Harré, 1966). The twin themes of geographical relocation and cultural dislocation through weakening tribal ties and intermarriage spawned representations of urban Māori as a culturally deficient but racially stigmatized group. In popular writings and contemporary commentaries on race relations, urban Māori were unfavourably contrasted against the *ahi kaa*, who remained in their tribal homelands, with cultural integrity intact.

Mercurial state policies also contributed to shifts in the opportunities and costs associated with being Māori. Policies targeted at Māori may be broadly described in terms of three chronological policy eras: amalgamation and assimilation (1840 to 1960); integration and adaptation (1960 to 1975); and rejuvenation and reform (1975 to 2004).[6] From the 1960s, integration was pursued in tandem with policies to facilitate Māori urbanization. This marked a deliberate shift from state benevolence and attempts to civilize Māori to an emphasis on equipping Māori to be economically productive citizens. Overt measures to culturally assimilate Māori were relaxed—language loss and the alienation and individualization of Māori land were already well advanced through assimilation measures—and the retention of symbolic, aesthetic Māori cultural forms were tolerated, though not actively encouraged.

From the late 1970s, and in common with other indigenous revival-
ist movements, Māori collective mobilization was brought to bear on the
government. Various measures were instituted to support the revival and
retention of Māori culture and language, address Māori socio-economic
disadvantage and make financial reparations for historical wrongdoings
and breaches relating to the Treaty of Waitangi.[7] These concessions paved
the way for the establishment of Māori educational, economic, and social
service initiatives and generated niche opportunities for Māori ethnicity to
be used as a strategic resource in the education and labour markets, particularly the public service. From the late 1980s and throughout the 1990s,
official state discourses emphasized biculturalism and the notion of Māori
and European as treaty partners and parallel, equal cultures. The reinstatement of tribal enumeration in the census coincided with a process of
"retribalization," in which tribes emerged as corporate actors with strongly
centralized structures to receive and administer financial settlements from
the Crown for historical wrongdoings (Rata, 2000; Webster, 2002).[8] Some
have argued that the so-called Māori Renaissance has both reified Māori
culture and obscured class differences within Māori society, enabling tribal
and urban elites to get ahead at the expense of the working-class majority. For those critics, tribal development is a mechanism for inscribing
new forms of inequality in the form of "neotribal capitalism" (Rata, 2000).
Others argue that state biculturalism has provided for the institutional
incorporation of Māori, but has left European privilege and power largely
intact (Maaka & Fleras, 2005).

Empirical research on inequality within the Māori population is scant but
revealing. A study of death registration and census data for 1976, 1986, and
1996 found significant social class differences in Māori and non-Māori mortality rates, with the effect of class differences markedly greater for Māori
(Sporle, Pearce, & Davis, 2002). Other research has attempted to identify
intra-Māori differences by comparing "sole" Māori and "mixed" Māori (see,
for example, Chapple, 2000). The general consensus is that individuals with
a stronger Māori identification have poorer outcomes across mainstream
indices of socio-economic and biomedical well-being (e.g., Blakely et al.,
2005; Callister & Blakely, 2004; Kukutai, 2004).

Intra-indigenous inequality is certainly not unique to New Zealand.
In the United States, for example, several studies have found that people

that appear to have strong ties to American Indian identity have poorer economic outcomes than those with thinner ties (Tafoya, Johnson, & Hill, 2004; Snipp, 1988). In Australia, work by Taylor and others have shown how Aboriginal peoples living in remote homeland areas are most disadvantaged (see Taylor, 2006). One of the challenges in analyzing dimensions of difference within indigenous populations is trying to capture the complexities of identity within the constraints of official data. It is to this we now turn.

MĀORI SEGMENTATION: AN EMPIRICAL ANALYSIS
Spatial Dimensions of Segmentation

We begin our analysis by examining the spatial dimensions of intra-Māori inequality. Our focus is on inter-regional differences for Māori, but we also include comparative data for Europeans. The following table shows quartiles and inter-quartile ranges of personal median income for Māori and European by region for 1986 and 2001. Unless otherwise stated, the Māori data refer to the MEG comprising all people who recorded Māori as their ethnicity, either alone or in combination with some other group. As noted, the period 1986 to 2001 was one of significant economic and social turbulence for the nation, and for Māori especially. For both groups, lower quartile incomes dropped in real value, while upper quartiles increased in most regions for Europeans, and in about a quarter of the regions for Māori. For both groups, and for every region, the distance between the lowest and highest earning quartiles increased—signaling an increase in income inequality—though the increase was larger for Europeans than for Māori.

Compared to other regions, Auckland and Wellington had higher incomes but also higher levels of inter- and intra-ethnic inequality. To illustrate, in 2001, a European residing in Auckland and falling within the upper quartile earned, on average, just over one-third more than an Auckland Māori in the same income quartile. The latter, however, earned more than triple the income of a Māori in the lowest quartile and living in the same region. Beyond Auckland and Wellington, inter-quartile differences for Māori were most apparent in regions where they were relatively few: Otago, Canterbury, and Southland. For Europeans, however, income inequality outside of Auckland and Wellington was highest in regions where the proportion of Māori was equal to or above the national average: Waikato, Bay of Plenty, and Taranaki.[9]

Table 18.1 Standardized Incomes (in 1996 Dollars) for Māori and European: Quartiles and Inter-quartile Ranges, by Region, 1986 and 2001

Regions	25th Percentile		75th Percentile		Inter-quartile range	
	European	Māori	European	Māori	European	Māori
	1986					
Northland	9,313	8,763	29,368	22,822	20,055	14,058
Auckland	10,525	9,998	33,809	26,078	23,283	16,080
Waikato	9,669	8,772	30,534	24,363	20,865	15,590
Bay of Plenty	9,830	9,021	30,418	24,642	20,588	15,621
Gisborne	9,601	9,034	29,417	21,810	19,816	12,776
Hawke's Bay	9,582	9,084	29,946	24,569	20,364	15,485
Taranaki	9,894	8,921	30,468	24,566	20,574	15,645
Manawatu-Wanganui	9,342	9,129	29,370	24,566	20,029	15,437
Wellington	10,813	10,490	35,820	27,557	25,008	17,067
West Coast	8,991	8,893	26,540	22,742	17,548	13,850
Canterbury	9,308	9,560	29,088	24,879	19,780	15,318
Otago	8,902	8,992	28,516	25,839	19,614	16,846
Southland	8,933	8,996	29,359	26,776	20,426	17,780
Nelson-Tasman	9,042	9,966	27,250	23,824	18,208	13,858
Marlborough	8,767	9,546	26,865	25,229	18,098	15,683
New Zealand	9,805	9,368	31,301	25,032	21,496	15,664
Range	2,045	1,726	9,281	5,747	7,459	5,004
	2001					
Northland	8,216	6,484	29,146	21,061	20,930	14,577
Auckland	10,006	8,159	39,417	29,104	29,410	20,946
Waikato	8,993	6,888	33,087	24,086	24,094	17,198
Bay of Plenty	8,877	6,850	31,541	23,424	22,664	16,574
Gisborne	8,366	6,610	30,240	20,734	21,875	14,124
Hawke's Bay	8,636	6,929	30,090	23,052	21,454	16,123
Taranaki	8,688	6,902	31,466	23,903	22,778	17,002
Manawatu-Wanganui	8,361	7,166	29,587	23,885	21,226	16,719
Wellington	9,874	8,400	38,883	29,259	29,009	20,860
West Coast	7,543	6,706	25,987	22,717	18,444	16,012
Canterbury	8,413	7,568	30,773	25,812	22,359	18,244
Otago	7,774	6,925	28,720	25,241	20,946	18,316
Southland	8,602	7,394	30,354	25,463	21,751	18,069
Nelson-Tasman	8,239	7,591	27,692	23,698	19,453	16,107
Marlborough	8,640	8,236	27,582	25,409	18,941	17,172
New Zealand	8,984	7,300	33,962	25,645	24,978	18,344
Range	2,464	1,915	13,430	8,525	10,966	6,821

Overall, Māori income inequality, within and across regions, was a muted form of more generalized economic segmentation. Over the focal period, inter-ethnic differences in earnings within each region either stayed around the same level or increased. In each region and at each time point, European incomes exceed those of Māori in all quartiles, with the greatest differences most apparent among higher earners. The differential typically increased over the period, even in those regions in which Māori incomes increased.

Shifting from income, we consider intra-Māori diversity with respect to fertility behaviour. Despite many years of interaction, both in terms of intimate and social relations, Māori and European have experienced quite different fertility and family transitions (for an overview, see Pool, 1991; Pool, Dharmalingam & Sceats, 2007). Though total fertility rates (TFR) are converging, with European rates just below and Māori just above replacement, major differences in patterns of family formation persist. For Māori, the force of reproduction continues to be skewed toward the youngest reproductive ages, and levels of childlessness are much lower than for Europeans. In 2001, 42% of the Māori TFR fell below 25 years, compared to just 20% for Europeans. In 2006, 80% of European women aged between 20 and 24 years were childless, compared to just over half of Māori women. Though most analysis has focused on Māori-European fertility differentials, intra-Māori differences along spatial and socio-economic lines were evident in the mid-1980s (Pool, 1991). Levels of childbearing and fertility (TFR) were low for South Island Māori but varied within the North Island, where the vast majority of Māori lived. Metropolitan zones in the Auckland region had the highest rates for any North Island region or subregion (South Auckland) as well as the lowest (North Shore). North Shore Māori, on average, had higher incomes and lived in neighbourhoods where other Māori were few, whereas South Auckland Māori were poorer and more likely to live in housing estates alongside other Māori (Pool, 1991: 200–202). Pool postulated socio-economic determinants confounded what had hitherto been a more homogeneous culturally-driven pattern.

To better understand these complexities, Table 18.2 employs data from the 2006 Census on childlessness among Māori and non-Māori women aged 30 to 34 years, taking account of labour force status, occupational category, and geographic residence. Childlessness captures the shifts in family formation to delayed childbearing, which has increased in New Zealand, resembling trends in other Western developed countries. The 30 to 34 age

Table 18.2 Percentage of Employed Women Aged 30–34 Years Who Are Childless, by Labour Force Participation and Occupation, Māori and European, Selected Regions, 2006 Census

		Labour Force Participation					
		Part-time			Full-time		
Geographic Area*		Managerial	Professional	All Occupations	Managerial	Professional	All Occupations
Auckland Region	Euro.	13	19	17	69	75	68
	Māori	19	18	14	44	48	39
Auckland City	Euro.	16	30	31	81	85	82
	Māori	21	31	21	65	62	55
Manukau City	Euro.	9	9	10	51	61	52
	Māori	20	12	12	24	35	27
Wellington Region	Euro.	13	17	16	67	77	79
	Māori	8	13	12	46	51	43
Wellington City	Euro.	20	24	26	78	84	80
	Māori	13	23	19	59	69	62
Gisborne Region	Euro.	7	7	7	47	53	45
	Māori	0†	7	5	21	28	23
North Island, small Urban Areas	Euro.	5	14	10	47	51	44
	Māori	5	11	9	29	21	21

* Regions are groupings of propinquitous districts. Auckland and Wellington Regions contain smaller districts and gazetted cities of the same name. Auckland and Wellington cities are urban, comprising the central business district and surrounding zones; Manukau is a suburban city. Among regions, Gisborne consists of a secondary urban area and an isolated rural zone. The small urban areas are minor towns, with no propinquity, located in the North Island.

† Small *n*'s may produce errors akin to those due to sampling.

group is the pivotal age group by which late and early starters can be distinguished, and where highly educated women in high-status occupations are most clearly confronted with choices between career and childbearing (Pool, Dharmalingham, & Sceats, 2007). Residence is defined to maximize variation, including Auckland and Wellington regions and their cities, the Gisborne region, and an aggregate of small urban areas in the North Island.

Table 18.2 clearly shows that Māori fertility behaviour (as measured by childlessness) is significantly mediated by labour force status, occupation, and geographic location. Within all regions, levels of childlessness were higher among full-time (versus part-time workers) and among professional and managerial women (versus employed women generally). The most pronounced differences, however, were spatial. Levels of childlessness were much higher in the metropolitan regions of Auckland and Wellington, especially in their central city zones. Within the Auckland region, significant differences between Māori women in different cities were also apparent, consistent with Pool's earlier findings. Differences cannot be attributed solely to occupational differences. Among Māori women managers, 65% residing in Auckland City (where Māori were 7% of the population) were childless, compared to just 24% in neighbouring Manukau City (where the Māori share was 15%). Interestingly, differences in levels of childlessness were also large among European managers in those cities, though not as pronounced as for Māori.

The patterns of childlessness among Māori women in Auckland and Wellington are important for several reasons. One is that the spatial concentration of highly skilled Māori women in Auckland and Wellington was marked by comparison with national trends—53% of Māori women managers and professionals lived in those two metropolis compared to 42% of the total population. Second, full-time work was nearly universal for employed professional and managerial Māori women in both regions (higher than 80%), slightly above that for professional and managerial European women. At an opposite extreme were regions with larger concentrations of Māori: Gisborne region, the minor urban areas, and suburban Manukau. In these areas, geographic propinquity with other Māori may be a factor in family formation norms. There may also be simple behavioural and institutional explanations—for example, the presence of whānau (kin) support networks that could provide props for reproduction. In sum, for the overwhelming majority of European and Māori women employed full-time in managerial and professional occupations, reproductive patterns reflected a trend occurring across all Western developed countries.[10] It needs to be emphasized, however, that regardless of region, levels of childlessness among full-time professional Māori women more closely resembled the level of the average full-time Māori worker than those of European professionals.

A Core–Periphery Model of Segmentation

Having considered the spatial features of segmentation, this section uses a core–periphery model to examine the potential associations between socio-economic status and ties to Māori identity as expressed in the national

Figure 18.1 The Multiple Boundaries of Māori Identity in the Census

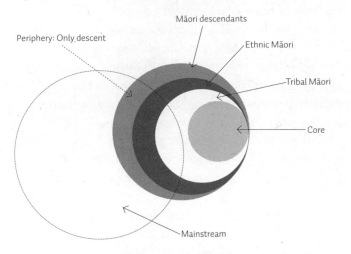

Māori descendants

Periphery: Only descent

Ethnic Māori

Tribal Māori

Core

Mainstream

census. All groups that see themselves as culturally distinctive hold ideas about their symbolic boundary and symbolic core (Kaufmann, 2000). The symbolic boundary is the most inclusive parameter and is typically delimited by the idea of putative descent in the form of race or ancestry. The symbolic core comprises the group's "ethnic mythomoteur" (e.g., symbols, myths, images etc.), which represent the group's ideal type and tends toward exclusivity (Kaufmann, 2000: 1106). Since 1991, the census has elicited information on three dimensions of Māori identity: ethnic group, ancestry, and tribe.[11] By combining these markers in various ways, we can construct different sorts of Māori identity categories to try and capture the multi-dimensionality of Māori identity, ranging from core to periphery. This is shown in Figure 18.1.

A population defined as Māori on the basis of ancestry or descent may be conceptualized as the symbolic boundary.[12] In the 2006 Census, 643,980 people recorded Māori descent. Māori descent is employed in some legal and administrative contexts as supposedly objective filter of group membership (Kukutai, 2004). In theory, only persons of Māori descent can enroll in a Māori electorate to vote in the national general election, lodge a claim with the Waitangi Tribunal, or apply for certain kinds of non-tribal educational scholarships. In practice, there is considerable elasticity in how these definitions are applied (for a more detailed explanation, see Kukutai, 2012). For many people who record Māori ancestry in the census, their ties to things

Māori may be merely symbolic, especially for those whose *only* tie to Māori identity is through ancestry.

Moving inward from the periphery, the ethnic Māori population (MEG) comprises people who recorded Māori as their ethnic group, either alone in combination with some other group. In 2006, this numbered 565,329. The ethnic group question is intended to capture a person's current ethnic identification, as distinct from the ethnicity of their ancestors. A further distinction can be made between those who identify exclusively as Māori (mono-ethnic Māori, n = 298,395), and those who choose Māori as one of several ethnic identifications (multi-ethnic Māori, n = 266,934). As Figure 18.1 shows, there is a considerable overlap between populations defined as Māori by ancestry versus ethnicity, though the relationship is asymmetrical. Ethnic identification is closely coupled with Māori descent, but about one-fifth of those that acknowledged Māori ancestry did not ethnically identify as Māori.

Tribal affiliation provides another criterion with which to construct boundaries.[13] As distinct from the concept of Māori, which was borne from the expediencies of cross-cultural contact, tribal affiliation is closer to customary conceptions of group membership based on *whakapapa*. Karetu (1990) has described whakapapa as the glue that connects individuals to a specific place or places, and locates them within a broader network of kin relations. *Whakapapa* also endows certain rights in terms of land succession and usufruct rights (e.g., shares in Māori land). Historically, residence near one's ancestral land was closely tied with *whakapapa*, but the majority of Māori now live outside their tribal area. In 2006, 535,233 people recorded a tribal affiliation. Finally, all three Māori identifiers can be combined to form a Māori core comprising those who identify as Māori by descent, exclusive ethnicity, and tribe. The number of people who met this definition was 243,642.

Drawing on Figure 18.1, the following analyses considers a range of socio-economic, demographic, and cultural indicators for the seven differently defined Māori categories, and a non-Māori comparator. Two caveats are made. One is that, with the exception of the "Māori by descent only" category, most people identified with a combination of identity markers; thus, there is a high degree of overlap between the categories (e.g., the core is fully subsumed in the mono-ethnic category). With the exception of the core, there is also a varying degree of overlap with the predominantly

Table 18.3 Key Indicators for Māori Categories Derived from the Census, 2006 Census

Indicator	Māori Core	Ethnic Māori	Tribal Māori	Māori Descent	Mono-ethnic Māori	Multi-ethnic Māori	Māori Periphery	Non-Māori
Median age	29.5	22.7	23.9	23.4	28.7	17.7	25.3	38.1
Adults (at least 15 yrs.)	72.6	64.6	66.0	65.5	71.7	56.8	67.8	80.8
Dependency ratio*	49.8	65.2	63.1	63.5	51.4	83.9	60.6	49.3
No formal qualification	45.3 (47.8)	39.9 (43.4)	37.1 (40.2)	37.3 (40.6)	47.6 (50.0)	29.8 (33.2)	29.2 (31.7)	23.0 (22.7)
Employment rate†	87.7 (87.8)	88.8 (89.7)	89.6 (90.3)	90.6 (92.2)	87.4 (87.7)	90.6 (92.2)	94.3 (94.7)	95.6 (95.1)
Managerial and Professionals	18.4 (18.9)	20.1 (21.1)	21.9 (23.1)	21.5 (22.8)	17.2 (17.9)	23.3 (25.6)	26.0 (28.0)	32.2 (34.2)
In a legal marriage	27.6 (30.2)	27.1 (32.6)	29.5 (34.6)	29.5 (35.1)	26.5 (29.5)	27.9 (38.1)	38.0 (43.0)	49.6 (48.2)
Partnered men with a non-Māori partner‡	36.1 (34.6)	48.4 (46.8)	52.6 (50.7)	57.5 (55.9)	37.0 (35.7)	66.2 (65.2)	90.1 (88.6)	94.9 (93.3)
Can speak Māori	37.9 (40.0)	26.98 (29.7)	26.1 (28.1)	22.4 (24.5)	35.9 (38.2)	14.2 (15.1)	3.9 (3.9)	0.8 (0.8)
Living in a high Māori TA§	44.6 (45.3)	37.6 (39.1)	37.0 (38.1)	34.9 (36.2)	43.9 (44.7)	28.8 (30.1)	23.7 (24.4)	14.7 (14.5)
Total (all ages)	243,642	565,329	535,233	643,980	298,395	266,934	117,975	3,294,834

Figures in parentheses are age standardized using the 2001 Total New Zealand population as the standard. All percentages are for the population aged 15 years and over and exclude unspecified responses. Shaded cells denote the lowest and highest standardized values.

* Population 0–14 years and 65+ years/Population 15–64 years x 100.

† Population employed 15–64 years/Population Employed and Unemployed 15–64 years x 100.

‡ Restricted to opposite sex couples living in the same household.

§ Territorial Authorities with at least 20% ethnic Māori.

European mainstream. For example, most of those on the Māori periphery identify exclusively as ethnic Europeans in the census. Second, these subgroups are statistical constructs based on aggregated individual-level responses to various identification options, rather than socially meaningful groups. The rationale for using non-exclusive groupings is to examine the benefits that might arise from analytically treating indigeneity as a continuous variable that extends from core to periphery, rather than identifying neatly bounded, discrete classes of Māori with peculiar characteristics. Data are shown for the 2006 Census and are age standardized.

The patterns in Table 18.3 are consistent with segmentation, showing systematic and significant differences in socio-economic, demographic, and cultural characteristics between the core and periphery. The mono-ethnic and core Māori categories display the poorest outcomes, as measured by educational attainment and employment status, and the strongest cultural ties as measured by Māori language ability, residency in areas with a high Māori concentration, and low levels of inter-ethnic partnering. Both categories also have the highest proportions of adults and the lowest levels of legal marriage. As expected, Māori on the periphery of Māori identity— whose ties are solely through ancestry—have characteristics that more closely resemble the non-Māori comparator. Multi-ethnic Māori—those who recorded both Māori and non-Māori ethnic groups in the census—are closer to the periphery than the core, though still significantly different from both. Across most dimensions, the singular categories delimited by tribe, ethnicity, or descent, have characteristics that locate them in a cluster somewhat closer to the core than to the periphery. Separate analyses not presented here also identified some important gender dimensions, with males in all categories faring unfavourably on the education and occupation indicators. Replication of the analysis using data from the 1996 and 2001 Censuses found that the patterns in Table 18.3 were systematic in direction and magnitude.

Given the regional differences identified in the preceding analyses, one might ask, to what extent are these patterns the result of spatial differ- ences? Attachments to Māori identity emanate from various sources including familial networks and the broader social environment. In the case of Māori identity, an important aspect of structural supports, and one already touched upon in earlier analysis, is geographic proximity to other Māori. The apparent disadvantage of the core might be due to residence in areas where Māori are strongly represented and, which we know from the literature, are more likely to be structurally disadvantaged. To tease out these relationships, Figures 18.2 and 18.3 show patterns of educational attainment and intermarriage by residential proximity to other Māori. The latter is approximated by a measure that captures residence in a territorial authority (TA) with low (0%–9.99%), medium (10%–19.99%), or high (20% or more) ethnic Māori concentration. Territorial authority is analogous to a

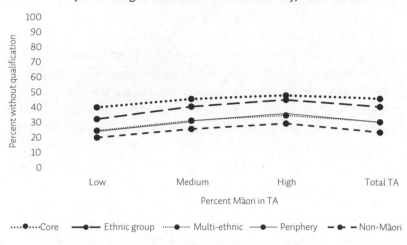

Figure 18.2 Percentage with No Formal Educational Qualification by Percentage Māori in Territorial Authority, 2006 Census

Low = 0%–9.99%; medium = 10%–19.99%; high = 20% and more.

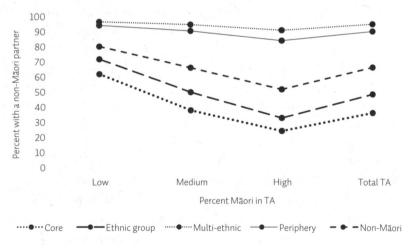

Figure 18.3 Percentage of Adult Men with a Non-Māori Partner by Percentage Māori in Territorial Authority, 2006 Census

Low = 0%–9.99%; medium ÷ 10%–19.99%; high = 20% and more.

county in the United States and is the level of aggregation most commonly used in social research in New Zealand. In 2006, there were 73 TAs, which ranged in size from 404,000 (Auckland City) to 3,621 (Kaikoura District).

To clarify patterns, only five categories are shown: Māori core, ethnic Māori, multi-ethnic Māori, Māori periphery, and the non-Māori comparator.

For each category, there are clear differences by geographic propinquity. As shown earlier, being located near the Māori core is associated with low levels of education generally, but this is especially pronounced when living in an area with a high Māori concentration. Differences between the core and periphery tend to be more pronounced in areas with either a low or high Māori concentration. Using out-marriage as an example, the difference between the core and periphery was 35 percentage points in areas where Māori were less than one-tenth of the population, but increased to 60 percentage points in areas where Māori were at least 20%. For those on the fringes of Māori identity and living in an area with few other Māori, partnering with a non-Māori was almost universal (94%). For those with multiple ties to Māori identity and living in an area where Māori were over-represented, marriage to a non-Māori was relatively uncommon (24%). Comparison across the extremes of the continuum—both in terms of ties to Māori identity and residential propinquity with other Māori—illustrates the great variation within the Māori population. Conventional analysis that uses only ethnic data to compare Māori with European or non-Māori (the two solid lines) masks a good deal of the variation that exists but can be exploited by conceiving of the Māori population in more complex ways (the dotted lines).

Our analysis has been descriptive, rather than predictive, and as such we make no attempt to infer causal relationships. Our goal was only to demonstrate that significant differences exist within the Māori population with regards to socio-economic position, cultural behaviours (e.g., language and partnering choices), and demographic characteristics, and that these differences appear to be related to attachments to Māori identity. Why these patterns can be observed is, of course, a much more difficult question to answer and beyond the scope of this chapter. We note, however, that there are likely to be unmeasured variables not entertained in our analysis that, once accounted for, might change some of the observed patterns. For example, ties to Māori identity may be less important than isolation from the mainstream and the associated benefits. Certain kinds of attachment (e.g., network ties) matter more than others, as well as the durability of such attachments over time (Kukutai, 2010). Though we have used more refined measures of Māori identity than have most studies, the measures are still simple proxies for the underlying latent construct of Māori identity. The use of surveys that contain multiple items on various kinds of ties or attachments (e.g., identity, networks, and behavioural), combined with more complex analytical techniques (e.g., latent class analysis), provide fruitful avenues for further study.

CONCLUSION

We have tried to make a case for greater reflection on the ways in which indigenous populations are constructed in the course of undertaking demographic analysis and the importance of attending to dimensions of difference within indigenous populations. Using descriptive analyses, we found evidence of significant intra-Māori differentiation with regard to expressions of Māori identification, material circumstances, and demographic statuses. We also found a general pattern that supported a segmented approach— with location in the Māori core tending to be associated with a higher level of disadvantage, even when taking account of geographic proximity with other Māori.

The findings confirm the presence of complex forms of differentiation within the Māori population. By combining markers of Māori identity in the census it is possible to gain a sense of how a core–periphery model might be applied within indigenous populations in settler states in ways that complement existing analysis. Future analysis that accounts for the potential effects of confounding variables, and provides more detailed measures of differences in the kinds, durability, and intensity of Māori attachments, will hopefully contribute to a more nuanced understanding of the multi-dimensionality of the Māori population and stratification processes.

The descriptive nature of our analyses cautions against causal inferences: the pattern may be directional and due to confounding factors related both to indigeneity and outcomes. The implication for demography is that it is increasingly problematic to analyze the Māori population in ways that suggest a group of people with a unitary set of cultural reference points and demographic experiences. The persistence of significant inter-ethnic differences confirms the continued need for analysis that both contextualizes the structural position of indigenous peoples within their national homelands, as well as a more critical evaluation of emergent forms of differentiation within indigenous populations.

AUTHORS' NOTE

The authors would like to thank Robert Didham from Statistics New Zealand for his generous assistance in providing us with the data used in this chapter.

NOTES

1. Throughout this chapter, the term "Anglo settler state" is used interchangeably with "settler state" to refer to nation-states in North America and Australasia that contained a pre-existing people who were subsequently colonized by an Anglo, typically British, power. Canada is included in this definition, though with the acknowledgement that French settlement has also been central to the nation's settlement history and contemporary political relations. The arguments presented in this chapter are limited in scope to the settler states, rather than indigenous populations globally.

2. The Māori term *Pākehā* is a historical term that evolved to describe British settlers and their descendants (King, 1999). Though a popular colloquial term, *Pākehā* has not been institutionalized as a statistical term. In the census, for example, the majority group is labelled "New Zealand European," and simply "European" at Level 1 of the Statistical Standard for Ethnicity (Statistics New Zealand, 2005). We use "European" throughout this chapter in order to maintain consistency with the statistical terminology.

3. In some countries, groups that would otherwise be considered politically and/or culturally dominant have come to see themselves as indigenous to a place—for example, Boers in South Africa (Barnard, 2006), descendants of British settlers in New Zealand (King, 1999), and the descendants of British and French settlers in Canada (Pryor, Goldmann, Sheridan, & White, 1992). Such claims are often treated with suspicion by those whom claim indigeneity on the basis of "first come" and non-dominance. This alternative notion of indigeneity is beyond the scope of this chapter.

4. "Colonialism" is a broader term that subsumes "colonization" (the establishment of settler colonies within the metropole's own population) as well as the ruling of existing peoples. Both terms are diffuse and multi-faceted theoretical constructs that defy statistical quantification. However, specific aspects of colonialism may be examined with respect to the demographic impacts on indigenous populations. The authors, along with Janet Sceats, have undertaken several substantial research projects investigating the short- and long-term demographic impacts of land alienation (a major component of colonialization in New Zealand) on *hapū* and *iwi* in the Central North Island and Heretaunga-Tamata regions of New Zealand (see, for example, Kukutai, Sceats, & Pool, 2002).

5. The format and complexity of indigenous identifiers in the censuses vary considerably in North America and Australasia. For example, the Australian

census simply asks, "Is the person of Aboriginal or Torres Strait Islander origin?" By comparison, the Canadian census asks three specific questions on Aboriginal status: "Is this person an Aboriginal person, that is, North American Indian, Métis or Inuit (Eskimo)?" "Is this person a member of an Indian Band/First Nation?" And "Is this person a Treaty Indian or a Registered Indian as defined by the Indian Act of Canada?" The ancestry question in the New Zealand census asks: "Are you descended from a Māori (that is, did you have a Māori birth parent, grandparent, or great-grandparent, etc.)?"

6. In New Zealand, as in other Anglo settler states, government assimilation policies had multiple meanings and rationales. In the early stages of colonization, assimilation referred mainly to the biological merging of Māori into the settler populace. After the Second World War, assimilation was more generally thought of in cultural terms. It was not unusual, however, for policies to imply both biological and cultural incorporation. Assimilation policies and sentiments received a degree of support from some prominent Māori politicians at different times, though often within a framework for improving the quality of life of Māori people. For more detailed descriptions of the consequences of particular policy eras, see Ward (1973), Hunn (1961), and Williams (2001).

7. The Treaty of Waitangi, signed in 1840 between Māori tribes and the Crown, has been described as the Māori "magna carta." The Māori version of the treaty guaranteed Māori protection of their lands and resources, *tino rangatiratanga* (self-determination), and the rights and privileges of British subjects. In return they ceded their governorship to the Crown. The Crown's failure to honour the terms of the treaty has long been the focus of Māori grievances relating to loss of land and political marginalization, although the establishment of the Waitangi Tribunal has made significant headway in addressing treaty-related concerns.

8. Two pieces of legislation were especially influential in fostering the centralization of *iwi* structures. The Runanga Iwi Act (1990) was key to the government's policy of devolving limited responsibility to Māori by conferring legal recognition to iwi authorities as treaty partners and preferred that organizations deliver social services to Māori. The act was repealed a year after its introduction, but the legacy of centralized *iwi* authorities endures. The Treaty of Waitangi Amendment Act (1985) allowed for Māori claims under the Treaty of Waitangi to be backdated to 1840. Barcham (1998) argues the act played an important part in defining modern *iwi* as the legitimate descendants of Māori society as it existed at the time of the treaty.

9. In 2001, the MEG comprised 14.1% of the total New Zealand population. The percentage of Māori in each region was Southland (11.3%); Otago (6%); Canterbury (6.8%); Bay of Plenty (27.9%); Waikato (21.2%); and Taranaki (14.7%).

10. The complex reasons for this are beyond the scope of this chapter but two are worth noting. First, families increasingly require all adult members to be employed because of pressures on family budgets and housing costs. In New Zealand, this last factor is particularly critical because of the lack of rental

housing stock. Second, because full-time work is often necessary to succeed on a career ladder, family formation appears to be an "impossible dream" for a significant number of women (Sceats, 2003). This conflict is more apparent among women in occupations requiring higher credentials, who have often studied for a significant period and who must attempt to fit family life to this career. It might also be that women in occupations not requiring managerial or professional skills may have started their families earlier, and thus will not be childless when working full-time in their thirties.

11. Since 1986, there have been major changes to how Māori identity has been treated in the census. The key change has been the replacement of a system based on quantum racial and descent measures with ethnic group identification. For a fuller discussion, see Kukutai, 2004.

12. The Māori descent question was introduced in the 1991 Census to meet legal requirements for determining electoral representation as the determination of electoral boundaries, and it depends, in part, on the size of the Māori descent population. Since its introduction, Māori descent data has not been widely used in research or policy.

13. Tribal identification in the census is based on self-reporting and multiple affiliations may be listed. There are various problems with how responses are coded under the official iwi classification system—for example, people who report place names and ancestral names may be erroneously coded as belonging to the local iwi. In contrast to the census, tribal registers require applicants to provide details of their whakapapa linkage, typically up to two generations, as well as the names of principal hapū (sub-tribe) and marae (meeting places). Applications must also be endorsed by a tribal kaumātua (elder). For more on tribal enumeration in New Zealand, see Walling, Small-Rodriguez, and Kukutai, 2009.

REFERENCES

Altman, J.C., Biddle, N., & Hunter, B. (2004). Indigenous socio-economic change 1971–2001: A historical perspective (Discussion Paper 266/2004). Canberra. Australian National University.

Andersen, C. (2008). From nation to population: The racialisation of Métis in the Canadian census. Nations and Nationalism, 14(2), 347–368.

Barcham, M. (1998). The challenge of urban Māori: Reconciling conceptions of indigeneity and social change. Asia Pacific Viewpoint, 39, 303–314.

Barnard, A. (2006). Kalahari revisionism, Vienna and the "indigenous peoples" debate. Social Anthropology, 14, 1–16.

Bedford, R., & Pool, I. (2004). Flirting with Zelinsky in Aotearoa/New Zealand: A Māori mobility transition. In J. Taylor & M. Bell (Eds.), Population mobility and indigenous peoples in Australasia and North America (pp. 44–74). London, UK: Routledge.

Blakely, T., Tobias, M., Robson, B., Ajwani, S., Bonné, M., & Woodward, A. (2005). Widening ethnic mortality disparities in New Zealand: 1981–99. Social Science & Medicine, 61, 2233–2251.

Chapple, S. (2000). Māori socio-economic disparity. *Political Science, 52*, 101–115.

Cornell, S. (1988). *The return of the native: American Indian political resurgence.* New York, NY: Oxford University Press.

Douglas, E.M.K. (1977). The new net goes fishing. In J. Caldwell (Ed.), *The persistence of high fertility* (pp. 661–678). Canberra: Australian National University.

Eschbach, K. (1993). Changing identification among American Indians and Alaska Natives. *Demography, 30*, 635–652.

Eschbach, K., Supple, K., & Snipp, C.M. (1998). Changes in racial identification and the educational attainment of American Indians, 1970–1990. *Demography, 35*, 35–43.

Fleras, A., & Elliott, J.L. (1992). *The "nations within": Aboriginal–state relations in Canada, the United States, and New Zealand.* Toronto, ON: Oxford University Press.

Gibson, C. (1973). Urbanization in New Zealand: A comparative analysis. *Demography, 10*, 71–84.

Guimond, É. (1999). Ethnic mobility and the demographic growth of Canada's Aboriginal populations from 1986 to 1996. In *Report on the Demographic Situation in Canada, 187–200* (Catalogue No. 91-209-XPE). Ottawa, ON: Statistics Canada.

Harré, J. (1966). *Maori and Pakeha: A study of mixed marriages in New Zealand.* London, UK: Institute of Race Relations.

Hopa, N. (1996). The torn Whariki. In J. Hawthorne, J. Jessop, J. Pryor, & M. Richards (Eds.), *Supporting children and parents through family change* (pp. 53–60). Dunedin, NZ: University of Otago Press.

Humpage, L., & Fleras, A. (2001). Intersecting discourses: Closing the gaps, social justice and the treaty of Waitangi. *Social Policy Journal of New Zealand, 16*, 37–53.

Hunn, J.K. (1961). *Report on the Department of Maori Affairs.* Wellington, NZ: Government Printer.

Jackson, N.O., Pool, I., & Cheung, M.C. (1994). Maori and non-Maori fertility: Convergence, divergence, or parallel trends? *New Zealand Population Review, 20*, 31–57.

Karetu, T. (1990, January). The clue to identity. *National Geographic, 5*, 112–117.

Kaufmann, E. (2000). Liberal ethnicity: Beyond liberal nationalism and minority rights. *Ethnic and Racial Studies, 23*, 1086–1119.

King, M. (1999). *Being Pakeha now: Reflections and recollections of a White Native.* Auckland, NZ: Penguin Books.

Kirch, P.V. (1989). *The evolution of the Polynesian chiefdoms.* Cambridge, UK: Cambridge University Press.

Kukutai, T. (2004). The problem of defining an ethnic group for public policy: Who is Māori and why does it matter? *Social Policy Journal of New Zealand, 23*, 86–108.

———. (2010). The thin brown line: Re-indigenizing inequality in Aotearoa New Zealand (Unpublished doctoral dissertation). Stanford University, Stanford, CA.

———. (2012). Quantum Māori, Māori quantum: Representations of Māori identities in the census, 1857/8–2006. In R. McClean, B. Patterson, & D. Swain (Eds.), *Counting Stories, Moving Ethnicities: Studies from Aotearoa New Zealand* (pp. 27–51). Hamilton, NZ: University of Waikato.

Kukutai, T., Sceats, J., & Pool, I. (2002). *Central north island Iwi: Population patterns and trends.* A Report prepared for the Crown Forestry Rental Trust. Wellington, NZ: Crown Forestry Rental Trust.

Maaka, R., & Fleras, A. (2005). *The politics of indigeneity: Challenging the state in Canada and Aotearoa New Zealand.* Dunedin, NZ: University of Otago Press.

McIntosh, I., Colchester, M., Bowen, J., & Rosengren, D. (2002). Defining oneself, and being defined as, Indigenous. *Anthropology Today, 18,* 23–24.

Metge, J. (1964). *A New Maori migration: Rural and urban relations in Northern New Zealand.* London, UK: Athlone.

Nagel, J. (1995). American Indian ethnic renewal: Politics and the resurgence of identity. *American Sociological Review, 60,* 947–965.

Pholi, K., Black, D., & Richards, C. (2009). Is "close the gap" a useful approach to improving the health and wellbeing of Indigenous Australians? *Australian Review of Public Affairs, 9*(2), 1–13.

Pool, D.I. (1963). When is a Maori a "Maori"? *Journal of the Polynesian Society, 72,* 206–210.

———. (1991). *Te Iwi Maori: A New Zealand population past, present & projected.* Auckland, NZ: Auckland University Press.

Pool, I., Baxendine, S., Cochrane, W., & Lindop, J. (2005a). *New Zealand regions 1986–2001: Industries and occupations* (Population Studies Centre, Discussion Papers, No. 59). Hamilton, NZ: University of Waikato.

———. (2005b). *New Zealand regions 1986–2001: Population geography* (Population Studies Centre, Discussion Papers, No. 54). Hamilton, NZ: University of Waikato.

Pool, I., Dharmalingham, A., & Sceats, J. (2007). *The New Zealand family from 1840: A demographic history.* Auckland, NZ: Auckland University Press.

Pryor, E.T., Goldmann, G.J., Sheridan, M.J., & White, P.M. (1992). Measuring ethnicity: Is "Canadian" an evolving indigenous category? *Ethnic and Racial Studies, 15,* 214–235.

Rallu, J., Piché, V., & Simon, P. (2006). Demography and ethnicity: An ambiguous relationship. In G. Casolli, J. Vallin, & G. Wunsch (Eds.), *Demography: Analysis and synthesis, vol. 3* (pp. 531–550). New York, NY: Academic Press.

Rata, E. (2000). *A political economy of neotribal capitalism.* Lanham, MD: Lexington Books.

Royal, T. (2003). *Indigenous world views: A comparative study.* Otaki, NZ: Te Wananga o Raukawa.

Sceats, J. (2003). The impossible dream: Motherhood and a career. *New Zealand Population Review, 29,* 155–171.

Snipp, C.M. (1988, June). On the costs of being American Indian: Ethnic identity and economic opportunity. *Proceedings of the Conference on Comparative Ethnicity: Vol. IV.* University of California, Los Angeles.

———. (1997). Some observations about racial boundaries and the experiences of American Indians. *Ethnic and Racial Studies, 20,* 669–689.

Sporle, A., Pearce, N., & Davis, P. (2002). Social class mortality differences in Māori and non-Māori Men aged 15–64 during the last two decades. *New Zealand Medical Journal, 115*, 127–131.

Statistics New Zealand. (2005). *Statistical standard for ethnicity 2005*. Wellington, NZ: Statistics New Zealand.

Steering Committee for the Review of Government Service Provision. (2009). *Overcoming indigenous disadvantage: Key indicators 2009*. Canberra: Productivity Commission.

Stokes, E. (1987). Māori geography or geography of Māoris? *New Zealand Geographer, 43*(3), 118–123.

Tafoya, S., Johnson, H., & Hill, L. (2004). Who chooses to choose two? Multiracial identification and Census 2000. *The American People*. New York, NY: Russell Sage Foundation / Washington, DC: Population Reference Bureau.

Taylor, J. (2006). *Population and diversity: Policy implications of emerging indigenous demographic trends*. Canberra: Centre for Aboriginal Economic Policy Research, Australian National University.

———. (2008). Indigenous peoples and indicators of well-being: Australian perspectives on United Nations global frameworks. *Social Indicators Research, 87*, 111–126.

———. (2009). Indigenous demography and public policy in Australia: Population or peoples? *Journal of Population Research, 26*, 115–130.

Te Puni Kōkiri. (2000). *Progress towards closing social and economic gaps between Māori and non-Māori. A Report to the Minister of Māori Affairs*. Wellington, NZ: Te Puni Kōkiri.

———. (2002). *Progress towards closing social and economic gaps between Māori and non-Māori. A Report to the Minister of Māori Affairs*. Wellington, NZ: Te Puni Kōkiri.

Thornton, R. (1997). Tribal membership requirements and the demography of "old" and "new" Native Americans. *Population Research And Policy Review, 16*, 33–42.

Tolbert, C., Horan, P.M., & Beck, E.M. (1980). The structure of economic segmentation: A dual economy approach. *American Journal of Sociology, 85*, 1095–1116.

Walling, J., Small-Rodriguez, D., & Kukutai, T. (2009). Tallying tribes: Waikato-Tainui in the census and Iwi Register. *Social Policy Journal of New Zealand, 36*, 2–15.

Ward, A. (1973). *A show of justice: Racial "amalgamation" in nineteenth-century New Zealand*. Toronto, ON: University of Toronto Press.

Webster, S. (1998). *Patrons of Māori culture: Power, theory, and ideology in the Māori renaissance*. Dunedin, NZ: University of Otago Press.

———. (2002). Māori retribalization and treaty rights to the New Zealand fisheries. *The Contemporary Pacific, 14*(2), 341–276.

Williams, D. (2001). *Crown policy affecting Māori knowledge systems and cultural practices*. Report for the Waitangi Tribunal. Wellington, NZ: Waitangi Tribunal.

Zuberi, T. (2000). Deracializing social statistics: Problems in the quantification of race. *The Annals of the American Academy of Political and Social Science, 568*(1), 172–185.

19

INDIGENOUS MINORITIES AND POST-SOCIALIST TRANSITION:

A REVIEW OF ABORIGINAL POPULATION TRENDS IN THE RUSSIAN NORTH[1]

Andrey N. Petrov

INTRODUCTION

The indigenous minorities of the Russian North have had a troubled history over the last two centuries (Diatchkova, 2001; Pika & Prokhorov, 1988; Shnirelman, 1994). Epidemics and poverty in the nineteenth century were complemented by hardships of collectivization, forced sedentarization, and intensive assimilation in the Soviet period (Poelzer & Fondahl, 1997; Skobelev, 2004). Resultant unstable population dynamics during the late Soviet times prompted some demographers to fear that many indigenous minority groups were nearing a complete extinction.[2] Along with assimilation, this phenomenon was attributed to an unusual demographic transition "stalemate": while fertility rates were slowly in decline, mortality failed to recede to the expected levels. Although better medical care and socioeconomic conditions predictably reduced infant mortality, extraordinary high death rates in the middle-age cohorts were responsible for the shrinking natural growth and low life expectancy. Although the most pessimistic scenarios have not materialized, the indigenous minorities still face serious challenges preserving their populations (Bogoyavlensky, 1994; Pika & Prokhorov, 1988; Ziker, 2002).

The main objective of this chapter is to review and discuss population dynamics of the indigenous minorities in the context of cultural, economic, and social transformations experienced by indigenous people in the post-Soviet period. This discussion will also inform a wider debate about the demographic viability of indigenous ethnic groups around the globe, and specifically in the Arctic. This chapter draws on the Russian Census of 2002 and annual statistical reports, as well as on the existing analytical studies.

DATA AND DEFINITIONS

The indigenous minority groups living in the Russian North are typically referred in Russian sources as "the Indigenous numerically small peoples of the North, Siberia and the Far East" (коренные малочисленные народы Севера, Сибири и Дальнего Востока). These groups are officially defined by the federal law (Federal'noe Sobranie RF, 1999) as "peoples of fewer than 50,000 individuals, which settle on the ancestrally occupied lands (homelands), maintain traditional lifestyle and activities and regard themselves as independent ethnic groups."[3] Given this definition, the group includes only numerically small indigenous ethnic groups. Larger indigenous peoples, such as Yakut, Komi, and Buryat, are not considered to be minorities and are not surveyed here.

Historically, the number of recognized indigenous minorities has not been constant. The changes were driven either by new ethnographic evidence, or by political decisions (Bogoyavlensky, 2004; Sokolovski, 2006). The post-Soviet period saw a substantial growth in the number of the officially recognized indigenous minorities in the Russian North. The Census of 2002 distinguished 35 indigenous minorities[4] (Goskomstat Rossii, 2002), up from 26 in 1989. In April of 2006, the government adopted a revised list of the indigenous minorities, which now includes 40 northern ethnic groups (Table 19.1).[5] These groups enjoy special indigenous minority rights and privileges (although, these are modest compared to other Arctic countries). The data available for longitudinal comparisons pertains to 26 ethnic groups used in both 1989 and 2002 Censuses (see Table 19.1). Most of the following analysis uses either 26 (as appeared in the 1989 Census) or 35 group designation (as used in the 2002 Census and in most annual post-Soviet statistics). In this text, I will make distinctions wherever necessary.

In contrast to the all-encompassing Census, the Rosstat (the Federal Statistical Agency of Russia) collects annual data only in the designated

Table 19.1 Census Population Count of the Indigenous Peoples of the Russian North, 1926–2002

	Censuses*							
	USSR (1929–1989)						Russia (2002)	
	Totals						Total†	Live in the North, Siberia, and the Far East
Year of Census	1926	1939	1959	1970	1979	1989	2002	2002
Northern Indigenous Peoples, total	132,549	143,359	131,111	153,246	158,324	184,448	208,980	198,745
including:								
Nenets	17,566	24,053	23,007	28,705	29,894	34,665	41,302	40,187
Evenk	38,746	29,666	24,151	25,149	27,531	30,163	35,527	34,610
Khant	22,306	19,160	19,410	21,138	20,934	22,521	28,678	27,655
Even	2,044	9,698	9,121	12029	12,286	17,199	19,071	18,642
Chukchi	12,332	13,835	11,727	13,597	14,000	15,184	15,767	14,109
Nanai	5,860	8,526	8,026	10,005	10,516	12,023	12,160	11,569
Mansi	5,754	6,315	6,449	7,710	7,563	8,474	11,432	10,572
Koryak	7,439	7,354	6,287	7,487	7,879	9,242	8,743	8,271
Dolgan	650	3,971	3,932	4,877	5,053	6,945	7,261	6,879
Nivkh	4,076	3,902	3,717	4,420	4,397	4,673	5,162	4,902
Selkup	1,630	6,441	3,768	4,282	3,565	3,612	4,249	4,056
Itelmen	4,217	1,706	1,109	1,301	1,370	2,481	3,180	2,939
Ulchi	723	n/d	2,055	2,448	2,552	3,233	2,913	2,718
Saami	1,720	1,836	1,792	1,884	1,888	1,890	1,991	1,769
Eskimo	1,293	1,309	1,118	1,308	1,510	1,719	1,750	1,553
Udege	1,357	1,743	1,444	1,469	1,551	2,011	1,657	1,531
Ket	1,428	1,243	1,019	1,182	1,122	1,113	1,494	1,189
Yukagir	443	507	442	615	835	1,142	1,509	1,176
Chuvan	705	611	n/d	n/d	n/d	1,511	1,087	990
Tofalar	415	410	586	620	763	731	837	723
Nganasan	-1	738	748	953	867	1,278	834	811
Orochi	647	n/d	782	1,089	1,198	915	686	426
Negidal	683	n/d	n/d	537	504	622	567	505
Aleut	353	335	421	441	546	702	540	452
Orok	162	n/d	n/d	n/d	n/d	190	346	298
Enets	n/d	n/d	n/d	n/d	n/d	209	237	213

Indigenous peoples added to the list of the Indigenous Numerically Small Peoples of the North, Siberia and the Far East after 1989‡

Shor	n/d	n/d	n/d	n/d	n/d	n/d	13,975	12,773
Veps	n/d	n/d	n/d	n/d	n/d	n/d	8,240	n/d
Todja	n/d	n/d	n/d	n/d	n/d	n/d	4,442	4,435
Kumanda	n/d	n/d	n/d	n/d	n/d	n/d	3,114	2,888
Soyot	n/d	n/d	n/d	n/d	n/d	n/d	2769	2,739
Teleut	n/d	n/d	n/d	n/d	n/d	n/d	2,650	2,534
Telengit	n/d	n/d	n/d	n/d	n/d	n/d	2,395	2368
Kamchadal	n/d	n/d	n/d	n/d	n/d	n/d	2,293	2,013
Tubalar	n/d	n/d	n/d	n/d	n/d	n/d	1,596	1,533
Chelkan	n/d	n/d	n/d	n/d	n/d	n/d	855	830
Chulym	n/d	n/d	n/d	n/d	n/d	n/d	656	643
Taz	n/d	n/d	n/d	n/d	n/d	n/d	276	256
Alutor	n/d	n/d	n/d	n/d	n/d	n/d	12	10
Kerek	n/d	n/d	n/d	n/d	n/d	n/d	8	3

* Data for different censuses are not equally reliable; n/d means no data available.
† Total is given for 26 ethnic groups included in 1989 and 2002 Censuses.
‡ Reflects changes effective April 17, 2006.
Sources: Rosstat, 2004b, vol. 4, vol. 13; Bogoyavlensky, 2004; RAIPON, 2007.

Indigenous homelands. The annual data pertains to all population living in the homelands, regardless of ethnicity. However, Indigenous minorities typically dominate there (particularly in rural areas), therefore providing a fairly accurate picture of Indigenous population characteristics. The list of Indigenous homelands (районы проживания коренных малочисленных народов Севера) at the *rayony* (county) level is approved by the Russian government. Since 1980, this list has been amended four times (1980, 1987, 1993, and 2000). In 1993, it was altered most significantly. As of 2013, the list includes all or most of the territories of Nenetskiy, Yamal-Nenetskiy, Khanty-Mansiskiy, Dolgan-Nenetskiy (Taimyrskiy), Evenkiiskiy, Chukotskiy, and Koryakskiy autonomous districts (*okrugs*) and parts of other regions in the European and Asiatic North.[6] Most of these are rural areas traditionally settled by indigenous peoples, where they dominate or constitute a sub-stantial proportion of population. Throughout this chapter, I will refer to the indigenous homelands in the official post-1993 interpretation and provide a special note in other cases if necessary.

Another important issue is the definition of ethnicity. According to the methodology adopted by the 2002 Census of Russia, the ethnicity question was open-ended and appeared on the form filled by 100% of respondents, who reported their ethnicity based on self-identification. The ethnicity of children was identified by parents. These principles were identical to previous Soviet censuses (Goskomstat Rossii, 2002).

The 2002 Census targeted 100% of individuals residing in the native homelands. It also gives 100% information on people's ethnicity elsewhere in the country.[7] All census respondents were asked to indicate their ability to speak Russian and up to three other languages (chosen by respondents).[8] This was a change from the 1989 Census where respondents were only requested to indicate their mother tongue—without specifying an ability to speak it. In 2002, to identify an ability of an indigenous respondent to speak a mother tongue, Rosstat assigned a corresponding native language to every indigenous group during the post-census processing: the ability of indigenous respondents to speak their native language was considered against the official list of mother tongues during the census data post-processing (Goskomstat Rossii, 2002: 560).

In addition to the census, this chapter incorporates information from the annually published statistical reports (Goskomstat Rossii, 1999; Rosstat,

2005). These annual datasets include information only on indigenous people
residing in their homelands. Moreover, many variables are available only for
the indigenous population residing in rural areas. This creates some problems with reconciling annual figures with census results.

GEOGRAPHIC OVERVIEW

Indigenous minorities of the Russian North are scattered across the vast
territories of Russia, both in the European and Siberian parts. Saami, Veps,
and Nenets constitute the indigenous minority groups west of the Urals.
Most of the indigenous peoples, however, settle in Siberia, along the Arctic
shore and deep inside the continent (Figure 19.1). Some groups are very
compact, while others (such as Nenets and Evenk) inhabit vast areas of
tundra and/or taiga, crossing physical and administrative boundaries. The
largest concentrations of Indigenous minorities are in the Republic of Sakha,
Khabarovskiy *kray*, and in the west, Siberia. Indigenous minorities are highly
heterogeneous in their ethnic origin, language, history, and culture, as well
as in their traditional way of life. They belong to four different language
families and form several isolated linguistic groups.

Indigenous homelands are located in 22 regions of the Russian
Federation. In contrast to the some other Arctic countries, Indigenous
minority groups do not constitute a majority in *any* of northern territories,

including indigenous autonomous districts (*okrugs*), in which they are titular nations. These administrative units were created in 1930 for ethnic groups with populations over 6,000, but most okrugs have since disappeared (two in the 1930s and three in 2007). There are, as of 2013, four remaining okrugs: Chukotskiy (of Chukchi), Khanty-Mansiiskiy (of Khant and Mansi), Nenetskiy (of Nenets), and Yamalo-Nenetskiy (of Nenets). The majority of population in northern regions is Russian, with substantial portions of Yakut, Buryat, Komi, and Karel in the respective republics. However, indigenous minorities frequently constitute a majority in rural areas, whereas non-indigenous population dominates in cities. This urban–rural majority–minority divide, in conditions of urban primacy and rural isolation, poses political and economic challenges for the indigenous people.

POPULATION DYNAMICS

The indigenous population of the Russian North has demonstrated growth over the last several decades (Table 19.1). However, throughout the Soviet period this growth has been unstable, and several ethnic groups experienced substantial population losses. From about 1950 to the 1980s, the indigenous minority population in the Russian North did not grow at the pace comparable to indigenous populations in Canada or Alaska. Among contributing factors to the slower growth, analysts point out a rapid decrease in the birth rate, stronger assimilation, and the high alcohol-related death rate (Gulevsky & Simchenko, 1994). In addition, a short life expectancy and high infant mortality reflected shortcomings of the health care system in the Soviet North. Whereas infant mortality dramatically declined from 180 per 1,000, according to 1926–1927 Polar Censuses, to 30–40 per 1,000 in the 1980s, it remained much higher than in the rest of Russia. Throughout the entire Soviet period, the indigenous life expectancy, albeit improved, was far behind the non-indigenous rate. A notable slowdown in population growth among the indigenous minorities occurred between the 1970 and 1979 Censuses (3.3% vs. 16.6% in 1959–1970), and resulted from falling birth rates and a mounting assimilation pressure (Bogoyavlensky, 2004; Gulevsky & Simchenko, 1994). In the 1980s, the dynamics were better, with higher population gains (Table 19.1), primarily due to the infamous "anti-alcohol campaign," improvements in health care, and a favourable demographic wave. Still, the population growth has been modest compared to other Arctic regions.

Figure 19.2 Sources of Change in the Indigenous Population, 1989–2002

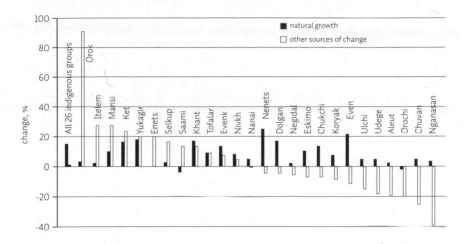

Source: Estimates by Bogoyalvensky, 2004.

POST-SOVIET PERIOD

In October 2002, the indigenous minorities (35) had 243,000 members, including 209,000 for the 26 groups continuously recognized by the 1989 and 2002 Censuses. The latter figure can be compared to 181,500 in 1989 and to 153,200 in 1979. The indigenous minorities of the North, however, constituted just 0.16% of Russia's total population.

As in the past, major drivers of the indigenous population dynamics were the natural growth and non-demographic "ethnic drift" (Figure 19.2). Non-demographic factors included legal changes and shifts in ethnic self-identification. Historically, the assimilation factor was remarkably strong for almost all northern indigenous minority groups. Some estimates show that assimilation reduced the population growth by 70% in 1970–1978 and by 12.0% in 1979–1989 (Bogoyavlensky, 2004). Some estimates demonstrate that the reclaim of the indigenous ethnicity and associated "non-demographic" factors contributed to the 5.5% increase in indigenous minority population in the post-Soviet period (1989–2002).

Indigenous minorities in Russia demonstrate very modest rates of population growth compared to their counterparts in North America. A slower population increase has been persistent in the last decades of the USSR and in the post-Soviet period. There are a number of fundamental

Table 19.2 Selected Indicators of the Indigenous Peoples Living in Home-lands (in the North, Siberia, and the Far East), Census 2002

	Population change 1989–2002*	Births per 1,000 women†	Percentage of urban, %	Percentage in working age, %	Employment in land-based economy, %‡	Employment in selected modern sectors, %‡	Employment rate, %	No secondary education, %	Ability to speak Native language, %
Aleut	-16.1	1,534	21.5	65.2	5.5	13.4	60.8	6.3	7.4
Chukchi	4.4	2,170	16.5	59.7	19.1	5.5	59.1	11.7	45.7
Chuvan	-21.5	1,835	29.8	58.7	12.7	12.4	65.4	7.7	8.9
Dolgan	10.3	2,038	16.9	56.5	29.4	5.2	60.9	13.7	64.1
Enets	19.7	1,919	12.2	61.9	18.9	8.2	46.3	15.5	33.5
Eskimo	2.7	1,993	25.7	62	9	10.9	60.5	6.5	15.4
Even	11.8	2,256	31.3	58.3	12.9	6.6	52.8	10.4	32.6
Evenk	18.8	2,131	22.8	58.6	11.2	7.5	49.5	10	19.7
Itelmen	30.9	1,921	34.4	63.3	5.1	6.2	46.7	6.4	5.3
Ket	37.8	2,304	16.7	60.1	3.8	5.2	54.2	16	30.7
Khant	28.7	2,109	33.2	58.3	11.1	7.5	49.7	16.6	44.2
Koryak	-2.2	1,953	28.6	61.3	9.8	7.3	44.4	12.1	29.3
Mansi	38.1	1,947	50.7	58	6.1	7	49.9	9.8	20.3
Nanai	2.3	2,130	28.3	64.1	7.5	4.7	40.0	8.5	26.5
Negidal	-3.4	2,210	22.8	61	11.4	3.5	39.3	11.4	6.3
Nenets	20.8	2,494	17	53.2	25.7	4.7	48.2	25.7	70.7
Nganasan	-33.9	2,158	18.1	56.5	18.6	3.9	42.2	13.2	50.1
Nivkh	11.5	1,986	46.7	62.9	9.8	5.1	48.2	10	9.8
Orochi	-22.3	1,974	35.2	62.9	23.5	5.6	55.5	6.8	4.3
Saami	8.5	1,813	38.4	61.6	13.9	8.4	47.9	11.9	32.1
Selkup	19.2	2,152	15.9	61.9	12.2	8.8	40.9	18.5	30.7
Tofalar	15.2	1,917	5.8	63.2	3.7	3.5	19.3	19.2	15.8
Udege	-12.9	2,298	22	63.2	12.3	3.6	44.2	13	9.1
Orok	93.2	1,748	56.7	65.8	12.2	5.1	34.4	9.4	3.7
Ulcha	-8.2	2,121	15.2	61.3	8.5	11.2	37.0	14.5	13.4
Yukagir	35.7	2,277	42	57.1	12.5	6.6	63.2	8.1	27.5

This table represents only 26 ethnic groups included in 1989 and 2002 Censuses.
* Data for all Russia.
† Calculated as the ratio between the total number of births and total number of women who reported having children (multiplied by 1,000), information for women 15 years of age and over.
‡ Land-based economy includes agriculture, hunting, fishing, forestry, and related industries.
"Modern" sectors include administration, security, finance, real estate, business, social services, transport, construction, and communication.
Sources: Rosstat, 2004b, vol. 13; Sokolovski, 2006.

reasons for such a slow dynamic, some of which I will discuss below in more detail. Analysts consistently identify five major reasons for small population gains among the indigenous minorities: rapid decline in fertility; high mortality (especially infant and alcohol-related); low level of socio-economic well-being; inadequate health care; and strong assimilation pressures (Bogoyavlensky, 2004; Donskoy Robbek, & Donskoy, 2001; Sokolova, 1995).

It must be pointed out that there is notable differentiation in population dynamics among the indigenous minorities (Table 19.1 and 19.2, Figure 19.2). Some groups experienced big population gains (e.g., Nenets, Khant, Evenk, and Mansi), while others demonstrated substantial losses (e.g., Nganasan,[9] Orochi, Aleut, and Ulchi). Population numbers of many groups remained essentially the same as in 1989. As becomes clear in the following analysis, this differentiation stems from dissimilarities in the natural growth and non-demographic factors among these groups. However, statistically, the inter-group differences are largely attributable to "non-demographic sources" of population dynamic (ethnic drift and legal changes). The latter explain 92.1% of variance, thus highlighting the strong impact of the post-Soviet institutional reforms.

Analyzing recent indigenous minorities' population change, Khruschev, Klokov, and Stupin (2008) identified several general patterns. First, the larger indigenous minorities post higher population gains and higher natural growth. Second, larger groups are less urbanized and are better in retaining their mother tongue. Third, indigenous populations living in autonomous territories have higher growth rates and greater native language retention rates. Fourth, rural population drives indigenous population growth (higher fertility, easier to find indigenous partners, and weaker assimilation), whereas urban indigenous populations have lower fertility and mainly grow due to migration from the countryside.

DEMOGRAPHIC TREND

Annual statistics indicate that over the period between 1989 and 2002 (Figure 19.2), only two of 26 northern indigenous nations experienced a natural decline. However, many minority groups exhibited a dramatic change in their demographic dynamics in the mid-1990s, after the post-Soviet socio-economic crisis fully unfolded. The analysis based on detailed statistical reports available since 1996 (Goskomstat Rossii, 1999; Rosstat, 2005), shows that 12 indigenous groups have experienced natural decline

Figure 19.3 Crude Birth and Death Rates (per 1,000) Among the Indigenous Numerically Small Peoples of the Russian North, 1989–2004

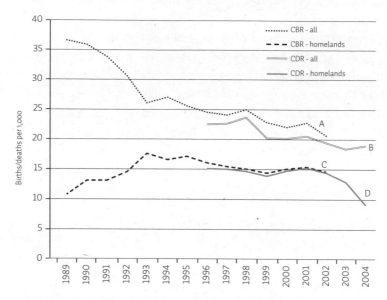

A. Crude birth rate for all 26 indigenous groups regardless of residence from 1989–2002 (an estimate by Bogoyavlenskiy, 2004).
B. Crude birth rate for indigenous minorities living in their homelands from 1996–2004 (Gokomstat Rossii, 1999; Rosstat 2005).
C. Crude death rate for 26 indigenous groups regardless of residence from 1989–2002 (an estimate by Bogoyavlenskiy, 2004).
D. Crude death rate for 35 indigenous minorities living in their homelands from 1996–2004 (Gokomstat Rossii, 1999; Rosstat, 2005).

between 1996 and 2004, including nine having persistent natural loss throughout these years.

As a result of high death rates and rapidly falling birth rates in the 1990s, the natural growth among indigenous minorities taken together declined from 19.7 in 1984–1988 to 5.9 per 1,000 in 1999–2002 (Bogoyavlensky, 2004). In other worlds, indigenous minority groups faced a threefold reduction of natural growth over merely one decade. This demographic shock was instigated by dramatic social and economic challenges of the post-Soviet transitional period. Below I survey fertility and mortality dynamics and discuss the unusual patterns of the demographic transition among the indigenous minorities.

FERTILITY

Indigenous fertility in the Russian North in the last few decades gradually declined. This is a common trend for Native peoples across the Arctic (AHDR, 2004), most of whom exhibit receding crude birth and fertility rates. It is also generally consistent with the pattern of the demographic transition. However, the fertility decline among the Indigenous minorities in the Russian North in the 1990s was exceptionally rapid and driven by socioeconomic cataclysms in the post-Soviet North (Fondahl, 1995; Semenov & Petrov, 2001). By the late 1990s, the crude birth rate dropped to 17.6 per 1,000 from 30.2 in 1984–1988 (Bogoyavlensky, 1994; 2004, data for 26 groups) or, according to a different source, from 31.9 in 1989 to 16.2 in 2003 (Klokov Petina, & Khruschev, 2004, includes 35 indigenous groups living in their homelands). Based on the annual statistics available for the indigenous homelands only (Goskomstat Rossii, 1999; Rosstat, 2004), during the late 1990s and early 2000s birth rates continued to fall, although at a modest pace. They dropped by about 3.0 points between 1996 and 2004, as the number of births continued to decline (Figure 19.3).

In comparative terms, the birth rate of the indigenous minorities of the Russian North is below the Arctic average of 19.7 (AHDR, 2004). However, it is much higher than in the rest of Russia (e.g., 10.2 in 2005 [Rosstat, 2006]). In fact, some indigenous minorities are among the most "fertile" ethnic groups in the country (Table 19.2): Nenets, Even, and Chukchi were among the top 20 in the number of children per woman (2.5, 2.3, and 2.2 compared to just 1.4 for ethnic Russians [Rosstat, 2004b]).

Similar to other Arctic regions (e.g., Romaniuc, 2003), there is evidence of links between the integrity of the traditional Indigenous culture (e.g., measured by the native language proliferation) and higher fertility (see detailed analysis in Petrov, 2008). To a lesser extent, high indigenous fertility can be associated with conditions of "underdevelopment," such as low levels of education and economic participation (particularly in the "modern" industries) among indigenous people, especially women. In fact, indigenous northerners are among the least educated Russian citizens: 41.5% lack high school education compared to 22.4% in the federation (Rosstat, 2004b). Indigenous people, again especially women, are also less economically active and have fewer employment opportunities than the non-indigenous population. According to the 2002 Census (Table 19.2), the Aboriginal employment rate is only 52.0% (Rosstat, 2004b). In addition, about 75% of indigenous people are rural dwellers (Table 19.2).

Although the underlying reasons for high fertility among the indigenous people in Russia are similar to indigenous populations elsewhere, the nature of rapidly declining fertility is rather complex and, largely, is not attributable to the "conventional" drivers of the demographic transition (e.g., "modernization," improvements in family socio-economic status, penetration of education, etc.), since none of these conditions can be observed. To the contrary, similarly to all Russia's citizens, indigenous northerners were affected by the economic crisis that unfolded after the collapse of the USSR (Donskoy Robbek, & Donskoy, 2001). Deteriorating economic well-being, diminishing social assistance, and a growing uncertainty in economic future forced families to engage in coping mechanisms, including delaying or foregoing childbirth. The crisis was particularly severe in the North, where price hikes and shortfalls in goods, fuel, and food supplies (due to the failures of the centralized delivery system) were accompanied by backlogs in wage payments. The post-Soviet economic shock was an especially powerful factor in the early 1990s, when the indigenous crude birth rate dropped from almost 40 to 26 per 1,000 over just a few years (Figure 19.3). However, studies demonstrated that purely economic factors did not entirely explain the overall fertility decline in the North (Petrov, 2006). Whereas the direct role of economic crisis was considerable, the decrease in fertility was also related to the rapid fertility transition amid deep changes in the traditional socio-economic organization and existential conditions of indigenous households (see "Economic Changes and Demographic Trends" section below).

In sum, the rapid fertility transition among the indigenous peoples was set off by a sudden economic crisis and institutional reforms, not by improving social and economic conditions. Changes in lifestyle and family behaviour, caused by the crisis, have long-term consequences. Even after the acute economic problems were partially resolved in the early 2000s (i.e., after the direct impact of the crisis was lifted), birth rates failed to increase (Figure 19.3), which indicates that the fertility transition is likely to be irreversible. This conclusion leads to a potentially paradoxical situation in the indigenous demographic dynamic, in which fertility transition is not accompanied by mortality transition. In other words, falling fertility coexists with high mortality. Thus, the indigenous population in the Russian North has experienced an unusual type of demographic transition, in which the decline in fertility outstripped the decline in mortality. If this distortion is not alleviated in the long-term (i.e., mortality does not eventually decline), it may lead to a true demographic crisis and trigger depopulation.

MORTALITY

In the past three decades, indigenous mortality in Russia was persistently high and was not declining, except for some short periods, most remarkably in the late 1980s during the anti-alcohol campaign (Fondahl, 1995). This trend illustrates a stalled mortality transition and contrasts with other northern indigenous nations, which experienced steady declines in mortality since the 1960s (AHDR, 2004; Romaniuc, 2003). From 1989 to 2002, the indigenous death rate in Russia increased by about 1.0 per 1,000 (see also Klokov, Pelina, & Khruschev, 2004), although by 2004 it receded to the pre-crisis levels (see Figure 19.3). The death rate peaked in the early 1990s (over 17.0 per 1,000!). Despite mortality among the indigenous minorities declining slightly during the early 2000s (Figure 19.3), it still drastically deviated from expected levels, given the young demographic structure of these ethnic groups. For the 26 minorities living in their homelands, the average death rate in 1996–2004 was 13.6 per 1,000 (Rosstat, 2005) compared to just 4.3 per 1,000 in Nunavut (Statistics Canada, 2006) and around 8.0 in Greenland (AHDR, 2004).

An increasing death rate in the middle-age cohorts is closely related to the growth in the unnatural causes of death among the indigenous people. The share of such causes (including accidents, poisoning, injuries, suicides, and murders) in the indigenous mortality reached 37%, as reported for the West Siberian nations (Bogoyavlensky, 2004). Ziker (2002) identified 60% of deaths, which occurred in the Taimyr community of Ust'-Avam between 1991 and 1997, as violent. This is true especially for indigenous men of working age. Although unnatural causes make an important contribution into the indigenous mortality elsewhere across the Arctic due to an array of social issues (e.g., Trovato, 2000; Romaniuc, 2003), their impact in Russia is much higher than anywhere else in the North (cf. in Greenland, 17.5%; in Alaska, 24.6% [AHDR, 2004], in Canada, 22% [Health Canada, 2000]). Alcohol addiction frequently is the underlying reason for unnatural deaths, as well as a strong contributor to morbidity. Annually, over 2,500 residents of the indigenous homelands are diagnosed with clinical forms of alcoholism (Rosstat, 2005). It has been speculated that as much as two-thirds of all deaths in some indigenous homelands can be directly or indirectly attributed to alcohol-related causes (Anisimov, 2002).

High mortality in the young and middle-age cohorts is associated with an extremely low life expectancy of Russia's indigenous minorities. Even prior to the breakup of the USSR, the indigenous life expectancy was only about 60 years, which was at least 10 years shorter than the national average in 1989 (AHDR, 2004). This also was approximately 10 years less than the life expectancy of Native Canadians (Romaniuc, 2003). In the 1970s and 1980s, by some accounts, the life expectancy of the indigenous population in Russia (especially males) was as much as 18 to 20 years less than of the non-indigenous northern population (Bakulin and Osipov, 1993). Thus, the life expectancy gap between the indigenous northerners and the non-Native population in Russia/USSR was substantially deeper than in other northern countries. Inadequate health care and social marginalization of indigenous minorities have often been cited as major factors influencing the life expectancy differential.

In the post-Soviet period, the life expectancy of the indigenous people of the North declined even further. The socio-economic crisis and the liberalization of hard liquor sales appeared to be strong contributing forces to this negative trend (Anisimov, 2002; Ziker, 2002). Some existing estimates suggest that the life expectancy of the indigenous northerners fell to 50 years by the mid-1990s. (For data on the Chukotka region, see Chernukha, Chernukha, Nikitin, & Voevoda, 2003. For the Evenkiya region, see Anisimov, 2002.) That is, life expectancy returned to the 1979 level (AHDR, 2004). For example, in 2005 the life expectancy at birth of the predominantly indigenous rural population in Chukotskiy okrug (Chukchi and Chuvan) was 50.8 years (46.9 for males and 55.4 for females), and in Koryakskiy okrug (mostly Koryak) it was 51.3 years (44.9 for males and 61.2 for females). In fact, the population of these two indigenous homelands demonstrated the lowest life expectancy in Russia, 13 years below the nation's average (63.8) for the rural population (Rosstat, 2006).

Encouragingly, however, between 1989 and 2002, indigenous infant death rates were in an unstable but persistent decline, while mortality in middle-age cohorts, especially among males, was on the rise. The drop in infant mortality from 41.1 in 1984–1988 to 27.6 per 1,000 in 1999–2002 (Bogoyavlensky, 2004), albeit good news, does not look impressive, given that infant mortality is close to 10.0 in most Arctic regions outside Russia

(AHDR, 2004). In remote northern autonomous regions (Chukotskiy, Koryakskiy, and Evenkiiskiy okrugs) infant mortality rates soared up to 52.8 per 1,000 in 1997 (Goskomstat Rossii, 1999). The structure of infant death causes reflects a deep social crisis and the lack of childcare and medical services in the Russian North (Semenov & Petrov, 2001). Many areas had high rates of infant injuries and accidents, perinatal deaths, and respiratory diseases.

POST-SOVIET ETHNIC DRIFT

Ethnic drift and assimilation have been factors of indigenous population dynamics for centuries, both in pre- and post-contact times. During the Soviet period, the pressure of Russian assimilation dramatically increased due to the mass in-migration of Russians (and other Russian-speaking ethnic groups) and the implementation of the Russian-based education system. Rising number of mixed marriages, declining traditionalism, and increased migration to cities were contributing factors in strengthening assimilation in the last decades of the USSR. For instance, between 1971 and 1990, the share of mixed marriages among Dolgan increased from 26.3% to 37.8%, among Nenets increased from 31.4% to 47.0%, and among Nandganasan increased from 15.1% to 59.0% (Skobelev, 2004). On occasion, Moscow exercised its right to officially amalgamate, split, or rename ethnic groups. All these processes slowed down the population growth and undermined the demographic vitality of indigenous populations in the Soviet North.

Ethnic drift and assimilation were important drivers of population dynamics in the post-Soviet period. The analysis conducted by Bogoyavlensky (2004), who compared census population figures and annual population estimates based on natural growth between 1989 and 2002, demonstrated that as many as 12 indigenous ethnic groups between 1989 and 2002 grew mostly due to "non-demographic" sources[10] (Figure 19.2), namely ethnic drift. Beneficiaries of ethnic drift were smaller indigenous groups, which experienced different degrees of "revival" in recent years (e.g., Saami). Other groups, especially living in oil-booming areas (e.g., Khant and Mansi), gained population from mass re-registrations amid the windfall of benefits for indigenous peoples.[11] Federal and regional laws supporting Native populations passed in the 1990s provided additional economic incentives for people to reclaim their indigenous status. The estimated effect of non-demographic factors on population growth in

1989–2002 (Bogoyavlensky, 2004) was remarkable for large groups such as Khant (43.4%), Evenk (34.5%), and Mansi (75.3%). No less important components of "non-demographic" change were legislative amendments (in particular, in respect to the legal recognition of certain ethnic groups as separate entities), as well as the confusion caused by past errors in data collection (e.g., Enets vs. Nenets, Orok vs. Orochi, Even vs. Evenk).

Other Indigenous minorities, however, remained under a strong assimilation pressure from both Russians and larger indigenous groups (Figure 19.2). Available estimates (Bogoyavlensky, 2004) show that 14 indigenous groups lost population due to ethnic drift. Among them, eight experienced net population loss between 1989 and 2002: Aleut, Eskimo, Orochi, Udege, Chuvan, Ulchi, Nganasan, and Koryak (Table 19.1). In all of these cases, the non-demographic loss overwhelmed the natural growth, except for Orochi, who had witnessed the natural decline in addition to ethnic drift. Assimilation tendencies will be considered in more detail in the following section on Indigenous languages.

An employment and existential separation of Indigenous men and women (reindeer herding semi-nomadic men and village-based women) is seen as a factor for an increasing share of mixed marriages and Métisation of the Indigenous minorities. In some areas children born in mixed marriages constitute the lion's share of the indigenous population growth: for example, in the Khabarovsk region, such children constitute 90% of all births delivered by indigenous women (Fauser, 2005). It is uncertain whether these offspring will maintain indigenous traditions or indigenous identities, especially given that they are likely to be detached from the traditional lifestyle and Native society.

NATIVE LANGUAGE PROFICIENCY AND ETHNIC DRIFT

It may be argued that Native language proficiency reflects the true level of belonging to Native cultures and may be a good proxy of an ethnic group's vitality. During the last Soviet decades, the recorded ability of indigenous minorities (all groups together) to speak their mother tongue progressively declined (by 0.5% in 1970, 4.6% in 1979, and 9.4% in 1989) with all ethnic groups but Aleuts losing the knowledge of a respective Native language, according to the 1989 USSR Census. Indigenous people living in their homelands and in rural areas demonstrated higher degrees of mother tongue preservation than their counterparts residing outside native homelands and in cities by approximately 20% in both cases (Gulevsky & Simchenko, 1994).

The census of 2002 indicated that the overwhelming majority of indigenous peoples in the Russian North spoke Russian. The figure varied from 88.4% for Nenets to 95%–100% for most Aboriginal nations (Rosstat, 2004b). Typically, urban indigenous populations had a near 100% ability to speak Russian, whereas rural residents had a noticeably lower likelihood to be Russian speakers, although in all cases the percentage of Russian speakers exceeded 80%. A strong penetration of the Russian language is, of course, not surprising given its dominant status in the education system, government, media, and other domains.

On the other hand, the 2002 Census revealed that Aboriginal languages were fading. If in 1989 over 60% the Indigenous people (26 groups) indicated a Native language as their mother tongue (Tishkov & Stepanov, 2004), by 2002 only 38.5% reported an ability to speak the Native language of their ethnic group (see Table 19.2). (But we should take note that these data are only for indigenous residents of the North, Siberia, and the Far East. Furthermore, the language questions in 1989 and 2002 were formulated very differently.) Smaller indigenous groups demonstrated the poorest knowledge of a mother tongue. In eight of them, less than 10% of the population was able to speak their Native language in 2002 (e.g., Orok, Aleut, Negidal, Orochi, Itelmen), while virtually all representatives of these ethnic groups reported to be Russian speakers. These are clearly endangered languages still spoken by only several dozens of people (e.g., Orok, 11 persons; Orochi, 18 persons, Aleut, 33 persons). However, this linguistic and cultural disintegration is not only a prerogative of the small indigenous peoples. Only 19.7% of Evenk, a second largest, although spatially dispersed ethnic group, spoke their mother tongue. This is partially due to a doubled assimilation pressure from both Russians and Yakut.

As I reported elsewhere, Native language preservation exhibited a positive and strong relationship with the level of engagement in a land-based economy. A positive correlation with the lowest levels of schooling reflects the destructive impact of the mainstream (Russian-based) education on Native languages. More populous indigenous peoples tend to maintain higher levels of Native language penetration than smaller ethnic groups (Khruschev, Klokov, & Stupin, 2008). Only 17.6% of indigenous people from minority groups with less than 5,000 members speak their mother tongue. This figure, by comparison, is 36.3% for midsize groups (5,000–15,000), and 44.1% for the largest ones (over 15,000). Place of residence also matters: the rate of Native language proficiency in the autonomous *okrugs* is almost three times higher than outside them (Khruschev, Klokov, & Stupin, 2008). At the same time, there is no apparent statistical relationship between indigenous language proficiency and population dynamics.

Among ethnic groups with low numbers of Native speakers (below 20%), there are two distinct categories: those that had population loss (e.g., Evenk, Udege, Chuvan, and Orochi) and those that experienced population gain (e.g., Orok, Itelmen, and Nivkh), both mostly due to ethnic drift. In the former case, the direction of the drift was toward assimilation, whereas in the latter case it was toward reclaiming the indigenous identity and ethnic revival. In both cases, though, the population base of these ethnic groups is quite unsustainable, and the future of indigenous cultures remains uncertain.

ECONOMIC CHANGES AND DEMOGRAPHIC TRENDS

As noted before, the introduction of the Soviet productions system (based on collective and state farms—*kolkhoz, sovkhoz, gospromkhoz,* etc.), and, later, the arrival of the market economy, have had profound impacts on vital characteristics of the indigenous population. Policies of collectivization and sedentarization launched in the 1930s dramatically transformed traditional activities and ways of life (Khruschev & Klokov, 2001). Nomadic reindeer herding became semi-nomadic with reduced seasonal migrations, and a traditional family nomadism gave way to a brigade-based form. The number of nomads was steadily declining throughout the late Soviet period, hitting the bottom in 1988–1989. However, even though women were partially restrained from living in the tundra, the state farm model of production retained some elements of the traditional subsistence activities (in both husbandry and hunting). In the 1970s and 1980s, both harvesting of wild reindeer and the size of domesticated herds increased (Glomsrod & Aslaksen, 2006).

Sedentarization affected demographic processes. First of all, it resulted in a decreasing family size. Available observations suggest that families permanently residing in settlements tend to be 20% to 30% smaller than nomadic families, reflecting lower levels of fertility. Interestingly, nomadic families also appear to be more prone to be two-parent families, as opposed to single-parent (usually single-mother) families in settlements. Most analysts agree that sedentarization, despite delivering more access to health care, better housing, and services, had an adverse effect on the demographic viability of indigenous peoples (Ulvevadet & Klokov, 2004).

After the downfall of the Soviet economic system, indigenous enterprises and households faced a sharp decline in government subsidies and favourable economic arrangements (e.g., a guaranteed purchase of a production output). On the other hand, indigenous people gained an opportunity to increase their private livestock, form communes, and return to a traditional and neo-traditional organization of economic activity. In the 1990s, nomadism regained its strength with a 30% growth just over the first post-Soviet decade (Khruschev & Klokov, 2001). Almost 50% of domesticated reindeer is currently in private hands, up from 11%–13% in the 1960s and 1970s (Ulvevadet & Klokov, 2004).

Overall, however, economic changes delivered by market reforms seem to have a negative impact on the traditional economy and demographic processes among indigenous people. As noted earlier, traditional division of labour and family organization of tundra reindeer herders, although substantially altered by Soviet economic reforms and forced sedentarization, were still partially preserved under the *kolkhoz/sovkhoz* system. Most families were still involved in nomadic or semi-nomadic reindeer herding, in which traditional roles of men and women were somewhat maintained (Klokov, Petina, & Khruschev, 2004). Institutional reforms of the 1990s resulted in the quick erosion of this system, especially for some ethnic groups (note that Nenets are the most remarkable exclusion from this trend). Indigenous families had to adjust to a deteriorating economic situation and diminishing state subsidies. One of the ways to adapt was to permanently resettle to villages and abandon reindeer herding in favour of more profitable employment for either or both genders (Glomsrod & Aslaksen, 2006). This move triggered fertility control mechanisms such as parity-related family limitation. Besides, the economic utility of children in non-nomadic settings diminished while the cost of raising them increased. In other cases, even if a complete sedentarization was not the case, there was a change in labour (and family) relations between genders. Men tended to continue with nomadic reindeer herding, whereas women (whose labour has always been underpaid in the *sovkhoz* system) became more prone to stay and find alternative jobs in villages. This "disintegrated family husbandry" effectively separated indigenous families. Furthermore, the separation of men and women negatively affected the probability to marry, and the number of never-married men and women substantially increased, as did the number of extramarital births and single-parent families (Fauser, 2005). All these processes, of course, had a decisively adverse impact on fertility among indigenous peoples.

The connection between fertility and traditional lifestyles is also evidenced by higher fertility rates among the indigenous minorities, which managed to expand the traditional economy. Nenets are the case in point with a 20% population growth, the highest fertility, and highly successful family-based reindeer herding (Klokov, Petina, & Khruschev, 2004). In addition, existing studies show a strong statistical relationship between traditional (nomadic) family reindeer husbandry, changes in number of reindeers, and population dynamics of indigenous ethnic groups (Khruschev & Klokov, 2001).

POPULATION STRUCTURE

The current population composition of the indigenous minorities reflects two major processes of the indigenous population dynamic: the demographic crisis (falling birth rates, increasing male and middle-age death rates, and low life expectancy) and the non-demographic change (assimilation or reclamation of the indigenous identity). The indigenous population structure, to some extent, mirrors the general patterns of demographic change in Russia (such as the presence of the baby-boom and echo waves). Population pyramids for northern indigenous minorities (aggregated for 26 groups consistently recognized by the 1989 and 2002 Censuses) and Russia's total population are presented in Figure 19.4. Census 2002 data reveal noticeable dissimilarities (or anomalies) that make indigenous nations distinct from the rest of the county's population. The following points are the most notable.

First of all, there was a weak effect of the first baby-boom wave in the cohorts between 40 and 55 years old. This circumstance may be explained by very high Aboriginal infant and child mortality rates in the 1950s and high contemporary death rates in these age cohorts. Besides, these generations, reaching their maturity in the 1970s, were deeply affected by assimilation, which was particularly strong in 1970–1979 (Bogoyavlensky, 2004).

Figure 19.4 Population Structure of the Russian Federation and the Indigenous Peoples of the North, 2002 Census

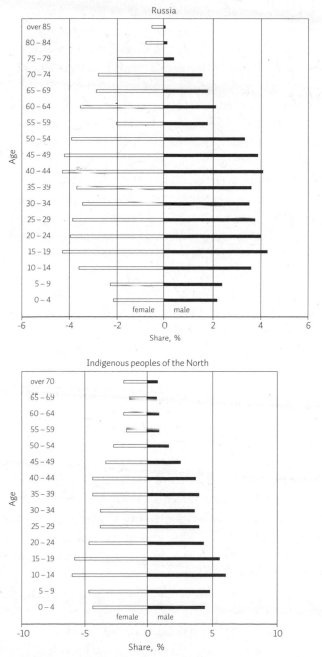

Source: Rosstat, 2004b.

Second, there is evidence that the social policies implemented in the 1980s had strong positive effects. Improvements in the social "climate," including child care and economic well-being among the "small nations," coupled with rapidly falling infant mortality, led to a strong showing of the second baby-boom wave. This wave is reflected in a high share of teenaged population (10–19 years old). In fact, teenagers comprised 24.1% of the indigenous population, compared to 16.0% across the nation. Needless to add, this wave in indigenous cohorts would have been even more profound if there had been no assimilation and miscegenation. Meanwhile, the number of mixed marriages in the 1980s was quite considerable and was rising.

Third, indigenous ethnic groups are female dominated. Women comprise 53.7% of the population (53.4% in Russia). Moreover, women prevail almost in all age cohorts staring at age 15, despite substantially trailing boys in early childhood (952.5 girls per 1,000 boys). A higher mortality of male children is an explanation here. The indigenous minorities are facing a male population crisis both in young and middle-age cohorts. At the age of 40–44, there are already 1,311.8 women per 1,000 men. Aboriginal communities lose their male population to devastating death rates. However, it must be noticed that the degree of female dominance is not the same for different "small nations." Most distorted sex composition is found for Evens (see Figure 19.5), Negidals, and Nganasans (more than 1,250 females per 1,000 males).

Notably, age structures substantially differed among indigenous ethnic groups, reflecting both their demographic "health" and varying assimilation pressures. For example (see Figure 19.5), Chukchis appeared to be more affected by the recent declines in fertility (proportionally smaller young-age cohorts) and had an older population than the Nenets (median age was 24.2 and 21.6, respectively). The Evens showed an exceptionally skewed sex structure. Perhaps the Negidals' pyramid may serve as an example of a strong assimilation effect: small bride-age female and middle-working age male cohorts coupled with relatively substantial share of elderly.

Because of high mortality and low life expectancy, indigenous minorities have a very small number of elderly; people over 60 years old comprise only 6.3% of the total indigenous population in contrast to 21.0% in Russia (Rosstat, 2004b). The Aboriginal elderly suffered throughout their lifespan from the hardships of the 1930s and 1940s, the social marginalization of the 1950s through the 1970s, and the economic and public health crises of the 1990s.

Figure 19.5 Population Structure of Selected Indigenous Ethnic Groups, 2002 Census

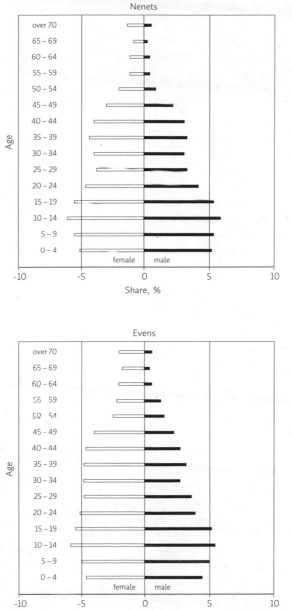

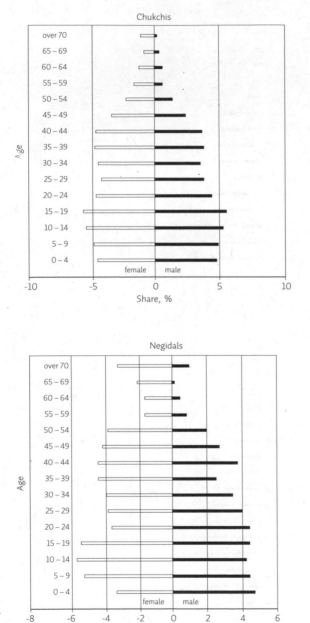

Source: Rosstat, 2004b.

Indigenous middle-working age cohorts (aged 40–59) are proportionally smaller when compared to Russia. The middle-age cohorts are subjected to several major negative demographic factors: high mortality, particularly from unnatural causes (stemming from social marginalization, alcoholism, and criminalization), and the virtual absence of the first baby-boom wave. Indigenous males were more affected by high mortality than women for various but mostly social reasons (Klokov, Petina, & Khruschev, 2004). Besides, this age group has experienced considerable assimilation pressures.

Unlike the national population structure, age cohorts between 20 and 26 are noticeably small. One explanation is assimilation given that the 1970s and early 1980s were decades of increasing miscegenation, acculturation, and migration to large cities (Bogoyavlensky, 2004). Many children were educated in boarding schools away from their families. In addition, the young northerners are exposed to assimilation by out-migrating for education or work.

Finally, the post-Soviet generation of indigenous northerners is numerically smaller than it could have been, if the trends of the 1980s had been preserved. The economic crisis and social problems left indigenous minorities with fertility levels below that of other Native peoples across the Arctic. In addition, the hardships of the 1990s eroded the social infrastructure, medical services, and child care support. The "children of the crisis" face additional challenges to ensure the survival of their ethnic groups.

CONCLUSION

Post-Soviet demographic trends among indigenous peoples of the Russian North give serious reasons to be worried about the future of the indigenous population, especially small ethnic groups. Whereas the indigenous population grew between 1989 and 2002, the indigenous minorities experienced nothing short of a demographic crisis with a rapid fall of fertility and high mortality. Both of these trends, in such form and sequence, were not expected under the conventional theory of demographic transition. They are also at odds with the trends observed in other parts of the Arctic. Much of the negative dynamic in the Russian North is directly attributed to dramatic economic, institutional, social, and cultural changes in the region after the collapse of the Soviet Union. Some of these changes were destructive to Native lifestyles and social well-being (and, in turn, to demographic trends), although others helped to raise an appreciation of indigenous identity. Formidable social and economic challenges to indigenous minorities are exacerbated by the deeply remote and isolated location of northern Aboriginal homelands. However, current problems did not appear instantly. Rather, they reflect the decades of demographic uncertainty associated with the Soviet economic and social reforms, which impacted well-being and health care, and also the strong assimilation pressures induced by the Soviet system.

The minority status, with the share of indigenous peoples in their homeland regions declining dramatically in the last 50 years, exacerbates the political and economic dependency of the indigenous people and undermines their ability to defend their rights and bargain for more privileges. The process of amalgamating autonomous okrugs into large, Russian-dominated provinces even further diminishes the level of fate control exercised by the indigenous minority groups. The indigenous minorities require practical attention from the federal and regional governments in Russia, not declarative statements in unenforceable laws, as it frequently is the case (Murashko, 2003). Indigenous minorities must be the subject of special socio-demographic policies, which are yet to be developed. Maintaining traditional economy and lifestyle is not only the way to achieve social justice and equality for the indigenous peoples but also the avenue to ensure the demographic vitality of these ethnic groups.

AUTHOR'S NOTE

I would like to thank Anatole Romaniuk and Frank Trovato for their determination and valuable comments.

NOTES

1. Parts of this chapter are based on A. Petrov, 2008, "Lost Generations? Indigenous Population of the Russian North in the Post-Soviet Era," *Canadian Studies in Population*, 35(2), 273–298.
2. At least 12 indigenous minorities of the North appear in *The Red Book of Russia: Disappearing Ethnic Groups in Russia* (http://www2.childfest.ru/good/42/02/redbook/index.htm).
3. Sokolovski (2006) provides a useful overview of historical change in defining indigeneity and in the legal recognition of the indigenous peoples in Russia.
4. At the time, Russia officially recognized 35 ethnic groups, but the census considered Alutor together with Koryak. Out of 35 peoples, however, only 28 are

geographically "northern peoples," while the other seven added ethnic groups reside in South Siberia regions.

5. As recognized by the Russian Association of Indigenous Peoples of the North (RAIPON) and in executive orders of the Russian Government (see Table 19.1).

6. In 2007, Evenkiiskiy and Taimyrskiy okrugs were amalgamated with Ktasnoyarskiy kray; and Koryakskiy okrug with Kamchatskaya oblast' (now Kamchatskiy kray).

7. Certainly, many experts expressed strong reservations about the accuracy of the 2002 Census. There are allegations of fraud and misrepresentation of results, as well as of failure to collect information about a substantial portion of Russia's population (see Heleniak, 2003).

8. The question (9.2) asks what language(s) does the respondent "master" (владеет), i.e., is able to speak.

9. Partly attributable to errors in the 1989 Census.

10. Unfortunately, the annual natural growth statistics for the entire period between 1989 and 2002 is not available. Bogoyavlenskiy used unpublished Goskomstat materials. Moreover, his analysis of natural growth included only Native home-lands, and, thus, tends to underestimate population numbers, especially for certain ethnic groups (e.g., Nanai, Udege). Consequently, this data should be used and interpreted with caution.

11. In post-Soviet Russia, people of mixed origin are granted an opportunity to freely change their "official" ethnicity. This was not the case in the USSR, where citizens had to permanently choose their "passport" ethnicity once, at the age of 16. A passage of new, more liberal legislation by regional governments in some instances had an effect of a sudden surge in indigenous population, similar to the aftermath of the Bill C-31 in Canada.

REFERENCES

Anisimov, N. (2002, December 26). Spasti severyan ot vymiraniya (Save Northerners from extinction). *Evenkiiskaya Zhizn'* 58(8371).

Arctic Human Development Report (AHDR). (2004). *Arctic human development report.* Akureyri: Steffansson Arctic Institute.

Bakulin V.V., & Osipov, V.A. (1993). Sovremennyi geodemograficheskii process korennogo naseleniya (Contemporary geo-demographic process of Indigenous population). In *Rossiya, Sever, More (Russia, North, Sea).* 5th Solovetskiy Forum (pp. 42–44). Arkhandel'sk.

Bogoyavlensky, D.D. (1994). Demograficheskie problemy malochislennykh Narodov Severa (Demographic problems of the numerically small peoples of the North). In A.G. Vishnevskiy & N. Rossii (Eds.), *Vtoroi ezhegodnyi demograficheskiy doklad* (pp. 144–160). Moscow: Evrasiya.

———. (2004). Vymiraut li Narody Severa? (Are Northern peoples dying out?). *Demoskop Weekly,* 165–166. Retrieved from http://demoscope.ru/weekly/2004/0165/tema02.php#4

Chernukha, A.D., Chernukha, A.A., Nikitin, Y.P., & Voevoda, M.I. (2003). Mediko-sotsial'nye i demograficheskie problemy narodnostei Aziatskogo Severa (Medico-social and demographic problems of the peoples of the Asian North). *Problemy sotsial'noi gigieny, zdravookhraneniya i istorii meditsiny*, 2(16).

Diatchkova, G. (2001). Indigenous peoples of Russia and political history. *The Canadian Journal of Native Studies*, 21(2), 217–233.

Donskoy, F.S, Robbek, V.A., & Donskoy, R.I. (2001). *Korennye malochislennye narody Severa, Sibiri i Dal'nego Vostoka Rossiskoi Federatsii v pervoi chetverti 21 veka: Problemy i perspectivy* (Indigenous numerically small peoples of the North, Siberia and the Far East of the Russian Federation in the first quarter of the 21 century: Problems and perspectives.) Yakutsk: Institut Problem Malochslennych Narodov Severa Sibirskolo Otdelenia Rossiiskoi Akademii Nauk (Institute of the Problems of the Indigenous Peoples of the North of the Siberian Branch of the Russian Academy of Sciences).

Fauser, V.V. (2005). Naselenie i demografichskoe razvitie Severa Rossii (Population and demographic development of the Russian North). In V.N. Lazhenzev (Ed.), *Sever kak ob'ekt kompleksnykh regional'nykh issledovanii* (pp. 96–106). Syktyvkar: Komi Science Center, Ural Branch of the Russian Academy of Sciences.

Federal'noe Sobranie RF. (1999). *O garantiyakh prav korennykh malochislannykh Narodov Rossiiskoi Frderatsii* (On the guarantees of rights of the numerically small peoples of the Russian North). *Federal Law adopted on April 30, 1999*. Moscow.

Fondahl, G. (1995). The status of Indigenous peoples in the Russian North. *Post-Soviet Geography and Economics*, 36(4), 215–284.

Goskomstat Rossii. (1999). *Sotsialno-ekonomicheskoe polizhenie v raionah prozhivaniya korennyh malochislennyh narodov Severa I priravnennyh k num mestnostyah* (Socio-economic situation in the regions of the habitation of the Indigenous numerically small peoples of the North and Equalized Areas). Moscow: Goskomstat.

————. (2000). *Rossiiskii statisticheskii ezhegodnik* (Russian statistical yearbook). Moscow: Goskomstat.

————. (2002). *Metodologicheskie Voprosy Vasrossiiskoi Perepisi Naseleniya 2002 Goda*. T. 13 (Methodological questions of the 2002 all-Russia population census, vol. 13). Moscow: Goskomstat.

Glomsrod, S., & Aslaken, I. (Eds.). (2006). *The economy of the North*. Oslo-Kongsvinger, Statistics Norway.

Gulevsky, A.N., & Simchenko, Y.B. (1994). *Economy of peoples of Russian North: History and contemporaneity*. Moscow: Institut Etnologii i Antropologii Rossiisskoi Akademii Nauk (Institute of Ethnology and Anthropology of the Russian Academy of Sciences).

Health Canada. (2000). A statistical profile on the health of First Nations in Canada for the year 2000. Retrieved from http://www.hc-sc.gc.ca/fnih-spni/pubs/gen/stats_profil_e.html

Heleniak, T. (1995). Economic transition and demographic change in Russia, 1989–1995. *Post-Soviet Geography and Economics*, 36(7), 446–458.

————. (2003). The 2002 census in Russia: Preliminary results. *Eurasian Geography and Economics, 44*(6), 430–442.

Khruschev, S.A., & Klokov, K.B. (2001). *Severnyi Nomadism v Rossii* (Northern Nomadism in Russia). St. Petersburg: St. Petersburg State University.

Khruschev, S.A., Klokov, K.B., & Stupin, Y.A. (2008). Regional'nye osobennosti dinamiki chislennosti i rasseleniya molochislennykh Narodov Severa Rossii (Regional aspects of population dynamic and settlement of the Indigenous minorities of the Russian North). *Izvestiya Russkogo Geograficheskogo Obschestva, 140*(3), 45–50.

Klokov, K.B., Petina, O.V., & Khruschev, S.A. (2004). *Semeinoye domokhozyaistvo v rayonakh prozhivaniya korennykh narodov Severa.* (Household economy in the regions of habitation of the Indigenous peoples). St. Petersburg: St. Petersburg State University.

Luffman, J., & Sussman, D. (2007). The Aboriginal labour force in Western Canada. *Perspectives on Labour and Income, 8*(1), 14–27.

Murashko, O.A. (Ed.). (2003). *Uchastie korennikh narodov v politicheskoi zhizni stran circumpolyarnogo regiona: Rossiiskaya real'nost' i mezhdunarodniy opyt* (Participation of the Indigenous peoples in the political life of the circumpolar countries). Moscow: IWGIA.

Petrov, A. (2006). *Geopopulyatsionnye processy na Rossiiskom i Kanadskom Severe v 90e gody 20 veka* (Geopopulation processes in the Russian and Canadian North in the 90s of the 20th century). St. Petersburg: Herzen State Pedagogical University of Russia.

————. (2008). Lost generations? Indigenous population of the Russian North in the post-Soviet era. *Canadian Studies in Population, 35*(2), 269–290.

Pika, A.I., & Prokhorov, B.B. (1988). Bol'shie problemy malykh narodov (Big problems of small peoples). *Kommunist, 16,* 76–83.

Poelzer, G., & Fondahl, G. (1997). Indigenous peoples of the Russian North: A decade of progress. *Cultural Survival Quarterly, 21*(3), 30–33.

RAIPON. (2007). Russian Association of Indigenous Peoples of the North. Retrieved from http://raipon.org

Romaniuc, A. (2003). Aboriginal population of Canada: Growth dynamics under conditions of encounter of civilisations. *Canadian Studies in Population, 30*(1), 75–115.

Rosstat. (2004a). *Rossiiskii statisticheskii ezhegodnik 2004g* (Russian statistical yearbook 2004). Moscow: Rosstat.

————. (2004b). *Vserossiiskaya Perepis Naseleniya. TT. 1–14* (All-Russia population census, Vol. 1–14). Moscow: Rosstat. Retrieved from http://www.perepis2002.ru

————. (2005). *Sotsialno-ekonomicheskoe polozhenie v raionah prozhivaniya korennyh malochislennyh narodov Severa i priravnennyh k nim mestnostyah* (Socio-economic situation in the regions of the habitation of the Indigenous numerically small peoples of the North and Equalized Areas). Moscow: Rosstat.

————. (2006). *Demograficheskii ezhegodnik Rossii, 2006* (Demographic yearbook of Russia, 2006). Moscow: Rosstat.

Semenov, S.P, & Petrov, A.N. (2001). Demograficheskiy krizis na Severe Rossii: Istoki i geografiya (Demographic crisis in the Russian North: Roots and geography). *Izvestiya Russkogo Geograficheskogo Obshestva, 133*(3), 89–91.

Shargorodsky, L.T. (1994). *Sovremennye etnicheskiye protsessy u Sel'kupov* (Contemporary ethnic processes of Selkup). Moscow: Institut Etnologii i Antropologii Rossiisskoi Akademii Nauk (Institute of Ethnology and Anthropology of the Russian Academy of Sciences).

Shnirelman, V.A. (1994). Hostages of an authoritarian regime: The fate of the "numerically-small peoples" of the Russian North under Soviet rule. *Études Inuit Studies, 18*(1–2), 201–223.

Skobelev, G.G. (2004, August). Demografia koremmykh narodov Sibiri v 17–20 vv. (Demography of the Indigenous people of Siberia in the 17–20th centuries). *Demoskop Weekly*, 165–166.

Sokolova, Z.A. (1995). Narody Severa: Vyzhivanie v usloviyakh rynochnoi ekonomiki (Peoples of the North: Survival in a market economy). In Z.P. Sokolova (Ed.), *Soisiali'no-ekonomicheskoe i kul'turnoe razvitie Narodov Severa i sibiri: Traditsii i sovremennost'* (Socio-economic and cultural development of the peoples of the North and Siberia: Traditions and modernity) (pp. 265–275). Moscow: Institute of Ethnology and Anthropology of the Russian Academy of Sciences.

Sokolovski, S. (2006, September 29–30). *Russian legal concepts and Indigenous peoples demography*. Paper presented at the International Workshop Indigenous Identity in Demographical Sources, Umeå University, Sweden.

Statistics Canada. (2006). Components of population growth, Canada, provinces and territories. Table 051-0004. Ottawa, ON: Statistics Canada.

Tishkov, V., & Stepanov, V. (2004). Rossiiskaya perepis' v etnicheskom izmerenii (Russian census in ethnic dimension). *Demoskop Weekly*, 155–156. Retrieved from http://demoscope.ru/weekly/2004/0155/index.php

Trovato, F. (2000). Canadian Indian mortality during the 1980s. *Social Biology, 47*(1–2), 135–145.

Ulvevadet, B., & Klokov, K. (2004). *Family-based reindeer herding and hunting economies, and the status and management of wild reindeer/caribou population*. Tromsø: Centre for Saami Studies, University of Tromso.

Ziker, J. (2002). *Peoples of the Tundra: Native Siberians in the post communist transition*. Prospect Heights, IL: Waveland Press.

APPENDIX A
CENSUS CONCEPTS AND DEFINITIONS PERTAINING TO CANADA'S ABORIGINAL POPULATION

1. CENSUS CONCEPTS AND DEFINITIONS PERTAINING TO CANADA'S ABORIGINAL POPULATION

For the longest time, ethnic origin was the ethnocultural characteristic most widely used in Canada to establish Aboriginal affiliation. With the exception of 1891, all Canadian censuses have enumerated Aboriginal populations by means of a question on ethnic origin. The concept of origin refers to the ethnic or cultural group to which a person's ancestors belonged. In theory, this concept could serve to identify the descendants of populations who lived in America when Europeans arrived in the sixteenth and seventeenth centuries (Robitaille & Choinière, 1987). In reality, however, since very few people have thorough and accurate knowledge of their ethnocultural genealogy, only a fraction of true descendants from pre-colonial Aboriginal peoples report an Aboriginal origin during a census. In addition to genealogy, census data on ethnic origin varies according to societal concerns in general (Isajiw, 1993; White, Badets, & Renaud, 1993) and the nature of the socio-political relations the Canadian society maintains (or not) with Aboriginal populations (as indicated by the absence of Métis in most censuses before 1981).

In Canada, the word "Aboriginal" includes many groups with unique heritages, languages, cultural practices, and spiritual beliefs, as well as distinct needs and aspirations. The Indian Act is the only Canadian legislative document that explicitly defines a specific Aboriginal group: Registered Indians (or Status Indians). The concept of Registered Indian was established to determine the right of residency on Indian reserves (Dickason, 2002: 263–265; Savard & Proulx, 1982: 131). The first version of the Indian Act in the confederative era dates back to 1876. Since then, the federal government has made several amendments to it. The latest amendments to the Indian Act were made in 1985[1] and 2010.[2] Section 35 of the 1982 Constitution Act of Canada recognizes three distinct groups of Aboriginal peoples: Indians (First Nations), Métis, and Inuit. Insofar as First Nations are concerned, Canadian legislation further distinguishes between Status Indians, who are registered as an Indian or are entitled to be registered as an Indian according to the Indian Act, and Non-Status Indians, who self-identify as Indian but are not eligible to be registered under the Indian Act. According to the Census of Canada, the population self-reporting as Registered Indian, as defined by the Indian Act, numbered at 623,780 persons in 2006.

Recent censuses allow for the Aboriginal population to be defined according to several criteria, including ethnic origin (ethnicity), identity (self-reported affiliation with an Aboriginal group), Registered Indian status, and band membership (see below). The census also allows for the population to be defined according to specific band affiliations (e.g., a particular Cree First Nation in Manitoba) or a particular linguistic group (e.g., Cree). The 1996 Census of Canada was the first Canadian census to collect information about membership in an Indian band or First Nation. There are 617 different Indian bands in Canada.[3] Since the 1985 amendments to the Indian Act, many Indian bands have exercised the right to establish their own membership codes, whereby it is no longer necessary for a First Nation or band member to be a Registered Indian according to the Indian Act. In 2006, 620,345 persons reported being a member of an Indian band or First Nation.

According to the 2006 Census (the most recent census at the time of this writing), the Canadian Aboriginal population numbered about 1,172,790, including 698,025 North American Indians or First Nation individuals (59.5%), 389,780 Métis (33.2%), 50,480 Inuit (4.3%), and 26,760 others who gave either multiple Aboriginal responses or did not report identity but did report Indian registration or band membership. The population reporting

Census Year	Principal Features and Instructions given to Enumerators/Respondents for Recording Ethnicity, 1961–2006[5]
1961	In the 1961 Census, the instructions to enumerators stated that descent was to be determined along patrilineal lines for all respondents. Mother tongue of the respondent, or the respondent's "ancestor on the male side," was to be used to determine ethnic or cultural group. The census collection staff was instructed to determine whether or not Indians were band members. Treaty Indians were to be coded as band members. Respondents of mixed white and Indian parentage were coded as Indian only if they lived on a reserve. If they lived off-reserve, they were coded according to patrilineal lines.
1971	Self-enumeration was introduced and the ancestry was determined along patrilineal lines. The ancestry question asked: *To what ethnic or cultural group did you or your ancestors (on the male side) belong on coming to this continent?*
1981	This census presented a major departure from the past with respect to the descent rules that were to be applied for ethnic origin. The decision on which method of determining ancestry was appropriate was left to the respondent. The ethnicity question was modified slightly, asking: *To which ethnic or cultural group did you or your ancestors belong on first coming to this continent?* Four categories were offered to Aboriginal respondents: Status Indian, Non-Status Indian, Métis, and Inuit. "Canadian" was accepted as a response when written in by the respondent.
1986	This was the first quinquennial Census of Canada that included comprehensive content. It was also the first census in which a separate question on Aboriginal identity was added to the questionnaire. No specific rules were imposed on how ancestry was to be established. The question on "Ethnic Origin" was rephrased to accommodate multiple responses: *To which ethnic or cultural group(s) do you or did your ancestors belong?* Four categories for the Aboriginal people were listed: Status Indian, Non-status Indian, Métis, and Inuit.
1991–2006	Starting with the 1991 Census, three questionnaires are now being used to collect the data from the on paper or electronically. These questionnaires are translated into 13 Aboriginal languages.
	Following each of these censuses, special post-censal surveys on Aboriginal peoples were conducted. Each of these surveys entailed extensive consultations to help determine the content, and special programs were introduced to encourage participation of the Aboriginal population.
	No specific rules exist as to how ancestry is to be determined. In each census, respondents were permitted to enter multiple responses for ethnic origin. In fact they were encouraged to do so by the wording of the question. The latest version population living in private households in Canada: short form (2A), a long form (2B), and a special version of the long form (2D) for people living in northern areas and on reserves. The on-reserve and northern residents are interviewed by enumerators, while other respondents are given an option to write in their responses to the ethnicity question, which asks: *What were the ethnic or cultural origins of this person's ancestors?* The question in the previous three censuses entailed essentially the same wording: *To which ethnic or cultural group(s) did this person's ancestors belong?* The Aboriginal identity question, first tried out in the 1986 Census, was repeated in the 1996 Census and in the subsequent censuses.
	In each census, persons with Aboriginal ancestry were asked to be specific in their response and to name the Aboriginal group to which they belonged, such as Cree, MicMaw, Ojibway, North American Indian, Métis, etc. Those who identified as Aboriginal were asked to indicate whether or not they had status under the Indian Act of Canada.

Indian registration numbered 623,780, which represents about 53.2% of the total population that reported Aboriginal identity. The Census of Canada shows that 1.678 million persons reported at least one Aboriginal origin in 2006.

Since the late 1990s, the concept of "Aboriginal identity" has become the preferred approach to defining affiliation with an Aboriginal group. Aboriginal identity is a subjective indicator of a person's current affiliation to an Aboriginal group. This concept was introduced in 1986 as a means to improve the enumeration of Aboriginal populations (Statistics Canada, 1989), in response to the growing ineffectiveness of objective indicators of cultural affiliation (such as "real" ethnic origins and mother tongue) for reasons of acculturation and exogamy.[4] According to the Census of Canada, 1,172,790 persons self-identified as Aboriginal in 2006.[5]

Although it is possible to go back to the historical definitions pertaining to the Aboriginal population used in the censuses of Canada prior to 1961, the list on the previous page begins with the 1961 Census, recognizing that that was the first census in which long- and short-form census question-naires were introduced and in which the ancestry question referred explicitly to ethnic and cultural origins.

2. QUESTIONS APPEARING IN THE 2006 CENSUS OF CANADA CONCERNING ETHNICITY, ABORIGINAL ANCESTRY, BAND MEMBERSHIP, AND INDIAN STATUS

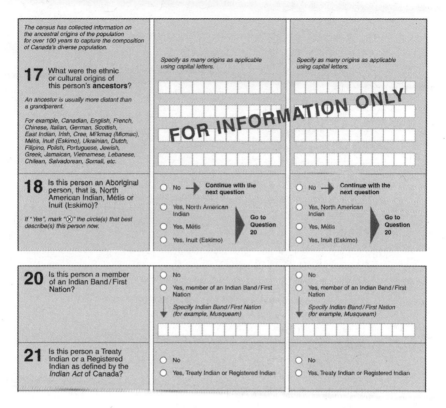

NOTES

1. The 1985 amendments to the Indian Act (Bill C-31) had the following three objectives: (1) to remove discrimination from the Indian Act for the future; (2) to restore rights to those who had lost them as a result of past discrimination; and (3) to recognize band control of membership as a step toward self-government. Changes introduced by Bill C-31 had significant demographic impacts on the Registered Indian population. See Clatworthy, 2001.

2. The 2010 amendment to the Indian Act (Bill C-3) provides Indian registration under the Indian Act (Section 6(2)) to any grandchild of a woman: (a) who lost status due to marrying a non-Indian; and (b) whose children born of that marriage had the grandchild with a non-Indian after September 4, 1951. See INAC, 2010, http://www.ainc-inac.gc.ca/br/is/bll/exp/est-eng.asp.

3. See Department of Indian Affairs and Northern Development, 2011, Catalogue No. R41-3/2011E-PDF, ISSN 1702-0964. Retrieved from http://www.ainc-inac.gc.ca/pr/sts/rip/rip07-eng.pdf.
4. The 1986 Census data on Aboriginal identity were never officially disseminated, partly because of reporting errors detected within the non-Aboriginal population (Crégheur, 1988). The data on the Aboriginal identity of populations of Aboriginal origin are considered reliable (Guimond, 1999).
5. See References for the Stastics Canada and Dominion Bureau of Statistics (1961) material used to develop this table.
6. The 2006 Census count of the population officially released by Statistics Canada on January 15, 2008, is 1,172,790. In addition to people self-reporting an Aboriginal identity to question 18, this figure also includes people who did not report to be part of an Aboriginal group, but who reported to be Registered or Treaty Indians under Canada's Indian Act (question 21), and/or who reported to be members of an Indian band or First Nation (question 20). See Statistics Canada, http://www12.statcan.ca/english/census06/reference/dictionary/pop001.cfm.

REFERENCES

Clatworthy S.J. (2001). *Re-assessing the population impacts of Bill C-31*. Report prepared for Research and Analysis Directorate, Indian and Northern Affairs Canada. Winnipeg, MB: Four Directions Consulting Group.

Dickason, O.P. (2002). *Canada's First Nations: A history of founding peoples from earliest times*. Don Mills, ON: Oxford University Press.

Dominion Bureau of Statistics. (1961). *The 1961 Census of Canada: Enumeration manual*. Ottawa, ON: Dominion Bureau of Statistics.

Guimond, E. (1999). Ethnic mobility and the demographic growth of Canada's Aboriginal Populations from 1986 to 1996. *Report on the demographic situation in Canada, 1998–1999* (Catalogue No. 91-208-XPE). Ottawa, ON: Statistics Canada.

Indian and Northern Affairs Canada (2010). *Gender equity in Indian Registration Act*. Ottawa, ON: Minister of Aboriginal Affairs and Northern Development Canada.

Isajiw, W.W. (1993). Definition and dimensions of ethnicity: A theoretical framework. In G.J. Goldmann & N. McKenney (Eds.), *Challenges of measuring an ethnic world: Science, politics and reality* (pp. 407–430). Washington, DC: United States Government Printing Office.

Robitaille, N., & Choinière, R. (1987). *An overview of demographic and socioeconomic conditions of the Inuit in Canada*. Ottawa, ON: Indian and Northern Affairs Canada.

Savard, R., & Proulx, J.-R. (1982). *Canada derrière l'épopée: les autochtones*. Montréal, QC: l'Hexagone.

Statistics Canada. (1973). *The 1971 Census of Canada: Population—ethnic groups* (Catalogue No. 92-723, Vol. 1, Part 3). Ottawa, ON: Statistics Canada.

———. (1976). *The 1971 Census of Canada, general review: Administrative report of the 1971 Census* (Catalogue No. 99-740, Vol. VI, Part 1). Ottawa, ON: Statistics Canada.

————. (1984). *The 1981 Census of Canada: Population – Ethnic origin* (Catalogue No. 92-911). Ottawa, ON: Statistics Canada.

————. (1989a). *The 1986 Census: Ethnicity, immigration and citizenship – The nation* (Catalogue No. 93-109). Ottawa, ON: Statistics Canada.

————. (1989b). *Profile of ethnic groups* (Catalogue No. 93-154). Ottawa, ON: Statistics Canada.

————. (1991). *The 1991 Census of Canada: Aboriginal Peoples procedures manual for canvasser reserve areas and Indian settlements* (Catalogue No. 92N0011E c.1). Ottawa, ON: Statistics Canada.

————. (1993). *The 1991 Census: Ethnic origin* (Catalogue No. 93-315). Ottawa, ON: Industry, Science and Technology Canada.

————. (1996a). *The 1996 Census of Canada: Ethnic origin procedures manual – automated coding* (Catalogue No. 92N0037XPE c.3). Ottawa, ON: Statistics Canada.

————. (1996b). *The 1996 Census of Canada: Indian Band/First Nation procedures manual – automated coding* (Catalogue No. 92-N0084-XPE c.3). Ottawa, ON: Statistics Canada.

————. (1997). *The 1996 Census: The 1996 Census handbook* (Catalogue No. 92-352-XPE). Ottawa, ON: Statistics Canada.

————. (2002). *The 2001 Census handbook* (Catalogue No. 92-379-XPB). Ottawa, ON: Statistics Canada.

————. (2003). *The 2006 Census content consultation report* (Catalogue No. 92-130-XPE). Ottawa, ON: Statistics Canada.

————. (2007). *The 2006 Census: A national overview – Population and dwelling counts, 2006 Census* (Catalogue No. 92-200-XPB). Ottawa, ON: Statistics Canada.

————. (2008). *The 2006 Census release topics: Aboriginal peoples* (Release No. 5: January 15, 2008). Ottawa, ON: Statistics Canada.

White, P.M., Badets, J., & Renaud, V. (1993). Measuring ethnicity in Canadian censuses. In G.J. Goldmann & N. McKenney (Eds.), *Challenges of measuring an ethnic world: Science, politics and reality* (pp. 223–269). Statistics Canada and US Bureau of the Census, Washington, DC: United States Government Printing Office.

CONTRIBUTORS

Chris Andersen
Associate Dean (Research), Associate Professor, School of Native Studies, University of Alberta. Dr. Andersen is an expert on sociological and social demographic aspects of the Métis population and on the administrative classification of the Métis. Recently published books include *Indigenous Statistics: A Quantitative Research Methodology* (with Maggie Walter, Left Coast Press) and *"Métis": Race, Recognition, and the Struggle for Indigenous Peoplehood* (UBC Press). He is currently the director of the Rupertsland Centre for Métis Research and is the editor of *aboriginal policy studies*.

Nicholas G. Biddle
Fellow, Centre for Aboriginal Economic Policy Research, Australian National University. Dr. Biddle is an expert on the social demography of Australian Aboriginal population. Between July 2011 and February 2012, Nicholas was a visiting scholar at the Center for Comparative Studies in Race and Ethnicity at Stanford University. He has also undertaken a research fellowship for the National Centre for Vocational Education Research (NCVER) and previously held a senior research officer and assistant director position in the Methodology Division of the Australian Bureau of Statistics. His research in this area spans many sociological and economic aspects of Aboriginal conditions in Australia, including preschool education, residential patterns, income inequality, and internal migration patterns.

Michael J. Chandler

Professor Emeritus, Department of Psychology, University of British Columbia. Michael Chandler is a developmental psychologist working at the University of British Columbia. His ongoing program of research involves an exploration of the role culture plays in constructing the course of identity development, shaping young people's emerging sense of ownership of their personal and cultural past, and their commitment to their own and their community's future well-being. Between 2002 and 2007, he was Canadian Institutes of Health Research (CIHR) distinguished investigator, and distinguished investigator with the Michael Smith Foundation. Professor Chandler's program of research dealing with identity development and suicide in Aboriginal and non-Aboriginal youth was singled out for publication as an invited monograph of the Society for Research in Child Development.

Stewart Clatworthy

Director, Four Directions Project Consultants, Winnipeg. Stewart Clatworthy operates Four Directions Project Consultants, a management consulting firm specializing in demographic and socio-economic research, population projections, and program evaluation. Since 1980, Mr. Clatworthy has completed numerous studies on Aboriginal demography and migration, the population impacts of the 1985 Indian Act, First Nations membership, and the socio-economic, housing, and employment conditions of Aboriginal peoples in Canada. Through this research, he has gained a national reputation as a leading scholar of Canadian Aboriginal socio-economic and demographic circumstances.

Senada Delic

PhD Candidate, School of Public Policy and Administration, Carleton University, Ottawa. Her published research focuses mainly on the social and labour market policies pertaining to the Aboriginal population in Canada. In her doctoral dissertation, she examines the link between Aboriginal identity and economic success in the Canadian labour market using mixed methods research.

James Frideres

Professor, Sociology, University of Calgary. Dr. Frideres holds the Canadian Ethnic Chair and directs the International Indigenous Studies program at the University of Calgary. He is the author of several books, including the ninth edition of *Aboriginal Peoples in Canada*, which has been in print since 1974. In addition, he has published numerous papers in a range of national and international journals, focusing on the socio-economic conditions of Aboriginal peoples in Canada.

Gustave J. Goldmann

Senior Fellow, Faculty of Social Sciences, University of Ottawa; Adjunct Professor, School of Public Policy, Carleton University. Dr. Goldmann is a social demographer specializing in Aboriginal demography, the settlement and absorption of immigrants and subjects related to ethnic groups and ethnicity. His recent publications include chapters focusing on the rural Aboriginal population, a demographic and demo-linguistic analysis of the Aboriginal population, and a historical demographic analysis of the Aboriginal peoples in Canada. Dr. Goldmann is a past manager of the Research Data Centre Program at Statistics Canada.

Eric Guimond

Aboriginal Affairs and Northern Development Canada, Strategic Research Directorate, Director. Eric Guimond is of French and Mi'kmaw descent and is a specialist in Aboriginal demography. His educational background includes demography, community health, physical education, and Aboriginal studies. He also possesses university research and teaching experience with expertise in projection models of population and Aboriginal groups. His PhD (Université de Montréal) focused on ethnic mobility of Aboriginal populations in Canada. He is also co-editor of *Restoring the Balance: First Nation Women, Community, and Culture* (University of Manitoba Press, 2009). Currently, Eric's role is to support policy making in Aboriginal and Northern matters through a program of survey development, policy research, and knowledge transfer.

Malcolm King

Dr. Malcolm King, a member of the Mississaugas of the New Credit First Nation (Ontario), is a health researcher at the University of Alberta, focusing on respiratory diseases. He is currently the scientific director of the CIHR Institute of Aboriginal Peoples' Health, and leads the development of a health research agenda aimed at improving wellness and achieving health equity for Aboriginal peoples.

Brenda Kobayashi

PhD Candidate, Department of Sociology, Western University. Her area of interest is criminology and her research focus is on young people in conflict with the law, particularly the relationship between the child welfare system and the youth justice system.

Tahu H. Kukutai (Waikato-Maniapoto, Te Aupōuri)

Senior Research Fellow, National Institute of Demographic and Economic Analysis, University of Waikato, New Zealand. She specializes in Māori population research and has written on issues of Māori identity, inequality, and population change for New Zealand and international audiences. Dr. Kukutai is currently working on two collaborative cross-national projects: one examining how governments around the world count and classify their populations by ethnicity; and the other looking at how colonization has impacted indigenous epidemiological transitions in New Zealand, Australia, and Sweden.

Ron F. Laliberté

Professor, Department of Native Studies, University of Saskatchewan. Ron Laliberté is a Métis person originally from Prince Albert, Saskatchewan, with family roots in Green Lake, Saskatchewan. From the early 1970s to the 1980s, he worked at a number of unionized labourer jobs. In 1982, he began his post-secondary education at the University of Saskatchewan. In 1998, he became a tenured faculty member in the Department of Native Studies, University of Saskatchewan, and in 2007 he received a PhD in sociology from the University of Calgary. His dissertation research focused on the transition of the migrant labour force from Aboriginal to Mexican workers in southern Alberta's sugar beet industry. His research interests include Métis issues and history, Aboriginal labour in western Canada, the history of the sugar beet industry in southern Alberta, and theoretical perspectives on migrant labour forces.

Roger C.A. Maaka

Professor of Māori and Indigenous Studies; Dean and Director, Māori Eastern Institute of Technology. Dr. Maaka's research interests include urbanization and indigenous peoples, Native studies as an academic discipline, post-treaty settlement development, the construction of contemporary indigenous identities, and indigeneity as a global social movement. He was the co-investigator of SSHRC grants investigating First Nations and Métis identities in cities, and he was instrumental in the establishment of an international network of scholars who study indigenous people in cities. He is also one of the regional representatives for the SSHRC-funded project "National Network for Urban Indigenous Economic Development."

Mary Jane Norris

Consultant and Researcher. Mary Jane Norris is currently a consultant specializing in Aboriginal research and demography. She has served in senior research positions within the Canadian government, including Aboriginal Affairs and Northern Development Canada, Statistics Canada, and Canadian Heritage. She has published extensively in the areas of Aboriginal demography, mobility and migration, urbanization, population projections, and the demographics of Aboriginal languages. Of mixed Aboriginal and non-Aboriginal ancestry, she is an off-reserve Registered Indian member of the Algonquins of Pikwàkanagàn (Golden Lake), in the Ottawa Valley. Mary Jane holds a master's in sociology and a BA honours in sociology and economics from Carleton University.

Evelyn J. Peters

Professor and Canada Research Chair, Urban and Inner City Studies, University of Winnipeg. Dr. Peters's research deals with Aboriginal urban geography, and she has published many scholarly articles on this topic. The focus of Dr. Peters's research has been First Nations and Métis people in cities. She has conducted research with a variety of community groups, including the Prince Albert Grand Council Urban Services Inc., the Saskatoon Tribal Council, the Saskatoon Indian and Métis Friendship

Centre, the Gabriel Dumont Institute, and the Central Urban Métis Federation Inc. Dr. Peters has authored a large number of works, including a special issue of *Progress in Planning*.

Andrey N. Petrov
Assistant Professor, Geography, and Director, Arctic Social and Environmental Systems Research Lab, University of Northern Iowa. Dr. Petrov is an economic and social geographer who specializes in Arctic economy, regional development, and post-Soviet society, with an emphasis on the social geography of indigenous populations of Russia. His current research is focused on regions of the Russian and Canadian North and concerns regional development, spatial organization, and restructuring of peripheral economies. He has also been a participant of the International Polar Year Arctic Social Indicators project (a follow-up to the Arctic Human Development Report). In the last few years, Dr. Petrov has published on issues pertaining to socio-economic crisis, development, and demographic dynamics of indigenous and non-indigenous populations in the North.

Ian Pool
Emeritus Professor, National Institute of Demographic and Economic Analysis, University of Waikato. Professor Ian Pool was appointed the chair in sociology at the University of Waikato in 1978 and was the founding director of Population Studies Centre between 1982 and 2003. His research spans all areas in demography. Throughout his career he has been called upon frequently by the United Nations Population Fund and other UN agencies to carry out research on their behalf in many parts of the world. Professor Pool's books, *The Māori Population of New Zealand 1769–1971* and *Te Iwi Māori: A New Zealand Population, Past, Present and Projected*, remain the definitive texts on Māori population dynamics. Currently, he is in the final stages of writing a new book on Māori population and development, 1769 to 1900.

Sarah Prout
Associate Professor, School of Earth and Environment, the University of Western Australia. Dr. Prout is a human geographer with research and teaching interests in population, development, and social policy in Australia and Africa. Her research focuses on the spatial, temporal, demographic, and socio-cultural characteristics of indigenous mobility practices and their interface with social policy and practice; the social geographies of urban-based indigenous populations; and the development of relevant, reliable, and representative indicators of indigenous well-being for reporting, monitoring, and planning purposes.

Norbert Robitaille
Professor, Demography Department, University of Montreal. Dr. Robitaille is an acclaimed scholar of Aboriginal demography, having published many studies in this area for well over 25 years. He has been in charge of the domain of population

projections in his department for more than 35 years, during which he projected many Aboriginal populations. He was also active in the domain of linguistic demography. He is presently working on the demography of Status Indians.

Anatole Romaniuk

Adjunct Professor, Sociology, University of Alberta. Formerly professor of demography at the Universities of Ottawa and Montreal, and research associate at the Office of Population Research, Princeton University, Dr. Romaniuk was for many years the director of the Demography Division at Statistics Canada. His published works intersect aspects of formal and social demography, covering various areas ranging from policy issues and challenges facing demographically mature societies to the analysis of fertility in Canada and social demographic conditions among Canadian Aboriginal peoples. He is the author of *Fertility in Canada: From Baby-Boom to Baby-Bust* and *La fécondité des populations congolaises*.

Sacha Senécal

Senior Research Manager, Aboriginal Affairs and Northern Development Canada. Sacha Senécal was born in the Mohawk community of Kahnawake. He holds a PhD in social psychology as well as an undergraduate degree in psychology. Since 2000, Sacha has been very active in the field of Aboriginal social statistics, holding analyst positions at Statistics Canada and in the First Nations and Inuit Health Branch (FNIHB) of Health Canada. He is currently a senior research manager with the Strategic Research Directorate at Aboriginal Affairs and Northern Development Canada in Gatineau. Sacha is also an adjunct research professor of sociology with the Social Sciences Faculty at the University of Western Ontario.

C. Matthew Snipp

Burnet C. and Mildred Finley Wohlford Professor of Humanities and Sciences; Director, Center for Comparative Studies of Race and Ethnicity; and Director of Institute for Research in Social Sciences (IRiSS) Secure Data Center at Stanford University. Dr. Snipp is a leading authority on the North American Indian population and Alaska Natives. His current research and writing deal with the methodology of racial measurement, changes in the social and economic well-being of American ethnic minorities, and American Indian education. For nearly 10 years, he served as an appointed member of the Census Bureau's Racial and Ethnic Advisory Committee. He also has been involved with several advisory working groups evaluating the US Census, and two National Academy of Science panels charged with designing the 2010 Census. He is also a member of the Board of Scientific Councillors for the Centers for Disease Control and the National Center for Health Statistics.

John Taylor

Professor and Director of the Centre for Aboriginal Economic Policy Research, Australian National University. For over 25 years, he has conducted research on demographic, social, and economic change among Indigenous Australians and has published widely on these issues in Australian and international books and journals. He is a member of the Australian Bureau of Statistics Advisory Group on Aboriginal and Torres Strait Islander Statistics and the Expert Group on Aboriginal and Torres Strait Islander Demographic Statistics. He is also board member of the Australian government's Closing the Gap Clearinghouse. He has been prominent in demonstrating the application of demographic analysis to Indigenous policy.

Frank Trovato

Professor, Sociology, University of Alberta, Edmonton. Frank Trovato is editor-in-chief of *Canadian Studies in Population*, the official journal of the Canadian Population Society. He is a past president of this association and a past director of the Population Research Laboratory at the University of Alberta. His research involves topics at the intersections of demography, sociology, and social epidemiology. His publications include a number of works concerning the health and mortality conditions of Canadian Aboriginals. His book *Canada's Population in a Global Contex: An Introduction to Social Demography* was awarded the Nathan Keyfitz Book Prize in 2012 by the Canadian Population Society.

Ravi B.P. Verma

International Consultant and Researcher; Adjunct Research Professor, Department of Sociology and Anthropology, Carleton University, Ottawa. Dr. Ravi P.B. Verma's areas of interest are applied demography, demographic and statistical modelling. He is an expert on population estimation and projections. He has been a senior population analyst, Development and Demographic Methods, Demography Division at Statistics Canada (1981–2009) and has served as a consultant at the Central Statistics Bureau, Government of British Columbia. He has also worked on a CIDA assignment in Bangladesh. Verma has published papers in the areas of immigrant adaptation, estimates of population for small areas, projections of fertility, mortality, and interprovincial migrations for total population and special groups such as visible minorities, Registered Indians, and other Aboriginal groups in Canada.

Cora J. Voyageur

Professor, Sociology, University of Calgary. Dr. Voyageur is a leading scholar on the socio-economic conditions of Canadian Aboriginals. Her research interests explore the Aboriginal experience in Canada, including leadership, employment, community and economic development, women's issues, and health. Among her recent works are *Firekeepers of the Twenty-First Century: First Nations Women Chiefs in Canada* and *My Heroes Have Always Been Indians*. She is currently writing on Aboriginal leadership in Canada and First Nations women and entrepreneurship. She is a member of the Athabasca Chipewyan First Nation from northern Alberta. She has given invited conference presentations across Canada and the United States, Britain, the Middle East, Australia, and Europe.

Paul C. Whitehead

Professor, Sociology, University of Western Ontario. Dr. Whitehead is a leading criminologist and an expert on the problem of alcoholism in First Nations communities. Some of his research in this area is policy options to fight this problem in Native communities. Among his many publications is *The Insanity of Alcohol: Social Problems in Canadian First Nations Communities* (with M. Hayes).

Mandy L.M. Yap

Research Officer, Centre for Aboriginal Economic Policy Research, Australian National University. As a researcher, Mandy has worked on a range of issues including aging, diabetes, women and fertility, income distribution and Australia's Indigenous peoples' socio-economic outcomes. Her research interest includes the role of gender equality in Indigenous development and quality of life measurements.

T. Kue Young

Dean, School of Public Health, University of Alberta. Dr. Young was previously Professor and TransCanada Chair in Aboriginal Health at the Dalla Lana School of Public Health, University of Toronto. Dr. Young is a leading authority on the health of Aboriginal Peoples. Among his many publications in this area are *The Health of Native Americans: Toward a Biocultural Epidemiology*, and *Health Transitions in Arctic Populations* (co-edited with P. Bjrerregaard).

INDEX

Canada Mortgage and Housing
    Corporation (CMHC)
    adjusted population, 81–82, 85t
    population growth projections,
        analysis, 80
    Statistics Canada, data comparison,
        84–86, 85t
Canadian Bill of Rights, 337, 344n11
Canberra, Australia, 426t, 431t
cancer and neoplasm
    education and, 218–21, 220t
    mortality rates, 30t
cancer and neoplasm, circumpolar
    areas, 220t
Canterbury, New Zealand, 451–52t,
    464n9
Cape York, Australia, 394, 401, 403, 405
Cardinal, Harold, 326
cardiovascular diseases, 30t, 199–201f,
    207–08
Carmagnani, A., 4
Carrier language, 307
Carr-Saunders, A.M., 11
casinos, 333–34, 344n8
categorical mobility, xxvi–xxvii, 275–80
    See also ethnic mobility
Cayugas, 61
Census Canada, 499–505
    overview, xiii–xvi, xviii–xix, 59–61, 74
    administrative reports, 62–63
    ancestry/origins/race categories,
        269–74
    census absence of Métis and
        Inuit, 70
    census sub-divisions (CSDs), 157n4
    comparability of data (1991–2006),
        80
    confidentiality policies, 266
    cultural change and, 59–60
    definition, Métis, 275–80, 280n1,
        280n3
    definition, North American Indian,
        287
    discontinuity in time series, xiv, 22,
        36, 38–39
    First Nation membership data,
        availability, 288

identity construction and, 285–86
identity homogenization and census
    questions, 287, 295, 298–99
identity of children in non-
    Aboriginal families, 273
legislation on, 62, 63, 70–71
lineality, 59, 70–71t, 270–72, 502
long-form census, elimination of
    mandatory (2011), 75n2
on- vs. off-reserve, 272
as political site, 63, 267, 286–87
Prairie provinces, quinquennial
    censuses, 75n1
public policy and categories, 285–87,
    299
reserve residency and categories,
    272
two survey components, 62
under- and overcoverage, 79, 81, 122,
    157n3
under- and overcoverage, defined,
    106
uses of data, 63
See also definitions and terminology;
    enumeration; multiple identities
Census Canada, pre-Confederation
    early censuses, 60–61, 75n3, 271
    first Census of the Canadas (1851), 61
    race questions, 270, 271
Census Canada, 1871
    lineality, 71t
    origin vs. place of birth, 65, 75n3
Census Canada, 1881
    lineality, 71t
    origin vs. place of birth, 65
Census Canada, 1885 (North West)
    origin vs. place of birth, 65
Census Canada, 1886 (Manitoba)
    Métis enumeration, 65
    origin vs. place of birth, 65
Census Canada, 1901
    Aboriginal terminology, first use, 65
    lineality, 65, 71t
    mixed ancestry, 65
    origins questions, 270
    tribal affiliation, 65

data inflation of improvement
indicators, xxvii, 110t–11, 268–69
deficit paradigm, xxviii–xxix, 252,
327, 442
demographic transition, xvii, xxxiii,
3, 23, 25, 37–38
demographic maturity, xviii, 48
ecological fallacy, xvi
ethnic mobility's impact on data,
xx, 110t–14
indigenous populations, criteria,
443–44
limitations of, xvi–xvii, 445–46
multivariate modelling, 218–21,
219f, 220t
population estimation by residual,
36, 94n3, 115n11, 266
populations vs. peoples, xvi–xvii,
443–46
segmentation, 442–43
standard hemispheric depopulation
ratio, 4–5
See also constructivism; definitions
and terminology; ethnic mobility; heterogeneity, Aboriginal;
identity, Aboriginal
Dene language, 311t
Denevan, William, 5
Denmark
overview, xxiv–xxv
administrative regions, 212t
fertility, teens, 223t
Greenland self-government, 213
health care, 226t
infant mortality, 217, 224t
life expectancy, 224t
mortality and morbidity, 224t–25t
population, 222t
population, density, 223t
population, indigenous percentage,
215, 223t
post-secondary education, 226t
SES indicators, 226t
tuberculosis, 225t
See also Greenland, Denmark
depopulation, 3–5, 13–16

descent rules. See lineality and
census questions
Dickason, Olive P., 4, 5, 18, 50, 237
digestive system diseases, 8, 30t
discrimination and gender in Indian
Act. See Bill C-3; Bill C-31
discrimination and stigma
juries' racial views, 338
overview of positive trends, 334–36
urban experiences, 288
See also legal issues; pride, shame,
and self-identification
diseases
overview, xxi, 30t, 225t
categories, RIs, 30t
epidemics, 8, 13–14, 16–17, 20
history, pre- and early contact,
8, 12–17
rates and categories, 27–33,
30t, 225t
social determinants of health and,
xxiii–xxiv, 203–08
See also cancer and neoplasm;
circulatory diseases; digestive
system diseases; respiratory
diseases; tuberculosis
diseases, circumpolar areas
incidence, 225t
multivariate modelling of outcomes, 220t
See also tuberculosis, circumpolar
areas
Dobyns, Henry F., 4
Dogrib language, 307, 311t, 313
Dolgan people, Russia, 471t, 475f,
476t, 483
Doohan, K., 388, 400–01
Dosman, E.J., 238
Drybones, R. v., 336–37
Dubbo, Australia, 426t–28, 431t

"eagle has landed" prophecy, 325, 343n2
economy
overview of positive trends, 331–34
businesses, 331–34
casinos, 333–34, 344n8
cultural tourism, 333–34